Terrorism and Public Safety Policing

Implications for the Obama Presidency

Terrorism and
Public Safety Policing

Implications for the Obama Presidency

JAMES F. PASTOR

CRC Press
Taylor & Francis Group
Boca Raton London New York

CRC Press is an imprint of the
Taylor & Francis Group, an **informa** business

CRC Press
Taylor & Francis Group
6000 Broken Sound Parkway NW, Suite 300
Boca Raton, FL 33487-2742

Printed in the United States of America on acid-free paper
10 9 8 7 6 5 4 3 2 1

International Standard Book Number: 978-1-4398-1580-9 (Hardback)

Library of Congress Cataloging-in-Publication Data

Pastor, James F., 1957-
    Terrorism and public safety policing : implications for the Obama presidency / James F. Pastor.
        p. cm.
    Includes bibliographical references and index.
    ISBN 978-1-4398-1580-9
    1. Terrorism. 2. Community policing. I. Title.

HV6431.P376 2009
363.325--dc22   2009015821

Visit the Taylor & Francis Web site at
http://www.taylorandfrancis.com

and the CRC Press Web site at
http://www.crcpress.com

To the Great God, may your protection, justice, and mercy be upon your people

Contents

SECTION I TERRORISM AND EXTREMISM: CONCEPTS AND ISSUES

SECTION II ELEMENTS OF PUBLIC SAFETY POLICING

SECTION III   LARGER ISSUES AND IMPLICATIONS

Preface

This book seeks to explain and illustrate a systematic change that is taking place in policing. Much of this transition stems from the threat of terrorism and the rise in extremist violence. These statements may seem out of place to some readers. At this moment in time, I accept the fact that most readers do not see any significant change occurring in policing. Indeed, most do not see a sustained threat of terrorism and extremist violence on the horizon. For those who do not recognize these issues, I can only ask that you read this book with an open mind. For those who see these trends, I hope you will view this book as a road map to help weave through the difficult roads ahead. Hopefully, it will also enable policy makers and practitioners to avoid the inherent difficulties related to any large-scale societal transition. Even better, this book can provide the narrative of the decisions that need to be made: who, what, where, why, and how questions that need to be addressed.

At the outset, let me commence by saying that this book is not designed to be a rendition of the "solutions" that need to be implemented. The key elements of the forthcoming policing transition are not without their own set of problems. This is not a panacea. Instead, this is a pragmatic answer to a series of vexing problems facing policing in America—or, more generally, in American society. In fact, the problems are grounded in public policy and public safety. The impact of such societal problems will directly affect policing. This is not unusual. Police agencies, for better or worse, are simply a reflection of the larger society. They are made up of and affected by the society they serve. Unfortunately for policing agencies, they are often the target of extremists in the larger society. This is part of "the job." I do not seek to "wish" this aspect of the job away. Indeed, I directly acknowledge this fact. In this regard, I offer a systematic response to these factors, albeit one with its own set of implications.

The main theme of this book is to present and discuss a new model of policing, that I characterize as *Public Safety Policing*. This "model" of policing will replace the *Community Policing* model. This model has dominated police, political, and academic circles for the past couple of decades. I realize this statement alone will be controversial to some circles. To these, I can only say let time be the judge. If my premises are wrong, then those who advocate *Community Policing* will prevail.

I will stake my professional reputation that my premises are not wrong. Read on. The trends, the data, and the logic do not lie. In my mind, it is the formation of the "perfect storm." The storm is on the horizon. We can ignore it and hope it does not affect us. Or, we can prepare for the coming storm. It is your choice. It is our choice. To those who prepare, the chances of a "successful" conclusion are better, much better. Plainly said, you can ride the wave, or it will blindside and shallow you.

My approach is to combine public policy analysis with an understanding of human nature. This framework is supplemented by experiences as a police officer, attorney, and professor. To get a sense of where I am coming from, please allow me to develop four short stories. Each of these stories had an impact on my thinking. Each of these stories has a moral that relates to this book.

As an undergraduate student in law enforcement administration at Western Illinois University, I remember watching the events leading up to the Iranian hostage situation with great interest. To refresh your memory, in 1978–1979 students protested daily in the streets of Tehran. The Shah of Iran was in trouble. This U.S.-backed leader was on the verge of losing power—and the country of Iran was teetering toward extremism. Each night on the news, U.S. diplomats and politicians gave various accounts of the circumstances. Typically the message was, "We have full confidence in the Shah and his government." Sitting in Macomb, Illinois, my roommates and I knew it was all over. We knew that the Shah did not have a chance to survive this uprising with his government intact. Nonetheless, each night U.S. government officials gave their "spin" as to why the "scene" we were seeing from 7,000 miles away was not "reality." Instead, these protesters were only some media-driven "perception." They did not have the ability to affect reality.

Of course, this message was wrong. The Shah was exiled and his government fell. The Islamic Republic of Iran came into being. The first demonstrable Islamic government since the Ottoman Empire was created. The moral of this story is that the government cannot always—if ever—tell you the full truth. Stated in a more positive way, the government has to err on the side of good public relations. This assertion, or its corollary, is the larger point. I am quite certain that government officials knew the Shah was history well before my friends and I did. They simply could not admit this in public. They had to "support" an ally even though they knew that he could not survive. Unfortunately, when the Shah fell, "student protesters" took American hostages. They used these hostages for their particular political and psychological ends.

The hostage situation lasted through the remaining days of the Carter Administration. Those who are old enough will remember that the American public was dismayed. The media saw the drama of this situation. The news documentary *Nightline* started from this hostage taking. Night after night, the show counted the days. Day five. Day twelve. Day thirty-five. Day one hundred. Day two hundred and fifty. Day three hundred and sixty. Each day, the show gave accounts of the hostage situation. Ted Koppel became famous with his hard-hitting, dramatic accounts of this circumstance. The American public was fixated to the circumstance—and the media account of such. This went on through the failed rescue attempt in an Iranian desert. There did not seem to be much hope for the hostages.

Enter Ronald Reagan. He was elected president in November 1979. The days of the hostage situation were now ending. On his inauguration day, after 444 days, the drama was finally coming to a close. The hostages were "miraculously" released. While I do not know for certain, simple logic says to me that much "back channel" communication took place from early November to that fateful day in January. Who can doubt that some very specific ultimatums were made? Who can doubt that the new administration took a stronger and more aggressive stance than the Carter Administration? Is it simply a coincidence that the hostages were released on inauguration day? In my mind, no reasonable person can believe this coincidence.

In the end, the moral of this situation is twofold: terrorism and the media are tied at the hip. They have a symbiotic relationship that is hard to deny. It is extraordinarily difficult to sever. Each needs the other. Each fuels the interests of the other. The second moral is more pointed and yet less accepted. That is, terrorists understand strength. In my mind this is a simple human dynamic. Remember the message we all heard as children: bullies are cowards. You must stand up to them or they will never leave you alone. The same message is relevant with terrorists. If you do not stand up to them, they will perceive you as weak. If you are perceived as weak, they have little or no respect for you. Without respect you are nothing.

This same message plays out on the streets in American cities. Day in and day out young, tough gang members intimidate and manipulate the weak and the frail. They are bold and strong as long as society tolerates their intimidating practices. In "civilized" society, we have forgotten the basic premises of life. On the street, the Darwinian theory controls: Only the strong survive! Because many "intellectuals" do not know this world, they will never get it. They reason. They advocate. They discuss. They seek to convince. What they do not understand is these techniques, while important, must be grounded on strength. If you do not have a solid founda- tion, you have nothing. If you do not have respect, you will never convince. If you are not prepared to assert strength—sustained and legitimate power—then the "bad" guys will simply play you like a fool. They may talk with you. They may take your money and your "goodies." They may even listen to you. They may do all these things, but they will not respect you. In the end, if they do not respect you, then you will not convince them or defeat them.

The terrorists come from a culture—or more accurately, a mindset—that respects strength and power. They understand these because they live them. They use them daily. They use them as the key means to their ends. Simply stated, they exert power to obtain power. It is their means—and their end. Our culture does not understand this. Our "politically correct" notions often seek the exact opposite. Do not offend anyone. Be tolerant of all people. Do not judge. Do not make waves. In the end, we are living in different worlds. Unless we understand their perspective, we will be hard-pressed to succeed. With the election of President Obama, I think we will move more toward the approach of Carter rather than Reagan. If history is any guide, we are in trouble.

As a result of this hostage situation, I graduated college in 1980 with a bachelor's degree and a fascination with terrorism. In a desire to work in federal law enforcement, I decided to attend graduate school to enhance my marketability. Shortly thereafter, I enrolled at the University of Illinois at Chicago. In these studies, I was extremely fortunate to have Dr. Richard Ward as a professor. Dick Ward was (and is) a legend in policing circles. He was a former NYPD detective who obtained his doctorate and engaged in a life of educational instruction. By the early 1980s, Dr. Ward was already an internationally recognized authority on terrorism. In this position, and as vice chancellor of the university, he held an annual terrorism conference. In this week-long conference, Dr. Ward would bring in experts from around the world, including key U.S. agencies, such as the FBI, CIA, DEA, ATF, and the State Department. As a young student, I attended these conferences with great interest. Sometime during the course of my studies, Dr. Ward also agreed to chair my thesis committee on terrorism.

In 1983, I joined the Chicago Police Department as a police recruit. After completing academy training, I was assigned to the 21st Police District. While some readers may not know the city of Chicago, this assignment was particularly relevant in my life. The 21st District contained the notorious "El Rukn" fort. The El Rukns were a Sunni Muslim organization that formed from the Black P-Stone Nation. The "Stones" were a radical and deadly gang. Their leader, Jeff Fort, was "inspired" to change the gang from the "Stones" to the Rukns. By any account, this change was not a transformation. To my knowledge, few, if any, individuals within the gang were changed from their life of crime. Instead, the gang was not a "gang" anymore. Now it was a "religion." With this newfound status, the "religion" was able to manipulate laws, gaining First Amendment freedom of religion, association, and related protections. Further, it gained legitimacy, or at least attempted to do so, as a "religion." No longer was this a criminal organization. They found Allah!

Please consider this dynamic. I am a young police officer patrolling the streets of the 21st District. I saw the El Rukns differently than other police officers. This is not because I was wiser or more astute. It was because I was exposed to the logic, data, and theories of terrorism. Studying and listening to this information made it clear to me that the El Rukns were indeed transformed—but not in the way they projected. The transformation was more political and strategic than religious. Please also consider the worldviews of my police friends. Many of these individuals were tough, Vietnam-era veterans. They had 10, 15, and even 20 years on the job. They had seen the El Rukns as the "Stones." The P-Stones were deadly and dangerous people. The "Stones" were killers and drug dealers. The "Stones" were criminals. They could not fathom the notion, however, that they would become terrorists. My assertions that they had graduated to "terrorists," rather than being simply gang members, fell on deaf ears.

In 1985, I completed my course work within the curriculum. I was working on my thesis titled, "A Critical Analysis of Terrorism." The gist of this document was that Marxist-oriented criminological theories—such as the critical theory of criminology—which asserted that *the system* was the causal connection to crime, would foster terrorism. The logic was that these theories—often advocated by the most respected criminologists—provided the intellectual groundwork to critique the system. This critique provided that the appropriate "solution" requires structural changes in society. While most of these theorists did not affirmatively state such, the logical conclusion, in my mind, was revolution. Indeed, in order to change the system to the degree needed to "cure" the structural components that caused crime, one would have to dramatically change the institutions that supported this supposedly corrupt and racist society. In my mind, this "logic" supported those disaffected and marginal members of society to advocate terrorism as a "solution" to bring down the capitalist system.

As we will see in this book, the ideologies developed by Islamist and Marxist thinkers would embrace these theories. I saw groups like the El Rukns as being ripe for this "logic." They were rebels. They were political. They advocated a radical brand of Sunni Islam. They would "graduate" to terrorism. During this same time frame, I had the good fortune to be transferred from the 21st District to the gang unit. This assignment to Gang Crime Enforcement was very important to me. The gang unit was the most prestigious and active enforcement group in the city—and one of the best in the entire country. I was assigned to Gang Crimes South—meaning the south side of Chicago. The unit provided tactical enforcement in the most crime-ridden areas of the south side. The individuals assigned to this unit were excellent police officers. They were tough, smart, and experienced. I was the youngest and least experienced person in the unit.

With this backdrop, I approached the administrative sergeant of the Gang Crime Unit to inquire about obtaining information and ideologies of the El Rukns. I introduced myself to the sergeant. I related to him that I was recently assigned to "Gang South." I explained that I was working on my masters thesis on terrorism. I further explained some of the details of the research and the overall approach. In doing so, I stated that I believed the El Rukns would be a terrorist group. He paused. The conversation seemed to become rather disjointed. He finally tilted his head, looked at me, and asked, "Are you living in the 60s kid?" Upon hearing this, I knew the conversation was not going to be fruitful. After a few pleasantries, I thanked him and walked out of the office with my tail between my legs. I was deflated. I knew that I had hit a dead end. After reframing my thesis, I deleted the section on the El Rukns due to my inability to get this information. I completed the thesis in 1988.

During the intervening years, I continued to attend the annual terrorism conference hosted by Dr. Ward. In addition, I was actively involved in gang enforcement. During an annual St. Jude parade (which honored fallen police officers), the gang unit hosted a breakfast after the parade. I happened to be seated at the same table as the administrative sergeant mentioned earlier. During the breakfast, he looked at me and asked, "Jim, did you ever finish that thesis?" I had to bite my tongue. I wanted to figuratively "slap" him. Parenthetically, this sergeant and I had become somewhat friendly over the two and a half years since this initial conversation. During this time, members of the El Rukns had been accused of obtaining monies from Libyan dictator Moammar Gadhafi. These individuals allegedly conspired to use this money to take down an airliner from O'Hare airport. The plan was to use a rocket launcher to shoot down a plane. Thereafter, the FBI along with key Gang Intelligence officers arrested members of the El Rukns with the rocket launcher. I participated in two subsequent raids on the "fort," which were joint federal, state, and gang unit operations. The "fort" was ultimately torn down. Members of the El Rukns were imprisoned and the "gang" was dismantled.

The moral of this story is this: we must change our paradigm. We must be ready to change the way we think about things—even things that we think we know. The members of the gang unit saw the El Rukns as gang members. They knew many of them personally. They engaged them in discussions and followed them in investigations. They locked them up. They saw them as criminals—not as potential terrorists. Conversely, I did not have a clue about who these individuals were. I had no preconceived notion of them. Instead, I saw the "big picture." I saw the logic of terrorism and applied it to them as a group. I did not know the details—the individuals, their notorious crimes, their organizational structure—but I did see the reasons why they would "graduate" to a terrorist group.

This same logic holds true today. In policing agencies, many police professionals live and work in the "guns, drugs, and gangs" paradigm. As problematic as these factors are, this paradigm will change. Those who spend their days focusing on these factors will soon learn the world has changed. Unfortunately, it is often the case that those closest to the issue are often so vested in the "status quo" that it does not enable them to see the forest for the trees. They become so focused on the individual trees that they cannot see the rest of the forest. They see the details so intimately they cannot see the larger picture.

While I was an "insider" as a tactical police officer in the gang unit, I had a "fresh" perspective because I was still young and unsullied. I had not bought into the way things are. I had not developed the mindset around particular worldviews. My mind was open to new possibilities and eventualities. Unfortunately, I think it is human nature to become conditioned to expect certain things. We become slaves to our routine. We think and live as if the status quo will last forever. We often forget that the only constant in life is change. When confronted with circumstances that are problematic, we remember this notion. We want change from problematic circumstances. As will be developed in the first chapter, this has been a critical factor in the election of President Obama.

I have been involved in policing and security in various positions and capacities for over 30 years. During much of this time, I have been an "outsider." While I was dealing in public safety matters, often I was not employed with a policing agency. I served as an attorney for the Chicago Police Department. I served as an attorney for two police unions. I served as an attorney for four security firms, including being the legal counsel/operational auditor for SecurityLink, which at the time was the largest privately held alarm firm in the country. In addition, I have taught police officers and police officials in both academic and training curricula. I have negotiated police bargaining unit agreements and litigated police disciplinary cases. In these experiences, I have engaged in numerous police "issues," yet I have not been on the "treadmill." Partly because of these experiences, I have kept my eyes on the big picture. These experiences have also enabled me to wrestle with the details. Understanding these details while maintaining an eye on the horizon has inspired me to develop this book.

Finally, the last personal story will tie up my experiences and the logic of this book. While operating my law practice, I worked on my doctorate in public policy analysis at the University of Illinois at Chicago. After many years of toil, I completed my dissertation titled, "The Functional and Constitutional Implications of Private Security Patrols on Public Streets." I was fortunate to assemble a committee of insightful and supportive individuals who not only cared, but were thoughtful about such an esoteric subject. I defended this dissertation on September 10, 2001. On that date, this subject was so far under the radar screen that few people, absent my supportive committee, would have cared about it. The next day the subject went from esoteric to relevant. While the issues related to this dissertation are still somewhat atypical, the momentum toward these issues had been inexorably set in motion on this infamous day. Largely because of such, I was able to publish the dissertation, which was subsequently reworked and retitled as "The Privatization of Police in America: An Analysis and Case Study." Some of the logic and data developed from this dissertation have helped shape and inform my thinking. Indeed, one of the key elements of the pending new policing model is framed from this thinking.

The moral of this story may be obvious. It is this: along with crisis comes opportunity. Indeed, in every crisis are resultant opportunities. Instructively, the Chinese language uses the same word to convey the concept of crisis and opportunity. These concepts are so ingrained together that they are interchangeable.

Please consider the possibilities as you read this book. I will outline the course for many difficult times ahead. Many pending predicaments are on the horizon. These will result in a dramatic change in the model of policing. It will result in some rather dramatic changes in the larger society. It will entail understanding larger movements in motion throughout the world. In the end, I trust the reader will see this book as combining the details along with a particular vision of the horizon. Hopefully, this book will be part of the policy-making process and the operational structures of policing agencies.

Part One is an overview of terrorism and extremism. In Chapter 1, I introduce the notion of *Public Safety Policing*. I will outline the elements of this new policing model in light of current societal circumstances. Of course, these circumstances are shaped and informed by the historic election of Barack Obama. These factors will come together in a big way. I hope you will agree that my approach is to objectively—and critically—examine extraordinary contemporary circumstances.

In Chapter 2, I develop and articulate the key factors related to terrorism and extremism. This chapter is packed with substantial concepts. I attempt to convey very complex concepts in a concise fashion. Admittedly, I attempt to tackle complicated issues in one chapter that some authors may develop in an entire book. As such, this chapter is not an exhaustive analysis of the substantive issues related to terrorism and extremism. Instead, it can be considered as a primer. I am confident, however, that the reader will view this chapter as very instructive and informational.

In Chapter 3, I present specific extremist groups with an explanation of their goals and ideologies. Given my premise that ideologies act as the fuel to fire extremism, I focus on the "logic" of these groups and their larger movements. In addition, I explain the societal application of extremism. In this sense, extremist thinking creates hardened positions. These positions are further exacerbated by bitter accusations. This results in violence. Violence begets more violence. This results in even more hardened positions. Radical groups grow. Their sympathizers increase. The middle—the moderates—get squeezed. In this dynamic, the police are targeted by both (or all) sides. This will result in dramatically changing the nature of policing—and the policing model.

In Part Two, the specific elements of *Public Safety Policing* are presented and analyzed. Chapter 4 presents the military weaponry and tactical operations element of the new policing model. Chapter 5 presents the intelligence methods and surveillance technologies element. Chapter 6 presents the order maintenance element of the new policing model. Chapter 7 presents the synergy of these elements into the larger *Public Safety Policing* model.

In Part Three, the book shifts gears toward the larger issues facing this country. Chapter 8 outlines the global—or universal—movement related to the notion of the "Holy War." This includes a discussion of the internal and external alliances related to this larger struggle. It also includes an overview of key theaters—and key concepts in the Holy War. Chapter 9 presents and examines critical public policy issues, which I contend act as "triggers" to extremist violence. In this discussion I take on critical issues in a manner that focuses on the potential to manifest violence. Pointedly, one of these issues is the notion that race, religion, and politics will act as an extremely volatile mixture.

Ironically, when I was finishing this book, the newly appointed attorney general, Eric Holder, asserted that Americans are a country of "cowards" in relation to race. In developing the logic and data related to this subject, I seek to directly address this notion. I do so in a provocative and pointed manner. I trust this will be seen as refreshing to some and inflaming to others. In my mind, this is the reason why this mixture is so volatile—and why it will lead to extremist violence. I say up front, I expect to be attacked because of such. I hope Mr. Holder will acknowledge that I am not one of the "cowards." Will I be trumpeted as an insightful thinker? Since I do not articulate the "politically correct" rhetoric, I do not expect this. This is not why I write. Instead, I write to warn of the consequences of the path we are on. Some will not like this analysis. Because we are so divided as a country, I expect attacks. Cowards, of course, do not desire attacks. Say what you want about my thoughts; one thing you cannot say is that I am a coward. Let's see how this plays out.

In any event, Chapter 10 presents some recommendations related to the new policing model—and the implications of such on American society. Hopefully, this chapter will provide a "road map" to address specific aspects of the new policing model. Please use this chapter to help model your operation and inform your thinking.

Beyond my words and recommendations, I trust the reader will acknowledge that this book attempts to paint the big picture and articulate specific details of such. This was a huge undertaking. I hope that these goals were achieved. You can be the judge. You can assess whether I "connected the dots" in a compelling and substantive manner. Even beyond your thoughts, I will be content to let time tell of the accuracy and insight of my vision. If you disagree with my premises and my vision, let's agree to let time act as the arbitrator of reality.

My vision and insight have been developed and framed in a number of ways. The experiences outlined above have significantly informed my thinking. Beyond these experiences, I have used numerous authoritative writings by respected terrorism authors. These writings have been read and reviewed for more than two and a half decades. In addition to these writings, I have developed much of the contemporary analyses by using a disciplined daily analysis of open source materials. I used daily source summaries provided by the following entities: the Department of Homeland Security (DHS Daily Infrastructure Report), the U.S. State Department (Overseas Security Advisory Council Daily Reports), Government Executive (Homeland Security reports), Southern Poverty Law Center (Hate Watch headlines), ASIS International (Security Management Daily Briefings), and the Institute of Terrorism Research and Response (Targeted Actionable Monitoring Center). These daily sources were then supplemented by links to specific media Web sites, both large and small, domestic and international. Further, I have regularly visited key Web sites, both media and professional, to delve deeper into contemporary issues.

These information sources were critical to inform my vision and my thinking. Possibly even more importantly, I am blessed to be an instructor to police officers around the world. I have worked for the renowned Northwestern University's Police Staff and Command instructional training program. I have instructed at the International Law Enforcement Academy, which is funded and delivered by a U.S. State Department program. Most importantly, however, I am a faculty member for Calumet College of St. Joseph. In this position, I have the distinct pleasure to stand before police officers from the Chicago metropolitan area. Most of these individuals are Chicago police officers. Others are from suburban and Northwest Indiana departments. I have great respect for these men and women. They are an inspiration to me. I am blessed to hear their stories—and their concerns. I am blessed to be privy to their insights and their thoughts. These individuals have helped me frame my thinking. They have been subjected to my lectures and PowerPoint presentations related to terrorism and the new policing model. I am extraordinarily thankful to each of you. Space is too short and memory too indistinct to name each of you. Please know that I respect your work and your insight. I am with you in word, action, and spirit.

There are numerous individuals who have contributed to this book, sometimes in ways of which they may not even be aware. While I cannot name and thank each person individually, please know that you have made a difference in my life. Of special note are certain people who directly made this book come to life. As mentioned earlier, Dr. Richard Ward, dean and director of Henry C. Lee College of Criminal Justice and Forensic Sciences at New Haven University, has from my earliest days as a police officer exposed me to the desire to grow academically and intellectually. In many ways, this is your book. You started this process. Due to your insight and tutelage, I have a much deeper sense of the gravity of terrorism in relation to public safety. Your insight and work product was and is an inspiration. I hope this book reflects well on your instruction. If it does not, it is my shortfalls, not your instruction, that are culpable.

In addition, I want to thank my doctoral dissertation committee for their help in framing my earlier work. This work has served as the framework for my life. Thanks so much to Drs. Wayne Kerstetter, Jess Maghan, Melissa Marschall, Evan McKenzie, and particularly the chairman, Richard Johnson. Your insights and direction were instrumental and most appreciated. Joseph N. DuCanto, Esq., also deserves special mention, as he provided a critical opportunity to me by serving as the general counsel of his security services firm. I learned a lot about the business of security and the legal exposures of such through the years I served your firm.

This same feeling relates to my friends and colleagues at Calumet College of St. Joseph. Of note are President Dennis Rittenmeyer, PhD; Vice President of Academic Affairs Daniel Lowery, PhD; Vice President of Development James Adducci, JD; Public Safety Program Chairman Michael McCafferty, JD; Public Safety Administration Director David Plebanski, PhD; Public Safety Management Director Dean Angelo, EdD; Assistant Professor Jeanette Shutay, PhD; Criminal Justice Program Director Allen Brown, JD; Paralegal Professor Michael Genova, JD; Public Safety Institute Director Geoff Anderson; Public Safety Institute Project Leader Nick Zivanovic; Director of Graduate Student Services Mary Severa; Director of Public Relations Linda Gajewski; Public Safety Management Academic Advisor John Battistella; former Academic Coordinator for Public Safety Roxann Brown; and Academic Coordinator for Public Safety Lynn Duimich. In addition, Professor Emeritus K. James McCaleb, PhD, deserves special note and consideration. Thanks to all of you!

To my friends and colleagues in security and policing, I wish you safety and Godspeed as you work to protect your clients, communities, and, ultimately, this country. There are simply too many people to name, but my respect and regards go out to you. In particular, my regards to those at the International Association of Professional Security Consultants (IAPSC), ASIS International, and the Illinois

Association of Chiefs of Police (IACP). I also want to personally thank a number of people I have the pleasure to work with at SecureLaw Ltd. These individuals include Thomas Elward; Steven J. Kovacik; Steven Scheckel; Doug Johnson; Daniel S. McDevitt; James Q. Gorman; Sean Ahrens; Anton Bommersbach; Thomas Braglia; Mark Brenzinger, PsyD; John M. Carpino; John E. Corey; Anthony DuCanto; Pete Floudas; Jack Halloran; S. Ronald Hauri; Arnette Heintze; James B. Jackson; David Jarmusz; Michael Mealer, JD; Edward Mirabelli; David E. Olson, PhD; Mark E. Powers; David Ramos; Tony Ramos; Anthony L. Richardson; Henry P. Rush; Vincent M. Russo, JD; William Shaver, JD; Todd Sherman; Scott Soltis; Garnett F. Watson; Howard Wood; and Rechelle Wooden. To these individuals I had the pleasure to work with, your work product and knowledge were both professional and insightful.

My regards, of course, to those at Taylor & Francis; I appreciate your confidence in this work. Of special consideration is Senior Editor Mark Listewnik, whom I had the pleasure to work with on two book projects. Mark, you are a thoughtful and dedicated professional. I enjoyed working with you. Finally, to Jay Margolis, project editor, and all other editors and support personnel, your help and work are most appreciated.

To my mother and family, thanks for all your help over the years. You have been instrumental in developing my career and my character. My regards are also with my late father, for his extraordinary work ethic. How can you ever adequately thank your family?

Finally, and most dearly, thanks to my wife, Rose Ann. You have been with me through many years of struggles. Only you know what this entails. It seems that each time we undertake another project, it challenges us to be better people and a closer couple. While it does not get any easier, I would not have done it any other way. Your help, encouragement, and support make it both possible and more worthwhile. My thanks and love are with you. God bless you Mi Amor!

James F. Pastor, PhD, JD
Lemont, Illinois

About the Author

James F. Pastor, PhD, JD, is a nationally recognized authority on public safety and security. He is the president of SecureLaw Ltd., a public safety and security consulting firm. He is also associate professor of public safety at Calumet College of St. Joseph.

Dr. Pastor is a frequent contributor to the media and has presented in numerous national and regional conferences on public safety and security issues. He also provides training, expert witness, and consulting services in premises liability, public safety management assessments, security policy development and audits, crisis and risk management, public–private policing, and terrorism. The common theme of these services relates to crime and misconduct and its attendant liability exposures. These topics are addressed in a critical and substantive manner, being conversant in both the conceptual and practical applications of public safety and security. Highlights of Dr. Pastor's experience and credentials include:

- PhD in public policy analysis, December 2001, from the University of Illinois at Chicago; dissertation titled "Assessing the Functional and Constitutional Implications of Private Security Patrols on Public Streets"
- JD from John Marshall Law School; licensed attorney in Illinois since May 1990
- MA in criminal justice from the University of Illinois at Chicago; thesis titled "A Critical Analysis of Terrorism"
- Associate professor in public safety programs at Calumet College of St. Joseph since June 2002
- Adjunct instructor for Security Technology at the International Law Enforcement Academy, which is a U.S. State Department funded program for police officials from countries throughout the world
- Eight years as adjunct faculty with Webster University (graduate program in security management where he teaches Legal and Ethical Issues in Security Management)
- Two years as adjunct faculty with Northwestern University–Center for Public Safety (Executive Management Program/Police Staff and Command where he taught several legal classes)

- Former legal counsel for two police unions (FOP and ICOPS), participating in hundreds of investigative interviews at OPS, IAD, and in other internal disciplinary forums, plus conducting approximately 300 depositions and 20 trials in police/fire commissions, merit boards, and the State Labor Board
- Former legal counsel for four security firms, including legal counsel/operational auditor for SecurityLink (which at the time was the largest privately held security alarm firm in the United States
- Former assistant department advocate for the Chicago Police Department dealing with police misconduct and discipline, including review of hundreds of use-of-force cases
- Former tactical police officer in the Gang Crime Enforcement Unit–Chicago Police Department
- Former security officer for The Art Institute of Chicago, The Ritz Carlton, the First Illinois Center, Lettuce Entertain You Restaurants, and several other environments
- Author of case book *Security Law and Methods,* Butterworth–Heinemann, 2006
- Author of *The Privatization of Police in America: An Analysis and Case Study*, McFarland and Company, 2003
- Author of chapter titled "Private Policing on Public Environments," in the ASIS International Protection of Assets (POA) manual, which is considered the "bible" of the security industry, published in January 2007
- Author of several articles on security, policing, and public safety

Contact:

SecureLaw Ltd.
Calumet College of St. Joseph
2400 New York Ave.
Whiting, IN 46394
Phone: 219-473-4353
Fax: 219-473-4356
www.CCSJ.edu
or
Phone: 312-423-6700
www.securelaw.info

TERRORISM AND EXTREMISM: CONCEPTS AND ISSUES

I

Chapter 1

Introduction

Obama Election and Attendant Circumstances

This book was largely drafted during the transition period between the historic election of Barack Obama and his inauguration as president of the United States. The election of Barack Obama was heralded worldwide as a transforming time for America. By any standard, this is true. Only in America can a man with Obama's obvious intellectual and political skills rise from almost obscurity into the position of the "leader of the free world." President Obama's personal story has inspired millions. He is a remarkable man with extraordinary skills. His election represents a rather dramatic shift from the insular, inarticulate, but incredibly focused Bush administration.

This history-making presidency will bring great excitement and great challenges. While economic issues dramatically rose in prominence during the final months of the presidential campaign, the significance of domestic and national security promises to be critical for the foreseeable future. Indeed, the economic crisis facing the United States may be a precursor for rising violence—and for the need to increase security. The devastating impact of the financial crisis coupled with economic woes in the banking system, auto industry, real estate, and the fate of the U.S. dollar will likely—and greatly—impact domestic and national security. These factors, and others, will drive an increase in the level of extremism that seems to be percolating just under the radar screen.

Even while these challenges play out, the U.S. population is extraordinarily excited about the prospects of the Obama Administration. While this excitement creates much momentum, it may lead to expectations that cannot be fulfilled. In fact, polling suggests that expectations are extraordinary. For example, a recent national poll suggested that most Americans think Barack Obama will make major accomplishments as president. Nearly two thirds of those questioned in a CNN/Opinion Research Corp. survey said President Barack Obama will change the country for the better. "The bar is being set awfully high for an Obama presidency," said CNN polling director Keating Holland, who added, "That's a pretty big to-do list." The internal data from the survey show that three quarters of those polled have a favorable view of Obama, with almost "perfect" support (99%) from black Americans, and a much less favorable rating (41%) from Republicans. Overall, Obama has a 75 percent favorable rating, making Obama the most popular president-elect in at least a quarter of a century.[1] The statistical impact of this phenomenon may be illustrated by doing a Google search for "great expectations" and "Obama". In doing so, about 229,000 references are found.[2]

In my mind, the basis for such support and these expectations are grounded in human nature. As humans, we crave for hope of a better life. Obama's campaign tapped into this craving. His campaign themes were basic, yet powerful: *hope* and *change*. These themes may demonstrate that the country has huge problems. The problems are so substantial that most intelligent people cringe at even attempting to articulate *the causes*. While it has become somewhat commonplace to "blame Bush," the reality is many of our contemporary problems are larger than Bush. Even assuming that Bush *is the cause* of our problems, I contend the solutions are so complex that to assume Obama is the "solution" is unfair to him or to any one person. Nonetheless, we all want justice. We all want prosperity. We all want peace. While it sometimes appears untrue, I believe we also want unity. We are seeking a strong leader to accomplish these needs. In Obama's election night speech, he directed us to these needs. He stated,[3]

> This is our chance to answer that call. This is our moment. This is our time—to put our people back to work and open doors of opportunity for our kids; to restore prosperity and promote the cause of peace; to reclaim the American Dream and reaffirm that fundamental truth—that out of many, we are one; that while we breathe, we hope, and where we are met with cynicism, and doubt, and those who tell us that we can't, we will respond with that timeless creed that sums up the spirit of a people.

The sentiment of this wonderful speech was awe inspiring. The crowd was in tears. People were happy. People were excited. It was truly an extraordinary time for America—even the world. In the end, the Obama campaign effectively turned the U.S. election into a *referendum* on hope. His victory, in my mind, is evidenced on just how strongly Americans yearn to invest in hope. The extent of this belief was illustrated in the weekend before the election. At a rally in Harlem, a state representative stumping for Obama led an enthusiastic crowd in this call-and-response:[4]

- "Who is going to lead us out of poverty?" *"Barack Obama!"*
- "Who is going to save the United States of America?" *"Barack Obama!"*
- "Who is going to save the entire world?" *"Barack Obama!"*

Beyond these worthy goals, the Obama campaign clothed itself in grandiosity. It seemed nothing was too complex to resolve. Indeed, the more eloquent the rhetoric and far-reaching the promises, the more his supporters hoped for his solutions. No problem was too great without a bold promise to solve it. Consider these promises from the campaign:[5]

> All nuclear material worldwide—safeguarded within four years. All nuclear weapons development—stopped. Afghanistan—solved. Al Qaeda—crushed. Darfur genocide—over. The Middle East peace process—brought to a safe, secure conclusion. World poverty—cut in half. Inner cities—revitalized. Immigration law—fixed. Health care—guaranteed for every American. Social Security—saved. Federal waste—eliminated. Taxes—cut for 95 percent of Americans. The economy—completely transformed. Carbon emissions—slashed. Energy crisis—solved.

While the reader may view these first few pages as a critique of the Obama campaign—or his presidency—the theme of this book is larger than Obama. My review of the campaign rhetoric is to illustrate that the problems are substantial. It is my intention to illustrate that the increase of hope may be related to the magnitude of the problems. In this sense, the *problems* become one of the themes of the book. The expectations of the American people, fairly or not, purposely or not, have become the mantle of the Obama Administration. In this way, the Obama campaign and his administration are impossible to ignore. This is due to both the historic nature of this campaign and the reaction of the American people. Many people see all this as great news. It certainly elicits high hopes. I hope these views are justified. It is my belief, however, we are on the verge of some very difficult and dangerous times. Due to the extent of problems facing this country, it is inevitable that reality will set in. Global crises will challenge the country and the administration. The financial meltdown will not go away any time soon. Indeed, I think it will get worse. The "fixes" will inevitably put the country into deeper and deeper debt. As Hilliker aptly said, "[W]hen these rains of adversity descend, and the floods and winds beat vehemently against people's hope, that hope will fall—because it is founded on sand."[6]

What changes are on the horizon in the Obama Administration and for America? I do not speak for the Obama Administration nor do I desire to portend the changes he will make. Instead, this book will discuss certain *implications* that I contend are inevitable. This is partly due to the historic nature of the Obama presidency, and partly due to the circumstances facing this country. In essence, I contend we are headed for the *perfect storm* that brings together historic events, a hostile worldwide movement, and a variety of extremist groups around domestic issues. Many, if not most, of the readers will not see this storm approaching. It is quite likely that many will view my vision as exceedingly negative—even fatalistic. Of course, my sense is that these negative terms are relative. I see future trends as simply explaining "reality." While my reality may differ from yours, let's agree on one obvious statement: Let the future events determine whose vision is correct, or at least, more accurate.

My vision is based on a worldview grounded on significant experiences and training. For example, I have been trained to assess "process." The term process is a shorthand way of describing the notion that things occur along a rather defined and often predictable path. In this way, the "secret" to seeing the future is to discern trends. Once trends are detected, the next assessment is to understand the likely causes of these trends, along with the implications of such. This process of identifying trends, their underlying causes (or at least likely causal factors), and the resultant implications are what shape my vision. In this sense, this public policy vision helps to discern the "big picture." I do not imply, however, that my vision is 20/20. Nonetheless, I attempt to paint the picture in a way that is both compelling and insightful.

Along with this public policy perspective, I have been trained as an attorney to focus on the details, and as a police officer to focus on the "street." From these varying levels, these experiences helped me become a "student of human nature." If one understands human nature, I believe you will understand what motivates and informs people. Simply stated, individual responses to stimuli are often quite predictable. In short, I will attempt to articulate the implications of increasing extremism that I see rising just below the surface of American society. Some of this extremist potential is based on international movements, while some are unique to America. In any case, I do not paint a pretty picture. To those with the "hope" of the Obama election resonating in your hearts and minds, this book may be difficult to swallow. I do not intend to upset or even disillusion any reader. Instead, I hope this book serves as a "wake-up call" to American society. This is especially true for those involved in policy making and to those who are involved in the provision of public safety services.

In this sense, this book looks to the basic motivators of people. From this perspective, people are predictable. When the rhetoric of the campaign ends and the policy implementation commences, then we will discern these motivations. Inevitably, policy decisions require "winners" and "losers." Who will benefit, who will be hurt? Since the problems are so great, this dynamic will intensify. Since the hope is so great, the expectations are magnified. In short, these historic times portend significant emotions and stakes. In the end, no matter what President Obama does, he will not be able to satisfy all. This is not new to politics. Indeed, the essence of politics is a battle of ideas. Many of these ideas are strongly held. As I will articulate later, there are many worldviews that are inherently conflicting. In my mind, these will result in conflict and violence. This violence will be increasingly founded on basic human distinctions: race, religion, and politics. Ironically, while many contend that the United States has entered into a "post-racial" society with the election of President Obama, I contend that some disconcerting trends are going in the opposite direction.

I will articulate how this will occur. I will articulate the likely "triggers" to such violence. I will articulate the response to such violence (and the threat of violence) from public safety providers. I will articulate the predictable societal response to this dynamic. In the end, I will illustrate the problem from the street or at the "target" level. At this level, the threat of extremist violence and terrorism may require a basic change in the nature of policing. As retractable as terrorism seems, we must remind ourselves that this problem also represents an opportunity for effective change. Consequently, this circumstance asks the reader to make a paradigm shift related to the nature of policing.

Those who have studied policing will agree that there is an age-old adage where the optimal level of security is to have a "police officer on every block." This "goal" is considered both desirable and unattainable. Indeed, during heightened threats we tend to look for police officers and other authority figures to calm our fears, and to provide a sense of security. This may explain why so many people have such great expectations for Obama. His leadership gives them hope for their future. This is based on the desire for a better life. However, in order to have a better life, one needs a stable and secure society. Unfortunately, we seem to live in an era where communicated threats and sensational media coverage of "successful" terrorist acts are commonplace. This is likely to continue—and become much more intense—for many years to come. The cumulative effect of this will have a great impact on how we understand and practice policing. In turn, it will have substantial societal implications.

Premises of the Book

This book addresses two predicted premises: terrorism and extremist violence will increase, and this increase will change policing. The change in policing will center on pragmatic responses to these larger trends. This dynamic has implications upon the larger society. Let me first explain the big picture, and then try to flesh out the details.

In developing this book, it is necessary to set the tone by articulating a number of premises. First, terrorism by its nature is political. This premise is based, at least partly, on the fact that all terrorism campaigns are designed to achieve some political end. The specific goals may be narrow, such as stopping abortion, or very broad, such as the establishment of a worldwide revolution or a worldwide caliphate. In any case, those who study and seek to stop terrorism will inevitably have different opinions as how to address it. Typically the "solutions" proffered by different thinkers or policy makers reflect their particular belief as to what is causing the violence, or how best to minimize or negate it. These differences help create divisions within the affected government, and in the larger society.

This brings us to the second premise. Terrorism is designed to foster division within society.[7] In this sense, they—the terrorists—are winning the "war on terrorism." Unfortunately, the American public is largely unaware of this assertion. I believe they fail to understand on two significant levels: conceptually and politically. Conceptually most people fail to realize that one key goal of terrorism is to divide people from each other, and the government from its citizens. If we truly understood this dynamic, I believe we would temper our thinking as it relates to terrorism. Part of the reason this fact has not been better understood is due to the second factor—politics. Because terrorism has become a "political lightning rod," people tend to see terrorism along ideological and political lines. Stated in a different way, Republicans see it one way, while Democrats see it another. It does not have to be this way. Indeed, for the sake of the country, it *should not* be this way. Unfortunately, we are in a time when it is hard to flesh out policy distinctions without being "political."

In saying this, let me attempt to broadly characterize the key distinctions between the parties. The respective parties tend to view terrorism in the ways shown in Table 1.1. Looking at these general distinctions, some explanation may be necessary to help communicate my points. One caveat is appropriate. I developed these distinctions with an understanding that they are not definitive. Instead, they seek to explain a tendency. Democrats tend to view terrorism as "crime," so their response is more likely to be based on police investigations, prosecution for illegal acts, and imprisonment, if convicted. The response to terrorist acts during the Clinton administration tended to fit this approach. Republicans, on the other hand, tend to see terrorism as war, using the military term "asymmetric warfare,"[8] to describe its overall approach. This distinction is illustrated by asking this question: Is terrorism a criminal justice problem or a national security problem? I believe this basic but profound distinction informs the response to the problem of terrorism. While this distinction does not imply a political orientation, yet in the contemporary society, it is often implied.

If you see it as "crime," you would quite naturally worry more about maintaining the "rights" of those charged with the offense. Similarly, you would worry about

Table 1.1　Political Distinctions

Democrats	Republicans
Crime	War
Defensive	Offensive
Rights	Security

Copyright, James F. Pastor, 2009.

the civil and constitutional rights of the larger society. Conversely, those who see it as "war" see policy preferences directed toward the security of the larger society. They are less concerned with the rights of the warriors, or even the rights of citizens. In this view, security trumps rights.[9] In the end, this distinction boils down to life being held as more critical, or valuable, than rights. Yungher calls this distinction between crime and war the "big dilemma." He argues that if you see it as crime, then the typical terrorist support network is extraordinarily difficult to resolve. Consider that these networks are made up of 30–50 people. They conduct such varying functions from financing, recruitment, intelligence, reconnaissance, transportation, weapons and explosive acquisition, and the actual attack. Yungher contends that the difficulties related to breaking up these networks through the justice process alone are immense. He adds this pointed assertion to the distinction:[10]

> [T]he tension between the restraints of law, and the desire to behave as
> if in a war is at the heart of the challenge of fighting terrorism because
> it threatens a free society's legalistic view of conflict management.

I think it is fair to say that much of the criticism of the Bush Administration deals with Bush's tendency to view terrorism as "war." With this worldview, Bush had a difficult time balancing the notion of crime versus war. This can partly explain the decision to keep prisoners in Guantánamo Bay. If your see "the war on terrorism" as war, this detention facility is simply a place where the enemy is kept until the war is over. Conversely, if you see terrorism as "crime," then you would worry about the rights of the prisoners. You would desire to adjudicate their case, prosecute them for their crimes—and imprison them if convicted. Of course, if the "evidence" is not sufficient to "convict" them, then they should be released from custody. In these very different worldviews the nature of the challenge is made clear. Are we fighting a war? Are we pursing criminals? Is it possible we are doing both?

Judge Richard Posner of the Seventh Circuit Court of Appeals, and professor at the University of Chicago Law School, attempts to "thread the needle" to achieve this delicate balance. He offers a thoughtful approach to the threat of terrorism. Posner argues that terrorist activity is sui generis—it is neither "war" nor "crime." Instead of these "either-or distinctions," he asserts that terrorism demands a tailored response, one that gives terror suspects fewer constitutional rights than persons suspected of ordinary criminal activity. He argues that when facing terrorism, the scope of constitutional rights must be adjusted in a pragmatic but rational manner. He advocates using a cost-benefit analysis. This analysis would balance the harm new security measures inflict on personal liberty against the increased security those measures provide. In this analysis, Posner comes down, in most but not quite all respects, on the side of increased government power.[11]

Now think about the "debate" in the country around this security versus rights distinction. A classic example of how this plays out can be seen in the executive order issued by President Bush, which allowed the National Security Agency to conduct eavesdropping of overseas calls.[12] In this arrangement, the essence of the eavesdropping was done by the use of sophisticated wiretaps. The Democrats, along with much of the media, articulated their "principled" defense of what they characterized as "domestic spying." The Bush Administration, as seemed consistent with his overall administration, presented a rather tepid defense of its own policy. The "explanation" of the policy was basically limited to a simple characterization of their approach: *terrorist surveillance.* Now take a step back. If you believe that the government was conducting "domestic spying," would you be inclined to support this arrangement? Conversely, if you believe that the government was conducting "terrorist surveillance," how much more likely would you be to support this policy decision? Consequently, in many cases, the key assessment of what is "good" versus what is "bad" is based more on rhetoric than substance. In the end, how the government, or the opposition party, characterizes its policy is likely to be based more on how it is communicated, and on the biases surrounding those who speak and hear the communication. This is the unfortunate nature of terrorism.

The defensive versus offensive distinction between the parties also relates to these biases. If you believe, as the Democrats typically do, that we should protect ourselves and avoid being enmeshed in foreign entanglements, then you would quite naturally seek a defensive posture against terrorism. In this worldview, the key is to defend American soil, and American interests, without being too aggressive against foreign states. Hence, the mantra of diplomacy and the avoidance of "unilateral" action inform their policy decisions. Conversely, if you believe the right approach is to "take the fight" to the terrorists, then an offensive, even preemptive policy is seen as the better approach.

In the end, I think understanding these tendencies helps to separate the notion that one party is "good" while the other party is "bad." These artificial and simplistic distinctions do nothing to further the debate, nor do they inform the populace in any meaningful way. Indeed, these distinctions are dangerous and help those who seek to divide and destroy this country. In this light, *neither* party is innocent. To those hard "Rs" or those hard "Ds," I ask you to get over yourself! If you believe that the other party is the enemy, then we have already lost the fight. In the end, whether you are a Democrat or a Republican matters little to those who view America as the "Great Satan" and its citizens as "infidels." You can die just the same! As I instruct my students, those who study and counter the threat of terrorism need to "keep their bias in check," while addressing the complicated remedies that seek the "right" balance.

In my mind, the key principles that are going to drive the debate—and future decision making—are the competing principles of security versus rights. Both of these principles are critical. Both are vital to this country. Regardless of what any politician or other "expert" may assert, the fact is you cannot achieve maximum levels of these principles. Indeed, at some point, the need for security will undermine the need for rights—and vice versa. Of course, this is nothing new to the American system. We have long understood, for example, that one cannot indiscriminately yell fire in a crowded theater. The limitation of an individual's First Amendment right to free speech must be balanced with the public safety of his or her fellow citizens. Finding the appropriate balance, however, has been difficult in the political and social climate around terrorism.[13] It will not get any easier. This is particularly relevant if we cannot even agree on who or what we are "fighting," and whether there is even a threat or an "enemy" to fight.

This brings us to another premise. This relates to the "war on terrorism." In my mind, one of the most critical lessons we need to understand is that terrorism is a "technique," it is not an enemy.[14] We cannot fight a technique. We cannot win a war against a technique. We cannot galvanize a population against a technique. We cannot sustain a generational conflict against a technique. Simply stated, we will not, nor cannot, fight against a technique. We are in a box. Indeed, this is a very deep and complicated box.[15] Let me try to flesh out why we got here and what we can do about it. Unfortunately, my explanation will be more helpful on the former point than on the latter.

In the days following 9/11, the Bush Administration had to make a very difficult decision. This decision was how to characterize the enemy or the offenders. Were we victims of a crime? Indeed, it was a very big, deadly, and devastating crime. This is how the Clinton Administration viewed the first World Trade Center attack—as well as each other terrorist attack during his administration. Conversely, were we attacked by a foreign enemy as an act of war? Significantly, Bush saw it as war. While I agree with this characterization, this does not end the dilemma.

It is clear that those who committed the tragic acts of terrorism on that day (assuming, of course, that you do not buy into the 9/11 conspiracy theories), the problem for the Bush Administration was how to explain the enemy to the American people. While those who committed the acts did so to advance a radical Islamic worldview, the administration could not simply state the war was against radical Islamists. One may ask, why not? Why not simply say who the enemy was? The answer is as follows. To name the enemy as such would "justify" those furthering the war that the battle was, indeed, against Islam. In essence, the radical Islamists *want* the war to be against Islam. This is one critical way they "sell" the need to fight the battle to the vast number of Muslims who reject the radical views of the Islamists. Hence, characterizing the war as against "radical Islam," as it rightly is, would have the detrimental effect of furthering the aims of the Islamists. To be clear, the Islamists are a small percentage of Muslims who desire to "cleanse" their religion—and the world—of practices and beliefs inconsistent with Allah's purpose. If we say that the war is against "radical Islam," the distinction between radical *and* Islam would be lost. The inevitable conclusion would be the war is against Islam. We cannot afford to allow this characterization to exist.

The Bush Administration *by inference* seems to agree with this assertion. In its *National Strategy for Homeland Security*, the document notes that "the 'War on Terror' is a different kind of war—not only a battle of arms but also a battle of ideas. Accordingly, we are advancing effective democracy as the antidote to the ideology of our enemies. ..."[16]

With this in mind, the Bush Administration made the decision to declare a "war on terrorism." This is not only wrong, it is dangerous. Let's start with being wrong. First, if we are in a war on terrorism, why have we not invaded Sri Lanka in order to stamp out the Tamil Tigers? If you ask the average American who or what the Tamil Tigers are, you will likely get a blank look. Indeed, I ask my police officer students the same question. Typically one or two students are able to correctly answer the question. A correct answer is that the Tamil Tigers have killed as many people, or more, than any other terrorist group in the world over the past three decades.[17] Most people would agree that a terrorist group with such a deadly history and capacity should be a focal point on the "war on terrorism." Of course, they are not a focal point in our war. Indeed, they are hardly on the radar screen.

The problem, therefore, rests on how to declare war on an enemy we cannot name, while simultaneously defeating this enemy. I do not have a good answer to this dilemma. Nor have I heard one from a politician—in either party. The best the Democrats seem to muster is to talk about "fighting" al Qaeda. As will be discussed in some detail, the problem is that the enemy is larger than al Qaeda. The enemy is a movement of radical Islamists. To characterize it any other way diminishes the nature of the enemy. Hence, the Democrats offer little in terms of a solution. Indeed, they tend to minimize the danger by characterizing the enemy as "al Qaeda."[18]

Unfortunately, we have been down this road before. Similar political rhetoric has been used in the "War on Poverty," the "War on Drugs," and the "War on Gangs." Each one of these "wars" is still being fought, without any end in sight. With these "shining" examples of political correctness, we enter into another "war" without a definition and without an end in sight. In an almost pathetic duplicity evidenced by the party that brought us the "War on Poverty," the leaders of the Democratic party complain about taking our eye off al Qaeda during the war in Iraq, and about the failure of the Bush Administration to articulate an "exit strategy" in Iraq. What is our "exit strategy" in the "War on Poverty"? Socialism? What is our "exit strategy" in the "War on Drugs"? Legalization? What is our "exit strategy" in the "War on Gangs"? Another march down another street? Consequently, the "answer" to the "war on terrorism" is as complex as the answers to these other "wars."

In a desire to conceptualize this dilemma, I developed the graphic shown in Figure 1.1 to illustrate the thinking of each party versus the realities of the situation. For example, on the left side of the graphic, the *enemy* to the Democrats is "al Qaeda," and the *enemy* to the Republicans as the ambiguous term "terrorists." In the middle of the graphic, the situation in *Iraq* is characterized by the Democrats as a "civil war,"[19] and to the Republicans as—again—the ambiguous term "war on terrorism." On the right side of the graphic, I believe the reality is as follows: The *enemy* in Iraq and in the larger world is the radical Islamic movement. It is conceptualized as a worldview, or as a "mindset." This movement is best illustrated by al

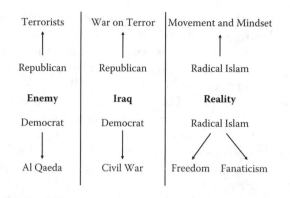

Figure 1.1 Political rhetoric versus reality.

Qaeda and Iran. But it is not limited to these alternatives. Indeed, it is a worldwide movement, with the two most prominent examples being al Qaeda and Iran. The solution to this dilemma is to further freedom over fanaticism. It is to advocate and advance the principles of freedom versus the chains of fanaticism. In Iraq and in the larger worldwide movement, the only solution, in my mind, is for freedom to prevail over fanaticism. How is this to occur? It requires a multifaceted approach that balances the key principles discussed above: security versus rights, crime versus war, defensive versus offensive. Of course, this also includes larger solutions relating to economics, public relations, foreign policies, and the like.

This leads me to the overall theme of this book, that is, terrorism and the rise of extremist violence will create many implications within American society—including changing the model of policing used to protect society. Before I delve into these implications, let me set the record on my approach to these issues. It is important for the reader to understand that I recognize my worldview informs my thinking of these complex subjects. For "full disclosure," my biases are as follows: conservative, security over rights, pro police, truth and righteousness over blood/race/party, American, and Christian. Specifically, I tend to think and vote conservative. Unlike some people, however, I do not believe the other side—read liberals or "progressives"—are bad people. Instead, they see the world differently than I do. I believe they are serious, but often wrong, in their worldview. Further, while I am an attorney, I tend to hold security more dearly than rights. This does not mean that I ignore my rights—or your rights. I simply tend to err on the side of security. This is particularly true when the threat of danger is real. I believe the threat is real. Hence, my "balance" will tilt toward security.

I also tend to give the benefit of the doubt to the police. I believe the police have an extraordinarily difficult job. They put their lives on the line each day. They have one of the few jobs in civil society where they are *expected* to confront dangerous people and situations. Unfortunately, poor decisions are sometimes made. Unfortunately, bad people are sometimes employed as the "police." Notwithstanding these facts,

I advocate for the police. I desire to help them achieve ever-increasing professionalism. Similarly, I advocate truth and righteousness over other "interests." That means my family, my race, my party, my country, and my religion are subordinate to what is true and what is right. While it is sometimes difficult to discern truth and righteousness, this principle must win the day. At the very least, I maintain an open mind to discern these goals. I believe we cannot have our minds clouded by interests—even when we so closely identify with them. Indeed, one of the reasons why I think this country is in trouble is due to our inability to see through the guise—and the selfishness—of our self-interests. If we are willing to subordinate our interests for the larger good, than we can get past these troubles. If not, we will balkanize ourselves around group interests. In this sense, I often ask the question, Are you part of the problem or the solution?

Finally, the notion of being a sovereign citizen of the American dream cannot be overstated. I have great faith in the American experiment. I have great regard for the millions of people who populate this country—and who have served and died for this country. Further, I realize that many people in the world do not like Americans. Unlike the current mantra, I do not believe this started with the Bush Administration. While Bush has certainly angered people around the world, he also has attempted to protect this country. Think back to 2004 when the war in Iraq was going badly. Bush was roundly criticized by Democratic leaders, the media, and by leaders from around the world—particularly our "allies" in Europe. Watch Europe in 2009 and beyond. The continent has taken a clear turn toward the right. The leadership of most countries is now conservative. I contend that they realize they are facing multiple threats. The continent is reacting. Hence, was the earlier criticism based on politics from leaders of a different political worldview, or was it based on something else?

I contend that because America is the "leader" of the world, people will inevitably criticize us. In this sense, I am informed by an old song by Three Dog Night titled *One*. Remember the familiar refrain, "One is the loneliest number"? The song implied that those on top are ostracized. It speaks to the negative side of human nature. We are "hard wired" to be jealous, envious, and resentful of those who are in a dominant position. Beyond these individual traits, universal competition is also fostered due to these same factors. In addition, other factors including political ideologies and partisan divisiveness also help create competition. These also include ethnic, racial, and religious distinctions. These distinctions are exacerbated by competition over limited resources, historical and geographic disputes, and a host of other factors. Indeed, like individuals, groups and countries tend to be self-interested. Despite the often simplistic mantras related to "diplomacy" and "communication," these factors leading to competition are more difficult to resolve than they are to mouth.

Unfortunately, most Americans tend to be myopic. We tend to see the world through an American perspective. Indeed, many Americans know very little of what is happening in this world. Many seem to not even care. This is partly because the media tells us what they want us to hear. The message from the media has largely been that it is the United States' fault (read Bush) for our international challenges. I think this is simplistic. All countries operate out of their self-interests. Do we have the ability to convince each country that their self-interests coincide with ours? I doubt it. In short, we have real enemies, both from states and from movements. Can the Obama Administration fix this situation? I say no. Not because of some deficiency of President Obama. Instead, the problem is our ability to operate in an increasingly complex and competitive world. Of course, this is a world that does not necessarily seek the interests of America and Americans.

Indeed, world leaders have already commenced criticism against Obama—before he is even sworn into office. Consider this example. Venezuelan President Chávez stated that Obama had "the same stench" as President Bush, who was a frequent target of Chávez's remarks. The Venezuelan leader contends that Obama is following orders from dark forces inside "the empire" (the United States). Chávez then offered this bombshell: "If he doesn't obey the orders of the empire, they'll kill him." Chávez offered this "pointed critique" of the then president elect without any details or proof. Does this sound like the start of a fruitful relationship? Are these bombshells a sign of things to come? These criticisms were in response to Obama's earlier assertion that Chávez had "been a force that has interrupted progress in the region." Obama also raised the issue of Chávez's relationship with the Revolutionary Armed Forces of Columbia (FARC).[20]

Finally, I am a Christian. I do not hide nor will I apologize for my faith. Indeed, my faith is my most powerful driver. I am motivated by God's purpose in my life. My faith, however, should not be confused with religion. Every organized religion has traditions and beliefs that need to be examined. I readily examine these. I also examine my heart and mind. I believe we all must do the same. However, since many in the United States have no sense of God—or actively deny that there is a God—I contend we are at a distinct disadvantage to those who not only acknowledge their God, but are willing to die for Him. Because many in this country are not cognizant of a greater being—a God—we will be hard-pressed to understand that the Islamists see the battle as a "Holy War." As will be fleshed out later, I believe the battle is, indeed, a "Holy War." While I understand this will make some uncomfortable—even offend some—I am a great believer in understanding one's enemy. We would be well served to follow this centuries-old adage.

In my mind, it is important to be up front on these biases, since the subject of terrorism is inherently subjective. The adage of "one man's terrorist is another man's freedom fighter," is consistent with the effects of bias on this subject. That being said, I try to live by my admonition to my students: "Keep your bias in check." In the development of this book, I did my best to adhere to this standard. You can be the judge as to whether I succeeded in objectively analyzing this subject.

While you assess my objectivity, I also ask you to assess your biases. We all bring our own set of experiences, opinions, and interests to this subject. We must acknowledge how our worldview and biases affect our thinking. I will challenge some basic aspects of contemporary American society. I do so because I believe that particular idiosyncrasies of American society will foster terrorism and extremist violence. I will make the best case I can to illustrate how certain aspects of American society will give rise to such violence. In doing so, I may make you uncomfortable, even angry. Although I do not intend to do so, in some manner, I do not care if I do. I believe there is simply too much at stake to "sugarcoat" the issue. As such, I will not worry about being politically correct. Indeed, I am not politically correct. I do not speak to the masses. I speak to those who are in the "trenches," including those who are fortunate enough to lead those in the front lines of this "war."

While you read this book, please be cognizant of your thinking. Are you being an objective and critical thinker? Do you think as an individual? Or do you see the world as member of some group? It does not matter if your "group" is racial, ethnic, political, religious, sexual, or gender based. If you practice "group think," then I respectfully assert that you are being manipulated by the media, the politicians, and other "leaders" who seek to advance their cause. This is often at the expense of your interests and of the larger society. Because terrorism and extremist violence are often used to advance these interests, it is important that you view the world with your "eyes wide open." Hopefully this book will help provide a perspective to distinguish and discern the critical issues facing this country.

To those who view terrorism simply by the tragic events of 9/11, this book will seem overly pessimistic, even gloomy. It is my belief that much of the American public, even many police officers, simply do not understand terrorism. Although this book relates to the effects of terrorism, I do not presume to characterize this book as an in-depth analysis of terrorism. There are many more substantive books on the subject of terrorism. Instead, the focus of this book is on the effects of terrorism and extremist violence on policing techniques, the policing model, and its implications for society. This is not to say that the reader will not be exposed to aspects of terrorism. I believe the analysis of terrorism contained in this book is important, even rather unique. With this said, let's look at the issues relevant to terrorism and policing.

Terrorism and Extremism Premises

Please allow me to establish some basic premises. These premises are designed to explain my thinking, building upon basic concepts contained in the terrorist literature. These premises can be outlined as follows:

- Terrorism is *not* just radical Islam.
- Radical Islam is larger than al Qaeda.
- Radical Islam is *a* or *the* trigger to increased extremism.
- Extremist ideologies are increasing.
- Extremist ideologies *will* foster increased violence.

■ Increased violence *will* result in counterviolence by opposing groups/ideologies.
■ Counterterrorism requires a "paradigm shift" in policing.

Each of these premises requires some explanation—as they form the intellectual basis of this book. First, the notion that terrorism is not just radical Islam should be self-evident to those with even a basic understanding of terrorism.[21] Numerous non-Islamic groups have been labeled as "terrorist" organizations. They range from left-wing groups such as FARC, the Weather Underground, Armed Forces of National Liberation (FALN), Shining Path, MS-13, and countless others. Right-wing groups also abound, such as the Ku Klux Klan (KKK), sovereign citizens, skinheads, militias, and various Nazi and/or national socialist groups. Other terrorist organizations and ideologies, such as single interest groups of Earth Liberation Front (ELF), Animal Liberation Front (ALF), and the Party of God, have a substantial capacity for direct action. Indeed, the Federal Bureau of Investigation (FBI) asserts that the most active terrorist groups in the United States are ELF/ALF.[22] Additional groups and ideologies include racial and nationalistic religious groups such as the Aryan Brotherhood, the New Black Panthers, and others. Simply stated, terrorists come in all colors, ideologies, and beliefs. They are most certainly not confined to a narrow "Islamic" worldview.

Similarly, those who view radical Islamic terrorism as al Qaeda are not accurately understanding the nature of this threat. The actions and ideology of al Qaeda do not preclude other groups with a similar Islamic worldview. Indeed, al Qaeda, which means "the base," was designed to act as the foundation of a worldwide movement of like-minded radical Islamic groups.[23] It was designed to serve as the umbrella organization for a worldwide network that includes many Sunni Islamic extremist groups, such as Egyptian Islamic Jihad, al-Gama'at al-Islamiyya, the Islamic Movement of Uzbekistan, and the Harakat ul-Mujahidin.[24] Other Islamic groups, some of which have more narrow—but related—goals, include Palestine Liberation Front (PLF), Hamas (Islamic Resistance Movement), Hezbollah (Party of God, aka Islamic Jihad), Palestine Islamic Jihad (PIJ), Jaish-e-Mohammed (JEM), Abu Sayyaf Group (ASG), and the Muslim Brotherhood, who in many respects was the "inspiration" of the contemporary Islam movement. Each of these groups is related to but separate from al Qaeda.[25] Indeed, the creed of the Muslim Brotherhood speaks volumes: "Allah is our goal, the Messenger is our leader, the Qur'an is our constitution, Jihad is our path, and death in the service of Allah our highest hope."[26] This creed is consistent with the basis ideology of numerous Islamic radical groups.

Based on these illustrative groups, even the casual observer would be hard-pressed to attribute "Islamic terrorism" to a simple characterization as "al Qaeda." Unfortunately, many in our society make this mistake. While the impact of al Qaeda upon American society has been substantial, I contend it represents more of the "symptom" as opposed to the source of the problem. The larger problem is the radical Islamic movement. As dangerous as this movement is, however, Islamic radical groups by themselves cannot achieve their larger goal: the destruction of the Great Satan (the United States) and the formation of a worldwide caliphate (Islamic government). It is my opinion that regardless of the dangers posed by radical Islamists, they need help to achieve these substantial goals. Their "help" is likely to come from the wide spectrum of extremist groups that have one underlying objective: take down the American government or, more generally, the worldwide capitalistic system.

This assertion fosters another threat: opposing and allied racial, ideological, and nationalist groups residing within America. This is where it gets "interesting." Because of 9/11, most Americans understand the threat of al Qaeda. The fact that al Qaeda is a radical Islamic group is also understood by some percentage of Americans who have some sense of the larger Islamic movement. However, the potential for inter-group conflicts with competing ideologies is largely invisible to the average American. Indeed, this vision is even missing from most of my students, who are mostly active police officers in Chicago and its metropolitan area. The evidence that group conflict is forthcoming is still rather vague. However, given the history of racial strife, given the combustive mixture of race, religion, and politics that underlies terrorist ideologies, I see inter-group conflict as not only likely, but inevitable. While I will have a lot more to say on this issue later in the book, some interesting connections between race, religion, and politics can be illustrated in these examples:

- During the presidential campaign of 2008, a number of conspiracies were uncovered that allegedly sought to assassinate Barack Obama. These include two men—one with ties to the Southern White Alliance, an offshoot of the Imperial Klans of America—who were arrested in October and charged with conspiring to threaten and kill African Americans. Daniel G. Cowart and Paul M. Schlesselman carried a short-barreled shotgun, a .357-caliber handgun, and cases of ammunition across state lines as part of the alleged plot.[27]
- William A. White, who calls himself the commander of the American National Socialist Workers Party, sent letters laced with racial epithets and swastikas to the homes of black tenants involved in a housing discrimination lawsuit, according to a seven-count indictment. Shortly before he was taken into custody in mid-October, White posted on his Web site a photo of Obama "with cross-hairs taking the form of a swastika" over his face.[28]
- Local police in southern California believe five recent attacks on minorities may stem from a backlash to the election of Barack Obama as the first black president in U.S. history. These attacks and rhetoric from a white supremacist group that was involved in the beatings are said to be part of a larger insurgence of hate groups throughout the nation.[29]
- Three men, one of who told investigators that he "was angry that the country was going to have an African-American president and that 'blacks and Puerto

Ricans' would now have more rights than whites" admitted to burning down the Macedonia Church of God in Christ, a predominantly black church.[30]

■ In February 2008, a Columbia, Tennessee, mosque was destroyed by a fire that appears to have been caused by arson. Investigators found drawings of swastikas and other graffiti at the Islamic Center of Columbia, said Special Agent Eric Kehn of the Bureau of Alcohol, Tobacco, Firearms, and Explosives. The graffiti included the words "white power" and "we run the world," said Daoud Abudiab, president of the center. The federal complaint asserts that two of the individuals arrested were members of the Christian Identity movement, an extreme doctrine that claims white people are God's chosen people.[31]

■ In September 2007, the Jena Six controversy in Louisiana led to significant racial strife, including some pointed language from a radical Web site:[32]

The harsh prison sentences hanging of the six are all too familiar for millions of working people caught up in the capitalist "justice" system. ... Racism permeates the entire capitalist system. In the workplace, the employers profit from paying Blacks less and forcing them into the dirtiest, most dangerous jobs. This discrimination helps drag down the working conditions of all workers. Bosses foster anti-Black prejudices in an attempt to keep the class divided and to prevent workers from fighting together for better conditions.

■ In response to this inflammatory rhetoric, a white supremacist Web site purported to list the addresses of five of the six black teenagers accused of beating a white student in the small town of Jena, and "essentially called for their lynching," an FBI spokeswoman said.[33]

■ In May 2007, al Qaeda operational leader al-Zawahiri stated,[34]

Al Qaeda is not merely for the benefit of Muslims, that's why I want blacks in America, people of color, American Indians, Hispanics, and all the weak and oppressed in North and South America, in Africa and Asia, and all over the world, to know that when we wage Jihad in Allah's path, we aren't waging Jihad to lift oppression from the Muslims only, we are waging Jihad to lift oppression from all mankind, because Allah has ordered us never to accept oppression, whatever it may be.

■ On September 17, 2001, just days after 9/11, in a sermon from Trinity United Church of Christ, Reverend Dr. Jeremiah A. Wright, the pastor and "spiritual advisor" of Barack Obama, stated,[35]

We bombed Hiroshima, we bombed Nagasaki, and we nuked far more than the thousands in New York and the Pentagon, and we never batted

> an eye. We have supported state terrorism against the Palestinians and black South Africans, and now we are indignant because the stuff we have done overseas is now brought right back to our own front yards. America's chickens are coming home to roost.

Some will surely argue that these examples are simply isolated incidents, having little consequence to the larger relations within society. I hope they are right. I doubt that they are. This is due to a couple of factors. First, these examples, while admittedly somewhat small in number, raise the possibility of significant divisions within society. These examples seek to "fuel the fire" of racial, religious, and political divisions, which unfortunately seem to lie much too close to the surface of American experience. Even if some say these examples are not meant to "fuel the fire," one is hard-pressed not to admit that some will inevitably view them as such. Indeed, one person no one will deny seeks to fuel the fire, Osama bin Laden, has clearly advocated an ideology designed to foster division within society—and against the capitalistic system.

Prior to Obama's election, the political and social framework was greatly divided. The last two presidential elections revealed an almost "perfect" split of the political parties. Even the Obama election did not substantially shift this divide. In my mind, the bitterness evidenced by the parties—and some key politicians—do not bode well for cooperation and cohesiveness going forward. To complicate an already combustible mix, the campaign of Barack Obama has created an almost unique set of circumstances in American history. On one hand, he is the forerunner of potentially many black individuals who have a legitimate chance to be the president of this country. This is truly a dramatic and historic part of the American narrative, illustrating how far we have come as a country. On the other hand, some in this country are not ready for this circumstance—on both sides of the fence. White supremacists will not like it. They are likely to become increasingly embittered. Conversely, black nationalists, coupled with a parade of "race hustlers," are likely to view Obama's public policy critics as "further evidence" of the widespread racism in American society.

One can get a sense of these potential implications by assessing the response from Trinity United Church of Christ (Dr. Wright's former church) following the criticism of his sermons. In its Web-based response, the church stated[36] (emphasis added),

> Reverend Dr. Jeremiah A. Wright's character is being *assassinated* in the public sphere because he has preached a social gospel on behalf of women, children and men in America and around the globe. This is an *attack* on the legacy of the African-American church, which led and continues to lead the fight for human rights in America and around the world. The African-American church community continues to face bomb threats, death threats, and their ministers' characters are *assassinated* because they teach and preach prophetic social concerns for social justice.

Please note the italicized words in this statement. While I italicized them for effect, I think it is fair to say that the language illustrates a defensive, even acute posture. Is there a way to reconcile pointed criticism of preacher with those of his church, who naturally desire to defend his views and his integrity? I cannot think of an easy solution to this circumstance. Some will argue that the criticism was taken "out of context" or was unjustified based on a long history of service to the community. Others will assert that Dr. Wright's statements were so inflammatory that Barack Obama should not have been associated with the pastor or his church. In short, the connection of Obama to this church will not be "forgotten" by some. The fact that John McCain—and the larger media—largely deemed this irrelevant during the campaign is, to some, also irrelevant. As I will articulate in detail later, the combustible mix of race, religion, and politics is likely to become increasingly important in the years ahead. This is true even if President Obama is deemed to "succeed" as president. In short, this mixture is likely to further exacerbate tenuous racial relations. These examples, of course, do not include the impact of any "direct action" against Obama. Any such action, whether by political maneuvering or in physical violence, would be a dramatic blow to the American system.

These examples, therefore, are but the "tip of the iceberg" of what this country is facing. Consider the impact that economic and societal factors will have on the country. For example, rising unemployment; rising costs of food, oil, gas, and other commodities; a shaky stock market and currency; underfunded pensions; falling housing market and home values; a neglected or even crumbling infrastructure; a faltering educational system; declining values and cultural standards; and the wars in Iraq and Afghanistan—to name but a few of the challenges currently facing this country. Please understand that I am not advocating that the country cannot overcome these challenges. Please also realize that I do not fancy myself as an expert on each of these diverse and complicated issues. Being trained in public policy analysis, however, I think I can see the "big picture" quite well. The picture does not look good. Can we, with the "right" approach and the "right" solutions, find a way to maneuver through the public policy challenges that befall this country? Sure we can. We have done it before. Does that mean, however, we can do it this time? This is particularly problematic given these daunting challenges have come together like the "perfect storm."

This book is not designed to "answer" these larger questions. It is designed to address the rise in terrorism and extremism. From my perspective, whether or not we are able to maneuver through the aforementioned public policy challenges, we will not do so without also having to deal with significant levels of terrorism and extremism. Obviously, this assertion complicates—possibly significantly—the challenges already facing us. Now factor in radical Islamic violence on American soil. Such violence may be from foreign nationals under the "banner" of al Qaeda, Hamas, Hezbollah, the Muslim Brotherhood, or any other radical Islamic group. Such violence may also stem from homegrown American "jihadists," who decide that their country is corrupt, racist, morally bankrupt, and/or any number of motivating conclusions leading to direct action. Either way, do you think that opposing groups will not stand up and fight back? Think of the Christian Identity members who decided that they needed to burn down a mosque. Are similar actions hard to imagine? In the event of another radical Islamic attack, a response of this type cannot only be imagined, it can be expected. Further, since you are reading this book, I do not doubt you believe we will be attacked again. Once attacked, a response from opposing groups is to be expected.[37] Consequently, I assert that radical Islamic violence will be *a* or *the* trigger toward increased terrorism and extremism in this country. Unless controlled at an early stage, such violence can beget more violence, leading to a spiraling effect, where a phenomenon known as the "climate of collapse" may challenge the viability of the government.[38]

Many examples of this dilemma can be found in contemporary America. While this book was being developed, two events occurred on the same day in New York and Chicago. These issues speak volumes of what we will face going forward. On April 25, 2008, a judge in New York City found three New York Police Department (NYPD) detectives not guilty in the Sean Bell shooting case. On the same day, Mayor Daley and the Chicago Police Department superintendent, Jody Weis, came out of a "crime strategy" meeting and announced that police officers in the city will be equipped with M-4 assault rifles. How do these two connect to each other, and what do they have to do with the theme of this book? They are pointed and powerful.

First, let's discuss the issues related to Chicago. This "strategic crime" meeting comes after a weekend in April where nine people were killed in a total of 36 shootings.[39] After this forum, the mayor and the superintendent announce that rank and file police officers will be equipped with M-4 assault rifles to counter the threat posed by heavily armed gang members.[40] Consider this development in light of the Sean Bell case. On the same day, the NYPD detectives charged with Bell's killing were found not guilty of murder charges. The Bell case has created substantial controversy in New York—and throughout the country. Bell was killed after a traffic encounter when his vehicle crashed with an NYPD police vehicle. After this the stories change. The end result is police fire 50 rounds at the Bell vehicle, killing Bell and injuring another occupant.[41] The decision by the criminal court judge created controversy and additional conflict.

Some may be asking, What are the common factors? First, consider the fact that Chicago seeks to counter increased gang violence with increased police weaponry. Consider that one of the controversial aspects of the Bell case is that police fired 50 rounds at an unarmed man. This event occurred with "normal" police weapons— semiautomatic pistols. The provocative question is whether police in New York with semiautomatic pistols and police in Chicago with M-4 assault rifles are disciplined enough to prevent a recurrence of these tragic events. The answer, of course, is that more tragic Sean Bell-type cases are likely to occur. Not necessarily because the police are "trigger happy" or that they are "racist," as some people will inevitably assert. Indeed, I believe these tragic events will occur because "the job" is getting more and more difficult.

Indeed, as the weaponry becomes more lethal, the resultant violence will increase. With these increasing threats, can we simply blame tragic deaths from high-volume expenditures of bullets as "murder," as was asserted by many regarding the Sean Bell case? More importantly, going forward can we assume that increased firepower by the police, although I believe it is needed, is going to change this dynamic? I think not. Simply put, the decision to use deadly force is politically and legally controversial. At the same time, while the weaponry has become much more deadly, the consequences of "wrong" decisions are likely to result in even greater controversies. Of course, those who have never faced the wrong end of a gun, or who have never had to subdue an offender with a gun, will never truly understand how difficult the "solution" really is. Indeed, many do not want to know. They are content to blame the police whenever their political interests and instincts say so!

Please ponder these thoughts. We will come back to the larger implications surrounding tragic police shootings. Suffice it to state at this point, such shootings act as catalysts to attack the capitalist system. In my mind, this is the desired consequence of some who exploit such tragedies for either personal or political agendas.

By now, some readers may be thinking that the picture I am painting is very negative. I agree it is not a pretty picture. Some may argue that this picture exacerbates, even creates the problem. With this thinking, I understand that by asserting extremist and inter-group conflict is likely—even inevitable—it creates a "self-fulfilling prophecy." This criticism, while seemingly logical, is nonetheless naïve. Let me try to flesh out why I say this.

Let's turn this criticism on its head. To those who believe that the potential for terrorism and group conflict can be resolved, I ask, How? Do we negate the factors leading to terroristic and group violence by maintaining the status quo? Can the Obama presidency—as the first "post-racial" candidate—end the racial divide? Are the current system of diversity, affirmative action, the "war on terrorism," "Bush bashing," and other politically correct "solutions" going to result in a peaceful, cooperative country and world? I think not. We will come back to these examples later in this book. For now, however, ponder how the Obama Administration will maneuver through these matters as a "post-racial" president.

While you ponder these questions, consider some statistics from the Equal Employment Opportunity Commission (EEOC). The EEOC reports that overall racial discrimination cases have risen from 3,075 in 1991 to more than 7,000 in 2007. Of these cases, more than 20 cases involved hangman's nooses in the workplace.[42] Some high profile cases related to nooses include Helmerich & Payne International Drilling, who settled a lawsuit for $290,000, and Pemco Aeroplex, who agreed to pay $300,000 for a hostile workplace suit for the display of nooses, swastikas, and KKK graffiti in work areas.[43] Of particular concern is the growing tendency to see such nooses in the workplace. Not only does the noose symbolically speak to a terrible part of American history, it also represents a key symbolic element of a right-wing terrorist group known as Posse Comitatus.

The cases and statistics can be explained in a number of perspectives. On one hand, it can be argued that this means discrimination and racial hatred still exist. One would be hard-pressed to argue against this assertion. This being said, the growing number of cases illustrates one of two alternatives: racial discrimination and hatred are growing, or some are using the legal system to embellish, or even manufacture, discrimination for their own ends. How do we know which of these alternatives is true? While it may be impossible to prove which assertion is correct, either way it is problematic. More importantly, how do we fix the problem? More aggressive litigation aimed at discrimination? How about additional diversity training? Some may answer yes to both questions. Others may say these have been attempted, and apparently they are not working. Who should decide? Or should we just maintain the status quo? I will provide substantial evidence to address these questions. For now, however, simply think about these questions as we highlight the impact of extremist and terrorist violence upon policing.

Impact on Policing and Public Safety Providers

It is my contention that the expected violence will have a dramatic impact on policing—and the policing model. This assertion is the primary focus of this book. As stated earlier, I contend that a new model of policing will develop in response to the threat—and incidence—of terrorism and extremist violence. How soon this policing model manifests itself will be dependent on the amount and impact of the violence. To be clear, however, I do not necessarily infer that there is a direct "cause and effect" relationship between these factors. What I do assert is that this does not matter to the average police officer who will become a target of a deadly "game" of revolutionary violence. This is what I meant when I mentioned earlier that *Public Safety Policing* is a "pragmatic" response to the threat and incidence of violence. Without trying to diminish the value of scientific processes and methods, the cold, hard fact is that if police become targets of random yet systematic violence,[44] they will defend themselves. This will entail the greater use of military equipment and tactics. It will also entail a very different "job" by contemporary policing standards. Selection, training, operational techniques, appearance, weaponry, and many other current "norms" will change. They will change not because the politicians and the academics desire such change, but because the police—and the citizens they protect—will require it!

This brings us full circle. Many will advocate *Community Policing* as sufficient to prevent, or at least minimize, the threats and implications of terrorism and extremist violence.[45] I respectfully disagree. I assert that the status quo will not be sufficient to deal with these coming threats. Let me try to flesh out my reasoning.

We are at the cusp of a largely unrecognized, yet fundamental shift that will change the nature of policing. This new policing model, which I term *Public Safety Policing*," will replace the *Community Policing* model, which is the current policing strategy of choice. As will be more fully developed later, I believe that the principles inherent in *Community Policing*, while appropriate for an earlier era, will soon be unsustainable. At the heart of this change will be a shift from the desire to change "hearts and minds" to one of "target hardening." Another way to say this is that policing will change from its current emphasis on "service" to an emphasis on "protection." Let me explain this crucial distinction.

Community Policing emphasized a "client-centered" focus. Its optimal goal was to prevent crime by changing the conditions that foster crime.[46] This was to be achieved by working with individuals within the community. In this way, strategic decisions in how the community is to be policed were to emanate from a partnership of police and community leaders. Even the more mundane daily tasks were to be derived from or influenced by community involvement. Underlying this level of police–community cooperation is the impression that crime can be prevented by a cooperative effort to remedy the conditions that cause crime. To achieve this goal, one critical effect of this model was to reorient the police to a more proactive and preventive approach to crime fighting.[47] In doing so, however, it has expanded the scope of the police mission by fostering the delivery of more and more services.[48]

This service orientation, heavily emphasized in *Community Policing*, will be unsustainable. While people—and communities—will continue to desire certain public safety services, the delivery of such by sworn police officers will substantially decrease. The data and logic beneath this assertion will be explained in detail later in this book. Suffice it to state at this point, the "protection" (or target hardening) emphasis of policing will stem from the threat—and the reality—of terrorism and increased extremist violence.

To defend myself from inevitable attacks, I need to make a clear point. I strongly advocate community involvement in policing. What I consider problematic is the notion that the police can change the root causes of crime—which logically results in seeking to transform "hearts and minds." As asserted earlier, this "hearts and minds" approach to policing requires that the police affect the "root causes" of crime. To illustrate the difficulties of this task, I often conduct a classroom exercise where I ask my students (who are active police officers) this question: What are the causes of crime? The inevitable answers are such things as poverty, lack of education, dysfunctional families, drugs and alcohol, teen pregnancy, gangs, racism, unemployment, opportunity, and the like. Upon listing these causes of crime, I then ask a follow-up question: Can police agencies control each specific cause of crime? We then rank the ability to control crime from 0 to connote "no control" to 5 to connote "complete control." As you may predict, the answers are almost universally in the 0 or 1 range, except for one specific cause of crime—opportunity. When assessing this "cause of crime," my police students invariably rank their ability to control as being 4 or even 5.

While this exercise is not meant to demonstrate a scientifically sound conclusion, it does provide key insights into the nature of policing. Please also consider that the above exercise illustrates an important underlying principle of *Community Policing*. I believe this creates a burden on the police that is unattainable. That is, police cannot positively affect the causes of crime. I am not alone in making this assertion. Indeed, one of the foremost proponents of *Community Policing*, Robert C. Trojanowicz, stated that "educating the public that the police can do little about the root causes of crime, such as poverty and unemployment, may help improve their overall credibility."[49] While police agencies may positively affect the conditions that foster crime through order maintenance techniques, the underlying causes of crime are more problematic. Most would agree that such factors as poverty, educational attainment, family life, teen pregnancy, unemployment, and even racism (excluding racial profiling) are beyond the ability of police agencies to control. Even gangs and drugs/alcohol, which are arguably within the scope of police control, are so widespread or endemic that it is inappropriate to expect the police to effectively control the inclinations and incentives of those who participate. Of course, community-policing advocates would argue that these causes of crime can be positively affected by police–community partnerships, which utilize a broad framework of social services.[50] While this may have been true in the past, I think it is unlikely or even impossible in contemporary times.[51]

There are two underlying factors that will drive the transition in policing. These are *fear* and *money*. As I develop the elements of public safety policing, it is inevitable that you may see reasons why this aspect or that aspect will not work. I accept these critiques. I agree that there are many roadblocks that will complicate the transition toward this new policing model. However, each time a roadblock surfaces or a rationale is framed, please ask yourself this question: How do fear and money affect this impediment? I believe each time an impediment appears it will ultimately be resolved in favor of fear and/or money.

When considering the impact of fear, it may be helpful to consider crime rates. One way to assess this is to consider historical relationships. In the 1960s, there were about 3.3 public police officers for every violent crime reported. In 1993, this ratio changed dramatically to 3.47 violent crimes reported for every public police officer.[52] While the crime rate has since been reduced, the net effect of these statistics is that each public police officer in contemporary America must deal with about 10 times as many violent crimes as police from previous eras. Walinsky notes that to return to the 1960s ratio of police to violent crimes, about five million new public police officers would have to be hired by local governments.[53] This will not occur. Indeed, what did occur during this time frame was an explosive growth of the security industry.[54] As will be shown below, monies have been flowing into the private security industry. Hence, people were willing to hire security, at least partly due to the impact of crime. Of course, crime can cause fear. Indeed, the relationship of crime and fear has been systematically developed in a number of studies.[55]

The undeniable growth of the security industry can be viewed by its involvement in businesses, homes, and communities throughout the country.[56] This includes such diverse services as alarm systems, security guard services, and investigative and consulting services. These services caused one observer to note, "We are witnessing a fundamental shift in the area of public safety. It's not a loss of confidence in the police, but a desire to have more police."[57] Indeed, comparisons are being made of the security industry in contemporary times in relation to the advent of public policing in the mid-1850s. One security firm owner stated that "this is a significant time for the private security industry. People are just beginning to realize its potential. I see private security much like what public law enforcement was in the 1850s."[58] This assertion seems even more relevant when one considers the threat of terrorism. In this sense, preparing for terrorism has "taxed" the nation's law enforcement agencies.[59]

While crime can cause fear, leading to the desire for more security, the impact of terrorism adds a qualitative dimension to this equation. Terrorism is *designed* to cause fear.[60] Consistent with this notion, Ganor pointedly asserts that "terrorism is psychological warfare pure and simple."[61] This is consistent with the long-standing notion that "terrorism is primarily theater." In this sense, it is the audience that is the true target of the terroristic attack.[62] With this logic, a terrorist attack is designed to create fear of those in the "audience." The audience is anyone who can see themselves as being the actual victim. It is those who "escaped" the attack, but may not be so fortunate the next time. This message, and this fear, is what those who advocate terrorism use to further their larger goals.

Given the damage that can be caused by terrorism, government is "forced" to respond in a manner that is, or at least is perceived as, strong. A strong response, of course, requires resources. Resources cost money. The costs include personnel and technology expenditures, infrastructure enhancements, convenience limitations, and the like. Depending upon the nature of the threat or of the "success" of previous attacks, the costs associated with an adequate security response may be substantial. In essence, the cycle looks this: threat-response-resource allocation-threat-response-resource allocation, etc. This cycle, or this "vicious circle" will ultimately impact the ability to provide for the security of the population. Since the ultimate "job" of government is to protect its citizens, many implications revolve around the inability to keep us secure. This entails financial, operational, and legal implications, to name a few.

As to the dual impact of money, one way to understand my thinking is to consider this common phrase: *follow the money!* On one hand, money is not limitless. Sooner or later, financial constraints will be felt. On the other hand, how (or where) people and government spend financial resources speaks volumes as to their priorities. In this light, consider the money sources. In just four years, from 1994 to 1998, Office of Community Oriented Policing Services (COPS) grant funds provided $5.3 billion to policing agencies around the country.[63] Thereafter, these community-policing monies continued to flow. In 2001, two events occurred. First, the Violent Crime Control and Law Enforcement Act, which created COPS grants, was scheduled to "sunset" (ending of the program). The second event was 9/11. These two events are now history. After providing over $8 billion in funding, the COPS program is now largely exhausted of its *Community Policing* funds.[64] Currently, the Department of Homeland Security (DHS) is the key funding source. Its approach to "policing" is significantly different from previous funding modalities. Consider these funding priorities in 2008 for the DHS:[65]

- More than $3 billion to bolster national preparedness and protect critical infrastructure
- $781 million to urban areas to address planning, operations, equipment, training, and exercise needs
- $400 million for terrorist prevention capabilities of state and local law enforcement
- $852 million earmarked for critical infrastructure protection, including ports, mass transit, highways, and rails

One would be hard-pressed to assert that these funds have little, if anything, to do with *Community Policing*. This data is just part of a larger trend. The trend shows public safety monies in relation to private or public sectors. In 1980, private monies accounted for $21.7 billion and public monies accounted for only $13.8 billion. In 1990, private monies accounted for $52 billion and public monies accounted for only $30 billion. In 2000, private monies accounted for $104 billion and public monies accounted for only $44 billion.[66]

These data illustrate a 20-year trend toward proportionally fewer expenditures of monies to policing, and proportionally more expenditures of monies to private security. While recent funding by the DHS has changed some of this dynamic, the monies derived from the DHS are largely designed toward technology—which, of course, is purchased in large part from private companies that manufacture the products. Hence, it can be inferred that the reliance on private sources of *public safety services* continues to increase. This same trend is illustrated by some substantial budgetary data in other countries. Consider the European Union. The European Commission has allocated about $60 billion for *security technology research* through 2013. The focus of this research will be on technologies that reduce risks from terrorism and organized crime, natural disasters, and industrial accidents. To those who wonder about the nature of these expenditures, the monies have been appropriated because the European Union "has been concerned about the radicalization of some populations either inside or outside Europe for a long time," says the acting head of the Security Research and Development unit.[67]

Both of these data sources illustrate a larger trend. That is, more monies are being spent on technology than personnel. While I do not necessarily advocate this trend, it is appropriate to acknowledge it. One consequence of this trend is that police agencies are increasingly being stretched thin with reduced numbers of police personnel. While police resources and personnel are being stretched, their service provision has not been proportionally reduced. Some relevant data can illustrate these assertions. For example, Richmond, California, experienced a 25% drop in police personnel, the Cleveland Police Department is 30% smaller than in 2002, and the Detroit Police Department is down 1,000 officers from 2001.[68] In addition, other departments have similar personnel deficiencies. Consider that New York City is seeking to hire 3,000 officers; Los Angeles police want to hire 1,000; Houston needs 600 officers; Washington, DC, is short 330 officers; Phoenix is down about 200 officers; and the Boston police force is about 100 officers below its 2000 level.[69] One possible implication of these financial constraints is that police departments appear to be struggling with rising rates of violent crimes. Table 1.2 illustrates violent crime increases in certain cities.[70]

Some attribute the increases in violent crime as a consequence of police resources and personnel being increasingly stretched. The provocative question raised by Mayor Douglas Palmer (Trenton, New Jersey) is whether "we are sacrificing 'hometown security' for homeland security."[71] The question can be asked another way: Can the police effectively combat crime and provide homeland security simultaneously? My short answer is no. The caveat to this answer is that police cannot perform both functions unless significant additional resources are provided. As stated above, this is not likely to be allocated any time soon. Los Angeles Police Department (LAPD) Chief William Bratton put the issue succinctly when he said,

Table 1.2 Recent Crime Milestones (2004–2006)

Alexandria, VA	Homicides doubled from 2004 to 2005
Boston, MA	Ten-year high for homicides
Cincinnati, OH	Twenty-year high for homicides
Fairfax, VA	Sixteen-year high for homicides
Nashville, TN	Seven-year high for homicides
Orlando, FL	All time high for homicides
Prince George's County	All time high for homicides
Richmond, CA	Ten-year high for homicides
Springfield, MA	Nearly 10-year high for homicides
Trenton, NJ	All time high for homicides

Source: Adapted from Rosen, Marie. *A Gathering Storm—Violent Crime in America*, Police Executive Research Forum, October 2006.

"It is a zero-sum game because every cop in the anti-terrorism division is one that is not in vice, narcotics or on gang activity."[72]

Because of this tension between policing crime and homeland security, some advocate shifting funding priorities. For example, an International Association of Chiefs of Police (IACP) report urges the next president (President Obama) to shift some funding from antiterrorism projects to police departments. Indeed, this seems appropriate, as since 2001 spending on local police has been cut by 81 percent.[73] Since 9/11, the IACP says 99,000 people have been murdered in the United States, and 1.4 million have been victims of violent crime each year. This situation has led an IACP official to assert, "In terms of day-to-day crime fighting, we're far worse off than we were before 9/11." Further, the dilemma related to crime, terrorism, and funding is pointedly argued by a statement issued by the U.S. Conference of Mayors. It states that "[i]f al-Qaeda were responsible for 34 deaths a day in the United States, the nation would do whatever was necessary to stop the deaths." Because of these statistics, many law enforcement and security experts argue that the government is spending hundreds of millions of dollars on antiterrorism equipment that is rarely used. All told, since 2003 the Department of Homeland Security has given out $22.7 billion to states and cities for emergency preparedness programs. A DHS official, however, disputed the notion that these monies are not being used—or that it is wasted. Their argument agrees that police may need more money. They contend, of course, that "we reject the view that enough has been done on homeland security."[74]

Regardless of how these funding questions are handled, my prediction is that given the financial struggles at all levels of government, the money to hire additional police officers will not be available. Even if monies are found to increase police funding, it is politically dangerous to move money away from the notion of homeland security. Indeed, since Democrats tend to be focused on the "protection of the homeland," I do not see a substantial shift away from homeland security funding priorities. In any event, I see no quick solution that would enable municipalities to hire significant numbers of needed police personnel. Even if the money was made available, through federal, state, or local sources, which is extremely doubtful given the current budgetary problems exhibited across governments at all levels, I believe it would be too little and too late to change current funding trends.

Looking at this issue from a larger perspective, one is struck by the impact of terrorism. It is becoming increasingly clear that terrorism is changing the way the military and public safety providers operate. As Figure 1.2 illustrates, the military, the police, and the security industry are being transformed. For example, the military is increasingly focused on special operations and tactical orientation. It is orienting itself around the desire to be smaller, lighter, and faster. Not only is the military 35% smaller than at the height of the Cold War, its approach to "war" is changing rather dramatically.[75] An excellent example of this transformation is with battleships, heavily armored tank divisions, and more traditional "Cold War" weapons systems. In an era of insurgency warfare, these have limited value

Figure 1.2   The impact of terrorism (Copyright, James F. Pastor, 2009).

to the military—and are costly to produce, deliver, and maintain. Indeed, Defense Secretary Robert Gates has urged the military services to stop spending money on costly weapons systems designed to fight big, conventional wars. He instead seeks to focus on training and preparing to better fight irregular wars and battle terrorist networks. In his pointed vision, Gates has said the military must better prepare to fight "brutal and adaptive insurgencies and terrorists." He further warned against a repeat of historical patterns where "bureaucratic nature" takes hold and the Army's "irregular [warfare] capabilities" are marginalized. This was an allusion to the post-Vietnam decline in counterinsurgency expertise. The defense secretary warned that even after a drawdown of forces in Iraq, American troops will continue to battle "violent jihadist networks" in other countries. He aptly stated, "To paraphrase the Bolshevik Leon Trotsky, we may not be interested in the long war, but the long war is interested in us."[76] This long war will not end in Iraq and Afghanistan. At some point, possibly sooner than later, it will take place—in a sustained manner—on American soil.

If, or when, the "war on terrorism" comes home, the police will increasingly adopt heavier, more military-like weapons. Along with these weapons, police agencies will also focus on counterterrorism and on tactical operations. Even now, prior to sustained terrorist actions in the United States, police agencies are using military-type weaponry, with more use of tactical teams and methods. Much of this change is the consequence of "normal" crimes and criminal gangs, who are often "outgunning" the police. This dynamic will be exacerbated when terrorist attacks occur. The police will be faced with being both targets and the first line of defense for civilian populations.

Finally, the security industry is increasing its scope, adopting a wider service provision. Much of this growth will be within the public realm. Indeed, the key growth market for security is in public areas. The focus of this wider public scope is oriented around order maintenance and the provision of public safety services.

To demonstrate the growth of the security industry since 9/11, consider the growth of security personnel in New York City. In September 2001, there were 104,000 security officers in New York City. In October 2003, the number of security officers rose to 127,006.[77] This is not atypical in the security industry. For example, in the United Kingdom currently, there are about 333,600 security personnel, compared to only 150,000 security personnel in 1996. Further, in South Africa, private security providers outnumber public police by a ratio of 5 to 1.[78] In addition, statistics in continental Europe reveal a substantial presence of security personnel. Recent estimates reveal that there are approximately 530,000 security personnel, with Germany having the largest concentration. Similarly, Australia witnessed an increase in security personnel from 22,975 in 1986 to 34,854 in 2001, accounting for a 52 percent increase, while police experienced only a 19 percent increase during the same time period.[79]

A good example of how security is being used in Europe was pioneered by the Swedish-based security firm Securitas. This firm has instituted "time-share" service to residential and commercial clients. This time-share concept provides patrol and other security services to numerous clients—essentially simultaneously.[80] Each client pays a proportionate share of the costs for the service provision. In essence, the time-share concept is similar to "buying" a fractional share of a condo unit, and in return the "owner" has the right to use the unit for a proportionate amount of time per calendar year. This service is provided in public places in various European locations, including in Trondheim, Norway, where Securitas security officers patrol a business district.[81]

The rise of private security in Western democracies may be a precursor of an early stage in the transformation of policing. Many countries in Europe, such as the United Kingdom and Sweden, are well into this transformation. For example, in London a program called Project Griffin was instituted within the city. This program has three components: training, communications, and the deployment of security officers in the event of a major incident. The training is conducted by metropolitan police officers for private security officers. The communication methods include a "bridge call" every week, where relevant information is shared by the police intelligence bureau to update security managers on current threats, recent crime trends, and upcoming events. The deployment of security officers to work alongside London Metropolitan Police occurs in the event of a major incident.[82]

Investigative and conviction data in England reveal that there is a significant potential for terroristic activity. For example, from April 2007 until March 2008, over 40 people were convicted of terrorist-related offenses as a result of Metropolitan Police investigations. These convictions resulted in prison sentences amounting to more than 600 years imposed on terrorist plotters. These convictions are only part of the story. The director general of the Security Service, MI5, Jonathan Evans, has said that he was aware of about 2,000 people involved in terrorist-related activity in the United Kingdom. The significance of this assertion was further developed by the home secretary Jacqui Smith, who previously noted there were 200 terror networks and 30 plots under investigation.[83] Consequently, the threat of terrorism in England appears to be demonstrably real. As evidenced by the elements of Project Griffin, police in the United Kingdom have developed an effective working relationship with private security firms.

Of course, prior to the threat of terrorism, most police agencies did not need—or want—help from private security. Things are changing. This change has been largely "under the radar." Most people have not connected the dots. This should not surprise the reader. More often than not, people do not see change because they are either too busy with other matters or they are too vested in the status quo to admit that change is afoot. This book seeks to describe and illustrate these changing circumstances.

Consider the implications of my assertions in light of terrorism. The authors of the National Policy Summit make the connection between the conflicting roles facing modern police departments. They contend that police are finding that, in addition to crime fighting duties, they now have significant homeland security duties. This assertion was well stated by Judith Lewis, a former captain with the L.A. County Sheriff's Department. She made this pointed statement:[84]

> The expectations of law enforcement as first responders for homeland security have put an almost unachievable burden on local law enforcement. Local law enforcement is not designed organizationally to support the cooperation needed, and its officers don't have the training and technology to do the job. … Currently, traditional law enforcement is being left behind.

Elements of *Public Safety Policing*

This brings us to the key elements of the *Public Safety Policing* model. I envision three, interrelated elements within this model: military weaponry and tactical operations, intelligence methods and surveillance technologies, and order maintenance provisions. As a way to introduce this new policing model, I will briefly highlight each of these elements. Prior to doing so, please consider the framework of this new policing model as seen in New York and in Los Angeles.

The two largest metropolitan cities seem to have adopted "kindred" counterterrorism strategies. Both have roving SWAT or Emergency Service Unit teams, equipped with gas masks and antidotes to chemical and biological agents. Both have set up "fusion" centers to screen threats and monitor intelligence sources, and both have started programs to identify and protect likely targets. In addition, both have tried to integrate private security into their model.[85] Each of these represents primary features of the public safety policing model.

The military weaponry and tactical operations element is the combination of heavier military-like weapons along with increased use of tactical operations. This includes heavy weapons/SWAT teams, gang and drug tactical teams, and saturation units, which are delivered by highly trained police officers.[86] This aspect of policing is likely to be much more militarized than what most people view as the role of the police. It entails a much different way of operating. While many casual observers may not recognize the basis for this statement, one can argue that policing agencies have been trending in this direction for years. In a journal article published in the summer of 2001, Bayley and Shearing insightfully argue[87]

> for all that heartening signs that public police are adopting community oriented crime prevention strategies, there are counter-indications that they are focusing more on threats to society at large [drugs and terrorism] ... and that military equipment and tactics are being used more often.

A shorthand characterization of this element can be called the "militarization" of policing. While much more needs to be said on this note, jurisdictions across the United States have been arming rank-and-file officers with high-powered assault rifles for a decade or more. Police officials say that the trend has accelerated in the past year because of a number of factors. These include greater numbers of shoot-outs, standoffs in which police were outgunned, the increasing number of officer deaths, and mass shootings of civilians by heavily armed gunmen. The justification for high-powered weaponry is powerfully advocated by Scott Knight, Police Chief of Chaska, Minnesota, and Chairman of the Firearms Committee for the International Association of Chiefs of Police (IACP). He stated, "If you get into a firefight, you want to be the winner." Knight further noted, "Our departments are moving to those weapons out of necessity across the country."[88] There is substantial additional data and evidence to support this militarization trend.

Intelligence methods and surveillance technologies is another key element of the new policing model. Part of this element embraces the notion of "intelligence-led policing," which is gaining momentum in policing agencies throughout the country. The logic of intelligence-led policing is sound. Two key advocates, William J. Bratton and George L. Kelling, define intelligence-led policing as "crime fighting that is guided by effective intelligence gathering and analysis."[89] In this style of policing, instead of relying solely on the federal government for intelligence, many state and local departments have now taken it upon themselves to create their own systems.

While I also embrace this policing style, I believe that the evolving policing model is larger than simply describing it as "intelligence-led policing." Indeed, I add another key aspect of "intelligence" by combining it with various surveillance and predictive technologies. The technological functions will also be greatly expanded as being from current policing practices. In this way, many commonly used security technologies will be emphasized within police agencies.[90] This includes the extensive use of networked cameras and access control systems, highly predictive crime mapping software, fusion centers, and integrated identification systems. These technologies will improve the "eyes and ears" of policing agencies to better respond to and even predict criminal or terrorist behavior. The key to this approach is surveillance designed for crime prevention, apprehension, and enforcement.[91]

With this thinking, police agencies have the responsibility to proactively establish a process that seeks to understand threats, criminal organizations, and crime targets within their communities. The key to this responsibility is to manage these crime threats and focus on *prevention*. Consequently, the overall purpose of this approach is to focus on crime prevention (read protection) through proactive technologies and tactics.

The order maintenance element borrows heavily on the "broken windows" theory.[92] Of course, order maintenance techniques were widely used in the community-policing model. While this theory has gained much acclaim, critics of the "broken windows" theory contend that order maintenance alone is not sufficient to reduce crime. For example, Harcourt argues that *surveillance* associated with order maintenance may be more important. Indeed, he asserts that "order maintenance probably contributes to fighting crime through enhanced surveillance."[93] Consequently, both order maintenance and surveillance are important elements of public safety policing.

Just as *Community Policing* borrowed various traditional policing techniques and "packaged" them into a new model of policing, I seek to adopt the order maintenance provision into *Public Safety Policing*. In *Community Policing*, the focus of order maintenance was "low level" crimes such as graffiti, loitering, public intoxication, and the like.[94] In *Public Safety Policing* these matters will still be important, but other factors will also be emphasized. These include the protection of critical infrastructure, more intense surveillance of mass transportation, and more extensive patrolling and monitoring of residential communities and business districts. Overall, the focus of order maintenance will be on the environment, attempting to prevent crime and terrorist incidents. The key will be to control the environment, and to focus on both physical and social incivilities.

In short, the difference between the two policing models can be summed up in one example: the difference between a mugging on a train compared to a suicide bomber on the train. While many of the same techniques used to secure the train in these examples are similar, many other differences exist. One key distinction is the growing use of "alternative service providers" to perform order maintenance functions previously performed by public police. Another difference is the amount and sophistication of technology designed to reduce the threat. Consequently, the new policing model will have a different order maintenance focus. It will also entail distinctions related to the methods and personnel used to achieve its goals.

The primary tasks of these service providers are to provide certain routine service functions, such as report writing, alarm response, traffic control, and "security."

Each of these tasks relate to either order maintenance or "observe and report" functions. In these ways, alternative service providers will also enhance the "eyes and ears" of policing agencies. As will be developed in detail, I believe that the majority of order maintenance functions will be conducted by private police employed by security firms. This work product, however, should be based on contractual provisions or be directly tied to the structure of the policing agency within the jurisdiction. While there are many potential problems and pitfalls related to the delivery of these services, I contend that the momentum toward this arrangement is strong, even unstoppable. It is the part of the "perfect storm" that cannot be stopped.

What is the proper function of private police? Should private police be relegated to private property and private accounts? Should they be a supplement for the public police? Is it necessary or proper for private police to replace public police? These questions result in many diverse answers. As will be presented later, some authors assert that the private sector will bear an increased preventive role, while public police will concentrate more heavily on violent crimes. Regardless of how these questions are ultimately answered, these two entities seem to be increasingly overlapping.

Each of these questions will be assessed individually, and as a cohesive whole. While we will delve into each element in detail, one additional caveat needs to be made clear. These elements reflect the "street level" structures of *Public Safety Policing.* That being said, the model assumes that police agencies will continue to conduct investigative work, testify in criminal prosecutions, provide administrative and policy oversight of the department, and a host of other "internal functions" that are beyond the scope of this model—and this book. In any event, the main features of future policing agencies are captured by this model.

The major premises of this model have an analogy in a successful movie. If you had the opportunity to see the movie *Minority Report,*[95] you were exposed to a very insightful, if not a bit far-fetched view of future policing. The premise of this movie is that future police techniques will include a "pre-crime" squad charged with the goal of stopping crime before the criminal can complete the act. With this approach, the pre-crime squad would not care about changing the criminal inclinations of the individual. Instead, the goal will simply be to affect the individual's opportunity to commit the crime. In doing so, these futuristic police officers will utilize various tactical, technological, and order maintenance methodologies. Without getting into where any similarities exist between the movie and my model, the structure looks as illustrated in Figure 1.3.

Figure 1.3   Elements of Public Safety Policing (Copyright, James F. Pastor, 2009).

Hopefully this explanation and Figure 1.3 provide enough information to give you a sense of where this book is going—and why. My intention at this point is to draw the big picture, then take you through the details. In this light, I will discuss the main tenets of terrorism and then describe in detail each element of the policing model. Thereafter, I will discuss the implications of the model and of the larger ramifications of terrorism and extremism. To be clear, my model is not intended to "solve" these larger trends. The model, instead, is a pragmatic response to these larger trends. As will be made clear, the "solution" is larger than the police. It rests in the citizens within this great society and, by extension, the society itself. To this end, I hope this book enables you to be part of the solution. To give the reader some sense of where this book is heading, it may be helpful to end this chapter with this thought:[96]

> Policing is changing today as profoundly as when Sir Robert Peel (the innovator of policing) put the first bobby on the streets of London in 1829.

Endnotes

1. Steinhauser, Paul (2009). "Poll finds great expectations for Obama." http://www.cnn. com/2008/POLITICS/11/13/poll.obama/index.html (retreived on January 17, 2009).
2. These results were found on January 17, 2009.
3. http://www.huffingtonpost.com/2008/11/04/obama-victory-speech_n_141194.html (retrieved on January 19, 2009).
4. Hilliker, Joel (2009). "Can He Deliver, Why There Is Reason for Hope," *Trumpet*, http://www.thetrumpet.com/index.php?q=5693.0.110.0 (retrieved on January 17, 2009).
5. Hilliker, Joel (2009) op. cit., 1.
6. Hilliker, Joel (2009) op. cit., 2.
7. For examples of the particular goals of terrorism, see http://www.isvg.org/ and www.txdps.state.tx.us.
8. Asymmetric warfare can be defined as the "quintessential weapon of the weak against the strong." Pillar, Paul R. (2001). "Is the Terrorist Threat Misunderstood?" *Security Management,* May. See also Hoffman, Bruce (2004). "Rethinking Terrorism and Counter-Terrorism Since 9/11," in *The New Era of Terrorism: Selected Readings,* ed. Gus Martin. Thousand Oaks, CA: Sage Publications, 11.
9. For a discussion on these distinctions, see Pastor, James F. (2003). *The Privatization of Police in America: An Analysis and Case Study.* Jefferson, NC: McFarland and Company, Inc.
10. Yungher, Nathan I. (2008). *Terrorism: The Bottom Line.* Upper Saddle River, NJ: Pearson/Prentice Hall, 248–49.
11. Posner, Richard (2006). *Not a Suicide Pact: The Constitution in a Time of National Emergency.* Oxford University Press.
12. For explanation of the Terrorist Surveillance Act, please see press release at http://www.usdoj.gov/opa/documents/nsa_myth_v_reality.pdf (retrieved on January 31, 2009).

13. Simon, Steven (2004). "The New Terrorism: Securing the Nation Against a Messianic Foe," *The New Era of Terrorism: Selected Readings*, ed. Gus Martin. Thousand Oaks, CA: Sage Publications, 171; and Poland, James M. (2005). *Understanding Terrorism: Groups, Strategies and Responses.* Upper Saddle River, NJ: Pearson/Prentice Hall, 2.

14. This assertion was echoed by John Lehman, the former secretary of the Navy and 9/11 Commission member, in a speech at the U.S. Naval Institute in May 2004.

15. For a pointed critique of this situation by a conservative political commentator, see Ingraham, Laura (2007). *Power to the People.* Washington, DC: Regnery Publishing, 99.

16. National Strategy for Homeland Security (2007), October:15.

17. For some information and statistics on the Tamil Tigers, see Simonsen, Clifford E. and Jeremy R. Spindlove (2000). *Terrorism Today: The Past, The Players, The Future.* Upper Saddle River, NJ: Pearson/Prentice Hall, 219–21.

18. Al-Qaeda is a "global network with broader political and ideological ambitions." See Tucker, Jonathan B. (2003). "Strategies for Countering Terrorism: Lessons from the Israeli Experience," *Journal of Homeland Security* March 26:3.

19. The term "civil war" was used extensively during 2005 to late 2007 or early 2008 by the media and many political leaders—usually from the Democratic party. Typically the mantra was "why are we involved in this civil war," and words to that effect. Ironically, with the success of the "surge," this term has largely disappeared from public discourse as of spring 2008 to the time this book was being drafted.

20. Forero, Juan (2009), "Obama and Chávez Start Sparring Early," *Washington Post*, January 19, A15. http://www.washingtonpost.com/wp-dyn/content/article/2009/01/18/AR 2009011802325.html.

21. This assertion is found in almost every book on terrorism, and is appropriately recognized in the *National Strategy for Homeland Security* (2007), October:10.

22. Richardson, Valerie (2005). "FBI Targets Domestic Terrorists," in *Violence and Terrorism*, ed. Thomas J. Badey. McGraw-Hill/Dushkin, 98.

23. Azzam, Maha (2005). "Al Qaeda: The Misunderstood Wahhabi Connection and the Ideology of Violence," in *Violence and Terrorism*, ed. Thomas J. Badey. McGraw-Hill/Dushkin, 153.

24. www.cdi.org/terrorism/terrorist-groups.cfm (retrieved on July 27, 2006).

25. www.cdi.org/terrorism/terrorist-groups.cfm (retrieved on July 27, 2006).

26. http://www.guardian.co.uk/egypt/story/0,129630,00.html (retrieved on July 19, 2007).

27. Johnson, Carrie (2009), "Bad Economy May Fuel Hate Groups, Experts Warn," *Washington Post*, January 11, A04.

28. Johnson, Carrie (2009) op. cit., A04.

29. Asbury, John (2009), "Racial Beatings in San Jacinto Valley Linked to Obama Election," *The Press-Enterprise*, January 18. http://www.pe.com/localnews/hemet/stories/PE_News_Local_S_hate18.44d722b.html.

30. Goonan, Peter (2009), "Affidavit Provides Details of Macedonia Church Fire Probe," *The Republican Newsroom* (MA), January 19. http://www.masslive.com/news/index. ssf/2009/01/affidavit_provides_details_of.html?category=Crime&category=Fires&cat egory=Springfield.

31. http://www.foxnews.com/story/0,2933,330504,00.html (retrieved on February 10 and 12, 2008).

32. http://www.themilitant.com/index.shtml (retrieved on September 23, 2007).

33. http://www.foxnews.com/story/0,2933,297731,00.html (retrieved on September 23, 2007).
34. http://www.foxnews.com/story/0,2933,270241,00.html (May 6, 2007, retrieved on April 28, 2008).
35. http://www.lewrockwell.com/blog/lewrw/archives/020008.html (retrieved on March 16, 2008).
36. http://elections.foxnews.com/2008/03/16/obama-pastors-church-fires-back/ (retrieved on March 16, 2008).
37. See, for example, Poland, James M. (2005). *Understanding Terrorism: Groups, Strategies and Responses*. Upper Saddle River, NJ: Pearson/Prentice Hall, 286, who states, "the growth of para-military groups to counter the actions of an indiscriminate terrorist campaign would intensify the violence."
38. Clutterbuck, Richard (1975). The Police and Urban Terrorism. *The Police Journal*.
39. http://www.houmatoday.com/article/20080422/APA/804221036 (retrieved on April 27, 2008).
40. Spielman, Fran and Frank Main (2008), "Cops to Get Rifles to Compete with Gangs," *Chicago Sun-Times*, April 26.
41. See various accounts of the Sean Bell case at http://www.nytimes.com/2008/04/28/nyregion/28bell.html?ref=nyregion and http://www.nydailynews.com/topics/Sean+Bell.
42. *Security Management* (2008) March:84.
43. *Security Management* (2008), op. cit., 84.
44. For an example of this violence, the movie titled *The Battle of Algiers* dramatically illustrated the widespread and systematic violence against Algerian police and the French military.
45. See, for example, Ortiz, Christopher W., Nicole J. Hendricks, and Naomi F. Sugie (2007). "Policing Terrorism: The Response of Local Police Agencies to Homeland Security," *Criminal Justice Studies* 20, no. 2 (June):91–109.
46. Oliver, W. M. (2004). *Community-Oriented Policing: A Systemic Approach to Policing*. Upper Saddle River, NJ: Prentice Hall.
47. Oliver, W. M. (2004), op cit., 32–46; and Kelling, G. (1995) "Reduce Serious Crime by Restoring Order," *The American Enterprise* May/June:17–18.
48. Pastor, James F. (2005). "Public Safety Policing," *Law Enforcement Executive Forum* 5, no. 6 (November).
49. Trojanowicz, Robert C. (1988). "Serious Threats to the Future of Policing," *Footprints, National Center for Community Policing*, Fall/Winter:2.
50. Oliver, W. M. (2004), op cit., 78–104; and Trojanowicz, Robert C. (1988), op. cit., 3.
51. Pastor, James F. (2005), op. cit., 13–14.
52. Walinsky, Adam (1993). "The Crisis of Public Order," *The Atlantic Monthly*, July.
53. Walinsky, Adam (1993), op. cit.
54. Cunningham, William C., and Todd H. Taylor (1994). "The Growing Role of Private Security," *National Institute of Justice*. Office of Justice Programs, U.S. Department of Justice, October.
55. See, for example, Lewis, Dan A., and Michael G. Maxfield (1980). "Fear in the Neighborhoods: An Investigation of the Impact of Crime," *Journal of Research in Crime and Delinquency*, July:160–89; Liska, Allen E., Joseph J. Lawrence, and Andrew Sanchirico (1982). "Fear of Crime as a Social Fact," *Social Forces* 60 (3):760–70; Moore, Mark H., and Robert C. Trojanowicz (1988). "Perspectives on Policing: Corporate Strategies for Policing," *National Institute of Justice*. Office of

Justice Programs, U.S. Department of Justice, No. 6, November; and Benson, Bruce L. (1990). *The Enterprise of Law: Justice Without State*. Pacific Research Institute for Public Policy, San Francisco, California.

56. Pastor, James F. (2003), op. cit.; Carlson, Tucker (1995). "Safety Inc.: Private Cops Are There When You Need Them," *Policy Review* 73 (Summer); and Goldberg, Ceil (1994). "New Roles for Private Patrols," *Security Management*, December.

57. Tolchin, Martin (1985), "Private Guards Get New Role in Public Law Enforcement," *The New York Times*, November 29.

58. Spencer, Suzy (1997). Private Security. Phoenix Mosaic Group. www.onpatrol.com/cs.privsec.html.

59. Office of Community Oriented Policing Services (2004). National Policy Summit: Building Private Security/Public Policing Partnerships to Prevent and Respond to Terrorism and Public Disorder, U.S. Department of Justice; Stephens, Gene (2005). "Policing the Future: Law Enforcement's New Challenges," *The Futurist* 39 (March/April); and Davies, Heather J. and Gerald R. Murphy (2002). "Protecting Your Community from Terrorism: Strategies for Law Enforcement, Working with Diverse Communities," *Community Oriented Policing Services* and *Police Executive Research Forum*.

60. Poland, James M. (2005), op. cit., 209.

61. Ganor, Boaz (2005). "Terror as a Strategy of Psychological Warfare," in *Violence and Terrorism*, ed. Thomas J. Badey. McGraw-Hill/Dushkin, 6.

62. The notion that terrorism is primarily theater is asserted by Poland, James M. (2005). *Understanding Terrorism: Groups, Strategies and Responses*. Upper Saddle River, NJ: Pearson/Prentice Hall.

63. Muhlhausen, David B. (2001). "Do Community Oriented Policing Services Grants Affect Violent Crime Rates?" The Heritage Foundation, CDA01-05, May 25.

64. For examples of community policing funding, see Johnson, Kevin (2003), "Federal, Local Cuts Pull Cops Off Streets," *USA Today*, December 2; Csepiga, Melanie (2004), "Local Director Says Grants are Drying Up and County Will Get No Money Without Plan," *NW Times*, November 24; and Laverty, Deborah (2003), "Merrillville Chief, Councilman Want More Cops," *The Times*, November 18.

65. *Intersec* (2008), March:42.

66. These data are from the Hallcrest Report by Cunningham, William C., John J. Strauchs, and Clifford W. Van Meter (1991). "Private Security: Patterns and Trends," National Institute of Justice. Office of Justice Programs, U.S. Department of Justice, August.

67. *Security Management* (2008), April: 40.

68. Rosen, Marie (2006), *A Gathering Storm—Violent Crime in America*, Police Executive Research Forum, October.

69. http://www.msnbc.msn.com/id/19116778/ (retrieved on August 24, 2007).

70. Rosen, Marie (2006), op. cit.

71. Rosen, Marie (2006), op. cit.

72. Rosenberg, Barry (2004). "Protecting the City of Angels," *Homeland Security*, March. www.mcgraw-hillhomelandsecurity.com.

73. Hall, Mimi (2008). "Rethink Spending on Anti-Terrorism, Report Says," *USA Today*, 1A. http://www.usatoday.com/news/washington/2008-10-01-terrormoney_N.htm (retrieved on October 3, 2008).

74. Hall, Mimi (2008), op. cit., 1.

75. Roberts, Marta (2004). "Working in a War Zone," *Security Management*, November.

76. Grant, Greg (2008), *Government Executive.com,* April 22. http://www.govexec.com/story_page.cfm?articleid=39835&dcn=e_ndw (retrieved on April 25, 2008); and Bender, Bryan (2008), "Gates: US Military Must Retool to Fight Terrorism," *Boston Globe,* December 5.

77. National Institute of Justice, Office of Community Oriented Policing Services (2004). National Policy Summit: Building Private Security/Public Policing Partnerships to Prevent and Respond to Terrorism and Public Disorder.

78. Sarre, Rick (2005). "Researching Private Policing: Challenges and Agendas for Researchers," *Security Journal* 18, no. 3:57–70.

79. Prenzler, Tim (2005). "Mapping the Australian Security Industry," *Security Journal* 18, no. 4:51–64.

80. See http://www.pinkertons.com/timesharing/timesharing1.asp (retrieved on March 12, 2003).

81. www.securitas.com (retrieved on June 10, 2008).

82. www.cityoflondon.police.uk (retrieved on June 10, 2008).

83. Gardham, Duncan (2008). "Counter Terrorism: Police Disrupt 13 Terror Networks in Last Year." http://www.telegraph.co.uk/news/uknews/2450020/Counter-terrorism-Police-disrupt-13-terror-networks-in-last-year.html (retrieved on July 23, 2008).

84. Stephens, Gene (2005). "Policing the Future: Law Enforcement's New Challenges," *The Futurist* 39 (March/April).

85. Miller, Judith (2007). "On the Front Line in the War on Terrorism: Cops in New York and Los Angeles Offer America Two Models for Preventing Another 9/11," *City Journal* (Summer). http://www.city-journal.org/html/17_3_preventing_terrorism.html (retrieved on May 9, 2008).

86. Pastor, James F. (2007). Private Policing in Public Environments, in *Protection of Assets Manual.* Alexandria, VA: ASIS International.

87. Bayley, David H. and Clifford D. Shearing (2001). "The New Structure of Policing: Description, Conceptualization and Research Agenda," *N.I.J.,* NCJ# 187083, U.S. Department of Justice, July.

88. http://www.foxnews.com/story/0,2933,340748,00.html (retrieved on March 23, 2008).

89. http://www.manhattan-institute.org/html/cb_43.htm (retrieved on October 16, 2007).

90. Bayley, David H. and Clifford D. Shearing (2001), op. cit., 19.

91. Pastor, James F. (2007), op. cit., 46.

92. Wilson, James Q. and George L. Kelling (1982). "Broken Windows," *The Atlantic* (March); Felson, Marcus (2002). *Crime and Everyday Life.* Thousand Oaks, CA: Sage Publications; and Kelling, G. L. and C. M. Coles (1996). *Fixing Broken Windows: Restoring Order and Reducing Crime in our Communities.* New York: Simon and Schuster.

93. Harcourt, Bernard E. (2002). "Policing Disorder: Can we Reduce Serious Crime by Punishing Petty Offenses?" *Boston Review:* 13.

94. Kelling, George and William H. Sousa (2002). "Do Police Matter: An Analysis of the Impact of New York City's Police Reforms," Manhattan Institute, Center for Civic Innovation, 22 (December); and Oliver, W. M. (2004), op. cit.

95. Goldman, G. and R. Shusett (Executive Producers) (2002). *Minority Report* [Motion Picture]. United States: 20th Century Fox and Dreamworks, LLC.

96. Bayley, David H. and Clifford D. Shearing (2001), op. cit., 39.

Chapter 2

Terrorism: Concepts, Influences, Structures, and Radicalization

This chapter provides an overview of these factors related to terrorism. Those who have studied terrorism realize that it is a comprehensive subject. Some books devote specific chapters to each of these factors. Instead, I seek to provide a simple, yet concise framework of these factors. One of the key aspects is to understand why people become terrorists and extremists. Hence, a key part of my approach is to focus on ideologies and other motivating influences. As Yungher asserts, the way to understand a group is to focus on the relationship between their values and their ideologies.[1] Hopefully this approach will enable you to apply key principles and issues related to terrorism to inform the policing model designed to combat it.

Definitions and Concepts

One of the problems with combating terrorism is that it is very difficult to attain consensus on any key principle. This is at least partly related to the notion that "one man's terrorist is another man's freedom fighter." This subjective aspect of terrorism extraordinarily complicates how affected societies understand and address it. The "it" is terrorism. But how do we know terrorism when we see it? More often then not, when the violence occurs, so do disagreements as to what it is and how we define it.

Consider Iraq. By almost any standard, the bombings and related violence against police, military personnel, and civilians would be considered terrorism. When was the last time you heard a media source characterize the violence as "terrorism"? The reluctance of the media to define an act as "terrorism" is, in the end, a political decision. Once you are labeled as a terrorist, then you are "bad." Instead of making this normative characterization, the media and many politicians avoid this label for political or financial reasons. Of course, the media contends that they desire to be viewed as "objective." This may be so. Maybe there are other reasons.

This is not just an academic problem. The failure to agree on how to characterize violence has profound implications. Consider this example. An individual is tragically killed by police, who are criminally tried and found not guilty. Because of the resentment generated by the affected community, some extremists within the community decide to kill a police officer as "retaliation" for the death at the hands of the police.[2] Is the killing of the police officer terrorism? Some will say this is clearly terrorism, as police officers are representatives of government. The attack on a police officer is an attack on the government. Correct? I think so, but I am not making the decision. Likely neither are you. I can say with definitiveness that some people will passionately argue that this example is *not* terrorism. Instead, it is a form of "self-defense." Maybe it is "justice"? Now what do we do? How do we convince those of the error in their thinking? It is a difficult task. It is a task we as a society are going to have to tackle.

As a starting point in the above-described definitional problem, it is helpful to look to the law. How does the law define terrorism? The FBI defines terrorism as[3]

> the unlawful use of force or violence against persons or property to intimidate or coerce a Government, the civilian population, or any segment thereof, in furtherance of political or social objectives.

While this definition may be useful for prosecutorial purposes, as is implied above, those who study terrorism understand the implications of consensus. Do we actually need consensus? According to Mahan and Griset, while terrorism is an ideological and political concept, it ought to be defined by the nature of the act itself.[4] Using this logic, it is not important to find a consensus on each particular act. It is only necessary to define the *nature* and *quality* of what is done. Hence, as a society, or as a culture, we can agree that exploding bombs in a market, which kills members of the civilian population, is terrorism. Similarly, killing a uniformed police officer by means of an ambush while the officer performs his or her duties is terrorism. Thus, as Cooper argues, "fighting for freedom may well be his or her purpose, but if the mission is undertaken through employment of terroristic means, a terrorist he or she must remain."[5] This assertion is echoed by Yungher, who makes the basic but profound distinction that "terrorism is never about the cause, it is always about the methods used."[6]

Since terrorism is a "naked struggle for power, who shall yield it, and to what ends,"[7] these distinctions are meaningless to terrorists. They want power. They seek to change the current system in order to obtain their power. While the American political system has maintained a delicate balance between the status quo and radical change, I am convinced that this balance is nearing a "tipping point." One of the reasons I say this is that the moral value system that has held this country together for so long is in danger of being undermined. Those on the left argue for "progressive" change. Those on the right argue for "conservative" stability. Extremists on both ends continue to "push the envelope." Each side will push. Each side will respond. Neither side is likely to relent. Indeed, the controversial public policy "triggers" provide little room for compromise (see Chapter 9). In this dynamic, violence will occur. Indeed, terrorists will justify their violence "by convincing themselves that the injustices of society outweigh the amount of harm caused by their actions."[8] Which one of these extremes will back off? What would it take to do so? It is very clear that both extremes have used violence in the past. What will prevent it in the future?

One effective way to deal with extremism is through the basic, yet powerful soothing impact of morality. Regardless of your political views, if you believe it is morally wrong to intentionally kill civilians, then the threat of extremist violence is greatly reduced. Unfortunately, contemporary American society appears to be particularly vulnerable to terroristic violence because a strong moral reference point is often lacking.[9] Think about the implications of this assertion. Is there a sufficient moral framework in this society to prevent extremist violence? Incidents such as Columbine, Virginia Tech, Northern Illinois, and numerous others reveal a disconcerting answer.

To those who seek simple solutions, the response is typically to add another law to the thousands of other existing laws. Each of the existing laws did not stop these violent acts. It is important to consider that those who advocate extremist violence do not accept laws and rules.[10] Indeed, terrorists and extremists seek to advance a "higher law," as they maintain that society's laws do not apply to them, or that they are subservient to their "higher" purpose. This is consistent with Yungher's assertion that "the duty to carry out God's will is more important than man-made laws, and therefore, the war becomes sacred and absolutist with total moral justification."[11] In this sense, there will never be consensus. This represents a fundamental problem in arriving at a definition of "terrorism" acceptable to all. This is due to the conflicting moral issues associated with terrorism.[12] Consequently, while the rule of law is critical to the battle against such violence, the law alone is not sufficient. As Cooper maintains,[13]

> terrorism thus becomes a battle for the moral high ground, with those in legitimate power trying to preserve their positions against opponents bent on dragging them into the gutter.

Notwithstanding the inherent difficulties of defining terrorism, in developing a framework to study the subject one must provide a basis to do so. The definition of terrorism I advocate has four basic elements:

- The calculated use of violence or the threat of violence
- To inculcate fear
- Intended to coerce or to intimidate governments or societies
- Toward goals that are political, religious, or ideological

Each of these elements has a specific purpose. First, there must be violence or the threat of violence. This violence is not mindless nor is it "random" in the true sense of the term.[14] The violence is a deliberate strategy to produce certain ends. On one level, violence is a way of strengthening the support for the organization, and of the movement it represents. In this sense, it can be described as a "marketing device" and a method for rousing the "troops," the sympathizers or even the larger audience.[15]

On another level, the violence is designed to speak to the external audience. When the bomb explodes or the attack takes place, people tend to view the incident as being "random." The terrorist act may seem "random" to those who were not involved in the decision. The fact is, it is usually carefully planned and assessed. In this way, it may be unpredictable and indiscriminate, but it is not random. The message that is conveyed is this: Anyone, anywhere, at any time may be the target of the next attack.[16] The psychological term for this is known as the "personalization of the attack."[17] It leads people to this conclusion: "It could have been me." In this sense, think about the attack on the World Trade Center. How often have you talked to people who said something like, "I (or my daughter, son, wife, husband, etc.) was just at the tower the previous day (or week, etc.)?" The logic of this thinking is that only time/place made the difference between life and death. In this way, Tucker contends terrorists seek to invoke a pervasive fear in the civilian population by "personalizing" the threat. He adds that this is designed "so that everyone feels vulnerable, regardless of the statistical probability that a given individual will be affected."[18] We can cope with this uncertainty much more effectively when such time/place variations involve accidents and acts of God. It is much more problematic when you add intentional, malicious human motives to the equation.

This concern may cause the civilian population to adjust their "normal" life. Daily routines may become fraught with anxiety. In the end, a campaign of terrorist violence aims to isolate the individual from the group, to break up society into frightened and fragmented groups.[19] While terrorist groups typically seek dramatic political, religious, and ideological change, the more realistic goal is simply to create chaos within the society. The chaos fosters divisions and balkanization. This, in turn, results in inter-group conflicts. These circumstances reveal the inability of the government to deal with the violence. This dynamic leads to a fearful, isolated, and fragmented society. An illustration of this dynamic is provided in Chapter 3.

Second, the violence must be designed to produce fear. To induce fear, the "target" of the violence must be larger than the actual victim. In order to "inform" the audience of their cause and that they (the audience) may be the next victim, the terrorists need publicity. They get their publicity from the media. Samuelson noted that this dynamic has made the media "unwitting accomplices" with the terrorists and that they risk being reduced to "merchants of fear … with the perverse result [being] that [the media] may become the terrorists' silent partner."[20] This caused Margaret Thatcher to say that "it is up to the media to deprive terrorists of the 'oxygen of publicity' on which they thrive."[21] This connection between violence and publicity has been termed "the propaganda of the deed." This concept recognizes that spectacular acts of terrorism are a dramatic and effective means for terrorist to publicize both their cause and their movement.[22] Propaganda of the deed can be boiled down to four basic points:

- Talk is cheap.
- Violence of the deed is *the message*.
- Violent messages speak volumes.
- Terrorists and the media benefit from the violence.

Third, the violence and the resultant fear must be intended to coerce or intimidate government or the larger society. Here the goal must be for a significant purpose, such as the train bombings in Spain, which led to the election of a socialist party president who almost immediately removed Spanish troops from Iraq. This is a classic example of a violent act causing fear, leading to an election of a new government, and the implementation of a new government policy.

Figure 2.1 shows the distinctions between the true "realities" of the government and of the terrorists. You will note that each "side" must communicate a particular message that speaks to the larger population—the audience. From the government's

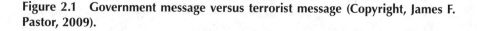

Figure 2.1 Government message versus terrorist message (Copyright, James F. Pastor, 2009).

point of view, they need to reinforce certain messages to the citizens. This is geared around the notion that you are "safe and secure." Although the government must communicate this message, one would be hard-pressed to quantify this assertion. Indeed, the reality of this message can be analogized to protecting citizens from "normal crime." No honest police or government official can say you "are safe and secure" from crime. The same logic holds true for terrorism. The need to reassure people that they are safe, however, is substantially more important than with "normal crime." This distinction is based on the perceived random nature of terrorism, coupled with its psychological effects and its potential catastrophic implications. Hence, in terroristic environments, government needs to be particularly cognizant to reassure populations that they are safe. This message is then contrasted with the message conveyed by the terrorists. They seek to make clear that the government cannot stop the violence. Underlying this message is the notion that government is incapable of controlling the violence. Indeed, the message is the government is weak, feeble, or ineffective. In essence, both messages are largely based on perception. One seeks to convey a message of safety and security; the other seeks to convey a message of inevitable attack.

In this same line of thinking, the government also seeks to convey it is prepared for any eventual attack. This message is communicated in a number of ways. For example, police agencies may have heavily armed police SWAT teams conduct drills. Alternatively, these SWAT teams may simply position themselves around a public facility as a show of strength. Similarly, specialized emergency response teams may conduct mock exercises to demonstrate—and practice—their skills. Each of these examples is partly designed to enhance performance in the event of an attack. They are also designed to speak to the audience. They do little to deter a group of committed terrorists. Instead, they say to the population, "We are here to help. We are prepared. We are ready." Conversely, the terrorists seek to convey they are operationally strong.

Think about the numerous bombings that have occurred in terroristic environments, such as Iraq. Each time a bomb is exploded, the message is "We are strong. We are capable of doing damage." These "deeds" are also reinforced by media coverage, showing the carnage and the death. Another way to supplement this message is to communicate a specific threat or demand through media channels. In this sense, both sides desire to communicate their message. Neither side can guarantee that their message is correct. Unfortunately, this is where the terrorists have the upper hand. The government can be prepared and still fail to stop the attack. This is where the statistical dilemma exists: the government has to be right 100% of the time, while the terrorists only have to "succeed" once. When the terrorists "succeed," they communicate that they are operationally strong—and that the government was not prepared to keep you safe!

The larger message by the government from this dynamic is to live a "normal" life. A classic example of this dynamic is when Bush urged people after 9/11 to "go shopping." While I agree with his desire to quickly foster normalcy back into society, I believe this message failed to articulate the larger sacrifices needed to counter the ideologies of an extremist movement. In contrast, President Obama seems to be cognizant of these needed sacrifices, when he stated,[23]

> What is required of us now is a new era of responsibility—a recognition, on the part of every American, that we have duties to ourselves, our nation, and the world, duties that we do not grudgingly accept but rather seize gladly, firm in the knowledge that there is nothing so satisfying to the spirit, so defining of our character, than giving our all to a difficult task. This is the price and the promise of citizenship.

Whether or not President Obama will articulate the nature of this sacrifice will be seen in the years to come. In any case he, along with other government officials, also must be able to articulate the need to live a "normal" life. This is truly a delicate balance. Think about the mixed messages that must be articulated. On one hand, the government must encourage people to go about their daily lives in a normal manner. On the other hand, the government must consistently remind the population that they need to be aware of the potential threat. Hence, these mixed messages may confuse people. They are being told to live a normal life, but they are also being told to be aware of the next explosion.

Conversely, the terrorist's message is "Be prepared to die!" When this message is conveyed after a "successful" attack, it has more impact. The more "successful" attacks, the more likely this message will be believed. In any case, the two messages are almost mirror opposites. One says to "live a normal life," the other says "be ready to die." This is an extremely interesting juxtaposition. It is based largely—even exclusively—on perception. As will be fleshed out in the last chapters of this book, how this message is communicated may have more to do with who is doing the communicating than with the actual substance of the message.

Fourth, the goal of the violence is political, religious, or ideological. This element usually separates the common criminal from the terrorist. Most criminals are motivated to commit crime for money, power, revenge, or a host of other reasons. Terrorists are motivated to commit crime (if they even acknowledge that it is a crime) for larger political, religious, or ideological purposes. For example, if a gang member sees opposing gang members on a street corner and shoots up the corner with an AK-47, is this a terrorist act? Typically the answer is no. Unless the gang member committed the crime for a political, religious, or ideological purpose, the characterization of the crime as a terrorist act is misleading.

In this example, one way to distinguish a criminal act from a terrorist act is illustrated in the columns in Table 2.1. While these should be considered only generalizations, they do help inform you on some important distinctions. These general characteristics have some value. For example, the typical criminal tends to take advantage of an opportunity that presents itself. This is not to say that some criminals do not plan their crime in advance. This is certainly true. Terrorists, at least at this point in time, have been known to be very focused and committed

Table 2.1 Criminal versus Extremist Distinctions

Typical Criminal Characteristics	Typical Extremist Characteristics
Opportunistic	Focused
Uncommitted	Committed
Self-centered	Team oriented
Undisciplined	Disciplined
Untrained	Trained
Escape oriented	Attack oriented

Copyright, James F. Pastor, 2009.

to their plans and their goals. Further, due to their desire for money and power, criminals tend to be self-centered, while the terrorists with their grand plans and goals tend to be more team oriented. Criminals are also usually undisciplined and ill trained, with terrorists tending to be more disciplined and trained. These factors are generally true at the time of this writing. Going forward, I believe that we will see some variance. It is likely that terrorists, particularly "lone wolves," will be less disciplined and less trained.[24] In addition, by isolating terrorist groups and preventing "sanctuaries," as in Afghanistan during the mid 1990s, the likelihood that we will see less disciplined and trained operatives is a distinct possibility. Indeed, if gang members "graduate" to terrorism, as I predict they will, it is likely they will be less trained than al Qaeda operatives currently are. Ironically, as will be articulated below, there is mounting evidence that a number of gang members have joined the U.S. military, enabling them to increase their training and discipline. Will these gang members reform themselves through their military experience? Or will they go home with skills and training to continue their life of crime? These provocative questions will be addressed below.

Finally, the key distinction between criminals and terrorists is their tendency to escape versus attack. Criminals typically desire to escape. When confronted by the police, most criminals will be oriented toward escape. This does not mean that all criminals will seek to escape. This also does not mean that some criminals will attack police in order to facilitate escape. Obviously these assertions are not universal. Similarly, some terrorists will not seek to attack, and instead will seek to escape. With these caveats, the two options: escape versus attack may be a useful distinction. They have significant implications on the police and public safety providers. I contend that the aggregate of this tendency will result in many more injuries and deaths to police and public safety providers. This fact alone will "trigger" a change in the policing model. This can be explained with the notion of "self-defense." If your safety is in jeopardy, you will take measures to protect yourself. The measures that police will take relate to weaponry, tactics, selection, training, and the like. In short, the policing model will change. The elements of this model will be presented in Chapters 4 through 7.

One of the main reasons police and public safety providers will be targeted is because they have a symbolic value to the terrorists. On one level, these individuals are the most obvious representatives of government. They enforce laws, maintain order, and seek to preserve the status quo. Each of these factors is adverse to the interests of terrorists. They do not respect the law. They seek to create chaos. They desire to change the status quo. On another level, by targeting police and public safety providers, terrorists communicate to the larger society that if they cannot protect themselves, how are they going to protect you? Individuals take note that the guns, badges, and paramilitary discipline do not protect them from being targeted. Since most people do not have anywhere near the same weaponry and capacity as police officers, how can they protect themselves from similar attacks? Consequently, the message is "The government cannot protect you." The larger implication is "Until you accede to our demands, you will not be safe."[25] Change the government, or be subject to more attacks.

Of course, police and public safety providers will not be the only targets of terrorist and extremist violence. Civilians have and will continue to die in terrorist attacks. The question of whether attacks against "innocent" civilians can be justified is a familiar theme. If you listen to the logic of al Qaeda, the answer is that it can. They demonstrated this answer on 9/11 in a very powerful manner. According to Azzam, the logic of attacking civilian populations is as follows: Citizens of this country elect their representatives. They pay their taxes, thereby providing the funds for the government to develop and execute its policies. Therefore, citizens are not innocent. In fact, they are responsible for the actions of their governments. Indeed, given our form of government, our citizens can be construed as being the actual decision makers of government policy.[26] This logic was echoed by Stern, who stated that the "target" audience is not necessarily the victims and their sympathizers, but instead it is perpetrators and their sympathizers.[27]

Terrorists view their enemies and assess where their vulnerabilities lie. This country has numerous vulnerabilities. It can be considered a "target-rich environment." The potential targets include

- Symbolic
- Governmental
- Financial
- Infrastructure/utilities
- "Soft targets"

While this target list is not exhaustive or definitive, it provides a useful vision of how wide open this country is. Symbolic targets include the Statue of Liberty, various government memorials, the Golden Gate Bridge, and any number of other significant sites throughout the country. Similarly, governmental targets include the White House, the Pentagon, Congress, the Supreme Court, and numerous other federal, state, and local government buildings. Financial targets include the World Trade Center (which also can be considered symbolic due to its symbol of American capitalism), stock exchanges, and any number of financial buildings and economic centers, such as business districts and "downtown" areas. Infrastructure/utilities include wide-ranging locations such as mass transportation, highways, bridges, airports, power grids, oil and gas refineries, educational institutions, water systems, ports and waterways, computer systems, radio and cellular phone towers, satellite communication systems, and numerous other structural or foundational networks that support the citizens of the country.

At the lowest level of difficulty and sophistication are the "soft targets." There are literally thousands or even millions of small businesses, such as cafes, restaurants, movie theaters, malls, convenience stores, buses, trains, and the like. In essence, there is no shortage of targets. While we may be able to secure these potential targets with certain security measures, such as detection systems, barriers, alarms, guards, and a highly visible patrol force, the best answer is still the age-old police formula of preventing crime: desire + opportunity = crime.[28] The new policing model developed in this book is designed to address this basic, but complex equation.

Influence of the Media

This section explains the role the media plays in influencing the perception of terrorism. Much of this "war" is being fought using the technique of terrorism. Indeed, this tactic is the key element of the military front of extremist groups. It is critical to their plan—and to their success. Unfortunately, because the "war" is based on this "covert" method, it has largely been conducted "under the radar screen." This is because people cannot, or will not connect the dots. They see each bombing or each attack as being an isolated case. They see each isolated case as being caused by some "crazy" group of misfits or extremist "outcasts." Indeed, many, if not most, of the terrorist acts around the world get little or no attention from the American media. Hence, the incident will not "exist" in minds of most people. This is why I asked in the earlier chapter about the existence of the "Tamil Tigers." Most people have not heard of them because they are irrelevant to their lives. Of course, they are not irrelevant to those whom they are attacking.

It is my belief that the current media climate has contributed to political divisions within this country. I say this not to imply that it is intentional—though some may argue that this is indeed true.[29] My contention is simply that media representatives—as any other individuals—view any issue from the worldview that they maintain. In this way, the "news" is shaped by the worldview of the person (and organization) that interprets, understands, and communicates the "facts."

Simply put, I reject the notion that journalists are unbiased. In my mind, it defies any understanding of human nature. It is a false premise to assume that people can completely separate themselves from their value systems and their worldview. This is particularly true of an industry that is based on discerning "truth" from an increasingly complex and competitive world. Hence, I assume reporting on world events will be based on a certain degree of subjectivity. The precise amount of the subjectivity is the key question.

It would be extraordinarily difficult to quantify the precise level of subjectivity that goes into the "news." Even if this were possible, I would not think it adds anything to wrestle with this matter. Suffice it to say, I see the "news" as divided into two very distinctive worlds. On one hand there is the traditional or "mainstream media" led by the *New York Times, Washington Post*, and the major TV networks, plus CNN. On the other hand is the conservative or "new media" represented by the *Wall Street Journal,* FOX News, and talk radio. Surrounding these competing worldviews are Internet blogs and sites, typically supporting one "school of thought" or the other. Admittedly, while these are generalizations, the essence of these worlds is rather simple but pointed: liberal (mainstream media) or conservative (new media). For those who dispute this assertion, I suggest you read the editorial columns of the *New York Times* and the *Wall Street Journal* for one month. The views coming from these papers are often mirror opposites. While these are indeed "editorials," it defies any rational explanation as to how these views do not affect the reporting of "hard news."

It is my assertion that these two worlds are becoming increasingly distinct. People who tend to see the world in liberal (or progressive) terms tend to read and watch traditional news sources. People who tend to see the world in conservative terms tend to read and watch (or listen) to conservative (new media) sources. This should not surprise anyone. I contend most people naturally gravitate to what they like and are familiar with. Hence, people tend to gravitate to what their worldview reinforces. This is especially true with adults, who have spent many years trying to make sense of a complex world. After people "figure out" the world they do not want to constantly reevaluate their conclusion. They may not be happy with their conclusion, but it is their way of seeing the world. The logic is: Do not "upset my apple cart" with new explanations of the world! This assertion, whether conscious or not, is often how people cope with the uncertainties and complexities of the world.

One may be asking, What does this have to do with terrorism? It is critical. This is so for a number of reasons. First, if I am correct in asserting that two distinct media camps exist, and that people gravitate to the news source with which they are most comfortable, then the reporting—and understanding—of terrorism will be bifurcated. That is, media institutions will likely report the "news" based on their respective worldviews. For example, liberal media may focus on the "freedom fighter" point of view. Or they may ignore threats—and direct attacks—from radical organizations as a means to minimize the notion that these groups actually pose a threat. Conversely, conservative news sources will likely trumpet the threats and attacks to manifest that the threat, indeed, is real. They will also be much more likely to characterize these individuals as "terrorists."

Implicit in these distinctions are numerous editorial decisions that strike at the heart of the information conveyed. In this context, I use the term "editorial decisions" broadly. I am not necessarily speaking of the editorial section of the newspaper. Instead, media organizations make numerous decisions about whether to run a story, how it will be presented, who they obtain background information from, what aspects of the story they will focus on, and why the story is deemed "newsworthy."

These editorial decisions affect whether to even publicize an "incident." It affects how the incident is presented. It affects the "spin" or the tone of the story. Numerous questions relate to this decision. For example, does the piece focus on the victim? Does it trumpet the cause of the extremists? Does the piece describe the tactical value of the incident? Does the piece explain how the incident fits into the larger strategic goals of the extremist group? Does the piece focus on the government response or some policy failure (or its failure to prevent the incident)? Does the story opine on the "proper" government approach to future incidents? Does the story provide context on the level or probability of the threat environment, or add context to the larger implications of the extremist movement? These and other aspects of the story are critical to the information conveyed to the "news consumer." In addition, the media source must assess whether or not to show videos of the incident, whether to communicate the body count, whether to characterize the "offenders" as "terrorists" (with its related negative connotation), as "insurgents" (with a more positive connotation), as "criminals" (implying that the act was a crime and not an act of war), as "freedom fighters" (as a positive connotation implying that the act relates to a larger war or cause), or whether to attach the religion of the offenders to the story[30] (so as to avoid the implication against the entire "brand" of religion).

These are difficult—and inevitable—questions that each news source must address. The point here is that, while each news source may address these questions in some context, the key is how they are addressed. What aspects are emphasized? What characterizations are used? What is the tone of the reporting? Does it provide context, such as who are these people, what do they want, why did they attack, how likely will another attack be? In short, I cannot overstate how important this reporting will be. It can swing the population—and its related emotions—for or against the government or the terrorists! It can facilitate swings in public opinion, for or against government policies or particular politicians. Of course, in an ideal world the purpose of the reporting is to communicate the "news." The substance of the "news," however, is much trickier. Objectively communicating "relevant facts" inevitably results in some editorial decision based on conflicting principles and opinions. Consequently, the best result is to help the population understand the issues surrounding terrorism. Unfortunately, due to the dynamics related to the current media climate—and of the complexities of terrorism—this is a very unrealistic expectation.

Second, assume again that I am correct about the distinctions of two diverse media "schools of thought." I think that these distinctions will inevitably divide the population. Let me explain this distinction by focusing on the result. The population will be divided in its "understanding" of the incident based on what media source it obtained its information from. For example, suppose a bomb explodes in a New York City subway, killing 40 people and injuring 60 others. The liberal (or progressive) media may play the story one way, while the conservative media may play it another. The liberals will likely focus on sympathy to the victims and in understanding the offenders. Further, depending upon who is in charge (Democrat or Republican) their tendency will be to blame the president or explain how the president is attempting to deal with the matter. Conversely, the conservatives will likely focus on the anger against the offenders, the threats from the offenders, and what should be done to avoid another attack. My point is, both aspects of the story are proper. Both need to be reported. However, if one media source reports with a certain "twist," and the other reports with another, the result is a population who is inclined to see the event based on where they obtained their "news." Consequently, the same incident may result in very difficult conclusions by large sections of the population.

What is particularly problematic is the aggregate of this dynamic. If this occurs often, as in Iraq, the result is a perception of the "problem" defined according to whom you listen to. Of course, once the problem has been defined, the "solution" follows. Hence, both the definition of the problem and the solution will be greatly impacted by the particular news source that helps shape your worldview. In this way, the possibility exists that the country will be divided by its tendency—liberal views from liberal news sources, and conservative views from conservative news sources. This is not just an academic explanation. It is not simply political science. It is potentially dangerous—and balkanizing. With high stakes and deadly consequences related to terrorism, people will not be thinking too clearly. They also will likely be thinking in accord with their worldview—which is validated by their media source! In this sense, it becomes a "vicious circle." People's views are shaped and validated by their news source. They then obtain their "news" from media sources in accord with this worldview. When they "understand" the problem they then desire "solutions" based on this thinking. Playing this thinking into the macro level, the potential for balkanization is great. As you think of this possibility, consider the implications of "group think" discussed in the "radicalization" section below. Consequently, the potential for severe "disagreements" over the nature of the problem, the appropriate solution, and who is to blame is greatly impacted by the current bifurcation of the media.

This potential internal conflict is exacerbated by the methods used to fight the "war on terror." It is fought using two methods: asymmetric warfare (terrorism) and the influence of "hearts and minds." The latter method includes psychological, cultural, political, and religious aspects of the "war." Please consider that it is not my desire to simply label this as "war." Indeed, those who are advocating this "war" have declared it as such. Once they declare war, we have two options. Ignore the declaration of war. We did this in 1998. We viewed each subsequent incident as a criminal event—until 9/11. Then we reevaluated this conclusion. Thereafter, the Bush Administration declared the "war on terror." It is likely that the Obama Administration will change this approach (see discussion of this in Chapter 8).

I wish the Obama Administration well. They have their hands full. I advocate that you closely watch and listen to the approach of his administration. I also hope that the mainstream media outlets will finally recognize the full scope of the threat facing America. My sense is that the "threat" will be communicated more than it was during the Bush years (absent of course, the media coverage of 9/11). This may be partly because the "war" will hit American soil—on the home front. In my mind, it will also be a function of the media's desire to advocate for a successful Obama Administration.[31]

The implications of this assertion can be illustrated by this rhetorical question: If a tree falls in the forest and no one is there to hear it, does it make a noise? Similarly, if a bomb goes off in Algeria and the American media does not cover it, did it really happen? This same question can be asked of terrorist attacks in a number of different countries. This is true for numerous countries, except in Iraq. For many months, the American public got the daily recitation of the number of bombings and attacks, along with the body count and the obligatory photos and video. In essence, we were fed the "propaganda of the deed" by our media for the benefit of our enemies. If you disagree with this assertion ask yourself, Who benefits from this coverage? Has it helped inform you of the strategic implications? Has it helped galvanize the American public of the nature of this "generational conflict"? Has it even informed you of the larger context of who is doing the bombing and why these events are occurring? I contend none of these questions are answered by the typical news coverage. Instead, the coverage strikes a deep emotional chord. No one, especially those with family members in the military, enjoys or benefits from these photos and videos. Of course, no one wants to hear of another soldier or marine killed in action. These are terrible and heart wrenching to see and feel. Unfortunately, this is exactly the point. These touch us deeply, at an emotional level. Do you think the terrorists are not cognizant of this? Do you think that the media does not understand this dynamic?

Consider again the concept of "propaganda of the deed." Acts of terrorism provide a dramatic and effective means of publicizing the larger message of the extremist group. When the media publicizes these deeds it facilitates the goals of the extremist movement. This is particularly true when the message provided by the media is typically limited to photos and videos of the carnage with little or no context. In the end, the violence of the deed is *the message*. These violent messages speak volumes to the intended audience. Indeed, the terrorists understand—and expect—the media to communicate the deed to the population. When these messages are conveyed, they speak volumes. They communicate the notion that the government cannot stop the violence. In the end, only the terrorists and the media benefit from the violence. I believe indiscriminate or irresponsible media coverage, as was evidenced in Iraq, does not help the population. It also does not help the cause of the mission.

Current terrorist groups, particularly with religious-oriented groups, typically plan to maximize casualties and media exposure.[32] The more blood shed, the more extensive the media coverage.[33] The phase "if it bleeds, it leads" is relevant in this context. It creates an ironic, yet complicated relationship between terrorists and the media. This relationship is powerfully characterized by Nacos, who said,[34]

> Terrorists and the media are not bedfellows, they are more like partners in a marriage of convenience in that terrorists need all the news coverage they can get and the media needs dramatic, shocking, sensational, tragic events to sustain and bolster their ratings or circulation.

Some will argue that the media has an obligation to report this "news." They are correct. There is no doubt that the media has an obligation to inform the public. No one could reasonably dispute this assertion. My main complaint is that the media skews the coverage to fit their particular agenda. A classic example relates to the coverage of Abu Ghraib by the *New York Times.* This Iraqi prison scandal was prominently featured for 32 consecutive days by this newspaper after the disclosure of the scandalous photos of the treatment doled out by U.S. military guards.[35] This speaks volumes about the purpose behind the stories. Think back to this event. Do you recall "new" information breaking daily from Abu Ghraib? Or do you remember, as I do, that once the story broke, most of the information was known from the initial publication of the scandal. In essence, the story was American soldiers abusing prisoners, evidenced by a series of photos. Indeed, the *photos were the story.* They were damning on their face. Once these photos were seen, over and over again, what else was gained from the story? I say little other than damning the military—and the cause of the war.

Ironically, during the same time this "story was being developed," another "story" was too terrible for the media to show you. This was the beheading of an American by Islamists, who were led by a Jordanian named al-Zarqawi, who was the leader of al Qaeda in Iraq. The American media, in this case, "policed themselves" by agreeing to not televise this sickening event. In essence, the media decided you did not "need" to see the video of the beheading. Instead, you "needed" to see numerous front-page stories of prisoners with women's panties around their head! Do you believe there is internal consistency with these two examples? I think the conclusion is obvious. Further, what makes the daily "propaganda of the deed" more problematic is that it comes with little, if any, critical analysis. There is little context. There is little emphasis on all the schools being built, the little girls being educated, or the repair of infrastructure that was neglected for decades. In essence, this good news is too boring! It also does not fit the "template" of the agenda, which is: We must leave Iraq!

After "reporting" (read advocating) this story for months when the story broke in 2004, the *New York Times* revisited the matter on October 13, 2007. On this date, the *New York Times* reported that Lt. Gen. Ricardo S. Sanchez, former Iraq commander, said the Iraq War has become "a nightmare." The *Times* asserted that Sanchez offered a "sweeping indictment of the four-year effort in Iraq," and called the Bush Administration's handling of the war "incompetent" and said the result was "a nightmare with no end in sight." The article further noted that Sanchez was replaced after the Abu Ghraib prisoner abuse scandal. The article also trumpeted that Lieutenant General Sanchez blamed the Bush Administration for a "catastrophically flawed, unrealistically optimistic war plan" and denounced the current addition of American forces as a "desperate" move that would not achieve long-term stability.[36]

This example raises a couple of important points about the media. First, consider the notion that the surge was a "desperate" move. While that may have been the "consensus" in the fall of 2007, I know of no one in early 2009 who maintained this same belief. Do you? When was the last time you heard this same criticism? An even a better question may be, When was the last time you heard anyone praise Bush for the surge? As of this writing, the Iraqi people just completed another "historic" election (on January 30, 2009). The election went off without any major incident. How many "breathless" news reports have you heard about the success of these elections?

Beyond the merits of the Iraqi election—or of the surge and even the larger war—my point here is that the *New York Times* article quoting Lieutenant General Sanchez left off a pointed critique of the media. Here is what Sanchez said that the paper did not see "fit to print." Please note that initially he seemed to be speaking specifically about Abu Ghraib, but after the second paragraph he spoke more broadly:[37]

> Almost invariably, my perception is that the sensationalistic value of these assessment[s] is what provided the edge that you seek for self-aggrandizement or to advance your individual quest for getting on the front page with your stories.
>
> As I understand it, your measure of worth is how many front page stories you have written and unfortunately some of you will compromise your integrity and display questionable ethics as you seek to keep America informed. ... For some, it seems that as long as you get a front page story there is little or no regard for the "collateral damage" you will cause. Personal reputations have no value and you report with total impunity and are rarely held accountable for unethical conduct.
>
> The speculative and often uninformed initial reporting that characterizes our media appears to be rapidly becoming the standard of the industry.

> An Arab proverb states—"Four things come not back: the spoken word, the spent arrow, the past, the neglected opportunity." Once reported, your assessments become conventional wisdom and nearly impossible to change ...
>
> All are victims of the massive agenda-driven competition for economic or political supremacy. The death knell of your ethics has been enabled by your parent organizations who have chosen to align themselves with political agendas. What is clear to me is that you are perpetuating the corrosive partisan politics that is destroying our country and killing our service members who are at war.

In my mind, any responsible and reasonable professional will assert that it is disingenuous—at best—to report Sanchez's criticism of the Bush Administration while ignoring his criticism of the media. Indeed, since he talked about the number of "front page" stories, it can be inferred that Sanchez's criticism was aimed directly at the very paper that reported his pointed criticism of Bush—the *New York Times*. I am hard-pressed to justify how one can report one aspect of Sanchez's criticism while ignoring the other. In the end, anyone who believes that the media plays these issues in an "unbiased" manner, I have a big, bright, and new bridge to sell. Are you interested? Before you answer this question, what do you think the media will say about this book?

Consequently, the mainstream media does not connect the dots, and many politicians—particularly Democratic leaders—have invested in using Iraq as a political strategy. At least partly because of this, the American people simply do not understand terrorism or the implications of the Iraq War—and the "war on terrorism." Let me emphasize the key point: The general public does not understand the issues or the implications of terrorism. Why should they? They are not experts on terrorism. They have their lives to worry about. They have more "immediate" concerns, such as paying their bills, raising their children, taking care of their jobs or their businesses, planning their vacations, and the like.

Instead of a critical analysis of terrorism, the media presents a daily recitation of an *agenda* that is being drummed into the deceived American public. Note when was the last time you saw a report on Iraq? Since the daily "propaganda of the deed" has ended, the constant stream of stories seemed to "disappear" into the diversion of "more important" news. In this light, when was the last time you saw a piece on the dangers posed by radical Islamist terrorism? Consider a cover story from *Life* magazine that was published in 1970. In this cover, a photo depicts numerous 8- to 10-year-old Arab youths with assault rifles across their chests.[38] Do you think similar photos and stories could be done today? If your answer is affirmative, when and where was the last time you saw similar stories? Most likely, if you recently saw such a story, it was in an "alternative" news source. I will leave it to your mind to answer the "whys" of these questions. Whatever your answer, I contend there are innumerable examples of similar stories in various parts of the world that could be played in the American media. Instead of being informed of these mounting threats, we are shown the "propaganda of the deed" of our enemies by our media and our enemies. If you think it is not an editorial decision, then I shudder to think about how one can understand the storm that is approaching.

This brings us to back to my initial point. This war is also being fought through a number of different mediums. As demonstrated by the "propaganda of the deed," the war is a war of ideas. It is a war of public relations. It is a war of disinformation. It is a war of political positioning. It is a war of international relations. But most of all, this is a war of ideology. It is battle of "hearts and minds." It is battle of one particular worldview (radical Islamist) against the current dominant worldview (modernity or capitalism).

Organizational Structures and Techniques

It is widely acknowledged that terrorist organizations are structured around "cells." Each cell is autonomous and separate from other cells. Typically, three to five people are contained in each cell. In order to maintain operational security, only one person in a cell may know of adjacent cell(s). This provides some level of protection for each cell. It also simultaneously enables leaders between the cells to communicate with each other. Overall, though, the key link from one cell to the other is by ideology. The reason they are part of the cell is to further the ideology of the group or, in some cases, the movement. In this sense, the ideology is the "glue" that holds the group together. Figure 2.2 represents the separate nature of these cells.

Each cell has a specific purpose. The benefit of segregating specific functions with specific cells allows each cell to specialize in a particular skill. It also provides for enhanced secrecy and operational security. Separating the tasks of cell members enables each member to isolate him- or herself from detection. For example, when the intelligence cell performs pre-incident surveillance, this will be the extent of his or her role. When the time comes for the attack, another cell member who will conduct the attack will not have been seen in the area previously. This greatly limits the ability of public safety providers to recognize the individual due to his or her absence from the scene until the day of reckoning. In this way, the operation is broken up in stages, conducted by different individuals who have little contact with each other.

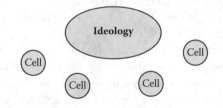

Figure 2.2 Typical terrorist cell structure.

While some groups have more or fewer levels of sophistication, it is fairly common to have four specific functional cells: intelligence, financial, logistics, and operational. The intelligence cell performs certain assessments of proposed targets, including videotaping, surveillance of security techniques, conducting reconnaissance, and testing the target to determine how security personnel and methodologies will perform.

The financial cell will provide the monies needed to perform the operation. This includes fundraising, money laundering, narcotics, and fraudulent schemes designed to collect money. A key goal of these money-making operations is not to raise suspicion of law enforcement. When crimes are committed for the purpose of financing a terrorist operation, they are commonly known as "precursor crimes." These can be defined as "unlawful acts undertaken to facilitate a terrorist attack or to support a terrorist campaign."[39] O'Neil illustrates a number of these crimes. For example, he asserts that narcotics are one of the most profitable fundraising commodities for terrorists. He noted in 2003 that there were $13 billion in profits at the production level, $94 billion at the wholesale level, and $322 billion at the retail level.[40]

Specific examples may help inform the reader. A Los Angeles-based terrorist group, known as Jamiyyat Ul-Islam Is-Saheeh (JIS), conducted a series of gas station robberies in order to fund their terrorist operation. This black Muslim group sought to attack U.S. military bases and Jewish facilities. Group members robbed gas stations in order to obtain the resources to carry out the planned attacks.[41] Fortunately, in 2005, police detectives captured the robbers before they could execute their plans. In doing so, they broke up the larger conspiracy. The benefit in this case was that the group had to commit other brazen and obvious crimes in order to fund the larger operation. In addition, the Islamic cell that was responsible for the Spain train bombings in March 2004 were financed by selling hashish and ecstasy.[42] Unfortunately, this drug selling operation was not detected prior to the direct action. In addition, a fraudulent insurance scheme by Karim Koubriti and Ahmed Hannon was disrupted by law enforcement in connection with an "economic jihad" designed to defraud insurance companies by falsely asserting vehicle accident claims.[43] Cell phone and phone card scams are also commonplace. Abdel-Ilah Elmardoudi was convicted in August 2006 of operating a phone card "shoulder surfing" scheme where he stole hundreds of calling cards.[44]

More established groups have much more sophisticated operations. For example, there is an extensive system of cigarette bootlegging and tax stamp fraud where the revenues are being used to fund terrorist groups. New York state officials estimate that one operation's fraudulent schemes generate between $200,000 and $300,000 per week, with a large percentage of the monies being diverted to Hezbollah, Hamas, and al Qaeda.[45]

Due to the extensive monies available from these schemes, law enforcement officials have been paying attention. A number of operations have been broken up.

In Charlotte, North Carolina, a criminal enterprise led by Mohamad Hammoud smuggled cigarettes from North Carolina, where the tax is 50 cents per carton, to Michigan where the tax was $7.50 per carton. Upon his conviction in 2002, law enforcement officials estimate that the group made about $8 million in about four years of operation. Approximately $100,000 of these monies was sent to Hezbollah.[46] In another case, 19 men were indicted in Dearborn, Michigan, for international racketeering. The indictment charged that from 1996–2004, the group trafficked contraband cigarettes, counterfeit rolling papers, tax stamps, and Viagra. Funds from the scheme were ultimately transferred to Hezbollah. It was estimated that the group was shipping $500,000 in cash per week.[47]

The third type of cell is the logistical cell. As the name implies, this cell is devoted to establishing safe houses, renting cars, providing documents, transferring cash/assets, and other necessary logistics. As mentioned above, it is very useful for these details to be conducted by individuals who will not participate in the actual attack.

Finally, the operational cell is in charge of conducting the attack—and specific preparatory measures prior to such. These include recruiting the members of the attack cell, establishing the timing and date of the operation, signaling the execution through established channels or networks, and then executing the act.

As these varying types of cells illustrate, the most effective terrorist organization probably consists of many clusters of sizes, functions, and complexity.[48] As illustrated above, individual clusters often find their own funding through licit or illicit businesses. These cells and clusters of cells are held together by trust and a shared mission. This is the "ideological glue" that keeps groups and movements together. As we will see below, the Islamist movement, partly through the organizational structures of al Qaeda, has helped guide and inspire the operatives.

Sophisticated organizations, such as al Qaeda, have developed training manuals that lay out in great detail the inner workings of how a cell should function. This sophisticated manual is designed for independent but affiliated al Qaeda operatives. This instruction is particularly true regarding the planning and execution of a direct action. As an example of the direction derived from this training manual, it states in pertinent part that[49]

> In every country, we should hit their organizations, institutions, clubs, and hospitals. The targets must be identified, carefully chosen, and include their largest gatherings, so that any strike should cause thousands of deaths. The strikes must be strong and have a wide impact on the population of that nation.

In addition, the manual articulates such directives and details as[50]

1. Gathering information about the enemy, the land, the installations, and the neighbors
2. Kidnapping enemy personnel, documents, secrets, and arms

3. Assassinating enemy personnel as well as foreign tourists
4. Freeing the brothers who are captured by the enemy
5. Spreading rumors and writing statements that instigate people against the enemy
6. Blasting and destroying the places of amusement, immorality, and sin
7. Blasting and destroying the embassies and attacking vital economic centers
8. Blasting and destroying bridges leading into and out of the cities

The level of detail shown in this document correlates with the organizational structure of the movement. As mentioned in the Chapter 1, when thinking about al Qaeda it is necessary to see them as a movement instead of a single group, or as a single threat. The structure of the organization speaks to this assertion. Consider the structure of the organization shown in Figure 2.3.[51]

In this hierarchal structure, bin Laden has created a worldwide network among various loosely knit terrorist cells.[52] The Shura Council acts as the board of directors and includes representatives from various terrorist groups in different parts of the world. In this capacity, this leadership appears to be functioning less as a group of commanders and more as inspirational leaders.[53] Though there is likely no single master plan, these cells are united in their Islamic vision. They view the movement as a larger crusade against the West, and against those governments viewed as puppets of the West.[54] This movement, through bin Laden's "logic" and inspiration, contends that American-led globalization has created and perpetuated the conditions that much of the world struggles with. They see the problems in the Muslim world as the result of the economic and political order. The United States is seen as the author of these conditions. Indeed, the United States is "anchor" of the status quo. Because of its influence, the United States is the "target" of much of the anger.[55]

When one compares this hierarchal structure to the cell structure, the similarities of their functions are evident. For example, the Finance Committee and finance cell conduct essentially the same purpose: finance terrorist operations. The Finance

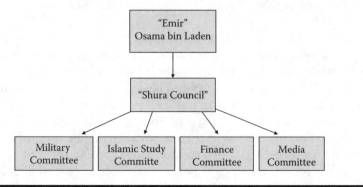

Figure 2.3   Al-Qaeda organizational structure.

Committee, however, has a much larger scope of operations (i.e., the world). The Military Committee is similar to the operations cell, whereby they both execute the attack. Once again, the Military Committee has a much wider scope of operations. The other two committees, Islamic Study Committee and the Media Committee, are more strategic in scope than the smaller cells. Cells are not generally equipped to conduct these strategic functions. For example, the Islamic Study Committee issues "fatwas" and other religious rulings, while the Media Committee publishes newspaper stories, conducts and distributes video/audio communications, and operates or fosters Web communications.[56]

In this discussion on the cell and hierarchal structure of terrorist organizations, however, I must caution that these structures are neither definitive nor universal. Examples of "lone wolves" abound.[57] These individuals are "inspired" by the ideology of the "cause." They are not connected to a larger organization. Instead, they act on their own for the larger cause. The same can be said for some right-wing, environmental, and Islamist individuals. These individuals act out of the notion of "leaderless resistance." These individuals do not need a leader to tell them what to do. They act from Web- or media-based pronouncements, such as a "fatwa" from the "emir." This approach has been adopted by radical environmental groups. They seek a strategy of "uncoordinated violence" by posting "hit lists" on their Web sites. Their advocates then select their own targets. This results in "membership by deed" where individuals become part of the "group" by their voluntary undertaking of violent act(s).[58] Consequently, while it is important to understand the cellular and hierarchal structures, one must be particularly cognizant of the larger ideological movements—as this is the glue of any sustained terrorist campaign.

Radicalization Process and Factors

We have briefly discussed some of the major concepts, influences, and structures related to terrorism and extremism. While this information is useful to understand how these groups operate, a more basic question needs to be addressed: Why do some people resort to extremist violence? The answer to this question is complex. As with most phenomena, the answer is not definitive. Nor does any one factor answer all circumstances. In order to address this question, we will explore some theories and data as to the predicted rise of extremism. This will also be tempered with reasoned arguments designed to shed light on a complex subject. Before we go on, one key principle needs to be emphasized. In order for terroristic and extremist violence to manifest itself, there first needs to be an ideological framework to foster the violence. Consequently, we will systematically examine the predicted rise of extremism from thought (mindset) to direct action (violence).

First, let's address the thought process that leads to extremism and then to violence. There are a number of avenues that inform or illustrate this process. For example, the New York Police Department (NYPD) tries to locate and neutralize pockets of militancy even before potentially violent individuals can form radical cells.[59] This "preventive" approach may be the most effective way that police departments can help fight terror. Implementing this approach requires fleshing out some premises that may be useful in understanding the process of radicalization:[60]

1. The consistency of the radicalization process provides a tool for predictability.
2. There is no useful profile to predict who will follow this trajectory of radicalization.
3. Radicalization occurs because the individual is looking for an identity and a cause, often finding them in extremist ideologies.
4. The radicalization process requires places where the ideology is transmitted to the affected individuals. These are known as "incubators" where the information and the techniques are needed to act out the violence.
5. "Group think" is a powerful catalyst to actually committing a terrorist act. This is spurred by the presence of a "spiritual sanctioner" and an "operational leader."

These factors merit additional discussion. Initially, it is important to note that these factors may enable the researcher, the investigator, or the policy maker to better understand the process of radicalization. While people intuitively understand that people do not wake up one morning and decide to become a terrorist, the actual process that brings someone to this decision is clouded by the disconnect that is foreign to most Americans. Most people do not know anyone who is willing to blow up a building, kill innocent humans, and die in a terrorist attack. These are foreign to almost all Americans. It is difficult to understand how one gets to the point where they are willing to conduct such dramatic attacks. The aforementioned premises, however, provide some consistency to the radicalization process. I do not imply these are definitive. Even if they are definitive, however, it is difficult to observe how a particular individual goes from "normal" to radical. Consequently, the most effective way to see this is from the aggregate (the macro level), instead of from the individual (the micro level). In this light, we will speak of tendencies, trends, and the resultant public policy implications.

The second premise follows the logic of the first, that is, there is no useful profile to predict who will follow this radicalization process. This means that it is impossible to predict precisely who will become radicalized. This does not mean, however, that there is no value in studying this process. Indeed, studying this process has great value. It provides a road map to understand how some (but not all) people gravitate to extremist ideologies and actions.

The third premise is when the process begins to take a more definitive shape. Those who are looking for an identity and for some larger purpose are a necessary precursor to extremist violence. Simply stated, people with an intense passion for something purposeful are many times more inclined to extremism than those who are not passionate. Said another way, someone who does not deeply care for something will not do anything dramatic about it. Those who are willing to be violent suicide bombers come to mind as a classic example of the impact of passion to this process. As Austrian author and playwright Arthur Schnitzler so cleverly notes, "Martyrdom has always been a proof of the intensity, never the correctness of a belief."[61] Understanding this factor makes the predictive nature of future extremism much more defined. In order to make this assessment, one needs to pay attention to the ideologies that are within the "marketplace" of ideas. If these ideologies advocate violence, and if these ideologies appear to be resonating with particular groups or segments of the population, then one can make a fairly accurate prediction of the likelihood of future extremist violence. As you will have concluded by now, I see many signs of increased extremism. This book is devoted, in part, to articulating these signs or indicators of future extremist violence.

The fourth premise takes the process one step further. Here the term "incubators" is added to the radicalization equation. Incubators are "places" (including virtual places such as the Internet) that serve to foster radicalization. They become pit stops, "hangouts," and meeting places where people develop the "logic" of radicalization. Generally these locations, which together comprise the radical subculture of a community, are rife with extremist rhetoric. Though the locations can be mosques, more likely incubators include such diverse things as:

- Cafes
- Student associations
- Cab driver hangouts
- Nongovernmental organizations
- Flophouses
- Hookah (water pipe) bars
- Prisons
- Butcher shops
- Bookstores
- The Internet

There are a number of insightful factors in this premise. As mentioned earlier, while it is difficult to predict who will radicalize, these incubators are places where like-minded individuals often congregate as they move through the radicalization process. One significant "incubation place" that the NYPD report emphasizes is the Internet. This "place," with its thousands of extremist Web sites and chat rooms, was called a "virtual incubator of its own."[62] The implications of the Internet are substantial. Terrorist groups distribute everything from extremist literature to bomb making instructions. They obtain photos of potential targets and real-time videos of security procedures, and they trumpet the aftermath of terrorist incidents. The impact of the Internet cannot be ignored. Nor should this valuable source of information be minimized. As Michael Doran, a terrorism expert at Princeton noted, "When we say al Qaeda is a global ideology, this is where it exists—on the Internet."[63]

The final premise, and I believe the most critical, relates to "group think." In the concept of group think are two critical factors: "spiritual sanctioner" and an "operational leader." These need to be fleshed out in some detail. Group think is an important contribution to the study of extremism. This concept has a profound effect on our ability to understand and counter the threat of extremism. Since the process of group think is complicated, I will simply highlight the process as follows.

Individuals who have certain characteristics in common, such as race, religion, political party, and culture, may find these similarities attractive. These similarities may foster relationships within a larger group. As individuals blend their personalities and identities into the group, a "group mind" begins to emerge. Due to the external pressures placed on groups who advocate, or even contemplate, violence, the individuals within the group gain solidarity. The solidarity is enhanced, at least partly, by the daily dangers and the sacrifices required of these individuals.[64] A frame of reference that most police officers will understand relates to gang membership. It is widely acknowledged that gang membership is galvanized around conflicts with other gangs, and by the threat of arrest by the police. These have the tendency to create solidarity within the gang. While this does not always result in solidarity, the tendency for such is expected, particularly in a group that has a strong ideological basis. This is especially relevant in well-developed extremist movements.

The impact of solidarity affects the belief system that the organization adopts, the nature of the targets chosen, and the members' commitment to self-sacrifice.[65] Each of these factors further galvanizes the group. Overall the appeal to a larger principle (or a group morality) enables terrorist organizations to indoctrinate their members to fight for what their adherents believe, and what may be noble principles. Hence, the drive for "important" principles helps to further indoctrinate their members to fight for their cause. Once they are convinced to fight for the cause, their willingness to kill and die for the cause becomes more likely. Whether this cause and its underlying principles are worthy of such sacrifice is open to objective analysis.

Yungher identified four factors that are characteristic of "group think."[66] First is that a *feeling of invulnerability* results in riskier courses of action than what an individual acting on his or her own would typically consider. This is similar to the "mob mentality" where the anonymous nature of the crowd causes some people to do things they would not do absent the mob. Second, the *certainty in the organization's morality* results in almost absolute confidence in the cause. This spurs individuals within the group to fight for the cause, thereby justifying all means to achieve such. Third, the *simplistic perception of the enemy as evil* is a powerful way to "dehumanize" the perceived opposition. What this mindset does is to create a "black" and "white" perception, where one side is good and the other is bad, without any "grey" area in between. One way to achieve this "dehumanization" is to turn the enemy into characterizations such as pigs, Jews, nips, monkeys, crackers, infidels, etc. These derogatory names are useful to inspire hatred against the enemy—and to enable them to be killed or injured without consequence or moral conflicts. Finally, group think fosters *intolerance toward any internal dissent.* In the application of this goal, the organization creates social and ideological unity that intentionally limits its members to a single way of interpreting events and processes. This requires consensus within the group. Any dissension, or even possible dissension, is often strongly repressed. The more repressive the group, the less likely dissent will result. Indeed, this approach is pointedly expressed by Yungher, who observes that "the way to get rid of the doubts [is] to get rid of the doubters."[67]

The underlying ideological basis of the group often determines the level of commitment of its members. A classic example of group distinctions is shown by comparing secular groups against religious groups. According to Hoffman, religious extremists see the world as a battlefield between forces of good and evil.[68] Similarly, Jurgenmeyer contends that all religious extremist groups share a common denominator, that is, their hatred for secular globalism. The fight against it gives meaning to their lives.[69] As these observations infer, religious groups tend to exhibit more intensity and passion for their goals. This is due to a number of factors, including:[70]

1. Religious extremists do not have the same inhibitions about mass death.
2. Religious extremists do not cater to a larger audience (except the co-religionists), as they act on behalf of God.
3. Religious extremists' purposes, methods, and targets are vividly clear, since they are based on historical precedent, scripture, or clerical guidance.
4. Religious extremists regard killing as a sacramental act and have little aversion to mass casualties as long as it advances the cause of faith. With this mindset, killing in the service of God is a righteous deed. Further, defeating the enemy is not sufficient. The enemy has to be completely eradicated.
5. Religious extremists are uncomfortable negotiating and compromising because doing so, in their eyes, means living with half-truths of man-made laws that contradict God's wishes.

These deep-seated convictions exhibited by religious extremist groups have an ironic twist. While secularism has famously proclaimed the death of religion, some religious groups desire to proclaim the death of secularism. For religious extremists, fighting secularism globally translates into an epic transnational war for the soul of the universe.[71] This is an all-or-nothing cosmic war between the contemporary evil forces and those "cleansing" forces seeking change. Indeed, this religious goal is so all encompassing that the "annihilation of everything else on its behalf may be justified."[72] A quote from an Islamist zealot may help to shed light on the intensity and commitment of their cause:[73]

> [W]e believe in the principle of establishing Sharia [Islamic moral/legal code] even if this means the death of all mankind.

This ideological framework is clearly articulated in al Qaeda's "training manual," which states that the "main mission is the overthrow of the godless regimes and their replacement with an Islamic regime."[74] As a result, this war is viewed as different from other, more typical conflicts. Again, the al Qaeda manual is instructive. It asserts that "Islam fights so the word of Allah can become supreme. Others fight for worldly gains and lowly inferior goals."[75] These are powerful motivators, indeed.

Consequently, this scenario sets up an ironic dynamic. The "religious" convictions and motivations of Islamic radicals are impossible for their enemies (the secular West) to fully comprehend. Indeed, secularists, almost by definition, do not have a sense of God—and of His purpose in this world. These groups are, therefore, unable to fully engage in effective communication. They are literally living in different worlds. Because of such, secularists should not be expected to comprehend the current worldwide struggle as a "Holy War." The fact that the Islamic radicals (and some right-wing groups) see it this way is of no avail to secular thought. These opposing worldviews have substantial implications on how we understand and address these movements. Before we address these implications, let's first assess how individuals become radicalized.

According to the NYPD radicalization report, the process requires four specific stages: pre-radicalization, self-identification, indoctrination, and jihadization. Stages in this process have certain "signatures" that can be discerned. It is important to note that this process does not necessarily entail that the individual will go from one stage to the next. An individual may move to one stage and then remain there. There is nothing in this process that would require, or even assume, that an individual will proceed through each stage of the process. Consequently, this process provides a good road map as to how people become radicalized. It does not, however, assert that an individual at any stage is, indeed, heading toward jihad.

The pre-radicalization stage is not really a part of the process. It simply signifies where the individual was prior to commencing the radicalization process. The report calls this the "point of origin" for individuals before they begin this progression. This is their life situation before they were exposed to and adopted the radical ideology.[76]

The self-identification stage is where individuals, influenced by both internal and external factors, begin to explore radicalized ideologies. In doing so, the individual gradually gravitates away from their old identity and begins to associate him- or herself with like-minded individuals. Here is where they begin to adopt this ideology as their own. The catalyst for this "religious seeking" is deemed a cognitive opening. It often results from a crisis that shakes one's certitude in previously held beliefs. This crisis may cause an individual to be receptive to new worldviews.[77] Many types of triggers may serve as the catalyst including:[78]

- Economic (losing a job, blocked mobility)
- Social (alienation, discrimination, racism—real or perceived)
- Political (international conflicts involving Muslims)
- Personal (death in the close family)

As validation for this aspect of the NYPD report, research conducted in prisons found similar triggers for religious conversion. These include personal crisis, security from gangs/peer pressure, influential world leaders, manipulative purposes, searching (serial converters), and genuine religious experience.[79] Of course, these factors are common attributes of life. At one time or another, people experience death in their family, they have various economic impediments, and they will inevitably face social disappointments and discrimination. Hence, why do some allow these factors to lead them down a bitter, resentful path? While this is a key question in the analysis, it is the most ill defined in terms of causation. Simply stated, there are so many personal factors and individual idiosyncrasies that it is almost impossible to make predictive assumptions at this stage of the process. However, the NYPD report provides what it terms "signatures," which may act as indicators for possible radicalism. These signatures include:[80]

- Being alienated from one's former life; affiliating with like-minded individuals
- Joining or forming a group in a quest to strengthen dedication to a particular ideology or religion
- Giving up cigarettes, drinking, gambling, and urban hip-hop gangster clothes
- Wearing traditional religious clothing; growing a beard
- Becoming involved in social activism and community issues

In assessing these "signatures," you will likely note that these are noncriminal, and generally "nondescriptive" behaviors. These behaviors are, in isolation, not particularly problematic. However, if three or four of these factors are seen in an individual, particularly during a relatively short period of time, then this should trigger some "red flags." Even with these indicators, however, this should not be considered a criminal predicate for intelligence purposes (for more on this connection see Chapter 5).

The third stage of the process is indoctrination. In this stage, the individual progressively intensifies his or her beliefs. At some point, the individual may wholly adopt a radical ideology. If this occurs, the individual may conclude, without question, that the conditions and circumstances require direct action to support and further the cause.[81] A key part of this phase is typically facilitated and driven by a "spiritual sanctioner." This person inspires the individual. He or she teaches and leads the tenets of the ideology. He or she instructs and explains the causes that have resulted in the current situation. He or she fosters and motivates the individual to sacrifice on behalf of the ideology. He or she gives inspiration and purpose for the benefits and blessings that will be derived from the individual's sacrifice. In short, the spiritual sanctioner gives the individual the "reasons" to do what needs to be done. This indoctrination is further supported, and even enhanced, by association with like-minded people as the process deepens. Consequently, these influences can be powerful. Indeed, they are instrumental—and necessary—for most people to "justify" extremist violence.

Ironically, once the individual becomes sufficiently indoctrinated by the spiritual sanctioner, often the individual will withdraw from those people who do not advocate taking action for the cause. In this regard, the report makes the following observations, which they refer to as indoctrination signatures:[82]

- Withdrawal from their support network
- Politicization of new beliefs
- Joining a group of like-minded extremists
- Holding meetings in private settings

From a sociological or psychological standpoint, I find it interesting that the individual seeks to avoid people from their social network. In thinking about this, however, it makes a lot of sense. The reasons cited by the report are that the individual becomes concerned that maintaining contact with the larger group may expose him to infiltration by law enforcement. Further, the individual may become suspicious of the motives of those who are not willing to kill and die for the cause. In addition, the individual may seek to protect the group from legal exposure, or other retribution, once he commits the direct action. In any case, the need for the individual to extricate himself from the group that helped radicalize him is a fascinating study in human nature. Whatever the cause, the individual now takes on the ideology and transforms it into a personal cause. The world for these individuals becomes divided into two sides: the enlightened believers (themselves) and the unbelievers (everybody else). The unbelievers become their archenemy.

The final stage in this process is called jihadization. This is when the individual enters the cell, or a cluster of cells, to accept his or her individual duty to participate in jihad. They have, in essence, graduated and self-designated themselves as holy warriors. Ultimately, the group will begin operational planning for the jihad or the terrorist attack. As they begin the operational planning for the attack, they typically conduct certain pre-incident indicators in preparation for the attack. These "acts in furtherance" include planning, preparation, and execution. As will be more fully developed later, this stage is when intelligence and law enforcement officers are most likely to develop the necessary criminal predicate to conduct surveillance and other investigative operations.

Once again, the report develops certain "signatures" or indicators of a pending attack. These include:[83]

Accepting jihad/decision to commit jihad
Training/preparation
  – Outward-bound activities (target shooting, paintball, etc.)
  – Mental reinforcement activities (Web sites, videos, draft will)
Attack planning
  – Researching the Internet (targets, capabilities, mode of attack)
  – Reconnaissance/surveillance (maps, videos, testing, dry runs)
  – Acquiring material/preparing devices (cell phones, explosives, weapons)
Actual attack

In assessing the radicalization process, there are many places that can be considered as incubators for potential extremism. This can be a tricky, complicated endeavor. There are a number of reasons for this. First, as the NYPD report asserts, there is no effective physical "profile" of a potential terrorist. Since there are so many "causes" or grievances that can lead to terrorist acts, there are an unlimited number of populations that extremist ideologies can draw from. Second, terrorism and security experts have long advocated that looking for particular physical characteristics is the better approach. Consequently, using known signatures (behaviors) and looking at particular incubators (places) is likely to have a much greater potential for success. Of course, in policing and in security, the key is to enhance the probability of either deterring or capturing the criminal. With this said, let's look at some data that may be useful to assess the likely sources of extremism.

It is my contention that an important source of future extremism will be found in gangs—particularly in gang members who have served time in prison. For a host of reasons, which will be presented, this is a ripe place for recruitment into extremist groups. Indeed, some notable examples are illustrative of this assertion. Jose Padilla was a gang member in Chicago, who was radicalized into al Qaeda within a Florida prison.[84] Similarly, John William King, who was convicted of the brutal dragging death of James Byrd on a Texas street, was radicalized into the KKK and the Aryan Brotherhood within a Texas prison. Richard Reid, the infamous "shoe-bomber" was radicalized into al Qaeda while serving time in a British prison. Kevin James, who ran Jamiyyat Ul-Islam Is-Saheeh (JIS) from his prison cell in a California state facility, was a former Crips gang member who founded his own terrorist group as an offshoot of the Nation of Islam. These are just a few of many examples. From these examples—coupled with other research—one can extrapolate potential trends that are on the horizon.

This country has plenty of gang members who can serve extremist agendas. There are two incubators that may foster these agendas. One is gangs within the military. The other is gangs in the prison system. Let's commence with gang members that serve in the military. Indeed, in one of the several disconcerting aspects of the current military conflicts, recent reports reveal that the military has identified a rather significant number of gang members who are serving in the armed forces. A report on the extent of this problem revealed that members of nearly every major street gang are in the military. Since 2004, the FBI and the El Paso Police Department have identified over 40 military affiliated Folk gang members at Fort Bliss. Since 2003, 40 gang members were identified on base at Fort Hood. Since 2005, nearly 130 gang and extremist group members were identified at Fort Lewis.[85] The obvious concern is that these gang members are learning how to kill. They are also learning how to use military weapons and military tactics. These skills, if not properly harnessed, can create substantial harm on the streets of this country.

Many gang members also do time in prison. Based on the nature of their activities, it would be typical that a large percentage of gang members ultimately spend time in prison. This implies many opportunities for radicalization. Chicago alone has an estimated 68 active gangs, with 600 different factions, totaling about 68,000 members.[86] The terrorizing impact of gangs was seen in Brazil. In São Paulo, gang members razed police stations, attacked banks, rioted in prisons, and torched dozens of buses. In addition, they shut down a transportation system serving 2.9 million people a day. A similar spate of violence occurred in Rio de Janeiro, where a copycat campaign by an urban gang called the Comando Vermelho ("Red Command") terrorized and essentially shut down the transportation system. In both cases, the gangs fomenting the violence did not list demands or send ultimatums to the government. Rather, they were flexing their muscles, testing their ability to challenge the government monopoly on violence. According to Robb, these gangs' rapid rise into challengers to urban authorities is something that we will see again elsewhere.[87]

In the United States it is becoming increasingly obvious that gang members are prime recruitment targets for extremist groups. For example, Ansar El Muhammad (AEM), a black Muslim extremist group, actively seeks members from black gangs who are recruited for the "purpose of creating Black unity." This group has engaged members of the Crips, Bloods, the 415s, and the Kumi into their fold. In addition, Islamic inmates have recruited members from the Latin Kings, Vice Lords, 5-Percenters, Black P-Stone Nation, and the Black Guerilla Family. These examples are part of what are known as a growing "crossover" trend. This entails "graduating" from gang member to extremism ideology. This trend is facilitated by charismatic inmates (read spiritual sanctioners) and the desire for status, attachment, and discipline. Along with these influences, the extremist recruiters are now adding an "ideological hook" into the equation.[88] In many cases, the ideological hook is a radicalized religion.

Research by Mark Hamm reveals some disconcerting trends. Consider these trends and data:[89]

- The fastest growing religion in prison is Islam.
- Eighty percent of all prison conversions are to Islam.
- Converts include African Americans, Hispanics, and whites.
- Annual prisoner conversions to Islam: 35,000.
- Percent Muslims in major prison systems: 18%.
- Prison conversions to Islam since 9/11: 175,000.

It is important to make clear that recruitment to Islam while in prison does not equate with extremism. However, when you consider the number of recruits into Islam from the prison system, one would be hard-pressed to assert that all such conversions were for altruistic reasons. It does not take a statistician to assert that some percentage of these conversions are for illicit reasons. What percentage? I do not know and will not venture to guess. However, given the previous examples of "prison conversions," coupled with my personal experience with the El Rukns, I will stake my professional reputation on the validity of my beliefs. To refresh your memory, a Chicago gang that previously called itself the Black P-Stone Nation was "inspired" to "convert" to a Sunni Islamic sect with the name of "El Rukn." Members of the group received $2.5 million from Libya's Mohamar Qaddafi to commit terrorist acts in the United States.[90] In conjunction with this revelation, I was personally involved in two raids on the El Rukn "fort" as a tactical officer in the Gang Crime Enforcement Unit with the Chicago Police Department.

The statistic from Hamm's research that is most troubling is that there have been about 175,000 converts to Islam since 9/11. Given the radical Islamist ideology that inspired this attack, one is struck that such a large number of prisoners would be attracted to Islam. As stated above, this is not inherently bad. Indeed, the attraction of Islam within the prison system is to be expected. For various reasons, over the past years, Islam has become a powerful force in the American prison system.[91] Prior to the rise of Islam, the ideologies with the most currency among prison minorities were revolutionary Marxism and varieties of black nationalism.[92] Overall, Aidi estimates that about 333,000 black prisoners are claiming affiliation with various sects or offshoots of the Islamic religion, including the Nation of Islam, Sunni Islam, the Moorish Temple, etc.[93] In this light, Aidi makes the provocative statement that the "prison system could supply a 'fifth column' to bin Laden and his ilk."[94] This assertion was echoed by Chuck Colson of the infamous Watergate case who converted to Christianity in prison, who stated that[95]

> America's alienated, disenfranchised people are prime targets for radical Islamists who preach a religion of violence, or overcoming oppression by jihad.

Hamm provides an interesting illustration of how prison gangs and radical Islamic religion influences a large number "conversions" to Islam.[96] He describes how traditional American Islam mutates to a more "pious" form of Islam within the prison. This radicalized version of Islam is then communicated to gang members within the system. It is important to note that many of these gang members are already disenfranchised from American society. Many live in isolated and angry subcultures. Many see little chance to change their circumstances. In short, they are young and angry, with little hope and few skills. With this mindset, they are "informed" about the racism, injustice, and economic discrimination within American society.

Ironically, many of these same "sins" are preached in Christian black nationalist churches, such as illustrated by Reverend Wright's sermons at the Trinity United Church of Christ. These same critiques of American society are also made by academics. For example, criminologists, like Jeffrey Reiman, assert that the criminal justice system in America leads to the imprisonment of certain classes of people. In Reiman's words, the criminal justice system[97] is morally indistinguishable from criminality insofar as it exercises forces and imposes suffering on human beings while violating its own morally justifying ideals: protection and justice.

Wherever they are preached, these messages have resonance to those who are embittered by their circumstances. These messages are then communicated to their friends in the gangs, which can subsequently result in affiliation of the "jihadi" movement (Figure 2.4). Ultimately it may lead to terroristic violence. Consequently, this "vicious circle" is both compelling and dangerous. I believe we are only at the genesis of its implications.

In this light, Hamm's research corresponds with many of the conclusions presented earlier. He found the following relevant findings:[98]

- Inmate conversions happen through friend and kinship networks.
- The main reasons for conversion are spiritual searching and protection.
- Riffs are increasing between traditional and radical elements of inmate Islam.
- Since 9/11, radicalized prisoners are very aware that people are interested in radicalized prisoners.
- Gangs are using religious groups for meetings.
- Religious groups are using gangs for protection.
- Among prisoners, there is a growing dissatisfaction with government.
- There is an increase in aggressive posturing.
- Some Muslim prisoners are susceptible to jihad.

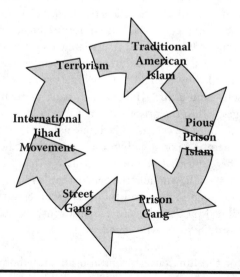

Figure 2.4   Prison Radicalization Process. Adapted from Mark Hamm, *Terrorist Recuitment and Radicalization in Prison,* **NIJ Conference, July 2007.**

While all of Hamm's conclusions are insightful, some have particular relevance to the thesis of this book. First, the assertion that riffs between traditional and radical elements are increasing points to one of the key factors identified in the "Holy War," which is there is an internal struggle taking place within Islam. This struggle is between moderates and radicals. The moderates desire to live a peaceful life, raise their families, go to work, and serve Allah to the best of their abilities. Conversely, the radicals want to change the world for Allah. They want all to submit to Allah and Sharia law. Those who fail to do so will be forced to do so by violence. The key to this struggle is to maintain the "modern" way of life. This is why I have discussed Iraq as part of this book. We must understand that the moderates in Iraq, who are supportive of the United States and are advocates of a democratic system, are key to this larger struggle within Islam. In short, if the moderates are abandoned in Iraq, they will be slaughtered by the radicals. If this occurs, the message to the Muslim moderates throughout the world will be, This is what you will get for backing the Great Satan!

Within the prison system, of course, individuals also convert to Islam in a quest to add meaning and direction to their lives. Disillusioned with mainstream society, these disaffected individuals are attracted to the sense of community and purpose that Islam offers. Consider the words of Akil, a former Crip gang member incarcerated in California for murder. He asserted, "Islam helped me set boundaries. It taught me to have respect for others. It taught me to understand the true nature of humanity. It keeps me from doing the bad things of my past." Assuming this sentiment is accurate, the influence of Islam within the system may be helpful. Numerous examples support the notion that prisoners can find fulfillment in their lives through Islam. If this reflects true conversion, then this is all for the better. If not, then it poses substantial concerns. Indeed, former French antiterrorism magistrate Jean-Louis Bruguiere has warned that Islamic converts are "undeniably the toughest" and most "radical."[99] How can these two examples be reconciled?

They can be reconciled by the fact that each person finds his or her own purpose through religion—and in life. This makes it particularly important to maintain positive messages within the prison system. Obviously, this is easier said than done. Nonetheless, we must be careful to facilitate religious instruction from moderate imams or teachers. As noted earlier, each potential radical needs someone who acts as his or her "spiritual sanctioner." This was reflected by DHS Senior Intelligence Officer Javed Ali, who told the Senate that "inmates have been radicalized through ... clerics, contractors, and volunteers who serve as religious authorities."[100] This was echoed by Donald Van Duyn, deputy assistant director of the FBI's Counterterrorism Division, who stated,[101]

> Particularly for Muslim converts, but also for those born into Islam, an extremist imam can strongly influence individual belief systems by speaking from a position of authority on religious issues. Extremist imams have the potential to influence vulnerable followers at various

locations of opportunity; can spot and assess individuals who respond to their messages; and can potentially guide them into increasingly extremist circles.

Unfortunately, there are numerous examples of prison imams who appear to be potential "spiritual sanctioners." For example, Marwan Othman El-Hindi, indicted in Ohio for plotting to kill U.S. soldiers in Iraq, had served as an imam at the Toledo Correctional Institution until he was fired for smuggling food to an inmate. In addition, FBI official John Pistole briefed Congress on another imam, Warith Deen Umar, the administrative chaplain for the New York State Department of Corrections. Pistole noted that Umar denied prisoners access to mainstream imams and materials. Significantly, Pistole asserted that Umar "sought to incite prisoners against America, preaching that the 9/11 hijackers should be remembered as martyrs and heroes." When Umar was subsequently banned from ever entering a New York State prison, New York Senator Charles Schumer issued a press release, revealing that "Umar has wielded tremendous influence over the 45 or so clerics or imams that currently preach within New York's prison system, almost all of whom subscribe to his brand of Wahhabi extremism." Senator Schumer reported the following incidents:[102]

> After the [9/11] attacks, the cleric was reported to have said that the attacks were punishments on the wicked and that the victims deserved what they got. At the prison in Watertown, the same cleric led what seemed to be a pro-Al Qaeda rally. At the Albion Correctional Facility for Women, a similar incident occurred when the cleric there praised Osama Bin Laden as a soldier of Allah.

Paying attention to imams is not the only concern. Another channel for radicalization is through charismatic, religiously radicalized inmates. This concern is driven by multiple factors, including the shortage of moderate prison imams, overcrowding, and prisoners' desire to exert influence. The Michigan Department of Corrections administrator explained, "No prisoner faith group ... wants volunteer support. Prisoners like the power of running their own religious groups." Moreover, another analyst pointed out that when "charismatic inmates ... assert themselves as unauthorized imams ... chaplains simply allow prisoners to lead the group."[103] Anyone who is familiar with the prison system knows we have no shortage of charismatic inmates.

Since the U.S. prison system has relatively less experience dealing with radical Islamic inmates, it may be helpful to consider circumstances in the other countries. For example, in England and Wales, where Muslims account for less than three percent of the total population, they represent approximately 11 percent of the inmate population. Accordingly to Lefkowitz, an internal British Ministry of Justice forecasts that in the next decade the number of terrorist inmates would skyrocket from 131 to over 1,600. The overwhelming majority of these prisoners will be high-security inmates. Just as in the U.S. system, a U.K. prison spokesman noted that there was an "emerging picture, based on anecdotal intelligence, that suggests terrorists may be linking into gang activities." In March 2008, Colin Moses, head of the Prison Officers' Association, urged "radical action" to stem radicalization efforts in the prison. As an example of this concern, French intelligence has estimated that approximately 17 percent of those who convert to Islam in prison join extremist groups after serving their time.[104]

Hamm's conclusions suggest that there is a growing connection between gangs and religious groups. This conclusion is echoed by DHS's Javed Ali, who reported that "radicalization within prison has occurred predominantly … among the African-American inmate population and those affiliated with gangs." Insight into the situation at a California prison comes from "Morino," an African American convert imprisoned for murder at Folsom. This prisoner was interviewed by Dr. Hamm for this research. When you read this quote, please consider the larger alliances that will be addressed in this book. Please also consider how potentially problematic things may become if gang members—with their gang mentality—are recruited into a radicalized version of Islam. In my mind, this is dangerous. You draw your own conclusion. Notwithstanding my editorial comments, Morino informed Hamm that[105]

> People are recruiting every day. It's a ripe climate for terrorism. It's scandalous. Everybody's glorifying Osama bin Laden. But these Muslims come to Islam with the same gang mentality they had on the streets. Same red rags, same blue rags [symbols of the Crips and Bloods]. The mentality is pure ignorance driving terrorism. There is recruiting feeding on the broken spirit and ignorance.

What is driving this radicalization of imprisoned gang members? It is not hard to understand how this would occur. Many of these gang members come to the prison system with little education and even fewer marketable skills. These youths typically grow up in environments infected with poverty, broken families, dysfunctional schools, illicit drugs, and a host of social ills. Coming from this environment—coupled with being convicted of a crime and imprisoned—can one expect them to be disillusioned with life and the larger society? I think it is not only typical, it should be expected. This view is echoed by Van Duyn, who contends that radicalized inmates[106]

> either feel discriminated against in the United States or feel that the United States oppresses minorities and Muslims overseas. The feeling of perceived oppression, combined with their limited knowledge of Islam, especially for the converts, makes this a vulnerable population for extremists looking to radicalize and recruit.

Along with the increased dissatisfaction with government comes the possibility of extremism and terrorism. Remember, a key element of terrorism is that the violence will be directed at or designed against the government. Can this dissatisfaction with government be tempered or even negated by the historic election of President Obama? In some ways I think it can. Many black youths may reconsider the notion that this society is racist. Many black youths may see his election as evidence that a black man can make it to the top of this society. As significant as this message is, however, for those who are incarcerated and without much "hope" of a viable career, the election of President Obama may be deemed "irrelevant" to their lives. Hence, we need to be cognizant of the increase in aggressive posturing—particularly within the prison system. As described earlier, this could result in a climate where Muslim prisoners are susceptible to jihad. These are critical themes of this book. On this note, consider the underlying basis for Aidi's notion of "jihadi's in the hood," who stated,[107]

> [T]he rise of Islam and Islamism in American cities can be explained as a product of immigration and racial politics, de-industrialization and state withdrawal, and the interwoven cultural forces of black nationalism, Islamism and "hip-hop" that appeal strongly to disenfranchised black, Latino, Arab and south Asian youth.

This research should make clear that prison officials—and by extension, the larger society—must deal with the potential of prisons being "radicalized cauldrons." While in prison, jihadists are distributing propaganda, planning jailbreaks, continuing to exercise operational control over their organizations, and even plotting attacks. In fact, as the Central Intelligence Agency (CIA) has noted, "Terrorists do not view prison as a major obstacle because they face similar challenges in the outside world—carrying out clandestine activity, facing a hostile security service, and creating or joining tight-knit groups to survive." This assertion is furthered by Jordanian researcher Hassan Abu Hanieh, who commented, "Things no longer end in prison anymore. In fact, increasingly they begin there."[108] This is not just a problem for foreign governments. Notably, in 2007 during Senate testimony, Department of Homeland Security Chief Intelligence Officer Charles Allen asserted that radicalization behind bars was "becoming increasingly common."[109] This sobering assertion was echoed in senate testimony by FBI Director Robert Mueller, who commented that "prisons continue to be fertile ground for extremists ..."[110]

In any event, there is evidence that the prison environment is already creating problems in the larger society. For example, some criminal justice researchers believe that recent increases in murder may be the result of "the rise of prison culture in the outside world." According to David Kennedy of the John Jay College of Criminal Justice, violence in prisons is often the result of a perception of disrespect, a trend that has risen on the outside. If this trend toward disrespect is coupled with a radical ideology, it does not take an expert to predict difficult times ahead. Given that about 700,000 convicts are released each year, simple arithmetic makes the future look problematic.[111]

With this backdrop, think about the implications of President Obama's executive order closing Guantanamo Bay.[112] While the executive order does not address how and where the prisoners at "Gitmo" will be handled, one can reasonably predict that some will be transferred to U.S. prisons. The executive order will rewrite American policy for detaining terrorism suspects, and will require an immediate review of the 245 detainees being held at Guantanamo. The Obama Administration will have to determine whether these detainees should be transferred, released, or prosecuted. The CIA would also have to stop keeping terrorism suspects in secret custody in undisclosed international locations. This practice has drawn heavy criticism from foreign governments and human rights groups. The agency will also be prohibited from using coercive interrogation methods, and will have to follow the same rules used by the military in interrogating terrorism suspects.[113]

Given the seemingly mounting problems within the prison system, what would be the implications of this decision on an already problematic environment? Is it possible that these prisoners would become "spiritual sanctioners"? Is it possible they may inspire other inmates to a radical worldview? Indeed, I contend they will be considered "superstars" by some inmates. In my mind, this is one of those policy decisions that seek to trumpet American values that will result in unintended consequences. Some may assert that our values are so important it is worth this risk. I acknowledge this point with one caveat. Many who boldly speak of the importance of our values may not feel the same way in a terroristic environment. This is not unusual. There are a lot of "committed" people during calm times. When the storm comes, however, it will separate the true believers from those who simply mouth politically correct mantras. To those who are true believers—those who are willing to die for the values of this country—my respect and regards are with you. To those who merely mouth mantras but are not prepared to deal with the consequences, I caution you to be careful what you ask for!

I offer little in the way of solutions to this dilemma. I only hope my message will serve as a pointed warning of its implications. As these examples and quotes imply, if prisoners are denied these sanctioners, then this reduces the chances that the radicalization process will occur. Instead, a moderating message must be communicated within our prison system—and in our country. We must facilitate moderate voices that resonate over the radicals. This is a challenge on a number of levels. We must address these challenges because it is clear that the message of anger and bitterness has an impact on disenfranchised youths.

Endnotes

1. Yungher, Nathan I. (2008). *Terrorism: The Bottom Line.* Upper Saddle River, NJ: Pearson/Prentice Hall, 42.

2. Indeed, this is not simply a hypothetical example. Consider that on March 5, 2007, a Riker's Island inmate offered to pay an undercover police officer posing as a hit man to *behead* New York City Police Commissioner Raymond Kelly and bomb police headquarters in retaliation for the controversial police shooting of Sean Bell. See "Terror Incidents in the U.S. Since the 9/11 Attacks" (2008). *Counter-Terrorism* 1, no. 1 (May/June):53.

3. Hoffman, Bruce (2006). "Defining Terrorism," in *Terrorism and Counter-Terrorism: Understanding the New Security Environment.* Eds. Russell D. Howard and Reid L. Sawyer. Dubuque, IA: McGraw-Hill.

4. Mahan, Sue and Pamela L. Griset (2008). *Terrorism in Perspective,* 2nd ed. Thousand Oaks, CA: Sage Publications.

5. Cooper, H. H. A. (2008). "Terrorism: The Problem of Definition," in *Terrorism in Perspective,* 2nd ed. Thousand Oaks, CA: Sage Publications.

6. Yungher, Nathan I. (2008), op. cit., 5.

7. Cooper, H. H. A. (2008), op. cit., 21.

8. White, Jonathan R. (2008). "A Theology of Anti-government Extremism," in *Terrorism in Perspective,* 2nd ed. Eds. Sue Mahan and Pamela L. Griset. Thousand Oaks, CA: Sage Publications, 200.

9. Poland, James M. (2005). *Understanding Terrorism: Groups, Strategies and Responses.* Upper Saddle River, NJ: Pearson/Prentice Hall, 4.

10. Laqueur, Walter (2004). "The Terrorism to Come," *Policy Review* 126:8. www.policyreview.org/aug04/laqueur_print.html (retrieved on November 1, 2004).

11. Yungher, Nathan I. (2008), op. cit., 78.

12. Poland, James M. (2005), op. cit., 5.

13. Cooper, H. H. A. (2008), op. cit., 22.

14. Poland, James M. (2005), op. cit., 19.

15. Stern, Jessica (2008). "The Ultimate Organization: Networks, Franchises and Freelancers," in *Terrorism in Perspective,* 2nd ed. Eds. Sue Mahan and Pamela L. Griset. Thousand Oaks, CA: Sage Publications, 167.

16. Ganor, Boaz (2005). "Terror as a Strategy of Psychological Warfare," in *Violence and Terrorism.* Ed. Thomas J. Badey. McGraw-Hill/Dushkin, 5.

17. Ganor, Boaz (2005), op. cit., 6.

18. Tucker, Jonathan B. (2003). "Strategies for Countering Terrorism: Lessons from the Israeli Experience," *Journal of Homeland Security* March 26:18.

19. Ganor, Boaz (2005), op. cit., 6.

20. Ganor, Boaz (2005), op. cit., 124.

21. Poland, James M. (2005), op. cit., 78.

22. Wilkinson, Paul (1986). *Terrorism and the Liberal State.* Washington Square, NY: New York University Press, 115; and Poland, James M. (2005), op. cit., 222.

23. President Obama inauguration speech. http://news.yahoo.com/s/ap/20090120/ap_on_go_pr_wh/inauguration_obama_text (retrieved on January 26, 2009).

24. Stern, Jessica (2008), op. cit., 170.

25. Ganor, Boaz (2005), op. cit., 6.

26. Azzam, Maha (2005). "Al Qaeda: The Misunderstood Wahhabi Connection and the Ideology of Violence," in *Violence and Terrorism*. Ed. Thomas J. Badey. McGraw-Hill/Dushkin, 154.

27. Stern, Jessica (2008), op. cit., 167.

28. Poland, James M. (2005), op. cit., 235.

29. See, for example, Coulter, Ann (2003). *Treason: Liberal Treachery from the Cold War to the War on Terrorism*. New York: Crown Forum.

30. For example, during the news reporting of the "beltway snipers," Ann Coulter noted that for three months, from October 2002 to January 19, 2003, the *New York Times* ran 128 articles about the shootings. In these articles, only nine mentioned the word "Muslim." See Coulter, Ann (2003). *Treason: Liberal Treachery from the Cold War to the War on Terrorism*. New York: Crown Forum, 281.

31. To those who doubt this assertion, research the "news" coverage of the campaign! Consider the fact that *Saturday Night Live* lampooned the media coverage of the Democratic debates. In these comedic pieces, most of the Democratic candidates were posed tough and even abusive questioning, while the "moderator" simply asked Barack Obama "if he was comfortable." For a more substantive piece on the media related to the campaign, please see Williams, Juan (2009). "Judge Obama on Performance Alone: Let's Not Celebrate More Ordinary Speeches," *The Wall Street Journal*, January 20. http://online.wsj.com/article/SB123249791178500439.html; and Phillips, Joseph C. (2008). "Barack Obama Can't Win as Long as He Continues to Play That Tired, Dog-Eared Race Card," http://www.blackamericaweb.com/site.aspx/sayitloud/phillips819 (retrieved on August 27, 2008). Other than these examples, it is beyond the scope of this book to critique particular news outlets. If you doubt my assertion, then I invite you to make the case. My email and contact information will be available with my publisher. I invite your comments!

32. Poland, James M. (2005), op. cit., 209.

33. Poland, James M. (2005), op. cit., 77.

34. Nacos, Brigitte (2005). "Terrorism as Breaking News: Attack on America," in *Violence and Terrorism*. Ed. Thomas J. Badey. McGraw-Hill/Dushkin, 125.

35. http://www.freerepublic.com/focus/f-news/1145998/posts (retrieved on February 3, 2009).

36. Cloud, David S. (2007). "Ex-Commander Says Iraq Effort Is 'a Nightmare,'" *The New York Times*. http://www.nytimes.com/2007/10/13/washington/13general.html (retrieved on February 3, 2009).

37. Warner, Frank (2007). "The *New York Times* Left Out Gen. Ricardo Sanchez' Attack on News Reporting That Results in Killing Americans" @ http://frankwarner.typepad.com/free_frank_warner/2007/10/the-new-york-ti.html (retrieved on February 3, 2009).

38. This cover appeared on June 12, 1970. A depiction of this can be found at http://elderofziyon.blogspot.com/2008_11_01_archive.html.

39. O'Neil, Siobhan (2007). "Terrorist Precursor Crimes: Issues and Options for Congress," *Congressional Research Service* May 24:1.

40. O'Neil, Siobhan (2007), op. cit., 10.

41. See example http://www.insideprison.com/prison_gang_profile_JUIIS.asp (retrieved on February 1, 2009); and O'Neil, Siobhan (2007), op. cit., 12.

42. Yungher, Nathan I. (2008), op. cit., 97.

43. O'Neil, Siobhan (2007), op. cit., 12.

44. O'Neil, Siobhan (2007), op. cit., 13.

45. *Tobacco and Terror: How Cigarette Smuggling Is Funding Our Enemies Abroad* (2008), Legislative Report Prepared by the Republican Staff of the U.S. House Committee on Homeland Security, U.S. Rep. Peter T. King (R-NY), Ranking Member, 5.
46. *Tobacco and Terror* (2008), 7.
47. Information related to the Dearborn, Michigan indictment can be found at a number of Web sites, including http://www.milnet.com/terr-prosecutions/2006-08-23_ybakri. pdf (retrieved on February 1, 2009).
48. Stern, Jessica (2008), op. cit., 171.
49. This information was obtained from the al Qaeda manual, also know as the "Manchester Document," where police in Manchester, England, captured the document, which was subsequently made available via the Internet.
50. Ibid with "Manchester Document."
51. This diagram was adapted from Stern, Jessica (2008), op. cit., 160.
52. Nedoroscik, Jeffrey A. (2005). "Extremist Groups in Egypt," in *Violence and Terrorism*. Ed. Thomas J. Badey. McGraw-Hill/Dushkin, 76.
53. Stern, Jessica (2008), op. cit., 170.
54. Nedoroscik, Jeffrey A. (2005), op. cit., 76.
55. Telhami, Shibley (2005). "Understanding the Challenge," in *Violence and Terrorism*. Ed. Thomas J. Badey. McGraw-Hill/Dushkin, 159.
56. Stern, Jessica (2008), op. cit., 160.
57. "Terror Incidents in the U.S. Since the 9/11 Attacks" (2008), op. cit., 53–54.
58. Smith, Brent L. and Kelly R. Damphousse (2002). "The American Terrorism Study: Patterns of Behavior, Investigation and Prosecution of American Terrorists," N.I.J., Final Report in Grant #1999-IJCX-0005, January 18, 2002.
59. Miller, Judith (2007). "On the Front Line in the War on Terrorism: Cops in New York and Los Angeles Offer America Two Models for Preventing Another 9/11," *City Journal* (Summer). http://www.city-journal.org/html/17_3_preventing_terrorism. html (retrieved on May 9, 2008).
60. NYPD Radicalization in the West: The Homegrown Threat (2007), 7–9.
61. Yungher, Nathan I. (2008), op. cit., 168.
62. NYPD Radicalization in the West: The Homegrown Threat (2007), 20.
63. Morgenstern, Henry (2008). "From Virtual Jihad to Real Jihad," *The Counter Terrorist* 1, no. 1 (May/June):27.
64. Yungher, Nathan I. (2008), op. cit., 43.
65. Yungher, Nathan I. (2008), op. cit., 43.
66. Yungher, Nathan I. (2008), op. cit., 44–45.
67. Yungher, Nathan I. (2008), op. cit., 45.
68. Yungher, Nathan I. (2008), op. cit., 73.
69. Yungher, Nathan I. (2008), op. cit., 76.
70. Yungher, Nathan I. (2008), op. cit., 75–76.
71. Yungher, Nathan I. (2008), op. cit., 77.
72. Lifton, Robert Jay (2005). "In the Lord's Hands: America's Apocalyptic Mindset," in *Violence and Terrorism*. Ed. Thomas J. Badey. McGraw-Hill/Dushkin, 145.
73. Lifton, Robert Jay (2005), op. cit.,145.
74. This information was obtained from the al Qaeda manual, also know as the "Manchester Document," at UK/BM-12.
75. "Manchester Document" at UK/BM-77.
76. NYPD Radicalization in the West: The Homegrown Threat (2007), 6.

77. NYPD Radicalization in the West: The Homegrown Threat (2007), 6.
78. NYPD Radicalization in the West: The Homegrown Threat (2007), 7.
79. Hamm, Mark S., "Terrorist Recruitment and Radicalization in Prison," NIJ Conference, July 2007.
80. NYPD Radicalization in the West: The Homegrown Threat (2007), 31.
81. NYPD Radicalization in the West: The Homegrown Threat (2007), 7.
82. NYPD Radicalization in the West: The Homegrown Threat (2007), 36–37.
83. NYPD Radicalization in the West: The Homegrown Threat (2007), 43–47.
84. Witkowski, Michael J. (2004). "The Gang's All Here," *Security Management* May:98.
85. Gang Activity in the U.S. Military. Report found at http://usmilitary.about.com/od/justicelawlegislation/a/gangs.htm (retrieved on July 27, 2006).
86. Main, Frank and Fran Spielman (2003), "New Police Gang Effort Comes up Big," *Chicago Sun-Times,* December 11.
87. Robb, John (2007). "The Coming Urban Terror: Systems Disruption, Networked Gangs, and Bioweapons," *City Journal* (Summer). http://www.city-journal.org/html/17_3_urban_terrorism.html (retrieved on May 16, 2008).
88. Islamic Radicalization in State and Local Prisons: NJTTF Correctional Intelligence Initiative Assessment of Radicalization and Recruitment (2006). FBI Counter-Terrorism Division, Intelligence Assessment, August 20:10.
89. Hamm, Mark S. (2007), op. cit.
90. Aidi, Hisham (2005). "Jihadi's in the Hood: Race, Urban Islam and the War on Terror," in *Violence and Terrorism.* Ed. Thomas J. Badey. McGraw-Hill/Dushkin, 128.
91. Aidi, Hisham (2005), op. cit., 132.
92. Aidi, Hisham (2005), op. cit., 132.
93. Aidi, Hisham (2005), op. cit., 132.
94. Aidi, Hisham (2005), op. cit., 128.
95. Aidi, Hisham (2005), op. cit., 128.
96. This graphic was presented by Mark Hamm at the NIJ conference in July 2007.
97. Reiman, Jeffrey (2004). *The Rich Get Richer and the Poor Get Prison: Ideology, Class and Criminal Justice.* Boston, MA: Pearson, Allyn and Bacon, 188.
98. Hamm, Mark S. (2007), op. cit.
99. Lefkowitz, Josh (2008). "Terrorists Behind Bars." www.nefafoundation.org (retrieved on May 5, 2008).
100. Testimony of Javed Ali, senior intelligence officer, Office of Intelligence and Analysis, Department of Homeland Security, before the Senate Committee on Homeland Security and Government Affairs, September 19, 2006.
101. Testimony of Donald Van Duyn, deputy assistant director, Counterterrorism Division, Federal Bureau of Investigation, before the Senate Committee on Homeland Security and Governmental Affairs, September 19, 2006.
102. Lefkowitz, Josh (2008), op. cit., 5.
103. Lefkowitz, Josh (2008), op. cit., 5.
104. Lefkowitz, Josh (2008), op. cit., 5.
105. Lefkowitz, Josh (2008), op. cit., 7.
106. Lefkowitz, Josh (2008), op. cit., 7.
107. Aidi, Hisham (2005), op. cit., 129.
108. Lefkowitz, Josh (2008), op. cit., 4.
109. Lefkowitz, Josh (2008), op. cit., 2.t10

110. Testimony of Robert S. Mueller, III, director, Federal Bureau of Investigation, before the Senate Committee on Intelligence of the United States Senate, February 16, 2005.
111. Fields, Gary (2008), "Murder Spike Poses Quandary," *Wall Street Journal*, May 6, A16.
112. President Barack Obama (2009). Executive Order—Review and Disposition of Individuals Detained at the Guantánamo Bay Naval Base and Closure of Detention Facilities. January 22, 2009. http://www.whitehouse.gov/the_press_office/ClosureOf GuantanamoDetentionFacilities/.
113. Mazzetti, Mark and William Glaberson (2009), "Obama Will Shut Guantanamo Site and C.I.A. Prisons," *New York Times,* January 22, A1.

Chapter 3

Extremist Groups, Ideologies, and Applications

This chapter provides an overview of various extremist groups, their ideologies, and some examples of violence attributable to them. I will present the groups along specific ideological frameworks. In this way, I will "classify" the group along its main ideological tenets: single interest, left wing, anarchist, right wing, nationalist/racial groups. A couple of caveats on this approach need to be made. First, some groups may fit into more than one classification. My classifications are not meant to "pigeonhole" any particular group into a specific, all-encompassing framework. Instead, it is simply my attempt to classify a group into a larger category. Second, this presentation is limited to groups who are considered "domestic" terrorist groups and to established international groups with a reach, infrastructure, or support within this country. Finally, once these groups and their ideologies are presented, I will illustrate how extremist "triggers" become applicable in society. With this approach established, it may help to initially provide a definition of domestic terrorism. The FBI defines "domestic terrorism" as[1]

> Domestic terrorism is the unlawful use, or threatened use, of violence by a group or individual based and operating entirely within the United States (or its territories) without foreign direction, committed against persons or

property to intimidate or coerce a government, the civilian population, or any segment thereof, in furtherance of political or social objectives.

Single-Interest Groups

- Extremists who seek to force the government or population to alter a specific grievance within the country
- Usually do not seek to overthrow or greatly alter the government
- Often represent a fairly popular point of view
- Currently most active in the United States

Antiabortionists

Antiabortionists are generally Christian oriented, with a small percentage advocating violence against abortion facilities and medical personnel. These groups generally point to four different approaches for their complaints: scriptural, legal, moral/philosophical, and medical.

The scriptural basis is often cited in the Old Testament legal code, such as Exodus 21:22–25, which states that[2]

> If men who are fighting hit a pregnant woman and she gives birth prematurely but there is no serious injury, the offender must be fined whatever the woman's husband demands and the court allows. But if there is serious injury, you are to take life for life, eye for eye, tooth for tooth, hand for hand, foot for foot, burn for burn, wound for wound, bruise for bruise.

The legal basis is to criticize the U.S. Supreme Court decision in *Roe v. Wade*. The argument against this decision can be summarized as:[3]

> *Roe v. Wade* violated standard legal reasoning. The Supreme Court decided not to decide when life begins and then … overturned the laws of 50 different states. Most of the Supreme Court's verdict rested upon two sentences: "We need not resolve the difficult question of when life begins. When those trained in the respective disciplines of medicine, philosophy, and theology are unable to arrive at any consensus, the judiciary, at this point in the development of man's knowledge, is not in a position to speculate as to an answer."

The medical basis can be summarized by asserting that "at conception the embryo is genetically distinct from the mother." This assertion was developed by Anderson, who stated,[4]

To say that the developing baby is no different from the mother's appendix is scientifically inaccurate. A developing embryo is genetically different from the mother. A developing embryo is also genetically different from the sperm and egg that created it. A human being has 46 chromosomes (sometimes 47 chromosomes). Sperm and egg have 23 chromosomes. A trained geneticist can distinguish between the DNA of an embryo and that of a sperm and egg. But that same geneticist could not distinguish between the DNA of a developing embryo and a full-grown human being.

The moral/philosophical basis can be summarized by asking this philosophical question: Where do you draw the line? When does a [fetus] being become a person? Anderson makes a pointed assertion that has relevance to animal rights advocates; he states,[5]

> The Supreme Court's decision of *Roe v. Wade* separated personhood from humanity. In other words, the judges argued that a developing fetus was a human (i.e., a member of the species *Homo sapiens*) but not a person. Since only persons are given 14th Amendment protection under the Constitution, the Court argued that abortion could be legal at certain times. This left to doctors, parents, or even other judges the responsibility of arbitrarily deciding when personhood should be awarded to human beings.

These arguments are presented for a couple of reasons. First, Anderson's arguments are well-founded and thoughtful presentations of his beliefs. I do not in any way assert that he is an extremist. Indeed, in reading his words he appears to be extraordinarily articulate and well meaning. Second, the logic and passion of his arguments have resonance for many different extremist ideologies. Again, this does not mean that Anderson is an extremist. It is to say, however, that extremist groups need to develop an intellectual and philosophical framework to further their cause. For example, as you will see below, the animal rights movement uses the logic of "rights" for the fetus, and they seek to apply it to animals. As will be presented below, applying "rights" to this cause has significant implications. In addition, anti-abortion advocates examine the question of when life actually begins. They do this in their desire to prevent the death of a fetus. One can also extend this assertion to its logical conclusion: If we can decide to kill a fetus, why should we be prevented from killing an infidel (or a pig, or a nip, or a Jew, or a monkey, or a cracker, or whatever). I present this to be provocative. I do not mean to connect abortion to these demeaning characterizations of people. The problem, however, is that some extremist groups will do just that.

One of the most active antiabortion groups is the "Army of God." This group considers itself as "Yahweh's Warriors." Its Web site calls Paul J. Hill, convicted for numerous bombings, an "American Hero." According to Hill, he did these deeds in "self-defense." In his words,[6]

> You have a responsibility to protect your neighbor's life, and to use force if necessary to do so. In an effort to suppress this truth, you may mix my blood with the blood of the unborn, and those who have fought to defend the oppressed. However, truth and righteousness will prevail. May God help you to protect the unborn as you would want to be protected.

The Army of God Web site also trumpets the "accomplishments" of Eric Rudolph, who was convicted of numerous bombings, including the Centennial Park bombing during the 1996 Olympics. Rudolph makes the following statement on his Web site, which pointedly illustrates the "logic" of extremists which de-legitimizes the government and the *law* because of its murder of children:[7]

> I am not an anarchist. I have nothing against government or law enforcement in general. It is solely for the reason that this government has legalized the murder of children that I have no allegiance to it nor do I recognize the legitimacy of this particular government in Washington.

With the election of President Obama, the antiabortion radicals will awaken their movement to direct action. In the past several years, these individuals have been relatively calm. I believe they desired to assess whether President Bush would appoint Supreme Court justices sufficient to change the balance of the court. This did not occur. With the Obama election, the balance will swing back in the other direction—toward more liberal "pro-choice" justices. This being said, those who seek to impose their will related to abortion have little legal means to do so. Consequently, those inclined to violence will come out with more frequent and more violent attacks. I believe if you understand the passion and commitment of this movement, this is a predictable assertion. This "prediction" is almost as sure as the sun rising in the east!

Animal Rights

The Animal Liberation Front (ALF), which migrated to the United States from England in 1979, has been the most active group claiming credit for attacks in this country. This group has committed over 1,000 attacks in the United States in the past 20 years, causing at least $45 million in damages. Most of the attacks, however, have been relatively minor, consisting of breaking windows, gluing locks, and spray-painting. Some attacks, though, have been violent and highly destructive. At least 90 of these incidents have caused $100,000 or more in damages, and some have resulted in damages that have run into multimillions of dollars. Some enterprises, including fur farms, have been driven out of business by these actions.[8] According to John Lewis, FBI deputy associate director for counterterrorism, groups like ALF and other "violent animal rights extremists ... pose one of the most serious terrorist threats to the nation."[9]

As stated earlier, the logic of this group is to create "rights" for animals. Once rights are created, then animals can be placed on a par with humans. Once this is achieved, then the next logical question results: How do humans have the right to capture, enslave, or kill animals? This thinking raises the provocative question of whether humans can be committing "terrorism" against animals. This can be illustrated by the following narrative:[10]

> Is it reasonable to speak of the "human terrorism" against the animal world?
>
> Virtually all definitions of terrorism, even by "progressive" human rights champions, outright banish from consideration the most excessive violence of all—that which the human species unleashes against all nonhuman species.
>
> *Speciesism* is so ingrained and entrenched in the human mind that the human pogrom against animals does not even appear on the conceptual radar screen. Any attempt to perceive nonhuman animals as innocent victims of violence and human animals as planetary terrorists is rejected with derision.
>
> But if terrorism is linked to intentional violence inflicted on innocent persons for ideological, political, or economic motivations, and nonhuman animals also are "persons"—subjects of a life—then the human war against animals is terrorism.
>
> Every individual who terrifies, injures, tortures, and/or kills an animal is a *terrorist*; fur farms, factory farms, foie gras, vivisection, and other exploitative operations are terrorist industries; and governments that support these industries are terrorist states. The true weapons of mass destruction are the gases, rifles, stun guns, cutting blades, and forks and knives used to experiment on, kill, dismember, and consume animal bodies.

Radical Environmentalists

Radical environmental or "eco" attacks date back more than 30 years. The Earth Liberation Front (ELF) has been one of the foremost extremist groups functioning in the United States during the past decade. These groups intend to force the government and the population to change the way particular aspects of the environment are used. They have made numerous direct attacks against businesses and the government during the past three decades. Around 60 of these incidents have caused over $100,000 in damages. One attack in 2003 caused about $50 million in damages to a housing complex under construction.[11] The FBI defines eco-terrorism[12]

> as the use or threatened use of violence of a criminal nature against innocent victims or property by an environmentally oriented, sub-national group for Environmental-Political reasons, or aimed at an audience beyond the target, often of a symbolic nature.

The logic and structure of the radical environmentalists can be found on ELF's Web site. The Web site states that "[t]he ELF is an underground movement with no leadership, membership or official spokesperson. The intention of this web site is to inform and chronicle issues related to E.L.F."[13] The Web site further asserts that:[14]

- There is no ELF structure; "it" is nonhierarchical and there is no centralized organization or leadership.
- There is no "membership" in the Earth Liberation Front.
- Any individuals who committed arson or any other illegal acts under the ELF name are individuals who chose to do so under the banner of ELF and do so only driven by their personal conscience.
- These choices are not endorsed, encouraged, or approved of by the Web site's management, Webmasters, affiliates, or other participants.
- The intention of the Web site is journalistic: to inform and chronicle issues related to ELF.

This group has recently become much more political in its orientation. It is difficult to state definitively when the political thinking came to the fore. Indeed, it is now apparent that the target of some eco-terrorists is capitalism. Hence, making the connection from the environment to capitalism is both ironic and problematic. While capitalism certainly has contributed to pollution and other environmental degradation, in my mind it is simplistic to only blame capitalism. Look at the pollution being caused by the industrialization in China. No one with any sense of political orientation could mistake China for a capitalistic system. Despite this "inconvenient truth," when you read the bin Laden quotation presented in Chapter 8, please consider these questions. When bin Laden cites the Kyoto Treaty and asserts that capitalism is the source of the world's problems, is it possible he was seeking allies with certain groups in this country? Surely you will agree he had a reason to criticize capitalism and to advocate the Kyoto Treaty. Who do you think bin Laden was talking to? In my mind, he was talking to leftist Americans, anarchists, and *environmentalists*. The ranting of bin Laden fits well with this quote from an environmental group. The connection in this thinking is reflected as:[15]

> Direct action is just one of the many fronts on which we need to attack our current system. Society will eventually be forced to rethink their

methods of living if these attacks occur. Over time, as the public learns what a money-fueled-government really looks like, it will become completely unacceptable.

A revolution will occur. It may not be a bloody one, taking place on the streets, but it will be one with equal or even greater force. One which will dry out the feed lots for greedy capitalists and their deadly ways. One which will end corporate rule and environmental destruction by man's thirst for wealth.

Left Wing (Marxism)

- Revolution of the workers, directed by revolutionary elite
- Seek to overthrow capitalism and create a socialist state
- No private property; means of production controlled by the workers

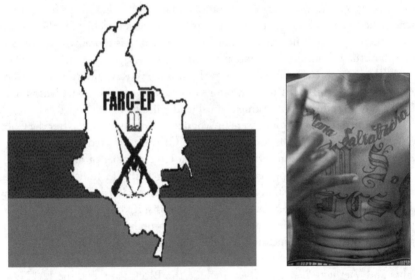

FARC   MS-13

Left-wing terrorists/extremists are often referred to as "Marxists" or "communists." In essence, left-wing extremists seek to eliminate capitalism, which would require a substantial overthrow—or overhauling—of the U.S. government. Ultimately, these groups desire a socialist system in which all people would be equal. In this system, people receive their basic needs and give according to their talents and skills, leading to a class-less nation where cooperation would be stressed over competition. The means of production would be owned in common. The multi-national corporations that presently exist would be eliminated. In the final stage of development, there would be little or no government. Any government that did exist would be weak and administrative in nature.

Leftist group ideologies vary as to the exact form that the new society would take. Traditional leftists believe that a transitional period would be required, during which the economic conversion is undertaken and people are educated in the new way of life. During this period, those with the insight necessary to accomplish the revolution would rule in a dictatorial manner. Communists often refer to this stage as the "dictatorship of the proletariat." Eventually, this period would end, and the strong government would cease to exist. However, many anarchists disagree with the need for a transitional period. They believe that if a capitalist state were overthrown, people could immediately live harmoniously with little or no government.[16] With this thinking, anarchists are more inclined to destroy without regard for the consequences.

One of the best examples of a "successful" terrorist campaign was with Narodnaya Volya in Russia from about 1869–1881. This group published the *Catechism of the Revolutionist,* which taught that the revolutionist has "only one science, the science of destruction ... His sole and constant object is the immediate destruction of this vile order ... For him, everything is moral which assists the triumph of the revolution. Immoral and criminal is everything which stands in its way."[17] This movement eventually led to the Bolshevik Revolution in 1917. When the communists took over Russia, millions of people died. The Soviet Union maintained a brutal, state-run government until its demise in 1990.

Communist-inspired groups were in "vogue" during the 1960s. After the Cuban Revolution in the late 1950s, Castro and Che Guevara inspired groups seeking to create a "people's revolution." They attracted a large number of followers. Groups dedicated to this cause appeared in Peru (Shining Path), in Italy (Red Brigades), in Germany (Red Army Faction), in Northern Ireland (Irish Republican Army), and in other countries. Many of the groups were inspired by *Manual of the Urban Guerrilla* by Carlos Marighella, who advocated a "scorched earth strategy, the sabotage of transport and oil pipelines, and the destruction of food supplies."

Numerous left-wing groups were active during the turbulent days of the Civil Rights and Vietnam War era. These include the Black Panthers, the FALN, and the Weather Underground. In essence, the Weather Underground was a Marxist group that sought to attack capitalism. It was credited with at least 35 bombings, including the U.S. Capitol, the Pentagon, police stations, and other government facilities.[18] The FALN, which sought independence for Puerto Rico, was "credited" with more than 130 bombings and arsons between the years 1974 and 1982. Members of this group attempted to assassinate President Truman in 1950 and shot up Congress in 1954.[19]

For various reasons, I believe that the ideologies of these groups, particularly the Weather Underground and the Black Panthers, will be more active in the months and years ahead. Ironically, a member of the Weather Underground, William Ayers, was associated with Barack Obama during the 1990s. While it appears this connection raised more partisan rancor than substance, it is still unclear what this connection is, or was. Partly due to the potential for partisan criticism, it is inevitable that the group will again be highlighted and come under contemporary scrutiny. Similarly, the New Black Panthers seem to be picking up where the old group left off. This group will be highlighted in the Nationalist/ Racial section of this chapter. Suffice it to say at this point, the thinking of these groups has not died. Indeed, they appear to be gaining steam in some quarters.

Notwithstanding this assertion, when the war in Vietnam ended, and with civil rights institutionalized in the country, the force of the radical groups lost much of its cause. With the fall of the Soviet Union, the movement lost additional justification for its existence. Currently, as noted in the last section, the environmental movement has a political, anticapitalist stripe, which appears to have some momentum. In addition, the connection between the radical Islamic movement and Socialist governments, such as Venezuela, is another indicator of concern. In any case, we will highlight two leftist groups, which I believe are prominent and dangerous.

FARC

This group has significant ties to the drug trade in this country. It has controlled the drug trade in Columbia for many years. It is estimated that the annual revenues from narcotics is $400 million, with almost 40 percent of it controlled by the 18,000 fighters of FARC.[20] This group has a significant paramilitary arm. The group started in 1964 with the stated goal of replacing the Columbian government with a Marxist regime. It was established as the military wing of the Colombian Communist party. Most of its activities occur in Colombia with some activities— extortion, kidnapping, logistics—in Venezuela, Panama, and Ecuador. This narco-terrorist group uses extreme force and violence against a government or population in order to enable a cartel to continue to function. Its affiliations include Venezuela and Cuba, which provide some medical care and political consultation.[21]

This group recently made international headlines with the resolution of a long-standing hostage situation, and its connection with Chávez from Venezuela. Information retrieved from captured and killed FARC members in March/April 2008 revealed that the Venezuelan government may have channeled $300 million to FARC.[22] It is important to note that if this is true, the implications of this relationship are far reaching. Consider this possibility. Is it possible that Chávez may engage leftist extremist groups, such as FARC, to further his socialist agenda throughout Latin America? Just as Chávez's apparent ally, Ahmadinejad from Iran, engages with terrorist groups like Hamas and Hezbollah as proxies, given the monies provided to FARC, is it possible we will see this occur in Latin and North America?

This concern is further evidenced by a disconcerting discovery in the spring of 2008. Open source reporting cited Colombian military officials who said that they recovered 66 pounds of uranium from the FARC raid. Colombian

Gen. Freddy Padilla tied the uranium to the seized laptops, saying one of the computer files mentions attempts by the FARC to buy uranium, apparently to resell. This discovery corresponds with earlier reporting in which Colombian officials claimed the rebels were seeking uranium to make a "dirty bomb."[23] In my capacity as an instructor for international police officials, I had the pleasure to ask Columbian police officials about their take on this discovery of the uranium—and the alleged plans to make a "dirty bomb." The response by the Columbian police officials was chilling. In essence, they acknowledged that these events occurred. They then pointedly asserted that FARC had no intention of using these materials in Columbia. They correctly noted that if they used a dirty bomb in Columbia, any support from the population would quickly dry up. Such a potentially devastating attack would be certain to alienate the very people they seek to influence. When I asked what they intended to do with the dirty bomb, they smiled and stated, "They would bring it north." Their body language and their inferences made it clear that the "target" of such an attack would be the United States. While I cannot prove this to be true, I would not doubt either the knowledge of these Columbian police officials or the deviant thinking of Chávez. In any event, it would be wise to pay attention to Venezuela and Columbia. These two countries currently represent mirror opposites: Venezuela is seeking to export socialist revolutions while Columbia is seeking to assert capitalist principles.

In this larger—and internal—conflict, the Colombian government has used a three-part strategy to fight FARC. The strategy consists of increased military pressure, rewards for the capture of top commanders, and incentives to surrender. This approach has had much success. As of May 2008, over 475 rebels have been captured and almost 500 have been killed since the beginning of 2008. This aggressive enforcement has hurt FARC's morale. It has also been hurt by high-profile desertions and internal fighting. For example, over 860 fighters have turned themselves in since the beginning of the year. In addition, a senior FARC leader, Iván Ríos, was killed in March 2007 by his own security guard, who turned himself in and collected a $1 million reward.[24] While these are significant successes, no one has declared FARC dead. It is a significant paramilitary and well-funded organization.

MS-13

In the 1980s civil war erupted in El Salvador, killing an estimated 100,000 people. Because of the unstable environment, about two million people have immigrated to the United States. These immigrant Salvadorian youth were subject to victimization by local gangs. A group of Salvadorian immigrants created a new gang, calling themselves Mara Salvatrucha, also known as MS-13.

It is believed they got their name from combining the name of "La Mara," a violent street gang in El Salvador, with Salvatruchas, a term used to denote members of the Farabundo Marti National Liberation Front. This was a group of Salvadorian peasants trained as guerilla fighters. The "13" was added to pay homage to the California prison gang the Mexican Mafia, to "13th Street" in Los Angeles, and the letter "M" being the 13th in the alphabet.[25] MS-13 members sport numerous tattoos on their bodies and faces, and wear blue and white colors taken from the El Salvadoran flag. Membership is believed to total about 6,000–10,000 in the United States, and over 100,000 worldwide.[26] Members typically range in age from 11 to 40 years old. Its members are dispersed over 31 U.S. states and several Latin American countries, and its proliferation continues unabated, despite close attention from law enforcement.[27]

The criminal activities attributed to the group include drug smuggling, gun running, people smuggling, killing for hire, theft, drug sales, and arson. Their progressive increase in violent activities and blatant disregard for the law (threats and attacks against law enforcement officials is common) has made them the most feared gang in the United States. According to Robb, MS-13 or a similar American gang may eventually find that it has sufficient power to hold a city hostage through disruption.[28] Their violent tendencies have been well recognized by law enforcement. Indeed, they have been known for their "signatures," which are more characteristic of a terrorist group than a gang. These signatures include having no fear of law enforcement, "booby-trapping" their drug houses, "announcing" their arrival into a new community with acts of violence, and "planting" females to surveil law enforcement personnel to note where they eat, exercise, drink, live, conduct business, and their daily routines. These activities, coupled with killing police and federal agents and threatening police with "green light" (target) notices, are characteristic of this group.

As illustrated by these signatures, I believe that MS-13's violent and political nature make it poised to "graduate" to terroristic violence. Indeed, the group has already committed a number of politically oriented violent acts. Consider these examples:[29]

- In 1997 the son of Honduras President Ricardo Maduro was kidnapped and murdered by MS-13 members. MS-13 members have continued to taunt Central American government officials. Members also left a dismembered corpse with a note for the Honduras president that "more people will die … the next victims will be police and journalists."
- In 2004, Guatemalan President Óscar Berger received a similar message attached to the body of a dismembered man from MS-13 members.
- After an increase in crime, Mexico began a campaign in 2004 to eradicate MS-13 when they arrested 300 members, calling them a "threat to national security."

Anarchist

Purist and idealistic anarchists do not believe that there should be any government. They feel that each person should function free of restraint. However, most people who claim to be anarchists are more opposed to big government and the capitalist system than they are to the basic concept of government itself. To accomplish this goal, some believe that the working class must unite to bring down capitalism. After this occurs, the workers will control the means of production. Workers will establish rules that will enable them to live in harmony with one another.

Anarchist philosophy had a significant impact on terrorist campaigns and groups. An early anarchist, Karl Heinzen, published a book titled *Der Mord* (translated from German as *Murder*), which justified terrorism on a grand scale. His thinking was quite blunt. He stated, "If you have to blow up half a continent and pour out a sea of blood in order to destroy the barbarians, have no scruples or conscience."[30] The desire to kill was strong. Anarchists were blamed for numerous notorious actions, including the assassination of President William McKinley in 1901; killing eight police officers in a bombing, which resulted in the Haymarket Riots in Chicago on May 4, 1886; and for the September 16, 1920, bombing on Wall Street in New York City. This attack killed 33 people, wounded 400 others, and caused approximately $2 million in damages.[31]

Contemporary anarchists are similarly interested in bringing down the capitalist system and government in general. During the 1990s, some anarchists engaged in violent protest demonstrations, usually staged by labor unions and other causes. Their typical approach is to dress in all black outfits and gather in "black blocs" to prepare for and function in these protests. These "black blocs" are not intended to be long-lasting organizations. Instead they exist solely for one event. The "Battle in Seattle" was a classic example of this violence at the World Trade Organization (WTO) meeting. The violence that was generated is potentially far reaching. This movement seeks to attack what is known as the "new world order." Consider the following quote from Louis Beam, a right-wing extremist, relating to the Battle in Seattle:[32]

> Mark my words this is but the first confrontation, there will be many more such confrontations as intelligent, caring people begin to face off the WACO thugs of the New World Order here in the U.S. The new American patriot will be neither left nor right, just a freeman fighting for liberty. New alliances will form between those who have in the past thought of themselves as "right-wingers," conservatives, and patriots with many people who have thought of themselves as "left-wingers," progressive, or just "liberal."

As this statement makes clear, the new world order is an attractive target to a surprising array of groups. As mentioned earlier, al Qaeda has criticized the capitalistic system—which is symbolized in the new world order. This mindset asserts that international corporations are controlling—and ruining—the planet. One consequence of this internationalization of business is that national identity and sovereignty will be greatly diminished or even abandoned. Because of their strong attachment to sovereignty, white supremacist and Christian Identity groups have applauded al Qaeda for their criticism of the new world order. According to Stern, these groups may eventually take action on behalf of al Qaeda in support of their mutual abhorrence to the new world order.[33] Each of these groups desires to "purify" the world through murder.[34]

The attraction for those who desire to attack the new world order also is strong for those who see themselves as oppressed. This message particularly resonates with racial and ethnic minorities who see the capitalist system as the cause of their troubles. These potential "converts" are not lost to al Qaeda leaders. Consider this assertion in light of al-Zawahiri's quote in Chapter 1, where he advocates that "the oppressed" join the Holy War against modernity—or capitalism! This message speaks to the disillusioned and disaffected of American society.

Right-Wing (Fascism)

- Stresses nationalism above individual rights.
- Some seek strong central government; others are strongly antigovernment.
- Foreigners and minorities are targets.
- Opposite of left-wing philosophy, but not necessarily along a straight line:
  1. Some oppose the U.S. government.
  2. Some believe government has been taken over.
  3. Some believe they are the government.

One would assume that right-wing terrorism would be the exact opposite of left-wing terrorism. To a certain extent it is. For example, neo-Nazi groups seek to establish a strong central government that would control the means of production, either directly or through corporate monopolies controlled by selected individuals. In this worldview, the country would be very nationalistic and militarily strong. Patriotism would be stressed. The white race, Aryan nationality, and a quasi-Christian creed would occupy a favored position. Other groups would face discrimination and would have their rights restricted.

While these tenets illustrate typical neo-Nazi thinking, there are other political philosophies (i.e., sovereign citizens, Freemen, Posse Comitatus) that are different from the neo-Nazi cause, yet are still characterized as right-wing philosophies. For this reason, it is difficult to categorize or classify right-wing extremist groups. No matter how they are categorized, there will be an overlap. There are many commonalities. The vast majority of these groups are antigovernment in philosophy. Almost all espouse an element of hate toward some other group of people.

One way to further distinguish these groups is to present two broad subcategories (antigovernment and racist/hate-based groups). These groups will be presented in this section, and another will be presented in the Nationalist/Racial section.[35] Notwithstanding this distinction, these groups are dangerous. Four police officers were killed by right-wing extremists in 2007 (the most since 1995). Since 1990, right-wing extremists are responsible for 500 murders and over 200 attempted murders.

"Power of the County"

Posse Comitatus

Antigovernment Groups

Posse Comitatus

Posse Comitatus is a conspiracy-oriented group, focusing on a "hidden history" and misinterpretation of laws to justify its beliefs. This group derives its name from the legal prohibition on using the military to enforce the law.[36] Its ideology believes the county is the highest level of government, with the sheriff as the highest elected official. However, they believe the county sheriff should never enforce unpopular laws. The definition of unpopular laws is essentially laws that the Posse does not like or those that allegedly violate biblical precepts or principles. Nor should the sheriff enforce orders from a judge. As inferred by this analysis, they view federal and state governments as illegitimate bodies. Laws from these bodies and from illegitimate courts need not be obeyed. Taxes imposed by these bodies also should be avoided—and ignored. Posse members claim that at one point in American history there were essentially no laws and every man was a king (or at least a sovereign citizen). In this thinking, from this point forward a long-standing conspiracy slowly replaced the true, legitimate (de jure) government with a tyrannical, illegitimate (de facto) government.[37]

The Posse also asserted that the Fourteenth Amendment was illegal. This amendment, which, among other things, gave citizenship to ex-slaves following the Civil War, also created an entirely new class of citizens. This new class of citizens was subject to federal and state laws and regulations. These citizens were different from sovereign citizens. According to this thinking, sovereign citizens did have to adhere to federal and state laws. However, these people could voluntarily (and unknowingly) become U.S. citizens by entering into "contracts" with federal or state governments (e.g., by using Social Security cards, driver's licenses, or ZIP codes). In short, two types of citizenship exist:

1. Sovereign citizens who are immune to almost all laws
2. U.S. citizens who are subject to government laws

Common Law Courts and Sovereign Citizens

Common law courts and sovereign citizens are direct ideological descendents of Posse beliefs. Both these groups use Posse thinking as a basis of their ideologies. Both also expand on the tenets developed by "posse logic." For example, these groups believe that an illegitimate government has replaced the lawful government. As such, sovereign citizens are subject only to the old common law. Adhering to this notion, they formed common law courts. Because of these courts, sovereign citizens refuse to "contract" with the de facto government, and believe they are exempt from paying taxes. Common law courts, often called Our One Supreme Court, were formed to hear sovereign citizen matters. They believe this is the *only* court that has jurisdiction over them. This court can take actions ranging from settling disputes among sovereign citizens, placing bogus liens on property of public officials and other targets, and issuing arrest warrants for both serious and sundry crimes, including treason. Sovereign citizens generally believe that the only enforceable laws pertain to crimes where someone was harmed, and they oppose any statutory law where there was no victim.[38]

Militias

Militias believe that citizen militias are authorized under the U.S. Constitution and/or early federal statutes, particularly the Second Amendment. This thinking goes back to the Revolutionary War. At that time, all adult males were considered part of the ready militia, subject to call should the nation require defense. Male citizens were expected to attend training sessions at their own expense. They were to provide their own uniforms and weapons. After the War of 1812, the need for a defense force diminished and became unpopular. To circumvent this federal law (requiring all males to be in the militia), the concept of having an "unorganized militia" was established. This allowed most males to simply be placed on a list to be called on only if the nation was under attack. Otherwise, these men did not attend any military training. In time, states began to create militia bodies that were paid and professional. These units became known as the National Guard in the early twentieth century.

Militia groups in the 1990s tend to be conspiracy oriented. These groups believe they are essential to protecting the people from a tyrannical government. This tyrannical government allegedly is becoming increasingly under the domain of the new world order and/or the United Nations. Stated another way, the U.S. government has become a puppet to these world-ruling organizations.

Beyond this thinking, most militia groups engage in paramilitary training. Some were involved in criminal activities, particularly with respect to the acquisition of weapons and explosives. Some also engage in violent activity. By the end of the twentieth century, the number of militias functioning in the United States had shrunk, and some became quite secretive. This was in stark contrast to the open and notorious way they had often functioned in the early 1990s. Of course, when the Oklahoma City bombing occurred, law enforcement agencies placed heavy emphasis on these groups. Militias continue into the twenty-first century. However, many are fairly small and clandestine in operation. Nonetheless, they present a threat that can suddenly emerge without warning.[39]

Racist/Hate Groups

Many right-wing terrorist groups are based on hatred of people of different races or ethnic origins. Indeed, for some organizations, the focus on racism is the primary reason they exist. These hate-based groups include racial hatred as a main plank of their agendas. The obvious example of this thinking is the KKK.

Ku Klux Klan

The Ku Klux Klan (KKK) has existed in three distinct waves in the United States. The group was initially started in the ex-Confederate states shortly after the Civil War. It was in response to Reconstruction, where state governments threatened the notion of white supremacy. It also served to protect white Southerners who had lost their citizenship following the war. Whites covered their faces to shield their identities, attacking blacks in an effort to make it impossible for them to enjoy the freedom granted by the Fourteenth Amendment to the U.S. Constitution. Numerous black people were menaced, beaten, and killed. Many black-owned businesses, residences, and churches were destroyed. The first KKK wave faded away as conservative white Southerners regained their citizenship and control of local and state governments.

The second KKK period began around 1915 in response to a number of social issues of the era. These included blacks moving north to work in factories, the Prohibition movement, labor struggles, the suffragist movement, immigrants—many of whom were Catholics from Ireland and Italy—entering the country in large numbers, and the unrest in Europe that led to World War I. The movie *The Birth of a Nation*, which depicted the KKK in a highly favorable light, also helped fuel its resurgence. Ironically, by the end of the decade it was politically expedient to seek KKK support—and even advocate or admit membership. Within a few short years, the Klan spread to every state in the Union and reached a membership in the millions. Although the KKK grew in size, it gradually lost its popularity in the late 1920s, and by the time World War II began, it had dwindled significantly in size. Soon it ceased to be a legitimate force.

The third period of the KKK commenced in the 1950s, largely in reaction to the issue of school integration and the Civil Rights movement. Although various KKK-related violent attacks against blacks and civil rights workers occurred during the 1950s and 1960s, the KKK never became a national, monolithic organization. Currently, the KKK is divided into a number of separate groups with little or no association with each other. Many of these entities have very small memberships. Only a few are known to be involved in terrorist/extremist violence. Some modern KKK groups spread their message through protest marches staged in areas where they know they will be met by counter-protesters. This, in turn, generates publicity and a variety of security problems for local law enforcement agencies.[40] Significantly, the basic beliefs of the KKK are:[41]

- *White race* is the irreplaceable hub of our nation, our Christian faith, and the high levels of Western culture and technology.
- *America first* before any foreign or alien influence, and a foreign policy of military nonintervention.
- *Constitution* as originally written and intended. The finest system of government ever conceived by man, which is based on the Holy Bible and Christian common law.
- *Free enterprise* of private property and business, but an end to high-finance exploitation (and opposes Federal Reserve Bank and "free trade").
- *Positive Christianity* illustrated by the right of the American people to practice their Christian faith, including prayer in the schools.

Consider these principles in light of "mainstream" American thought. Except the first *white race* assertion, many people in the United States would advocate for this thinking. Much of this rhetoric can (or will) have broad appeal. This is particularly true during difficult economic times. In addition, the focus on the Christian faith and biblical principles may portend a direct conflict with Islamic and secular groups. As such, there are a number of possible "Holy War" components this domestic terrorist group will emphasize in direct opposition to radical Islamists.

KKK

Neo-Nazis

Neo-Nazi groups arose in the United States after World War II. In contemporary America, some neo-Nazi groups want to establish a national socialistic regime. Generally, however, most neo-Nazi groups have diverged considerably from the German Nazi ideology of the 1930s and 1940s. Other groups simply focus on the symbolism and white supremacy aspects of Nazism.[42]

The National Socialist Movement, founded in 1974, is the most explicitly "Nazi-like" of neo-Nazi groups. This movement emulates the uniforms and paraphernalia of the Third Reich. Typically, these groups adhere to a paramilitary structure, with military ranks for its members. Its ideology calls for a "greater America" that would deny citizenship to Jews, nonwhites, and homosexuals. Significantly, some neo-Nazi groups have ties with various Klan, racist skinhead, and other white supremacy groups.[43]

An affiliated biker gang known as the Nazi Low Riders (NLR) was first organized as a gang in the early to mid-1970s among inmates housed by the California Youth Authority. Their ideology is built around white supremacy. Much of the group's rise to power can be attributed to its alliance with another, older prison gang: the Aryan Brotherhood (AB). This alliance helped build NLR's brutal and ambitious reputation. It also created new criminal opportunities unrelated to the AB. The Nazi Low Riders champion its "whiteness," especially when recruiting members from skinhead gangs and among new inmates. However, it is primarily driven by criminal profit. Much of this funding stems from narcotics trafficking, extortion, and armed robbery. At the same time, NLR members have been responsible for a number of infamous racist attacks during the past decade. They are based primarily in Southern California and are scattered among other states, including Arizona, Colorado, Florida, and Illinois. Their symbols include swastikas, SS lighting bolts, and "NLR."[44]

National Alliance is a white-supremacist, anti-Semitic, and anti-United States movement. It was initially founded by Dr. William Pierce and evolved from an earlier group known as the National Youth Alliance, which was created to protest the New Left movement on college campuses during the late 1960s. In 1978, under the pseudonym Andrew MacDonald, Pierce wrote a novel called *The Turner Diaries*, which sold hundreds of thousands of copies. It is regarded as a kind of "bible" for right-wing extremists. Both Robert Mathews of The Order and Timothy McVeigh of Oklahoma City bombing infamy were heavily involved in the promotion of this book. Indeed, the name of Mathews' group came from the novel. It is also widely believed that the outline for McVeigh's attack on the Murrah Federal Building was modeled after an attack described in the publication. The National Alliance has had a significant influence on right-wing philosophy in the United States. Those holding right-wing extremist, hate, and antigovernment views continue to exist, but often lack large groups to join. Instead, they tend to form smaller, clandestine cells around these extremist ideological premises. Some follow the leaderless resistance philosophy and may foment violence on their own.[45]

Another right-wing threat is derived from skinheads, who are often described as a movement, rather than a group or even a political ideology. The movement began in the British Isles and eventually spread to Europe, Canada, and the United States. Some skinheads are deeply involved in music, substance abuse, and are typically apolitical. Others have a political agenda, usually with a white-supremacist or anti-immigrant bent. As is characteristic, many skinheads adorn their bodies with tattoos. Some engage in violence toward minorities and wear boots that they use to kick and stomp their victims. Ironically, many in the right-wing movement view skinheads as the hope for the future of their cause. They openly court them with literature or through Web sites, personal contacts, and music. Significantly, the skinhead culture appeals to both the World Church of the Creator (WCOTC) and to the National Alliance. These groups are likely allies.

Nationalist/Racial Groups

- Individuals of common ethnic origin seeking to establish or regain a homeland
- Usually exist in conjunction with a broader racial, religious, or political ideology

These groups represent a major source of potential extremist violence. As previously described, I believe that groups formed along a nationalist bent, coupled with a broader racial, religious, or political ideology, will foster violence in "defense" of their particular race. Two groups, the New Black Panther Party and the Aryan Brotherhood, will be key drivers in the years ahead.

New Black Panther Party for Self-Defense

The New Black Panther Party for Self-Defense (NBPP) is the proper name of this group. It was founded by Aaron Michaels in 1990. Its ideology combines black nationalism, Pan-Africanism, racism, and anti-Semitic bigotry. Its influences are the original Black Panthers, Black Panther Militia, and the Nation of Islam. The current leader is Malik Zulu Shabazz.

As an example of the heated rhetoric associated with this group, during an NBPP demonstration in front of the B'nai B'rith building in Washington, DC, Shabazz led chants of "death to Israel," "the white man is the devil," and "jihad." He also said, "Kill every goddamn Zionist in Israel! Goddamn little babies, goddamn old ladies! Blow up Zionist supermarkets!" In addition, protestors held large posters that read, "The American Israeli White Man is the Devil" and "The State of Israel Has No Right to Exist."[46]

In its Web site, the group provides a very clear picture of its ideology.[47] Its "ten point" ideology includes some interesting premises and some dangerous language. In my mind, any reasonable reading of this "ten point platform" will manifest an ideology that is devoid of "compromise" with "white racists." As with the white racial ideologies presented above, this platform is formed around extremist notions of race. While I truly hope that I am wrong, these conflicting ideologies are so extreme there does not seem any hope of real compromise. Indeed, neither this ideology nor the white racist rhetoric leave much room for compromise. This ideology is as presented below, almost in its entirety, with the emphasis in the original:

1. We want freedom. We want the power to practice self-determination, and to determine the destiny of our community and THE BLACK NATION. We believe in the spiritual high moral code of our Ancestors. We believe in the truths of the Bible, Quran, and other sacred texts and writings … We believe that Black People will not be free until we are able to determine our Divine Destiny.

2. We want full employment for our people and we demand the dignity to do for ourselves what we have begged the white man to do for us.

   We believe that since the white man has kept us deaf, dumb and blind, and used every "dirty trick" in the book to stand in the way of our freedom and independence, that we should be gainfully employed until such time we can employ and provide for ourselves. We believe further in: POWER IN THE HANDS OF THE PEOPLE! WEALTH IN THE HANDS OF THE PEOPLE! ARMS IN THE HANDS OF THE PEOPLE!

3. We want tax exemption and an end to robbery of THE BLACK NATION by the CAPITALIST. We want an end to the capitalistic domination of Africa in all of its forms: imperialism, criminal settler colonialism, neo-colonialism, racism, sexism, zionism, Apartheid and artificial borders.

   We believe that this wicked racist government has robbed us, and now we are demanding the overdue debt of reparations … as restitution for the continued genocide of our people and to in meaningful measure and repair the damage for the AFRICAN HOLOCAUST (Maangamizo/Maafa).

   We believe our people should be exempt from ALL TAXATION as long as we are deprived of equal justice under the laws of the land and the overdue reparations debt remains unpaid. We will accept payment in fertile and mine rally rich land, precious metals, industry, commerce, and currency. As genocide crimes continue, people's tribunals must be set up to prosecute and to execute.

The "Jews" were given reparations. The Japanese were given reparations. The Black, the Red and the Brown Nations must be given reparations. The American white man owes us reparations. England owes us reparations. France owes us reparations, Spain and all of Europe. Africa owes us reparations and repatriation. The Arabs owe us reparations. The "Jews" owe us reparations. All have taken part in the AFRICAN HOLOCAUST and the slaughter of 600 million of our people over the past 6,000 years in general and 400 years in particular. We know that this is a reasonable and just demand that we make at this time in history.

4. We want decent housing, fit for shelter of human beings, free health-care (preventive and maintenance). We want an end to the trafficking of drugs and to the biological and chemical warfare targeted at our people.

    We believe since the white landlords will not give decent housing and quality health care to our Black Community, the housing, the land, the social, political and economic institutions should be made into independent UUAMAA "New African Communal/Cooperatives" so that our community, with government reparations and aid (until we can do for ourselves) can build and make drug-free, decent housing with health facilities for our people.

5. We want education for our people that exposes the true nature of this devilish and decadent American society. We want education that teaches us our true history … and our role in the present day society. We believe in an educational system that will give our people "a knowledge of self." If we do not have knowledge of self and of our position in society and the world, then we have little chance to properly relate to anything else.

6. We want all Black Men and Black Women to be exempt from military service. We believe that Black People should not be forced to fight in the military service to defend a racist government that holds us captive and does not protect us. We will not fight and kill other people of color in the world who, like Black People, are being victimized by the white racist government of America. We will protect ourselves from the force and violence of the racist police and the racist military, "by any means necessary."

7. We want an immediate end to POLICE HARRASSMENT, BRUTALITY, and MURDER of Black People. We want an end to Black-on-Black violence, "snitching," cooperation, and collaboration with the oppressor. We believe we can end police brutality in our community by organizing Black self-defense groups (Black People's Militias/Black Liberation Armies) that are dedicated to defending our Black Community from racist, fascist, police/military oppression, and brutality. The Second Amendment of white America's Constitution gives a right to bear arms. We therefore believe that all Black

People should unite and form an "African United Front" and arm ourselves for self-defense.

8. We want freedom for all Black Men and Black Women held in international, military, federal, state, county, city jails and prisons.

    We believe that all Black People and people of color should be released from the many jails and prisons because they have not received a fair and impartial trial. "Released" means "released" to the lawful authorities of the Black Nation.

9. We want all Black People when brought to trial to be tried in a court by a jury of their peer group or people from their Black Communities, as defined by white law of the Constitution of the United States. We believe that the courts should follow their own law, if their nature will allow (as stated in their Constitution of the United States) so that Black People will receive fair trials. The 6th Amendment of the United States Constitution gives a man/woman a right to an impartial trial, which has been interpreted to be a "fair" trial by one's "peer" group. A "peer" is a person from a similar economic, social, religious, geographical, environmental, historical, and racial background. To do this, the court will be forced to select a jury from the Black Community from which the Black defendant came. We have been and are being tried by all white juries that have no understanding of the "average reasoning person" of the Black Community.

10. WE DEMAND AN END TO THE RACIST DEATH PENALTY AS IT IS APPLIED TO BLACK AND OPPRESSED PEOPLE IN AMERICA. WE DEMAND FREEDOM FOR ALL POLITICAL PRISONERS OF THE BLACK RED AND BROWN NATION!

    We want land, bread, housing, education, clothing, justice and peace. And, as our political objective, we want NATIONAL LIBERATION in a separate state or territory of our own, here or elsewhere, "a liberated zone" ("New Africa" or Africa), and a plebiscite to be held throughout the BLACK NATION in which only we will be allowed to participate for the purposes of determining our will and DIVINE destiny as a people. FREE THE LAND! "UP YOU MIGHTY NATION! YOU CAN ACCOMPLISH WHAT YOU WILL!" BLACK POWER!

    History has proven that the white man is absolutely disagreeable to get along with in peace. No one has been able to get along with the white man. All the people of color have been subjected to the white man's wrath. We believe that his very nature will not allow for true sharing, fairness, equity and justice.

    Therefore, to the Red Man and Woman, to the Yellow and to the Brown, we say to you: "The same rabid dog that bit us bit you too." All power to the people! "THE SAME RABID DOG THAT BIT U, BIT US TO!" ALL POWER TO THE PEOPLE!

New Black Panther Party

If the ideology of the New Black Panthers was based on a fringe and limited segment of the population, it would not be as disconcerting as I perceive it to be. To illustrate this point, as will be presented in Chapter 9, many of these racial-based premises were echoed in Reverend Wright's Trinity United Church of Christ. Indeed, when one compares the "ten-point platform" of the New Black Panther Party with the 12-point "black value system" of Trinity United Church of Christ, one is struck by the overwhelmingly racial orientation of both groups. While the New Black Panther Party has a much more hostile and confrontational edge, it is obvious that Trinity United Church of Christ's value system is also demonstrably based on race. I am confident that some would assert that racial pride is a necessary and positive force within the black community. On one level, I would agree. Racial pride, particularly when connected to positive values, is beneficial to the community—and to the country as a whole.

The larger question, in my mind, is that ideology of racial nationalism, as clearly illustrated by the New Black Panthers, is not connected to positive values. In my mind, this represents a real and present danger. This decisive "group think" and inflammatory rhetoric will inevitably result in violence. As an example of the potential for violence, the desire to bring the Crips and the Bloods together was trumpeted in the New Black Panthers' Web site. Is this an attempt to end "black on black" violence? I hope it is. When one reads their "ten point platform," one can come to a different conclusion.

The potential connection between black nationalist groups, such as the New Black Panther Party, and black nationalist churches is not limited to "Christian" churches. According to Aidi, the first African American scholar to advocate an alliance between global Islam and Pan-Africanism was Edward Blyden. He was convinced that Islam was suited for people of African descent due to racial prejudice, the doctrine of brotherhood, and the value placed on learning Islam.[48] Blyden's contemporary counterpart in the Arab world was Dusé Muhammad Ali, who created the Universal Islamic Society in Detroit in 1926. This group was the precursor and inspiration for the Moorish Science Temple and the Temple of Islam—both of which predated the Nation of Islam.[49] In Nation of Islam doctrine, Arabs are seen as a "sign" of future people, a people chosen by God to receive the Koran (Quran). However, since Arabs strayed, God selected American blacks as his people to spread Islam to the West.[50]

Another group, known as the "Five Percenters" (or 5% Nation), has adopted a particularly hostile ideology. It was founded by Clarence Smith (also known as Father Allah), who was a former Nation of Islam (NOI) member. Smith formed this group in New York City in 1964 after he was expelled from the NOI for disagreeing with the group's teachings. While the Five Percenters do not consider their beliefs a religion, they do follow nontraditional variants of Islam.

They believe that blacks are the original people of Earth. As such, blacks founded all civilization. Because blacks founded all people, the "Blackman" is god. They also believe that whites have deceived the whole world. Whites have used their influence to cause the world to honor and worship false gods and idols. In this regard, the symbolism of the Five Percenters is instructive. The five-pointed star symbolizes knowledge and children. The crescent moon symbolizes wisdom and black women, with the number seven symbolizing Allah because it is allegedly the mathematical terminology for the creator of the universe (and the seventh letter of the alphabet, G, stands for God). The white background symbolizes the deceptions and lies practiced by white people. The sun symbolizes truth and light, and the points around the sun are the symbol of the universe.[51]

Some Five Percenters profess their beliefs through rap and hip-hop music. There are some very successful hip-hop performers, such as Busta Rhymes, Wutang Clan, and Mobb Deep, who further this message. Though these performers may not be affiliated with the jihadi movement, some striking similarities are present. These include the language of Islam and of the hip-hop culture, which often express anger at structures of domination, government indifference, and U.S. foreign policy. This connection—and the implications of such—were powerfully asserted by Aidi, who stated,

> the cultural forces of Islam, black nationalism and hip-hop have converged to create a brazenly political and oppositional counter-culture that has powerful allure.[52]

The potential for direct action by an interrelationship with gangs and radical-ized black Muslim groups can be seen in some examples. The group that became known as the Liberty City Seven allegedly intended to destroy Chicago's Sears Tower and bomb FBI buildings to ignite a guerrilla war. This war was suppos-edly designed to overthrow the U.S. government and pave the way for an Islamic regime. FBI investigative tapes purportedly show that they planned to use street gangs as soldiers who would stage attacks. These attacks ranged from large-scale bombings of major buildings to poisoning saltshakers in restaurants, said Assistant U.S. Attorney Richard Gregorie. Batiste, a 33-year-old construction worker who was leading the Miami chapter of a sect called the Moorish Science Temple, was allegedly the ringleader of this group.[53]

Many will also recall the Beltway snipers during three weeks in October 2002. John Allen Muhammad and Lee Boyd Malvo killed 16 people and critically injured three others. In their trial, evidence presented showed an affinity to the cause of Islamic Jihad.[54] To the general public, it should not be surprising to learn that the "motivation" for the crimes was unclear. In the three months following the capture of the Beltway snipers, the *New York Times* ran 128 articles about the shootings—and only nine even mentioned the word "Muslim." Despite the failure of the media to connect the dots, the fact is Muhammad was a member of the Nation of Islam. He "coincidentally" registered the getaway vehicle on the first anniversary of 9/11, writing the time of the registration at 8:52 am (the precise moment the first plane hit the World Trade Center).[55]

There are a number of other examples to illustrate the connection of black Muslims to jihadi activities. These include Portland, Oregon; Virginia Jihad Network; Elshafay and Siraj in the Republican Convention; Kevin James and JIS; and the Kennedy Airport case, to name some notable cases.

Aryan Brotherhood

The Aryan Brotherhood is the other side of the racist coin. The Aryan Brotherhood (AB) originated in 1967 at San Quentin prison. Originally, this gang was estab-lished to provide protection for white inmates from black and Hispanic groups. Although the Brotherhood is a white supremacist organization, for most AB mem-bers crime is their priority and racial hatred is a secondary goal. Since 1972, the Aryan Brotherhood has had an alliance with the Mexican Mafia. The AB also uses religion to further their "cause." They often use the Odinist religion to con-duct gang meetings and disguise illicit business practices.[56] This "religion" views Christianity as defective since it allows blacks, Hispanics, and other nonwhites in the congregation. This religion is derived from the pagan god of Odin (Odinism). A key symbol of this religion is three intersecting triangles (known as volknut or valknut). In white supremacist groups, wearing these triangles signifies the person is willing to give his life to Odin in battle. It symbolizes that the person is a chosen warrior, who is willing to give his life at any time he desires.[57]

This group is affiliated with numerous like-minded groups, such as neo-Nazis, the National Alliance, and various racist organizations. There are some specific requirements to be affiliated with the group. These include lifelong allegiance, a "blood in, blood out" oath must be taken, and often a "hit" or significant act of violence is required before full membership is earned. Prior to being considered, candidates for membership must serve a year or more in some probationary status. As would be expected, membership in the AB has traditionally come from white male inmates.[58]

The group uses certain symbols and methods, such as shamrock cloverleaf, the initials "AB," swastikas, double lighting bolts, and the numbers "666." The number "666" has biblical significance as being symbolic for the "Antichrist" in prophecy. The group is also known to use Gaelic (old Irish) symbols as a method of coding communications. The overall creed of the Aryan Brotherhood illustrates the racial attachment of the group. Their creed is:

> I will stand by my brother
> My brother will come before all others
> My life is forfeit should I fail my brother
> I will honor my brother in peace as in war

While the precise number of Aryan Brotherhood members and associates is not known, the gang has chapters in virtually every major state and federal prison in the country. Estimates of AB's total strength vary widely, but nearly all exceed 15,000 members and associates nationwide. Roughly half are in prison and half are on the outside.[59] They have traditionally nurtured a deep hatred toward black individuals and members of black groups/gangs, such as the Black Guerrilla Family (BGF), Crips, Bloods, and the El Rukns.[60]

Unlike the New Black Panther Party, the Aryan Brotherhood does not maintain a Web site that announces its beliefs and ideologies. However, like radical black groups, radical white extremists also have certain "religious" components to their ideology. Aryan Brotherhood members throughout the country have typically joined Aryan Nations under its alter-ego name, Church of Jesus Christ Christian. This "church" is a purveyor of the "Christian Identity" religion preached by late Aryan Nations founder and head pastor Richard Butler. His "prison ministry" promoted the doctrine that nonwhites are "mud people" and Jews are the literal descendants of Satan.[61] This racial nationalist thinking was based on the larger movement known as Christian Identity.

Christian Identity evolved from an eclectic set of beliefs known as British-Israelism (or Anglo-Israelism) that began in the eighteenth century in England. This theory held that the people of the British Isles were direct descendants of the "chosen people" of the Bible. These people were carried off from the Promised Land by the Assyrians around 730 BC. This ideology reasoned that the people of England (and later the white Christian people of Europe) were, in fact, the chosen people for whom the Bible was written. This philosophy spread to the United States, where it evolved and changed during the early twentieth century.

Christian Identity differed from British-Israelism in that it taught that God had created the white man in His image and gave him a soul. He also created man-like creatures of various colors that were not really human. Instead these "creatures" were actually animals. They did not possess a soul. These people are known to Christian Identity followers as "mud people." This "religion" also teaches that the devil came to Eve in the Garden of Eden and impregnated her. The result of this pregnancy was the birth of Cain. This child eventually committed the first murder when he killed his "half brother," Abel, who was fathered by Adam. Christian Identity teaches that the bloodline of Cain continues to exist today in the form of people who now call themselves "Jews." Christian Identity churches exist in many parts of the country and are usually small. Nationally, probably fewer than 50,000 people adhere to Christian Identity beliefs. However, this is still a large and dangerous movement.[62]

This mindset has ironic similarities with radical Islamists. For example, some Islamists await the 12th imam, which can be analogized as an "Islamic Messiah." Hence, both these worldviews have a strong adherence to the prophetic event of Armageddon. For these people, Armageddon will take place when the second coming of Christ ushers in a cosmic war between the white race and the "forces of evil." This apocalyptic belief corresponds with those radical Islamists who desire to provoke worldview chaos designed to usher in the Islamic messiah. Is it possible that both will attempt to facilitate this cosmic battle? According to Yungher, the true believers of Christian Identity remain a potent terrorist threat as they bide their time awaiting some "political, economic or security calamity to impact the American political landscape to unleash their holy war."[63] Inherent in this statement is the desire for chaos. Think again about current circumstances. If economic circumstances get worse, and if direct action results, is the possibility for chaos out of the question?

An additional comment is related to the potential for racial, religious, and political conflict (for more on this please see Chapter 9). I realize this presentation may have been hard to read for some people. I do not mean to create distress. However, I believe it is critical that we see things as they are. In this sense, we all contribute to this dynamic. Some are part of the solution. Some are part of the problem. I suspect we all are partly the former, partly the latter. In any case, please look at Figure 3.1. Where do you place yourself in this continuum? I assert if you are not as close as possible to the middle, then you may be more part of the problem than the solution.

Application of the Triggers

Given the ideologies outlined in this chapter, it may be helpful to assess how these ideologies may result in violence. In Chapter 9, I provide a number of specific issues

Where do You Come in?

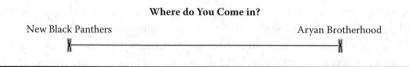

Figure 3.1 Solution or problem?

I call "triggers" that can inspire people to violence. Regardless of your personal beliefs, it is fair to say that many people have strong views on abortion, energy and the environment, police shootings, and the sovereignty of American society. Further, deteriorating economic circumstances are a factor that cannot be ignored. The prolonged impact of a poor—or failing—economy is hard to discount as a potentially significant "trigger." Finally, the volatile mix of race, religion, and politics—which was briefly introduced in this chapter—may provide substantial incentive and "inspiration" toward extremist violence. In my mind, each of these are taken as a "given." In order to conceptualize this process, please see Figure 3.2.

I ask the reader to think about each trigger in relation to this figure. On your left is the term "radicals." This term is meant to apply to those individuals who seek to change the status quo. It is not meant to imply a negative connotation. Instead, it means an individual with great passion for a particular issue—who seeks to forward that issue. Next to this is the somewhat larger group called "sympathizers." These people care about the issue but they are not willing to forward it with the passion of a radical. These people may be too old, frail, or simply not confrontational by nature. They also may hold positions where they do not desire controversy—or they need to avoid controversy. In any case, this larger group of sympathizers desire for the issue to be forwarded but they want someone else to do the "heavy lifting." In order to help, however, they may be willing to donate money, encouragement, votes, and any number of other "contributions."

On the other side of the figure is the term "loyalists." This term applies to those individuals who seek to maintain the status quo. This term does not imply a positive connotation. As with the term "radical," there is no intention to imply some normative meaning. Instead, I simply apply this term to those who desire to hold

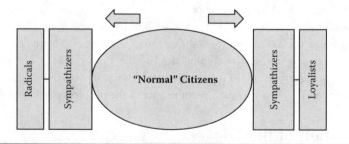

Figure 3.2 Social dynamic in "normal" circumstance (Copyright, James F. Pastor, 2009).

on to or maintain the status quo. In any event, the group next to the "loyalists" is their sympathizers. These people are the same as the sympathizers of the "radicals." They care about the issue at some level, but for one reason or another they are not willing to do the "heavy lifting."

The middle is the large segment of society that really does not care about the issue. People in this group either do not know enough to care, are too busy to care, are uninspired by nature—or by this issue—or because they simply do not want to get involved in a public policy debate. These people are the key to the stability of society. In my mind, this is how most Americans currently see the world. Most are disengaged or disconnected to the larger issues facing society. This could change—possibly dramatically.

I contend the key to this potential change in the middle relates to the impact of the particular issue. As long as life for those in the middle is "normal," chances are they will stay disengaged. However, if circumstances begin to deteriorate, for example, if the economy remains sluggish for a long period of time—or if it gets worse—people will start to pay more attention to what is happening. When they do this, they will also make some judgments as to who is to blame and what are the causes of their situation.

Now think about how this plays itself out. One "side" blames the other. One party, race, or group blames the other. Similarly, the "other side" blames the opposite side. As these sides blame each other, their respective positions harden. This is particularly true if either side personally attacks the other. Indeed, such attacks are inevitable. It is extraordinarily difficult for people—particularly if they are frustrated and passionate—to stay focused on the substantive aspects of the debate. Inevitably, the debate will turn increasingly hostile. If violence ensues, it serves to harden the sides even more. Particularly if injuries or deaths occur, the lost of loved ones "die hard." Their loss serves to spur others to fight harder. It also serves to inspire deeper levels of commitment from the participants. As these commitment levels deepen, the respective sizes of the groups change. The extremes grow, the sympathizers grow—and the middle decreases. Figure 3.3 illustrates this change.

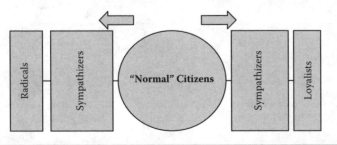

Figure 3.3 Social dynamic in "heightened" circumstance (Copyright, James F. Pastor, 2009).

Now take this a step further. Consider the impact of sustained violence. If violence is used as a strategy, then the dynamic changes considerably. In this scenario, the radicals and loyalists grow larger and bolder. However, it is likely that these extreme groups never get too large, as the limitations of killing and dying are inherently limiting to only certain characteristic individuals. Generally speaking, this is limited to particular personalities, age groups, genders, and those most directly impacted by the violence. Conversely, the sympathizers on both sides grow proportionately larger. In this process, the group most affected by this dynamic is the middle—the normal citizens (Figure 3.4). This group, which is the most critical to a stable society, is also the group that is most difficult to maintain. If violence gets too troublesome, the tension between the competing sides becomes too intense to maintain a "middle ground." In essence, this tension forces people to "pick sides." The dynamic is this: if you are not with us, then you are against us. This creates a circumstance where even people who do not want to be involved are forced to be involved because the status quo becomes increasingly tenuous to maintain. This thinking is even illustrated in counterinsurgency. Consider this dynamic: Speaking about tribal groups in Afghanistan, Johnson and Mason provided insight into the nature of fear and violence in the human dynamic. They stated that village "elders won't commit to opposing the Taliban if they and their families are vulnerable to Taliban torture and murder, and they can hardly be blamed for that."[64]

Consequently, the impact of this dynamic separates society based on issue—or more likely, group identity. Whether that group is racial, religious, or political, it is a powerful, cohesive factor. This is especially true if people are effectively forced to identify with the group, or risk being accused of being a traitor, sympathizer, or worse. Hopefully the reader can extrapolate some of the ongoing events in society and consider how these can become so emotional as to turn violent. If violent events occur, the tendency will be for the other side to respond in kind. This violent response, in turn, may inspire additional violence. Each time this occurs, it gets more difficult to stop. Each time this occurs, it gets more difficult to maintain "neutrality." Each time this occurs, the stability in society becomes more tenuous. Each

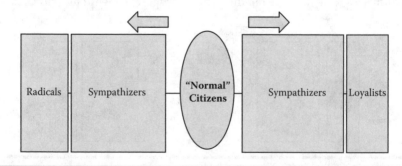

Figure 3.4 Social dynamic in "volatile" circumstance (Copyright, James F. Pastor, 2009).

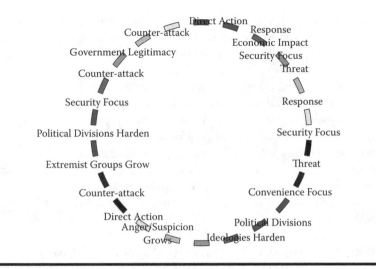

Figure 3.5 Climate of collapse (Copyright, James F. Pastor, 2009).

time this occurs, the police are placed in the middle—and often are targeted by the violence. Each time this occurs, the government is placed in a more and more difficult position. The government seeks to balance the need to stop the violence while at the same time avoid draconian police tactics.

The end result of this dynamic is a spiraling cycle of violence and its resultant implications on society. As you review the cycle in Figure 3.5, please consider each aspect of this "process." Start at the top with the words "direct action." Think of this as 9/11. With this as your starting point, go clockwise around the cycle. Following this event, the government's response was strong. National Guard troops secured airports. Police were on high alert. People were afraid. The attack also had substantial economic impact. On the heels of the attack, people slowed their buying habits. People were uncertain about their future. During this time, President Bush urged people to "go shopping." Notwithstanding this admonition, the population was focused on security. Thereafter, the anthrax attacks occurred. This kept the threat level high. People were afraid to open their mail. People called the police with any shred of "evidence" of anthrax. This kept the security focus of the population. Over time, the DC sniper incidents reemphasized the security focus, which, one year after 9/11, was beginning to wane.

Over the period of time since 9/11, the emphasis of the population has shifted from a security focus to a convenience focus. People who happily waited in long airport lines, over time became less tolerant for such inconveniences. People began to feel less fearful. As their fear levels reduced, their desire for convenience—and rights—increased. This dynamic was further exacerbated by political divisions. Conservatives tended to see an ongoing need for security—as they tend to see the threat of terrorism as real and substantial. Liberals increasingly tended to see the threat of terrorism with suspicion. Many conspiracy theorists of the 9/11 attacks percolated. Others who would not buy into these conspiracies, nonetheless, were suspicious of the approach taken by the Bush Administration. Some saw the policies of the Bush Administration grounded in an underlying desire to impose draconian tactics on innocent people. This belief resonated widely.

Now add the Iraq War into this dynamic. The controversial decision to invade Iraq caused much political division. As a consequence, political positions harden. Widespread antiwar protests gained great media attention. Bombings in Iraq coupled with the number of U.S. deaths were reported on a daily basis. The daily "death toll" along with the videos of burning vehicles, damaged buildings, and dead bodies filled the news reports. Over time, the Iraq War became widely unpopular. This created more and more anger as the Bush Administration refused to relent on its policy. Anger fueled anger. The political positions became increasingly hardened. Suspicion of the parties grew more pervasive.

The election of Barack Obama has changed some of this dynamic. The population is much more hopeful. His election victory was not as close as the last two elections. President Obama has—at least temporarily—changed the dynamic. The question, as raised in Chapter 1, is how long will this last? In terms of the aforementioned cycle, I think we are at the anger/suspicion stage (at above seven o'clock, near the bottom of the cycle). While we now seem to be less angry and less suspicious, I believe these emotions are still present. They have been tempered but they have not disappeared. We are now in the "calm before the storm." How long this calm will last is dependent on the introduction of some dramatic event. A number of events can trigger substantial emotion. This is because people are on edge. In any event, the storm will commence when the next direct action occurs. When (not if) this occurs, watch to see what happens. If the country comes together, waving flags and caring for the victims, then we as a country have an opportunity to weather the storm.

If, on the other hand, groups in society blame the president, blame the policies of his administration, and/or blame the other side for the attack, then we are in trouble. In this case, a counterattack by an opposing group is likely. If this occurs, extremist groups will harden and increase. This will result in even more hardened political divisions. Throughout this violence, the population will revert to a security focus. This is particularly true if multiple attacks and counterattacks occur. This violence, in turn, will create the balkanization of groups (as described above). This balkanization will also be reflective of the inability of government to stop the spiraling violence. People will be afraid—and they will be angry. They will be angry at those who created the violence, who will be blamed on the other side. They will also be angry at the government for failing to stop the violence. The process, known as the "climate of collapse," can create its own momentum where the ongoing cycle becomes increasingly difficult to stop. The consequences of this cycle may be accelerated based on the magnitude of the attacks. For example, attacks with weapons of mass destruction (WMD) would foster widespread disruption and the resultant breakdown in society. The potential impact of this process is substantial. I trust the reader sees this discussion as a dispassionate analysis of an extraordinarily complex situation. This analysis is based on sound logic and reasoning. Unfortunately, if this process begins, there will be little logic utilized. People will think with their emotions. This is why we must understand and address this potential during the periods of calm. If we fail to address these potentialities during calm times, we will not be able to deal with them during turbulent times. The last chapter, therefore, attempts to address the key issues related to this potential. Hopefully, this will help prepare us for such an extremist climate. This is my underlying purpose for drafting this book.

At this point, we will transition to part two of the book. This section will delve into the elements of *Public Safety Policing*. Initially, we will examine military weaponry and tactical orientations of the police. The subsequent chapter will examine intelligence methods and surveillance technologies. Thereafter, we will examine order maintenance provisions. Finally, I will attempt to illustrate how these elements synergize into the larger policing model.

Endnotes

1. http://www.fbi.gov/congress/congress02/jarboe021202.htm (retrieved on May 2, 2008).
2. Anderson, Kerby. "Arguments Against Abortion." http://www.leaderu.com/orgs/probe/docs/arg-abor.html (retrieved on May 2, 2008).
3. Ibid. http://www.leaderu.com/orgs/probe/docs/arg-abor.html.
4. Ibid. http://www.leaderu.com/orgs/probe/docs/arg-abor.html.
5. Ibid. http://www.leaderu.com/orgs/probe/docs/arg-abor.html.
6. http://www.armyofgod.com/Paulhillindex.html (retrieved on May 2, 2008).
7. http://www.armyofgod.com/EricRudolphHomepage.html (retrieved on May 2, 2008).
8. State and Local Anti-terrorist Training (SLATT) Manual, Domestic Terrorist Groups, 13. :\content\section3domestic\pdfs\narrative.pdf.
9. Yungher, Nathan I. (2008). *Terrorism: The Bottom Line.* Upper Saddle River, NJ: Pearson/Prentice Hall, 129.
10. Best, Steven and Anthony J. Nocella. "Defining Terrorism" http://www.criticalanimalstudies.org/JCAS/Journal_Articles_download/Issue_2/DefiningTerrorism.doc (retrieved on May 2, 2008).
11. SLATT Manual, Domestic Terrorist Groups, op. cit., 14.
12. http://www.fbi.gov/congress/congress02/jarboe021202.htm (retrieved on May 2, 2008).
13. http://www.earthliberationfront.com/main.shtml (retrieved on May 2, 2008).
14. Ibid. http://www.earthliberationfront.com/main.shtml.
15. http://www.salvationinc.org/archives/2004_08.html (retrieved on May 2, 2008).
16. SLATT Manual, Domestic Terrorist Groups, op. cit., 2.
17. Mahan, Sue and Pamela L. Griset (2008). *Terrorism in Perspective,* 2nd ed. Thousand Oaks, CA: Sage Publications, 7–8.
18. SLATT Manual, Domestic Terrorist Groups, op. cit., 3.
19. SLATT Manual, Domestic Terrorist Groups, op. cit., 4.
20. Yungher, Nathan I. (2008), op. cit., 92.

21. www.cdi.org/terrorism/terrorist-groups.cfm (retrieved on May 2, 2008).
22. *Intersec* (2008), 18, no. 4 (April):41.
23. http://www.csmonitor.com/2008/0328/p07s03-woam.html (retrieved on May 16, 2008).
24. Brodzinsky, Sibylla (2008). "Is Colombia's Revolutionary Armed Forces of Colombia on the Ropes?" *Christian Science Monitor* May 21:6.
25. http://www.knowgangs.com/gang_resources/profiles/ms13/ (retrieved on June 12, 2007).
26. Quirk, Matthew (2008). "How to Grow a Gang," *The Atlantic* May:24.
27. Robb, John (2007). "The Coming Urban Terror: Systems Disruption, Networked Gangs, and Bioweapons," *City Journal* (Summer). http://www.city-journal.org/html/17_3_urban_terrorism.html (retrieved on May 16, 2008).
28. Robb, John (2007), op. cit., 3.
29. http://www.knowgangs.com/gang_resources/profiles/ms13/ (retrieved on June 12, 2007).
30. Mahan, Sue and Pamela L. Griset (2008), op. cit., 6.
31. SLATT Manual, Domestic Terrorist Groups, op. cit., 4–5.
32. Stern, Jessica (2008). The Ultimate Organization: Networks, Franchises and Freelancers. *Terrorism in Perspective,* 2nd ed. Eds. Sue Mahan and Pamela L. Griset. Thousand Oaks, CA: Sage Publications, 173.
33. Stern, Jessica (2008), op. cit., 172.
34. Stern, Jessica (2008), op. cit., 175.
35. SLATT Manual, Domestic Terrorist Groups, op. cit., 5.
36. Yungher, Nathan I. (2008), op. cit., 126.
37. SLATT Manual, Domestic Terrorist Groups, op. cit., 6; and Yungher, Nathan I. (2008), op. cit., 126.
38. SLATT Manual, Domestic Terrorist Groups, op. cit., 6.
39. SLATT Manual, Domestic Terrorist Groups, op. cit., 7–8.
40. SLATT Manual, Domestic Terrorist Groups, op. cit., 10–11.
41. www.kkk.com/intro.htm (retrieved on August 17, 2007).
42. SLATT Manual, Domestic Terrorist Groups, op. cit., 11.
43. www.adl.org (retrieved on August 17, 2007).
44. www.adl.org (retrieved on August 17, 2007).
45. SLATT Manual, Domestic Terrorist Groups, op. cit., 12.
46. www.adl.org (retrieved on July 27, 2007).
47. http://www.newblackpanther.com (retrieved on May 5, 2008).
48. Aidi, Hisham (2005). "Jihadi's in the Hood: Race, Urban Islam and the War on Terror," in *Violence and Terrorism*. Ed. Thomas J. Badey. McGraw-Hill/Dushkin, 129.
49. Aidi, Hisham (2005), op. cit., 129.
50. Aidi, Hisham (2005), op. cit., 129.
51. www.adl.org (retrieved on August 17, 2007).
52. Aidi, Hisham (2005), op. cit., 134.
53. http://www.startribune.com/484/story/1459843.html (retrieved on October 9, 2007).
54. "Terror Incidents in the U.S. Since the 9/11 Attacks" (2008). *The Counter Terrorist* 1, no. 1 (May/June):53.
55. Coulter, Ann (2003). *Treason: Liberal Treachery from the Cold War to the War on Terrorism.* New York: Crown Forum, 281.
56. http://www.knowgangs.com/gang_resources/profiles/ms13/ (retrieved on June 12, 2007).
57. Wood, Laurie (2007). *Intelligence Report* Fall:56–57.
58. http://www.dc.state.fl.us/pub/gangs/prison.html (retrieved on May 5, 2008).
59. http://www.splcenter.org/intel/intelreport/article.jsp?aid=569 (retrieved on May 5, 2008).

60. www.adl.org (retrieved on August 17, 2007).
61. http://www.splcenter.org/intel/intelreport/article.jsp?aid=569 (retrieved on May 5, 2008).
62. SLATT Manual, Domestic Terrorist Groups, op. cit., 8.
63. Yungher, Nathan I. (2008), op. cit., 125.
64. Johnson, Thomas H. and M. Chris Mason (2008). "All Counterinsurgency Is Local," *The Atlantic* October:38.

ELEMENTS OF PUBLIC SAFETY POLICING

Chapter 4

Military Weaponry and Tactical Operations

This chapter explores the trend toward the increasing use of military-style weapons and tactical methods by civilian police departments. The shorthand way to describe this phenomenon is the "militarization" of the police. This phenomenon is defended by some, attacked by others, and ignored by most. I will attempt to take a "middle ground" on this issue. I do not see it with alarm. I see it as a pragmatic "solution" to some vexing issues facing the police. However, I do acknowledge the criticism. Is the prospect of heavily armed police officers on American streets problematic? My answer is, yes—but it is or will be necessary! In this light, I will address the data, the logic, and the implications of this trend.

In order to quickly see where I believe policing is evolving, a few basic premises may shed light on my thinking. The first premise is that police will be targets of terroristic and extremist violence. One needs to look no further than Iraq to see this dynamic. Regardless of your view of Iraq, it is clear the "insurgent" violence is often aimed at police, civil defense, and military targets. For example, while the exact number of deaths is hard to validate, the number of deaths of Iraqi police and military personnel since April 28, 2005, is 6,573.[1] The number of dead prior to this date is almost impossible to estimate. The same problem is occurring in Afghanistan. The Taliban regularly attack Afghan police. In 2007 alone, more than 900 police were killed in such attacks. These rising death tolls, coupled with the fact that Afghan police often face superior firepower of attacking Taliban fighters, make it hard to fault them for their tendency to retreat.[2]

The reason for targeting of police and military is grounded in the "logic" of terrorism. The message and the logic are: If we can kill police and military, we can kill civilians. This conveys a profound meaning. If the police and military cannot protect themselves from attack, how can average citizens do so? Indeed, without the weapons and the training, citizens have little hope to protect themselves! This message also speaks to these public safety personnel. It says that they must do more to protect themselves. This may entail better training, tactics, weapons, and any other "self-defense" methods.

This leads to the second premise: Police and other public safety providers, like any other people, are going to protect themselves when threatened with attack. While we will flesh this out in more detail below, suffice it to assert that people will innovate when targeted. They will not simply wait to die. They will find ways, sooner than later, to protect themselves from attacks. Indeed, since part of the "job description" of public safety providers is to provide "security services," it stands to reason that they will seek to secure themselves. One obvious way to provide "force protection" is to counter the attack with similar—or superior—weapons and tactics.

It is particularly interesting that new acronyms are helping to change the "job description" of police officers. Consider the acronym PAIN (pre-attack indicators). This relates to specific indicators that typically occur prior to a terrorist attack. In addition, RAIN is another disconcerting acronym. This relates to the potential for weapons of mass destruction (WMD) attacks. The acronym stands for:[3]

- *R*ecognize the hazard/threat
- *A*void the hazard/contamination or injury
- *I*solate the hazard area
- *N*otify the appropriate support personnel

Finally, the impact of being targeted, and in countering the attacks, has potentially profound psychological implications on public safety personnel. Since much, if not most, of the terroristic violence is unpredictable (in terms of time, place, and method), the impact of this violence is difficult to cope with. Of course, at its core is the underlying goal of terrorism: kill one, frighten thousands. This fear is directed not only at the "civilian" audience, it is also aimed at the audience of public safety providers who see their comrades wounded and killed. Indeed, these public safety providers are supposed to be ready for this violence—since it is part of their job. Nonetheless, they are not immune from the ill effects of seemingly random—and deadly—violence. Our military personnel returning from Iraq have experienced many adverse psychological and physical effects from such violence. The uncertainty and unpredictability of this violence is extraordinarily difficult to cope with.[4] While this book is not designed as a psychological analysis of the effects of violence, one cannot seriously think of terrorism without accounting for such. In this sense, this chapter can be viewed as a prediction on how terroristic and extremist violence will "trigger" a reciprocal response from American police. Further, one can presume that the psychological impact of such violence experienced by American military personnel will also impact American police and public safety personnel.

Current Data and Circumstances

As is inferred above, a good starting point may be to simply ask the question, Why militarization of police? Militarization is a broad term that refers to using military-style weapons, tactics, training, uniforms, and even heavily armed vehicles and equipment by civilian police departments.[5] There are two aspects to the militarization phenomenon. First, some view the American tradition of civil-military separation as breaking down. This is, at least partly, the result of Congress assigning more and more law enforcement responsibilities to the armed forces. Second, as will be made obvious, state and local police officers are increasingly emulating the war-fighting tactics of soldiers. Most Americans are unaware of the militarization phenomenon simply because it has been creeping along imperceptibly for many years.[6]

According to some media sources, jurisdictions across the United States have been arming rank-and-file officers with high-powered assault rifles for a decade or more. Police officials say that the trend has accelerated due to a number of factors including increases in shootouts, more lethal weaponry, increases in officer deaths, and increases in mass shootings.[7] These factors will accelerate. As these become more and more problematic, police will increase the trend toward militarization.

Anecdotal evidence appears to confirm this assertion. This trend is appearing in small towns, large urban cities, and in college or university environments. Some examples include the following departments. The Jasper, Florida, police department, with only seven officers, is now equipped with fully automatic M16s.[8] Similarly, the small town department of Chaska, Minnesota, arms its police officers with assault rifles, each with two 30-round magazines. Campus police at Arizona's three large public universities are now armed with assault rifles. In large cities like Miami and Los Angeles, arming its police officers with assault rifles is also deemed necessary. Miami authorized its patrol officers to carry AR-15s because of an increase in assault rifles used by criminals. The LAPD issues AR-15s to its officers due, in part, to the Bank of America shootout (as described below). Commenting on the need for such weapons, Miami Police Chief John Timoney stated, "This is a national problem. Police agencies all over the U.S. are going to bigger weapons." His agency has about 50 AR-15s and expects to get 150 more.[9] Further, Indianapolis Metro Police has issued at least 218 M16 assault weapons, and the Marion County Sheriff's Department issued at least 49 AR-15s to patrol officers.[10] In addition, Jody Weis, the superintendent of the Chicago Police Department, announced in April 2008 that all 13,500 police officers would soon be equipped with M-4 assault weapons.[11]

In describing this trend, it may be helpful to present some aggregate data of police tactics and weaponry in agencies around the country. In a study of paramilitary techniques by police, Kraska and Kappeler found that 90 percent of police departments with populations over 50,000 had paramilitary units. The smaller departments, with populations under 50,000, show a slightly smaller tendency to use paramilitary units. Still, fully 70 percent of those departments use paramilitary units.[12] Additional data from this study revealed that from 1995 to 1997 at least 1.2

million *pieces* of military hardware were given by the military to police agencies. This included[13]

- 75 grenade launchers
- 112 armored vehicles
- 600 M16s (LAPD alone)

It is instructive to note the timing of these weapons and equipment transfers to policing agencies from the military. In 1995, the terrorist attack in Oklahoma City occurred. In 1997, the North Hollywood shootout occurred. Is it a coincidence that this large transfer occurred during this time frame? While I cannot definitively answer this question, it is clear that police agencies are taking advantage of what is called "the 1033 Program." This program enables the military to give surplus weapons and equipment to policing agencies. This is done without charge. The only cost to the police agency is delivery or transportation charges to get the weapons and equipment to the department. This type of equipment, including military-grade semiautomatic weapons, armored personnel vehicles, tanks, helicopters, airplanes, and other equipment designed for use on the battlefield, is now being used on American streets.[14]

Cash-strapped law enforcement agencies are lining up to take advantage of the Pentagon's generosity. About 16,000 departments obtained more than 380,000 pieces of equipment in the 2005 budget year alone.[15] In California, more than $30 million in excess military hardware has been distributed—mostly free of charge—to more than 200 law enforcement agencies since November 1996. Nationally, a total of 43,253 items originally valued at $204.3 million went to more than 11,000 government law enforcement agencies in all 50 states over a one-year period. Incredibly, these include such things as bayonets, used as weapons of deadly hand-to-hand combat! Consequently, police agencies have taken part in a "massive flow of surplus military gear."[16]

Additional data from this program illustrate the growing utilization—or the perceived need—for the military hardware. Consider the data from Table 4.1.[17] This chart and the accompanying data illustrate a rather significant trend toward increased militarization of police. This trend is not just with weaponry. It also includes tactical operations. This can entail the formation and deployment of SWAT teams. It can also entail increased use of tactical operations. For example, the Chicago Police Department has approximately 80 different tactical units. This includes a combination of gang teams, gun teams, narcotics teams, directed response teams, mission teams, and other initiatives in its 25 police districts and its five police areas.[18]

The purpose and mission of these tactical units are to proactively find and arrest criminals. They are not there to take reports after the crime has occurred. They are to look for gangs, guns, and drugs—and arrest those who participate in such. In addition, for the first time in history, the Chicago Police Department has a full-time

Table 4.1 Value of Military Equipment to Power Agencies

Fiscal Year	Value of Military Hardware
2006	$146 Million
2005	$116 Million
2004	$120 Million
2003	$ 94 Million
2001	$ 98 Million

SWAT team that trains—and waits—for an incident to respond. The small number of officers in Chicago's heavy weapons team, however, pales by comparison to the 2,000+ officers assigned to the NYPD counterterror unit, and the 300 assigned to the LAPD counterterror unit. Beyond these tactical operations, it is now common for urban departments to have this and other similar tactical equipment:

■ Bomb disposal unit
■ Bomb robots
■ Bomb scanning devices
■ Radiation detection devices
■ K-9 units for explosive detection
■ Incident deployment trucks with SWAT gear, protective gear, and crowd control devices
■ Emergency service teams, equipped with gas masks and antidotes to chemical and biological agents
■ Tactical helicopters, drones, and even submarines

In a recent and classic example of this trend, consider the raid on the polygamous Yearning for Zion (YFZ) ranch community in Texas on April 3, 2008. When the police raided the YFZ ranch, they were armed with a search warrant, automatic weapons, helicopters, plus dozens of police vehicles—including an armored personnel carrier.[19] The raid was conducted without incident. In my mind, this operation portends the type of policing that will be much more common in the months and years to come.[20]

The level of SWAT operations is already significant. An early estimate asserted that 40,000 annual deployments of SWAT-type units occur in this country.[21] More recent estimates reveal an even higher level of SWAT deployments: from 3,000 deployments a year in the 1980s to 50,000 a year in 2006.[22] The vast majority of these SWAT raids are for routine warrant service.[23] Some criticize this as "mission creep."

The typical criticism is as follows. Inactive SWAT teams have a "strong incentive" to expand their original "emergency" mission into more routine policing activities. In this thinking, they do this to justify their existence.[24] This thinking contends that police will use the military-style equipment when it is not necessary. While I acknowledge the tendency to "use it because you have it," I contend the issue is more basic than this criticism. For example, I disagree with the characterization of raids or warrant service as "routine." Indeed, I contend these functions are "routine" only when the subjects within the facility surrender peacefully. Further, it can be argued that heavily armed and trained SWAT units are excellent "motivators" for those within the facility to surrender without incident. Consequently, once again, I see things differently from those in the "audience." They write about what *should be done.* From the perspective of the "audience," it is much easier to see raids and warrant service as *routine.* Those who have to "go through door," however, understand the dangers posed by this work. They want to go home after their shift. This is not to imply the use of excessive force or to advocate inappropriate police tactics. It is to say, however, that heavy weapons and tactics help level the playing field against individuals who often have no rules or morals.

There are two competing "schools of thought" on this matter. In some circles, represented by Ms. Weber, "armored personnel carriers and machine guns, should not be a part of everyday law enforcement in a free society."[25] On the other hand, a police official stated that "police officers working in patrol vehicles, dressed in urban tactical gear and armed with automatic weapons are here—and they're here to stay."[26] This "here to stay" assertion seems to have some credence. In my mind, it is likely that the number of SWAT "patrols" will rise in the future.

The survey conducted by Kraska and Kappeler asked this question: Is your department using the tactical operations unit as a proactive patrol unit to aid high-crime areas? One hundred and seven departments indicated they used tactical units in this manner. Fully 61 percent of all respondents thought it was a good idea. In fact, 63 percent of the departments in that survey agreed that SWAT units "play an important role in community policing strategies." The research of Kraska and Kappeler also revealed that SWAT units are often trained alongside, or with the support of, personnel from military special forces. They found that of 459 SWAT teams across the country, 46 percent acquired their initial training from "police officers with special operations experience in the military." Another 43 percent acquired their initial training with "active-duty military experts in special operations."[27] Almost 46 percent currently conducted training exercises with "active-duty military experts in special operations," and 23 respondents indicated that they trained with either Navy SEALs or Army Rangers.[28]

Because of their close collaboration with the military, some contend that SWAT units are taking on the warrior mentality of our military's special forces. In this view, the so-called war on drugs and other martial metaphors are turning high-crime areas into "war zones," citizens into potential enemies, and police officers into soldiers. The civilian law enforcement officer, on the other hand, confronts not an "enemy" but individuals who, like him or her, are both subject to the nation's laws and protected by the Bill of Rights. Although the police officer can use force in life-threatening situations, the Constitution and numerous Supreme Court rulings have circumscribed the police officer's direct use of force, as well as his or her power of search and seizure.

A typical criticism of SWAT teams is that they accept the military as a model for their behavior and outlook. This approach is said to be distinctly impersonal and elitist. From this perspective, American streets are viewed as the "front" and American citizens as the "enemy." Those who advocate SWAT teams will discount this assertion. It is likely that the truth is somewhere in between these two extremes. It is often the case, though, that SWAT team officers consider themselves members of an elite unit with specialized skills. They typically have more of a military ethos than the normal police culture. Hence, it can be argued that the sharing of training and technology by the military and law enforcement agencies has (or will) produced a shared mindset.

Critics argue this "warrior mindset" is not appropriate for the civilian police officer charged with enforcing the law.[29] In this thinking, the soldier confronts an enemy in a life-or-death situation. The soldier learns to use lethal force on the enemy, both uniformed and civilian, irrespective of age or gender. The soldier must sometimes follow orders unthinkingly, act in concert with his comrades, and initiate violence on command. That mentality, which new recruits are strenuously indoctrinated with in boot camp, can be a matter of survival to the soldier and the nation at war. As we will discuss throughout this book, the question of whether terrorism is war or crime relates directly to this notion. Again, in my mind, the answer is that it is a blend of both. Sometimes it can be viewed—and addressed—as war, other times it is more appropriately viewed as crime. In any case, the interplay between these two approaches is instructive.

The Fresno SWAT unit, for example, sends its 40-person team, with full military dress and gear, into the inner city "war zone" to deal with problems of drugs, gangs, and crime. Another example is found in a Midwestern community with a population of 75,000. This policing agency uses aggressive tactical patrols. These patrols include military-type uniformed officers patrolling within a military personnel carrier. The armored vehicle, according to the SWAT commander, stops "suspicious vehicles and people. We stop anything that moves. We'll sometimes even surround suspicious homes and bring out the MP5s (machine gun pistols)." Another department described its use of SWAT teams in the following way:[30]

> We're into saturation patrols in hot spots. We do a lot of our work with the SWAT unit because we have bigger guns. We send out two, two-to-four-men cars, we look for minor violations and do jump-outs, either on people on the street or automobiles. After we jump-out the second car

provides periphery cover with an ostentatious display of weaponry. We're sending a clear message: if the shootings don't stop, we'll shoot someone.

On the other hand, despite this increase in police weaponry and tactics, and prior to any sustained terrorist campaign on American soil, we are starting to see the impact of "criminals" outgunning the police. Some data may help make this case. According to Alcohol, Tobacco and Firearm (ATF) data, AK-47s and similar assault-type weapons seized or connected to a crime has grown from 1,140 in 1993 to 8,547 in 2007.[31] This 800% increase has been attributed almost exclusively to the weapons being used by gang members. This circumstance led an International Association of Chiefs of Police (IACP) spokesman to say that police departments are "in an arms race" with criminals.[32] The consequence of this assertion has led spokesman Peter Hamm from the Brady Center to Prevent Gun Violence to assert that "police officers need to be able to defend themselves and the rest of us, and they need the weapons to do so." Since the Brady Center is devoted to gun control laws, it is rather surprising to note that they are advocating heavier weaponry for the police.

Some serious thinkers are addressing this dilemma. Most of those who weigh in on this issue do so from the perspective of being concerned about freedom or liberty. With this approach, the question is not militarization, but instead is, What will militarization do to my freedom? This is reflective of the larger society. To most people, this issue is less about police weaponry and tactics, and more about how it will affect the liberties and freedoms that this country stands for (Figure 4.1). At this level, this is a fair and fundamental question. How this question is typically addressed, however, is to highlight particular incidents where citizens were "terrorized" by heavily armed police. This approach makes the issue more about emotion than substance. It is my desire to make this a substantive analysis.

Notwithstanding the desire to assess this issue from a substantive standpoint, the emotional impact—or better said, the perception—raised by militarized police weapons and tactics must be taken into account. Critics say that the appearance of armored vehicles may only increase tensions by making residents feel as if they are under siege.[33] While this is a legitimate concern, from the perspective of the police it is also problematic. Should police die because they did not have the equipment and weaponry to counter a gang member or a terrorist? Regardless of the answer to this vexing question, as we have seen from the above examples, militarization of the police is "marching forward." This has been fostered by widespread political acceptance—even prior to 9/11—where the military is encouraged to share training, equipment, technology, as well as the mentality with state and local police. Conversely, to some observers, police militarization threatens civil liberties, constitutional norms, and the well-being of all citizens—thereby sending an alarm to people of goodwill from across the political spectrum.[34]

Figure 4.1 Public Safety Policing model (Copyright, James F. Pastor, 2009).

Security and Safety versus Freedom and Rights

To address the critical principles impacted by the militarization of policing, one must have a defined, structured way to think about it. It is my belief that two underlying principles are instructive: security (safety) versus freedom (rights). Indeed, these principles are the key variables in the larger *Public Safety Policing* model that I contend is being advanced throughout this country. In each element of this model, these principles will be debated, contrasted, and assessed. In my mind, there is no clear answer to these often competing principles. Indeed, it depends on where you stand or, more specifically, who you are—as your worldview holds the key. Like many complex issues, there are strong arguments on both sides of the issue. This is because we see the world from our perspective. We see the world from our vantage point. Within this worldview, our opinions reside.

With this backdrop, let's look at the interplay of these critical principles. First, much of the criticism of the militarization of policing revolves around the principles of freedom and rights. This interplay is both substantive and emotional. Allow me to flesh out these distinctions. As to substantive issues, it is fair to assert that heavily armed police may create an environment where individual rights may be violated. This could occur from use of force inflicted by police against citizens. It could also occur from other constitutionally violative police practices stemming from an increase in the tactical orientation of policing. Each of these concerns is well founded. Consider Balko's pointed assertion that[35] innocent American citizens had the sanctity of their homes invaded by agents of the government behaving more like soldiers at war than peace officers upholding and protecting our constitutional rights.

The potential for increased use of force incidents is clearly problematic. Those who criticize the militarization trend typically argue that police will be inclined to use force because their weaponry and tactics foster such. This is a legitimate argument and a legitimate concern. The logic of this criticism is that more aggressive police practices are likely to result in a more aggressive attitude by individual police officers. The more aggressive the practices and attitudes, the more likely the use of force incidents become. I think this logic holds true. Indeed, I would expect more use of force incidents by police. I also realize this dynamic will result in more controversial police shootings (see Chapter 9 for a discussion on police shootings).

Let me first say that I do not advocate increased violence. Just as I hope that my predicted increase in terrorism and extremist violence is wrong, I hope my prediction of increased police use of force incidents will also be flawed. However, assume for the sake of argument that I am correct about my first premise, that there will be a generalized increase in terrorism and extremist violence. If this premise is correct, then the correlating premise is also likely to be correct, that use of force by police will increase in response to a generalized increase in violence. The consistency of this logic is particularly relevant when the *target* of much of this predicted increase in terrorist and extremist violence will be targeted toward *police* and *other public safety providers*. This assertion and this relationship will be more fully developed below. For now, however, one must be cognizant of the impact of violence generally. If, as it currently appears, criminals and terrorists will use more deadly and sophisticated weaponry, then it stands to reason that the police will do the same. To be clear, I hope this does not come to pass. As was shown in the above discussion, of course, it is already happening!

Figure 4.2 illustrates this logic. While each of these ideologies has its own natural enemies as well as its potential allies, the common theme is that each sees the police and first responders as being both a threat and a detriment. The police are a detriment because they represent the larger society. Indeed, they are the most visible representatives of government. They also are a threat to these groups because they stand for stability and, hopefully, law and order. In this role, they are a threat to extremist and terrorist groups because they arrest, prosecute, and sometimes kill their members. In this way, these groups cannot achieve their goal of illicit power without defeating the police.

Consequently, I am not going to offer what I perceive to be simplistic "solutions" to complex problems. It would be easy to simply say such things as we need better gun control laws, or police should not use heavy weaponry! While I do not oppose restricting the sale of assault weapons, for example, one must be cognizant that tens of thousands of these weapons are already within the market—and in the hands of criminals. To think critically and logically about this as being *the solution* is simplistic—even

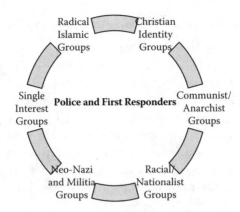

Figure 4.2 Police and first responder implications (Copyright, James F. Pastor, 2009).

naïve. I expect that these weapons will be increasingly used. I also expect the police to "arm up" to the level of weaponry that the criminals will exert. While this may be perceived by some as "fighting violence with violence," I respectfully acknowledge this point. This is clearly problematic. When one thinks about any viable alternatives, however, I am struck by the lack of any answers. Indeed, the answer to some is to simply "hope" it will not happen. I do not believe that "hoping" is a policy. I do not believe it will change the dynamics that have been taking root—for years. The seeds of this violence have been playing out for decades. To quote the good Reverend Wright, "Your chickens are coming home to roost." While I do not agree with the basis of his assertion, I do agree that difficult times lie ahead. Since neither Wright nor I can change the past, I think we agree that the future portends increased violence and extremism. We will not wish this away. We will not solve it by gun control laws. We will have to confront it on the streets, and in public and private environments throughout the country. While I do not discount any factor that will contribute to the "solution," I also realize that those who foster violence will have to be confronted.

While I agree that the substantive concerns offered by critics of militarization of the police are often well founded, I contend that the "solution" is not simply to ignore the obvious—that this trend is coming, like it or not. If it is indeed coming, then my answer has more to do with changing the dynamics—not simply "hoping" it does not occur. By changing the dynamics, I mean changing the selection, training, policies, and attitudes of police officers and public safety professionals. This entails cultural and organizational initiatives geared toward much greater levels of discipline, which can only be fostered through revamping the way police agencies do business. I will delve into these factors in Chapter 10. Suffice it to state at this point, future policing agencies must find ways to both protect their officers and to limit the use of force to only those circumstances that require it. Correctly implementing this delicate balance—often in split-second decisions—is an extraordinarily difficult distinction to achieve.

Police Weaponry and Tactics

With this backdrop, now look at the issues around police weaponry and tactics. Since most do not see these issues from the perspective of the police, I think it is appropriate to provide some perspective from the viewpoint of street police officers. Since I have served in this capacity, and since I have represented police officers as an attorney and teach them as a professor, I believe I am well qualified to "speak for the police." I say this, however, with a caveat. I do not pretend that "the police" are some monolithic organization that has only one perspective. Clearly, there are many different voices and perspectives on this complex subject. My perspective on how police see this issue is that of one voice of many. That being said, I believe this perspective will resonate with most police officers.

An effective way to introduce this perspective is to think about the North Hollywood shootout in February 1997. To refresh your memory, two heavily armed bank robbers entered a Bank of America branch in North Hollywood. They were equipped with AK-47s and other assault weapons, full body armor, and thousands of rounds of ammunition.[36] The bank robbers fired hundreds of rounds through various assault weapons, while responding police officers took cover and returned fire with revolvers and semiautomatic handguns. During the shootout, police officers were forced to enter a local gun store to obtain heavier weapons. At the end of the incident, an LAPD SWAT team showed up and engaged the last offender, who surrendered but later died from wounds suffered in the shootout. Based on both the courage of the responding officers and some good fortune (the assault weapon of one of the offenders jammed), this incident ended with only the offenders dead. According to a recent account, law enforcement officials say the trend toward issuing assault rifles to regular patrol officers started after this shootout, where 11 police officers were injured along with six civilians.[37]

This incident was a wake-up call for police agencies throughout the country, especially in large urban police departments. Two years later, police began rethinking their typical tactical strategy when dealing with hostage situations. Typically, the practice was to secure the perimeter and wait for negotiators and SWAT teams. The Columbine school shooting in Littleton, Colorado, changed this approach. In this incident, two teens killed 13 people and wounded two-dozen others while police response focused on protecting the perimeter. Later, the tragic events at Virginia Tech, Northern Illinois, various mall and school shootings, and numerous other incidents have changed the thinking of many police administrators.

These incidents take us back to an early era when the Los Angeles Police Department formed the first SWAT team and, it is said, originated the acronym SWAT to describe the elite force. The Los Angeles SWAT unit acquired national prestige when it was used successfully against the Black Panthers in 1969 and the Symbionese Liberation Army in 1973. What is the possibility that extremist groups like these will reappear in contemporary America? I believe it is inevitable.

Indeed, the Mumbai terrorist attack in November 2008 is illustrative. Ten terrorists armed with AK-47s, grenades, and bombs caused havoc throughout the financial capital of India.[38] In the Mumbai attacks, the gunmen arrived in the city by boat and attacked several targets, including two hotels, a local train terminal, and a Jewish center. Miami Police Chief John Timoney said that the attacks were notable because they involved crude methods instead of spectacular tactics such as crashing planes into buildings or using large bombs. In the wake of the attacks, police departments across the country are taking steps to ensure that similar incidents do not happen in their cities. For instance, the New York City Police Department will participate in live exercises that simulate scenarios in the Mumbai terrorist attacks. In addition, the NYPD will hold a briefing for 400 corporate security officials from businesses throughout the city. Meanwhile, the Boston Police Department has increased surveillance around the city and is monitoring hotels more closely.[39]

Many fear that this approach will be a model for future terrorist attacks. According to former White House homeland security adviser Ken Wainstein, U.S. cities are vulnerable to a Mumbai-type attack, which resulted in the deaths of 179 people. "You can envision that happening in any American city, and it's chilling when you think about it," said Wainstein. Security and public safety experts are concerned that the success of this low-technology attack may spur similar attacks by terrorist organizations. This is because of the extraordinary difficulties involved in securing an entire urban area against an attack by a team of gunmen.[40]

Before we go into the larger impact of these incidents, please put yourself in the shoes of the typical police officer. Police officers, like any other employee, typically desire to "do their job and go home." While this job is different than most, the people who do this work have needs just like any other employees. They desire job security; they have to pay their mortgage, raise their children, juggle their bills, and go home to be with their family. In short, they have human needs and dreams. Due to the work they perform, however, they tend to be more cognizant of their safety than most other occupations. This is both a defensive and coping mechanism. It is defensive because the focus on "officer safety" fosters more thoughtful and tactical orientations to the job. Simply stated, by being aware of safety issues, police officers are better able to do their job. This makes them more prepared for the numerous scenarios they face daily. These range from street and traffic stops, "in-progress" and many other disturbances, alarms, and crime-related calls. Awareness of officer safety techniques also helps officers cope with the inherent dangers of the job. This thinking, training, and experience help enhance the courage and commitment to enter situations when other people are going the opposite way. Indeed, when police officers go *toward* a man with a gun while civilians are moving in the opposite direction, it would not be surprising that police and civilians see the world differently. The civilian's "job" is to call the police. The police officer's job is to engage the offender.

When considering the "militarization" of the police, one must understand what it is like to face weaponry that you cannot counter. Using the North Hollywood example, the offenders had weaponry that far outgunned those used by the police. One does not need to be a police officer to understand how this must make you feel. This fact, however, does not simply impact police. I would venture to say that the civilians who were injured and at risk that day would have greatly appreciated if the police could have effectively responded to the incident. Indeed, everyone involved had a "vested interest" in "neutralizing the threat" on that sunny day in February. Hence, those who write and fret about the "militarization of the police" were likely not at the Bank of America during the shootout. The implications of this point are made plain by Captain Phil Burton of the Marion County (Indiana) Sheriff's Department who explained the reason why his department was equipping its officers with assault weapons. He stated,

> [W]e felt the need ... to equip ourselves, for lack of a better term, to meet force with force in order to provide safety to the public.[41]

In my mind this is a natural and pragmatic consequence of being targeted: humans (read police) will respond with increased self-defense and self-preservation techniques. One of the self-defense techniques is weaponry. In short, the North Hollywood example illustrates that being outgunned is a lonely—and helpless— feeling. It does not help the police, or the community, to be outgunned by ill-intended criminals.

Admittedly, the aforementioned description just broke my rule: to stay focused on the substantive, not emotional, aspects of the issue. In reality, one cannot completely separate the substantive from the emotional. While we all want to be—and sound—substantive, the reality is that when one comes face to face with violent offenders, it is extraordinarily difficult to remove emotion from the mix. When you see it from the perspective of the responding police officer, one is hard-pressed to dismiss out of hand the legitimate human need for self-defense. Of course, some people will simply say that is "their job." When this cavalier response is mouthed, note who is saying it. More than likely those who worry more about their rights (and conveniences) than the lives of public safety providers are the same people who never had to face an armed offender.

Consequently, it is easy to talk like an enlightened, freedom-loving disciple while never having to actually engage a heavily armed individual who would rather kill you than go to jail. Fortunately, this type of threat does not exist on a daily basis for police officers. However, one such experience is sufficient to change your perspective. Indeed, even the possibility of this occurring is enough to get your attention. "We live on being prepared for 'what if?'" said Pittsburgh Sergeant Barry Budd, a member of the SWAT team.[42] Many in this country have never had to even envision this possibility. To the average police officer, this notion is of little comfort.

Contemporary police are far more likely to have to deal with violence than the average citizen. This includes violence where citizens are the actual victims. Please understand my thinking. Crime victims must face tragic consequences. These consequences are real and significant. The police, however, are also involved in this process. They inevitably are present at the scene of the crime, even if it is too late to stop the crime. While crime victims are directly and profoundly affected by the crime, police officers are also tangentially affected by the aggregate of all crimes they see and deal with. In this way, the police are exposed to crime in a qualitatively different manner than the rest of society. This aggregate effect has trended upward for a generation. For example, in 1960, there were 3.3 public police officers for every violent crime reported. This ratio of police officers to violent crimes was turned upside down in one generation. It changed to 3.47 violent crimes reported for every public police officer by 1993.[43] The net effect is that each public police officer in contemporary America must deal with many more violent crimes than police from this previous era.[44] As the economic crisis plays out, violent crime rates are likely to increase in the years ahead. I contend that crime, particularly extremist and terroristic violence, will also increase in the years ahead.

This brings us to my initial premise: police officers see security and safety differently than most civilians. This is due to the nature of the job. However, the job is changing. As dangerous as it may have been in previous eras, I believe these eras will pale by comparison to the years ahead. This assertion, of course, is based on the predicted increase in extremist and terroristic violence. Put aside, for a moment, the merits of my assertion and simply view terrorism from a clinical perspective. In any review of terrorist campaigns, in different parts of the world and during different time frames, one key target of this violence is the police. One needs to look no further than Iraq to observe that police and civil defense forces have been frequent targets of terrorists. This is not novel. Indeed, examples of terrorist attacks against police officers and police facilities are undeniable, both in contemporary and historical times. One consequence of this reality is that police will be forced to protect themselves as they protect the community. This dynamic will result in the police adopting more paramilitary tactics and weaponry, which will be notable attributes in the coming *Public Safety Policing* model.[45]

Implications of Terroristic Violence

Prior to addressing the implications of terroristic violence on the policing model, it may be helpful to assess the underlying basis for this transition. Key questions relating to the "militarization of policing" can be explained by two critical factors: the Posse Comitatus Act,[46] and terrorism as *asymmetric warfare*. Both of these factors, while interrelated, provide the impetus toward increasing militarization of policing.

First, the Posse Comitatus Act (Section 1385, Title 18, United States Code), passed in 1878, prohibits the U.S. military from being used to enforce laws entrusted to civilian law enforcement authorities.[47] A brief history of this act may be instructive. After the Civil War, Congress imposed martial law in the rebel states. To shield the military's reconstruction policies from constitutional challenges, Congress passed this landmark piece of legislation, namely, the Posse Comitatus Act. In essence, the Act was passed to curb police and judicial powers of the Army during the Reconstruction period in the South. It prohibited the use of armed forces in the execution of civilian law enforcement. It remains in force today, with several statutory limitations. This law provided:[48]

> Whoever, except in cases and under such circumstances expressly authorized by the Constitution or by Act of Congress, willfully uses any part of the Army as a posse comitatus or otherwise to execute the laws shall be fined no more than $10,000 or imprisoned not more than two years, or both.

Despite the language of this law, the U.S. Army was used to restore order in industrial disputes in the late nineteenth and early twentieth centuries. Army troops were sometimes used to accomplish other objectives—after which they were immediately withdrawn. For example, federal troops and federalized National Guardsmen were called upon to enforce the desegregation of schools in Little Rock, Arkansas, in 1957; in Oxford, Mississippi, in 1962; and in Selma, Alabama, in 1963.[49] The military was also used in the Watts riot in Los Angeles in 1965, the Cleveland riot of 1966, the Detroit riot in 1967, and the L.A. riots in 1992.[50] These are just a few instances in which federal troops deployed to help quell civil disturbances beyond the control of local police. Indeed, the involvement of the military is extensive. The Army was involved in 125 interventions between 1877 and 1945, and participated in 29 situations in the twentieth century.[51]

Over the past 20 years there has been a dramatic expansion of the role of the military in law enforcement activity. The military has participated in "special security events," such as the Super Bowl and presidential inaugurations, suggesting a trend toward pragmatically relaxing the Act. Those who advocate the military's involvement argue that the military is the only organization with the training, equipment, and expertise necessary to address terrorist threats. Counterterrorism, as previously discussed, is simply another type of warfare. Finally, this school of thought notes that the Department of Defense (DOD) has emphasized defense of the homeland through an active and layered defense strategy. The *Strategy for Homeland Defense and Civil Support* specifies certain lead roles for the DOD. "Through its deterrent force posture and capabilities, the Department seeks to convince adversaries that they cannot achieve their objectives through attacks on the U.S. homeland." Moreover, the strategy suggests that protecting the homeland is the most important responsibility of the U.S. government.

This thinking has evolved from congressional amendments to the Posse Comitatus Act. In 1981 Congress passed the Military Cooperation with Law Enforcement Officials Act (2310 U.S.C. Section 371–74). This law amended the Posse Comitatus Act insofar as it authorized the military to "assist" civilian police in the enforcement of drug laws. Under this act, Congress directed the military to make equipment and facilities available to policing agencies in the antidrug effort. This act also authorized the military to share information acquired during military operations with civilian police agencies. In 1994 the Department of Justice and the Department of Defense signed a memorandum of understanding (MOU), which has enabled the military to transfer technology to state and local police departments. As a result, police departments began to acquire more sophisticated tactical equipment. Taken together these legislative acts encouraged the military to

1. Provide equipment, weapons, and research facilities to police;
2. Train and advise civilian police on the use of the equipment and weapons; and
3. Assist law enforcement personnel in keeping drugs from entering the country.

These examples of military-police cooperation leads to this question: Has the procurement of military weapons and equipment changed policing? More pointedly, some ask the question this way: Has the enemy abroad begun to resemble law enforcement's enemy at home? In my mind, police are—and will increasingly—confronting threats that more and more resemble asymmetric warfare. For example, not long ago most police administrators—and those in the "audience"—worried about such things as robberies in a subway. This type of crime, while problematic, pales in comparison to the suicide bomber on a train. As such, police weaponry and tactics will change accordingly. This is due to the changing nature of criminals, the destructive nature of their crimes, and the lethality of their weapons. In response, police officers now have at their disposal an array of high-tech military items previously reserved for use during wartime.[52] The procurement of weapons and equipment has been outlined above. For photos of what "the police" may increasingly look like, please see the provided links.[53]

The amendments to the Posse Comitatus Act seem to be driving the incremental development toward a more militarized policing model. This prompts the posing of these questions: Should the Posse Comitatus Act be amended again? Should it be abandoned? Should the military be allowed to "police" the streets of the United States? While I think the police will be hard-pressed to handle an active terroristic environment, I think using the military is even more problematic.

Consider the use of the British Army during the active days of the Irish Republican Army (IRA) in Northern Ireland. From 1971–1976, the British Army conducted over 250,000 home searches and inspected 5,000 vehicles a day. The overall effect of these repressive tactics was the alienation of the population. As a result, the military was considered ineffective as a law enforcement tool. Significantly, the failures of the military helped transform the police into a more "military-like" organization.

Taking note of the failures of the British military, the Royal Ulster Constabulary (RUC) transformed itself into a "formidable, militarized security force." The RUC maintained an arsenal of offensive equipment resembling army units. Officers patrolled combat-style in armored land rovers equipped with high-power weapons, and trained in counterinsurgency tactics. Additionally, they formed military-trained mobile support units for surveillance, rapid strike operations, and support for other RUC units. Intelligence units also oversaw and coordinated intelligence and police operations. Thereafter, the Army accepted the role of aiding the civil power and providing support to the police. Following the switch to *police primacy*, the number of incidents and fatalities resulting from terrorism markedly decreased when compared to the period when the military controlled the streets. The reduction of civilian deaths was the result of improved security force personnel and tactics, improved intelligence, and special emergency powers granted to the police.[54]

According to Thurston, we can learn much from the failures of the counterterrorism effort against the IRA. First, the British Army was not prepared for a lead role in law enforcement in Northern Ireland. It lacked training, intelligence, and knowledge of the sectarian nature of the violence. Instead of a direct role, the Army should have been used in a support role to the RUC. In extreme circumstances, the Army could help serve in a crowd control capacity by supplying troops so that minimum force could be utilized against rioters. Second, conventional military tactics are ineffective against terrorism. Since the military lacked training in counterinsurgency, they relied on conventional tactics. Yet conventional tactics are designed to counter another army. As a result, the British Army acted very harshly in their encounters with civilians. It failed to realize the damage its techniques would have on the mission. While such tactics might suppress the violence that day, or win the battle, these actions alienated the Catholic community and rallied support for the IRA. Indeed, this illustrates that complex problems elude a classic military solution. In short, simple suppression of troublemakers is insufficient to address the underlying causes of an insurgency.[55]

It is also important to note that the RUC took on many characteristics of the British military. While it is clear in my mind that the U.S. military would have similar problems as their British counterparts, the larger theme of this chapter is that the RUC used many military weapons and tactics. Regardless of any well-founded criticisms, my belief is that security concerns—both of the police and of the public—will necessitate sustaining and increasing this incremental transition in policing. This is not a novel assertion. History provides us with some pointed examples. Following "draft riots" during the Civil War, the Massachusetts Assembly granted the police the right to carry firearms. During the 1920s and 1930s, in response to growing violence, police introduced the use of machine guns for its officers.[56] With the current—and anticipated—rise in violence, police agencies will "innovate" as they did to previous threats. Some examples of this assertion may be instructive.

First, notwithstanding the examples of the British in Northern Ireland, the U.S. military expects to have 20,000 uniformed troops inside the United States by 2011. These military personnel will be trained to help state and local officials respond to a nuclear terrorist attack or other domestic catastrophe, according to Pentagon officials. Of course, critics express concern that the new homeland security emphasis threatens to strain the military and possibly undermine the Posse Comitatus Act. Before the terrorist attacks of September 11, 2001, dedicating 20,000 troops to domestic response "would have been extraordinary to the point of unbelievable," said Paul McHale, assistant defense secretary for homeland defense. McHale added that the realization that civilian authorities may be overwhelmed in a catastrophe prompted "a fundamental change in military culture."[57]

This policy stemmed from a series of plans forwarding the role of the military within the United States. For example, in 2005 a homeland defense strategy emphasized "preparing for multiple, simultaneous mass casualty incidents," such as the detonation of a nuclear bomb in a U.S. city. Later, in 2007, a Department of Defense directive approved more than $556 million over five years to set up the three response teams, known as Consequence Management Response Forces (CBRNE). This response force assumes incidents could lead to thousands of casualties, more than one million evacuees, and the possible contamination of as many as 3,000 square miles. In the fall of 2008, government officials agreed to begin a $1.8 million pilot project funded by the Federal Emergency Management Agency (FEMA) through which civilian authorities in five states could tap military planners to develop disaster response plans. Each of these states will focus on a particular threat—pandemic flu, a terrorist attack, hurricane, earthquake, and catastrophic chemical release. Finally, in December 2008, Defense Secretary Robert Gates ordered defense officials to review whether the military, National Guard, and reserves can respond adequately to domestic disasters.[58]

Even military officials see this trend with some reservations. According to Bert B. Tussing, director of homeland defense and security issues at the U.S. Army War College's Center for Strategic Leadership, the Pentagon approach "breaks the mold" by assigning an active-duty combat brigade to the Northern Command for the first time in history. Of course, many civil libertarians are also concerned. Domestic emergency deployment may be "just the first example of a series of expansions in presidential and military authority," or even an increase in domestic surveillance, said Anna Christensen of the ACLU's National Security Project. In addition, the Cato Institute's vice president, Gene Healy, warned of "a creeping militarization" of homeland security.[59] Despite these concerns, it is inevitable that homeland security will be increasingly "militarized." While I advocate "police primacy" instead of extensive military involvement, the notion that a more warrior approach is inevitable. According to Chief of Police Eugene Hernandez of Chino, California, "I see increased community pressure to return to a warrior officer who suppresses, through legal mandate, more civil liberties in response to homeland security."[60]

Second, another related response that Americans may find appropriate is to utilize National Guard forces to help deal with this threat. This is not uncommon. Consider after 9/11, National Guard troops were used in airports and assisted police in various public environments. The sustainability of this approach, however, is questionable. How long can National Guard troops actively perform such functions on American soil? While these troops have been used any number of times following weather emergencies, riots, and for other civil protests, they have not been used in any sustained manner. Some states, including Rhode Island, have prepared for the implementation of specially trained commandos—whose mission is to assist first responders in an event of terrorist attack. These commandos are a full-time unit ready for rapid deployment to support local, state, and federal authorities in responding to any attack involving weapons of mass destruction. This unit, while well trained and highly regarded, has only 22 members, who have completed a three-year training period.[61] There is little evidence that a group of this size could have any long-term sustainability.

Third, an illustration of what the future portends may be found in Mexico. For the past couple of years, Mexican police and army have been in pitched battles with narco-gangs. In 2007, Mexican officials sent more than 20,000 troops throughout the country to battle the drug cartels. The response from the mafia kingpins was spectacularly swift and bloody. All told, the death toll eclipsed 2,500 in 2007. Given this violence, the Mexican government increased the number of troops to deal with the drug cartels. Yet, the death toll in 2008 set new records. November was the bloodiest month of 2008, with 943 murders. By the beginning of December 2008, the death toll was 5,376, a rise of 117 percent from the same period the previous year.[62]

Throughout 2008, Mexican President Felipe Calderón dispatched more than 2,000 soldiers to a troubled border city where execution-style murders remain commonplace. In this violence, heavily armed drug cartels battled for control of lucrative drug-smuggling routes into the United States. In one city, Ciudad Juárez, at least 15 law enforcement officers have been killed. Consider this assertion of Tony Payan, an expert in drug cartels, who stated, "Even for a violent city like Juárez, this is pretty amazing. … It's unprecedented."[63] In response to this violence, the Mexican government has replaced local officers with 27,000 federal police officers and 30,000 troops. They, too, have paid a price. At least 449 deaths from this violence since late 2006 have been officers and soldiers.[64]

The drug cartels' weapons of choice include AR-15s, .223-caliber assault rifles, AK-47s, FN 5.57-caliber pistols, rocket-propelled grenade launchers (RPGs), and .50-caliber machine guns.[65] Most of these weapons originated from the United States. In an effort to confront these gangs, the United States and Mexico entered into an antidrug program known as the Mérida Initiative (from a city in Mexico), where the United States provides $306 million to fund counter-narcotics, counter-terrorism, and border security operations. Despite this level of funding, the intelligence and evidence-sharing network with Mexico has been "overwhelmed" by the flood of weaponry—and the resulting violence.

While these are disconcerting circumstances, two other events that occurred in early 2009 may illustrate that even greater problems are on the horizon. These events were the attack of a media station in Mexico coupled with the planned "surge" to protect the U.S. border from this drug violence.

The attack of the news station was coordinated and brazen. On January 6, 2009, the commando-type assault by gunmen occurred. They fired on the Televisa network news offices in Monterrey, Mexico, shooting at the building's front doors and throwing a hand grenade into the parking lot close to a reporter and her cameraman. While no one was injured during the incident, the attackers left a message that stated, "Stop reporting only about us, also report about the narco-officials. This is a warning." They drove a red Pontiac with Texas license plates. As brazen as this incident was, it is the latest in a string of attacks on journalists in Mexico. This incident and the accompanying message demonstrate a strategic change in the "drug war." According to University of Texas at El Paso professor Howard Campbell, he believes that the drug cartels are no longer interested in killing their enemies and the cops, but are instead trying to control whole regions of Mexico.[66]

As you ponder the significance of this, please also consider a plan released by governmental officials in their attempts to keep this violence from spilling into the United States. On January 7, 2009, Homeland Security secretary Michael Chertoff said that the federal government has developed plans for a "surge" of police—and possibly military personnel—along the border with Mexico. Consider some details of the plan. It involves aircraft, armored vehicles, and special teams of civilian law enforcement officials who would be deployed to trouble spots along the border. Significantly, the plan provides for the military to "back up" the police if they are "overwhelmed."[67] While DHS officials say it is "unlikely" that the military would need to get involved, I think this is overly optimistic—or simply "spin." The military will be used along the border. It is simply inevitable.

Overall, these examples provide some pointed insight into the future of policing and of homeland security. Taking the common themes of these examples, this logic and data pose a couple of provocative questions:

1. If the Mexican army and police cannot deal with the violence of drug cartels, what would make us think that American police can handle extremist and terrorist groups?
2. Given the level of violence currently taking place in Mexico, are we to assume that this will not occur in the United States?

In my mind, the answer to these questions is obvious. As the war against cartels escalates in 2009, so will the threats, particularly against U.S. officials and other Americans, said U.S. Ambassador Tony Garza. The threats are a result of "growing frustration" among cartel leaders and the internal dynamics of cartel organizations.

An intelligence official described the drug gangs as "transnational, with deep financial, cultural and social ties to Mexican and U.S. cities." Indeed, Philip Heymann, a Harvard law professor and expert on terrorism, characterized the ongoing violence in Mexico as "narcoterrorism, given the tactics used," including beheadings and efforts to silence and intimidate society through threats, gruesome videos, and text messages. According to Dr. Heymann, "… the situation in Mexico is very, very dangerous for everyone, including the United States." He added, "The situation hasn't yet registered in the mindset of Americans, but it will, especially when Americans become the target. All you need are two, three Americans killed and the issue will suddenly become important." Indeed, Ambassador Garza echoed this sentiment:[68]

> Drug trafficking, the capacity to corrupt, and the violence inflicted by these cartels presents a real threat to public security across the Americas. … We're talking about a hemispheric security issue. [President] Bush gets it. Calderón does, too. We either pony up and partner up with Mexico and others in the region or face a far less secure future.

The result of this situation is plain. The Mexican cartels "are the dominant distributors of wholesale quantities of cocaine in the United States, and no other group is positioned to challenge them in the near term," according to the Department of Justice's 2008 National Drug Threat Assessment.[69] If this "war" spills out into the United States, police will face substantial increases of violence. When confronted with such lethal weaponry, police will respond. This will entail a dramatic change in weapons and tactics. Even with this change, it will still require great sacrifice— in blood and liberty—to overcome such violence. As difficult as this may sound, I believe many police officers will die in the years ahead. Their deaths will be very traumatic to the American society—and its psyche. Of course, it will greatly affect the police and families of the police. The social and psychological dynamics of this level of violence is very disconcerting. We will discuss some of the implications in Chapter 9. In any case, suffice it to state at this point, society will have to change. Just how greatly will depend on the level and sustainability of the violence.

These examples lead us to the question of terrorism as *asymmetric warfare*. In essence, asymmetric warfare poses the weak against the strong. The "weak" (read the terrorists) declare "war" on the strong. The tactics used in this war are largely terroristic. The "strong" (read the United States) have superior weaponry, technology, resources, and personnel. These advantages are, nonetheless, constrained by a number of factors, including legal and moral considerations, public relations, operational capabilities, and the like.[70] The weak are not constrained by such niceties. When the "strong" are not able—or willing—to use their superior advantages, the battlefield in this "war" is leveled, sometimes even favoring the "weak."

The impact of asymmetric warfare has created a number of implications for the military. As stated in Chapter 1, the military is reorienting its approach.

Battleships and armored tank battalions are much less important in an asymmetric war compared to a traditional war. As described in this chapter, those charged with protecting public safety will resemble the military—as asymmetric warfare has implications for both the military and the police. The "right" response requires some balance between the notion of war and crime. Police will need to "arm up," while simultaneously being cognizant of civil rights and principles. As we observed in Northern Ireland—and in Iraq—the military had a very difficult time achieving this delicate balance.

If American police must deal with a terrorist environment, the psychological implications upon policing will be substantial. The psychological effects of war have been given many labels, including "soldier's heart" in the American Civil War, "shell shock" in World War I, and "battle fatigue" in World War II. As this relates to contemporary times, the key concern to police officers—and to the larger society—will be the increased potential for posttraumatic stress disorder (PTSD). PTSD is essentially a disorder of physical and emotional arousal brought on by the experience of traumatic events. It typically involves assessing three clusters of symptoms and behaviors. Each of these may be relevant in the event police are faced with unpredictable and extreme levels of violence. These symptoms and behaviors include[71]

- *Intrusion*—in the form of intrusive thoughts, nightmares, or flashbacks. This entails sudden, vivid memories accompanied by painful emotions, which take over the person's attention. The person may feel like he or she is actually reliving the traumatic experience.
- *Avoidance*—of close emotional relationships with family, friends, and colleagues and of activities and situations that remind the person of the traumatic event. Also included in this category is the inability to feel or express emotions at all. Depression and feelings of guilt over having survived while others did not may also be present.
- *Hyperarousal*—which includes being easily startled and constantly feeling that danger is near. Other reactions in this category include anger and irritability, loss of concentration, and disturbed sleep. Flashbacks and startle reactions can be prompted by the sound of gunshots or a truck backfiring, or by any of the sights, sounds, smells, and tastes that an individual closely associates with a particular traumatic event.

In Webster's study of police officers who served in Iraq and Afghanistan, she found that personnel deployed to Iraq have exhibited significantly higher rates of PTSD than those deployed to Afghanistan. Almost 35 percent of U.S. military personnel who serve in Iraq seek help for mental health concerns through military programs. These concerns are linked to trauma exposure and are strongly associated with intense and prolonged combat. The key concern of her study was that many service personnel in Iraq particularly (but this was also true in Afghanistan) have little respite from daily exposure to death and life-threatening events. For example,

Iraq veterans often mention the sight of objects lying by the roadside. Similarly, the smell of wet drywall became unbearable for one first responder who pulled bodies from the Pentagon following the September 11 terrorist attacks.[72]

This psychological impact was also found in first responders following Hurricane Katrina. The Centers for Disease Control and Prevention (CDC) conducted an assessment of New Orleans police and firefighters after Katrina. Of the 912 police officers who completed the questionnaire, 19 percent reported PTSD symptoms and 26 percent reported major depressive symptoms. Of the 525 firefighters who completed the same questionnaire, 22 percent reported PTSD symptoms and 27 percent reported major depressive symptoms.[73] In addition to these statistics, public safety professionals comprise 10 percent of National Guard and reservists deployed to Iraq. Inevitably, these officers will come back to the police "job." How do they cope when they come back? Further, future police recruits will also include military service members who were active in these wars. Some who conduct psychological screenings have identified this as a serious issue. What does this mean for police departments? As one Iraq War veteran explains, "Not everyone [returning from war] is damaged, but everyone is changed."[74]

The research by Webster and the CDC illustrates that the impact of catastrophes like Hurricane Katrina and the September 11 attacks on first responders is significant. However, we do not fully understand the long-term implications of a sustained terroristic environment. The intensity and duration of exposure to this type of trauma may be severe. This impact is not limited to the first responders. Casualties may also include family members, friends, coworkers—and the larger society. This impact is partly related to the fact that first responders may work long hours for weeks or months after a significant event. At the same time they must deal with the disaster's personal impact on their own life circumstances.

Beyond these factors, think of the impact of having to be overly protective for your own safety, as you must be constantly prepared for the next attack. These factors led Webster to advocate future research on reducing the risk of PTSD and other long-lasting psychological problems associated with traumatic experiences. These questions—and others—are raised throughout this book.

In addition, one less obvious consequence related to the "war on terror" has been the growing use of private security personnel in contracted roles with the military. For example, many military bases in this country are guarded by private security personnel, thereby freeing up soldiers for overseas assignments.[75] This is not new. The use of private security personnel has predated the current wars in Iraq and Afghanistan. Since 1994, the State Department has been using contract "policing operations" in various countries, including Haiti, Bosnia, Croatia, Kosovo, Macedonia, Serbia, East Timor, Liberia, and now Iraq and Afghanistan. The level of funding for these contracts has been substantial. Consider the contract amounts to just one company, DynCorp (Table 4.2), over a six-year period:[76]

These figures tell only part of the story. Some additional data may help. In Iraq, private contractors are the second largest contributor to coalition forces after the

Table 4.2 Private Security Military Contracts

Year	Amount
2003	$91 Million
2002	$63 Million
2001	$75 Million
2000	$81 million
1999	$40 Million
1998	$21 Million

U.S. military. Stated another way, there are more private security contractors in Iraq than any other country's military, except the United States. Further, the percentage of security personnel has grown exponentially since the first Gulf War. In 1991, there were 100 U.S. troops for every private contractor. In 2003/2004, there are only 10 U.S. troops for every private contractor.[77] In total, there are about 20,000 private security contractors in Iraq at any time.[78] This 10-fold increase amounts to $30 billion for private security services in Iraq.[79] These services include operating weapons systems such as Predator drones, Global Hawks, and B-2 bombers. It also entails training for Iraqi army and police forces. In addition, the pentagon sought to "pursue additional opportunities to outsource and privatize," said former Defense Secretary Donald Rumsfeld.[80] According to the *New York Times*, the privatization of certain military functions is partly by design—the desire to transform the military into a leaner, more lethal fighting force. This is effected by the outsourcing of tasks "not deemed essential to war-making."[81] The solicitation for security services for a $100 million annual contract to guard the "Green Zone" in Baghdad is illustrative of the military approach. The solicitation proposal states,[82]

> the current and projected threat and recent history of attacks directed against coalition forces, and thinly stretched military forces, requires a commercial security force that is dedicated to provide Force Protection security.

More than 1,100 private contractors have been killed since the war began.[83] These are numbers published at the end of March 2008. The current numbers are likely to be even higher. Over 180,000 private contractors have served in Iraq, performing some of the most dangerous tasks, such as guarding State Department convoys. Of course, there have been problems with the deployment of security contractors. One firm seems to symbolize the controversy around such deployments. For example, Blackwater security personnel were killed and later hung from a bridge during a March 2004 ambush in Fallujah, Iraq. Subsequently, the firm was accused of killing a number of Iraqi citizens. These examples have made headlines and have triggered congressional action.[84] The work of these contractors, however, is critical. Consider the assertion from Tahseen Sheikhly, an Iraqi official, who admitted that removing security contractors would produce a "security vacuum" that would force Iraq to withdraw field troops to perform security functions.[85]

In December 2007, the Pentagon and the U.S. State Department reached an agreement that gives the military more control over government contractors, with specific provisions regarding the scope of the military's authority. The agreement provides that all security contractors must now give detailed information about air and ground movements to the chief military command in Iraq. Significantly, however, the agreement continues to provide the discretion for private security personnel to act on their own judgment if they are in a hostile or perilous situation.[86] In this critical aspect of their work, the military has no real control over these security firms. This concern has led Representative Jan Schakowsky (D-IL) to assert, "I think we have to have some uniform rules, particularly when these security guys are walking around fully armed. ... Who are they accountable to?"[87] While the new agreement between the Iraqi and U.S. governments transfers control of accountability to the Iraqi government, the use of private security personnel, by any account, was significant.

There are a number of concerns raised by the use of private security personnel within "war zones" as war by proxy—as one observer called "imperialism lite." Other concerns include critical questions such as loyalty. Who are the security personnel loyal to: the country, the contractor, the mission, the money, or some combination thereof? Further, the question of accountability is raised, as the Blackwater example illustrates. Next, some are concerned about the ideology of the security personnel. Finally, others question whether these arrangements are in our best national interest.[88] While I agree that these are legitimate questions, I believe the use of private security personnel in foreign countries to supplement the military is a precursor to the use of private security personnel to supplement American policing agencies. The impetus to using private security to supplement American police is the same as in Iraq. Simply stated, the military cannot perform the necessary security provisions without private contractors. As will be more fully developed in this book, this same assertion will be made in America as it relates to policing. Suffice it to say at this point that the turbulent twenty-first century will have direct implications for the *private military/security industry*. Experts acknowledge that military and civilian interests may converge into a symbiotic dynamic thanks to the expertise of private military contractors. The extent of these relationships is seen by the scope of this business. More than 150 private military companies operate worldwide, and the global industry generates between $20 billion and $100 billion each year.[89]

In the end, the level of violence will drive the widespread implementation of these contracted arrangements. Indeed, a growing number of merchant fleets are interested in hiring private security firms such as Blackwater to protect them in the pirate-infested shipping lanes off the coast of Somalia. The trend has even been encouraged by the U.S. Navy. "This is a great trend," said Lieutenant Nate Christensen, a spokesperson for the U.S. 5th Fleet, who later added, "We would encourage shipping companies to take proactive measures to help ensure their own safety." However, some say that the trend toward using private security firms could make the current situation even more dangerous than it is now. Among the critics is Cyrus Mody, the manager of the International Maritime Bureau, who contends that the presence of armed guards on ships could encourage pirates to use their weapons against a ship or spark an arms race between pirates and shipping companies. Others worry that security contractors could be overzealous in protecting merchant fleets and accidentally open fire on fishermen.[90]

In example after example, the struggle for security must be weighed against the need for human and civil rights. In essence, the dilemma is: the distinction between defense and offense is being blurred. When security forces fire on "bad guys" (such as pirates and terrorists), most people applaud their courage—and their desire to provide security. On the other hand, when security forces fire on "innocent" people, the condemnation is swift and sure. The problem, in the real world, is discerning the difference. The problem is doing so in a timely manner— meaning, before you die. This dynamic creates a very difficult circumstance. As stated earlier—and as illustrated by Blackwater—the police will be a prime target for extremist and terrorist violence. As a target, police should be expected to defend themselves. This entails heavier weaponry and tactics. The amount of force used, however, must be constrained. It must be used only when aimed at the "bad guys." In this sense, the police have been placed in the most delicate social balance to protect and serve American citizens.[91] It will only be harder to achieve this balance when the "protectors" are in fear of their safety—from increasingly dedicated threats and increasingly lethal weaponry.

Attempting to achieve this delicate balance, however, is clearly problematic. According to Laqueur, "Experience teaches that a little force is counter-productive ... the use of massive, overwhelming force, on the other hand, is usually effective."[92] Hence, Laqueur cautions against governments launching antiterrorist campaigns, unless they are "able and willing to apply massive force."[93] Given the many examples presented in this chapter, one is struck by the seemingly constant scrutiny of those who use force. While it is certainly appropriate to examine these incidents, the ability to do so within a terrorist environment is extraordinarily difficult. Under these circumstances, being "able and willing" to launch such an antiterror campaign is extremely questionable. Putting aside the political, legal, and public relations arguments, it is questionable that the police have the operational capability to perform massive antiterror operations. Indeed, Poland agrees that massive force would be necessary, and he adds that[94]

[u]nquestionably, a campaign of prolonged terrorism in the U.S. would result in the federal government assuming direct police powers; and the

temporary suspension of civil liberties would be deemed necessary to maintain order and locate offenders.

As would be expected, any notion that the police (plus security forces and/or the military) would respond to terrorist campaigns is disconcerting in some circles. Consider Balko's testimony before a Congressional subcommittee, who argued that[95]

> the military has a very different and distinct role than our domestic peace officers. The military's job is to annihilate a foreign enemy. The police are supposed to protect us while upholding our constitutional rights. It's dangerous to conflate the two. … It's time we stopped the war talk, the military tactics, and the military gear. America's domestic police departments should be populated by peace officers, not the troops of an occupying military force.

It is hard to imagine two completely different views of the world. Poland argues for massive force. Balko is adverse to force, as he desires "peace" officers. In the end, people will offer solutions based on how they see the problem. Those who see the problem differently are not likely to see eye to eye. In short, some see the problem of police having too much force, too much weaponry, and too much authority. Others see the extremists and the terrorists as being too dangerous, too well armed, and too great a threat to combat with traditional policing modalities.

Either way, this debate will be heated and controversial. We have barely scratched the surface of the intensity of the coming controversy. To some, police will be seen as "shock troops,"[96] while others will desire the perceived protection from heavily armed police. The "right" approach will be much debated and fluid. The challenge will be to balance the security and safety principles desired by the police and the public, with the often-competing principles of rights and freedom. Depending upon the level of violence, this balance will weigh in favor of security and safety when violence (or the threat) is high. Conversely, it will weigh in favor of rights and freedom when violence is diminished.

Achieving an "optimal balance" will always be subject to disagreement. This is due to the fact that consensus will never be achieved on either the threat posed or the solutions to the threats. This is due to the different experiences, perceptions, and beliefs people use to "filter" their decisions. In this sense, their worldview determines the "right" approach. While we will have more to say on this note in Chapter 10, it is critical that this issue be debated "before the storm." Simply stated, we cannot engage in a substantive public policy debate of this magnitude—and be filled with this amount of emotion—while faced with high levels of violence. Our minds are simply unable to cope with both reasoned analysis and high levels of emotion at the same time. Hopefully, this book will spur such debate. In the meantime, please consider how your particular worldview shapes your sense of the militarization of the police.

Endnotes

1. http://icasualties.org/oif/IraqiDeaths.aspx (retrieved on June 7, 2008).
2. Johnson, Thomas H. and M. Chris Mason (2008). "All Counterinsurgency Is Local," *The Atlantic* October:38.
3. "Weapons of Mass Destruction Student Manual AWR-160," *U.S. Department of Homeland Security*, Preparedness Directorate, Office of Grants and Training, Center for Domestic Preparedness, 15–16.
4. An excellent analysis of the psychological effects of violence is provided by David Grossman, who has published various research projects and developed books and presentations, including *On Killing* and *The Bullet Proof Mind*, which can be found at http://www.killology.com/index.htm.
5. Balko, Radley (2007), in his testimony "Our Militarized Police Departments" before the House Subcommittee on Crime, June 21. http://www.reason.com/news/show/121169.html (retrieved on May 6, 2008).
6. Weber, Diane Cecilia (1999). "Warrior Cops: The Ominous Growth of Para-Militarism in American Police Departments," *Cato Institute*. August 26. http://www.tysknews.com/Depts/The_Law/paramilitarism_in_police2.htm (retrieved on May 6, 2008).
7. http://www.foxnews.com/story/0,2933,340748,00.html (retrieved on March 23, 2008).
8. Miller, Joel (2002). "Cops at War: The Drug War and the Militarization of Mayberry," posted on December 30. http://www.rutherford.org/oldspeak/articles/law/oldspeak-cops.asp (retrieved on May 6, 2008).
9. http://www.foxnews.com/story/0,2933,340748,00.html (retrieved on March 23, 2008).
10. Spalding, Tom (2004), "IPD to Arm Officers with M-16's," *Indianapolis Star*, August 27.
11. Weber, Diana Cecilia (1999), op. cit.
12. Weber, Diana Cecilia (1999), op. cit.
13. Weber, Diane Cecilia (1999), op. cit.
14. Balko, Radley (2007), op. cit.
15. http://www.usatoday.com/news/washington/2007-01-26-militarygiveaways_x.htm (retrieved on May 6, 2008).
16. Farah, Joseph (1997). "The Militarization of the Domestic Police," WorldNetDaily.com posted on November 6. http://www.wnd.com/news/article.asp?ARTICLE_ID=14363 (retrieved on May 6, 2008).
17. *Star-Telegram* (2007), February 26. www.dfw.com/mld/dfw/news/16786386.htm (retrieved on August 17, 2007).
18. Spielman, Fran and Frank Main (2003), "Elite Police Unit to Flood Streets in City's Hot Spots," *Chicago Sun-Times*, June 24.
19. Perkins, Nancy and Amy Joi O'Donoghue (2008). "Heavily Armed Sect Raid Pleased Officials," *The Desert Morning News*, posted on April 16, 2008. http://www.policeone.com/police-products/vehicles/specialty/articles/1684847-Heavily-armed-sect-raid-pleased-officials (retrieved on May 6, 2008).
20. For an image of a police armored vehicle see http://www.foxnews.com/story/0,2933,351408,00.html (retrieved on April 16, 2008).
21. Balko, Radley (2007), op. cit.
22. Robb, John (2007). "The Coming Urban Terror: Systems Disruption, Networked Gangs, and Bioweapons," *City Journal* (Summer). http://www.city-journal.org/html/17_3_urban_terrorism.html (retrieved on May 16, 2008).

23. Balko, Radley (2007), op. cit.
24. Weber, Diane Cecilia (1999), op. cit.
25. Weber, Diane Cecilia (1999), op. cit., 11.
26. Weber, Diane Cecilia (1999), op. cit., 8.
27. Kraska, Peter and Victor Kappeler (1997). "Militarizing American Police: The Rise and Normalization of Paramilitary Units," *Social Problems* 44:5–6.
28. Weber, Diane Cecilia (1999), op. cit.
29. Balko, Radley (2007), op. cit.
30. Weber, Diane Cecilia (1999), op. cit.
31. Sedensky, Matt (2008). "AK-47s Are Turning Up More in US," *Newsweek* March 26.
32. Sedensky, Matt (2008), op cit.
33. Plushnick-Masti, Ramit (2007). "U.S. Police Departments Deploying Heavy Armor," posted on May 13. http://www.policeone.com/police-products/vehicles/specialty/articles/1244834-U-S-police-departments-deploying-heavy-armor (retrieved on May 6, 2008).
34. Weber, Diane Cecilia (1999), op. cit.
35. Balko, Radley (2007), op. cit.
36. For a gripping account of this incident, please see Twentieth Century Fox Film Corporation (2003). *44 Minutes: The North Hollywood Shoot-Out.*
37. Ridler, Keith (2008). "Arms Race with Criminals Has Police Toting Heavy-Duty Rifles," reported on March 23. http://www.signonsandiego.com/news/nation/20080323-0837-policeweapons.html (retrieved on May 6, 2008).
38. See example of an explanation of the Mumbai incident and its implications at Ist, Ians (2009). "Mumbai Attacks Call for New Counter Terrorism Strategy: Obama," *Economic Times of India,* January 12.
39. Johnson, Kevin and Frank Thomas (2008). "Mumbai Attacks Refocus U.S. Cities," *USA Today*, December 5, 1A.
40. Mikkelsen, Randall (2009). "Mumbai-Like Attack Could Happen in US—Bush Aide," *Reuters* (UK), January 8; Johnson, Kevin and Frank Thomas (2008), op. cit.; and Robb, John (2007), op. cit.
41. Spalding, Tom (2004), op. cit.
42. Plushnick-Masti, Ramit (2008), op. cit.
43. Walinsky, Adam (1993). "The Crisis of Public Order," *Atlantic Monthly* July.
44. Pastor, James F. (2003). *The Privatization of Police in America: An Analysis & Case Study.* Jefferson, NC: McFarland & Company, Inc; and Walinsky, Adam (1993), op. cit.
45. Pastor, James F. (2005). "Public Safety Policing," *Law Enforcement Executive Forum* 5, no. 6 (November):14.
46. Black's Law Dictionary (1983) (St. Paul: West) at page 606 defines the term "posse comitatus" as a "group of people acting under authority of police or sheriff and engaged in searching for a criminal or in making an arrest." It continues describing its history by stating, "In ancient Rome, governmental officials were permitted to have retainers accompany and protect them on their travels throughout the Empire. This practice was known as 'comitatus.' In medieval England, the sheriff could require the assistance of able-bodied men in the county over the age of fifteen in suppressing small insurrections and capturing fugitives. This civilian force was called the 'posse comitatus,' deriving its name from the old Roman practice."
47. State & Local Anti-terrorist Training (SLATT) Manual, Domestic Terrorist Groups, 5. :\content\section3domestic\pdfs\narrative.pdf.

48. Weber, Diane Cecilia (1999), op. cit.

49. Weber, Diane Cecilia (1999), op. cit.

50. As a pointed example of the difference in police officer versus military training was described by Delk, James D. (1995). *Fires & Furies: The L.A. Riots.* Palm Springs, CA: ETC Publications, 221–222: "Police officers responded to a domestic dispute, accompanied by marines. They had just gone up to the door when two shotgun birdshot rounds were fired through the door, hitting the officers. One yelled, 'cover me!' to the marines, who then laid down a heavy base of fire … The police officer had not meant 'shoot' when he yelled 'cover me' to the marines. [He] meant … point your weapons and be prepared to respond if necessary. However, the marines responded instantly in the precise way they had been trained, where 'cover me' means provide me with cover *using firepower* … over two hundred bullets [were] fired into that house."

51. Thurston, Timothy W. II (2007). The Military's Role in Domestic Terrorism. Unpublished master's thesis at Naval Postgraduate School, Monterey, California, December 2007.

52. U.S. Department of Justice and U.S. Department of Defense (1997). Department of Justice and Department of Defense Joint Technology Program: Second Anniversary Report. Washington: U.S. Department of Justice (February), 8–18.

53. http://www.berkeleydailyplanet.com/photos/04-14-06/webSWAT.jpg, depicting Berkeley police; http://cache.daylife.com/imageserve/0bVd9yh7hLfIN/610x.jpg, depicting Los Angeles police; http://blogs.kansascity.com/crime_scene/images/2008/ 01/16/police.jpg, depicting Kansas City police; http://cache.day-life.com/imageserve/ 079t8Pl961960/610x.jpg, depicting Chicago police; http://cache.daylife.com/imageserve/0e790kTb2heHT/610x.jpg, depicting Tampa police; and http://www.roswellpolice.com/images/photos/swat.jpg, depicting Roswell, NM, police.

54. Thurston, Timothy W. II (2007), op. cit.

55. Thurston, Timothy W. II (2007), op. cit.

56. Wadman, Robert C. and William Thomas Allison (2004). *To Protect & To Serve: A History of Police in America.* Upper Saddle River, NJ, Pearson/Prentice Hall, 116–117.

57. Hsu, Spencer S. and Ann Scott Tyson (2008). "Pentagon to Detail Troops to Bolster Domestic Security," *Washington Post,* A01. http://www.washingtonpost.com/wp- dyn/content/article/2008/11/30/AR2008113002217_pf.html (retrieved on December 2, 2008).

58. Hsu, Spencer S. and Ann Scott Tyson (2008), op. cit., 1.

59. Hsu, Spencer S. and Ann Scott Tyson (2008), op. cit., 2.

60. Stephens, Gene (2005). "Policing the Future: Law Enforcement's New Challenges," *The Futurist* 39 (March/April):5.

61. Vernon-Sparks, Lisa (2006). "Special Guard Squad's Debut Showcases Commando-Style Protection," *Providence Journal.* Posted on August 3, 2006. http://www.projo.com/ri/coventry/content/projo_20060803_cv3team.1ee9eeb.html (retrieved on August 3, 2006).

62. "Mexico Drug Gang Killing Surge" (2008), *BBC News,* posted on December 9. http://news.bbc.co.uk/2/hi/americas/7772771.stm (retrieved on December 9, 2008).

63. Root, Jay (2008). "Mexican Army Can't Stop Drug Lords' War on Cops," *McClatchy Newspapers,* posted on May 8. http://www.mcclatchydc.com/226/story/36404.html (retrieved on May 8, 2008).

64. Blumenthal, Ralph (2008). "What the Mexicans Might Learn from the Italians," *New York Times*. http://www.nytimes.com/2008/06/01/weekinreview/01blumenthal. html?_r=2&ref=americas&oref=slogin&oref=slogin.

65. An "Iron River of Guns" Flows South (2008). *Security Management* June:48.

66. Booth, William (2009). "Gunmen Attack TV Offices in Mexico," *Washington Post*, January 8, A9.

67. Archibold, Randal C. (2009). "U.S. Plans Border 'Surge' Against Any Drug Wars," *New York Times*, January 8.

68. Cruz, Claudio (2009). *Associated Press*. Mexichttp://www.dallasnews.com/shared-content/dws/news/world/mexico/stories/DN-mexviolence_04int.ART.State. Edition2.4a508fe.htmlo.

69. Schwartz, Jeremy (2008). "Drug Violence in Atlanta Tied to Several Cartels," *Atlanta Journal-Constitution*, July 31.

70. Laqueur, Walter (2004). "The Terrorism to Come," *Policy Review*, no. 126:8. www. policyreview.org/aug04/laqueur_print.html (retrieved on November 1, 2004).

71. Webster, Barbara (2008). "Combat Deployment and the Returning Police Officer," U.S. Department of Justice, Office of Community Oriented Policing Services and Institute for Law and Justice, 2005-HS-WX-K005, August.

72. Webster, Barbara (2008), op. cit., 4.

73. Webster, Barbara (2008), op. cit., 23–25.

74. Webster, Barbara (2008), op. cit., 23–25.

75. Wayne, Leslie (2004). "Security for the Homeland, Made in Alaska," *New York Times*, August 12.

76. Higgins, Andrew (2004). "Contract Cops: As It Wields Power Abroad, US Outsources Law & Order Work," *Wall Street Journal*, February 2.

77. Traynor, Ian (2003). "The Privatization of War: $30 Billion Goes to Private Military, Fears Over Hired Guns' Policy," *The Guardian (UK)*, December 10.

78. Barstow, David (2004). "Security Companies: Shadow Soldiers in Iraq," *New York Times*, April 19, A-1.

79. Traynor, Ian (2003), op. cit.

80. Traynor, Ian (2003), op. cit.

81. Barstow, David (2004), op. cit., A-11.

82. Barstow, David (2004), op. cit., A-11.

83. Herbeck, Dan (2008). "Private Army of Contractors Carries a Heavy Load in Iraq," *Buffalo News*, March 31.

84. See, for example, Cole, August (2007). "Private Security Providers Become a Pentagon Focus," *Wall Street Journal*, September 27, A9; Mroue, Bassem (2007). "Blackwater License Being Pulled in Iraq," *Associated Press*, September 17; and Lardner, Richard (2007). "Who Watches US Security Firms in Iraq?" *Associated Press*, September 19.

85. Zavis, Alexandra (2007). "Iraqi Official: Blackwater Exit Not Feasible," *Los Angeles Times*, September 24.

86. Burns, Robert (2007). "Tighter Control of Blackwater Agreed," *Associated Press*, December 6.

87. Zavis, Alexandra (2007), op. cit.

88. Traynor, Ian (2003), op. cit.

89. Valero, Rafael Enrique (2008). "Hired Guns," *National Journal*, January 7.

90. Houreld, Katharine (2008). "Private Security Firms to Take on Pirates," *Associated Press*, October 27.

91. Wadman, Robert C. and William Thomas Allison (2004). *To Protect & To Serve: A History of Police in America.* Upper Saddle River, NJ, Pearson/Prentice Hall, 159.
92. Laqueur, Walter (2004), op. cit., 9.
93. Ibid. Laqueur, Walter (2004), op. cit., 9.
94. Poland, James M. (2005). *Understanding Terrorism: Groups, Strategies & Responses.* Upper Saddle River, NJ: Pearson/Prentice Hall, 286.
95. Balko, Radley (2007), op. cit.
96. Miller, Joel (2002), op. cit.

Chapter 5

Intelligence Methods and Surveillance Technologies

This chapter presents the intelligence methods and surveillance technologies element of *Public Safety Policing*. It is important to note from the start that while one of the current "buzzwords" within policing circles is intelligence-led policing (ILP), this is a necessary but not sufficient way to describe contemporary policing practices. The below discussion explains this point.

Current Issues and Circumstances

Many thought leaders in policing, like Bratton and Kelling, argue for the merits of ILP. I believe they are correct. ILP practices are critical to public safety. However, as commonly explained, ILP does not sufficiently account for the dramatic increase of police militarization (Chapter 4), and of the growing emphasis on order maintenance (Chapter 6). It also does not adequately explain the dynamics of interfacing and collating information from public camera systems, crime mapping, predictive software, access control systems, and similar technologies. These are critical to the provision of public safety services. They are also key sources of information that can be used within the intelligence process. This chapter brings together these and other technologies to provide a fuller, more robust view of what this element of public safety policing will look like as we move forward.

In 2007, the Department of Homeland Security's Urban Area Security Initiative offered grants to help local police strengthen their ability to collect and analyze intelligence. These grants are designed to enhance the intelligence capacities of state

159

and urban policing agencies. These funds should be considered in conjunction with two Homeland Security presidential directives. A driving force behind intelligence-based policing has been Homeland Security Presidential Directive No. 6. Its stated goal is to integrate and use information to protect against terrorism. Specifically, the goals are to

- Develop, integrate, and maintain accurate information about individuals known or suspected of preparing for, or in aid of any terrorist acts on U.S. soil
- Use that information for prosecution to the fullest extent of the law
- Support federal, state, county, tribal, and local visa screening processes

Similarly, in Homeland Security Presidential Directive No. 11, the goal is to develop comprehensive terrorist related screening procedures. Specifically, these goals are to

- Detect, identify, track, and interdict foreign or domestic citizens that pose a threat to homeland security
- Safeguard legal rights, including freedoms, civil liberties, and information privacy guaranteed by federal law

One way to bring this element of *Public Safety Policing* into a structural assessment is to consider the acquisition of information. Inherent in policing, and for that matter almost any industry, is the need to obtain, process, analyze, and disseminate information. In the old days, this was rather straightforward. A crime was committed; it was observed by a citizen who yelled for help. The police came and arrested the offender based on the statement of a witness. This "information flow" was sometimes enhanced by observations of the officer, or by statements made by the offender. Over time, various technological enhancements made the acquisition of information more readily obtainable. Police moved in vehicles enabling them to observe much more "data" from the street as they drove from location to location, from beat to beat, from beat to sector, and from sector to the larger community. Telegraphs, "call boxes," and then radios within the vehicle, and later handheld radios, greatly increased the acquisition of additional information. Telephones used to report crimes facilitated this information flow. Other technologies like burglar and holdup alarms helped transmit information from the protected facility to monitoring centers, to police dispatch centers, then to responding police vehicles. These and many other technologies have fostered rapid flows of information designed to prevent crime or capture the criminal.

As a society, we are awash in data. The amount of data and information transmitted within society is overwhelming. It is data overload. Police are processing substantial amounts of information from seemingly ever-increasing sources. Indeed, one of the "innovations" of *Community Policing* was to cultivate the flow and quality of human information by emphasizing relationships within the community. In this way, foot patrols enabled police to observe details of crime indicators that may go unnoticed by rapid vehicle patrols.[1] Walking also helped facilitate conversations with citizens and business owners designed to foster relationships so data and information flows would be enhanced. Beat meetings were also said to open up the dialog to a larger audience, enabling community concerns to be aired. In these meetings, the information flow was to go both ways: from the community to the police, and from the police to the community. Other more strategic information flows were fostered with community and political leaders at regularly scheduled meetings.

Internally, police agencies developed information reports and special attention notices that are read at roll calls. More generalized—and sometimes more important—information is transmitted via bulletins, teletypes, and other electronic means. Accountability sessions are held to assess the effectiveness of tactical and strategic remedies designed to impact crime patterns and trends. These patterns and trends are facilitated by increasingly sophisticated data analysis methods, by crime mapping software, by "real-time" information transmitted by such technologies as cameras and alarms, and by an overall increase of technologies designed to transmit and discern information.

These technological enhancements, like those in the larger society, have resulted in "information overload." Seemingly ever-increasing sources of information, more sophisticated layers of data, and the rapid transmission of both have created operational dilemmas within police agencies. Added to this dilemma is the fact that failing to "connect the dots" from any information source can result in a tragedy like 9/11. Indeed, reading the 9/11 Commission Report, one is struck by the failure to make sense of numerous pieces of information. These range from pilot training patterns, immigration and identification data, intelligence reports—and the like—that were missed or fell through the cracks. Consequently, police agencies are in the process of reorienting themselves around better use of the vast amount of data and information that are available. This desire is at the heart of ILP. In this way, the problem for American policing is not so much getting the intelligence, but making sense of it and sharing it with those who can use it.

As stated earlier, prior to 9/11 significant amounts of information in the possession of law enforcement was noncriminal in nature (i.e., pilot training that did not emphasize landing skills). By itself, such information did not provide the basis of reasonable suspicion of a terrorist or criminal conspiracy. Traditionally, police have been trained to focus on criminal behavior. The threat of terrorism, however, requires police to focus their attention on data or observations that *do not necessarily indicate criminal intention or conduct.* Consequently, information sharing is the cornerstone of the intelligence process! A couple of real examples may help clarify the difficulties of "connecting the dots," particularly when the actions do not constitute a crime, or are only minor crimes, and involve multiple jurisdictions.

Example #1: In the San Francisco Bay area, ferryboat services provide tours around the bay. In the summer of 2003, a citizen called police to report the following: three Middle Eastern-looking men boarded a ferry and immediately separated. One individual went to the back (fantail) and appeared to be recording times of the ferry's movements. Another went to the wheelhouse area and appeared to be examining the locking mechanism. The third went to the engine room and seemed to be trying to enter the room. Around the same time, in another bay area city, a citizen reported a vehicle break-in. In the burglary, manuals on navigation of the bay, a ferryboat engineer's uniform, and an ID card were stolen. In addition, at another location, an individual described as "Middle Eastern" attempted to rent a boat at a bay area yacht club. When the boat owner checked the man's credit card against his driver's license, a discrepancy became apparent. Discovering that the transaction was going badly, the man fled the yacht club. The boat owner retained the credit card and driver's license and called police.

In the initial encounter, no crime occurred. In police parlance, the assignment was easy to "blow off" because it did not seem important. In the second encounter, the incident involved only a minor crime. It would have been typical to take the report and go to the next assignment. Simply stated, there was little reason to spend a lot of time on a minor crime. Finally, the third encounter also involved a minor crime. Here again, the typical approach would be to take the report and go to the next assignment. In each encounter, taken individually, there appeared to be no big deal. Connected together, the three encounters may indeed be a big deal! In terms of "connecting the dots," what is particularly significant is the fact that these events each took place in different jurisdictions.

Example #2: Two men were fishing in the Everglades west of Miami. A state law enforcement agent, whose job it is to enforce antipoaching laws in the Everglades, detained the two men. The officer requested that they show him their car. There were no alligators in the vehicle. In the back seat, however, were maps of Miami International Airport, including travel and departure time of airlines. Significantly, the Everglades form part of the flight pattern of flights into and out of Miami. A rocket propelled grenade (RPG) could bring down an airliner from this location. The officer completely missed the signs, released the men and wrote up a report.[2] The moral of these examples is to recognize indicators, and report them in a timely and thorough manner, thereby enabling the intelligence personnel to "connect the dots."

Attributes of Intelligence-Led Policing

A useful starting point is to provide a definition. According to the *National Strategy for Homeland Security*, intelligence-led policing is[3] a management and resource allocation approach to law enforcement using data collection and intelligence analysis to set specific priorities for all manner of crimes, including those associated with terrorism. ILP is a collaborative approach based on improved intelligence operations and community-oriented policing and problem solving, which the field of law enforcement has considered beneficial for many years. Today it is being adopted by a variety of law enforcement entities.

One basic distinction between ILP and traditional police investigations is the concept of information and intelligence. Information is unprocessed (raw) data. It is gathered or collected in its original form by the agent or officer. Information can be gleaned from a number of sources including informants, documents, surveillance, wiretaps, observations, cameras, alarms, and the like. The need to process and interface these information sources is critical. Processing this information, however, does not transform it into intelligence. Intelligence is much more defined and refined. It is the output of analysis, generated by applying the intelligence process by a trained analyst. More pointedly, intelligence is the analysis of information that is assessed for validity and reliability, through inductive and deductive logic. In short, this equation is illustrative: information/data + analysis = intelligence.

These terms can be further broken down into the following distinctions. Data can mean raw print, image, or signal. It can be *classified*, such as technical intelligence signal intercepts, or *unclassified*, such as fliers distributed during a demonstration or posts on Internet message boards. Information is data that have been collated and processed in order to produce a document that is of generic interest, such as a police report. Intelligence is those products that allow a specific group or organization to make an informed decision, such as an intelligence briefing.[4] Overall proper intelligence is built with information that:

- Has an appropriate crime predicate
- Has originated from a verified and evaluated source
- Is enhanced by research and analysis

Obtaining intelligence requires the systematic exploitation of information. It is the process of putting together several, often disjointed and seemingly unrelated bits and pieces of information.[5] An excellent analogy is to picture intelligence much like putting together a puzzle. The difference, however, is a puzzle has a picture of what it should look like when completed. Hence, the disadvantage of intelligence is not being able to have an advance "picture" of the completed puzzle. In this way, intelligence is a collaborative philosophy that starts with information gathered at all levels of the organization that is analyzed to create useful intelligence and an improved understanding of the operational environment. In the end, intelligence is designed to assist leadership in making the best possible decisions with respect to crime control strategies, allocation of resources, and tactical operations.[6]

It is important to note that police agencies have the responsibility to proactively establish a process that seeks to understand threats, criminal organizations, and crime targets within their communities. In this way, intelligence is not about merely reacting to issues as they develop. It is being proactive. It requires discerning and preventing crimes/events before they happen. The significance of contemporary threats can be illustrated by a mugging on a train or suicide bomber on a train. The key to this responsibility is to manage these crime threats and focus on *prevention*. As such, intelligence is destined to play a key role in twenty-first-century policing. Instead of relying solely on the federal government for intelligence, many state and local departments are taking the initiative to create their own systems. In this way, intelligence-led policing is crime fighting that is guided by effective intelligence gathering and analysis.[7]

Since the intelligence process starts with information, where information comes from is of some consideration. Information is typically subdivided into two categories: open source and covert. According to Central Intelligence Directive 2/12, the definition of "open source" is "publicly available information (i.e., any member of the public could lawfully obtain the information by request or observation), as well as other unclassified information that has limited public distribution or access." As much as 95 percent of all information is open source. Examples of open source information include:[8]

- Business directories
- Media reports (newspapers, magazines, television, other publications, radio)
- Internet searches, chat rooms, databases, and Internet Web sites
- Telephone directories and people finders
- Commercial information providers
- Credit bureaus
- City, county, and state agencies (public records)
- Court records (unless sealed)

It is important to note that open source information about individuals must meet the criminal predicate requirement to be retained in agency intelligence files. This legal standard will be presented below. Suffice it to say at this point, the key is not the source of information but *what is being retained* by a law enforcement agency.[9] Conversely, covert or "private" information sources include:

- Law enforcement records and reports
- Schools records and reports
- Public utilities records and reports
- Employment records and data
- Banking and financial institutions records and data
- Military records and reports
- Arrest and warrant evidence/information/statements

- Interviews, public contacts, traffic stops, etc.
- Police operations
    - Undercover operatives (confidential source or informant)
    - Physical surveillance (either remotely via videotape or in person)
- Electronic surveillance

One way to appreciate the difference between intelligence reporting and police investigations is to distinguish the goals of each. Investigations are typically based on leads and evidence associated with a particularly defined criminal act. The investigation is designed to identify and apprehend offenders for prosecution. Intelligence collection, conversely, is designed to capture information based on reasonable suspicion of criminal involvement. This intelligence can be used in developing criminal cases, identifying crime trends, and protecting the community by means of intervention, apprehension, and/or target hardening. In this way, while intelligence may lead to criminal prosecutions, it is more often exploratory and more broadly focused than a criminal investigation.[10] This type of reporting is premonitory (advance notice), with prosecution not being the main objective. It is directed toward potential criminal activities, though the reporting of such is typically not expected to meet rigorous standards for formal investigative reporting. They may, however, require focused investigations or tactical responses.

A useful way to line up the key attributes of investigations and those of intelligence is shown in Table 5.1.

The intelligence cycle has five separate but interrelated elements. I will briefly identify and summarize each element. A more detailed explanation will follow below. Before doing so, it is important to consider that all steps of this cycle should be focused on the needs of the end user. The end users can be police administrators,

Table 5.1 Investigation versus Intelligence Distinctions

Key Attribute	Investigation	Intelligence
Function	Crime Driven	Threat Driven
Primary Goal	Arrest and Prosecution	Prevent and Warning
Operational Emphasis	Narrow — on perpetrator	Broad — on potential threat
Orientation	Facts and Evidence to support burden of proof (Court based)	Facts and Probabilities to generate intelligence products (Prevention based)

Copyright, James F. Pastor, 2009.

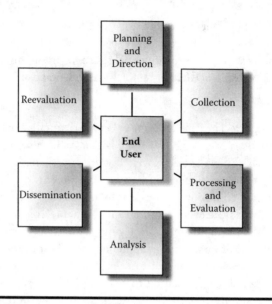

Figure 5.1 Intelligence cycle.

criminal investigators, patrol officers, political leaders, and even the general public. The end users need to embrace the process so that they will participate. Similarly, the end users need to understand both the great potential and the limitations of intelligence operations. The elements of the intelligence cycle are (Figure 5.1):

- Planning and direction: develop incident reporting processes by establishing policies and procedures.
- Collection: develop information and submit it through predetermined channels, where the intelligence personnel receive and process the information.
- Analysis: results in development of intelligence assessments through the application of scientific testing.
- Dissemination: reports are tendered or disseminated according to protocols and guidance.
- Reevaluation: assess how to enhance the process to best counter the threat.

The planning and direction element is the foundation that the entire process is built upon. The functions of this part of the process are to develop and prioritize goals and objectives. As mentioned earlier, goals and objectives must take into account the needs and desires of the end users. It is to provide and then manage resources to meet these goals. While assessing these goals, it may be useful to ask the following questions:

- Why do we need this?
- What resources and guidelines will the unit need to function?

- What will be the operating budget?
- Can we obtain the necessary resources through external sources, such as the legislative process?

In this way, the organizational framework for intelligence is created. This would entail outlining authority and responsibility within the unit, and the placement of the unit within the overall department. From an external perspective, it is critical that partnerships and information-sharing arrangements are formulated. These partnerships can be made with any organization that helps provide resources and/ or actively contributes to the intelligence activities. Each such partnership must have a shared responsibility for operations.

In addition, rules and regulations must also be developed. These must adhere to 28 CFR Part 23. Since statutory requirements form the basis of all intelligence projects, it may be useful to describe key requirements of 28 CFR Part 23.2. The legislative purpose of this law articulates both the need for intelligence and the potential implications for abuse. It states,[11]

> The exposure of such ongoing networks of criminal activity can be aided by the pooling of information about such activities [need]. However, because the collection and exchange of intelligence data necessary to support control of serious criminal activity may represent potential threats to the privacy of individuals to whom such data relates, policy guidelines for federally funded projects are required [abuse].

As a guide to 28 CFR Part 23, the below bulleted items can be viewed as summary requirements. Each of these is required for law enforcement agencies that operate multi-jurisdictional criminal intelligence systems *using federal monies*. Those agencies that do not use federal monies would be exempt from these requirements. However, it is prudent to comply with these guidelines, regardless of whether or not federal monies are used. In any event, the guidelines are:

- Submission and entry of criminal intelligence information
- Secure storage
- Inquiry and search capability
- Controlled dissemination
- Periodic review, validate, and purge process

The second element is the collection component. This provides the raw resources from which the final product is produced. The overall goal of the collection process is to gather information that is accurate, timely, and relevant. The collection component also involves some planning. Typically these relate to questions like, what resources are available to gather information, what available resources would be the most effective, and when would be the best time to deploy those resources?

Information can come from a wide variety of sources and therefore can come in through many different conduits. As mentioned earlier, the information can come from a variety of open sources or it can derive from covert methods. Regardless of the source, the collection of information must be done in a systematic and consistent fashion. Typically the information will be reported in "information" or "activity" reports. These can be done in both hard copy and electronic formats. Some guidelines may serve to enhance the systematic consistency of information.

When possible, each report should address only one subject or event. In this way, each report should be geared toward a specific purpose. Second, each report should typically reflect the statement of one source. Third, the reports should reflect a consistent, clear, and aesthetic format. Fourth, each report should be carefully sourced. Fifth, the reports should segregate background information from collected intelligence. Sixth, the reports should consider the "end user" and strive to contain all critical information the "consumer" needs without superfluous information. Finally, the reports should be carefully phrased to guard against inadvertent disclosure of sensitive sources and/or collection methods.

An excellent example of the development of a standardized reporting system was recently developed by the LAPD's Counter Terrorism and Criminal Intelligence Bureau. This bureau revised the investigative report officers complete for actual or suspected crimes. The report was amended to add a section used to describe different kinds of potential terrorist-related activities. These reports are required when officers observe suspicious activity, whether or not a crime was committed. In order to facilitate standardization, all LAPD officers are trained in the types of suspicious activities to look for. This is based on a 65-item checklist. The checklist includes activities such as conducting surveillance on a government building, trying to acquire explosives, openly espousing extremist views, or abandoning a suspicious package. In this way, the standardized reporting not only tells officers what to look for, it also helps to connect dots that may have been overlooked in the past.[12]

The collection methods not only need to be standardized, they need to be legal. According to 28 CFR Part 23, when an officer has reasonable suspicion that supports the belief that information relates to criminal activity, it may be collected, analyzed, stored, and shared. Of course, the agency shall not include in any criminal intelligence system information that was obtained in violation of any applicable federal, state, or local law or ordinance.[13] A useful way to assess the reasonable suspicion standard is to ask these questions:[14]

- Has the subject committed crimes in the past?
- Is the subject committing or conspiring to commit crime?
- Does the subject have intent (or motivation) to commit crime in the future (but be careful of entrapment!)?

Key operating principles of the legal standards are set out in 28 CFR Part 23.20.[15]

- Reasonable suspicion must exist that an individual is involved in criminal conduct/activity *and* the information collected is relevant to such activity [23.20 (a)]
- Cannot collect or maintain information on political, religious or social views, associations, or activities of any individual or group unless reasonable suspicion exists involving the individual or group in criminal conduct or activity [23.20 (b)]

An example of how these laws are applicable may be relevant in this patrol situation. A police officer observes an individual photographing a bridge. When the individual notices the presence of the police officer, he gets into his car and drives away. The officer pulls behind the individual and notices an inoperable taillight. The officer pulls the vehicle over, notifies the driver of the violation, and engages him in discussion about his actions. If this stop leads to an arrest (as articulated in *Whren v. United States*), courts will not assess the police officers' subjective motivation for making the stop (unless race was motivating factor). If this stop does not lead to an arrest, but the police officer can articulate reasonable suspicion to establish the criminal predicate standard, the information gained by the encounter can be used to open an intelligence file. If the police officer cannot articulate reasonable suspicion, he or she may still be well advised to complete an information report. Consequently, this situation may lead to any of these legal options. The key is to maintain the legal basis for any subsequent action.

Another way to establish a criminal predicate is to assess what is known as a potential threat element (PTE). According to the Department of Homeland Security, PTE is defined as

> "any group or individual in which there are allegations or information indicating a possibility of the unlawful use of force or violence, specifically the utilization of a Weapon of Mass Destruction, against persons or property to intimidate or coerce a government, the civilian population, or any segment thereof, in furtherance of a specific motivation or goal, possibly political or social in nature.[16]

This would be accomplished by articulating motivations involving political, religious, racial, environmental, or special interest extremism. The key element is to assess the potential for a group or individual to commit terrorist acts.[17] The specific elements of PTE are:[18]

- Any group or individual
- Allegations or information
- Unlawful use of force or violence, specifically WMD
- Against persons or property
- Intimidate or coerce government or civilians

■ Specific motivation or goal (political, religious, racial, or social)

Because of the rather complicated legal constraints, it is highly recommended that all agency personnel receive training as intelligence gatherers. This is because intelligence collection has many legal and administrative pitfalls. Some typical concerns relating to intelligence collection are:

■ Maintenance of noncrime information
■ Evidence of political, sexual, and racial materials
■ Constitutional violations (association, religious, social, etc.)
■ Trespass/invasion of privacy violations
■ Secrecy, spying, and entrapment
■ Failure to timely purge intelligence files

In addition to the potential for constitutional and tort claims, two federal statutes should be considered. One is the Federal Privacy Act and the other is the Freedom of Information Act (most states have similar statutes, so it is advisable to check these as well). The Federal Privacy Act allows an individual to review almost all federal files (but does not specifically apply to state records) pertaining to him- or herself. It places restrictions on the disclosure of personally identifiable information, and specifies that no secret record systems on individuals may be kept by the federal government. In addition, it compels the government to reveal its information sources. While criminal records are generally exempt, it requires the information to be:

1. Accurate
2. Complete
3. Relevant
4. Current

The Freedom of Information Act provides that any person has a right, enforceable in court, of access to federal agency records, except to the extent that such records (or portions of the records) are protected by a specific exemption. In order to obtain these records, the individual must follow proper procedures and must reasonably describe records being sought. Once a proper request is made, the agency has 10 days to respond to the records request. This applies to records only, not tangible items or objects.

The third element is the processing and evaluation component. In this phase, the information is organized, evaluated, and stored. These functions are accomplished so that the information can be brought to the refinement stage when needed. The goals of this phase are threefold:

1. Evaluate the information to determine its reliability, validity, and value.
2. Sort and organize the information into categories and into a logical order.
3. File the information so that it can be retrieved at a later time.

Proper filing of information is critical because the system must have adequate security to prevent unauthorized access. It also must be open enough to allow the flow of information to the end users. Certain requirements relating to the filing and safeguarding of information must be maintained. These include administrative, technical, and physical safeguards (including audit trails). These safeguards must be adopted to insure against unauthorized access and against intentional or unintentional disclosure. Further, the information shall be labeled to indicate levels of sensitivity, levels of confidence, and the identity of submitting agencies and control officials.[19] Additional requirements imposed on the agency ensure that all information that is retained by the agency has relevancy and importance.

Once collected, the information cannot simply sit in a file for infinity. The agency must periodically review the information, and destroy any information that is misleading, obsolete, or otherwise unreliable. All information retained as a result of this audit must reflect the name of the reviewer, date of review, and explanation of the decision to retain. If changes were made pursuant to these audits, the agency shall notify any recipient agencies of such changes that involve errors or corrections. Finally, information retained in the system must be reviewed and validated for continuing compliance with system submission criteria before the expiration of its retention period, which in no event shall be longer than five years.[20]

As a summary of the relevant maintenance of records requirements, it is advisable to set policies and procedures designed to:

- Ensure physical security of files
- Segregate "classes" of files
  1. Active investigations
  2. Intelligence files
  3. Temporary/working files
- Establish an official custodian of record files
- Limit the information placed in each file according to the type or reason for the file (Figure 5.2)

The fourth phase of the intelligence process is the analysis component. It is often said that analysis is the heart and soul of the intelligence cycle. It is the refinement

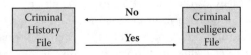

Figure 5.2 Criminal history records versus criminal intelligence records.

of the raw information into a usable product. The goals and objectives of the analysis component are to provide additional meaning to raw information by linking individual pieces of raw information into a cohesive intelligence assessment. In essence, the analysis should answer this key question: What does the collected information mean? There are various techniques used to facilitate this analysis. These include time event charting, link analysis, crime analysis, criminal profiling, and behavioral evidence analysis. These analytical assessments can be quite sophisticated. As such, an explanation of these techniques is beyond the scope of this book.

The fifth phase of the intelligence process is the dissemination component. As critical as the merits of the analysis are, it stands to reason that intelligence that is not shared has little value. Said another way, intelligence is worthless if it is not timely disseminated to those who need it or can use it. Hence, the dissemination component is the distribution of the final product. The end product should consider the following factors:

- Identify the target audience;
- Convey information clearly and in a manner understandable to the target audience;
- Provide a time parameter where the information provided is actionable;
- Provide a recommendation for action; and
- Allow for feedback

Like every other phase of the intelligence cycle, the dissemination of information has legal standards and consequences. When assessing whether or not to disseminate the information, consider these critical questions:

- Is the request legitimate?
- Can the requestor be trusted?
- Can the information be legally released?

In order to guide this decision, the agency must establish written definitions for dissemination. These relate to the "need to know" and "right to know" standards. Generally, dissemination is appropriate only where there is a need to know and a right to know the information in the performance of a law enforcement activity. In addition, criminal intelligence information should only be disseminated to law enforcement authorities who shall agree to follow procedures regarding information receipt, maintenance, security, and dissemination that are consistent with these principles.[21] Significantly, the "Third Agency Rule" ensures that any recipient of intelligence is prohibited from sharing the information with another (third) agency. This affords some degree of control and accountability, yet may be waived by the originating agency when appropriate.[22] Finally, the most relevant exception to these dissemination requirements is when dissemination is allowed to a government official or to any other individual, when necessary, to avoid imminent danger to life or property.[23] Of course, the spirit of this exception is to allow dissemination of information to private sector entities, such as security personnel, when an imminent danger exists.

In addition, the agency is responsible for establishing the existence of an inquirer's need to know and right to know the information being requested either through inquiry or by delegation of this responsibility to a properly trained participating agency. This process must also be subject to routine inspection and audit procedures established by the agency. In the event dissemination of information is allowed, the agency must maintain records indicating who has been given information, the reason for release of the information, and the date of each such dissemination.[24]

The reevaluation component is the quality control aspect of the cycle. The goals and objectives of this phase are as inferred from the title. The agency should seek out and obtain feedback from the end user and each individual component of the process. This is designed to improve the end product. This information should process feedback into a usable form for the planning and direction component. Each component must critique the information provided to them in order to determine what can be done to make the process more efficient. In addition, each component part and each end user must critique the information to assess these questions:

- Was the information useful?
- Was the information timely?
- Was the information in a form/format that was easily understood?
- How can the end product be improved?

Having reviewed the intelligence process in some detail, it may be useful to assess the types of intelligence and their respective purposes. The distinction between types of intelligence is generally based on where the information was obtained from, and how the intelligence product is to be used. The initial level of intelligence is known as indicative intelligence. Indicative intelligence is essentially information from a variety of sources that provides a view from street level, often for immediate enforcement action. It is the most common type of intelligence activity in policing in that it requires minimal resources. Examples of this intelligence may indicate the presence of new criminal groups or existing groups planning new criminal activities. It is geared toward specific criminal activity with the immediate goal of neutralizing it. Hence, the perspective is generally short ranged. This is ideal for identifying gangs, drug dealers, known criminals, sex offenders, etc. Key features of this approach include being used to:

- Build data files/dossiers
- Provide front-end analysis of a problem
- Assess certain pre-incident indicators
- Provide basic data/information about specific suspects
- Provide investigative leads, direction, and support

Tactical intelligence is information developed by law enforcement through case research and analysis of direct sources such as surveillance, countersurveillance, covert operations, informants, and eavesdropping. This type of intelligence is operational and ongoing. This information is designed to generate targets and investigations by collating and assessing information. It seeks to identify key problem areas, suspects, and/or groups. It may also be developed through analysis of indicative intelligence.

Strategic intelligence is the culmination of both indicative intelligence and tactical intelligence, providing a broader perspective. It is a more thorough examination of data and events. It is used to evaluate and analyze critical issues, factors, and organizations, such as street gangs or terrorist groups. It involves a predictive component by identifying evolving or emerging trends and patterns. Because of its strategic value, this type of intelligence is often used for policy-making decisions, operational planning, and crime prevention strategies. It can also be used as a management evaluation tool or as an "internal consultant."

Finally, evidentiary intelligence is designed to foster criminal prosecutions. In this way, it is similar to traditional criminal investigations. Since the information may be used in court, procedural and constitutional collection requirements will take on a heightened sense of legitimacy. Of course, any information obtained in violation of the law will not be admitted into the trial. In addition, the sources and methods of the intelligence gathering process may be scrutinized by the court system. Consequently, as with any other investigation, it is necessary to avoid any and all "shortcuts" throughout the intelligence process. One never knows what case will result in prosecution. The best practice, of course, is to perform each intelligence case file as if it may appear in court.

The graph in Figure 5.3 developed by Ratcliffe provides an excellent illustration of the value of intelligence. Start by looking at the "intelligence" image. This depicts an attempt to interpret the environment. In this sense, environment means the information coming from the target location. This could be a particular group or community, or a larger city, and even the world. Sometimes this information could involve incidents or threats. Sometimes the information could be trends or ideologies. Whatever the source and type of information, the goal of intelligence is

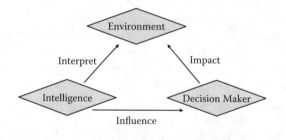

Figure 5.3 3i-Intelligence-led police model. Adapted from J.W. Radcliffe, *Intelligence-Led Policing,* **2008.**

to make sense out of an issue. Thus, while any number of factors may contribute to the issue at hand, intelligence is designed to help the end user understand these factors. Similarly, this understanding is also designed to influence the policies of decision makers. If the intelligence is an accurate understanding of the environment, the policy maker is benefited with an assessment that can help frame appropriate decisions. On the other hand, if the intelligence is not accurate, then the decision maker will be hampered by erroneous information. The policy decision is then used to impact the environment. Consequently, the likelihood of making favorable policy decisions is a function of the accuracy of the intelligence.

Surveillance Technologies

This section of the chapter is devoted to what I consider the "other" facet of intelligence-led policing. In some ways the technologies we will discuss are beyond the scope of what is typically considered ILP. This is one of the reasons why I believe the term "intelligence-led policing" does not accurately reflect overall trends in policing. As such, we will discuss some initiatives within policing that go beyond the notion of ILP. A brief list of these technologies includes, but is not limited to:

- Networked camera systems
- Remote traffic enforcement
- Predictive crime mapping
- Identification systems
- Access control systems
- Facial recognition systems
- Infrared/night vision systems
- Explosives detecting scanners
- Global positioning systems
- License plate readers
- Sensor systems
- Fusion centers

The scope and extent of technologies used within policing are substantial. In many ways, the federal government is leading the way toward these technologies. As of 2006, the U.S. government had spent over $3 billion on antiterrorism technologies.[25] The level of technology is so widespread, this chapter can only highlight certain key aspects. As such, I do not pretend to provide a comprehensive analysis of policing technologies. Instead, my desire is to provide a sense of how policing is changing in relation to the dual threats of extremist and terroristic violence. The impact of technology on policing can be summarized in the following quote from Ron Huberman, a leader in the implementation of technology with the Chicago Police Department. He pointedly stated,[26] technology enabled our troops to succeed because it acted as a force-multiplier. It allowed our armed forces to have more eyes, more ears and to be in more places than they otherwise could be were it not for that technology.

As briefly described in the Attributes of Intelligence-Led Policing section, the most obvious connection between technology and terrorism is fusion centers. In essence, fusion centers are designed to bring information from various sources, assess and analyze this information, and provide insight and direction to police policies and operations. As a concept, fusion centers are designed to bring together representatives from all aspects of government, including federal, state, and local. The fusion center framework is built around the National Operations Center (NOC), which serves as the nation's nerve center for information sharing and domestic incident management. This center provides real-time situational awareness and monitoring of the homeland, and coordinates incidents and response activities. In conjunction with the Office of Intelligence and Analysis, the NOC also issues advisories and bulletins concerning threats to homeland security, as well as specific protective measures. The NOC operates 24 hours a day, seven days a week, 365 days a year, coordinating information sharing to help deter, detect, and prevent terrorist acts and to manage domestic incidents. Information on domestic incident management is shared with emergency operations centers at all levels through the Homeland Security Information Network (HSIN).[27]

The NOC is comprised of two sections based on the clearance level of its personnel. The "high side" is occupied by agents and analysts from every federal intelligence agency including the FBI, Secret Service, and the Defense Intelligence Agency. Assignees to the high side must possess Top Secret security clearance. They analyze intelligence that is gathered from every corner of the globe. The "low side" consists of law enforcement personnel who are "detailed" (temporarily assigned) from agencies such as FEMA, National Oceanic and Atmospheric Administration (NOAA), Environmental Protection Agency (EPA), CDC, Immigration and Customs Enforcement (ICE), and numerous law enforcement agencies including LAPD, New Jersey State, U.S. Capital Police, Florida, and Chicago. Each "detailee" must possess the minimum of Secret clearance.[28]

While detailees typically view this as an important assignment, the activity level often can be minimal. During periods of inactivity, most officers produce a daily intelligence briefing report for their agency. During situations of local or national concern, the detailee acts as a liaison between DHS and their department or agency. Most detailed officers are employed for four to five weeks. For some of this period, the detailees spend their time getting familiarized with the system and handling administrative requirements. The officers and agents assigned to the NOC also communicate with fusion centers around the country.

As an overview, it may be useful to have some basic data about fusion centers. There are approximately 58 fusion centers around the country.[29] While many, if not most, were designed to address terrorism, according to a report by the Congressional Research Service, approximately 40 percent of fusion centers focus on "all-crime."[30] This means that these fusion centers are not limited to only terrorism prevention. They are also used to address "normal" crime.

In this "all crime" approach, centers like Chicago's Crime Prevention Information Center (CPIC) gather intelligence from national, state, and local levels to deal with all criminal activity during lulls in threats of terrorism. This is rather typical. Since we have not had a significant terrorist incident on American soil in years, it stands to reason that fusion centers will expand their scope to address "normal" crime. Indeed, I view this approach as a way to enhance the practices of the fusion center. Providing the "all crime" approach serves to develop the operational capacity of these fusion centers. By addressing crime issues, these fusion centers are serving as a resource for police agencies. They are seeking to become part of the police culture. Like all cultures (and operations) it takes time to demonstrate their value. It requires time and effort to be relevant. As these fusion centers expand and perfect their operations, they will be seen more and more as a resource that street level police officers can rely on.

For example, the Indiana Intelligence Fusion Center's approach is illustrative of my assertions. According to Indiana Code 10-19-10-2, the duties of the Indiana Intelligence Fusion Center are established to gather "criminal intelligence information and other information to support governmental agencies and private organizations in detecting, preventing, investigating, and responding to criminal and terrorist activity in compliance with applicable state and federal laws and regulations."[31] Hence, the legislative language for this fusion center specifically provided applicability for both criminal and terrorist activity. Indeed, given my premise that extremist violence—including gangs—will greatly increase, the attention given to criminal activity by fusion centers is appropriate.

In my mind, the key is that the information flow to and from the "end users" is both timely and accurate. Critical end users include street police officers, security firms, and corporations—particularly those who have a role in the critical infrastructure. This concern was mentioned due to the fact that a majority of state fusion centers are failing to receive critical infrastructure information from companies in the private sector. This concern was reflected in a recent report by the Congressional Research Service (CRS). The report stated that fusion centers have been unsuccessful in partnering with private sector owner-operators. This was due to a "lack of appreciation" of the information they could supply, failure to identify the infrastructures most susceptible to risk, and a lack of guidelines on how fusion centers and private companies should work together. The article noted that businesses are also hesitant to disclose sensitive information to fusion centers, and that the amount of information to divulge and analyze can be intimidating. To address this disconnect in information flow, the CRS report recommended that a national plan be implemented to bridge communication and information sharing between businesses and fusion centers.[32]

As can be inferred from this discussion, fusion centers may represent a "double-edged sword." On one hand, counterterrorism professionals typically view the network of intelligence fusion centers as an important tool for helping all levels of government collect and exchange information on potential criminal and terrorist activity. On the other hand, civil libertarians say they conflict with citizens' rights to privacy. An interesting interplay between these two principles was noted in certain legal disputes. For example, in Virginia, government proceedings and documents are open to public view under the state's Freedom of Information Act (FOIA). These requests must be honored unless government officials can demonstrate a reason for an exemption, such as a critical matter of public safety. Another law, the Government Data Collections and Disseminations Practices Act (GDCDPA), bans secret databases and forbids the government from using personal data for purposes other than that for which it was originally collected. GDCDPA further guarantees citizens the right to query government agencies to find out what personal data is held by the agency. This privacy act also requires that agencies must correct any errors found in their database. Interestingly, in their Fusion Center Guidelines, issued in 2006, the FBI and the DHS provide that fusion centers should leverage and "obtain access to an array of databases and systems." The guidelines list possible data assets, but cited as examples only publicly held assets, such as state motor vehicle databases and government data exchanges. Earlier this year, however, the *Washington Post* reported that state fusion centers contract with private data brokers to obtain broad access not only to public records but also to private information, such as unpublished cell phone numbers, or data held by private credit agencies.[33] Consequently, there is some measure of controversy with fusion centers. I contend, however, that they are critical to the new policing model.

While much more can be said about fusion centers, suffice it to assert that these technological- and intelligence-driven approaches are substantial. They are not going away. Indeed, these centers will be increasingly seen as a valuable—even indispensable—tool to combat extremism and terrorism. That being said, the value of these centers is only as good as the information they receive. An old adage seems relevant: garbage in, garbage out! The information gathering process described in the previous section is a key to obtaining useful and valuable information. So is the information that is obtained from cameras and other technological systems. With this being established we will now present certain other technologies and attempt to "connect the dots" as they relate to the *Public Safety Policing* model.

The most obvious technologies being introduced to address crime and terrorism are the installations of cameras into the public domain. Cameras in the private sector have been commonplace for decades. The private sector began using cameras (closed-circuit television [CCTV]) in the early 1960s in banks and commercial buildings. By the 1970s CCTV was deployed in hospitals and all-night convenience stores. In the 1980s video recorders were introduced, and in the 1990s digital technology followed.[34] In contemporary society, estimates of an astonishing 30 million cameras exist in the United States, shooting about four billion hours of footage every week.[35] While cameras have been used in the security industry for decades, the introduction of camera systems in public environments is a relatively new development.

The first generation of cameras installed in public environments involved wide-angle cameras that were targeted toward crime hot spots. The second generation of cameras brought remote access by using a joystick and zoom capabilities. The third generation uses software for facial and license plate recognition, and for motion detection systems.[36]

It can be argued that some technologies, such as predictive and behavioral based systems, constitute the fourth generation of security systems. The scope and implications of this development still remain to be seen. However, I contend that "the sky's the limit" as it relates to security and camera systems. Stated another way, we are only at the front end of the trend toward public camera and surveillance systems.

In considering this assertion, please take note of the level of camera systems in the United Kingdom. The United Kingdom has approximately 75 cities with about 1.5 million public environment cameras.[37] In total, it is estimated that over 4 million cameras have been "networked" throughout the United Kingdom.[38] One city, London, is viewed as the most "surveilled" city in world! Why? I contend the answer is three words: Irish Republican Army (IRA). The IRA has actively prosecuted its direct action for decades. Because of this violence, the British have innovated to defend the public safety of its citizens. One key innovation has been the widespread implementation of cameras. Years later, this system of public surveillance is so pervasive that some view it as a "fifth" utility, joining water, gas, electricity, and telephones as an "essential public service."[39] Indeed, the July 7, 2005, train bombers were identified through camera systems. So were the individuals who planned the July 21, 2005, and the June 2007 attempted bombings. Many of the offenders were identified and arrested, at least partly based on camera systems. British police searched more than 18,000 hours of camera footage to track down and arrest the plot's operatives.[40]

The camera networking system in the United Kingdom is seen as the "gold standard" for surveillance camera systems. It is drawing increasing attention in both the United States and elsewhere in Europe, including France, where President Nicolas Sarkozy has announced his own "vast plan" to deploy CCTV cameras on public transport. In Paris, a network of about 2,000 cameras protects the city's subway system and suburban train network. Similarly, New York City officials intend to place cameras aboard hundreds of buses in Manhattan and install 1,000 cameras along with 3,000 motion sensors to protect the city's subway and commuter rail stations. In Germany, the failed train-bombing plot in the summer of 2007 convinced officials to increase the number of surveillance cameras protecting train stations, harbors, and airports.[41]

This approach is gaining prominence in the United States. Consider that the Chicago Police Department is developing a networked system of cameras that will enable an officer in the squad car or the dispatch center to monitor such diverse conditions as gunshots on street corners to unattended briefcases within a protected facility. The implementation of this camera system, dubbed "Operation Disruption," involves cameras outfitted with night vision and digital optical lenses that can pan 360 degrees to zoom in on activity as far as two city blocks. It will record activity 24 hours a day. Officers can operate the cameras from remote locations, using a monitor and a joystick.[42] The project was trumpeted as a central part of Chicago's response to the threat of terrorism, as well as an effort to reduce the crime rate in the city. According to Ron Huberman, then emergency management executive director, the video images from the cameras will be instantly available to the police dispatch center, which has the ability to tilt or zoom the cameras to react to the events on the street. Huberman adds,[43]

> what we're doing is a totally new concept, this is a very innovative way to harness the power of cameras. It's going to take us to a whole new level.

Surely many more cities will implement CCTV systems sooner than later. Of course, private firms have used cameras and other security technologies within their protected facilities for decades. My point is that such technologies are now being used by public police agencies in the public way. This is a qualitative change that will change the way policing agencies operate. According to Chicago Mayor Richard M. Daley, "Cameras are the equivalent of hundreds of sets of eyes ... they're the next best thing to having police officers stationed at every potential trouble spot."[44] This assertion seems to have been widely accepted. The below list illustrates the extent of camera systems in public locations—which is only a partial list of cities that have done so.[45] Consequently, coming to "street corner" near you—is a camera![46]

- New York, NY
- Redlands, CA
- Houston, TX
- Columbia, SC
- Dallas, TX
- Boston, MA
- Stockton, CA
- Tampa, FL
- Virginia Beach, VA
- Palm Springs, CA
- Washington, DC
- Brentwood, CA
- Crown Point, IN
- Sacramento, CA
- Moline, IL
- Phoenix, AZ

- San Francisco, CA
- New Orleans, LA
- Baltimore, MD
- Bellingham, WA
- St. Louis, MO
- Chicago, IL
- Calumet City, IL
- Merrillville, IN
- Gary, IN
- Cicero, IL
- Chelsea, MA
- Louisville, KY
- Milwaukee, WI

While this list is by no means exhaustive, it is reflective of a larger trend. Even small towns, like Calumet City, Illinois, are using surveillance to record video images from highly visible, bulletproof cameras. These images are monitored in the police communication center.[47] Similarly, in Gary, Indiana, city officials approved $295,000 to purchase six camera "pods" equipped with ShotSpotter technology, which will connect to the police dispatch center and then to laptop computers in the squad cars. This technology is designed to detect the sound—and location—of gunshots where dispatchers can pinpoint for police response.[48]

West Palm Beach, Florida, implemented a wireless video surveillance network in several neighborhoods. Initially, 13 video cameras were installed in areas that have high crime rates. The cameras were connected to police headquarters, allowing officers to look for prostitution, drug deals, and gangs. The cameras also feature a wireless access point that allows police officers to look at camera feeds from laptops in their cars. The initial program was so successful that the police department is launching "City-Cam," which will greatly increase the number of cameras. This program includes training and supervision of volunteers. These volunteers will monitor the cameras and notify police of any crimes. The city has partnered with businesses and homeowner associations to garner the necessary funding to purchase these cameras.[49] Police in Boca Raton, Hallandale Beach, and Fort Lauderdale have also spent hundreds of thousands of dollars in recent years to mount cameras on roofs, utility poles, and buildings in order to monitor parking lots, shopping centers, and other areas where crimes occur.[50]

In Seattle, Mayor Greg Nickels proposed an $850,000 budget for a one-year trial of public cameras. These cameras are monitored and controlled by the police, enabling them to tilt, zoom, or pan for viewing specific locations. Video is recorded 24 hours a day and stored for two weeks. It can also be kept longer if it is needed in an investigation.[51] Similarly, in Stockton, California, 24 cameras were installed to record and transfer images via a fiber optic line to a security monitoring center where they are monitored by security personnel. Police and city officials lauded the security cameras as the "next big thing for law enforcement," because they allow police to be aware of numerous locations simultaneously, without having to pay for manpower. In line with the thesis of this book, Stockton Police Chief Mark Herder stated,[52]

> society has changed to where it's become more acceptable for police to monitor key public areas ... because people want to know they are safe.

In New York, spurred by 9/11 security concerns, the video surveillance industry is growing at a rate of 15–20 percent a year. The New York Police Department (NYPD) monitors at least 200 cameras surveying public places, plus 5,000 cameras in public housing developments. These government camera systems, however, are dwarfed by privately owned cameras. The ACLU calls this the "little brother" phenomenon. They note increases in private cameras—that are publicly visible—in three locations (Chelsea, Times Square, and the lower East Side) from 1998 to 2004. In 1998, these locations had 67, 98, and 21 cameras, respectively. By 2004, cameras at these locations increased to 368, 258, and 125, respectively.[53] These camera systems did not include the New York Metropolitan Transportation Authority, which installed more than 1,000 surveillance cameras, 3,000 motion detectors, and an integrated access control system since 2002.[54] New York has also installed cameras on at least 400 buses, and 70 cameras in subway stations.[55] Since these camera systems are designed to reduce the threat of terrorism, it may be interesting to note that the NYPD reported 22 bomb threats and 32 intelligence leads related to subway bomb attack plots. This was for only a little more than two months in the year 2007.[56]

Newark is the first major city to integrate an assortment of technologies on a large scale. Newark currently has 111 cameras installed and plans to add more technology. This includes a new citywide broadband wireless network that allows police officers to make police reports from their vehicles. By the end of 2008, the city intends to have an audio sensor system installed that is capable of determining where gunshots were fired.[57]

In another futuristic arrangement, city officials and a private technology company are working together to make Hoboken, New Jersey, the first city in the United States to have a citywide wireless audio/visual system. The Office of Emergency Management and Hoboken-based PackeTalk have set up 75 wireless locations around the city, linking over 50 surveillance cameras around town. PackeTalk is also testing a community alert loudspeaker system that will be linked through the wireless network. The speaker system will allow emergency officials to provide localized information to different areas of the city during a crisis. PackeTalk officials said that the system can be securely accessed from a remote laptop. The network is encrypted and protected by a variety of security measures, including fingerprint recognition software. Additionally, since the system relies on its own infrastructure, it will not be impacted by a systems crash at an Internet service provider or telecommunications company.[58]

As this arrangement illustrates, an interesting yet intrusive enhancement includes audio capabilities to camera technology. I believe that "audio intelligence" will increase as more people adopt network video systems. Audio can expand a system's coverage beyond a camera's field of view, alerting camera operators of an audio alarm or audible request for help. Further, intelligent audio solutions have the ability to instruct a pan-tilt-zoom or dome camera to provide a visual of the area where the audio originated from. Audio can also be used by security personnel to communicate with visitors or intruders, alerting them that security is on the way. More advanced technology will even allow audio surveillance systems to detect tone of voice or the use of certain words that are generally a precursor to violent incidents.[59]

In an extensive—possibly unprecedented—operation in May 2008, Washington, D.C. launched a new system that will link thousands of city-owned surveillance cameras. The D.C. Homeland Security and Emergency Management Agency will monitor the closed-circuit video systems run by nine city agencies, including the Transportation Department and the D.C. Housing Authority. In its initial phase, the program will include 4,500 cameras installed in sensitive areas around the city, including the areas around schools and government buildings. The D.C. Police Department will not be able to directly access the new system, but the monitoring office will have the ability to transmit video to police if a crime is detected. Officials hope that the new system will increase efficiency, as the current system requires Homeland Security and Emergency Management to formally request camera feeds from other agencies.[60]

The operators who monitor the cameras will be aided by analytic software that can alert operators to dangerous situations. The completed system will link over 5,200 cameras under the Video Interoperability for Public Safety (VIPS) program, which will be fully operable by 2009.[61] To get a better sense of the scope and sophistication of this system, the following cameras (and their locations) are expected to be integrated into the VIPS program, linking a total of 1,388 cameras in outside environments and 3,874 cameras inside buildings:[62]

- DC Housing Authority: 720
- DC public schools: 3,452
- Department of Parks and Recreation: 181
- Department of Transportation: 131
- Metropolitan Police Department: 92
- Department of Corrections: 218
- Property Management/Protective Services Division: 468
- DC Homeland Security: 4

On a smaller scale, Baltimore revealed a pilot video surveillance program in downtown areas through the CityWatch program. Security personnel serve to monitor images from over 400 cameras throughout Baltimore and five of its public housing projects at the Atrium Control Center. Many of the permanent cameras and mobile cameras are atop light poles and provide around-the-clock surveillance via images and video. There also are five police monitoring stations that receive wireless video and image data from easily deployable, in-box cameras. Suspicious activity is monitored by staff members, who can dispatch police to the scene and brief the officers on the events. The program boasts that several arrests have been made by video surveillance.[63]

Similarly, the Department of Homeland Security (DHS) awarded funds to the city of Springdale, Ohio, for the installation of surveillance equipment around the Tri-County Mall. DHS awarded the money after designating the country's shopping malls as high-risk areas, due to the high volumes of traffic and scant security. With the funds, Springdale police plan to install the cameras close to several intersections around the mall. These cameras are capable of identifying the car and license plate number of any crime suspect. "We are going to record all the events on these cameras. We are not going to monitor it," said Captain William Hafer, Springdale's assistant police chief. "This is not a Big Brother thing. This is strictly an investigative tool."[64] This statement illustrates that this arrangement has a critical deficiency. The fact that the cameras will not be monitored means that they will only have value *after* the incident. This is consistent with two themes: lack of resources to conduct the monitoring and privacy concerns. As will be fleshed out in detail later, these dual deficiencies must be resolved or any "security" provided by the cameras will be illusory.

The impact of cameras is also seen at large public events. For example, surveillance police cameras across Denver nearly quadrupled for the Democratic National Convention (DNC). Now those cameras are taking aim at daily crime. Denver police used 13 cameras before the DNC convention came to town. The convention resulted in the acquisition of an additional 50 cameras. The cameras cost about $25,000 each. Each has a range of about a city block and can zoom in with great clarity, Senator Martinez said, and he added, "We'll redeploy cameras ... to high-crime areas," in part based on "calls for service." Police plan to use civilians to monitor the cameras so they do not tie up officers. Typically one person will monitor the cameras. Each camera digitally records information 24 hours a day and stores the data for up to 30 days.[65]

In Dallas, the police department launched a pilot project involving the installation of video surveillance cameras in the busy Deep Ellum area of the city. After just four months of operation, the project was credited with significantly reducing the number of crimes in the area. Thereafter, the police department sought to expand the program to install a wireless video surveillance system in the central business district. The goal of these cameras was to reduce crime in hot spots by 30 percent. In January 2007, the new system was deployed, covering about 30 percent of the downtown area with around-the-clock monitoring. The functionality of this system allows operators to change the direction of the cameras. The system also allows officers to redeploy cameras as needed to increase monitoring capabilities at special events or in other downtown locations. Based on these results, the police department now plans to increase the number of cameras deployed around the city by threefold.[66]

Other cities are using cameras for both crime deterrence and enforcement. For example, Washington, D.C., uses infrared cameras to scan license plates to identify drivers with outstanding parking tickets, and the city is considering three different parking enforcement systems.[67] Chicago has installed cameras in at least 30 intersections for red light enforcement, and has over 2,000 cameras linked to the Emergency Command Center.[68]

Similar technology on a smaller scale was installed in Merrillville, Indiana. Police Chief John Shelhart presented a plan to install mobile cameras equipped with speed monitors at stop signs or along streets to take photos of passing vehicles that fail to stop or fail to obey the speed limit. The camera would take a photo of the license plate and fine the registered owner. Since the police chief noted that they were 20 officers short on their allocated personnel, he emphasized that the agency did not have the time to "catch traffic violators." As is the typical "sales pitch" for cameras, the police chief downplayed the notion of "Big Brother," and instead focused on "increasing safety."[69]

The city of Manchester, England, has installed automatic number plate recognition cameras, which will take pictures of about 600,000 cars that travel through the city each day. Police officials believe the photos will help fight terrorism, crime, and car theft. The system works as follows: After a camera snaps a picture of a car, it records its license plate number, color, and the time. This information is then sent to a central computer, which stores it for five years. The information is also checked against data contained in the Police National Computer, a license database, and other police intelligence databases. This system can detect stolen automobiles, search for cars driven by terrorists or other criminals, and even locate people who have not paid their car tax or insurance.[70]

When one considers interfacing public and private camera systems, the ability to "connect" approximately 30 million cameras used in the private sector with those being installed in the public sector, the impact of these "intelligence" sources would be substantial. Imagine if these cameras were interfaced, and then feed in "real time" to police or public safety personnel as they approach the scene. This is the breakthrough approach that many cities are trying to achieve. The advertised features of this technology are diverse and substantial:[71]

- Real-time view and archived video playback from all surveillance cameras
- Tracking of global positioning system (GPS)-enabled vehicles and personnel
- Monitoring of alarms and tracking of targets using a map-and-floor plan interface both in-house and in the field
- Securely delivers live or stored video images to mobile devices
- Enables responding personnel on foot patrol or in a vehicle to request specific views of any camera

- Enables responding personnel to remotely control the functions of any camera independent of the command center
- Enables responding personnel to retrieve archived data independent of the command center
- Enables the command center to "bookmark" archived data for retrieval by the responding personnel
- Employs a graphical user interface enabling responding personnel to call up and display maps, floor plans, and alarm points on his or her mobile device
- Enables management to set access permissions for remote devices and users

The protection of critical infrastructure is an important consideration to both intelligence-led policing and surveillance technologies. By way of example, the following arrangements illustrate where technology is being used to bolster the security of critical sites. For instance, intelligent surveillance cameras are being implemented around the port city of Richmond, California, to deter both terrorists and copper thieves. These include 82 cameras at the port and 34 in high-crime areas. Each camera can be programmed to detect suspicious activities, known as "exceptions." For example, if somebody jumps a fence or is loitering, the exception will signal an alarm. The alarm alerts security officials that there is something they may want to investigate. The video footage can be monitored in real time, so authorities can witness a crime while it is occurring.[72] In addition, the Transportation Security Administration (TSA) is running a test at a North Carolina ferry terminal of a 21-foot-high arch-like machine that shoots low-intensity x-rays at cars as they pass through. The technology, called backscatter x-ray, is in use at several airports to screen passengers.[73]

Similarly, radiation detection devices are being used at seaports. The purpose of these devices is to scan cargo containers for materials that could be used to construct a nuclear device or "dirty bomb." The scanners provide a graphic visual profile of a container, activating an alarm if radioactive materials are present. The devices are already operating at the 22 largest ports in the country, which handle 98 percent of all cargo that enters the country by sea. Congress mandated a goal of scanning 100 percent of cargo by 2012. Customs officials are working to make other security improvements to complement the radiation portals. In addition, the main gate of the harbor is being reconfigured to reduce the number of inbound lanes, each of which will be monitored by a radiation detector.[74]

The Washington State Patrol is testing a program for the state's ferry system in which all the vehicles loaded onto the ferries will have their license plates read by the Automatic License Plate Recognition System. The readers run the data from the plates against listings of current "amber alerts," stolen automobiles, and individuals wanted for crimes. It also assesses whether the plates are wanted on DHS' "terror watch list." The pilot program has been launched in Seattle. If successful, it will be introduced throughout the entire Washington State ferry service. In addition to this system, security is also being beefed up throughout the British Columbia ferry system, as fences and closed-circuit security cameras are being installed at high-traffic terminals.[75]

A similar technology, but in a different environment, was recently implemented at the University of Minnesota in Minneapolis. This technology allows security guards to better monitor activity at a campus bridge through near-real-time footage. Using 11 cameras positioned along the bridge and the surrounding steam tunnels, a software program detects aberrant movement on the bridge, such as people standing alone or objects left unattended. These and other aberrant indicators will alert security guards to pay attention. Approximately 1,000 cameras on the Twin Cities and Duluth campuses are monitored 24 hours a day. In the past, employees have struggled to monitor so many cameras. With the "intelligence software" capabilities, monitoring these cameras is much more efficient and less labor intensive.[76] This technology is consistent with research in explosives detection and facial recognition software, which can pinpoint distress in a crowd to hone in on erratic body movements.[77]

An illustration of the use of infrared technology can be shown by the Reno, Nevada, Police Department. In 1997, this agency acquired four helicopters, and night vision goggles and sensors from the military (from the 1033 Program discussed in the last chapter). In addition to other functions, each helicopter is equipped with 30-million-candlepower spotlights and global positioning systems. These technologies formed the basis of the Regional Aviation Enforcement Unit (RAVEN), which is designed to respond to critical incidents—and to enhance police operations during evening hours.[78]

Examples of even more cutting-edge technologies are making news. For example, the Transportation Security Administration will test new heat-sensing cameras that can be used to screen people at a train or bus station without requiring a mandatory wait at a security checkpoint. These cameras can be placed anywhere in a station, where they will be able to screen people as they walk by. The cameras can take a thermal image of the body from up to 20 yards away. This image highlights materials colder than body temperature, signifying objects such as metals, plastics, and ceramics. Objects that fit certain criteria will set off a red light, prompting a screener to do a more thorough search. Of course, some people are skeptical of such cameras. The typical concern is that the technology is not advanced enough and will result in the search of innocent people. "Lots of things look like guns or explosives. It's going to result in people being needlessly searched or worse," said Barry Steinhardt of the American Civil Liberties Union. These concerns will be addressed more fully in Chapter 10. Despite the concerns, the manufacturer hopes that the cameras will eventually be used in a variety of settings, including military bases, arenas, and landmarks.[79] Of course, if the technology is proven effective, detecting only actual threats, it will have widespread application.

In addition, researchers are seeking to develop cameras capable of seeing hidden objects under a person's clothes from up to 25 meters away. This technology may be the newest device used to stop terrorists from committing attacks in public places. The Thruvision camera, which does not emit any radiation, picks up terahertz rays (also know as T-rays) that are emitted by all objects. T-rays are able to pass through fabric and walls. Using T-rays, the camera can detect metallic and nonmetallic objects under a person's clothes such as explosives, liquids, narcotics, weapons, plastics, and ceramics. A person's body detail will not be exposed during the process. Since the camera screens people in large, open areas, people may not even be aware of when they are being screened. The camera could speed up security at border crossings and security checkpoints and is already being used in London's Canary Wharf financial area.[80]

In other examples of "Brave New World" technologies, the DHS is working to develop technology that detects improvised explosive devices (IEDs). One camera system seeks to identify a person in possession of a bomb by analyzing the way the person moves. Another system would make use of sensors that could identify chemicals used to make bombs. Experts contend, as I do, that terrorists will eventually attempt to use IEDs in the same manner as they have been used in Iraq. "Iraq has been an invaluable battle lab for the terrorists," said security expert Randall Larsen. "We should expect to see these extraordinarily lethal devices in future attacks ..." In addition to bomb detection, DHS is advising companies that sell chemicals that could be used in bombs to train employees in "bomb making awareness" in an effort to prevent terrorists from acquiring an IED. The DHS is also developing advanced computer programs that could analyze communication and bank information to identify possible terrorist behavior.[81]

In another innovative camera technology, the DHS is investigating new video surveillance technology that would allow agents in public places to film suspicious people or activities. The DHS plans to spend $700,000 on tests before submitting this RealEyes program for review. If it passes privacy measures, security agents would then be able to covertly film people in airports, border crossings, and other high-risk areas. These live video images can then be instantly shared with other government enforcement officials. Homeland Security spokesperson Amy Kudwa says that "dozens or hundreds of authorized users" could use the live feeds to unite law enforcement agents in the pursuit of criminal suspects, lost children, or disaster victims.[82]

This technology is similar to research being conducted by Ohio State University (OSU) researchers. This research seeks to develop a "smart" surveillance system that will distinguish between a "lost" and a "suspicious" person. The goal of the research is to create a network of smart video cameras that will allow officers to quickly and efficiently observe and monitor a wide area. OSU professor James W. Davis stated that "we've always tried to develop technologies that would improve officers' situational awareness, and now we want to give that same kind of awareness to computers." Davis says the goal is to analyze and model the behavior patterns of people and vehicles moving through a scene. "We are trying to automatically learn what typical activity patterns exist in the monitored area, and then have the system look for atypical patterns that may signal a person of interest," he says.[83]

This system will focus on how a person moves and what they do. The first step is to expand the small field of view of traditional pan-tilt-zoom cameras. This entails providing a series of snapshots from every direction within a camera's field of view. These photos are then combined into a 360-degree, high-resolution panorama. The operator can then click anywhere on the picture and the camera will pan and tilt to that location for a live image. The program will also map locations onto an aerial map of the scene and then calculate where the view spaces of the security cameras overlap. The overlap will determine the geo-referenced coordinates of each ground pixel in the panoramic image. Another functionality of the system will use aerial and panoramic views for tracking people based on their behaviors.[84]

These "smart" technologies are also being researched by the DHS and the Justice Department, who have made enhancements to their respective biometric systems—the Automated Biometric Identification System (IDENT) and the Integrated Automated Fingerprint Identification System (IAFIS). The goal is to improve the interoperability of the two systems, and to enhance the information-sharing process. IDENT and IAFIS interoperability is the cornerstone of Secure Communities, which is a comprehensive plan to identify and remove criminal aliens from local communities. In collaboration with the Department of Justice (DOJ) and other DHS components, the plan is to expand this capability to more than 50 state and local law enforcement agencies throughout the nation by spring 2009.[85]

In possibly the most elaborate—and frightening—technology, the DHS is working on Project Hostile Intent (PHI). This research has the ambitious goal of projecting "current or future hostile intentions" among the 400 million people who enter the country each year through remote behavior analysis systems. The PHI technology, if perfected, seeks to identify physical markers (body temperature, heart rate, respiration, blood pressure, facial expressions, etc.) associated with hostility or the desire to deceive. These assessments would then be applied toward the development of "real-time, culturally independent, non-invasive sensors" that can spot such behaviors. These sensors could include infrared light, heart rate, and respiration sensors; eye tracking; laser; audio; and video. As a precursor to this technology, since 2003 the Transportation Security Administration (TSA) has been using the Screening Passengers through Observation Techniques (SPOT) program to detect suspicious people through study of micro-expressions—involuntary facial telltales that indicate attempts to deceive. This process, however, is costly and arduous. It also requires specialized training. The automation of the SPOT program, with computers instead of people screening for micro-expressions and other suspicious bodily indicators, is the impetus behind PHI. Such a complex system, if capable of being developed, would center on the ability to identify hostile micro-expressions in a potential terrorist.

The qualitative difference in this technology is that most preventive screening looks for explosives or metals that pose a threat. The MALINTENT system turns this approach on its head. This Orwellian-sounding machine detects the person—not the device—set to wreak havoc and terror. MALINTENT searches your body for nonverbal cues that predict whether you mean harm. But this is no polygraph test. Subjects do not get hooked up or strapped down for a careful reading. Instead, the sensors do all the work without any actual physical contact. As an analogy, this technology is like an x-ray for bad intentions. In this sense, it is the "mind reading" element of the pre-crime squad illustrated in the movie *Minority Report*. As discussed earlier, the basis for the movie is playing out in the evolving *Public Safety Policing* model.

The system works to recognize, define, and measure seven primary emotions and emotional cues that are reflected in contractions of facial muscles. MALINTENT identifies these emotions and relays the information back to a security screener almost in real time. When the sensors identify any of the above-mentioned cues, they transmit warning data to analysts. The analyst then decides whether to flag passengers for further questioning. The next step involves micro-facial scanning, which involves measuring minute muscle movements in the face for clues about mood and intention.

This technology, also known as Future Attribute Screening Technology (FAST), is not easily fooled. It is said to be good enough to tell the difference between a harried traveler and a terrorist. Even if you sweat heavily by nature, FAST technology will not mistake you for a terrorist. "If you focus on looking at the person, you don't have to worry about detecting the device itself," said Bob Burns, MALINTENT's project leader. Indeed, while the success rate of this technology is classified, an undersecretary at the DHS declared the experiment a "home run." Indeed, as cold and inhuman as the electric eye may be, one benefit is that the scanners are unbiased and nonjudgmental. "It does not predict who you are and make a judgment, it only provides an assessment in situations," said Burns. "It analyzes you against baseline stats when you walk in the door, it measures reactions and variations when you approach and go through the portal."[86]

The DHS is planning an even wider array of screening technologies, including an eye scanner in 2009 and pheromone-reading technology by 2010. The team will also be adding equipment that reads body movements, called "illustrative and emblem cues." According to Burns, this is achievable because people "move in reaction to what they are thinking, more or less based on the context of the situation." FAST may also incorporate biological, radiological, and explosives detection, but for now the primary focus is on identifying and isolating potential human threats. Supporters argue that the application of FAST is almost limitless because it is a mobile screening laboratory. It could be set up at entrances to stadiums and malls, and in airports, making it ever more difficult for terrorists to live and work among us.[87]

These technologies pose both promise and frightening implications. The most obvious initial question is, do they work? Do they actually prevent crime or terrorism? Can such malicious intent or hostile indicators be spotted in time to stop a terrorist incident?

Alternatively, do they pose privacy ramifications? In addition, what will be the reaction of "innocents," who may be highly emotional or aggravated due to stress caused by being flagged as potential terrorists?[88] These questions, and others, will be addressed in Chapter 10. Notwithstanding potential implications, the data and examples presented in this chapter demonstrate this country is witnessing an explosion of public camera and surveillance systems. While I see these systems as a pragmatic response to a demonstrable threat, I also acknowledge the privacy and public policy concerns raised by some. The widespread use of camera and security systems, in my mind, is most troublesome because it has been done without any real debate. Hopefully, this book will help inform any such debate.

Endnotes

1. Wadman, Robert C. and William Thomas Allison (2004). *To Protect and To Serve: A History of Police in America.* Upper Saddle River, NJ, Pearson/Prentice Hall.
2. Morgenstern, Henry (2008). "From Virtual Jihad to Real Jihad," *The Counter Terrorist* 1, no. 1 (May/June):27.
3. "National Strategy for Homeland Security" (2007). Homeland Security Council, Office of the President of the United States, October.
4. *Law Enforcement Prevention and Deterrence of Terrorist Acts*, Version 1.0. Department of Homeland Security, 2/9.
5. SLATT, 25.
6. Practical Guide to Intelligence-Led Policing (2006), New Jersey State Police.
7. http://www.manhattan-institute.org/html/cb_43.htm (retrieved on October 16, 2007).
8. *Law Enforcement Prevention and Deterrence of Terrorist Acts*, 2/10.
9. SLATT, 31.
10. SLATT, 24.
11. 28 CFR Part 23.2.
12. http://www.latimes.com/news/local/la-me-counterterror14apr14,1,5682393.story (retrieved on April 16, 2008).
13. 28 CFR Part 23.20 (d).
14. *Law Enforcement Prevention and Deterrence of Terrorist Acts*, 7/15.
15. 28 CFR Part 23.20.
16. *Law Enforcement Prevention and Deterrence of Terrorist Acts*, 2/14.
17. *Law Enforcement Prevention and Deterrence of Terrorist Acts*, 2/30.
18. *Law Enforcement Prevention and Deterrence of Terrorist Acts*, 2/13.
19. 28 CFR Part 23.20 (g).
20. 28 CFR Part 23.20 (h).
21. 28 CFR Part 23.20 (f) (1).
22. 28 CFR Part 23.20 (e); and SLATT, 36.
23. 28 CFR Part 23.20 (f) (2).
24. 28 CFR Part 23.20 (g).
25. "Video Cameras on the Lookout for Terrorists," found on www.cnn.com. http://edition.cnn.com/2006/tech/08/07/terrorism.technology.ap (retrieved on September 1, 2006).
26. Spielman, Fran and Frank Main (2003). "City Deploys High Tech Cameras to Fight Crime," *Chicago Sun-Times,* July 11.
27. Homeland Security Act (HSA) of 2002, Pub. L. No. 107-296, 116 Stat. 2135 (November 25, 2002).
28. Personal interview with Todd Sherman, who served as a "detailee" at NOC. The interview took place on November 20, 2008.

29. Rozas, Angela (2007). "Anti-Terror Center Adds Crime Focus," *Chicago Tribune,* December 28.
30. Ibid. Rozas, Angela (2007), op. cit.
31. Indiana Code 10-19-10-2.
32. Fusion Centers Should Work With ISACs (2007). *Security Management* 51, no. 11 (November):34.
33. Straw, Joseph (2008). "Fusion Centers and Civil Rights," *Security Management.* http://www.securitymanagement.com/article/fusion-centers-and-civil-rights-004447 (retrieved on September 12, 2008).
34. GAO (Government Accounting Office) (2003). Video Surveillance: Information on Law Enforcement's Use of Closed Circuit Television to Monitor Selected Federal Property in Washington, D.C. GAO-03-748, June:6–7.
35. "Video Cameras on the Lookout for Terrorists," found on www.cnn.com. http://edition.cnn.com/2006/tech/08/07/terrorism.technology.ap (retrieved on September 1, 2006).
36. GAO (2003), op. cit., 5–6.
37. GAO (2003), op. cit., 9.
38. Leicester, John (2007). "British 'Big Brother' System of CCTV Surveillance Impresses Neighbors in Europe and in the U.S.," *Associated Press,* July 11.
39. GAO (2003), op. cit., 22.
40. Leicester, John (2007), op. cit.
41. Leicester, John (2007), op. cit.
42. Konzol, Mark J., Allison Hantschel and Alice Hohl (2003). "The Police Are Watching: Chicago Force Unveils Camera System that will Record Activity on the Streets," *Daily Southtown,* July 11, 9.
43. Kinzer, Stephen (2004). "Chicago Moving to 'Smart' Surveillance Cameras," *New York Times,* September 21.
44. Kinzer, Stephen (2004), op. cit.
45. These examples are taken from open sources collected by the Department of Homeland Security and are disseminated in its daily security briefings. Also see Shenk, D. (2003). "Watching You: The World of High-Tech Surveillance," *National Geographic* November:4–29; and GAO (2003), op. cit.
46. Pastor, James F. (2005). "Public Safety Policing," *Law Enforcement Executive Forum* 5, no. 6 (November):19.
47. Ayi, Mema (2004). "Cal City Police Use Cameras, Surveillance to Cut Crime," *Northwest Indiana Times,* August 30.
48. Grimm, Andy (2005). "Gary Approves Surveillance Camera Purchase," *Post-Tribune,* June 17.
49. Hamblen, Matt and Patrick Thibodeau (2008). "IT Deputized to Help Take a Bite Out of Crime," *Computerworld,* March 3.
50. Fooksman, Leon and Barbara Hijek (2008). "Cameras Keep Digital Eye Out of Trouble," *Fort Lauderdale Sun-Sentinel,* January 15, A1.
51. Young, Bob (2008). "Surveillance Cameras Installed in Seattle's Cal Anderson Park," *Seattle Times,* April 22.
52. Ioffee, Karina (2005). "Cameras Aim to Boost Sense of Security." www.recordnet.com (retrieved on April 10, 2005).
53. Lee, Jennifer (2005). "Caught on Tape, Then Just Caught," *New York Times,* May 22.
54. *Security Management* (2007). May:26.

55. Lucadamo, Kathleen and Pete Donohue (2007). "Bloomberg: Get Surveillance Cameras for Buses, Trains," *New York Daily News,* October 3.

56. Eisenberg, Carol (2007). "NYC Counter-Terror Chief Urges Stiffer Subway Protection." www.newsday.com (retrieved on March 7, 2007).

57. Ante, Spencer E. (2008). "Newark and the Future of Crime Fighting," *Business Week,* August 25.

58. Carroll, Timothy J. (2008). "Hoboken Gets First-of-Its-Kind Security System," *Hoboken Reporter,* October 13.

59. SecurityInfoWatch.com. "Eye on Video: Adding Audio Intelligence" (retrieved on July 22, 2008).

60. Sheridan, Mary Beth (2008). "D.C. Forging Surveillance Network," *Washington Post,* May 1, A1.

61. Emerling, Gary (2008). "5,000 Monitoring Cameras Opened to D.C. Police," *Washington Times,* April 9.

62. Emerling, Gary (2008), op. cit.

63. "Innovative Surveillance" (2007). *Security Technology and Design* 17, no. 11 (November):79.

64. Weathers, William A. (2008). "Terrorism? Zoom In," *Cincinnati Enquirer,* February 28.

65. Nicholson, Kieran (2008). "Denver Weighs Security vs. Privacy as Cops Focus Cameras on Crime," *The Denver Post.* http://www.denverpost.com/news/ci_10613181 (retrieved on October 3, 2008).

66. Levin, Gregg (2007). "Dallas PD Fights Crime with Video Surveillance," *Security Technology and Design* 17, no. 7 (July):52.

67. Hamblen, Matt and Patrick Thibodeau (2008), op. cit.

68. Keen, Judy (2006). "Daley Wants Security Cameras at Bars," *USA Today,* February 14.

69. Cole, Bradley (2003). "Merrillville Cop Chief Wants OK for Camera to Nab Traffic Violators," *Post-Tribune,* December 11.

70. "City Cameras to Catch Every Car" (2008). *BBC News,* May 20.

71. http://www.airvisual.com/intelliviewer.htm (retrieved on April 7, 2008).

72. Bulwa, Demian (2008). "Richmond Installs 'Smart' Cameras," *San Francisco Chronicle,* May 15.

73. http://www.usatoday.com/news/nation/2008-09-17-car-scanner_N.htm?csp=34 (retrieved on September 19, 2008).

74. Sanchez Jr., Jose L. (2008). "Radiation Detection Devices to Be Installed at Harbor," *Ventura County Star* (CA), June 6. http://www.venturacountystar.com/news/2008/jun/06/radiation-detection-devices-to-be-installed-at/.

75. Nuttall, Jeremy (2008). "Ferry Rides to See Tougher Security," *Globe and Mail* (CAN) http://www.theglobeandmail.com/servlet/story/LAC.20080722.BCFERRIES22/TPStory/National (retrieved on July 22, 2008).

76. Shelman, Jeff (2007). "To Deter Crime at U, These Eyes Never Blink," *Star Tribune (MN),* November 24.

77. "Video Cameras on the Lookout for Terrorists," found on www.cnn.com. http://edition.cnn.com/2006/tech/08/07/terrorism.technology.ap (retrieved on September 1, 2006).

78. O'Malley, Jaclyn (2005). "Homeland Security Grants Adds Infrared Gear," *Reno Gazette-Journal,* March 1.

79. Thomas, Frank (2007). "TSA to Test New Thermal Cameras in Rail Stations," *USA Today,* October 4.

80. Newton, Paula (2008). "New Security Camera Can 'See' Through Clothes," *CNN International,* April 16.

81. Hall, Mimi (2007). "Feds Work on Detecting Bombs in USA," *USA Today,* November 27, A3.
82. Hall, Mimi (2008). "Surveillance System Raises Privacy Concerns," *USA Today,* February 29, 3A.
83. Gorder, Pam Frost (2009). "Smart Cameras Are Watching You," *The Lantern* (Ohio State University). http://media.www.thelantern.com/media/storage/paper333/news/2009/01/09/Campus/smart.Cameras.Are.Watching.You-3582772.shtml (retrieved on January 9, 2009).
84. Gorder, Pam Frost (2009), op. cit., 1.
85. Kouri, Jim (2008). "Homeland Security and Justice Departments Providing More Info to Local Officers," *National Ledger* (NC). http://www.nationalledger.com/artman/publish/article_272623792.shtml (retrieved on November 16, 2008).
86. Barrie, Allison (2008). "Homeland Security Detects Terrorist Threats by Reading Your Mind," *Fox News.* http://www.foxnews.com/story/0,2933,426485,00.html (retrieved on September 23, 2008).
87. Ibid. Barrie, Allison (2008), op. cit.
88. Marks, Paul (2007). "Can a Government Remotely Detect a Terrorist's Thoughts," *New Scientist* 195, no. 2616 (August 11):24.

Chapter 6

Order Maintenance Provisions

This chapter discusses the third element of *Public Safety Policing*: order maintenance. This element is not new. Indeed, it is as old as policing itself—even older. What makes this element distinctive in the new policing model can be answered in a few descriptive words: who, what, where, why, and how. Each of these factors is explained in detail below:

Who—entails the notion of a division of labor, where different types or levels of workers perform different tasks.
What—entails the kinds of work that will be performed.
Where—entails the locations of the work product.
Why—entails the reason a division of labor needs to be applied, and the reason why certain types of workers should or will perform these tasks.
How—entails the methods and the focus of order maintenance provisions.

Consequently, while order maintenance is as old as *law and order,* there are rather new or—more accurately—innovative aspects of order maintenance that will be applicable in the new policing model. In contemporary times, the goal of the terrorist or the extremist is to create chaos. The goal of civilized society is to maintain order through the rule of law. The dynamics on how these conflicting "goals" are achieved is the essence of the new model of policing, that is, the desire to protect the homeland. Thus, while I advocate using long-standing order maintenance provisions, the reasons these functions are performed entail innovative approaches. In order to better understand how this will come about, let's consider the notion of order maintenance.

Theoretical and Historical Perspectives

Order maintenance is designed to control the environment in a way that makes the commission of crime—or terrorism—more difficult to accomplish. Order maintenance techniques and their relationship to the physical environment are relevant in this new model of policing for several reasons. First, from the perspective of "normal crime," order maintenance—widely utilized in *Community Policing* —may prove beneficial in both reducing crime and in reducing the level of incivility or disorder.[1] With this thinking, many researchers believe that an area often undergoes a transition from relatively few crimes to one with a high incidence of crime or a heightened fear of crime, caused, in part, by lack of order.[2]

The theory underlying order maintenance contends that crime problems initially occur in relatively harmless activities. Drinking on the street, graffiti on buildings, and youths loitering on street corners are common activities in certain areas. These are often considered relatively harmless activities. If these activities go unchecked, however, the level of fear and incivility begins to rise. Left to fester, more serious crimes such as gang fights or even drive-by shootings may take place. In this sense, the presence of disorder tends to reduce the social controls previously present in the area. This results, at least in theory, in increased crime. Increased crime, particularly serious crime, in turn contributes to the further deterioration of the physical environment and of the economic well-being of the community.[3]

The development of order maintenance theories can be traced to a line of thinking that initially focused on conditions in cities, particularly in the "slums." In these areas, conditions such as "physical deterioration, high density, economic insecurity, poor housing, family disintegration, transience, conflicting social norms, and an absence of constructive positive agencies" were deemed as contributors to criminal behavior.[4] Over time, researchers started to shift their focus from socioeconomic factors toward the physical characteristics of the community or, in other words, the "environment." Focusing on the physical characteristics of the location where crime occurred resulted in a substantial body of scientific research. For example, Cohen and Felson argued that the completion of a crime requires the convergence in time and space of an offender, a suitable target, and the "absence of guardians capable of preventing the violation."[5]

This focus on environmental factors was found in a number of other studies. In keeping with the theme of this book, Gibbs and Erickson argued that the daily population flow in large cities "reduces the effectiveness of surveillance activities by increasing the number of strangers that are routinely present in the city, thereby decreasing the extent to which their activities would be regarded with suspicion."[6] The implication of their conclusion is obvious: the more people in a given geographic area, the less likely strangers would be noticed. From this thinking, natural surveillance from community residents is reduced, leading to more crime.

Lewis and Maxfield took this logic to the next level. These authors focused on specific physical conditions within the environment, seeking to assess their impact on crime and the fear of crime. Their research assessed such things as abandoned buildings, teen loitering, vandalism, and drug use. They believe these factors draw little attention from police partially because the police have limited resources to effectively deal with these problems.[7] The researchers noted that such problems are important indicators of criminality within any community.

This conclusion has been echoed by a number of other authors. For example, Kelling maintained that citizens regularly report their biggest safety concerns to be things like "panhandling, obstreperous youths taking over parks and street corners, public drinking, prostitution, and other disorderly behavior." Each of these factors was identified as precursors to more serious crime. Moreover, the failure to remedy disorderly behaviors may be perceived as a sign of indifference. This indifference communicates that "no one cares"—which may, in turn, lead to more serious crime and urban decay.[8] Consequently, the key to crime control is to address both the physical and social conditions that foster crime. By controlling or correcting these conditions, they will not fester into more serious levels of crime and decay.[9]

The implications of these studies were clear. When faced with disorderly conditions, individuals tend to feel a greater exposure to risk, and have loss of control over their immediate environment. This leads to being more aware of the consequences of a criminal attack.[10] This thinking advanced the concept of "situational crime prevention." This assessment takes into account the "intersection" of potential offenders with the opportunity to commit crime. In this analysis, researchers argued the commission of a particular crime could be avoided through certain preventive measures designed to reduce the offender's ability (or even propensity) to commit crimes at specific locations.[11]

Implicit in these findings is the desire to prevent crime, or reduce the conditions or factors that foster crime. These conclusions have been embraced by both public police and private security. A key component of these preventive methods, in both the public and private sectors, is known as order maintenance. Order maintenance is designed to improve conditions within a specific geographic area. This can be accomplished in a number of ways, including the rehabilitation of physical structures, the removal or demolition of seriously decayed buildings, and by the improvement of land or existing buildings by cleaning and painting. Other relatively simple environmental improvements are recommended, such as planting flowers, trees, or shrubs. These are designed to enhance the "look and feel" of an area.[12] These physical improvements, coupled with efforts to reduce or eliminate certain antisocial behaviors, such as loitering, drinking and drug usage, fighting, and other disorderly behaviors, are critical components of an order maintenance approach to crime prevention. Of course, the goal is to correct these conditions and behaviors before more serious crimes occur.

Viewed in this broad manner, "security" can encompass diverse factors, from trash collection to planting flowers to private police patrols. Each is designed to improve conditions within the area. With the logic derived from this line of thinking, the need to control physical conditions and public activities is paramount.

The threat of terrorism will magnify this environmental focus. For example, an unattended package left on a street corner may actually be a lethal bomb. Similarly, an unidentified vehicle may become a tragic and lethal explosion. With these demonstrated tactics of terrorists, the importance of an orderly and clean environment cannot be overstated. While these perceived or potential threats are difficult to remedy, this focus on the environment has been echoed by Kaplan, who views the environment as *the* security issue of the early twenty-first century.[13]

Discouraging crime by manipulating the environment has many facets. In the security industry, Crime Prevention through Environmental Design (CPTED) has been used successfully for years. This approach seeks to change certain features of the environment to reduce the incidence of crime. With this approach, natural surveillance is emphasized. With this thinking, the environmental design is structured so that users can see farther and wider. In addition, CPTED encourages territorial behaviors and natural access controls. As with the larger notion of order maintenance, proper care and control of the facilities are critical.[14] An example of CPTED can be found in newly developed parking garages designed to make people feel safer and curb crime. The garages boast glass-enclosed elevators and stairwells designed to bolster visibility and security. These glass structures also reduce opportunities for criminals to hide. The parking structures also are typically equipped with security cameras and emergency phones, and with lighting fixtures that propel light up into the ceiling and down to the floor. This focus on lighting was supported by a National Institute of Justice study that deemed lighting the most significant security feature in parking garages.[15]

Another example of a CPTED strategy was used to deter loitering. One author suggests clearly defining the borders of a property by using grade changes, low walls, gateways, or distinct paving for walkways. To eliminate potential sleeping spaces, benches should have seat dividers, and low walls should be covered with strips of raised material about 2 inches high spaced 18 inches apart. Green areas should feature unwelcoming plants like Russian olive, red barberry, crown of thorns, or Siberian pea shrub. Other measures include monitored surveillance cameras, regular patrols, and installing card readers or punch-code locks on bathrooms. Stairwells and garages should be enclosed with fencing or gating. Outside utility areas like sprinkler rooms, loading docks, and transformer rooms should have bolt locks and monitored alarm contacts. Light and sound deterrents include the use of low-pressure sodium lights and sound effects like mechanical beeps or cats fighting.[16] While one may criticize the nature of these methods, their effectiveness in deterring crime should be weighed against any such critique.

As stated earlier, in public policing the use of order maintenance techniques was emphasized in *Community Policing*.[17] In this sense, the core goal of *Community Policing* is to extend beyond the traditional goal of crime fighting to focus on fear reduction through order maintenance techniques. In this way, preventing crime was more important than capturing the offender after the crime had been committed.[18]

In the private sector, the focus on prevention, as opposed to enforcement, has traditionally dominated the decisions of security industry officials.[19] The similarity of private security and *Community Policing* techniques can be narrowed to one core goal: both are intended to utilize proactive crime prevention that is accountable to the client or the citizen, respectively. The "client focused" emphasis on preventing crime traditionally used by the security industry—not merely making arrests after a crime has occurred—directly relates to this approach. Private security, indeed, is particularly well suited to perform an order maintenance function. At least partly because of its crime prevention focus, private security personnel have long since replaced public police in the protection of business facilities, assets, employees, and customers. Private security personnel provided what the public police could not accomplish. Specifically, security firms provided services for specific clients, focusing on the protection of certain assets, both physical and human, as their primary and even exclusive purpose.[20]

In light of the criminological theories outlined above, a substantial body of law has grown around the notion of the environmental aspects of crime. At least partially due to such thinking, tort causes of action, known as either premises liability or negligent security, have provided explosive business for personal injury attorneys. This legal exposure helped create a significant consequence. Property and business owners were motivated to institute security measures within and around their property or business location. This can be viewed as both a carrot and a stick. The carrot is a safe and secure place to do business, and to live or work in. Of course, a safe and secure environment will not hurt the reputation of the business, or the viability of the property. Conversely, the stick is substantial potential liability, with significant jury awards. In addition, media exposure stemming from crime, coupled with the reputation and public relation damages associated with the incident, each provide particular motivation to secure the premises from criminals. Consequently, security began to be seen as an asset and crime control as a duty. Both of these often supersede merely relying on public police for protection.[21]

The result of this carrot and stick approach was a growing use of security personnel and methodologies. Business and property owners started to think and worry about security, becoming more proactive in their approach to a safe and secure environment. For security firms, it created opportunities. It brought security closer and closer into the realm of the average citizen. Security personnel began to be routinely used at businesses and large corporations, now often focusing on the *protection of employees and clients*, instead of simply focusing on asset protection. In this sense, security became more commonplace and mainstream. Consequently, the security industry moved into the lives of average people. No longer was it just the public police who serviced the people. This relationship of the security industry to mainstream society also increased the scope of the services provided by private police.[22]

As liability for security increased, the perimeters of security expanded farther and farther from the "protected facility." Indeed, it is now becoming common for security patrols for properties and businesses to extend into the streets and other public areas. These extended perimeters seek to prevent crime by providing a secure environment. In this sense, private police can be deemed as another security layer, or as an extension of the security perimeter into the public domain.

Conversely, as stated elsewhere in this book, public police are faced with an increasingly difficult task incorporating crime prevention or homeland security services. This is based on the broader societal mission to universally enforce laws throughout society, as well as the need to preserve democratic and constitutional ideals. Considering that the already overburdened public police are also faced with economic and operational constraints, it is not unreasonable to conclude that the role of private security will continue to increase. For these reasons, many have advocated that private police play a larger role in the prevention of crime in areas traditionally and exclusively patrolled by public police.[23] The use of order maintenance techniques will prove to be an increasingly important function of private policing, particularly in a terroristic climate.[24]

As security professionals appreciate and understand, the provision of security and public safety services is not the exclusive domain of government. Indeed, as the below statistics will illustrate, the majority of those individuals charged with security and public safety services are employed by private firms. Of course, this does not minimize the substantial role that public police officers contribute to public safety. The key point is that security and public safety are not exclusive to government, as security professionals throughout the world can attest to.[25]

While this fact is commonly accepted within the security profession, the introduction of private police into the public domain may cause concern, or even alarm, to some people. This is understandable, particularly in Western countries. Most contemporary observers view police agencies as "normal," as if this were the natural state of law enforcement. It is not. Many do not realize that public policing is a rather new phenomenon. When the first police department was organized by Sir Robert Peel in London in 1829, many people viewed this with concern, or even alarm. This was due to a dramatic change in "policing." In this way, the introduction of private policing can be viewed as *back to the future*, whereby private citizens will contribute more time and effort to the safety and security of their communities.[26]

For centuries, people in the community acted as "security" within the community. The "job" of security was not even a job. There were no "police" to call. Instead, it was the duty of all able-bodied men to protect their homes and their community.[27] Thus, the people acted in self-defense or in defense of their community. Viewed in this manner, security has historically been the provision of the people. This assertion was even reflected in one of Peel's guiding principles: *the people are the police, the police are the people.*[28]

This brief historical perspective explains that the advent of private policing in public environments is not new. It is a variation of an age-old principle: *security is the province of the people.* In contemporary times, "the people" typically pay others for protection. Citizens pay taxes for municipal policing. Clients pay contracted fees for security services from firms.[29] Both of these methods are accepted as contemporary norms. However, there is a new dynamic developing. When citizens hire security firms for protection within the public realm, a sort of *back to the future* circumstance occurs.

Contemporary Circumstances

This subject is both comprehensive and complex. This chapter attempts to balance the complexity of these issues in a manner that is both comprehensive yet within the scope of this book. This is not an easy task. The goal is to delve into each issue in a manner that leaves the reader with a sense of how order maintenance provisions will be delivered in the new policing model. In doing so, consider this work as both a primer and a resource to those professionals interested in this emergent and important topic.

As these statements portend, I contend the movement toward a *Public Safety Policing* model is inevitable. This begs the question, why now? The answer is, following the terrorist acts of 9/11 many things have changed. With the enactment of the Department of Homeland Security in the United States, the Afghan and Iraqi wars, and other significant terrorist actions in Mumbai, Bali, London, and Spain, the desire for increased levels of security is obvious. These factors, however, must be viewed in the larger socioeconomic and political context. Hopefully, the above discussion demonstrates that the security industry has played an increasingly larger role in crime control services. In this sense, terrorism is not the only trigger for the new policing model. As significant as it is, terrorism alone would not require a transformation of policing. The following additional factors, both independently and in combination, have brought us to this point.

Prior to delving into the substantive analysis of this subject, it is important to establish a few caveats:

■ First, using alternative service providers, such as private police, in order maintenance provisions in no way advocates the elimination, or even the diminishment, of public policing. Indeed, one consistent theme of this book illustrates that the expansion of security personnel into the public realm is due to forces outside the control of policing agencies. As such, the growth of private police is not a reflection of poor public policing.
■ Second, the use of private police is designed to supplement already overworked, and often understaffed, law enforcement officers. In this way, the work product of public and private police should be viewed in a "division of labor" perspective.
■ Third, as will be more fully articulated later, the provision of private policing has certain market-based benefits when compared to government-based service providers. I believe the widespread introduction of private police serves the interests of more highly trained law enforcement officers, as well as the community—or the clients—served by these public safety service providers.

A useful way to conceptualize this arrangement is to view it in light of other professions. Three or so decades ago, the introduction of "paralegals" and "para-medics" created a great deal of controversy in their respective professions. Many in these professions viewed the introduction of "paramedics" and "paralegals" as an offensive and even dangerous intrusion into the standards maintained within the industry. The legal bar worried about lowering the "value" of the licensed attorney. Similarly, doctors worried about the quality of medical services that their clients would receive from medical paraprofessionals. Nonetheless, market and fiscal constraints necessitated the development of supplemental service providers to act as paraprofessionals for the higher-skilled licensed professionals. In this way, paramedics and paralegals contribute to client service delivery, while simultaneously supporting the professionals in a structured "work sharing" or division of labor relationship.[30] In contemporary times, these paraprofessionals play important roles in these professions. This working relationship is manifested in different functional and cognitive roles. In this sense, alternative service providers can be analogized as "para-police."[31] A useful way to characterize these paraprofessionals was developed by McLeod. He stated,[32]

> para-professionals generally support the host profession by offering a restricted menu of services by technicians who may be trained for shorter periods of time, but are thus more financially affordable to the public. … Every mature profession invites the rise of para-professionals.

My conclusion is that municipal police and private security will become increasingly interrelated in the public safety industry (Figure 6.1). In order for this to occur, however, private police must exhibit increased professionalism at the patrol level, which can only be accomplished by a requisite increase in training, wages, and accountability. Consequently, if "para-police" are to function within the public realm, they must be prepared to appropriately contribute to the order maintenance and service needs of the community, thereby taking on the supportive

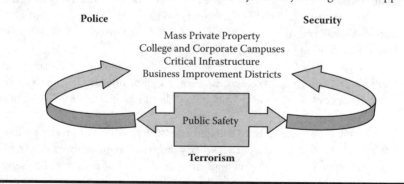

Figure 6.1   Police and security converge.

"paraprofessional" role of municipal police departments. Consequently, because of the extended scope of private police within public and semipublic property, the need for professionalism within the industry has dramatically increased.

The "Who" of Order Maintenance

With the threat of terrorism and extremism, the delivery of order maintenance services to a given community or within a given environment will change. The days of police officers answering barking dog and noise complaints, guarding crime scenes, directing traffic, responding to alarms, and similar order maintenance services are ending. Simply stated, municipal police departments will not be able to afford employing highly trained and relatively highly paid police officers to perform such routine functions. I believe that alternative service initiatives will be an increasingly viable alternative for such routine functions.

Order maintenance provisions will be done by many different types of workers. Some will be done by police. Most of this work, however, will be accomplished by others. A descriptive view of how this may look is shown in Figure 6.2. This diagram splits the provision of order maintenance into three specific areas: police officers, alternative service providers, and volunteers/service workers. As stated above, police officers will continue to perform order maintenance tasks. However, the amount or the percentage of this work will likely decrease—possibly significantly. This depends on a number of factors, such as the level of terrorism and the resultant fear, operational considerations, and financial constraints. These factors will be discussed below.

Suffice it to say at this point that order maintenance provisions will be performed by many workers and by volunteers. Many volunteers (such as truck drivers) are

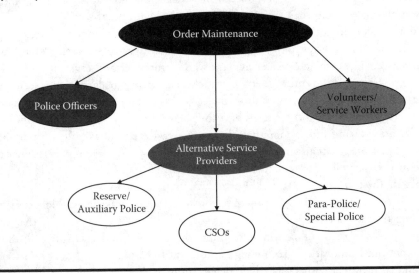

Figure 6.2 Order maintenance provisions (Copyright, James F. Pastor, 2009).

being trained to be aware of indicators of terrorism, how to help prevent an attack, and how to respond in the event of an attack. These programs include the following examples. The Community Emergency Response Team (CERT) program educates people about disaster preparedness.[33] Citizen Corps embraces the individual citizen's responsibility to be prepared. This entails first aid and emergency skills training, and volunteering to support local emergency responders, disaster relief, and community safety.[34]

In addition, many service workers who do not perform public safety services, such as firefighters and transit employees, are being trained in terrorism awareness programs. For example, the DHS is working with the Fire Department of New York City to establish a threat-information-sharing system between first responders and security officials. DHS officials also want to train firefighters to look for and identify signs of terrorist activity. If the program is successfully implemented in New York, it could be expanded to include fire departments across the country.[35] If this test program proves successful, personnel from the city's fire department and emergency medical workers will report suspicious behavior occurring in homes of private residents. The firefighters are told that when entering private homes, they should report persons who are hostile or uncooperative; persons who express open hatred toward the United States or the government; ammunition, firearms, and other weapons; blueprints and surveillance equipment; and homes with little or no furniture besides a bed.[36] Each of these may be indicators of potential terrorist activity.

In addition, New York City transit workers are also being trained in antiterror seminars sponsored by the DHS. These training sessions are three hours long and are designed to acquaint the workers with terrorist planning, selection, surveillance, and attacks. Eventually all 28,000 transit workers will be trained.[37] While these programs have merit, they are not sufficient to deal with the threat of terrorism. It will take more focused work—from people dedicated to order maintenance.

In my mind, the key to this approach is alternative service providers. Alternative service providers are, in essence, civilians who perform certain service functions—ranging from parking enforcement to crime scene security to alarm response. These services are cost-effective. They also reduce the service provisions required of police officers. While some of these tasks have long ago shifted away from police officers, there are growing indications that alternative service providers will substantially increase. I predict that innovative initiatives utilizing private police personnel to perform basic police services, including order maintenance functions, will be widespread. These arrangements will be attractive for many reasons.

As the threat—or the reality—of terrorism grows, so will the need for security. Using the past several years as an indicator, it is reasonable to presume that the impact of terrorism will continue to strain governmental budgets. This will result in continued innovation. Technology and tactical techniques will only go so far. Cameras on street corners may help deter criminals, but will they deter the committed terrorist? Tactical and heavily armed police officers may help prevent terrorist attacks, but they cannot be everywhere. What is needed are more "eyes and ears" on the public way.

Those "eyes and ears" will increasingly be attached to alternative service providers. These individuals will perform many service and order maintenance functions—on the public way—that public police officers are unable or unwilling to perform. These functions include controlling loitering, public drinking, and rowdy behavior; providing "street corner security" in business or mixed commercial/residential districts; and responding to burglar alarm calls. These and other such tasks are critical for a secure, orderly environment.

Most would agree that the police are responsible for managing crime and its effects. However, if the police cannot prevent crime, then one logical response is to hire individuals, either through contracts or as employees, to help control the environment. In this way, alternative service providers can be viewed as an additional layer of security. The work of these alternative service providers can be considered as a division of labor.[38] This division of labor should include structural components that would enable the entities to blend the delivery of public safety services through operational and administrative processes. Consider Bayley and Shearing's view of this model of policing. They view public police as increasingly specializing in "investigations and counterforce operations, while private police [are] becoming decentralized, full service providers of visible crime prevention."[39] This could be accomplished by focusing sworn police officers on tactical functions and shifting service and order maintenance functions to alternative service providers.

Two options for alternative service providers exist: either they are employed by government or they are employed by private firms. For example, Chicago has recently greatly increased its Traffic Management Authority, shifting much of the traffic control work from sworn officers to civilian employees. There is much cost savings related to this. Consider the pay rates: civilians are paid $15.59 per hour, while police were paid $31.90 per hour. City spokesperson Monique Bond explained it well. She stated, "It'll allow us to transition out of using sworn officers … we're reducing costs, identifying streams of revenue and deploying our police resources in a smarter way that focuses on neighborhood beat assignments and high crime areas." Of course, not everyone agrees. Police union president Mark Donahue countered by articulating a key theme of this book, stating,[40]

> they [the city] feel they can replace the presence of law enforcement with part time *kids*. In a post 9/11 society, people would like a greater police presence" (emphasis added).

As these quotes illustrate, each type of supplemental service has its own strengths and weaknesses. There are legitimate arguments on both sides of this issue. Regardless of the merits of these arguments, the fact is policing agencies will be forced to use various types of alternative service providers. Drawing your attention back to the figure, those civilians employed by government are referred to as Community Service Officers (CSO). The "auxiliary/reserve" category is typically sworn police officers who work part-time, usually without benefits.[41] Each reduces costs in that they entail less expense than full-time police. While each will be used, private police have particular appeal because property or business owners can directly contract with them. In this way, these public safety service provisions are *outside* of municipal budgets. In short, they cost government little or nothing.

Consequently, while each type of "alternative service provider" will coexist, I predict that private firms will be the preference. The clear benefits of private firms provide cost savings to municipal budgets. This is achieved through lower salaries. Other cost reductions include little or no pension and medical costs, overhead savings, more discretion for job actions (due to lack of unions or contract provisions), and other similar factors. Indeed, some privatized arrangements are exclusively funded by voluntary real estate tax increases by business and property owners. These have clear benefits to already overburdened municipal budgets. Table 6.1 provides some sense of the complexities of these options.

One critical factor derived from this table is that alternative service providers are related to a larger distinction: civilianization or privatization. This distinction is illustrated by competing theories—one based on government and one based on the market. From a market or economic perspective, advocates of privatization argue that the use of private firms will result in lower costs for the same—or better—service as compared to those derived from government.[42] The authors cited maintain that private firms are able to pay lower wages and are more able to terminate inefficient workers. Consequently, private firms are able to deliver better quality service at a lower cost. While this may not be universally true, there is substantial evidence that labor costs (including benefits, training, etc.) have a direct relationship to service quality.[43] The logic is, if labor costs are high then service quality would be high (or better).

Table 6.1 Attributes of Civilianization versus Privatization

Type	Civilianization	Privatization
Control	Sovereignty	Market forces
Economic principle	Monopoly	Competition
Contract basis	Union contract	Services contract
Benefits and overhead	City pays directly	Shared or firm pays
Budgetary	Annual/always	Others often pay

While this may not be definitive, there is ample evidence to support the assertion that private firms can deliver more efficient services for less cost. Cost savings are typically based on:[44]

1. More flexible use of labor
2. A richer array of incentives and penalties
3. More precise allocation of accountability
4. Less constraint on process, more focus on results

Proponents of privatization argue that market competition results in more efficient service delivery, especially when many similarly situated firms are ready, willing, and able to provide such services. Conversely, the absence of competition within the public sector allows for complacency, with little incentive to provide better service at the lowest cost possible. Consequently, while privatized services do not guarantee that market forces will lower costs and increase service quality, these economic principles support this notion.

For example, some maintain that the private police perform tasks in a cost-effective manner and are more flexible.[45] Cost savings include lower wages and more consistency of services. This consistency stems from security personnel spending nearly all allotted time "on post" or "on beat." Conversely, police officers spend a much higher percentage of their allotted time making arrests, doing paperwork, testifying in court, running errands, and the like.[46] An additional flexibility of contracted arrangements allows for property owners to assign guards to specific locations, without having to leave to answer service calls, as is required of the public police.

Opponents of privatization see it differently. They argue that reduced labor costs are illusory because they are achieved through hiring less qualified and less trained personnel, providing inadequate benefits to employees, using hiring practices that focus on part-time employees, and even by using creative accounting methods. Opponents further argue that even the cost of contract bidding and administration must be assessed, as it adds to the "bottom line" and may even invite corruption.[47] Aside from these factors, other authors contend that without adequate competition, the ill effects of monopolies will result.[48]

These opposing viewpoints demonstrate the nature of the issues related to privatization. As these views make clear, the use of privatized service providers does not guarantee either lower costs or even better service quality. In my mind, however, the benefits of a limited privatization arrangement far outweigh the negatives. This is especially true in the case of public safety services, where the failure of law enforcement to protect society is potentially measured in thousands of lives. When viewed from the perspective of terrorists with weapons of mass destruction, the concerns voiced by privatization opponents seem pale. Nonetheless, many of their criticisms are well taken. It is critical to maintain competition within private sector vendors. It is critical to maintain accountability within privatized arrangements. It is critical to develop and maintain appropriate standards for the selection, training, and hiring practices of private security firms. All that said, the need for security may override these criticisms. As will be asserted in the "why" section, fear and money will trump all other factors in a sustained terroristic environment.

Another way to distinguish public and private police is by the roles they play or functions they perform. The distinctive aspects of these policing functions were laid out by Chanken and Chaiken, and are illustrated in Table 6.2.[49] This table illustrates that the functions of public and private police vary in a rather dramatic fashion. One of the most profound distinctions regards the "input." This asks, For whom is the service designed or intended? In public policing, the citizen or society is the client. In private policing, the bill payer is usually deemed the client. This is so because the property or business owners typically pay for the patrol services, and are also citizens within the protected area. Because patrol services—in a public policing context—often result in arrests and investigative stops, it is expected that private police will conduct themselves in a similar manner, thereby resulting in the enforcement of laws or the assertion of legal authority. Consequently, some property owners may be paying for protection, while others may be paying to be arrested! While this ironic situation can be analogous to paying taxes to public police, which inevitably results in taxpayers being arrested, the link between the payment and the arrest is less direct, or at least more of an accepted norm.

Most people would recognize that this "input" distinction explains a great deal about the service orientation of the two entities. The need to "please the client" cannot be underestimated. In essence, private security firms tend to view behavior in terms of whether it threatens the interests of the client.[50] The ability to please or even discern the motivation(s) of the client is a critical determination of any

Table 6.2 Public, Private Policing Characteristics

Policing Function	Public Police	Private Police
Input	Citizen	Client
Role	Crime response	Crime prevention
Targets	General	Specific
Delivery system	Government	Profit-oriented enterprise
Output	Enforcement/arrest	Loss reduction/asset protection

Source: Adapted from Marcia Chanken and Jan Chaiken (1987). "Public Policing-Privately Provided." National Institute of Justice, Office of Justice Programs. U.S. Department of Justice (June).

firm. This is so because the goal, or input, drives how the security firm performs its duties. It is my assertion that when people are fearful, they will desire aggressive and extensive security. Inherent in this desire is to prevent problems—and crime. Such a role could entail aggressive enforcement of criminal laws through proactive law enforcement, and crime prevention techniques such as order maintenance. In essence, the underlying factor is the motivation or the desire of those who hire private patrols. Are the privatized patrol officers expected to "act like the police," thereby enforcing laws and public order? This may become a major focus of their work.[51] Conversely, public police have less incentive to "prevent crime" since they are expected to produce arrest statistics and other quantifiable measures.[52] The result is an operational incentive geared toward waiting for crimes to be committed in order to make the arrest.

Another important aspect of the traditional functions regards the "output" of the service. The traditional (though not necessarily historical) output for private policing is focused on loss reduction or asset protection. The role of private police (or private citizens) changed from a desire to address and prevent crime within the community as a whole to a more focused desire to protect specific business and property owners.[53] This latter focus has become the "traditional" view of private security. However, it is my belief that private security may be shifting back to its historical roots. That is, private policing will renew its enforcement orientation, through law and order functions.

Perhaps the most important issue relative to the function of private police versus public police is the delivery system. For private police, the delivery system is profit-oriented firms or corporations. For public police it is government. This distinction is critical. A key factor is competition versus monopoly. Most people acknowledge that competition drives better service and value. Conversely, monopolies, such as police departments, tend to be less efficient, even complacent. If the security firm is not performing or is not providing good value, it can be fired. Of course, citizens do not have this option with the police. They cannot terminate the services of the police department. While they may petition political leaders for redress, this is not nearly as effective as a 30-day termination clause, as is common in the security industry.

Typically, labor union contracts include many provisions designed to protect workers. While this is not in itself problematic, when compared to the 30-day cancellation clause typically found in security contracts, one is struck by the fact that nonperforming firms can be "fired" much more simply than nonperforming public employees. For this reason alone, government officials may find this an attractive option.

In addition, one distinct advantage of private policing is that the monies used to provide these services are obtained from business or property owners, either derived from special taxing initiatives or more directly from contracts with property or community associations. With these funding sources, private policing services could be sustained with little or no municipal expenditures. Consequently, the economic benefits derived from privatized service providers can help relieve already strained municipal budgets.[54] Given the current economic circumstances, it seems apparent that financial constraints will necessitate more "creative" service provisions. This assertion is pointedly echoed by economist Diane Swonk. When you read this quote, please keep in mind this was written years prior to the financial collapse in 2008. In any event, she stated,[55]

> almost half of all states were already in a budget deficit and trying to cut back prior to 9/11, and by allocating more funds toward security after 9/11, they would be forced to make some very difficult and counter-intuitive decisions about the fiscal situations in the months that followed.

Only time will tell how the current economic woes and public safety concerns will coalesce. However this plays out, the need for security coupled with the budgetary constraints facing government will result in privatized arrangements being viewed as attractive alternatives. At the core of these arrangements is the choice between labor union contracts versus firm service contracts.

Finally, obtaining public safety services from private firms typically entails the contracting party being a property or homeowner association. Obtaining these services from a taxing initiative usually involves the creation of a special taxing district that has its powers derived from a governmental entity, such as state or city legislation. This district acts as a political subdivision of the legislative entity that created it. Depending on the purpose of its creation, the political subdivision could be conferred broad powers—usually to promote economic development or stability—through the assertion of health, safety, and environmental improvements. The specific source of the monies can be a tax on real property or even a sales tax levy. Since the tax is confined to a certain geographic area, the local property or business owners usually maintain control over the authority vested in the district. This control enhances the accountability on the taxing levels and revenues derived from the district. Participation in this authority usually requires specific connections to the geographic area, such as being a property owner, working in or owning a business within the district, or owning stock in a corporation within the district.[56]

The "What" of Order Maintenance

The focus of this section is "what" kinds of work will be performed. In this function, the key will be to control the environment. As illustrated in the historical section, this requires focus on both physical and social incivilities. Going forward, this work will be increasingly accomplished by the use of technologies (as described in Chapter 5) and by the use of alternative service providers. The primary tasks will focus on certain routine service functions, such as report writing, alarm response, traffic control, and "street corner security." Each of these tasks relate to either order maintenance or other services. In these ways, alternative service providers will also enhance the "eyes and ears" of policing agencies.

Table 6.3   Private Policing Functional Characteristics

Function Type	Number of Incidents	Total Incidents (%)
Observe and report	791	32.0
Order maintenance	1,281	51.5
Law enforcement	413	16.5
Totals	2,486	100

Copyright, James F. Pastor, 2009.

Considering the significance of this question, I conducted extensive research on alternative service providers. This included riding in a patrol car as the private police officers performed their duties. As one of the few—if not the first—to perform such ride-along research of private policing, I had a bird's eye view of this new policing model. The study demonstrated that private police officers will perform many service and order maintenance functions. The research also revealed that even law enforcement functions, such as arrests for gun possession and serious crimes, were performed by private security personnel—as they patrol public streets. It also demonstrated that constitutionally violating searches and seizures would occur and that questionable legal authority will complicate their patrol functions.[57]

Specifically, my research addressed a key element of this new policing model: the use of private police patrols on public streets. As Table 6.3 illustrates, I found that order maintenance was the dominant function performed by private police (51.5%). This is consistent with the "client service" focus of private security and with a key premise of *Community Policing*—reducing disorderly conditions results in less crime. The remaining functions by the private police officers were observe and report (31.8%) and law enforcement (16.6%). These findings reveal that private police focus on certain "lower" level police functions, such as order maintenance and as the "eyes and ears" of the police (the "observe and report" function). In this way, private police demonstrate that they could perform these functions—thereby allowing municipal police departments the ability and resources to focus on higher-level concerns or threats.

The "Where" of Order Maintenance

When one considers the provision of public safety and security services, it is useful to think in terms of location and provision (Table 6.4). In this table, the location is broken down as either private or public, and the provision is divided as either a substitute or a supplement. Looking at such tasks in a conceptual manner, it is useful to think of the location of the services in relation to the service provision.

Table 6.4 Private Policing Provision and Location Characteristics

		Provision	
		Substitute	*Supplement*
Location	Private	Corporate security	Corporate campuses College campuses Shopping malls Sporting facilities Gated communities
	Public	Reminderville, Ohio Sussex, New Jersey	Communities Business districts Buses/trains and stations Critical infrastructure

Copyright, James F. Pastor, 2009.

In the private/substitute cell, the typical provision is where the security personnel, either contract or proprietary, provide the majority (if not all) of the security services. Traditionally, security firms have operated almost exclusively within private environments. In this sense, security personnel act as the "sheriff" within their environment. They typically do so with little or no support from the public police. The practice in this environment is that security personnel act as a "substitute" for police agencies, providing most, if not all, of the security services at the particular location. This does not mean that public police officers do not nor cannot enter into these facilities. It simply means that public police do not routinely enter or patrol private facilities and properties. For example, public police typically do not stand guard at the entrance of a manufacturing plant. Instead, private facilities typically perform their own dedicated patrols or other crime prevention services. Of course, if a crime occurs, police are often called to the private property. In this way, the cell is not a complete substitute. It is *largely* a substitute, and for some firms an almost exclusive substitute. Consequently, this cell represents the norm in the security industry.

In the public/substitute cell, the towns of Remainderville, Ohio, and Sussex, New Jersey, fired their police officers and hired security personnel as substitutes. When this occurred, the security officers patrolled the town, answered calls for service, took reports, and made arrests. In this sense, the private security personnel acted as a substitute for the public police. These services were provided within the public domain, as if they were "the police." This highly unusual and controversial substitute arrangement was terminated after a short period of time. Simply stated, there are too many problematic issues tied to this type of an arrangement. Although this arrangement proved unsustainable, it represents the extreme of privatization— being the actual "sheriff" within the town. To be clear, I do not advocate such an extreme approach. I do, however, advocate the use of privatized patrols as supplements in both private and public environments. This is where the focus will be as we go forward.

In the private/supplement cell, there are many examples of security firms acting as a supplement to the public police. These often occur in private, gated communities. In these instances, the "protected communities" are separated by perimeter fencing coupled with private security patrols within the area. There are countless examples of contracted security services within gated communities.[58] One author estimated that by the mid 1990s between three and four million people in the United States lived in gated communities.[59] Later data reveals that this number has increased to seven million, with over 50,000 gated communities.[60] A survey of gated communities in South Africa revealed some extraordinary data. Of the 117 municipalities that responded to the survey, fully 20 percent had enclosed neighborhoods and 23 percent had large security estates.[61] Some authors who study gated communities, such as Blakely and Synder, contend that security is the driving force for all gated communities.[62] In this sense, gated communities may represent a *fortress mentality* growing in America and in some Westernized countries. Much of this occurred prior to 9/11.

In this private/supplement cell, there is overlap between the service provision of public and private entities. In this cell, the focus is on supplementing or enhancing the public safety provision already provided by policing agencies. For example, on college campuses there are often undefined or loosely defined boundaries between the "campus" and the larger community. In these areas, the public police may regularly, or at least semi-regularly, patrol the gated community and the college or corporate campus. The involvement of public police in these areas is usually more than in the private/substitute areas, and substantially less than public streets, parks, and the like (i.e., in the public realm). Consequently, the provision of security services by private firms in this cell (private/supplement) is already quite extensive.[63]

In these locations, private security firms provide patrol and other "quality-of-life" services that the police are unable or unwilling to perform. Most of the functional service provision is manifested in "observe and report" and order maintenance tasks. In this sense, these arrangements combine the traditional "observe and report" function of private security with the order maintenance role traditionally reserved for public police.

The same can be said of the substantial growth of shopping malls. The extent of growth coupled with the potential for terroristic attack make the notion of securing shopping malls critical. The economic and psychological impact of such an attack would be great. Indeed, attacks and planned attacks of shopping malls may become "common."[64] This same desire for security is also driving private policing in public environments. Performing such functions in the public domain, however, raises important public safety and public policy questions. Notwithstanding the potential for both benefit and abuse, these private patrols have been relatively unstudied within academic research and largely overlooked by policy makers.

An increasingly common approach in private policing is acting as a supplement to public police. This illustrates the public/supplement realm. It is this aspect of privatization of police services that has the most growth potential. Many of these arrangements are contained within business improvement districts (BID). Indeed, there are over 40 of these districts in the city of New York alone. There are more than one thousand across the United States.[65] In addition, the need to secure critical infrastructure is clearly part of this order maintenance function. The security of ports, utilities, transportation, water and sanitary systems, farms and food supplies, and a host of other critical aspects of a functioning society must be secured. For example, the DHS distributed $844 million in fiscal 2008 grants for protection of ports, transit systems, and other components of the nation's critical infrastructure. This funding is intended to support terrorism and disaster prevention, protection, and response and recovery capabilities. "With this year's funding, the department will have provided roughly $3 billion in grants for securing the nation's critical infrastructure and transportation systems," Homeland Security Secretary Michael Chertoff said in a press release. "As capabilities mature, we're encouraging state and local governments and the private sector to prioritize prevention and protection, communications capabilities, information sharing and regionally based security cooperation."[66] In these environments, the typical provision of security services is from private firms. Indeed, approximately 85% of the critical infrastructure is owned and secured by private firms.[67]

Accurate statistical information on the current scope of private policing is difficult to pinpoint, as there is no reference source that collects information on these arrangements. In any case, the examples in the next chapter illustrate a larger approach that some may view as a trend. As a means to introduce these examples, it may be helpful to think about the roles of private police and those of public police. Remember that much of the traditional literature on policing distinguishes public police as being focused on "law enforcement," while private police focus on "observe and report." Partly due to the impact of *Community Policing*, these traditional roles appear to be changing, with both groups being concerned with order maintenance functions. In this sense, it may be difficult to distinguish the work of the public police from the work of the private police.

The scope and details of these arrangements vary widely. In rare cases, private security has *replaced* public police within a given jurisdictional area. In most private policing initiatives, some level of "partnership" or some supplement with local police agencies form the basis for the arrangement. These partnership arrangements have a particular logic, especially when one considers the characteristics of public and private policing. Both have many similar goals—usually designed to reduce crime and fear through an environmental or order maintenance approach. Hopefully, the commonality of goals may serve to foster cooperative efforts in the "spirit of public safety." One way this could occur is when public police rely on private police to carry out tasks they prefer not to undertake. In return, public police provide some needed service, such as expeditious response to calls for assistance. Most public police officials welcome a fuller partnership with private security, if contracting would free up their officers for crime fighting.[68]

The "Why" of Order Maintenance

The prospect for alternative service providers—particularly private policing—conducting order maintenance functions can be derived from two basic factors: *fear* and *money*. Both of these factors will independently contribute to the market need for these services. Both of these factors, in combination, will increase the need for private policing in public environments. There are a number of ways that these factors are manifested. A useful characterization may include:

- Economic and operational issues (*money*)
- Crime and terrorism (*fear*)

Economic and Operational Issues (Money)

The relative cost of salaries is a significant factor between public and private policing. Of course, labor costs and benefits have a substantial price tag. From a purely financial perspective, alternative service providers, such as private security firms, provide certain cost savings. Estimates place the median annual income of security guards at $20,320 with the highest 10 percent paid at $33,270.[69] This is consistent with salary surveys. For example, a compensation survey conducted by the Bureau of Labor Statistics found the cost of hourly pay for security personnel ranging from an average of $6.82 in the Tampa/St. Petersburg metro area to $12.82 per hour in Denver.[70] More recent data reveal that the hourly wages for security personnel vary according to function and employment. Table 6.5 illustrates these variables.[71]

Compare these data to public police. Even rather dated police expenditures reveal that it costs at least $100,000 per year per police officer when salary, benefits, and overhead expenses were calculated into the equation.[72] Further, Miranda cited personnel expenditures as the single largest municipal budgetary line item. For example, two groups—police and fire—represent over 55 percent of the total expenditures for the city of Chicago. Personnel costs included salaries or wages, pensions, and fringe benefits. These costs, adjusted for inflation, increased 63 percent over the 10-year period.[73] These are straining municipal budgets and operations. This has caused the police union in Chicago to file a lawsuit against the city related to the denial of compensatory time. In his decision, U.S. District Judge Schenkier found that the Chicago Police Department operated 22 of the 25 police

Table 6.5   Private Security Salary Structures

Proprietary Security	Low (Dollars)	High (Dollars)
Unarmed	11.00	16.00
Armed	14.00	21.50
Console operations	12.50	15.00
Investigators	22.00	31.00
Contract Security	*Low (Dollars)*	*High (Dollars)*
Unarmed	10.00	15.00
Armed	15.00	20.00
Console operations	12.00	15.00
Investigators	25.00	32.69

Source: 2006 ASIS Security Industry Salary Survey.

districts with fewer than the authorized number of police officers, with an aggregate shortfall of 8.04 percent fewer officers than authorized. In his decision—which was ironically issued on September 11, 2007, Judge Schenkier concluded that the city deprived police officers their statutory right to use compensatory time. He asserted that[74]

> there is evidence that the city [Chicago] regularly assigned fewer personnel to the various units and district than authorized by the budget. … We do not presume to tell the city how many police personnel it must hire, or how to balance the challenging budgetary and public safety concerns that the city must confront.

Similar economic constraints have been reflected in academic research. For example, Savas found about 90 to 95 percent of police budgets go to personnel costs.[75] His study of New York City revealed that over a 25-year period, the number of public police officers rose from 16,000 to 24,000. However, the total annual hours worked by the entire force actually declined. He noted that the entire increase in the city's police force (fully 50 percent) was devoted to personnel benefits, such as shortening the workweek, lengthening lunch periods and vacation time, and providing more holidays and paid sick leave.[76] This assertion is echoed by Youngs, who stated, "Police in today's environment typically spend less than 20% of their time on crime related matters."[77] This circumstance is just the tip of the iceberg. These conflicts between costs and operations reveal greatly strained financial circumstances.[78]

Based on these statistics, a large proportion of the expenditures of policing—and of municipalities—are allocated to pay salaries and benefits of public police officers. These statistics raise the logical question, can this pay structure be sustained? As asserted earlier, this is doubtful.

While public police departments experience budget constraints, private security firms have dramatically expanded their relative size and scope. As presented earlier, studies of the "public safety" industry reveal a growing disparity between public and private policing. Over time, this data reveals a growing trend toward monies being spent on private security as compared to public police. By the year 2000, the ratio of dollars invested in private compared to public policing reveals that about 70 percent of all money invested in crime prevention and law enforcement is spent on private security.[79] Based on the spending patterns after 9/11, more and more monies are being spent on security technologies. As illustrated in the previous chapter, DHS funding has largely focused on security technologies. There is nothing to suggest that this will not continue.

Going forward, a market research firm predicts that the U.S. demand for private contracted security services will grow 4.3 percent a year to $48 billion in 2010, according to a report by analyst Jennifer Mapes of the Freedonia Group. According to the report, the security sector should benefit from the sharp focus on safety and security on the part of government, corporations, and consumers. These estimates also reveal that by 2017 a staggering $81 billion will be spent annually on a range of security services.[80] Indeed, the federal government alone has spent $41 billion on homeland security funding in 2004, which is double the amount in fiscal year 2001.[81] How long can the government continue this level of funding? Of course, this increase in security spending and investments is attributed to terrorism—and to people wanting to feel safe. Despite falling crime rates, consumers are worried about crime and overburdened public safety agencies, according to Mapes. "The aftermath of 9/11 has created a continuing and accelerating backdrop for revenue in the security companies, whether they be military related or homeland security related or ultimately commercially related," said analyst Jeffrey Kessler of Lehman Brothers.[82]

Beyond the salaries, benefits, and investments, a number of authors have argued certain operational functions drive up the costs associated with public safety services. For example, for decades citizens have been urged to call "911." This computerized call-taking system has resulted in huge increases in workloads in police departments. Years of urging citizens to call "911" has contributed to a culture where people call the police for more and more service-oriented requests. Calls for such things as barking dogs, streetlight repairs, noisy neighbors, unruly children, alarm response, and the like have created a difficult "unintended consequence" for police agencies already strapped with resource constraints.[83] This "unintended consequence" was aptly described by Scott and Goldstein, who stated, "Citizens [are] bringing problems to the police that the police may not be best suited to address."[84] Attempts to resolve the increasing level of service calls had some success, such as using "311" (nonemergency police response), and call stacking (prioritizing calls for dispatch based on level of seriousness).[85] However, these have not resolved the basic dilemma—servicing the community through the resources allocated to the department.

Added to these operational costs is the expense associated with a proactive crime prevention strategy. This proactive approach is in keeping with the *Community Policing* model now in vogue within policing. A proactive crime control strategy is costly to administer and is very labor intensive.[86] In purely financial terms, *Community Policing* has created additional tasks for police agencies.[87] These tasks include beat meetings, crime prevention missions, accountability sessions, and other service- and communication-oriented tasks. Most readers would agree that proactive problem-solving tasks take to time to accomplish. As a result, these tasks have contributed to the budgetary and operational constraints now facing municipal police agencies. Since most, if not all, of the federally funded *Community Policing* monies are now exhausted, the ability to maintain this level of service seems unrealistic.

This circumstance illustrates a basic problem with fully implementing *Community Policing*. Simply stated, the resources, operational constraints, and personnel levels associated with these tasks have resulted in overburdening policing agencies. The threat of terrorism has exacerbated this situation. Ironically, this may provide an impetus for public police to transfer to or supplement forces with private security personnel. As stated earlier, crime prevention and order maintenance have been the forte of private security. With these functions in mind, private policing will play an increasingly larger role in public safety. The form of this new policing model may mirror the *Community Policing* approach, which is premised on client service designed to achieve crime prevention and control. In this sense, private police will be used to supplement public police in service and order maintenance functions. This allows public police officers more free time to devote to more serious crimes, including terrorism prevention and response. Carlson asserts that communities are certain to follow this approach because "they may have to." He draws the analogy with medical care in that hospitals were "forced" to give more responsibility to nurses due to rising medical costs. Carlson emphasized his point in this way:[88]

> Cities may find that sworn police officers whom they must train, pay relatively well and sustain pensions—are too expensive—for fighting and deterring certain types of low-level crimes. To maintain basic civic order, rent-a-cops may be a better deal.

Instead of considering private police officers as "rent-a-cops," the more appropriate way to characterize their role is as "alternative service providers." Many needed and valuable services can be performed at a far reduced cost, as compared with public police officers. Importantly, by using these alternative service providers, it frees up police resources and personnel for more serious matters, such as gang and drug activities, tactical operations, criminal investigations, terrorism prevention, and intelligence gathering. In turn, there are numerous service-oriented tasks that can be performed by private police. Contracting certain service tasks can be equated to "outsourcing," which is common in business.[89]

The budgetary and operational dilemma for law enforcement officials may be best illustrated by alarm response. Alarm response refers to police being dispatched to burglar, fire, or panic alarms from commercial, industrial, and residential facilities. To understand the impact of this service provision, it may be helpful to cite some statistics. Nationwide, alarm calls comprise 10–12 percent of all calls for service. In the year 2000, Blackstone and Hakim estimate the annual costs for this service at $1.8 billion. This figure is equivalent to paying 35,000 police officers.[90] According to the Seattle Police Department, alarm response accounts for the second largest resource allocation. In just one year (2003), Seattle police officers responded to over 22,000 alarm calls, averaging about 62 alarms a day at a total estimated cost of $1.3 million per year.[91] Similarly, in 1995, the Charlotte-Mecklenburg Police Department received more than 500,000 calls for service. More than 100,000 were alarm calls. Of these alarm calls, 98.6 percent of them were "false alarms" (meaning no crime occurred). The department estimated that 70,000 "officer hours" were spent responding to these calls.[92] In an astonishing statistic, the Los Angeles Police Department responded to more than 120,000 alarm calls in one calendar year—which lead to only one arrest.[93] Partly due to this circumstance, the executive director of the L.A. Police Commission, Joe Gunn, asserted that "we [the city] lost 15% of the patrol time responding to false alarms."[94]

Often the problem with alarm response is attributed to the high rate of false alarms, which is as high as 95 percent or more.[95] This is only part of the problem. Consider that in the 1980s, only two to five percent of residences had alarm systems. This figure increased to 10 percent in the 1990s, and to about 20 percent by the year 2000.[96] Consequently, as the market for security alarms increased, the burden of alarm response for police agencies has also increased.

Many police agencies are looking for ways to deal with this problem. For example, using fines against property owners for excessive false alarms is common throughout the country.[97] While these have some merit, some argue that the police agencies still have to bear the operational burden of responding to false alarms, without directly receiving the revenue from the fines (which go to the overall city coffers).[98] At least partly based on this reality, some cities have instituted "verified response." This entails police *not* responding to alarms unless the call is verified by some third party (owner, clerk, witness, security, etc.).[99] In this policy, the call must be proven to be "bonafide" (an actual crime is occurring or has occurred). Salt Lake City instituted this policy in 2000. It reduced police responses by 90 percent, resulting in substantial cost reductions for the department.[100] In addition, this policy had other benefits to the department. For example, police response time to other emergencies decreased and police availability increased.[101] Importantly, it was also noted that the response times by private security to these calls were shorter than the response times by the police.[102] Unfortunately, this policy also resulted in a 13.7 percent increase in burglaries over a four-year period.[103]

While the reader can discern the obvious dilemmas related to alarm response and "verified response," the fact is, given the financial and operational constraints for policing agencies, private response is inevitable. Consider Johannesburg, South Africa. Partly due to resource constraints and response-time deficiencies, there is a growing market for alarm response conducted by private firms. As with the United States, this service provision evolved from the public's lack of confidence in the responsiveness of the police. In this sense, people looked to the private sector for more responsive protection. The result is more than 450 registered companies serving about 500,000 clients. These firms employ about 30,000 private officers who provide alarm response services. These officers are equipped with 9 mm weapons, and bulletproof vests, but have only citizen arrest powers. The average response time to the protected facility is five minutes. According to Davis, these services were done in a professional manner. He drew this conclusion by measuring citizen complaints, use of force incidents, and the average response time for alarm calls.[104]

These examples result in one overriding conclusion: since public police response was deemed not acceptable, citizens looked to the market for more responsive protection. While some services such as alarm response may be necessary, the compelling conclusion is that municipalities will not be able to afford the status quo.[105] Partly as a result of this situation, the Toronto Police Department reported that more than 60 percent of all calls to the police are handled by "alternative response" units, which include private police acting as a supplement to public police departments.[106]

The data and analysis presented in this section illustrate that public police are overburdened with many service-oriented functions, as well as by the economic and operational costs of providing these services to the public. Private police can help resolve these functional and economic constraints. Indeed, the threat of terrorism will only exacerbate these constraints—thereby accelerating the need for alternative service providers. When terrorist attacks occur—and they will—private police will increasingly move into many public spaces, including business and residential communities. This chapter shows how private police services, financed through alternative funding sources, have been used to address economic and operational constraints that burden police departments.

Finally, the overriding implication drawn from this section is that private police will be increasingly utilized to combat or respond to crime. Numerous authors have predicted or shown that private security personnel are being hired in response to the incidence of crime.[107] This assertion is echoed by Stephanie Mann, the author of *Safe Homes, Safe Neighborhoods*, who asserted that "[p]eople need to take responsibility for their safety. ... Citizens are the law and order in a community, not the police."[108] It can be argued that the private security industry is responding to the demand from individual citizens, businesses, and even communities due to the incidence and fear of crime. These views were advocated as a result of the impact of "normal" crime. With the threat of terrorism, it seems particularly appropriate to assert that government cannot implement the necessary remedies to deal with crime and terrorism (including the attendant fears) without the contribution of the private sector.

Crime and Terrorism (Fear)

As demonstrated above, the relationship between crime and fear has been systematically developed in numerous studies.[109] Similarly, other authors assert that crime has led to a generalized increase in fear levels in certain demographic subsections, as well as in the larger society.[110] From both perspectives, the conclusions were similar and compelling. The consistent conclusion was that crime has created a concern, often rising to what could be construed as fear. This fear of crime is exacerbated by signs of criminal activity. Criminal activity, such as disorder or incivility, has an impact on people's perceptions of crime. In this sense, incivility is equated with disorder, in that both purport to represent chaotic conditions that result in more serious criminal activity.

This leads to the conclusion that the *combination* of concern with crime and incivility (or disorder) affects neighborhood fear levels. The levels of fear are greatest where *both* crime and incivility coexist. Hence, objective crime rates are mediated by *perceptions* of neighborhood incivility. Ironically, if incivility (or disorder) is not perceived to be a problem, then residents may be able to cope with higher rates of crime. This conclusion has important implications. Communities must deal with both the crime rate *and* the physical and social indicators that lead to the perception of incivility and disorder.[111]

Now add terrorism to the equation. It is important to remember this key distinction: while crime causes fear, terrorism is *designed* to cause fear. Anyone who studies terrorism understands that terrorist acts are designed to play to the audience. Think of this distinction. If you are mugged on a subway, it is likely that the offender was interested in one thing: your money. He does not desire publicity. He does not want acclaim for his actions. Instead he wants to spend your money. He certainly does not want his "deed" to appear on the news. Now consider a terrorist act. Generally, the victims of the act are irrelevant. By that I mean the victims are typically a means to a larger end—unless the victim is intentionally assassinated, such as former Pakistani Prime Minister Bhutto. Usually, however, the victims are simply a way of communicating the "deed." The message is, pay attention to us because you may be next! Remember, when the media takes that message and communicates the deed to the masses, the "propaganda of the deed" is achieved.

This dynamic speaks volumes. It will create a need for more security. It will explain "why" police methods need to be changed. It will convey a deep message that the government (read the police and law enforcement) may not be able to protect you. This will increase—potentially substantially—the movement toward engaging more alternative service providers (read security personnel and technologies).

A couple of international examples may help to illustrate this dynamic. The private security industry is booming in Mexico City, where residents are taking steps to protect themselves from an increase in violent crime. A recent study showed that 25 percent of Mexico City residents reported being the victim of a crime in 2005. The country has a higher per-capita rate of violent robbery than the United States or any country in Europe. The traditional security measures employed by civilians include private guards, closed-circuit surveillance systems, and alarms. One expert reported that many Mexico City homes are also protected by electric fences. In order to meet the increased demand for security solutions, many companies are offering innovative new products. Consider these examples. Uno Technology has received 600 orders for a surveillance system that can send live video feeds to clients' cell phones, allowing them to constantly keep track of their home, business, or car. FLIR Systems recently began selling thermal infrared imaging cameras to commercial clients. The technology, which can detect a potential intruder's body heat, was traditionally used by law enforcement and the military. *Xtrem Secure*, a Mexican magazine covering the security industry, reported that many firms are seeing annual revenue increases of around 25 percent.[112]

This response has come from "normal" crime. The response to crime related to organized gangs and terrorism is even more problematic. As Mexico's drug cartels become increasingly violent, it has led to higher demand for security services in Mexico. Up to five percent of Mexico's gross domestic product is being spent on security, and the market for electronic security technology in Mexico is growing between 10 percent and 15 percent annually, according to the Latin American Security Association trade group. Terrorism in Mexico also became a concern after al Qaeda urged terrorists to attack oil facilities in Mexico and elsewhere. There are 400,000 security guards in Mexico, and outdoor surveillance camera networks have been implemented in 16 of Mexico's 31 states.[113]

In addition, after the terrorist attacks in November 2008 in Mumbai, an increasing number of citizens are turning to private-sector security and emergency services because local authorities failed to stop the terrorist attacks. The terrorist attacks caused many Mumbai residents to feel vulnerable for the first time. Rajeev Sharma, president of the security firm Topsgrup, said, "There has been an unprecedented rise in inquiries," when asked about his services since the attacks, and he has run out of armed guards. The company employs more than 40,000 guards nationally. Private emergency services also are expecting more attention because of the attacks. Sweta Mangal, the chief executive of a Mumbai ambulance service company, said its vehicles arrived at some of the attack sites before the police did.[114] *When* attacks like Mumbai occur in America, the result will be similar. Consequently, please consider this significant dynamic derived from the dual yet basic factors of *money* and *fear*.

The "How" of Order Maintenance

"How" entails a very different approach to order maintenance. As developed in the theoretical/historical section, the traditional desire of order maintenance was to change physical and social conditions in order to reduce crime. In this approach, often called the "broken windows" theory, the focus was on abandoned buildings, littering, graffiti, and other physical conditions within the environment.[115] This approach also focused on social aspects such as drinking, loitering, prostitution, and disorderly behaviors. Both the physical and the social cues created the perception that the people in the community do not take care of the neighborhood. As such, the environment was said to be conducive to more serious crime. While these concerns will still be relevant in the public safety era of policing, they will be subordinated to an overall desire to protect. A descriptive, shorthand way of describing this approach is to focus on *protection* instead of *service*.

This requires a different purpose underlying order maintenance provisions. For example, in the *Community Policing* era the purpose was to *clean* the environment of physical and social incivilities in order to combat crime. In the public safety era the purpose will be to *control* the environment in order to protect the community. Due to the potential devastating impact of terrorism, this desire to control the environment will be based on the following formula: order + surveillance = control. As seen in the last chapter, the use of surveillance technologies will be a critical element of this new policing model. These technologies, coupled with an "enhanced" order maintenance approach—with more eyes and ears on the street—will result in an almost "clinical" focus on the environment.

The application of a "clinical" environmental approach at improving security can be illustrated by recent changes implemented in British railroad stations. These stations will soon have additional security standards with more thorough screening, including the use of biometric identification. Civilian employees will also be trained by terrorism experts on how to conduct searches and identify suspicious behavior. In addition, the number of security service personnel is projected to ultimately double what it was in 2001. "While no major failures in our protective security have been identified, companies responsible for crowded places will now be given updated and more detailed advice on how they can improve their resilience against attack, both by better physical protection and greater vigilance in identifying suspicious behavior," said British Prime Minister Gordon Brown.[116]

An excellent—yet dramatic—example of this clinical focus on the environment is illustrated by a recent proposal devised by the New York Police Department. It advocates placing the new World Trade Center into a "security zone." Only specially screened taxis, limousines, and cars would be able to enter the site through "sally ports," or barriers guarded by police officers. Approximately 12 guard booths will be erected at popular street corners where pedestrians or automobiles may try to access the site. Service and delivery trucks will be required to pass through the underground bomb screening center, and buses will not be allowed to leave the underground security center and garage until each passenger has returned. In addition to these security measures at this site, each automobile that comes into Manhattan will also have its picture taken and its license plate scanned by the NYPD. The data will be stored for at least one month. This plan is part of the NYPD's Lower Manhattan Security Initiative (more about this plan in the next chapter), which aims to increase security in the area by deploying armed officers, closed-circuit television cameras, license plate readers, and explosives trace detection systems.[117]

Beyond this environmental focus, other order maintenance strategies have been proposed. For example, Chief Bratton is promoting the idea of "policing terrorism" in Los Angeles, much the same way he embraced the "broken windows" strategy in New York City. He advocates focusing on small crimes before they turn into big ones. The key is to shift police officers away from the idea that they are only first responders and train them on prevention techniques.[118] Getting police oriented toward prevention, of course, is consistent with the tenets of *Community Policing*. While I agree that much of the focus of police should be on prevention—or what I think is better characterized as *protection*—the reality is police will need help. I believe this help will come from military weaponry, technology, and alternative service providers.

These alternative service providers will include civilian governmental employees, volunteers, and, most importantly—and controversially—private police officers. Given the data and analysis contained in this chapter, one can reasonably assert that the majority, if not the vast majority, of order maintenance functions will be conducted by private police employed by security firms. There are numerous order maintenance functions that can be accomplished by these lower skilled, less paid workers. The tasks of these alternative service providers may include, but are not limited to:[119]

- ◾ Traffic accidents
- ◾ Traffic control
- ◾ Parking tickets
- ◾ Abandoned vehicles
- ◾ Vehicle lockouts
- ◾ Building checks
- ◾ Alarm response
- ◾ Animal complaints
- ◾ Funeral escorts
- ◾ Paperwork/subpoena services
- ◾ "Cold call" follow-ups
- ◾ Vandalism complaints/reporting
- ◾ Theft/burglary/lost and found reporting
- ◾ Crime scene security
- ◾ Prisoner transports/security
- ◾ Missing persons assistance
- ◾ Shoplifting arrests
- ◾ Special event security

I close this chapter with the acknowledgment that "combining" police and security into a larger "public safety" policing model will not be easy. There are numerous pitfalls and complications to this transition (see Chapter 10 for this discussion). The dangers inherent in this work and within this transition are real. Consider, for example, an incident in Cincinnati where a private police officer was shot at while on patrol. According to police, the private officer was not seriously harmed by the gunfire, but bullets struck his vehicle. He was fired on multiple times by three separate shooters. When he called 911, he was put on hold by the operator. The private police officer, Blankenship, says that he had to call the operator from his cell phone because the city does not provide private officers with radios. If he had a police radio he could have called for backup during the shooting. This officer was part of the Cincinnati Special Police, who are sworn and commissioned officers through the city of Cincinnati. They attend the same training as Cincinnati police officers; however, they are not employed by the city.[120] Obviously, they are not equipped with police radios.

Admittedly, this example reveals that it may be a tall task, with many roadblocks and obstacles in the way. When you identify or encounter these obstacles, remember two words: *fear* and *money*. These will be the drivers toward this transition. I contend these two basic premises will overcome any obstacle. In addition, many have already worked long and hard to develop "partnerships" and other relationships between professionals in security and policing. These will go a long way in facilitating this new model of policing.

Endnotes

1. Pastor, James F. (2003). *The Privatization of Police in America: An Analysis and Case Study*. Jefferson, NC: McFarland.
2. Covington, Jeanette and Ralph B. Taylor (1991). "Fear of Crime in Urban Residential Neighborhoods: Implications of Between and Within Neighborhood Sources for Current Models," *The Sociological Quarterly* 32, no. 2:231–49; Lewis, Dan A. and Michael G. Maxfield (1980). "Fear in the Neighborhoods: An Investigation of the Impact of Crime," *Journal of Research in Crime and Delinquency* July:160–89; and Kelling, George (1995). "Reduce Serious Crime by Restoring Order," *The American Enterprise* May/June.
3. Pastor, James F. (2003), op. cit.
4. McLennan, Barbara N., ed. (1970). *Crime in Urban Society*. London: Cambridge University Press.
5. Cohen, Lawrence E. and Marcus Felson (1979). "Social Change and Crime Rate Trends," *American Sociological Review* 44:588–607.
6. Gibbs, Jack P. and Maynart L. Erickson (1976). "Crime Rates of American Cities in an Ecological Context," *American Journal of Sociology* 82:605–20. Also see Reppetto, who concluded that social cohesion and informal surveillance declines when a large number of people live in a given area, in Jackson, Pamela Irving (1984). "Opportunity and Crime: A Function of City Size," *Sociology and Social Research* 68, no. 2:173–93.
7. Lewis, Dan A. and Michael G. Maxfield (1980), op. cit.
8. Kelling, George (1995), op. cit.

9. These "theoretical" concepts have been widely recognized in police operations. For example, numerous physical and social factors contributing to crime reduction and problem solving are enumerated in policies and procedures by municipal police departments, such as "Community and City Services Problem Strategies" (2000), in *Chicago Alternative Policing Strategy (CAPS)*. Chicago Police Department, December 12:1–14.

10. Fisher, Bonnie and Jack L. Nasar (1995). "Fear Spots in Relation to Microlevel Physical Cues: Exploring the Overlooked," *Journal of Research in Crime and Delinquency* 32, no. 2:214–39.

11. Pastor, James F. (2003), op. cit.

12. Pastor, James F. (2003), op. cit.

13. Kaplan, Robert (1994). "The Coming Anarchy," *The Atlantic Monthly* February.

14. Felson, Marcus (2002). *Crime and Everyday Life.* Thousand Oaks, CA: Sage Publications; and Atlas, Randy I. (2008). "Fear of Parking," *Security Management* February:54.

15. Adams, Duncan (2008). "In Its Garages, Roanoke Aims to Stop Threats—Real or Imagined," *Roanoke Times* (VA), July 21.

16. Fenton, Mike (2008). "Discouraging Loiterers by Design," *Security Management* 52, no. 5 (May):68.

17. See, for example, Moore, Mark H. and Robert C. Trojanowicz (1988). "Perspectives on Policing: Corporate Strategies for Policing," National Institute of Justice, Office of Justice Programs. U.S. Department of Justice, no. 6 (November); Palango, Paul (1998). "On the Mean Streets: As the Police Cut Back, Private Cops Are Moving In," *MacLeans* 111, no. 2 (January 12); Seamon, Thomas M. (1995). "Private Forces for Public Good," *Security Management* September; Kolpacki, Thomas A. (1994). "Neighborhood Watch: Public/Private Liaison," *Security Management* November; Cox, Steven M. (1990). "Policing into the 21st Century," *Police Studies* 13, no. 4:168–77; Johnston, Les (1992). *The Rebirth of Private Policing.* London: Routledge; Kelling, George L. and Catherine M. Coles (1996). *Fixing Broken Windows: Restoring Order and Reducing Crime in Our Communities.* New York: Simon and Schuster; and Schmerler, Karin, Matt Perkins, Scott Phillips, Tammy Rinehart, and Meg Townsend (2002). "Problem Solving Tips: A Guide to Reducing Crime and Disorder through Problem-Solving Partnerships," Office of Community Oriented Policing Services. U.S. Department of Justice (June).

18. Muhlhausen, David B. (2001). "Do Community Oriented Policing Services Grants Affect Violent Crime Rates," *The Heritage Foundation* May 25:4.

19. See, for example, Chanken, Marcia and Jan Chaiken (1987). "Public Policing-Privately Provided," National Institute of Justice, Office of Justice Programs. U.S. Department of Justice (June); Shearing, Clifford D. and Philip C. Stenning (1983). "Private Security: Implications for Control," *Social Problems* 30, no. 5:493–506; and Cunningham, William C., John J. Strauchs and Cliffiord W. Van Meter (1991). "Private Security: Patterns and Trends," National Institute of Justice, Office of Justice Programs. U.S. Department of Justice (August).

20. Pastor, James F. (2003), op. cit.

21. Pastor, James F. (2006). *Security Law and Methods.* Burlington, MA: Butterworth-Heinemann.

22. Pastor, James F. (2006), op. cit.

23. See, for example, Benson, Bruce L. (1990). *The Enterprise of Law: Justice Without State.* San Francisco, CA: Pacific Research Institute for Public Policy; McLeod, Ross (2002). *Para-Police.* Toronto: Boheme Press; Chanken, Marcia and Jan Chaiken (1987), op cit.; and Palango, Paul (1998), op. cit.

24. Pastor, James F. (2003), op. cit.; and Pastor, James F. (2006), op. cit.

25. Pastor, James F. (2005). "Public Safety Policing." *Law Enforcement Executive Forum* 5, no. 6 (November):13–27.

26. Pastor, James F. (2006), op. cit.

27. Pastor, James F. (2003), op. cit.

28. Oliver, Willard M. (2004). *Community-Oriented Policing: A Systematic Approach to Policing.* Upper Saddle River, NJ: Prentice Hall; and Pastor, James F. (2003), op. cit.

29. Pastor, James F. (2006), op. cit.

30. Hyde, David (2001). "A Theory of Evolution," *Canadian Security* 23, no. 5 (June/July).

31. McLeod, Ross (2002), op. cit.

32. McLeod, Ross (2002), op. cit., 15 and 61.

33. See http://www.citizencorps.gov/cert/ (retrieved on February 1, 2009).

34. See http://www.citizencorps.gov/ (retrieved on February 1, 2009).

35. Meserve, Jeanne and Mike M. Ahlers (2007). "FDNY Anti-Terror Plans Spark Fears of Witch Hunts," CNN (retrieved on December 5, 2007).

36. DeStefano, Anthony M. (2007). "New Role for the Bravest," *Newsday* (retrieved on November 24, 2007).

37. www.nydailynews.com (retrieved on October 11, 2007).

38. This division of labor approach was characterized as "blended policing" by McLeod, Ross (2002), op. cit., 129.

39. Bayley, David H. and Clifford D. Shearing (2001). "The New Structure of Policing," *NIJ* July.

40. Spielman, Fran (2004). "Daley Wants Bigger Traffic Management Corps," *Chicago Sun-Times,* November 12.

41. Bourque, Julia (2004). "Chief: More Officers Mean Less Crime: Calumet City to Lure Reserve Police Officers," *Northwest Indiana Times,* July 2.

42. Wessel, Robert H. (1995). "Privatization in the United States," *Business Economics* October; Donahue, John D. (1989). *The Privatization Decision.* New York: Basic Books; Tolchin, Martin (1985). "Private Guards Get New Role in Public Law Enforcement," *The New York Times,* November 29; Clotfelter, Charles T. (1977). "Public Services, Private Substitutes and the Demand for Protection Against Crime," *The American Economic Review* 67, no. 5:876; Miranda, Rowan A. (1993). "Better City Government at Half the Price," in *Chicago's Future in a Time of Change,* ed. Richard Simpson. Stipes; Carlson, Tucker (1995). "Safety Inc.: Private Cops Are There When You Need Them," *Policy Review* 73 (Summer); Benson, Bruce L. (1990), op. cit.; Morgan, David R. (1992). "The Pitfalls of Privatization: Contracting Without Competition," *American Review of Public Administration* 22, no. 4:251–68; and Clemow, Brian (1992). "Privatization and the Public Good," *Labor Law Journal*: 344–49.

43. Linowes, David F. (1988). "Report of the President's Commission on Privatization," in *Privatization: Toward More Effective Government.* Washington: U.S. Government Printing Office; Wessel, Robert H. (1995), op. cit.; Benson, Bruce L. (1990), op. cit.; and Donahue, John D. (1989), op. cit.

44. Donahue, John D. (1989), op. cit.

45. Carlson, Tucker (1995), op. cit; and Patterson, Julien (1995). "Forging Creative Alliances," *Security Management* January.

46. Benson, Bruce L. (1990), op. cit.

47. Hebdon, R. (1995). "Contracting Out in New York State: The Story the Lauder Report Chose Not to Tell," *Labor Studies Journal* 20, no. 1:3–24; Donahue, John D. (1989), op. cit.; and Chanken, Marcia and Jan Chaiken (1987), op. cit.

48. Bilik, Al (1992). "Privatization: Defacing the Community," *Labor Law Journal*:338–43; Shenk, Joshua Wolf (1995). "The Perils of Privatization," *The Washington Monthly*, May; Schine, Eric, Richard S. Dunham, and Christopher Farrell (1994). "America's New Watchword: If it Moves, Privatize It," *Business Week*, December 12; Donahue, John D. (1989), op. cit.; and Hebdon, R. (1995), op. cit.

49. Chanken, Marcia and Jan Chaiken (1987), op cit.

50. Shearing, Clifford D. and Philip C. Stenning (1983), op. cit.

51. Pastor, James F. (2003), op. cit.

52. Benson, Bruce L. (1990), op. cit.

53. Benson, Bruce L. (1990), op. cit.

54. Pastor, James F. (2003), op. cit.

55. Swonk, Diane (2003). *The Passionate Economist: Find the Power and Humanity Behind the Numbers.* New York: John Wiley and Sons.

56. Pastor, James F. (2003), op. cit.

57. For an explanation of this research and its findings, please see Pastor, James F. (2003). *The Privatization of Police in America: An Analysis and Case Study.* Jefferson, NC: McFarland.

58. See Farnham, Alan (1992). "U.S. Suburbs Are Under Siege," *Fortune*, December 28. He reported that in Los Angeles, 35 neighborhoods have asked local governmental permission to separate from the surrounding communities by installing gates and hiring security firms. In suburban Detroit, the 2,300-home East English Village Association hired a private security force to supplement patrols of local police. The reasoning behind this decision is illustrated by a statement from the president of this property association: "We figured if we wanted to keep this neighborhood stable, we couldn't stick our heads in the sand and say the police should take care of it. We realized there's only so much they can do." Also see Cruickshank, Ken (1994). "Frenchman's Creek Provides the Ultimate in Security," *Manager's Report* 8 (November), who described a property association in the Frenchman's Creek development in Florida that hired a "mini-swat team" (called S.T.O.P.—Special Tactical and Operations Personnel). This specially trained tactical team "roams the grounds every night dressed in camouflage face paint to stay as unobtrusive as possible and give them the edge on any intruder." The author asserts that this "tactical team" stays sharp by conducting exercises with sophisticated equipment, including high-tech night vision gear and infrared body heat detectors that distinguish a human body from the surrounding vegetation. The security force also includes a marine patrol and enforces speed limits by ticketing violators.

59. Blakely, Edward J. and Mary Gail Snyder (1997). "Gating America." www.asu.edu/caed/proceedings97/Blakely (retrieved on October 28, 2004).

60. McGoey, Chris E. (1999). "Gated Communities: Access Control Issues." www.crime-doctor.com/gated.htm (retrieved on June 20, 2006).

61. Landman, Karina (2003). "National Survey of Gated Communities in South Africa." www.gatedcomsa.com (retrieved on June 20, 2006).

62. Blakely, Edward J. and Mary Gail Snyder (1997), op. cit.

63. The trend toward more extensive policing on college campuses was discussed in Parry, Marc (2008). "New View of Campus Watch," *Albany Times Union* (NY), March 8, A1. The author noted that the SUNY effort occurs as numerous campus shootings have forced U.S. colleges to take a closer look at their security protocols. The peace-

officer upgrade also signifies what HVCC public safety director Fred Aliberti calls a trend toward the expanded professionalization of campus security departments. This was also cited by Reid, Betty (2008). "Security at County Colleges to Begin Carrying Guns," *Arizona Republic,* January 7. She noted that police officers assigned to provide security to the Maricopa County Community College District in Arizona will carry guns starting in the spring semester. At least 36 armed officers will be deployed to 9 of the district's 10 campuses. The officers received firearms training in December 2007 and will carry .45-caliber handguns. The community was forced to arm its campus police because of a new state law that requires sworn police officers to carry guns. The law went into effect in October 2007, six months after 32 students were shot and killed by another student at Virginia Tech. The campuses will still have an additional force of unarmed campus security personnel. Also see supplementing police forces with security officers in Abbas, Rohma (2008). "Security Guards Hired for Early Morning Hours," *Stony Brook Independent,* October 30.

64. See, for example, Meserve, Jeanne, Eliott McLaughlin, and Kelli Arena (2007), "Malls Debate How to Protect Shoppers From Violence," CNN, December 6, who note that the killing of eight people at an Omaha, Nebraska, mall has raised security questions at malls across the country. Security officials at the 1,200 malls and 50,000 shopping centers in the United States are expected to consider adding more security measures and updating their emergency plans. Security should watch people as they enter the mall, looking for suspicious behavior that could signal a violent act is about to take place. Focus groups conducted by the International Council of Shopping Centers showed that shoppers would accept additional security measures, such as bag checks and magnetometers, only if the national threat advisory system was raised to level red. Malls are doing more to train their guards after a 2006 study revealed that only a few states require training or minimum hiring standards. The council worked with George Washington University to create a training video that has been seen by an estimated 6,000 security guards over the past year.

65. Davis, Robert C. and Sarah Dadush (2000). "The Public Accountability of Private Police: Lessons from New York, Johannesburg, and Mexico City," *Vera Institute of Justice*, August.

66. http://www.govexec.com/story_page.cfm?articleid=40050&dcn=e_hsw.

67. Simeone, Matthew J. (2006). "The Power of Public-Private Partnerships P3 Networks in Policing," *The Police Chief* May; Cooke, Leonard G. and Lisa R. Hahn (2006). "The Missing Link in Homeland Security," *The Police Chief* 73, no. 11 (November); and National Policy Summit: Building Private Security/Public Policing Partnerships to Prevent and Respond to Terrorism and Public Disorder (2004). Office of Community Oriented Policing Services. U.S. Department of Justice.

68. Pastor, James F. (2003), op. cit.

69. U.S. Department of Labor Statistics from May 2004 cited in Security Director's Report (2006), March:7. www.ioma.com.

70. IOMA (2001). Security Director's Report, May.

71. 2006 ASIS Security Industry Salary Survey cited in *Security Management* August:20.

72. Reynolds, Morgan O. (1994). "Using the Private Sector to Deter Crime," *National Center for Policy Analysis*, March; and Pastor, James F. (2003), op. cit.

73. Miranda, Rowan A. (1993), op. cit.

74. *Hans Heitman and Thomas Linnane v. City of Chicago*, 04 C 3304, U.S. District Court for Northern District of Illinois, Eastern Division, order issued on September 11, 2007.

75. Spitzer, Steven and Andrew T. Scull (1977). "Privatization and Capitalist Development: The Case of the Private Police," *Social Problems* 25, no. 1:18–28.

76. Savas, E. S. (2000). *Privatization and Public-Private Partnerships*. New York: Chatham House.

77. Youngs, Al (2004). "The Future of Public/Private Partnerships," *FBI Law Enforcement Bulletin* January.

78. For examples of contemporary financial constraints, please see Chapter 9.

79. Carlson, Tucker (1995), op. cit.; and H.B. 2996: *Law Enforcement and Industry Security Cooperation Act of 1996* (104th Congress), February 29, 1996.

80. "Private Security Services" from the Freedonia Group, Inc., cited in *Security Management* (2008), November:22.

81. Uchitelle, Louis and John Markoff (2004). "Terrorbusters, Inc: The Rise of the Homeland Security Industrial Complex," *The New York Times,* October 17.

82. "Aiming to Protect and Serve" (2007). *Investor's Business Daily* August 17.

83. A pointed example of this dilemma was discussed by Kelling and Coles where they cite data from Boston. From 1975 to 1991, the total number of 911 calls rose about 33 percent. In 1975, the "non-index" calls were 350,000. By 1991 they rose to 600,000. See Kelling, George L. and Catherine M. Coles (1996), op. cit., 91; Hyde, David (2001), op. cit., 14; and Pastor, James F. (2005), op. cit.

84. Scott, Michael S. and Herman Goldstein (2005). "Shifting and Sharing Responsibilities for Public Safety Problems: Problem Oriented Guides for Police Response," Guide Series no. 3, Office of Community Oriented Policing Services. U.S. Department of Justice (August):1–53.

85. "Call stacking" is a process that the computer system performs where nonemergency, lower priority calls are ranked and held ("stacked") so that higher priorities are continually dispatched first. For most busy departments, call stacking and delayed response have become the norm. For analysis of this process, see McEwen, Tom, Deborah Spence, Russell Wolff, Julie Wartell, and Barbara Webster (2003). "Call Management and Community Policing: A Guidebook for Law Enforcement." Institute for Law and Justice. U.S. Department of Justice (February).

86. Pastor, James F. (2003), op. cit.

87. Moore, Mark H. and Robert C. Trojanowicz (1988). "Perspectives on Policing: Corporate Strategies for Policing," National Institute of Justice, Office of Justice Programs. U.S. Department of Justice, no. 6 (November); and Trojanowicz, Robert C. and David L. Carter (1990). "The Changing Face of America," *FBI Law Enforcement Bulletin* January.

88. Carlson, Tucker (1995), op. cit.

89. Youngs, Al (2004), op. cit.

90. Blackstone, Erwin A. and Simon Hakim (2002). "A Market Solution for False Alarms," *Reason,* November 11.

91. www.seattle.gov (retrieved on November 22, 2004).

92. Lowrey, Michael (2003). "Incentives, Privatization Help City Police: Charlotte Addresses Burglar Alarm Abuse through Creative Program," *Carolina Journal Online,* November 17. www.carolinajournal.com/issues/display_story.html?id=1197 (retrieved on March 7, 2004).

93. This statistic was cited from an editorial in the *Los Angeles Times* in January 2003 by Betten, Michael and Mitchell Mervosh (2005). "Should Police Respond to Alarms?" www.securitymanagement.com (retrieved on June 8, 2005).

94. Garza, Mariel (2002). "Alarm Plan: Police May Quit Reacting," *L.A. Daily News,* December 2. www.freerepublic.com (retrieved on May 13, 2004).
95. Olick, M. (1994). "Private Response: The No Response Solution," *Security News,* December; Benson, Bruce L. (1990), op. cit; and Cunningham et al. (1991), op. cit.
96. Litsikas, Mary (1994). "Security System Installations Up in 1994," *Security Distributing and Marketing,* September; and Cunningham et al. (1991), op. cit.
97. See Lowrey, Michael (2003), op. cit., 1, for an example of this system.
98. Blackstone, Erwin A. and Simon Hakim (2002), op. cit., 2.
99. Lowrey, Michael (2003), op. cit., 2.
100. Lowrey, Michael (2003), op. cit., 2; and Scott, Michael S. and Herman Goldstein (2005), op. cit., 27–28.
101. Betten, Michael and Mitchell Mervosh (2005), op. cit., 3; and Lowrey, Michael (2003), op. cit., 2.
102. Betten, Michael and Mitchell Mervosh (2005), op. cit., 3; and Lowrey, Michael (2003), op. cit., 2.
103. Lowrey, Michael (2003), op. cit., 2.
104. Davis, Robert C. and Sarah Dadush (2000), op. cit.
105. Pastor, James F. (2003), op. cit.
106. Palango, Paul (1998), op. cit.; and Pastor, James F. (2003), op. cit.
107. Meadows, Robert J. (1991). "Premises Liability and Negligent Security: Issues and Implications.," *Journal of Contemporary Criminal Justice* 7, no. 3:112–25; Spencer, Suzy (1997). "Private Security." Phoenix Mosaic Group. onpatrol.com/cs.privsec. html; Benson, Bruce L. (1997). "Privatization in Criminal Justice." National Institute of Justice, Office of Justice Programs. U.S. Department of Justice; Tolchin, Martin (1985), op. cit.; Cunningham, William C., John J. Strauchs and Clifford W. Van Meter (1991), op. cit.; Walinsky, Adam (1993), op. cit.; and McLeod, Ross (2002), op. cit.
108. Litsikas, Mary (1994), op. cit.
109. Smith, Lynn Newhart and Gary D. Hill (1991). "Victimization and Fear of Crime," *Criminal Justice and Behavior* 18, no. 2:217–40; Lewis, Dan A. and Michael G. Maxfield (1980). "Fear in the Neighborhoods: An Investigation of the Impact of Crime," *Journal of Research in Crime and Delinquency* July:160–89; Liska, Allen E., Joseph J. Lawrence, and Andrew Sanchirico (1982). "Fear of Crime as a Social Fact," *Social Forces* 60, no. 3:760–70; Benson, Bruce L. (1990), op. cit.; and Moore, Mark H. and Robert C. Trojanowicz (1988), op. cit.
110. West, Marty L. (1993). "Get a Piece of the Privatization Pie," *Security Management* March; Farnham, Alan (1992), op. cit.; Walinsky, Adam (1993), op. cit.; and Litsikas, Mary (1994), op. cit.
111. Lewis, Dan A. and Michael G. Maxfield (1980), op. cit.
112. Hawley, Chris (2007). "Security Business Booms in Mexico," *Arizona Republic,* May 3.
113. Avila, Oscar (2008). "Mexico City's Crime Rate Is Like Gold for Security Firms," *Chicago Tribune,* May 20.
114. Bellman, Eric (2008). "A Traumatized Mumbai Seeks to Protect Itself," *Wall Street Journal,* December 18.
115. Davis, Robert C. and Sarah Dadush (2000), op. cit.; and Felson, Marcus (2002), op. cit., 111 and 114.
116. Lyall, Sarah (2007). "Britain Plans New Security Measures," *New York Times,* November 15.
117. Bagli, Charles V. (2008). "Police Want Tight Security Zone at Ground Zero," *New York Times,* August 12.

118. http://www.dailynews.com/news/ci_8527308 (retrieved on March 17, 2008).

119. McEwen, Tom, Deborah Spence, Russell Wolff, Julie Wartell, and Barbara Webster (2003), op. cit., 38–39; and Youngs, Al (2004), op. cit.

120. Howard, Jacqueline (2008). http://www.wcpo.com/news/local/story.aspx?content_id=0123b69a-aa51-4c74-a0d9-de485f871737 (retrieved on January 23, 2008). See also where a security guard killed two attempted armed robbers reported by the *Dallas Morning News*, "Police: Security Guard with Assault Rifle Kills 2 Suspected Robbers" on October 4, 2007. A Dallas security guard fatally shot two of the three men holding him up at gunpoint in a strip mall parking lot. According to Dallas Police Sergeant Ray Beaudreault, the three men approached the guard around 11:30 pm, pointed a gun at him, and asked him to step out of his car, after which the guard fired on one man with an assault rifle and immediately killed him. The second attacker fled by foot, said Beaudreault, and the guard shot and killed the third man as he drove away because he feared being attacked. Beaudreault says the case will go before a grand jury, but he does not believe the security guard will face any charges.

Chapter 7

Public Safety Policing—
Model Synergy

Discerning What Does Not Exist

By this point in the book, the reader should have made some observations—or even conclusions—as to the merits of my proposed policing model. I have attempted to develop the reasons why the policing model will change and what it will look like. This exercise has been largely based on making sense of a complex world, where seemingly disparate examples may illustrate a larger trend. In this sense, I analogize this exercise as like putting together a puzzle—without the benefit of the completed picture. As such, the attempt to articulate a future policing model is like the intelligence analyst trying to discern and predict a particular terrorist attack.

The last three chapters have been devoted to fleshing out the specifics of each particular element. In the "military weaponry and tactical operations" element, the data, the logic, and the framework—in my mind—demonstrate that police will "look and act" more and more like the military. In the "intelligence methods and surveillance technology" element, intelligence process techniques combine with increasingly sophisticated technology. The goal is to discern and interdict crime before it occurs. When crime does occur, these intelligence processes and the related technologies will also be used for identification and prosecution. The "order maintenance" element illustrates that the focus on the environment will become increasingly important, with innovative attempts to provide more "eyes and ears" for public safety. The end goals of these elements are to control the environment—and the population—in a manner that will facilitate the protection of the homeland.

All three elements are critical. Each must contribute to the larger goal—*protection*. The dual purpose of *service* will often be subordinate to this overriding focus. Each element must be cognizant of these traditional dual goals. Stated another way, the application of each element must be cognizant of the desire to protect and the desire to serve. This is a difficult balance to achieve. As will be evident in the discussion below, it is likely that the alternative service providers will focus on order maintenance for both service and protection. This approach will be developed in this chapter.

Related to this assertion is the need for each element to work in tandem with the other elements. Since the application of this model is still more conceptual than real, being able to illustrate actual examples of these elements working together will be difficult. This is so for at least two reasons. First, there is little, if any, research that attempts to bring together these disparate elements into a "policing model." There is evidence of individual elements. For example, some manifestation of the "militarization" of the police is apparent. As noted in Chapter 4, the data—and the related concerns—are evident. Further, there is a clear desire for "intelligence-led policing" by thought leaders in policing. Also, much has been written about camera systems in public environments. In addition, there has been discussion around the use of private police in public environments. However, no one, to my knowledge, has "connected the dots." No author, researcher, or policy maker has advocated bringing these seemingly disparate pieces into a cohesive model.

Second, because there is no existing cohesive "model," there is little ability to demonstrate the development of the model. In this sense, it is like the age-old question, what came first, the chicken or the egg? In this case, the answer is easier than the chicken or the egg question. In my mind, the answer is the elements come first. The "model" is subsequently discerned. Of course, it is easier to explain the existence of particular elements than it is to explain how and why they can—or will—work together. In the end, this discussion must attempt to communicate the synergy using two approaches: show developing examples of each element working together, and show specific examples of each element in isolation. The logic of this approach is then further articulated by illustrating the "connection" of the elements through actual and hypothetical examples. In any case, I trust this chapter will build on—and hopefully bring together—what in my mind is a discernable trend toward *Public Safety Policing*.

"Model" Synergy

Based on the aforementioned model elements, and from the issues presented in this book, I contend that a new model of policing is emerging. Although this model is in its infancy, certain assumptions can be made on what a future model of policing will look like. Before describing this model, two core questions need to be answered:

1. Can municipal police departments perform both as a first responder for homeland security and with a community service orientation?
2. What role will alternative service providers have in the delivery of public safety services?

The answer to the first question should seem apparent. A number of factors answer this question in the negative. First, while it is still an unsettled question, it would be reasonable to conclude that terrorism will be a fact of life for years to come. If this is true, then police agencies will not only have to deal with the carnage associated with terroristic violence, but they will also be prime targets of the violence. Any study of terrorism will result in this inescapable conclusion. For example, the classic movie *The Battle of Algiers*, based on terrorist violence in Algeria, powerfully demonstrates the systematic assassinations of police officers. Indeed, contemporary times reveal horrendous violence against Iraqi police and civil defense forces.

Based on these assumptions, it seems reasonable to conclude that terrorism will have a great effect on the operations of police departments. This will likely result in many police fatalities. As cold as this may sound, the realities of being both a first-line responder and a target will create an environment that is extraordinarily complex, both in operational and in human terms.

The second part of this question is that *Community Policing* is about to end. This statement may be subject to criticism from police, academic, and political circles. The fact is that the federal funding used to support *Community Policing* programs is largely exhausted. Without additional monies to support this policing model, it will be slowly de-emphasized into extinction. Since the vast percentage of available resources is earmarked for terrorism- and homeland security-related matters, an old adage seems appropriate: *follow the money*. If the money for *Community Policing* is gone, and it is now directed at homeland security, then police agencies will redirect their mission to account for this funding rationale. Simply put, police agencies will increasingly focus on the first responder mission, with *Community Policing* ending in its current form. However, because of their responsiveness to the client (i.e., citizen), and due to the nature of the service provision, private police may prove to be an excellent provider of *Community Policing* services.

The answer to the second question follows from this assertion. With the future focus of police on terrorism and violent crime (including street gangs that are likely to "graduate" to terrorism), the need for alternative service providers becomes extraordinarily important. As stated in the previous chapter, alternative service providers will be the paraprofessionals of the police departments. These include private police, civilian employees of police agencies, and auxiliary (part-time) officers. While it is likely that all three types of alternative service providers will coexist in some form, the most likely and beneficial option is private police officers. Due to the economic and operational aspects of private police (as previously discussed in the last chapter), this model is likely to predominate.

This book is not the only advocate for enhanced cooperation and connection with the public and private sectors around the notion of public safety. For example, the *National Strategy for Homeland Security* clearly sets this underlying principle. It states that "homeland security is a shared responsibility built upon a foundation of partnerships. ... The private and non-profit sectors also must be full partners in homeland security."[1] While this document does not directly advocate the specific elements of *Public Safety Policing*, the principles set forth are consistent with my vision. Similarly, "Operation Cooperation" advocates increased use of the private sector into homeland security strategies. This advocates various interactive public–private approaches, including contractual, goodwill, and umbrella programs. The resources and skills of these entities need to be fully utilized. In short, this Justice Department sponsored approach seeks to[2]

> improve the crime prevention capabilities of private security and reduce crime in public and private places by reviewing the relationship between private security systems and public law enforcement agencies, and by developing programs and policies regarding private protection services that are appropriate and consistent with the public interest.

Other countries with more "experience" dealing with terrorism have developed similar public–private cooperative models. These models utilize the key elements of pubic safety policing. The United Kingdom, for example, has dealt with the IRA for many decades. One approach used by the United Kingdom was to develop an extensive network of four million closed-circuit security cameras. This was instrumental in helping authorities investigate three separate terrorist attacks or attempted attacks in recent years. These include the failed July 21, 2005, London transit bombing plot where U.K. police used 18,000 hours of camera footage to track down and arrest the offenders.[3] In addition, an excellent example of public and private arrangements is illustrated by Project Griffin. As previously noted, this arrangement was initially instituted in the United Kingdom. From its success in England, it has been imitated in Australia, Hong Kong, Singapore, and in New York City (NYPD SHIELD). This program has three key elements.[4]

The first element is called "Awareness Days." This consists of a full-day training seminar for private security personnel. The curriculum is delivered by police experts. It includes the history of terrorism, the nature of terrorism, and terrorism indicators and tactics. It also includes specific responsibilities of security personnel in the event of a crisis. Specifically, the instruction provides guidance for vehicle- and person-borne bombs and bomb structures. It also includes detecting hostile reconnaissance and suspect packages, persons, and vehicles. The security officers who complete the training are highly sought after. In short, they are considered more professional than other security personnel.[5]

The second element is called "Bridge Calls." These are weekly teleconferences providing up-to-date threat assessments. This information is provided to private sector companies and security personnel. It is then filtered down to the security personnel who previously completed the above-mentioned training. In addition, the security personnel are encouraged to contact the police with information they discern. The police, in turn, are instructed to use this information in their ongoing threat assessments. Indeed, an individual involved in the program asserts that[6]

> the success of the program depends absolutely on the working relation-
> ship between police and the security industry, and on the intelligence
> that the security industry can gather and get to the British police.

The third element is called "Cordon Support." This entails using these trained security officers to help provide perimeter security during a crisis. Classic examples of this approach were demonstrated on two different occasions. Following the train bombings in July 2005, fully 6,000 "Griffin trained" security personnel fanned out across the city. Again in June 2007, Griffin trained security personnel were partly responsible for spotting the car loaded with dynamite that was subsequently suc-cessfully defused. According to Harwood, this has led to great confidence in these security personnel—and has resulted in a high level placed on them in the market-place.[7] Consequently, it may be wise to consider duplicating this approach. As will be shown later in this chapter, the New York Police Department is doing so.

It should not surprise the reader to learn that early evidence of the *Public Safety Policing* model is being manifested in large U.S. municipalities. The cities of New York, Los Angeles, Chicago, Houston, Philadelphia, Washington, D.C., Miami, and other large cities are on the forefront of this trend. This is so for several rea-sons. These are the most likely targets of terrorism. Further, these cities have been traditional leaders in policing innovation. This is either because they are blessed with more resources and/or have more dynamic and educated leaders. It also may be because these cities tend to have substantial crime problems, thereby requiring more innovation and resources to combat crime. In any event, these cities are mov-ing forward with aspects of this new policing style. For example, Miami police are using "in your face" shows of force in public places, with random, high-profile security operations designed to keep terrorists guessing about where officers might be. "We want that shock. We want that awe ... we need them [citizens] to be our eyes and ears," said Deputy Chief Frank Fernandez of the Miami Police.[8]

It should also not surprise anyone to learn that of all the cities mentioned, New York is farther along the path toward the application of each of these model ele-ments. The devastating attacks on 9/11 obviously have forced New York to directly deal with terrorism. While other cities can "hope" that terrorism does not touch them, New York cannot simply "hope" away the threat.[9] They have implemented a number of protection-based initiatives. For example, the NYPD coordinates with the numerous agencies that operate the city's massive public transportation system, with its 6.5 million daily riders. The city is also spending $250 million to install cameras in its subway and transit system.[10] Transit officials say that they are exploring the potential installation of cameras on subway cars and are running a pilot program with cameras on 400 buses. The transit system has also recently installed new cameras in 70 subway stations, and has a contract with Lockheed Martin to install an additional 2,000 new cameras in the network.[11] In addition, other specific examples of what New York is doing illustrate how policing is changing.

New York City

The mission statement of the NYPD speaks volumes in terms of its approach to terrorism. In reading the details of this policy, one is struck by the focus on all three elements of *Public Safety Policing*. Specifically, note the emphasis placed on tactical weaponry, intelligence and surveillance technologies, and on order maintenance. Indeed, the language speaks for itself. It states, in pertinent part,

> NYPD is the primary local authority defending against a terrorist attack in New York City. Built upon the realization that the City could not rely solely on the federal government for its defense, the Counterterrorism Bureau was created by Police Commissioner Raymond W. Kelly in 2002 as the first unit of its kind in the nation. *Since then, the Counterterrorism Bureau has been at the forefront of this new aspect of municipal policing: counterterrorism for local law enforcement.* The mission of the Counterterrorism Bureau is to develop innovative, forward-looking policies and procedures to guard against the threat of international and domestic terrorism in New York City. One such policy puts uniformed counterterrorism executives in the rank of Inspector in positions to lead borough and citywide counterterrorism activities. Furthermore, the Joint Terrorism Task Force (JTTF) has been enhanced with a dramatically larger complement of NYPD investigators and supervisors[12] (emphasis added).

The mission statement further notes that the NYPD:

> has transformed the role of local police at all levels of the Department in an effort to protect the city's 8.2 million residents from terrorism. The Counterterrorism Bureau accomplishes this through its Borough Counterterrorism Coordinators... and operational liaison with the Intelligence Division and Patrol Services and Transit Bureaus. Patrol officers draw on their understanding of the neighborhoods they patrol

to report any potentially terrorism-related developments. They protect critical infrastructure and conduct high visibility deployments to disrupt terrorist planning and surveillance based on real-time intelligence.[13]

The department's strategic and continuous counterterrorism deployments include:

1. Teams of Emergency Service Unit (Hercules): Officers with heavy weapons and canines who conduct directed patrols at city landmarks and critical infrastructure. These tactical deployments are designed to deter attacks, detect terrorist threats through surveillance and other means, protect the public, and raise awareness for both law enforcement and the public. In short, the objective of these deployments is to establish a heightened security presence in the city and deter terrorists through a show of force. This entails "mustering" at a central location and deploying to various soft-target locations. Prior to deployment, officers are briefed on current terrorism intelligence and tactics.
2. Critical Response Vehicle (CRV): Uniformed officers from each of the city's 76 precincts in marked vehicles meeting at strategic locations in a massive show of force for deployment around the city at bridges, transportation facilities, and other highly critical and sensitive locations.
3. Transit Order Maintenance Sweeps (TOMS): Teams of officers stopping, boarding, and inspecting subway trains and subway container inspection and explosive trace detection, in which officers examine bags and other containers carried by passengers entering the subway system to detect explosives.[14]

These approaches correspond to the elements of pubic safety policing. Other common aspects are as follows. The Counterterrorism Division is charged with wide-ranging capabilities and responsibilities—which also reflect elements of this new policing model. For example, the NYPD has a robust intelligence system seeking to connect the dots to interdict potential terrorist acts. The Counter Terrorism Bureau's 205 officers analyze worldwide threats to determine how and where officers should deploy, provide training for all members of the force, assess risks to targets, and develop plans for protecting key sites in and near the city. Interestingly, the division has 23 civilian intelligence analysts with master's degrees and higher from leading universities. Some analysts come from leading think tanks, even from the CIA. The division also employs "field intelligence officers," one assigned to each of the NYPD's 76 precincts. The function of these intelligence officers is to maintain information on people, crimes, and arrests that might have terrorism links. In addition, the department employs "core collection officers" who develop confidential informants and give early warning about people being radicalized by militant associates or Web sites. The department has even sent liaison officers overseas to work alongside police departments in some of the cities most frequently targeted by terror, including Amman, London, and Singapore.[15]

In addition to these specialized positions, the NYPD employs over 870 civilian and uniformed speakers of Albanian, Arabic, Bengali, Farsi, Pashto, Turkish, and Urdu. Of the 470 or so in uniform, more than 200 are master linguists in "high-priority languages." Some of these linguists work for the division's Cyber Intelligence Unit, a 25-person group situated in unmarked headquarters in a Chelsea industrial building. Others are assigned in the Prison Intelligence program. These officers work with officials from the probation department, the New York State Police, and other agencies to monitor the spread of militancy within the prison and probation systems. In addition, New York's "fusion center," the nation's first, includes counterterrorism representatives from approximately 40 local, state, and federal agencies. Overall these efforts are the cutting edge of the NYPD's antiterrorism efforts. According to Chief Ray Kelly, much of "their approach is analytical work. ... It's all about prevention."[16] Additional similarities with the elements of *Public Safety Policing* are seen in the Counter-Terrorism Division, which is divided into seven subunits:[17]

- The Terrorism Threat Analysis Group performs strategic intelligence gathering and analysis and disseminates this information, both open-source and classified, to the appropriate recipients in the department, the private sector, the U.S. intelligence community, and other law enforcement agencies.
- The Training Section develops and delivers counterterrorism training to the patrol force and to other law enforcement agencies and private sector entities.
- The Critical Infrastructure Protection Section and the Transportation Security Section identify critical infrastructure sites throughout the city and develop protective strategies for these sites.
- The CBRNE Policy and Planning Section researches and tests emerging technologies used to detect and combat chemical, biological, radiological, nuclear, and explosive weapons, and develops plans and policies for their use.
- The Special Projects Unit plans and deploys physical security measures for special events and conducts undercover "red cell" investigations to assess vulnerabilities within the city.
- The NYPD SHIELD Unit manages the department's public-private security partnership, providing training and information to the private sector and addressing concerns from the private sector (more on this initiative below).
- The Emergency Response and Planning Section is the department's interface with the New York City Office of Emergency Management.

Specific examples of these initiatives will further illustrate elements of *Public Safety Policing*. For example, the elements of the model are illustrated by the following:

Joint Terrorism Task Force (JTTF) was augmented after the 9/11 attacks from 17 to 125 officers. These personnel are assigned to the operational control of the Counterterrorism Bureau. These officers partner with FBI agents on terrorism investigations in the New York metro area and around the world. The NYPD's partnership with the FBI through the JTTF not only provides the NYPD with access to national level classified intelligence, but it is also a means by which the NYPD can disseminate its own intelligence and analysis at the federal level and to other policing agencies.

NYPD SHIELD is an umbrella program for a series of current and future department initiatives that pertain to private sector security and counterterrorism. It is a public–private partnership based on information sharing. It acts as a "central destination" for private sector security managers to obtain information and engage police department resources. A critical mission of NYPD SHIELD is to help area businesses assess and revise their security procedures. The NYPD also provides training services to assist public–private sector entities in defending against terrorism. NYPD SHIELD keeps the private sector partners informed of developing situations in the city, preparations for upcoming events, and new intelligence and threat information. This approach is similar to Project Griffin in London.

The program also shares unclassified intelligence and security tips with private security firms. "Shield is all about sharing with the private sector on a real-time basis," said NYPD Chief Kelly. A recent session, with more than 500 in attendance discussed the chlorine bombs that American forces have faced in Iraq.[18] Information dissemination to a particular sector or neighborhood is transmitted directly to those affected by one of several methods:

- In-person intelligence and threat briefings conducted by Counter Terrorism Bureau and Intelligence Division personnel
- Informal conferrals with Patrol Borough Counter-Terrorism Coordinators
- NYPD Web site postings
- Shield Alert e-mail messages

This approach recognizes that information dissemination is a "two-way street." The key to success is for information to flow in two directions. In doing so, NYPD SHIELD also seeks information from private sector partners to assist in its efforts to keep the city safe. Note the policy also recognizes that private sector personnel are well situated to serve as *eyes and ears* of the NYPD, and that *order maintenance* techniques are effective in preventing against terrorism (and crime):[19]

> We ask your assistance in the fight against terrorism by reporting suspicious behavior as soon as possible. In addition, we recognize that our private sector partners are uniquely qualified to assist NYPD personnel during counter-terrorism deployments. Your personnel know your buildings, blocks and neighborhoods from a different perspective. You know what belongs and what is out of place. We urge you and your staff to speak with the police officers you see on the street, particularly

those assigned to posts in the vicinity of sensitive and critical locations. Sharing your perspective can help us be more effective.

Operation Nexus is an example of soliciting a "volunteer" nationwide network of businesses and enterprises joined in an effort to prevent another terrorist attack. NYPD detectives have conducted over 30,000 visits to firms in this mutual effort. Members of Operation Nexus are committed to reporting suspicious business encounters that they believe may have possible links to terrorism.[20] Operation Nexus is explained in pertinent part as:[21]

> Terrorist attacks do not occur in a vacuum. They require planning and preparation, such as the acquisition of certain materials or training in targeted activities. Terrorist operatives will try to obtain these in the private sector, from businesses both inside and outside of New York City's geographic boundaries. ... [The] NYPD believes terrorists may portray themselves as legitimate customers in order to purchase or lease certain materials or equipment, or to undergo certain formalized training to acquire important skills or licenses Through Operation Nexus, the NYPD actively encourages business owners, operators, and their employees to apply their particular business and industry knowledge and experience against each customer transaction or encounter to discern anything unusual or suspicious and to report such instances to authorities.

Operation Atlas entails increased deployments of Harbor, Aviation, and Emergency Service units. In addition, the Transportation Bureau works closely with the MTA and the Port Authority to ensure counterterrorism precautions are in place. This involves deploying critical response vans to events, or simply to stop at certain locations, like hotels, restaurants, landmarks or tourist attractions. The decision to deploy to a specific location is derived from daily assessments. The ongoing goal is to determine which hotels, museums, landmarks, and other attractions merit additional protection. In addition, the financial district is under intense 24-hour coverage. Each of these protective deployments is achieved through specialized patrols comprised of heavy weapons, canine, and intelligence units.[22]

Lower Manhattan Security Initiative is designed to secure key financial sites like the New York Stock Exchange plus the headquarters of leading companies and financial institutions in lower Manhattan. This initiative is directed through a counterterrorism "nerve center," whose exact location has not been disclosed. The center quietly began operating in November 2008—the first phase of a $100-million project. The project will rely largely on 3,000 closed-circuit security cameras covering roughly 1.7 square miles in and around the financial district. By the end of 2008, about 150 cameras were in place, with 250 more coming on line by the end of 2009, with the remainder by 2011. The 33 officers assigned to the nerve center monitor the live feeds from the cameras. As the volume of images increases, the NYPD hopes to incorporate "smart surveillance" software programmed to automatically detect possible signs of trouble. As described in Chapter 5, this may include an unattended bag, an unauthorized vehicle, an activated alarm, or a suspicious person. In addition, 30 police cars with two roof-mounted cameras have begun reading license plates of passing and parked cars. An additional 96 stationary readers will also be installed. Computers check the scanned plate numbers against a database of stolen and suspicious cars, while interactive maps help officers pinpoint their locations and track their movements. Eventually, the command center will also receive data from devices designed to detect any radiological and biological threats posed by cars and trucks. Significantly, the program was modeled in part after the "ring of steel" surveillance measures in London's financial district. NYPD officials said, however, that the Lower Manhattan Security Initiative will exceed that effort in scope and sophistication.[23]

Operation Sentry has as its goal to forge counterterrorism partnerships within a 200-mile radius of New York City. Recognizing that the 9/11 attacks began not in New York but in Boston and Portland, Maine, Chief Kelly has invited law enforcement officials from counties and cities as far away as Baltimore to discuss such issues as the radicalization of Muslim youth and what New York has learned about how to identify terrorism-related conduct. Francisco Ortiz, New Haven's police chief, calls Operation Sentry "invaluable." Through Operation Sentry, he now gets updates on regional threats as they unfold, as well as invitations to bimonthly sessions in New York featuring the latest threat assessments and training courses on improving security at sensitive sites. These training classes are delivered by NYPD officers to over 250 security personnel who protect 31 key buildings. The training consists of a 40-hour curriculum, including subjects on terrorism prevention and indicators.[24] "They're helping us become a better listening post in Connecticut for New York," Ortiz said. He also noted that he will start a version of New York's Nexus program to sensitize New Haven businesses to potential threats.[25]

These programs developed by New York City for "terrorism prevention" can also be utilized and incorporated into "crime prevention" programs developed during the *Community Policing* era. Examples of public–private arrangements that inform my vision of the order maintenance element of *Public Safety Policing* are provided below.

Grand Central Partnership (GCP) is an area within the city of New York consisting of more than 6,000 businesses, comprising upward of 51 million square feet.[25] Consistent with the funding model articulated in the last chapter, each property owner contributes monies from property taxes to support this arrangement. All of the tax revenue is returned to the district management association, which administers the program and hires security personnel.[26] The revenues and cooperative efforts with city officials provide many diverse services, including private street sweepers and trash collectors, garbage cans, street lighting, and flower boxes. It is also used to provide multilingual tour guides, homeless shelters, and uniformed security guards.

Obviously, the scope of this project goes beyond what is traditionally viewed as "security." This should not surprise the reader, as the concept of "security" involves more than physical protection. As mentioned earlier, security often includes the perceptions of people, the physical environment, and the human desire for order and safety. This is why the overall environment and the perception of people within the environment had to be changed. This logic stems from order maintenance. This arrangement was accomplished with the use of private police paid for with specific taxing initiatives from property owners. Carlson contends that the arrangement was successful, transforming the area "from a chaotic mag [sic] of threatening streets into one of the safest sections of Manhattan."[28]

The reasons for the success of this arrangement are consistent with the theory of order maintenance. For example, a retired New York City detective in charge of the GCP operations asserted, "Police are involved with other matters, they cannot concentrate on the quality of life crime when they have major crimes. We are the eyes and ears of the police department ... they appreciate our work because we try to solve some problems ourselves, without police intervention."[29] This assertion was echoed by another GCP staffer who stated, "We don't do homicides, we don't do rapes, but we do other quality of life things. ... We do the work the police have trouble getting [to] because they are so busy."[30]

Unmistakably, both of these statements reflect an order maintenance approach. Statistics also demonstrate this focus. This can be shown, at least partly, by the workload handled by the security personnel. In one calendar year, the security personnel responded to 6,916 incidents, with only 624 requiring police assistance and only 122 resulting in arrest.[31] This statistic is significant. The security personnel handled more than 6,000 incidents without the involvement of New York City police. This frees up the police to concentrate on other matters. Indeed, the result of this cooperative effort is that police are able to focus on more serious crimes, with the bulk of the service and order maintenance duties shifted to security personnel.[32] The selection characteristics of the security personnel are not substantially dissimilar to public police. They include these requirements:[33]

- At least 18 years of age
- No recent felony convictions
- Reasonably upstanding and sober citizen
- High school graduate
- Preference for military service
- Pass psychological examination
- Pass a drug-screening test

The training of the security personnel lasts about seven days. It focuses on operational and legal issues. Weekly follow-up training, usually on "use of force" issues and security procedures, is also conducted. In addition, discipline within the ranks is strictly enforced. According to Carlson, absenteeism or lateness, sloppy dress, smoking in public, and even minor rule violations are not tolerated. This level of discipline is particularly important because the security personnel wear distinct uniforms, intentionally designed to resemble those of New York City police. They—like the police—also wear radios and bulletproof vests.[34]

Metro Tech Area is another New York City arrangement that provides supplemental private security and sanitation services. This business improvement district (BID) also focuses its efforts on an order maintenance approach. It seeks to control crime and disorder by reducing signs of physical and social disorder. This is achieved through street cleaning and improvement coupled with regulating people's behavior.[35] The underlying purpose of these services is to help people feel safe. This is achieved through order maintenance techniques. These include the use of private police patrols, by minimizing signs of disorder within the environment, and by discouraging the presence of vagrants, rowdy youths, and street peddlers. In addition, surveillance is considered a significant aspect of this approach. The arrangement installed sophisticated CCTV systems with 26 cameras that are monitored by security personnel. To enhance the security of the environment, NYPD radio dispatches are also monitored by security personnel.[36]

This BID employs 28 private police officers. The candidate selection is highly competitive, selecting only one of 25 applicants. Each applicant must be 21 years old, pass drug tests and psychological exams, submit to random drug tests, have a clean felony record, and have no history of drug activity.[37] Each officer receives 96 hours of training at the NYPD academy. Training includes such topics as conflict resolution, communication skills, legal topics, court procedures and testimony, investigative techniques, and report writing. These officers also receive in-service training at roll calls, and annual training in CPR and baton use. They do not carry firearms, but they do possess arrest powers. Approximately six arrests are made per year—but only when the private officers witness the crime. Typical incidents handled by these officers usually relate to social disorder and providing assistance to citizens.[38]

Some level of internal accountability is structured into this arrangement. Each private officer must pass written exams each year. These exams focus on such matters as code of conduct, post orders, and rules required in the arrangement. Merit increases are based on professional performance. In addition, the conduct and activities of these officers are subject to CCTV surveillance and internal investigation complaints. There have been only six abuse allegations in nine years. These complaints are overseen by the BID's public safety committee and the board. Finally, Davis notes that external accountability is accomplished by the court system, the Department of Business Services, the New York Police Department, and by their clients.[38]

Starrett City illustrates that the use of private security is not confined to business districts. The Starrett City housing development in Brooklyn is located in the 75th Precinct, which consistently has one of the highest murder rates in New York City.[40]

The management company that administers the development hired private police officers. At that time, 60 private police officers were employed. About 40 of these officers are armed. Each private police officer carries the "special police" designation, and has full arrest powers. The average salary is about 70 percent of the average salary of a police officer. Their contribution to the community is significant. Each year, these private police personnel handle about 10,000 service calls.[41]

Carlson noted that 20 years after hiring these security officers, Starrett City remains as safe as any affluent neighborhood. In 1994, this community of 20,000 people reported only 24 car thefts, 12 burglaries, 6 aggravated assaults, and no rapes.[42] In the same year, Carlson noted that the complex reported only 67 robberies. This compares favorably to the 2,548 reported in the neighborhood just outside its boundaries.[43] Further, the overall crime rates in New York City were substantially higher than in Starrett City. New York averaged 84 felonies reported per 1,000 residents, while Starrett City reported just 7 felonies per 1,000. Similarly, in the 75th Precinct, a residence was 38 times more likely to be burglarized than within Starrett City.[44] Significantly, there are no physical boundaries or barriers separating Starrett City from other residents within the 75th Precinct. The only real "physical" distinction is the private security personnel. The difference between the neighborhoods is so distinct that a Starrett City security supervisor described the complex as "an oasis in a vast wilderness."[45]

This belief is apparently widespread among Starrett City residents. In a survey conducted by Penn State University, almost 90 percent of the residents said that they felt "somewhat or very safe" living in the complex. Only 40 percent felt similarly secure outside its boundaries.[46] This survey further found that 90 percent of the residents believed the complex would not be safe without its private security personnel. Significantly, over 50 percent said they would leave the area if the private police were not employed.[47] As another indication of the commitment to private security, 78 percent of the residents said that, if assaulted, they would call security before calling the police. Indeed, the complex receives only part-time coverage from two police officers. This is so even though the complex accounts for about 16 percent of the population in the 75th Police Precinct.[48] The authors concluded that without private policing, Starrett City would not be a secure residential environment.

Los Angeles and Northern California

While the Los Angeles Police Department (LAPD) does not have as robust a counterterrorism and homeland security approach as New York, it is clear that Los Angeles is heading in this direction. The organizational structure supporting this assertion can be found as follows.

In the LAPD, the Counter Terrorism and Criminal Intelligence Bureau is comprised of a Major Crimes Division and an Emergency Services Division. The Major Crimes Division is comprised of Criminal Conspiracy, Criminal Investigations, Intelligence Investigations, Surveillance, and Liaison sections.[49] Simply by assessing the titles of these units, one gets the sense that the functions are similar to the elements of *Public Safety Policing*. Note the emphasis on intelligence, surveillance, and liaison functions. In addition, the Emergency Services Division is comprised of Field and Community Support, Emergency Planning, Operations, and Hazardous Devices sections. In short, the overall Counter Terrorism Bureau is responsible for planning, response, and intelligence. Each of these is designed to deal with the threat of terrorism, both prior to an incident and in the aftermath of an incident.

LAPD Chief Bratton has added 75 officers permanently to the group of 33 who worked on terrorism before 9/11. At least 44 more will be assigned. Beyond these counterterrorism officers, the Joint Regional Intelligence Center (JRIC) is held up as a model for fusion centers. It was launched with a $4 million DHS grant and opened in 2007 within a concrete building. The center has 16 LAPD staffers and some 30 designees from other law enforcement and public-safety agencies. The interior has a vast open working space, countless computer screens, and wall-mounted television monitors showing various American and foreign-language news broadcasts. The JRIC's analysts do not conduct investigations. Instead, they vet tips and leads—about 25 new ones per week. Once vetted, the JRIC's "threat squad" of some 20 analysts from federal and local agencies assess whether the danger is real. Some statistics reveal their effectiveness. The LAPD has arrested some 200 American citizens and foreigners with suspected ties to terrorist groups since September 11th. At present, the division has 54 open intelligence cases, involving at least 250 "persons of interest."[50]

In articulating the actual function of the Major Crimes Division, its commanding officer noted that it is the prevention component of the city's antiterrorism effort. It is connected to several other functions related to intelligence information. This connectivity includes the first responders, crisis managers, and data centers such as the Los Angeles County Terrorist Early Warning System and the California Anti-Terrorism Information Center. These functions are an integral part of the city's crisis management process, which also includes recovery and community outreach programs. The Major Crimes Division has also developed excellent working relationships with many federal agencies. It is because of those ongoing relationships and a well-developed infrastructure that critical intelligence information is shared appropriately.[51] Of course, these functions are critical to and part of the larger *public safety* approach to policing. This larger approach can be illustrated by Operation Archangel (which is a particularly appropriate name given that it "protects" Los Angeles in the "Holy War").

Operation Archangel is considered a "pillar" of the LAPD's counterterrorism effort. It is funded by Homeland Security monies, and uses sophisticated computer software to identify, prioritize, and protect vulnerable targets. These targets range from Disneyland to nuclear plants. Archangel personnel ask owners and operators of these sites to provide current structural information. This includes floor plans, air-conditioning and electrical system locations, entrances and stairwells, and the like. This information is then recorded into a massive database. A software program then assesses vulnerabilities and devises deterrence and prevention strategies. It also provides basic emergency response plans. "We're basically doing what we did before, but on steroids," says Tom McDonald, the LAPD lieutenant who runs Archangel. He advocates, as many federal officials do, that Operation Archangel should be emulated by other cities.[52]

In addition to this approach, the LAPD has implemented sophisticated technology that can detect the radioactive signature of "dirty bombs." One of these devices is utilized from a helicopter. It is allegedly able to locate an unexploded dirty bomb from 800 feet above the ground. The department has utilized DHS funds to purchase a bomb-response truck with a robot that can be remotely operated from one mile away. In addition, the department uses a mobile response truck for police public information officers, to function as a portable center for communicating data through news media.[53] Beyond these initiatives, the Los Angeles mass transit system has plans to install 379 gates and surveillance cameras on subways and various light-rail lines. The gates will serve dual functions as chemical and bomb detectors. The first test gate will be up and running by September of 2009 and, if it yields results, the rest will be installed by 2010.[54]

These technological initiatives are being supplemented with large-scale tactical teams designed to respond to terrorist incidents. What is known as Urban Shield, the country's biggest homeland security drill, took place in September 2008. This training exercise involved teams of 25 separate tactical situations, including airplane attacks and bank heists. The two days of intensive training were designed to test officers' abilities in highly stressful, tiring conditions. A police official explained that this training commenced following the Columbine High School shooting in April 1999, and it became especially imperative after the 2007 Virginia Tech shooting. In conjunction with the tactical exercises, officers used cameras situated around buildings, which were interfaced with cameras attached to their helmets. These cameras were used so that the teams can study their performance on film and devise training to deal with issues that occur during the drill.[55]

The Hollywood and Sunset business improvement districts (BIDs) are excellent models of public-private policing. Both of these arrangements are operated by Andrews International, Inc. Each BID is about 3.5 square miles. They contain some of the most famous Hollywood landmarks, such as the "Walk of the Stars." The private police patrols are comprised of 20 officers, each of whom are retired, former, or off-duty police officers. The officers are uniformed in navy blue pants and polo shirts. The shirts contain security patches, the company logo, and the words "BID PATROL" on the back. Each officer is armed, either with 9-mm or .45-caliber handguns, along with typical police equipment such as handcuffs, ammunition, pepper spray, and the like. They drive white SUVs marked with the company logo. The officers also walk foot patrols. These patrols are designed for direct community contact, observable patrol presence, and the enforcement of "quality of life" infractions.[56]

The firm maintains a robust training curriculum for the patrol arrangement. The officers receive firearms training at least every other month. They are trained in the proper use of pepper spray and receive ongoing legal update training including L.A. city attorney briefings. In addition, numerous members of the homeless outreach community brief the officers. Training subjects also include search and seizure, trespass, workplace violence, public relations, company policies, terrorism, cultural diversity, being a good witness, telephonic bomb threats, ethics and code of conduct, bomb threat protocol, handcuffing, making a good impression, drug-free workplace, and powers of arrest.[57] Based in part on this training, coupled with the police backgrounds of the private police officers, LAPD Captain Beatrice Girmala stated that "these officers are different. They are not trying to be the police. Instead, they are acting in a support role. The level of professionalism and training earn them respect from both LAPD and the citizens."[58]

This training is supplemented with various systematic communication methods with the LAPD. The BID patrol supervisors attend LAPD crime control meetings every week. In these meetings, current crime trends are analyzed and strategies to combat them are planned. The BID arrangement also strives for total transparency and accountability. This includes a computer tracking system that maps each arrest. This enables tracking times, dates, locations, and types of arrests that occur throughout the BID areas. It also facilitates identification of crime trends, with corresponding timely adjustments of personnel staffing. This database also contains the arrest report, a photograph, and other detailed information about the suspect. This system is also used to track graffiti. The arrangement also maintains 24/7 video coverage of the "arrest bench" in their security office in order to ensure that all suspects are treated properly while in custody.[59]

Data from these bids are instructive. In the Hollywood BID, the work product of the private police officers was substantial. In 2007, the private police officers made a total of 2,349 arrests. In 2008, they made a total of 1,707 arrests. Of the 1,017 total arrests, 593 were for drinking in public, 99 were for urinating in public, 114 were for narcotics violations, 38 for trespass, 21 for illegal vending, 19 for battery, 16 for blocking the sidewalk, 11 for theft, 11 for vandalism, and 44 for various misdemeanors. Of course, each of these reflects order maintenance functions. In addition, they made 51 arrests for various felonies. Further, the patrol teams also made 2,615 outreach referrals, made contact with 3,919 citizens, handled 1,412 radio calls for service, and conducted 2,382 business checks.

In the Sunset BID, a total of 690 arrests were made. These break down as follows: 327 for drinking in public, 84 for urinating in public, 27 for narcotics, 17 for trespass, 9 for illegal vending, 5 for battery, 17 for blocking the sidewalk, 10 for theft, 3 for vandalism, and 161 for various misdemeanors. Again, these are critical order maintenance functions. In addition, they made 30 arrests for various felonies. The patrol officers also made 1,318 outreach referrals, made contact with 2,127 citizens, handled 709 radio calls for service, and conducted 1,255 business checks.[60]

In a two-year period, the private patrol officers conducted substantial work. They made a combined total of 3,933 homeless referrals and 6,046 citizen contacts, handled 2,121 radio calls for service, and visited 3,637 businesses. In addition, the breakdown of their arrests clearly illustrates an order maintenance approach. The approximate percentages of arrests break down as follows:[61]

53 percent—alcohol related
12 percent—miscellaneous misdemeanors
11 percent—urinating in public
8 percent—narcotics
5 percent—felonies
3 percent—trespass
2 percent—blocking sidewalk
2 percent—battery
2 percent—illegal vending
1 percent—theft
1 percent—vandalism

A mixture of order maintenance and technology implemented in a new development in Brentwood, California, is illustrative. In this arrangement, developers, local officials, and law enforcement developed a security plan for a retail development. This plan is to incorporate lighting, video surveillance, and various vehicle, foot, and bicycle patrols throughout the shopping center. The development will also employ patrol cars with noise meters that detect loud music. It will also employ a curfew to enforce safety, if necessary, and the Brentwood Police Department plans to staff a substation nearby.[62]

Similarly, in Oakland the city council approved the hiring of armed security officers to monitor commercial districts in the eastern part of the city. As in other cities, Oakland set up special tax zones called business improvement districts, where the affected property owners agree to pay a special assessment tax to fund private security and other initiatives designed to make the area safer and to spur economic development.[63] The security officers will supplement Oakland police officers, as the department is experiencing staff shortages. As a consequence of these shortages, storeowners have complained that police are unable to respond to reports of drug dealing or loitering. Some residents believe that it has been difficult for police officers to develop an understanding of the community's problems because of staff shortages resulting in police constantly being shifted around. "We hope by spending this money that these security guards will at least be on the job long enough so there will be a positive impact," said Art Clark, a member of a the citizen advisory board. The city will also spend money on a campaign to teach business owners safety techniques, and on installing security cameras and better lighting.[64] According to a reporter from the *San Francisco Chronicle*, the new security personnel are being hired to do "what public police used to do, public order policing. ..."[65] This function took on additional significance due to rioting following a police shooting (for discussion of this incident coupled with larger implications, please see Chapter 9). In an attempt to secure the downtown area, Oakland Mayor

Ron Dellums announced that the city will hire unarmed private security guards to patrol the area and supplement the police department.[66] Of course, this approach is consistent with the framework of *Public Safety Policing.*

In San Francisco, in what may be the most unique private policing arrangement in America, the San Francisco Patrol Special Police patrol the city as a supplemental public safety force. This arrangement dates back to the gold rush days. It was initially formed in 1847 by business owners to combat the insurgence of criminals, such as the infamous Barbary Coast pirates. The Patrol Special Police is a separately chartered law enforcement group that works under the supervision of the San Francisco Police Department (SFPD). Patrol Special officers are governed by rules and procedures set by the San Francisco Police Commission. The Commission is empowered with the authority to appoint Patrol Special Police officers, and may suspend or dismiss them after a fair and impartial hearing on charges duly filed with the commission. The Police Commission also may establish requirements and procedures to govern the position, including the power of the chief of police to supervise these special police officers.

Each Patrol Special Police officer shall be at least 21 years of age at the time of appointment. They must pass an extensive police background investigation, complete training at the San Francisco Police Academy, and possess such physical qualifications as required by the commission. These requirements are consistent with those from the California Commission on Peace Officers Standards and Training, and include medical standards reflective of the San Francisco Police Department. In addition, these officers receive training on an annual basis from the San Francisco Police Department. They must also qualify with firearms at the police department's range. They wear uniforms approved by the Police Commission, carry a firearm, and use two-way SFPD radios. Each of these factors illustrates an excellent example of structural interaction with the San Francisco Police Department, including specific accountability measures designed to ensure proper and consistent service.[67]

The unique aspect of the Patrol Special Police officers is that they are considered *the owner* of their certain beat or territory. As the owner of a beat or territory, it is considered "property" that may be bought, sold, leased, bequeathed by will, or otherwise conveyed. This makes the ownership of the beat very unique and potentially very valuable. The "beat" property may be conveyed to a person of good moral character, who is approved by the Police Commission and eligible for appointment as a Patrol Special Police officer. The beat ownership, however, may be rescinded by the commission.

According to its Web site, the San Francisco Patrol Special Police officers strive to make the communities they serve better places in which to live and work. These private police officers are committed to *Community Policing* with an emphasis on problem solving and community outreach. These goals are achieved through various tasks including walking the "beat" and getting to know people on an individual basis. They also attend community meetings and work closely with the police department and other city agencies to find resolutions to everyday neighborhood concerns.[68] This emphasis on *Community Policing* clearly reflects the need to service clients and to perform order maintenance functions.

In yet another example, in Renton, Washington, Visitor Information and Downtown Assistance (VIDA) hired private security as part of a broader city public-safety initiative to reduce crime and promote a sense of safety. The program hosts the unarmed guards, who walk or ride bikes through the downtown area during afternoon and evening hours wearing easily identifiable yellow and black uniforms with a VIDA logo.[69] "Public safety is the cornerstone of a civil society and it is our responsibility to ensure that we do everything possible to make our neighborhoods and community feel safe," said Mayor Denis Law. "We are the eyes and the ears for the police here," said one of the security officers while riding a bike through downtown Renton. The purpose of these patrols is for the officers to provide information, report vandalism and graffiti, deter criminal activity, and extend a helping hand when needed. These services are part of a comprehensive plan to reduce criminal activity and enhance overall safety. The plan includes additional security, increased patrols, security cameras, enhanced code-enforcement efforts, and a significant emphasis on traffic safety.[70]

Chicago

As described in Chapter 5, Chicago has a robust camera system. This system corresponds to the larger mission statement of the Chicago Police Department as it relates to terrorism:[71]

> While the specific day-to-day duties of the department's various units and personnel vary, each member shares in a collective responsibility for the effectiveness of the department's response to potential terrorist threats and to actual terrorism incidents. Ensuring an effective response requires the coordinated use of its administrative support, planning, training, patrol, investigative, and intelligence resources.

In the operation of this mission, Chicago is also instituting its Private Sector Video Domain (PSVD), which seeks to access private sector cameras to monitor them by its Office of Emergency Management. Toward this end, this approach is designed to incorporate private camera systems into the police communications system. Consider this application. A "holdup" alarm goes off at a downtown bank. The cameras within the bank are then activated, sending a wireless video feed of the camera to the police dispatch center. This feed is then transmitted to the police vehicle that is assigned to the call. The officers in the responding vehicle can assess the scene prior to arriving. This enhances employee, officer, and even vehicular safety. This also could reduce the number of "false alarm" calls, as the dispatcher can monitor the video even prior to assigning the call.[72] The potential usage of this technology is almost limitless.

In addition to this technological innovation, residents of a Chicago neighborhood developed a special district that implemented a private policing arrangement. The Marquette Park Special Service District was initially developed in the early 1990s due to concerns over gang activity. The special service district is part of the 8th Police District, which is segmented into 16 different beats and is one of the largest districts—both in terms of land area and population—within the city of Chicago. A special service district is a separate taxing entity within the city of Chicago.

Prior to the formation of the special service area, community groups petitioned for a ballot referendum. At issue was whether property owners would vote to increase their real estate taxes for the purpose of hiring private security patrols. These private patrols would supplement the police department, seeking to reduce crime and to minimize the conditions that foster crime.[73] Once the special services district is established by the city council, the alderman in the affected ward selects individuals for the governing commission. Those eligible for selection to the commission must either be residents or business owners in the community. The commission also contains three nonvoting members, including the commander of the police district and two officials who represent the city of Chicago Department of Planning and Development. These nonvoting members are supposed to provide guidance and advice to the voting members of the commission. This governing commission is charged with the oversight of the special services district, including preparing a budget, conducting periodic community meetings, and arranging all applicable administrative matters to operate the private police patrols.[74]

The private police officers are equipped with handguns, handcuffs, flashlights, and other police equipment. Each private police officer wears "civilian dress" clothing that makes them appear almost identical to tactical police officers. Despite their appearance as "the police," these officers are not afforded any "police" powers. While a few of these officers are off-duty police, the vast majority have only private citizen arrest powers.

My research of these officers was to assess three basic, yet critical, questions related to the privatized police services. Initially, the main thesis related to the functional tasks of the private police officers. In answering this question, three functional categories were identified as they relate to policing and security: observe and report, order maintenance, and law enforcement. After utilizing three data sources (ride-alongs, interviews, and document analysis), the conclusions were as follows: The preponderance of their functional work product was *order maintenance* (51.5%). Of course, this conclusion reflects both the criminological theories and the other models previously presented. The other functional findings were *observe and report* (32%) and *law enforcement* (16.5%), respectively.[75]

Notwithstanding these conclusions, the examples in this chapter provide compelling illustrations of the elements of the new policing model. They illustrate the continued and growing need for cooperative efforts between private and public police.[76] Such cooperative efforts have been successful in combating crime and enhancing the environment within the patrol arrangement. In this sense, these examples show that security and police create a natural combination of talent and resources. The crime prevention mission within the security industry, coupled with the ability of the police to arrest and prosecute offenders, provides a dynamic combination of skills and resources. Consequently, the homeland security focus within policing may act as a precursor toward the widespread establishment of privatized public safety services. Some additional examples may help to illustrate this approach.

Public–Private Policing Arrangements

Philadelphia

Another example of a supplemental public safety arrangement is within the city of Philadelphia. In 1991, the city council approved the Center City District (CCD), a private not-for-profit group responsible for administering the business improvement district. For years prior to this arrangement, the downtown Philadelphia site exhibited significant criminal activity. The police district, which serves the downtown area, reported 37 percent of its workload coming from this area.[77] In addition—or possibly as a consequence of the crime rate—the area experienced increases in vacant commercial properties, unregulated vendors, homeless citizens, and trash accumulating on the streets and sidewalks. This supplemental arrangement was designed to address these incivilities through enhanced order maintenance techniques.

The district covers 80 square blocks, with 2,087 property owners each paying a property tax surcharge from the real estate levy. The budget is allocated to the following privately contracted services:[78]

- 53 percent allocated to street cleaning and trash pickup
- 33 percent allocated to public safety
- 7 percent allocated to administration
- 7 percent allocated to marketing

These budgetary allocations illustrate that to impact crime the concept of security must be broadly defined. Again, these services reflect the order maintenance approach. In accordance with these functions, the CCD set up its daily operations to foster collaboration with the police department. This entailed assigning police officers to the CCD. It also entailed security officers, called community service representatives (or CSR) sharing headquarters with police officers. This included joint locker facilities, conducting joint roll calls, and facilitating ongoing communication relating to crime trends.[79] The security personnel are unarmed and uniformed. They act as public "concierges" and as neighborhood "watchers." They are equipped with radios that are interconnected with the police. The security personnel also use a computerized crime mapping system designed to enhance crime prevention methodologies.

The CCD security force consists of 45 to 50 officers. The training curriculum is wide ranging, including such subjects as problem solving and customer service techniques, hospitality methods, use of force, radio communications, first aid, CPR, and victim assistance.[80] The minimum standards are significant. Recruits must possess two years of college, be at least 21 years old, and pass a background investigation. These standards make the security personnel meet higher standards than typical guards within the security industry.

St. Louis

In a similar supplemental arrangement, the St. Louis Metropolitan Police Department contracts with uniformed security personnel to patrol the central city. The private security force is operated through a special tax district that was initially created in the late 1950s. The tax district encompasses all of downtown St. Louis. It is administered by Downtown St. Louis, Inc., a private not-for-profit chamber of commerce. Property owners within the district pay a tax surcharge, which is collected by the city and state, then redistributed to the district. The focal point of the tax revenues is to provide security protection to businesses. The revenues are also used to pay for the following services:[81]

- ■ Market the area's attractions
- ■ Provide special events
- ■ Provide private security

The business district is divided into 12 different beats, with a particular allotment from both security and the police. The security personnel consist of a patrol force of 6 to 30 officers, depending on the time or the particular event. In addition, some off-duty police officers serve on the security force. Partly because of the interrelationship between the security force and the police, the security personnel have the same arrest powers as police. Just like the police, security officers wear uniforms and walk their beats—using reasonable force when necessary to stop a crime.[82]

The selection criteria are more varied and sophisticated than in previous examples. For example, the selection criteria includes factors such as an outgoing personality, knowledge of the St. Louis metro area, two years prior experience in the security industry, a psychological test, and several personal interviews. The training consists of a 16-hour course designed and administered by the St. Louis Police Department. The training stresses police policies and procedures. The security firm also conducts a 16-hour course focusing on public relations. When the training is completed, the security officers are licensed by the St. Louis Police Department, and are given arrest authority by the city's police board.[83] In this sense, the private police officers are vested with "special police" powers.

Minneapolis

Downtown business leaders have joined with police and city officials to create the Downtown Security Collaborative. This arrangement commenced following a dramatic 21 percent increase in serious crime.[84] In conjunction with other improvements, a "safety ambassador" program was initiated where unarmed security provide a "security presence" in addition to helping people with information and other services. The plan provides 11 unarmed security guards, two supervisors, and five "ambassadors." This arrangement, as most others, is ultimately designed to enhance public safety. Indeed, in the words of the director of economic development for Minneapolis, this program "arises from the business community's call to action."[85]

Seattle

The city implemented a security arrangement as part of the Metropolitan Improvement District (MID). As with many of the other programs, this district is funded by self-imposed property taxes on downtown real estate. It hired 35 uniformed security officers to patrol the streets. These security officers, also called "safety ambassadors," work with and are largely trained by the Seattle Police Department. The training consists of 90 hours, with its curriculum focusing on such subjects as report writing, radio codes, ordinances, and customer service instruction. This safety ambassador program was created because there "weren't enough beat cops to walk the streets in the intensity we wanted," said MID Director Bill Dietrich.[86]

Houston

The Greater Green Point Management District (GGPMD) encompasses a 12-square-mile section within Houston, Texas. This district has a mix of residential and commercial properties. Prior to this initiative, increases in crime and the general deterioration in the conditions within the district were manifest. At least partially due to these factors, local property owners within the district petitioned the state legislature to create the district. The state legislature approved the district and levied a tax on the assessed property value for each parcel of real property. The district is administered by a 22-member board of directors appointed by the governor. Included in the board is an executive director who is in charge of operations, and a security manager who is in charge of security and public safety.[87]

Surveys conducted within the district revealed that business owners were in "absolute terror" due to the growing crime problem. Among other results was the realization that police response times ranged from 14 to 15 minutes for emergency calls, and almost two hours for nonemergency calls.[88] This created a substantial and compelling need for more responsive services. The solution was to enact a series of initiatives aimed at reducing crime and improving the conditions in the district.

The initiative included hiring additional police officers and supplementing these officers with private security personnel. The district was to pay all costs and salaries associated with the increases in public safety personnel. Further, the district opened a new police substation, which was donated by a large shopping mall. The police and security personnel were stationed at this facility. These initiatives—and others—were said to have contributed to a significant reduction in crime. The crime rate in the district dropped 25 percent in the year following the implementation of the initiatives. Further, the occupancy rate of business units within the district rose to one of the highest in the city of Houston.[89] In short, the arrangement was deemed to have contributed to the betterment of the overall environment in the city.

Dallas

In another Texas-based arrangement, business owners hired 31 private police officers to patrol the downtown business district. The patrols cost about $1.5 million a year, with each officer earning $12.50 per hour.[90] These private police officers wear blue police-like uniforms, carry pepper spray, and use radios. They also exhibit a friendly, courteous approach while patroling. The patrols are both on foot and on bicycles. Training of these officers lasts three weeks or about 120 hours. One deputy chief of the Dallas Police Department noted that this new force will work as extra "eyes and ears" of the police. The stated goals of this patrol force are to reduce crime and to increase the perception that the area is safe.[91] As such, the patrols illustrate the order maintenance approach. Significantly, these officers are considered "public safety officers," which is consistent with my assertion of a *Public Safety Policing* model.

It is interesting to note that the author of one police magazine article discussed these private patrols in a somewhat negative manner. She stated that "inexplicably" the Dallas police brass seem to be in favor of "losing department jobs to the private sector." She characterized this arrangement as "the front" in the "privatization war."[92] While it is unfortunate to view this public safety initiative with such harsh language, the merits of these supplemental arrangements are sure to survive the arrows of some critics.

Atlanta

A rather robust private policing approach can be traced back to the 1996 Summer Olympics. In anticipation for the huge number of visitors, Atlanta's Downtown Improvement District (ADID) put together its 65-person "private police" force called the "Ambassadors."[93] Central Atlanta Progress President A. J. Robinson credits the Ambassador Force with providing a formidable law-enforcement presence in Atlanta. Partly based on this success, another BID, the Midtown Alliance, added its "Midtown Blue" security patrol teams in 2000.[94]

The Atlanta Downtown Improvement District has a nine-member board of directors, representing law enforcement and private businesses. This board oversees the work of the Ambassadors, who are to serve both public safety and public relations functions.[95] They patrol approximately 120 square blocks. Ambassadors patrol the sidewalks looking for people who need assistance—giving directions and medical assistance, assisting with emergency response for building evacuations and fire drills, and assisting with crowd control. Beyond these functions, they are to provide a public safety presence.[96] In essence, they are to be seen, and they are to help when they can. They serve as the *eyes and the ears* of Atlanta. They escort downtown employees to and from cars. They report broken streetlights. They try to deter aggressive panhandling, but not by force. Instead they steer people who are down on their luck to agencies that can help.[97]

Each Ambassador carries a two-way radio, providing access to the Atlanta Police Department radio frequency, called COMNET. This gives them simultaneous emergency communication between the ADID, businesses, and public safety personnel. This communication network is fostered by monthly meetings, where law enforcement and the private industry discuss crime, homeland security, security technologies, and relevant events. In addition to their patrol duties, they also maintain and monitor 13 surveillance cameras that record images from public areas. Another 18 employees, called the Clean Sweep Team, pick up trash and keep the area clean.[98] Of course, these surveillance and order maintenance functions are critical aspects of *Public Safety Policing*. As such, these Ambassadors are a great example of *Community Policing* by the private sector—and dramatically illustrate the new policing model.

The interrelationship of these elements—and the relevant parties—was pointedly illustrated by a mock terrorist exercise on MARTA (local transportation system). These exercises involved ADID, law enforcement, fire officials, business leaders, and private security personnel.[99] These exercises were related to a larger program known as Operation Shield. This program is designed to create "force multipliers" where private security serves to enhance the public safety presence in the community. This program has three parts:[100]

1. CityWorkSite—A Web-based information-sharing network that allows the police department to send information about crimes and/or other critical events directly to private security personnel. This information is sent via text messages, e-mail, pager, and fax.
2. COMNET radio system—As explained earlier, the private security personnel are connected to the Atlanta police through this radio system. This enables them to communicate directly.
3. Surveillance—The camera system is monitored by both private security and Atlanta police, thereby providing a network of surveillance within a technological framework. In this way, being the *eyes and ears* involves more than human senses. In addition, the surveillance system intends to

expand to "smart" video analytics, such as automatic object detection, gunshot detection, and facial recognition components (as described in Chapter 5).

Critical Infrastructures

The use of private security to provide public safety services is not limited to business districts, or even housing projects. For example, in a recent transformation, security personnel will be used to guard three nuclear power plants in New Jersey. The security personnel will replace National Guardsmen and the New Jersey State Police. The belief is that private security coupled with a new video monitoring system will provide sufficient levels of security. The video monitoring system has thermal imaging capabilities and provides views of the property's perimeter. It feeds images directly to a Regional Operations and Intelligence Center. National Guardsmen have patrolled outside these nuclear plants since October 2001. During the last seven years, the facilities have spent more than $82 million combined on capital security improvements.[101]

Another way to get a sense of how these arrangements are developing is to look at specific critical infrastructures and locations. In this light, there are initiatives in the transportation sector that illustrate a growing interrelationship between the key elements articulated in my model. When one considers the breadth of the U.S. transportation sector, the "job" of securing this critical infrastructure is daunting. Northwestern Professor Joseph Schofer provided some data to illustrate the gravity of this undertaking. He stated that our highway system consists of four million miles of interconnected roads. The freight networks extend more than 300,000 miles, and commuter and urban rail systems cover some 10,000 miles. When presenting these statistics, Professor Schofer made the obvious, yet profound, assertion that the "nature of the U.S. transportation system is to be open, and in that respect we're at serious risk."[102]

Despite the magnitude of this undertaking, there is some movement to secure transportation facilities. For example, the St. Louis Metro has increased the number of security guards at several rail stations. The effort to improve security is a response to recent high-profile *criminal* attacks. In addition to increasing the number of private security guards, the Metro hired additional fare officers and convinced the county to provide more police officers. Metro officials said that they implemented these security upgrades even though statistics show that riders are safe. Riders claim that they have seen fewer disruptive passengers since the additional security guards were placed on trains and at stations.[103]

Another example is illustrated by Wackenhut Security and the Durham Transit Authority's agreement to provide security services on transit buses in Durham, North Carolina. This arrangement followed a series of shootings on transit authority buses. These private police officers are vested with the same arrest powers as police officers. This includes extensively trained and armed private police. They wear "police style" uniforms (but different in appearance to the local police). This service proved successful in that crime was reduced, ridership increased, and people's satisfaction with the bus system improved.[104]

Similarly, security officers ride buses traveling in and around Aspen, Colorado. They carry stun guns to ensure the safety of passengers and drivers during unruly late-night and weekend shifts. The guards, employed by Colorado Protective Services, are contracted by the Roaring Fork Transportation Authority (RFTA) at $38 an hour. Each guard has completed formal training at police academies. In another similar contracted arrangement, a new security policy in Aspen provides for security officers employed on buses during weekend nights to monitor dense and often inebriated passenger loads.[105]

The implementation of a *tactical* approach to public safety is illustrated by a couple of transportation providers. Amtrak is taking a much more aggressive security posture in its operations. They are expanding security sweeps to stations across the country. These "security sweeps" entail counterterrorism teams screening passengers, conducting random security checks, and scanning luggage for explosives. The random security checks are voluntary. However, anyone who declines will have their ticket refunded and be forced to leave the station. In addition to the counterterrorism teams, Amtrak has undercover agents throughout the station to scan the crowds for suspicious activity.[106] Similarly, the Metropolitan Transportation Authority (MTA) is increasing police patrols on commuter trains and in stations to guard against terrorist attacks. In these patrols, riders will see more officers from the authority's police force walking through trains, checking bags, and patrolling platforms. In addition, Metro officers will conduct random searches of backpacks, purses, and other bags. Metro officials say this policy will protect riders and also guard their privacy and minimize delays.[107]

The use of technology to secure transportation facilities is also illustrated by the Transportation Security Administration (TSA) deployment of heat-sensing cameras that can be used to screen people at a train or bus station without requiring a mandatory wait at a security checkpoint.[108] Similarly, radiation portals will be used in ports and other critical infrastructure in an attempt to detect the presence of WMD.[109] Of course, this technology is not limited to critical infrastructure. For example, NYPD personnel have manned checkpoints with radiological monitoring equipment in response to dirty bomb threats.[110] In these checkpoints, police screen trucks to assess evidence of radiation, fertilizers, explosives, and chlorine. Trucks or drivers who lack identification or paperwork are removed from the road. Further, dump trucks and cement trucks receive extra attention because they are capable of smashing through security checkpoints.[111]

"Soft Targets"

Beyond critical infrastructure, the need to secure "soft targets" is getting more attention from public safety professionals. Some of this is driven from "normal" crime, while others are concerned about the threat of terrorism. Ultimately, soft targets will be the targets of choice for terror attacks—particularly those targets that have high casualty count possibilities. These include but are not limited to shopping malls, hotels, popular night spots, sporting events, business districts, and government buildings and complexes.

Beyond the arrangements developed above, a number of cities are drafting legislation that requires security measures in nightclubs and entertainment facilities. For example, the New York City Council has passed legislation requiring that nightclubs install security cameras at the entrance and exit doors to their establishments. The footage from the cameras must be kept in a secure area and would be privy only to authorized personnel. "In recent months the city's nightlife industry has been marred by a number of high-profile tragedies and acts of violence—many of which were linked to problems with club security and management practices," said Council Speaker Christine Quinn. "This package of nightlife safety legislation aims to help solve those problems and to ensure that nightlife in New York City is safe and secure."[112]

Chicago has similar legislation requiring security cameras, trained security personnel, comprehensive security plans, and minimum lighting requirements at nightclubs.[113] Houston has similar legislation requiring certain security methods. These include registering each store in a citywide database, and installing color digital surveillance cameras, panic buttons, and drop safes. Each establishment must also display "no trespassing" and "no loitering" signs. All obstructions in front of the cash register also must be removed so it is visible from the parking lot.[114] In Dallas, the city council enacted similar rules intended to boost safety at convenience stores and give law enforcement the right to detain trespassers and loiterers. The new law requires that the 950 convenience stores in the city must be equipped with "high resolution cameras, silent alarms, and drop-down safes" by May 2010. It also requires store owners to register with the city and sign an affidavit permitting law enforcement to implement no trespassing rules. This gives the police the power to arrest loiterers and panhandlers.[115] Numerous other cities as diverse as Wichita, Kansas; West Covina, California; Toledo, Ohio; and Milwaukee, Wisconsin also have legislation requiring security at nightclubs and retail facilities.[116]

Security in nightclubs is also being assessed in a terroristic climate. For example, the Los Angeles Police Department (LAPD) is conducting security assessments at Hollywood nightclubs due to the discovery of car bombs targeting a nightclub in the United Kingdom. Noting that Hollywood has the most nightclubs of any U.S. city, LAPD Police Chief William Bratton said that the comprehensive "terror assessment" would include several dozen high-profile, high-volume nightclubs. The security assessment will focus on the ways terrorists might target nightclubs and the means by which security for patrons can be increased. Some club owners and employees downplayed the need for antiterrorism measures, but LAPD officials point out that the crowds of patrons who line up outside trendy Hollywood nightclubs provide a target-rich environment for car bombers.[117]

Similarly, in the United Kingdom, the National Counter Terrorism Security Office (NCTSO) is drafting two protective security guidance booklets for the hospitality and entertainment businesses. This is in response to fears about terrorists attacking congested public areas. Owners of these companies will be advised to review their firm's weaknesses and draw up contingency plans for employees in case there is an attack. The police-led security office will also launch counterterrorism training exercises for these businesses.[118]

Two "interesting" examples of real incidents that occurred in 2008 illustrate the complexities and dangers posed in contemporary America. Neither of these examples received much press. Both—in my mind—demonstrate the need to maintain an almost "clinical" approach to order maintenance. In early June, Prince George's County police found explosives material in a stolen car near Andrews Air Force Base. The vehicle contained commercial-grade and military-grade explosives.[119]

Another incident allegedly occurred on July 3. A thief broke into a red van in Brooklyn. He was stunned when he looked inside. The van was filled with gas cans and Styrofoam cups containing a mysterious white substance with protruding wires and switches. What caused police to become aware of this van was that, upon noticing these items and realizing that he may have been riding in a very "explosive" situation, the thief notified the NYPD. Although still unconfirmed, a Web site citing a "highly credible source" stated that there were C-4 explosives possibly attached to a battery found inside the van.[120]

While there is no reason to "connect" these two incidents to any common group or cause, the potential impact of these examples is profound. As stated earlier, there is no legitimate reason to believe—at least in my mind—that incidents such as these will not occur in the United States. Indeed, they are inevitable. Once they occur, the movement toward *Public Safety Policing* will accelerate. I think it will do so in direct response—and in direct correlation—to the perceived threat.

Think again of the two basis premises: *fear* and *money*. When fear prevails, people will spend money to protect themselves. It is important to note that people will spend money on any entity to protect themselves. It does not matter if the FBI saves your life. It does not matter if the NYPD saves your life. It does not matter if the Atlanta Ambassadors save your life. It does not matter if a security camera saves your life. All that matters is that you are safe. This assertion is aptly made by an astute security officer who stated, "A lot of people are scared. They want security and are willing to pay for it."[121] This assertion is almost verbatim with a statement made by an academic, Mary Clifford, who stated, "People are afraid, and they are willing to pay to feel safer."[122] She partly validates this assertion by noting that Maslow's hierarchy of needs recognizes that[123]

> the need for stability in the area of safety and security is so important
> to humans, both as individuals and within social groupings, that they
> are not expected to proceed to higher levels of psychological develop-

ment until fundamental aspects of these needs for safety and security are fulfilled.

As the threat grows, the expenditures by government get increasingly difficult to maintain. Each time a bomb threat shuts down a building, it requires resources to investigate and possibly neutralize the threat. Please consider the aggregate implications of this data. In preparation for writing this book, I began to collect data on bomb threats. From July 2004 to approximately July 2007, I searched for bomb threats and actual incidents through various media open sources.[124] I found 198 incidents where bomb threats were made, suspicious items caused closures and/ or evacuations, an explosive device was found, an explosion occurred, and an object posed some perceived threat. This figure did not include numerous "white powder" (suspect anthrax) incidents. It did not include other biological, chemical, or other threats. It simply included bombs—and bomb threats. Even with these caveats, based on my flawed research and on the nature of reporting, I am quite confident the number of such events is much higher than my data reveals. It is the proverbial "tip of the iceberg." The key point, however, is not whether my numbers are correct—because they are not.

The key point that I think can be extrapolated from this data is that each of these "incidents" required some response by government. Since each of these "incidents" had made "news," chances are that some disruption or even some commotion resulted. These disruptions caused people to miss appointments, get tied up in traffic jams, evacuate their office, or simply to "sit and wait" while authorities investigated. Each of these incidents caused some loss of money, time, and even confidence in the police. Each of these incidents resulted in some frustration, anxiety, or even fear. The aggregate of these incidents damages individual or business productivity—and even adversely affects the larger economy.

The good news is that most of these "incidents" were not bonafide—to use police terminology. That is, the threat posed was usually false. Because this conclusion was not known at the time, the authorities must appropriately respond. The response, therefore, must occur. Threats and suspicious items or persons must be taken seriously. The larger point is government will become increasingly challenged and financially constrained to deal with the threats—or these realities. They need help. As this chapter—and this book—demonstrates, there are options available to help deal with the threats. Technology and alternative service providers will be a critical aspect of this new policing model.

As one internalizes this approach, it may be useful to again consider the notion of "division of labor" or the paraprofessional analogy used in the last chapter. These photos and related tasks, however, are not meant to imply that security personnel will be limited to unarmed functions. Indeed, even prior to any terroristic climate in the United States, there is a discernable trend toward arming security personnel.[125] For example, when an armed robbery was foiled at a Wisconsin theater, security executives noted that the era of the "night watchman" with no weapon is giving way to a more highly trained, armed security officer. Jim Mankowski, a security firm president, echoed sentiments about the professionalization of the security business. "We want to provide a more advanced security officer, a high end security officer. The security officer that's trained in defense and arrest tactics, trained in public relations, trained in report writing, trained in vehicle contacts, high risk situations, and of course firearms, is going to be more marketable."[126] Indeed, both police chiefs and industry executives said security guards are often the first on the scene of a burglary, a break-in, and other crimes. Another security professional said high-risk situations have increased for his security personnel: "There's been more response by our security officers to serious crime situations in the past two years than in the previous ten."[127] This assertion will be widely recognized in the years to come. In this light, think about the extensive use of highly trained security personnel by the military. The "market" for these services will inevitably be manifest in the United States.

Beyond these specialized security providers, the use of private police has also been trumpeted by some as an effective way to reduce crime. For example, the private patrol arrangements in two Los Angeles–based BIDs, Hollywood and Sunset, boasted significant levels of crime reductions. The LAPD Hollywood Division ended 2008 with a 10.2 percent reduction in crime and led all LAPD divisions in crime reduction. In 2007, the private police officers made a total of 2,349 arrests. In 2008, they made a total of 1,707 arrests. Since the reduction of arrests occurred as the crime rate fell by over 10 percent, officials with Andrews International asserted that this shows their dual goals to decrease arrests continue along with continued decreases in the crime rate. In this thinking, arrests will be reduced because there is less crime.[128]

Consequently, I will close this chapter with two pointed quotations. Both quotes are relevant to the application of this new policing model. The first is by Brian M. Jenkins, a well-respected terrorism expert from the RAND Corporation. In explaining the significant role that the police will play in the "war on terror," he stated that[129]

> [a]s this thing metastasizes, cops are it. We are going to win this at the local level. Federal agencies are not built to be the eyes and ears of local communities, but local law enforcement—with the right training and support—can be. There is still much work to be done to enlist state and local officials in the war on terror.

The second is by Elizabeth E. Joh, an attorney and researcher on private policing. She sees, as I do, that the police (or even government) cannot by themselves protect the homeland. It will require a combined, multifaceted approach as reflected by the elements of *Public Safety Policing*. Although Ms. Joh concludes that private police will be necessary, she is somewhat—or even passionately—opposed to the involvement of private police in the public realm. While I will flesh out my concerns on this issue in the last chapter, suffice it to state at this time that private police are here to stay. Indeed, surveys of security professionals reveal they believe that private security will emerge as a "major policing body," and that joint police-security efforts will increase in the future with the "boundaries" between public and private policing eventually vanishing.[130] While this is a substantial statement, I believe the evidence developed in this book demonstrates that things are changing. Whether the boundaries of public and private police will actually vanish is for future consideration. I see them coming together around a new policing model.[131] Joh appears to agree. She states that "the private police are considered the first line defense in the post 9/11 world."[132] This notion is consistent with the theme of this book. In any event, her larger point is:[133]

> Increased pressures on the public police spurred by the war on terrorism will undoubtedly lead to greater reliance on the private police to act as their partners and supplements.

Endnotes

1. "National Strategy for Homeland Security" (2007). Homeland Security Council, Office of the President of the United States, October.
2. "Operation Cooperation," (2004). Bureau of Justice Assistance, U.S. Department of Justice, the Institute of Law and Justice, and Hallcrest Division of Science Applications International Corporation. www.ilj.org/securitypartners/coop_paper_old.html (retrieved on October 28, 2004).
3. Leicester, John (2007). "British 'Big Brother' System of CCTV Surveillance Impresses Neighbors in Europe and in U.S," *Associated Press,* July 11.
4. Harwood, Matt (2008). "Fighting Terrorism in the U.K.," *Security Management* January:48–55.
5. Harwood, Matt (2008), op. cit., 54–55.
6. Harwood, Matt (2008), op. cit., 55.
7. Harwood, Matt (2008), op. cit., 55.
8. CBS News reported "Miami Police Take New Tack against Terror," November 29, 2005.
9. For example, New York City has been targeted by terrorists on several occasions, most notably the 1993 and 2001 attacks against the World Trade Center. Other plots have been thwarted, such as the attempt to bomb the Atlantic Avenue subway station in 1997 and the 1993 Landmarks plot that targeted key sites, such as the Lincoln and Holland Tunnels, the United Nations, and 26 Federal Plaza.
10. Miller, Judith (2007). "On the Front Line in the War on Terrorism: Cops in New York and Los Angeles Offer America Two Models for Preventing Another 9/11," *City Journal* Summer. http://www.city-journal.org/html/17_3_preventing_terrorism.html (retrieved on May 9, 2008).
11. Lucadamo, Kathleen and Pete Donohue (2007) "Bloomberg: Get Surveillance Cameras For Buses, Trains," *New York Daily News,* October 3.

12. http://www.nypd.org (emphasis added) (retrieved on December 2, 2008). http://www.nypd.org (retrieved on December 2, 2008).
13. http://www.nypd.org (retrieved on December 2, 2008).
14. http://www.nypd.org (retrieved on December 2, 2008).
15. Miller, Judith (2007), op. cit.
16. Miller, Judith (2007), op. cit.
17. http://www.nypd.org (retrieved on December 2, 2008).
18. Miller, Judith (2007), op. cit.
19. http://www.nypdshield.org/public/about.aspx (retrieved on December 2, 2008).
20. Miller, Judith (2007), op. cit.
21. http://www.nypdshield.org/public/nexus.nypd (retrieved on December 2, 2008).
22. http://www.nypdshield.org/public/initiatives.nypd (retrieved on December 2, 2008).
23. "NYPD Opens New Counterterrorism Nerve Center" (2008). http://www.wjla.com/news/stories/1108/570988.html, November 18.
24. "City Launches Security Training." www.nynewsday.com (retrieved on April 27, 2005).
25. Miller, Judith (2007), op. cit.
26. Carlson, Tucker (1995). "Safety Inc.: Private Cops Are There When You Need Them," *Policy Review* 73 (Summer).
27. Goldberg, Ceil (1994). "New Roles for Private Patrols," *Security Management* December.
28. Carlson, Tucker (1995), op. cit.
29. Carlson, Tucker (1995), op. cit.
30. Carlson, Tucker (1995), op. cit.; and Pastor, James F. (2003). *The Privatization of Police in America: An Analysis and Case Study.* Jefferson, NC: McFarland.
31. Carlson, Tucker (1995), op. cit.
32. Pastor, James F. (2003), op. cit.
33. Carlson, Tucker (1995), op. cit.
34. Carlson, Tucker (1995), op. cit.
35. Davis, Robert C. and Sarah Dadush (2000). "The Public Accountability of Private Police: Lessons from New York, Johannesburg, and Mexico City," *Vera Institute of Justice* August.
36. Davis, Robert C. and Sarah Dadush (2000), op. cit., 14–16.
37. Davis, Robert C. and Sarah Dadush (2000), op. cit., 11–12.
38. Davis, Robert C. and Sarah Dadush (2000), op. cit., 12.
39. Davis, Robert C. and Sarah Dadush (2000), op. cit., 17–18; and Pastor, James F. (2003), op. cit.
40. Walsh, William F., Edwin J. Donovan, and James F. McNicholas (1992). "The Starrett Protective Service: Private Policing in an Urban Community," *Privatizing the United States Justice System,* eds. Gary W. Bowman, et al. Jefferson, NC: McFarland, 157–77; and Carlson, Tucker (1995), op. cit.
41. Carlson, Tucker (1995), op. cit.
42. Walsh, William F., et. al (1992), op. cit.
43. Carlson, Tucker (1995), op. cit.
44. Walsh, William F., et. al (1992), op. cit.
45. Carlson, Tucker (1995), op. cit.; and Pastor, James F. (2003), op. cit.
46. Carlson, Tucker (1995), op. cit.; and Pastor, James F. (2003), op. cit.
47. Walsh, William F., et. al (1992), op. cit.
48. Walsh, William F., et. al (1992), op. cit.
49. http://www.lapdonline.org/search_results/content_basic_view/6502, January 3, 2009.

50. Miller, Judith (2007), op. cit.
51. Parks, Bernard C.; Captain Joseph Curreri as updated by Captain Gary S. Williams, Commanding Officer of Major Crimes Division. "Terrorism and the Municipal Police Department." http://www.lapdonline.org/search_results/content_basic_view/27421 (retrieved on January 3, 2009).
52. Miller, Judith (2007), op. cit.
53. "LAPD Buys 'Dirty Bomb' Detectors" (2007). *Daily Breeze,* September 10.
54. Doyle, Sue (2008). "Metro Gets $16.1 Million for Gates," *Los Angeles Daily News,* July 15.
55. Widdowson, Anna (2008). "Urban Shield Tests Police Ability," *Daily Californian,* September 15.
56. Andrews International, Inc. (2007). "A Private Police Success Story," *Andrews International, Inc.* March:1.
57. Seyler, Stephen (2008). "2008 Final Report for Hollywood and Sunset Business Improvement Districts," Andrews International, BID Security Director, 1-1-08 through 12-28-08.
58. Personal interview with Captain Girmala, January 27, 2009.
59. Seyler, Stephen (2008), op. cit., 2.
60. Seyler, Stephen (2008), op. cit., 6.
61. Seyler, Stephen (2008), op. cit., 7.
62. King, Paula (2008). "Tight Security Promised for Streets of Brentwood," *Mercury News,* November 4.
63. Spadanuta, Laura (2008). "Patrols Gone Private," *Security Management* August:20–22.
64. Heredia, Christopher (2008). "Oakland May Hire Armed Security Guards," *San Francisco Chronicle,* April 16, B2.
65. Hazelkorn, Bud (2003). "Privatization of Police: Making Crime Pay," *San Francisco Chronicle*, August 17.
66. Jones, Carolyn (2009). "Expecting More Protests, City to Hire Guards," *San Francisco Chronicle,* January 16, B5.
67. www.sfpatrolspecpolice.com (retrieved on December 10, 2008).
68. www.sfpatrolspecpolice.com (retrieved on December 10, 2008).
69. "Renton, Wash., Beefing Up Downtown Security" (2007). *Puget Sound Business Journal* (Seattle), November 25.
70. Radford, Dean (2008). "Renton Transit Center beefs up security with guards on bikes," *Renton Reporter,* July 16. http://www.pnwlocalnews.com/news/25411819.html, July 16.
71. "Homeland Security and Anti-Terrorism Preparations," Chicago Police Department, General Order 04-04, December 6, 2004.
72. As a natural "enhancement" of this technology, a *Chicago Tribune* article titled, "Private Security Cameras Could Join Chicago's Video Surveillance" (July 23, 2008), described how security cameras at companies and private homes may be connected to the Chicago 911 center's large network of video surveillance if a new proposal is approved. With the owner's consent, city emergency personnel would have access to the camera footage and would only monitor them in the event of an emergency, like a car accident or crime. Chicago has the capacity to take information from "thousands" of cameras and obtains the feeds via encrypted Internet transmissions.
73. Pastor, James F. (2003), op. cit.
74. Pastor, James F. (2003), op. cit.
75. Pastor, James F. (2003), op. cit.

76. An example of this trend can be found in Atlanta. Although the city police force has expanded from 1,433 sworn positions to 1,833 over six years, companies have hired private security guards to monitor commercial areas. In addition, almost 3,000 private security officers have been hired by Atlanta businesses. These statistics were reported by Williams, Dave (2008). "Businesses Face Crime Wave," *Atlanta Business Chronicle,* July 28.

77. Seamon, Thomas M. (1995). "Private Forces for Public Good," *Security Management* September.

78. Seamon, Thomas M. (1995), op. cit.

79. Seamon, Thomas M. (1995), op. cit.

80. Seamon, Thomas M. (1995), op. cit.

81. Mokwa, Joseph and Terrence W. Stoehner (1995). "Private Security Arches Over St. Louis," *Security Management* September.

82. Mokwa, Joseph and Terrence W. Stoehner (1995), op. cit.

83. Mokwa, Joseph and Terrence W. Stoehner (1995), op. cit.

84. McKenzie, Sarah (2005). "Business, City Join to Fight Crime Downtown," *Minneapolis/St. Paul Business Journal.* www.msnbc.msn.com/id/7541911/ (retrieved on April 17, 2005).

85. McKenzie, Sarah (2005), op. cit., 1.

86. Kearney, Pat (2000). "Going Private Downtown: Businesses Hire Their Own Police," *The Stranger* 9, no. 49. www.thestranger.com (retrieved on May 1, 2004).

87. Robinson, Frank W. (1996). "From Blight to Bliss," *Security Management* February.

88. Robinson, Frank W. (1996), op. cit.

89. Robinson, Frank W. (1996), op. cit.

90. Brown, Cynthia (2004). "Outsourcing Police Jobs: Cops Replaced by Civilians to Cut Costs," *American Police Beat* 11, no. 12 (December).

91. Brown, Cynthia (2004), op. cit., 16.

92. Brown, Cynthia (2004), op. cit., 16.

93. Williams, Dave (2008), op. cit.

94. Williams, Dave (2008), op. cit.

95. Anderson, Teresa (2008). "Cooperation Rules," *Security Management* September:95–106.

96. http://www.atlantadowntown.com/ambassador.asp (retrieved on November 12, 2008).

97. http://findarticles.com/p/articles/mi_qa3676/is_/ai_n8805715 (retrieved on November 12, 2008).

98. Anderson, Teresa (2008), op. cit.

99. Anderson, Teresa (2008), op. cit.

100. Anderson, Teresa (2008), op. cit.

101. *Cherry Hill Courier-Post* (New Jersey). http://www.courierpostonline.com/article/20081227/NEWS01/812270323/1006, December 27, 2008.

102. Lindell, Rebecca (2003). "Traffic Nightmare," *Kellogg* Summer.

103. Leiser, Ken (2008). "Guards' Visibility Reassures Riders," *St. Louis Post-Dispatch,* September 21.

104. Operation Cooperation: Guidelines for Partnerships between Law Enforcement and Private Security Organizations (2006). Bureau of Justice Assistance, Office of Justice Programs. U.S. Department of Justice.

105. Colson, John (2008). "RFTA Bus Security Armed With Stun Guns," *Aspen Times,* January 10.

106. Hall, Mimi (2008). "Amtrak Expands Security Sweeps," *USA Today,* July 11, 1A.

107. www.ebscohost.com (retrieved on March 26, 2008).

108. Frank, Thomas (2007). "TSA to Test New Thermal Cameras in Rail Stations," *USA Today,* October 4.

109. http://www.venturacountystar.com/news/2008/jun/06/radiation-detection-devices-to-be-installed-at/, June 6, 2008.

110. http://www.reuters.com/article/wtMostRead/idUSN1026252120070811, August 14, 2007.

111. Hays, Tom (2007). "New York City Police Eye Trucks as Potential Vehicles for Terrorists," *Seattle Times,* June 12.

112. http://www.thebostonchannel.com/news/11143266/detail.html, March 1, 2007.

113. Municipal Code of the City of Chicago Section 4-60-130, and General Provisions Section 4-60-205.

114. Feibel, Carolyn (2008). "Houston Will Tackle Convenience Store Crimes," *Houston Chronicle,* March 10.

115. Daniels, Rhianna (2008). "Dallas Passes Convenience Store Security Ordinance," *Security Director News,* September 10.

116. Woods, Christina M. (2008). "Club Safety May Draw New Laws," *Wichita Eagle* (KS), September 8; McLain, Jennifer (2008). "Police: Beef Up Security at Club," *San Gabriel Valley Tribune* (CA), September 29; Sandler, Larry (2008). "Police May Now Order Security Cameras in Milwaukee Bars," *Milwaukee Journal Sentinel,* September 16; and Griffin, Joel (2008). "Toledo Requires Closed-Circuit Television Systems in C-Stores, Small Restaurants," SecurityInfoWatch.com, June 2. The language of the Toledo ordinance is reflective of this trend. It requires owners of convenience stores and small restaurants to equip their businesses with closed-circuit television systems. The law requires the camera systems to monitor the cash register or other areas where currency is exchanged; be properly maintained and have a light that shows the system has been activated; take "recognizable, color, retrievable, enlargeable, and reproducible photographic images of persons" so that they can easily be identified; and allow the police department's crime lab access to the images. Businesses are required to make sure that tapes of recorded images are stored for 30 days. They also must have a sign informing people that the property is under video surveillance.

117. Winton, Richard and David Pierson (2007). "LAPD Reviews Terror Threat at Nightclubs," *Los Angeles Times,* July 4.

118. Kirkup, James (2008). "Police Prepare Terror Attack Warning for Restaurants and Cinemas," *London Telegraph,* August 4.

119. http://www.washingtonpost.com/wp-dyn/content/article/2008/06/04/AR2008060401636.html, June 5, 2008.

120. http://www.theyeshivaworld.com/article.php?p=20633 (retrieved on July 4, 2008).

121. Hazelkorn, Bud (2003), op. cit., 3.

122. Clifford, Mary (2004). *Identifying and Exploring Security Essentials.* Upper Saddle River, NJ: Pearson/Prentice Hall.

123. Clifford, Mary (2004), op. cit., 70.

124. Let me admit up front that this research had two obvious flaws. First, while I conducted daily research, some days time constraints and other commitments precluded such. Second, and more importantly, my research was not all-encompassing. I am quite sure that my typical information sources did not "find" each threat (or even incident). Further, some incidents may have been subtle or even concealed so that the media may

not have even been informed. With these caveats established, my research found that in the approximately 32 months that I collected data (three years minus the months of March–June 2006), I found 198 bomb threat incidents.

125. See, for example, Hopkins, Kyle (2008). "City Plans to Arm Security Guards," *Anchorage Daily News,* February 26, where the author notes that officials in Anchorage, Alaska, are pushing to have armed guards at City Hall and all Assembly meetings. The city's contract with Securitas Security Services USA will call for an armed guard to be stationed at City Hall. The city assembly has also proposed a resolution to have armed guards at all of their meetings. Officials cited a recent shooting at a city council meeting in Kirkwood, Missouri, as evidence that armed guards are needed. In that incident, two police officers and three city officials were shot at a meeting, which was protected by a single unarmed security guard. Also see Correll, DeeDee (2007), "Colorado Springs May Change Gun Rules for Guards," *Los Angeles Times,* December 15, A17, who notes that since semiautomatic weapons are available to purchase in Colorado Springs, the city's officials may repeal an outdated regulation and allow security guards to also carry semiautomatic guns. Currently, armed security guards may carry revolvers with up to eight rounds of ammunition, and acceptable handguns include .38s, .38 Specials, and .357 magnums. City legislators have been considering the change for several months, but attention to the issue has accelerated in the wake of recent shootings at the city's New Life Church. Security firms are pushing to update the law and give guards more powerful weapons to match what a potential shooter might carry. Others, like Paul Helmke of the Brady Campaign to Prevent Gun Violence, think a total ban on assault weapons would deter more violence. "We allow ordinary citizens to carry these things around. … If we're going to allow that, we're probably forcing the hand of security guards to do the same," Helmke says.

126. WKOW.com (Madison, Wis.) "Armed Security Guards Becoming Industry Standard" http://www.wkowtv.com/global/story.asp?s=8794528&ClientType=Printable, August 5, 2008.

127. Ibid, WKOW.com.

128. Seyler, Stephen (2008), op. cit.

129. http://www.manhattan-institute.org/html/cb_43.htm, October 16, 2007.

130. Cooke, Leonard G. and Lisa R. Hahn (2006). "The Missing Link in Homeland Security," *The Police Chief* 73, no. 11 (November).

131. As additional evidence of this assertion, please consider that Youngs reported that police departments in 18 states currently use, or plan to use, private security to fill support roles. This was noted in 2004. Based on the evidence presented in this chapter, one could reasonably conclude this number has increased. See Youngs, Al (2004). "The Future of Public/Private Partnerships," *FBI Law Enforcement Bulletin* January.

132. Joh, Elizabeth E. (2004). "The Paradox of Private Policing," *The Journal of Criminal Law and Criminology* 95, no. 1:49–132.

133. Joh, Elizabeth E. (2005). "Conceptualizing the Private Police," *Utah Law Review* October:574–617.

LARGER ISSUES AND IMPLICATIONS

Chapter 8

Internal and External Alliances—The Holy War

This part of the book takes the focus away from the policing model outlined in the past four chapters. In the next three chapters, we will look at the big picture to get a sense of how contemporary issues may impact our future. This chapter will transition from the earlier emphasis on extremism to illustrate how larger forces shape our understanding of terrorism. These forces include the possibility of alliances that are (or will be) forming, and the implications of the universal—or cosmic—Holy War that some desire. Before doing this, it may be helpful to first take a step back to assess how we got where we are. This approach recognizes that explaining past circumstances is a considerable exercise. Thus, it is beyond the scope of this book to provide a historical account of this complex subject. Instead, I will simply discuss the underlying "logic" and key contemporary incidents.

Incidents and Implications

Terrorism is as old as ancient history. Most people think of Aristotle (384–322 BC) as a great thinker. Yet he believed violent resistance to a despotic ruler was not a crime. Instead, he believed it was a civic duty! This thinking "justified" violence against a corrupt leader. This "logic" contributed to the assassination of Julius Caesar (44 BC), which was viewed by some as a civic duty. The same thinking led to the assassination of Abraham Lincoln by John Wilkes Booth, who yelled, "Thus always to tyrants." This act manifested Aristotle's ancient belief to kill "corrupt" leaders. Numerous other extremist groups appeared over the years. Groups that practiced this "technique," which became known as "terrorism" during the French Revolution, have wide-ranging political views. They include anarchist, Communist, fascist, and Islamist movements. These movements alternatively appeared, dominated, and then receded.

The modern day Islamist movement gained great momentum during the Afghan War with the Soviet Union. When the Mujahidin (the holy warriors) prevailed against the Soviet Union, this proved "ideologically intoxicating."[1] In doing so, radical Islam claimed credit for not only winning the war, but also for destroying the Soviet Empire.[2] It is hard to underestimate the significance of this victory—and of the larger declaration. Once they won the war and brought down the empire, they believed that they could do the same to the other empire: the United States. Following this tremendous victory, literally anything was possible. Indeed, the belief was powerful: Allah willing, Islam will prevail! From this point forward, many with this worldview declared jihad against Western infidels, particularly the Great Satan.

The first direct attack on U.S. soil against American interests was the first World Trade Center bombing. This took place in 1993. The response to this bombing was based on the "crime" approach to terrorism. The investigation, indictments, and subsequent prosecution of those responsible were an illustration of the excellent work product of American criminal justice officials. Unfortunately, this work product did not dissuade any other jihadist from planning and executing future attacks.

Following this incident, the United States was "awakened" by a dramatic act of terrorism conducted by "homegrown" extremists, inspired by the right-wing militia movement. According to Lifton, this group, including Timothy McVeigh, was dedicated to bringing a "new world" into being—part of a "secular crusade," guided by the book, *The Turner Diaries*.[3] This book sought to "empower" a revolution of "white patriots" against the U.S. government, which had come under the evil influence of Jews and blacks. Among other "offenses," the U.S. government was attempting to take guns away from whites, in order to subject them to these "defiled races."[4] The dangers inherent in this ideology, coupled with the devastating action, led law enforcement and policy makers to focus their attention on right-wing groups. For the rest of the decade, much of the attention was devoted to the dangers of militias and other right-wing extremists. This emphasis was well founded. In July 1996, during the Olympics, the Centennial Park bombing occurred, resulting in two deaths along with 111 injured. In addition to this bombing, a number of antiabortion bombings occurred around the country. These incidents gave additional credence to the threat posed by these groups. Each of these bombings was investigated using the "crime" approach discussed earlier.

Just a month prior to the Centennial Park bombing, a U.S. military compound in Saudi Arabia was bombed, resulting in 19 dead and hundreds injured. Since this attack occurred against a military installation on foreign soil, it had little political or public relations impact. Again, the FBI went to work on investigating this act, which was conducted by an Islamist group—sometimes attributed to al Qaeda, sometimes attributed to other groups.

On February 23, 1998, bin Laden issued his now infamous "fatwa" in which he declared war on the U.S. In this "religious ruling," bin Laden called for Muslims to kill Americans and Jews anywhere in the world. The fatwa concluded, "[W]e—with God's help—call on every Muslim who believes in God and wishes to be rewarded to comply with God's order to kill Americans and plunder their money wherever and whenever they find it." The fatwa was issued under the name of the "International Islamic Front against the Jews and the Crusaders." Along with bin Laden, it was signed by members of the Egyptian Islamic Jihad, Egyptian Al-Gama'a Al-Islamiya, Jamiat-ul-Ulema-e-Pakistan, and the Jihad Movement in Bangladesh. Following this written "declaration of war," bin Laden was interviewed by ABC News correspondent John Miller. In this interview, bin Laden repeated his declaration of war against the United States. This "declaration of war" was received by the American public with a large yawn.

On August 7, 1998, two simultaneous car bombs destroyed the U.S. embassies in Kenya and Tanzania. In total 234 were killed (12 Americans) and about 5,000 wounded. Most of the wounded were Muslim. Again Islamist groups, probably al Qaeda, were considered the source of the attack. Following this attack, the Clinton Administration lobbed Tomahawk missiles at Somalia and Afghanistan, marking the first time this administration used military tactics against terrorist groups. Ironically, Clinton was criticized for this response by Republicans for this "wag the dog" approach. Here some saw the response as a means to divert the public from the impeachment trial sparked by the Monica Lewinsky controversy. During this same time, the Clinton Administration twice cancelled planned military strikes against bin Laden and his group due to concerns over "collateral damage."[5]

Less than two years later, in October 2000, another terrorist attack occurred, this time against the USS Cole, which was refueling in a Yemen port. In this attack, 17 U.S. sailors died and 39 were injured. This attack was conducted by the use of a "boat bomb." Neither President Clinton in the latter days of his presidency, nor President Bush, when he came into office in late January 2001, made any military response to this attack. Instead, the incident was investigated by the FBI. Eight years after the attack that nearly sank the USS Cole, however, all those jailed for their role in the incident have escaped from prison or had been freed by Yemeni officials.[6] What does this say about the "crime" approach to terrorism? This question is particularly ironic due to the strong words used by President Clinton following the attack. He vowed to hunt down the plotters and promised "justice will prevail."[7]

Less than one year later, on September 11, 2001, the long-planned attack against the United States on American soil occurred.[8] The rest, as they say, is history. The Afghan War commenced shortly thereafter. The Iraq War commenced in March 2003. Both of these wars continue as of the writing of this book. In my mind, both these wars are critical to the larger "Holy War." I contend they are the most critical theaters of this worldwide war.

In the years following 9/11, these wars have resulted in much blood and treasure being expended. I have great respect for members of the military who have volunteered for this "generational conflict," as was characterized by President Bush. As described earlier, I do not think Bush effectively communicated this conflict. Further, my sense is that the media and academic and political elites will never fully grasp the notion of a "Holy War." This is because America has become very secular in its "elite class." While some talk of religion, most will never understand why people will kill themselves for their god. Neither will they truly understand the larger intent and implications of a Holy War. That is one major reason why I believe America is in deep trouble.

Since the Obama Administration is now entering this dynamic, it will be interesting to assess how the president's policies will look going forward. Since the Obama Administration will likely focus on the "hearts and minds" option, let's analyze how these options may play out.

First, the hearts and minds methodology is both "enlightened" and complicated. As with any war, one critical aspect of the "battle" is to influence the population using various economic, psychological, religious, political, and cultural influences. Since these influences are often very subtle, they are sometimes hard to detect. For example, when Islamist advocates use *zakat* (the method of tithing or charitable giving) to funnel monies to certain groups, it often appears completely innocent. If these groups take the money and divert it to extremist groups, such as Hamas and Hezbollah, it becomes more complicated. Since "one man's terrorist is another man's freedom fighter," those who receive this money will view it as entirely proper and legitimate. They will also rightly assert these are legitimate and necessary charitable contributions. Of course, in making these contributions, the extremist group gains converts. In this way, Hamas, Hezbollah, and almost every extremist group in the world uses some of its funds to help the needy, feed the poor, and to provide shelter for the homeless. According to Undersecretary of State James Glassman, these groups are of growing concern because they combine social services, local governance, national politics, along with extremist attacks.[9] These services are obviously appreciated by those who receive them. This, in turn, creates loyalty to the organization—even if they happen to kill certain people. Indeed, if they kill the "right" people, it only serves to deepen the sense of commitment to the organization. Consequently, these are excellent means to enhance public relations to the affected population.

Indeed, this approach is not new. Growing up in Chicago (as with most other cities), I learned as a child that Al Capone regularly gave to the needy, that the Black Panthers had many community outreach functions, and that the political machine had jobs and "goodies" for those who voted. This is not meant to equate each of these on one moral or normative plane. Instead, it is an acknowledgment that almost all groups do some "good." Obviously the more good that a group does, the more likely their popularity will increase. The problem for those who seek to confront extremist groups is that the public relations component of the "battle" has to be robust and effective. The Bush Administration did a lame job of communicating this aspect of the "war." As a consequence, Bush did a poor job in explaining the overall nature of the war. While he made some effective presentations (such as following 9/11), Bush generally failed to take the message to the people in a consistent and compelling manner. By almost any account, President Obama will clearly outshine Bush in this aspect of the "war."

The Obama Administration is likely to focus on ways to foster the "hearts and minds" approach in this larger "war." He will seek ways to communicate with representatives of extremist groups. He will seek to contribute aid and other benefits to "at risk" populations in the Muslim world. While the Bush Administration also did these, Obama will focus more attention on this aspect of the "war." The media will also likely trumpet this approach. While this is necessary and proper, it is also delicate. Consider this possibility. Let's use real examples to illustrate this point. Since the Obama Administration views Afghanistan as the "centerpiece" of the war, the president must seek to change the dynamic in the lawless, tribal areas in northwest Pakistan. This region has been widely acclaimed to be a key supply route to Afghanistan—of materials, weapons—and fighters.

Let's agree that Obama will attempt to provide various benefits to the population of this area. This could include "incentives" to tribal leaders, and food and materials to the local populations. This may also entail deals with national leaders in Pakistan, and various other ways to engage the "hearts and minds" of the region. Now consider also that despite these best efforts, certain segments of this population will be true believers. They are radical believers in the Islamist worldview. These people will not be convinced that the United States is not the Great Satan. They desire to kill and die for their cause. With this worldview, the "hearts and minds" approach will not work for them.

Take this to the policy level. While the larger desire is to utilize this "hearts and minds" approach, those engaged in the "war" realize certain people need to be captured—or killed—as they are not likely to be changed. What can you do to "engage" these people? Your options are limited. On one extreme, you can seek to isolate them from the larger population. As you reward and benefit the larger population, you hope that these people put peer pressure on the radicals in an attempt to convince them to change. Of course, the opposite can also be true. That is, the radicals can change the larger population—despite the benefits derived from the "enemy." In this sense, the benefits can be seen as a way to take advantage of the enemy, without actually buying into the larger goal—understanding and compassion toward the United States and its policies. To use the adage, "Why look a gift horse in the mouth?" In this sense, why turn down money and other goodies?

Going beyond this question, the possibility exists that the dynamic between the radicals and the moderates may turn violent. If the moderates are rewarded and benefited by the "Great Satan," what is to stop the radicals from taking the benefits away from the moderates? Since the moderates are, almost by definition, less inclined to use violence, will they be able to protect themselves and fend off such attacks? Will the Pakistani military do this for us? Or will this ultimately fall on our shoulders? Regardless of the answer to this question, it is likely that any attempt to reward moderates will be met with resistance and violence. If we meet this violence with violence, what happens when the martyred from these incidents are trumpeted within the village? Do you think the tribal leaders and elders will not be challenged—if they support the United States? Do you think they will not be angered—if they do not? Even if they are sympathetic toward the United States, can they support the notion of killing members of the tribe by the hated enemy?

The other policy extreme is to put pressure on—or target—the radicals while continuing to reward the larger population. The complication in this approach is, how do you achieve this delicate balance? In essence, the balance is as follows. Can you use force—even if it is a "surgical" application of force, without adversely impacting the larger population that you desire to positively influence? Consider this example. You have intelligence from local leaders that certain radicalized individuals are helping the Taliban and al Qaeda. What do you do? Do you hope that these individuals are marginalized by the larger population? Of course, this supposes that the larger population is, indeed, sympathetic toward the United States. This assumption, in some parts of the Muslim world, is optimistic and even naïve. Indeed, this is particularly true for the region in northwest Pakistan. This being said, let's assume that policy makers conclude that these individuals need to be targeted. Let's further assume that the military, or the CIA, attempts to kill or capture these individuals. The military or CIA action, unfortunately, results in killing these individuals—and numerous other family members and friends.

What are the implications of this incident? Do you think that killing these "innocent" people will be easily forgotten by the larger community? Does it negate the previous "good will" that the "hearts and minds" approach attempted to develop? Can you negate these implications by doing "damage control?" Can you negate these implications by delivering more money and goodies? Can you negate these implications by blaming military and intelligence officials for their "failed" action? Do you negate these implications by promising to halt any future actions? I trust the reader can see the difficult implications of this dynamic. If this were only one isolated example, it would be far less problematic. Unfortunately, this example is literally the "tip of the iceberg." Please think back to the "hearts and minds" graphics in Chapter 3. Consider how the pressures imposed on people "push" them in one direction or the other. Particularly, when violence and death are part of this dynamic, the positioning of moderates is made more tenuous. Many "blame Bush" for this dynamic—caused by his policies. The cold, hard fact is it has more to do with the nature of terrorism—and counterterrorism—than it does Bush. Since Bush emphasized asymmetric warfare more than "hearts and minds," it would not be surprising that more of these incidents would occur. Conversely, if the policy focused on "hearts and minds," it would not be surprising that much of the attempts to "convert" people would fail. In either approach, there are downsides. Consequently, despite what many assert, neither approach is inherently "correct."

Going beyond these distinct policy approaches, the reality is, some aspects of both approaches are inevitable. Simply stated, it is impossible to maintain an exclusively "hearts and minds" approach. Indeed, while some may propose this approach, it defies any understanding of the world—and of terrorism. That said, how do you "balance" these two approaches? As described above, this is exceedingly difficult.

Even before President Obama took office, he advocated going into Pakistan to ferret out Osama bin Laden. Specifically, Obama said, "If Pakistan is unable or unwilling to hunt down [Osama] bin Laden and take him out, then we should."[10] Almost without hesitation, the demands to rebuke this assertion were raised. Pakistani Americans and antiwar advocates delivered a letter to Obama's campaign office, calling on him to support a halt to U.S. bombing of terrorist targets in Pakistan. The letter stated in pertinent part, "You must understand the sweeping dismay that your avowed support for U.S. military incursions into Pakistan ... has elicited among untold numbers of Pakistani-Americans and peace activists across the country."[11] This was not the first rebuking directed against Obama for his campaign rhetoric. Earlier on in the campaign, he asserted that if he were elected he might order military strikes against terrorists hiding in Pakistan. The Pakistani foreign minister responded that this was a "very irresponsible statement, that's all I can say." He added, however, that "as the election campaign in America is heating up, we would not like American candidates to fight their elections and contest elections at our expense."[12] Note that shortly after this statement, Obama, Bush, and Congressman Tancredo had their effigies burned by protestors in Pakistan. The protestors called for "Deth [Death] to Obama of America."[13] As described earlier with Chávez, is this the start of another fruitful relationship?

These examples illustrate that even during the campaign, trying to balance legitimate American interests against the interests of tribes, movements, and countries is difficult indeed. Since we can all agree that it is harder to govern than to campaign, these examples represent very difficult challenges for the Obama Administration—and for America. For those who are inclined to simply "leave them alone," I trust you will agree that did not work so well during the 1990s. Throughout that decade, the Clinton Administration largely left the Taliban and bin Laden alone in Afghanistan. How did that work out? After 9/11, Bush decided to take away the sanctuary that allowed radical Islamists to train and plan for their Holy War. While I do not have any definitive knowledge, my sense is the Obama Administration will attempt to balance the approaches of the last two presidents. He will be more aggressive than Clinton. He will be more inclusive than Bush. Based on the discussion above, attempting to achieve this "hearts and minds" approach is difficult. Given the difficulties inherent in this balance, I am not optimistic that Obama—or anyone else—can thread this needle. Simply stated, it is extremely difficult to find the middle ground in a terroristic environment. It is particularly difficult to do so when dealing with committed adversaries in a Holy War.

Second, another aspect of this Holy War that makes it difficult to manage is based on a covert or asymmetric type of warfare. It would be much easier to see the nature of the threat if large armies lined up for battle. This is not how this war is or will be fought. Because of this fact, many will never "connect the dots." Each time a bomb explodes, the almost reflexive thought is "another crazy person." In this manner, the focus is on the criminal, the fanatic, the group, or the extremist. The focus, in my mind, should be on the movement, the ideologies, and the larger goals. Since most people have not focused on the study of terrorism, they are too busy to delve into the writings of extremist groups. They are not interested in seeking out alternative or international media sources. Instead, they hear about the explosion. They see the photos. They learn of the "body count." They may pause to pray for the victims. They may get angry with the criminals—or the extremists, the insurgents, or whatever "label" the media gives them. They may blame the administration. In the end, the response from people is limited. All they can do is get active, organize, and vote.

Now that the election is over, the difficult part of the job is just beginning. Remember at its root, this conflict is a war of ideas. It is a war of public relations; it is a war of disinformation; it is a war of political positioning; and it is a war of international relations. In the end, this is a war of ideology. It is battle of "hearts and minds." It is a battle of one particular worldview (radical Islamist) against the current dominant worldview (Western capitalism). In this war, like any other war, there is the need to "ally" with other like-minded ideologies. Indeed, some-times-allied ideologies are not directly connected with each other. They may even be somewhat conflicting in their interests and/or their worldviews. They may be united, however, by a common enemy. Said another way, they may see their frustrations, or their problems, as being connected to a particular source. Remember: the enemy of my enemy is my friend.

Terrorism Alliances and Incidents

In contemporary times, a number of ideologies see the source of their problems as capitalism. Unquestionably, the leader of worldwide capitalism, also referred to as "globalization," is the United States of America. As mentioned earlier, there is an "interesting" mixture of seemingly diverse ideologies galvanizing around the notion that capitalism is the enemy. For example, Ayman al-Zawahiri, the second in command of al Qaeda, contends that this "new world order" is a source of humiliation for Muslims. He believes it is better for the "youth of Islam" to carry arms and defend their religion with pride and dignity than to submit to this humiliation.[14] He argues that "violence restores the dignity of the humiliated youth." This assertion is similar to the rhetoric of communist thinkers, such Franz Fanon, who advocated that violence is a "cleansing force" that frees the oppressed youth from his or her "inferiority complex" of despair and inaction. In short, violence makes the youth fearless and restores his or her self-respect.[15]

To those who pay attention to their enemies, this "logic" should not be a surprise. To those who have waited for the media to inform you of the enemy's rhetoric, then you may be a bit surprised, even shocked to read various quotes from "the enemy." Although we will flesh out ideological sentiments in some detail, please read the below statement from bin Laden, which was published around the sixth anniversary of 9/11. Please read this quote in light of the potential for internal divisions within American society. Also consider the larger "alliances" forming around the globe. In particular, consider how this rhetoric may be designed to foster resentment toward and even destruction of the capitalist system. Without further editorial comment, he said,[16]

> People of America: the world is following your news in regards to your invasion of Iraq, for people have recently come to know that, after several years of the tragedies of this war, the vast majority of you want it stopped.
>
> Thus, you elected the Democratic Party for this purpose, but the Democrats haven't made a move worth mentioning. On the contrary, they continue to agree to the spending of tens of billions to continue the killing and war there, which has led to the vast majority of you being afflicted with disappointment.
>
> And here is the gist of the matter, so one should pause, think and reflect: why have the Democrats failed to stop the war, despite them being the majority …
>
> So in answer to the question about the causes of the Democrats' failure to stop the war, I say: they are the same reasons which led to the failure of former president Kennedy to stop the Viet Nam war. Those with real power and influence are those with the most capital.
>
> And since the democratic system permits major corporations to back candidates, be they presidential or congressional, there shouldn't be any cause for astonishment—and there isn't any—in the Democrats' failure to stop the war. And you're the ones who have the saying which goes, "Money talks." And I tell you: after the failure of your representatives in the Democratic Party to implement your desire to stop the war, you can still carry anti-war placards and spread out in the streets of major cities, then go back to your homes, but that will be of no use and lead to the prolonging of the war.
>
> However, there are two solutions for stopping it. The first is from our side, and it is to continue to escalate the killing and fighting against you. This is our duty, and our brothers are carrying it out, and I ask Allah to grant them resolve and victory. And the second solution is from your side. It has now become clear to you and the entire world the impotence of the democratic system and how it plays with the interests of the peoples and their blood by sacrificing soldiers and populations to achieve the interests of major corporations.
>
> And with that, it has become clear to all that they are real tyrannical terrorists. In fact, the life of all mankind is in danger because of the

global warming resulting to a large degree from the emissions of the factories of the major corporations ... [citing failure to observe Kyoto accord] ...

This greatest of plagues and most dangerous of threats to the lives of humans is taking place in an accelerating fashion as the world is being dominated by the democratic system, which confirms its massive failure to protect humans and their interests from the greed and avarice of the major corporations and their representatives.

And despite this brazen attack on the people, the leaders of the West [Bush, Blair, Sarkozy, and Brown] still talk about freedom and human rights with a flagrant disregard for the intellects of human beings. So is there a form of terrorism stronger, clearer and more dangerous than this? This is why I tell you: as you liberated yourselves before from the slavery of monks, kings, and feudalism, you should liberate yourselves from the deception, shackles and attrition of the capitalist system ...

And before concluding, I tell you: there has been an increase in the thinkers who study events and happenings, and on the basis of their study, they have declared the approach of the collapse of the American Empire.

Any reading of bin Laden's words can result in only one conclusion: the enemy is capitalism. Why should he characterize the enemy as capitalism instead of the "Great Satan"? The answer in my mind is clear. If he asserts the Great Satan as the enemy, then his allies are likely limited to radical Islamists. Conversely, if he asserts that capitalism is the enemy, he has now connected with a much broader set of allies. This connection plays out both in domestic politics in America and in larger international relations.

First, consider the world scene. Can you doubt that the numerous face-to-face meetings between Ahmadinejad from Iran, Putin from Russia, and Chávez from Venezuela are geared toward an Islamic-Socialist alliance? Do you think it is possible they are talking about oil? Ironically, this may be the focus of their initial "battle." Is it unreasonable to conclude that they would seek to manipulate oil to their strategic interests? While the left throws allegations at "big oil," these players seem to go under the radar screen. This is not to say that "big oil" does not deserve some oversight, regulation, and when appropriate—criticism. My assertion is that the issue is much larger and more complicated than "blood for oil," which seems to suffice in some circles. This being said, for our purposes the issue is not the price of oil. The issue, instead, is the framing of an Islamic-Socialist strategic alliance. I believe it is real and dangerous. Indeed, Russia is arming Iran and Venezuela with military weapons and technology. The Russian navy conducted its first maneuvers since the days of the "Cold War" in the Caribbean Sea in the fall of 2008. Could it be that the Islamic Republic of Iran and the socialist-leaning governments of Russia and Venezuela see their interests intersect in a strategic alliance against the United

States? However this potential plays out, it is clear that the goal of Islamist violence is a worldwide jihad, designed to:[17]

1. Topple all governments in the Middle East in order to create a united, wealthy, and powerful Islamic caliphate
2. Destroy Israel
3. Recapture all lands previously under Muslim control
4. Keep pushing the West until the whole globe is dominated by Islam

Second, these international agendas are (or will) play themselves out on U.S. soil. Think again of the Sean Bell case. The larger issue relating to this case is the interesting connection between the disaffected black community and the socialist-inspired revolutionary movements. This is, in my mind, more complicated than the tragic police shooting it was supposed to represent. If you consider who has been adversely affected by this tragic case, two conclusions come to mind. Of course, initially the family of Sean Bell must be considered. While I understand the dynamics that go into a shooting incident, one must sympathize with the family. From a larger perspective, however, this incident has furthered a notion, whether true or not, that police are more willing or likely to shoot black people. While I will have more to say on this point in the next chapter, the more disconcerting implication is that this case has furthered a growing black-socialist movement. This movement has been furthered by the New Black Panther Party, which rails against the white, capitalist system.[18]

These high profile police shootings foster an "interesting" connection between the black community and socialist organizations. Are these connections relevant to the possibility of terrorism and extremist violence? Only time will truly answer this question. My answer is that the connection is deep and profound. In my mind, this will result in a cooperative movement, not unlike the connection between Ahmadinejad, Putin, and Chávez, with an interesting twist. This connection was described by Azar Nafisi. She argued that some contemporary Islamic traditions maintain as "much from the crassest forms of Marxism as [they do] from the religion ... with [their] leaders influenced by Lenin, Sartre, Stalin, and Fanon as they are by the prophet."[19] Consider this statement in light of the advocacy of al-Zawahiri who seeks to elicit the "oppressed" to join the Holy War:[20]

> Al Qaeda is not merely for the benefit of Muslims, that's why I want blacks in America, people of color, American Indians, Hispanics, and all the weak and oppressed in North and South America, in Africa and Asia, and all over the world, to know that when we wage Jihad in Allah's path, we aren't waging Jihad to lift oppression from the Muslims only, we are waging Jihad to lift oppression from all mankind, because Allah has ordered us never to accept oppression, whatever it may be.

Will these "connections" actually be manifested? I think they will. In contemporary America, one likely connection is "black nationalist" Christian churches aligning with revolutionary Socialist movements to further their respective interests. Indeed, there is evidence to maintain that "black nationalist" churches, such as Trinity United Church of Christ, will connect with Islamic thought. Indeed, Dr. Wright's church declared Nation of Islam leader, Louis Farrakhan, "man of the year" in their magazine. In addition, Imam Mohammad Ali Elahi, head of the Islamic House of Wisdom in Dearborn Heights, said he plans to "condemn the unfair treatment" that he says Wright "received by some media members who are ignoring this faith leader's decades of dedication and services to this country and nation."[21]

To be clear, the fact that some Muslims have sympathy and connection with black nationalistic churches is not inherently problematic. What is disconcerting is as group ideologies harden, as I believe will occur, the likelihood that extremists within opposing and allied groups will resort to violence. Indeed, following the verdict in the Sean Bell case, supporters of Bell chanted "murderers, murderers!" and shouts of "KKK" rang out on the courthouse steps.[22] Since the three police officers were black, white, and black Hispanic, the notion that they were part of the KKK is both inflammatory and ridiculous. Hopefully, as this book makes clear, facts are often subordinated to the ideology of the group. Consequently, I pay particular attention to what groups are saying, as their ideologies are an important, if not the most important, precursor to violence. This is why I highlighted the ideologies of various extremist groups in Chapter 3.

On the other side of this dynamic is the possibility that right-wing extremist groups will ally against this black, socialist, and Islamist coalition. This side of the "fence" could include a mixture of white supremacist groups, such as the KKK forming alliances with neo-Nazi and Confederate "rebels." Each of these groups is banded along race and tends to be conservative in their political philosophy. Helping to band them together, as stated previously, was the election of Barack Obama. Further, another way these groups may find common ground is through variants in Christianity. This "religious" connection may be derived from the Christian Identity movement, and/or through the Creativity Church (the Creators). In any event, if either of these two opposing sides form a coalition, it becomes much more likely that the "other side" will do the same.

If my premise is correct, the incidence of inter-group conflict will be the result of and response to increased extremist ideologies. Currently, I contend that extremist ideologies are percolating just underneath the social and political framework of the country. What does it take to trigger a rise in extremist ideologies? As stated above, radical Islam is, in my mind, clearly a factor. How significant is this factor? How soon will this occur? These are the key questions. Assume for a moment that radical Islam does not conduct another terrorist attack on American soil for the next five years. Are we then in the clear? Have we dodged the proverbial bullet? I think not. Of the expected increase in extremist violence, I assert that radical Islam is a factor, possibly being the most critical factor. It is by no means, however, the only threat capable of fostering this circumstance. Indeed, this country's history, which some people cannot or will not let go, can create ample "ammunition" for extremist ideologies. While we will explore the potential for this eventuality, suffice it to say at this point that certain groups are poised to impose their radical agendas through direct action. In my mind, who acts first, when they act, what they do, how opposing groups and the larger society respond, and whether public safety forces can control the violence are the only real questions. Consequently, it is not whether extremist violence will increase, but how and when it manifests itself.

As an illustration of what this may look like, Figure 8.1 may help to conceptualize the pending threats. Note that some of these groups may directly oppose each other, while some groups may ally with each other. To illustrate these potentialities, I show arrows from one circle to another. Sometimes this can represent a potential ally. Sometimes it may represent a potential adversary. Other times, the line is contained within the circle. For example, racial and nationalist groups are the most likely to exclusively oppose each other. This is because their respective interests leave little room for even tactical cooperation. To illustrate this, the line is contained within the circle.

Groups such as neo-Nazis and leftist/anarchist groups are likely to be natural enemies. Others, such as radical Islamic and Christian Identity groups, possess numerous inherent conflicts, not the least of which stem from their interpretations of the Koran and the Bible. However, some assert that their common, mutual foe—the Jews—may inspire some tactical cooperation against their mutual enemy. In thinking about these potential inter-group conflicts, it is critical that you deeply

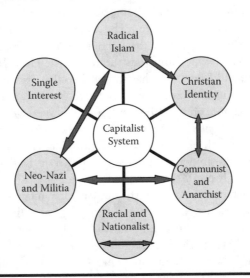

Figure 8.1 Extremist ideologies versus capitalism (Copyright James F. Pastor, 2009).

internalize the notion that "the enemy of my enemy is my friend." If you get this notion, then you will be able to imagine how groups can cooperate at one time, and then oppose each other at another time. In either case, they could still be true to their ideological beliefs. In the end, however, each one of these groups, from religious to political to racial/nationalist, all have one common theme: the destruction of the government or, more broadly, the capitalistic system.[23] The impact of this fact is wide ranging—and extraordinarily problematic—for policing agencies and public safety providers. The reason for this, of course, is that the most visible representatives, and symbols, of government are the police and other public safety personnel.

With these provocative assertions established, focus your attention on the substantial international issues facing the Obama Administration. Let's try to connect the dots regarding the Islamist movement, the Iraq War, and the "war on terrorism." Hopefully this brief recitation will help give some additional context to the theme of this book.

Theaters in the Holy War

This section highlights certain "theaters" in the Holy War. This analysis, however, is not meant to be a definitive explanation of a very complicated world. All I seek in this presentation is to provide an overview of the many theaters in the world where radical Islamists are operating. This war is being fought on a number of different fronts. These fronts—or theaters—range from Algeria to Tanzania, from Pakistan to the Philippines, from Somalia to Egypt, from Gaza to Glasgow, from Lebanon to Libya, from Yemen to Germany. In each theater, Islamists are actively pursuing their goals to further their caliphate throughout the Middle East and the world.

The above map represents numerous theaters in the Holy War. Take a look at Afghanistan, Iran, and Iraq. Note that Iran is directly between Afghanistan and Iraq. I believe one crucial reason why the United States commenced the war in Iraq was to place pressure on Iran from both sides. While the Bush Administration did not admit this as a basis for the war, the strategic basis for doing so is clear. In essence, it could destabilize the mullahs in Iran by implanting "democracies" on both of its borders. It is important to note that much of the population in Iran is young, with a generally pro-Western outlook. The logic of this approach is that the establishment of democracies outside the borders of Iran could stir the pro-Western youth to rebel against their theocratic government. Of course, Iran understands this as much as the Bush Administration. In response, Iran has actively sought to destabilize Iraq (see discussion below). Iran has also played a role, but to a lesser extent, in arming and supplying the war in Afghanistan.[24] Syria, a close ally of Iran, has also sought to destabilize Iraq, from the opposite border. Each country, therefore, is fostering destabilization through porous borders that enable Islamist fighters to enter Iraq. Of course, the impact in and from Pakistan

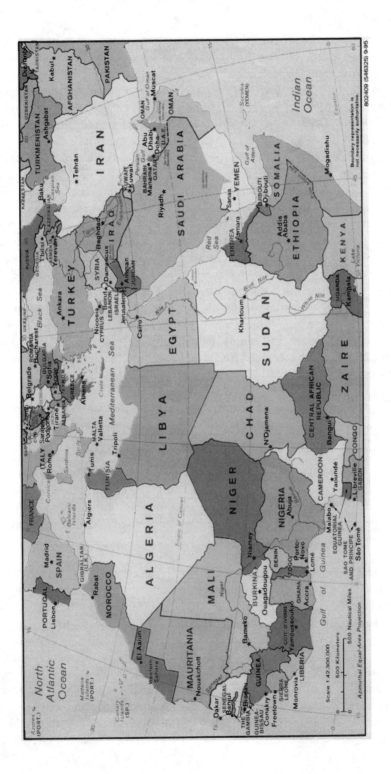

into Afghanistan is also of critical importance. Consequently, the Islamists see the opportunity to "triangulate" Afghanistan and Iraq, just as the United States sought to do with Iran.

Admittedly, this picture simplifies a complex world. Of course, the complexities of international relations are woven with historical, regional, geopolitical, and religious implications. I seek to simplify this complex puzzle for a number of reasons. First, much of the contemporary threats facing the United States have their roots in this region. The nationalities of the 9/11 hijackers speak to this assertion. Second, related to the realities of 9/11, the region represents a seemingly never-ending supply of potential radicals. Simply stated, many children learn from their earliest days that their plight is due to the corruption of the United States (or the Great Satan). While this may be difficult to prove, I believe that Bush attempted to change this dynamic by implanting democracies into the region. While some may legitimately argue this was a foolish endeavor, I contend the "wisdom" of this decision will only be assessed by the benefit of time and historical context. Even assuming this was a foolhardy decision, what was our alternative? Shall we await the next suicide bomber that will inevitably come out of this region? Shall we instead seek to change the dynamics in the region by more aid, better education, more effective public relations? Are these "hearts and minds" factors sufficient? Indeed, one can argue none of these are sufficient. Fouad Ajami wrote about this "impossible" American predicament in the Middle East. He stated,[25]

> Policy can never speak to wrath. Step into the thicket [get involved] and the foreign power is blamed for its reach. Step back [stay out of the region] and Pax Americana is charged with abdication and indifference.

When you are indoctrinated that your problems are the result of the policies of a particular country, this creates the incentive to lash out against the source of your problems. Whether this is real or imagined, many in the Middle East have been brought up with this mindset. This reality was reflected in President Obama's inauguration speech. He stated,[26]

> To the Muslim world, we seek a new way forward, based on mutual interest and mutual respect. To those leaders around the globe who seek to sow conflict, or blame their society's ills on the West—know that your people will judge you on what you can build, not what you destroy.

Third, since this region is also the source of much of the world's energy supply, the importance of this region cannot be underestimated. While I "hope" that we can wean ourselves from Middle East oil, my analysis in the next chapter leaves me doubting whether this transaction will occur quickly enough to secure our national interests. Finally, the most relevant reason why I devoted attention to the Middle East in this book is due to the theme of this book—terrorism. It should be readily apparent that I contend that radical Islam will be *a* or *the* trigger toward increased extremism in the United States. Since the source of radical Islam stems from this region, one would be negligent to ignore this vital region.

Of course, terrorism occurs outside the Middle East. Indeed, my thesis is the "Holy War" is a worldwide struggle. It is important to know that Northern Africa has several countries with active Islamist geopolitical struggles. These include Egypt, Morocco, Libya, and Algeria. The bloody "civil war" in Algeria is a case in point. During the 1990s, Islamists engaged in a bloody war for control of Algeria. This war pitted Islamists who sought to impose Sharia law against those who desired a more secular government. The war lasted 15 years, and had killed as many as 200,000 between the army and groups trying to set up a purist Islamic state.[27] Indeed, this war still rages, albeit in a less direct conflict. Now the war is largely limited to bombings and occasional firefights between Islamists and Algerian police and military units. The situation, however, is not by any means resolved. For example, after one recent suicide bombing, Algerian President Bouteflika blamed Islamist rebels, denouncing them as "criminals" trying to scuttle his policy of national reconciliation. In December 2007, car bombs exploded minutes apart in central Algiers. The bombings were directed at the United Nations offices. They were heavily damaged. In addition, the facade was ripped off the wing of a new government building. Officials said 45 people were killed and dozens more injured.[28] To those who desire to blame every grievance on the United States, answer this rhetorical question: What did the United Nations do wrong to the Islamists?

The theater in Morocco is also problematic. For example, on July 6, 2007, Moroccan authorities raised the terror alert level to its highest level, citing a current, serious threat of terrorism. A statement from the Ministry of the Interior stated the alert "indicates a serious threat of a terrorist act and demands extreme mobilization by the bodies concerned." Analysts speculate that the threat may have been raised in part due to continued calls for attacks by senior al Qaeda leadership, as well as recent attacks throughout North Africa by al Qaeda in the Land of the Islamic Maghreb (AQIM).[29]

In Libya, the dynamic of the "Holy War" can be seen with a different strategy. Libyan leader Gadhafi was recently criticized by al-Zawahiri accusing him of being an "enemy of Islam." The al Qaeda leader threatened a wave of attacks against Libya because it has improved relations with the United States. Significantly, this criticism followed Gadhafi's voluntary admission to give up his WMD program after the United States invaded Iraq. Moreover, al-Zawahiri also announced in an audiotape ironically titled, "UNITY OF THE RANKS," that the Libyan Islamic Fighting Group was joining ranks with al Qaeda. The audiotape stated that "the Islamic nation is witnessing a blessed step ... the brothers are escalating the confrontation against the enemies of Islam: Gadhafi and his masters, the Washington Crusaders."[30]

Of course, this is the same Gadhafi who was blamed for the bombing in the German disco in the 1980s. It is the same Gadhafi who had conspired in the mid 1980s with a Chicago street gang known as the El Rukns to blow up an airplane from O'Hare Airport. I had the distinct pleasure of taking part in two raids of the El Rukn "fort" as a police officer in the Gang Crime Enforcement Unit of the Chicago Police Department. Those who think that the Middle East does not matter should consider that the world is "much smaller" than it was over two and a half decades ago. Is it possible another Middle East-inspired terrorist attack will occur on U.S. soil?

In Somalia, Islamists have been fighting U.S.-backed African Union and Ethiopian troops for years. As early as 1994, Islamists in Somalia sought to exploit America's "Vietnam complex," due to its fear of being bogged down in a real war.[31] Along with this notion, Islamist demands include the destruction of churches, and Jewish and Buddhist temples.[32] The tide of this conflict appears to be turning in favor of the Islamists. In the fall of 2008, members of al-Shabaab have consolidated their hold on southern Somalia, meting out punishments on the population based on their interpretation of Islamic law.[33] Later, in January 2009, the last Ethiopian troops left Somalia's capital after a two-year deployment. In their absence, Islamist militiamen immediately took control of their bases. It remains unclear whether the Ethiopian troops who have been shoring up the country's weak transitional government will leave the country. Or will they redeploy in other parts of Somalia? This question is fueling fears that Islamists could try to expand their power in the lawless Horn of Africa region. Once these forces were redeployed, various Islamist factions began to battle each other for control. For example, the Union of Islamist Courts fought against al-Shabaab after the former signed a peace agreement with the government.[34]

As you read this account, please remember that it is not unusual for one radical faction to fight another radical faction. The fight for control is not limited to radical Islamists versus modernity (or the West, or the United States, or another religion). Remember the key principle: *the enemy of my enemy is my friend*. It should be expected that some radical groups will vie for control against other radical groups. Indeed, these groups tend to understand one fact—violence. Once this "internal" conflict is resolved, however, they will fall in line to battle their common enemy: the West, or the United States, or another religion (depending upon the context and the theater). Significantly, Ethiopia's prime minister said he could not predict what would happen when his troops leave Somalia. He expects the extremist Islamic group, al-Shabaab, and others to try to seize control. Al-Shabaab, which the United States considers a terrorist organization with links to al Qaeda, says it wants to establish an Islamic state in Somalia.[35]

This same approach is taking place in Sudan, Yemen, Lebanon, and in numerous other countries. The common theme is a battle for control between moderate Muslims and Islamists. In each theater, Islamists further their cause with violence. Of course, no discussion of terrorism and the Middle East can ignore the impact of Israel and Palestine. As this book is being drafted, the Israeli Defense Force (IDF) has moved into Gaza. In Gaza, the IDF and Hamas engaged in heavy fighting, with Hamas taking the brunt of the casualties.[36] This fighting was sparked by rocket attacks into Israel by Hamas. While this conflict alone can fill many books, one important point to consider is that Hamas has a significant infrastructure within the United States. They will inevitably strike the U.S. homeland!

The deeper problem with this conflict—and with much of the Arab-Israeli relations—is the dilemma over Jerusalem. Ironically, Jerusalem is known biblically as "the city of peace." This city has witnessed an extraordinary amount of violence over its long history. Regardless of all the attempts to diplomatically resolve the Arab-Israeli dispute, the question of the sovereignty of Jerusalem will make this difficult to achieve. In short, the "Holy War" cannot be resolved until sovereignty of Jerusalem is resolved. The significance of this city is clear. All three major religions view Jerusalem as special, even unique. The Jewish religion views the Wailing Wall (Temple Mount) as its holiest site. The Muslim religion views the Dome of the Rock as the third most sacred site in Islam. Similarly, Christians view Jerusalem with its connection to the life and death of Christ as critical. In short, many believe God chose Jerusalem.[37] The biblical admonition makes this clear. "Pray for the peace of Jerusalem: May those who love you be secure."[38] Based on these deeply held beliefs, one would be wise to watch Jerusalem in the months and years ahead.

Of course, this overview just scratches the surface. The number of terroristic incidents throughout the world is substantial. Obviously, there is much more to this story. This is a very complicated international chess game! Paying attention to the world, however, gives you perspective. These world theaters get precious little substantive attention from the U.S. media. Based on my analysis of the media in Chapter 2, I contend that you will not get a perspective of this conflict from the major U.S. media. Instead, you will have to search out international media sites, law enforcement, and security reporting systems. It may be helpful to study U.S. DHS, State, and Defense Department daily briefings. If you do "your homework," you will be informed. In my mind, those who see the storm approaching will be most able to prepare. Hence, the purpose of this brief international "analysis" is that it foretells what will occur in the United States. When it does occur, the media will report the violence in a big way. By then, it may be too late. In any case, most of these incidents are under the radar of the U.S. news reports. If they are reported, they are rarely linked to the larger "Holy War." As stated earlier, that is because the media does not get it! Or they have decided to diminish the nature of the threat for ideological, political, or other reasons. However, as articulated below, the media was consistent with its reporting in Iraq. Or more accurately, it was consistent *before* the level of violence dramatically decreased. When this happened, they lost interest.

Most Americans—even Democrats—continue to advocate the advancement of the Afghan War. Indeed, part of the mantra from leading Democrats was that "we took our eyes off al Qaeda when we started the Iraq War." If you believe the enemy is limited to al Qaeda, then this assertion has some merit. This is because the connection of al Qaeda to Iraq prior to the war was tenuous, at best. The assertion, repeatedly made, by antiwar activists is a pointed criticism of the Bush Administration and of the war. Before we deal with some of the issues raised by Iraq, let's first provide an overview of the Islamists' approach to the Afghan War.

According to U.S. intelligence officials, a national intelligence assessment released in 2007 said al Qaeda had regenerated its leadership and ability to conduct attacks in the ungoverned tribal region of western Pakistan. Because of this, Afghanistan has grown increasingly violent. The alliances in Afghanistan combine close ties and collaboration between the Pakistan tribes, the Taliban, and al Qaeda. The Afghan War continues to attract new fighters to fight U.S. forces in Afghanistan, and radical Internet sites that provide religious justification for attacks and violent anti-Western rhetoric are spreading.[39] This does not bode well for the future of this war. Indeed, if President Obama's inauguration address is any indicator, he seemed to focus on "peace" instead of "victory" in Afghanistan. While this may be simply rhetoric, he stated,

> We will begin to responsibly leave Iraq to its people, and forge a hard-earned peace in Afghanistan.[40]

Since most of the antiwar attention is placed on Iraq, most do not seem to know, or refuse to acknowledge, that the tactics used in Afghanistan are remarkably similar to those used in Iraq. Both wars pit radical Islamists against the United States and its allies. Both wars are largely waged by "asymmetric" means, that is, terroristic tactics by a militarily weaker, but determined, foe against a stronger military. Part of this approach is to intimidate coalition governments to remove their troops from Afghanistan. For example, Taliban and al Qaeda fighters have used hostage taking as a strategy to compel troop withdrawals. In numerous examples, Austria and Germany were threatened unless their troops were removed. Similar threats were made against Spain, Italy, and the United Kingdom.[41]

While these incidents made "big news" in Europe, the amount of coverage in American media was almost nonexistent. One can argue that this is due to the fact that the hostages were European. With this logic, of course, the coverage was more extensive in Europe. While that is a fair statement, I do not believe it tells the whole story. I believe if the whole story were told, it would have to acknowledge that the very same assertions made in Iraq by Islamists are also being made in Afghanistan. That is, get your troops out of the Muslim land. These are not the only examples. In July 2007, 23 South Korean missionaries were kidnapped by the Taliban.[42] Once again, threats were made against the hostages unless South Korea removed its troops from Afghanistan.[43] While some may argue that these are simply isolated examples, I contend they represent a larger strategy designed to intimidate Western countries into submission. To those who argue that these examples are only isolated incidents, I can only say, *when* we leave Iraq, you will see a lot more threats against the United States until we remove our troops from *Afghanistan*. Quite simply, this is inevitable. Because many refuse to "connect the dots," we will continue to assume that the next threat is the last. In my mind, this is both foolish and dangerous.

This brings us to the most controversial question: Iraq. There are legitimate arguments over how viable and imminent the WMD threat in Iraq was prior to our invasion (see Appendix). Whatever the answer, now that we are in Iraq, I believe that precipitous withdrawal is not a solution. I strongly contend that the implications of the Iraq War are critical to the "Holy War." Simply stated, if we fail to win in this theater, as defined by a stable, moderate, and friendly Iraq, then we will live to regret it. While our "enemies" view the war as critical, even the *centerpiece* of their worldwide effort,[44] many advocate leaving Iraq "immediately." If we do, we will leave it to the radicals. I believe this will result in the Iranian domination of the country and the region. Since Iran is one of the foremost advocates of terrorism around the globe, it seems simplistic, at best, to allow this to occur. This book, however, is not designed to speak to this decision. It is designed to speak to the implications of such. One observer noted that the implications are substantial. Azar Nafisi makes a passionate plea to the American people by saying,[45]

> Democracies in the West have to support the aspirations of those fighting for democracy in the Muslim world, and, if Americans have become too cynical to do so out of idealism and compassion, then they should do it for the urgently pragmatic reason that their own survival, it is now unmistakably clear, is also at stake.

Briefly stated, my analysis of the circumstances in Iraq is as follows: I see this conflict as part of the "Holy War" being conducted against the West. Inside the "Holy War" is another war—this one for the control of Islam. Both of these conflicts are being played out in Iraq. The internal conflict is between moderates and the radicals. The radicals are lead by al Qaeda (Sunni) against al-Sadr and his Mahdi Army (Shiite). Both these radical groups sought to foster a civil war in Iraq. This *civil war* was not necessarily between native Iraqis. Instead, much of the fighters were of foreign nationalities, or were native Iraqis funded by foreign governments. While the commonly held notion that Sunni and Shiite are traditional rivals is accurate, remember chaos is the "friend" of the extremist and the terrorist. In this sense, I ask the provocative question, could this be a battle for domination of Islam?

The internal conflict in the country is *not* a civil war. This is another tired—and wrong—mantra trumpeted mindlessly by so many "leaders" and media elites. Consider the following: According to the U.S. military, the overwhelming majority, approximately 90 percent, of suicide attackers in Iraq are foreigners. The spokesman for Multinational Forces in Iraq added that "Iraqis are religiously and socially opposed to suicide, requiring al-Qaeda to recruit foreigners to carry out their terror." Records seized from al Qaeda by the military show that 40 percent come from North African countries such as Libya and Algeria, and 41 percent from Saudi Arabia.[46] If this was a civil war, why are so many suicide bombers foreigners?

Partly because of its indiscriminate use of violence, the prospects of al Qaeda's success in Iraq have been severely affected. Following the "surge" of the U.S. military instituted in spring 2007, the level of violence in Iraq declined dramatically. While the military troop levels have played a key role in the reduction of violence, another factor must be considered, that is, Sunni groups have turned *against al Qaeda*. Indeed, there is evidence that this violent strategy used by al Qaeda in Iraq is backfiring. Top U.S. counterterrorism officials have recently said al Qaeda is "imploding." These counterterrorism experts added that its violent tactics have turned Muslims worldwide against the organization. "Absolutely it's imploding. [Al Qaeda is] imploding because it's not a message that resonates with a lot of Muslims," said Dell Dailey of the State Department.[47] This is part of the "interesting" dynamic of terrorism. Sometimes the terrorists overplay their hand. Sometimes they use too much violence. While violence is critically important to the terrorist campaign, terrorists must use it wisely. If they indiscriminately exercise violence, at some point the populace, even their sympathizers, may stand up and fight back. Consequently, this notion is consistent with data offered by U.S. State Department officials. They contend that vastly more Muslims than Westerners are killed by al Qaeda car and suicide bombs, particularly in Iraq where local tribes have largely turned against al Qaeda.[48]

This assessment was initially made known in the summer of 2007. It was manifested when U.S. troops visited safe houses of former Iraqi insurgents that were identified by CLN ("concerned local nationals"). The cooperation between the Sunni fighters and American forces was driven as much by political aspirations as by a rejection of the brutal methods of *al Qaeda in Iraq*. This assertion was made by U.S. officers and former insurgents.[49] An example of this dynamic may be instructive. In September 2007, more than 1,500 mourners attended the funeral of an American ally, Abdul Sattar Abu Risha, who was killed in a bomb attack in Anbar province. At this funeral, mourners chanted, "We will take our revenge," and, "There is no God but Allah and *al-Qaeda is the enemy of Allah*" (emphasis added). A leader of this tribe said, "The killing will give us more energy ... to continue confronting al-Qaeda members and to dispose of them."[50]

In response to this threat from pro-U.S. Sunnis, al Qaeda warned it will hunt down and kill Sunni Arab tribal leaders who cooperate with the United States and its Iraqi partners. The al Qaeda front group [the Islamic State of Iraq] said in a Web site posting that it had formed "special security committees" to track down and "assassinate the tribal figures, the traitors, who stained the reputations of the real tribes by submitting to the soldiers of the crusade. ... Today we are on the door steps of a new era. ... Today we witness the fallacy of the Western Civilization and the renaissance of the Islamic giant."[51] This statement is consistent with the larger strategy of al Qaeda. A July 9, 2005, letter from al-Zawahiri to al Zarqawi (then leader in Iraq) makes their goals clear. The four main goals of al Qaeda were stated as:[52]

1. Expel the Americans from Iraq.
2. Establish an Islamic authority and develop it into a caliphate, extending influence over as much Iraq territory as possible.
3. Extend the jihad to Iraq's secular neighbors.
4. Extend the jihad to Israel.

These assertions by al Qaeda should dispose of any notion that the conflict in Iraq is a "civil war." Indeed, al-Zawahiri's letter went on to urge the leader of al Qaeda in Iraq to *not* attack Shiites and to *minimize excessive violence*.[53] At least partly due to al Zarqawi's failure to heed this advice, the violence between radical Shiites and al Qaeda continued to spiral for a few more years. Over time the excessive violence—and the implementation of the military surge—changed the dynamic toward the moderates against the radicals. Consequently, it may be helpful to consider the conflict in Iraq—and in the global jihad—as a conflict on two levels: between radical Islamists and moderate Muslims, and between al Qaeda (Sunni) versus al-Sadr (Shiite) backed by Iran.

In thinking about this assertion, also consider the impact of Iran's ruling theocracy. It emphasizes martyrdom and jihad, and threatens to galvanize Muslims into a furious anti-Western campaign against the infidels and the Muslim regimes allied with them.[54] While these tactics and goals are similar to those of al Qaeda, other differences between these groups make internal cohesion challenging. Most likely, there will be more conflict between these groups until a resolution is formed. In any event, it is clear that Iran is dominated by Shiites, and a large section of Iraq, particularly the southern oil-rich regions, are also dominated by Shiites. Indeed, it is unmistakable to all but the naïve, or the blind ideological "purists," that Iran is heavily involved in Iraq. Some pointed examples include:

- U.S. troops detained two suspected weapons smugglers who may be linked to Iran's elite Al-Quds force. The suspects and a number of weapons were seized during a raid on a rural farm compound in eastern Iraq, near the Iranian border. "The suspects may be associated with a network of terrorists that have been smuggling explosively formed projectiles (EFPs), other weapons, personnel and money from Iran into Iraq," a military spokesperson said.[55]
- Attacks on U.S.-led forces using a lethal type of roadside bomb said to be supplied by Iran reached a new high in July 2007. EFPs were used to carry out 99 attacks last month and accounted for a third of the combat deaths suffered by U.S.-led forces, said Lt. Gen. Raymond Odierno.[56]
- Rockets fired at a U.S. military base near Baghdad were manufactured in Iran, showing again Iran's continued support for insurgents inside Iraq. The seized rocket is the 40th Iranian manufactured rocket that soldiers have captured in the last four months, the military said.[57]
- Shiite militants were hammering the U.S.-protected Green Zone with rockets and mortars in April 2008. American military officials say the attacks

are coming from breakaway factions of al-Sadr's Mahdi Army. The groups are believed to be funded and trained by Iran. Of course, Iran denied the allegations.[58]

■ The top U.S. commander has shifted the focus to Iranian-backed "special groups" as the main threat to Iraq— a significant change that reflects both the complexity of the war and its changing nature. The role of the "special groups" remains unclear. U.S. officials say they are breakaway factions of the Mahdi Army that no longer take orders from al-Sadr. Such talk about the threat posed by the special groups casts the internal Shiite conflict as a proxy war between the United States and extremists controlled by Iran.[59]

To those who are still not convinced, please do not listen to me. I have never been to Iraq. While I conducted substantial research on the merits of my "case" involving Iraq, I am not an expert on what is happening on the ground. In this sense, it may be wise to deeply consider the above assertions by U.S. military leaders and spokesmen. If you distrust the military, then consider the words of al-Zawahiri, who has accused Iran of seeking to extend its power in the Middle East, *particularly in Iraq* and through its Hezbollah allies in Lebanon. Al-Zawahiri said the insurgent umbrella group led by al Qaeda, called the Islamic Nation of Iraq, is the "*primary force opposing the Crusaders and challenging Iranian ambitions*" in Iraq (emphasis added).[60]

In an amazing and ironic twist, here is one terrorist group (al Qaeda) complaining that an opposing force led by Iran is trying to "extend its power" in the Middle East. In my mind, this should leave no doubt about what is really going on—and what is really at stake. The struggle is for control of the Middle East through proxy wars in various countries, including Iraq, between al Qaeda and the Iranian-led terrorists. These proxy wars are key fronts in the Holy War. Each proxy war is a theater within the larger conflict. Who will win the proxy war in Iraq? In essence, there are three choices: Iran, al Qaeda, or an Iraqi government backed by the United States. If either Iran or al Qaeda dominate Iraq, then they are on their way to dominating the Middle East. I predict Iran will win—if the Obama Administration leaves too soon. Unfortunately, this will be likely. Now that the campaign is over, his supporters will demand that he adhere to his campaign pledge—that he made over and over again. I hope that he will see that the stakes in Iraq are greater than campaign pledges. Either way, keep this adage in mind: *the enemy of my enemy is my friend!*

One final point on Iraq is worth noting. Since I view this war as critical to the implications of future terrorism within the United States, it may be helpful to consider Dr. Henry Kissinger's assessment of Iraq and the larger radical Islamic movement:[61]

The Islamic jihad is, in a way, only at the beginning. We're just seeing the symptoms of it in one part of the world [the Middle East] … pointing to huge potentially disaffected Muslim populations in India, Indonesia, and in the West.

When people talk about Iraq and talk about American withdrawal, they have to understand that the war we're fighting happens to be located in Iraq today, but it will not end in Iraq. It's an assault on the institutions in the region, and on the international system. It's deeply funded and it's run by dedicated people.

If this radical element develops the idea that they defeated the Soviet Union in Afghanistan and the Americans in Iraq, that will not be the end of the process. It will be the beginning of a whole new kind of crisis … the script for a much more serious crisis down the road.

This is not something we can win by a decision to leave. We can only win it by demoralizing the terrorists and keeping them from achieving their goals and by building up the leadership structures to resist them. … Making a decision to leave would only produce a "temporary quiet."

In this analysis, I do not want to seem like an apologist for the Iraq War. We have made many costly mistakes—both in lives and in treasure. If we could redo the past, I would count off numerous mistakes, including the number of invasion troops, decommissioning the Iraqi army, and letting al-Sadr operate his militia in the early months of the "reconstruction" of Iraq. These and other mistakes have greatly complicated our ability to "succeed" in this conflict. Indeed, I am not optimistic about the outcome. This is not because of the ability of the U.S. military or even the Iraqi military and government. In the end, we are in trouble because the will and the resources to conduct the war are about exhausted. It is up to President Obama to find a way to resolve these difficult circumstances.

Unfortunately, I believe that once the war ends, the Islamist movement will have a huge rallying cry: they defeated another superpower! Just as the USSR was defeated in Afghanistan, if the radicals defeat the United States in Iraq, it will set in motion a momentum we will live to regret. Remember the Mujahidin! If they defeat the Great Satan in Iraq, the theater of the "Holy War" will soon switch focus to the U.S. homeland. Indeed, those good citizens of Iraq who supported the notion of democracy—and who relied on the United States—will be slaughtered. Once this occurs, the radical Islamists will coalesce around Iranian leadership (Shiite), and the "moderate" and secular governments in the Middle East (Egypt, Lebanon, Algeria, Kuwait, Pakistan, Morocco, Saudi, etc.) are in trouble.

As partial validation to this prediction, a recent U.S. State Department report labeled Iran as the "most active" and "most significant" state sponsor of terrorism. The report said Iran helps Palestinian terrorist groups like Hamas, Hezbollah, militants in Iraq, and Taliban fighters in Afghanistan achieve their "common regional goals." The report also stated that Iran uses terrorism as a defense mechanism by "deterring United States or Israeli attacks, distracting and weakening the United States, enhancing Iran's regional influence through intimidation, and helping to drive the United States from the Middle East."[62] Indeed, this report corresponds to the *National Strategy for Homeland Security.* It asserts that al Qaeda will likely intensify its efforts to place operatives in the United States. Further, Hezbollah may increasingly consider attacking the U.S. homeland if it perceives the United States as posing a direct threat to the group, or to Iran, its principal sponsor.[63] I think both these reports speak volumes.

"Holy War" versus "Cold War"

The specific attributes of the "Holy War" can be illustrated by an appropriate comparative analysis. Since many people have compared Iraq to Vietnam, I think it would be instructive to compare the "Holy War" to the "Cold War." In order to get a handle on the significance of these conflicts—and the larger worldwide war— Table 8.1 was developed to show relevant comparisons and contrasts. The table may require some explanation. Before I do so, however, it may be instructive to assess bin Laden's message to Americans. As you read his words, please consider the extent of condemnation that he places on us. This has political, moral, legal, military, and even religious underpinnings. Also, consider that these words were published *before* the Iraq War. For those who believe that our exit from Iraq and even Afghanistan is a "solution" to the conflict with radical Islamists, you must ignore these words. While I realize it is "fashionable" to believe these nonsense "solutions," you have a choice to make—sooner or later. You can believe the media and our "leaders," or you can believe the "enemy." In any event, here is an edited, and relevant, version of bin Laden's words:[64]

> In the Name of Allah, the Most Gracious, the Most Merciful,
> Permission to fight (against disbelievers) is given to those (believers) who are fought against, because they have been wronged and surely, Allah is Able to give them (believers) victory. [Quran 22:39]
> So fight you against the friends of Satan; ever feeble is indeed the plot of Satan. [Quran 4:76]
>
> Some American writers have published articles under the title, "On what basis are we fighting?"
> Here we wanted to outline the truth—as an explanation and warning—hoping for Allah's reward, seeking success and support from Him.
> While seeking Allah's help, we form our reply based on two questions directed at the Americans:
>
> (Q1) Why are we fighting and opposing you?
> (Q2) What are we calling you to, and what do we want from you?
>
> As for the first question: Why are we fighting and opposing you? The answer is very simple:

(1) Because you attacked us and continue to attack us.

   (i)   Palestine, which has sunk under military occupation for more than 80 years. The British handed over Palestine, with your help and your support, to the Jews, who have occupied it for more than 50 years; years overflowing with oppression, tyranny, crimes, killing, expulsion, destruction, and devastation. The creation and continuation of Israel is one of the greatest crimes, and you are the leaders of its criminals. ... The creation of Israel is a crime that must be erased. Each and every person whose hands have become polluted in the contribution toward this crime must pay its price, and pay for it heavily.

  (ii) It brings us both laughter and tears to see that you have not yet tired of repeating your fabricated lies that the Jews have a historical right to Palestine, as it was promised to them in the Torah. ... When the Muslims conquered Palestine and drove out the Romans, Palestine and Jerusalem returned to Islam.

      ...

      (b)   You attacked us in Somalia; you supported the Russian atrocities against us in Chechnya, the Indian oppression against us in Kashmir, and the Jewish aggression against us in Lebanon.

      (c)   Under your supervision, consent, and orders, the governments of our countries, which act as your agents, attack us on a daily basis.

   (i)   These governments prevent our people from establishing the Islamic Sharia, using violence and lies to do so. ...

   (v)   The removal of these governments is an obligation upon us, and a necessary step to free the Ummah, to make the Sharia the supreme law and to regain Palestine. And our fight against these governments is not separate from our fight against you.

      ...

      (d)   You steal our wealth and oil at paltry prices because of your international influence and military threats. This theft is indeed the biggest theft ever witnessed by mankind in the history of the world. ...

      (e)   Your forces occupy our countries; you spread your military bases throughout them; you corrupt our lands, and you besiege our sanctities [sic], to protect the security of the Jews and to ensure the continuity of your pillage of our treasures. ...

      (g)   You have supported the Jews in their idea that Jerusalem is their eternal capital, and agreed to move your embassy there. With your help and under your protection, the Israelis are planning to destroy the Al-Aqsa mosque. ...

(2) These tragedies and calamities are only a few examples of your oppression and aggression against us. It is commanded by our religion and intellect that the oppressed have a right to return the aggression. Do not await anything from us but Jihad, resistance, and revenge. Is it in any way rational to expect that after America has attacked us for more than half a century, that we will then leave her to live in security and peace?!!

(a) This argument contradicts your continuous repetition that America is the land of freedom, and its leaders in this world. Therefore, the American people are the ones who choose their government by way of their own free will; a choice that stems from their agreement to its policies. ... The American people have the ability and choice to refuse the policies of their Government and even to change it if they want.

(b) The American people are the ones who pay the taxes which fund the planes that bomb us in Afghanistan, the tanks that strike and destroy our homes in Palestine, the armies which occupy our lands in the Arabian Gulf, and the fleets which ensure the blockade of Iraq. These tax dollars are given to Israel for it to continue to attack us and penetrate our lands. So the American people are the ones who fund the attacks against us, and they are the ones who oversee the expenditure of these monies in the way they wish, through their elected candidates.

(c) Also the American army is part of the American people. It is this very same people who are shamelessly helping the Jews fight against us.

(d) The American people are the ones who employ both their men and their women in the American Forces that attack us.

(e) This is why the American people cannot be not innocent of all the crimes committed by the Americans and Jews against us.

(f) Allah, the Almighty, legislated the permission and the option to take revenge. Thus, if we are attacked, then we have the right to attack back. Whoever has destroyed our villages and towns, then we have the right to destroy their villages and towns. Whoever has stolen our wealth, then we have the right to destroy their economy. And whoever has killed our civilians, then we have the right to kill theirs.

The American Government and press still refuse to answer the question: *Why did they attack us in New York and Washington?*

(Q2) As for the second question that we want to answer: What are we calling you to, and what do we want from you?

(1) The first thing that we are calling you to is Islam.

    (a)   The religion of the Unification of God; of freedom from associating partners with Him, and rejection of this; of complete love of Him, the Exalted; of complete submission to His Laws; and of the discarding of all the opinions, orders, theories, and religions which contradict with the religion He sent down to His Prophet Muhammad. …

(2) The second thing we call you to is to stop your oppression, lies, immorality, and debauchery that has spread among you.

    (a)   We call you to be a people of manners, principles, honour, and purity; to reject the immoral acts of fornication, homosexuality, intoxicants, gambling's, and trading with interest.

    (b)   It is saddening to tell you that you are the worst civilization witnessed by the history of mankind.

        (i)   You are the nation who, rather than ruling by the Sharia of Allah in its Constitution and Laws, choose to invent your own laws as you will and desire. You separate religion from your policies, contradicting the pure nature which affirms Absolute Authority to the Lord and your Creator.

        (ii)   You are the nation that permits Usury, which has been forbidden by all the religions. Yet you build your economy and investments on Usury.

        (iii)   You are a nation that permits the production, trading, and usage of intoxicants. You also permit drugs, and only forbid the trade of them, even though your nation is the largest consumer of them.

        (iv)   You are a nation that permits acts of immorality, and you consider them to be pillars of personal freedom.

            Who can forget your President Clinton's immoral acts committed in the official Oval office? After that you did not even bring him to account, other than that he "made a mistake," after which everything passed with no punishment.

        (v)   You are a nation that permits gambling in its all forms. The companies practice this as well, resulting in the investments becoming active and the criminals becoming rich.

(vi) You are a nation that exploits women like consumer products or advertising tools calling upon customers to purchase them. You use women to serve passengers, visitors, and strangers to increase your profit margins. You then rant that you support the liberation of women.

(vii) You are a nation that practices the trade of sex in all its forms, directly and indirectly. Giant corporations and establishments are established on this, under the name of art, entertainment, tourism and freedom, and other deceptive names you attribute to it.

(viii) And because of all this, you have been described in history as a nation that spreads diseases that were unknown to man in the past. Go ahead and boast to the nations of man, that you brought them AIDS as a Satanic American Invention.

(ix) You have destroyed nature with your industrial waste and gases more than any other nation in history. Despite this, you refuse to sign the Kyoto agreement so that you can secure the profit of your greedy companies and industries.

(x) Your law is the law of the rich and wealthy people, who hold sway in their political parties, and fund their election campaigns with their gifts. Behind them stand the Jews, who control your policies, media, and economy.

(xi) That which you are singled out for in the history of mankind, is that you have used your force to destroy mankind more than any other nation in history; not to defend principles and values, but to hasten to secure your interests and profits.

(xii) Let us not forget one of your major characteristics: your duality in both manners and values; your hypocrisy in manners and principles. All manners, principles, and values have two scales: one for you and one for the others.

(a) The freedom and democracy that you call to is for yourselves and for white race only; as for the rest of the world, you impose upon them your monstrous, destructive policies and Governments, which you call the "American friends."...

(e) You have claimed to be the vanguards of Human Rights, and your Ministry of Foreign affairs issues annual reports containing statistics of those countries that violate any Human Rights. However, all these things vanished when the Mujahideen hit you, and you then implemented the methods of the same documented governments that you used to curse.

In America, you captured thousands of Muslims and Arabs, took them into custody with neither reason, court trial, nor even disclosing their names. You issued newer, harsher laws.

What happens in Guatanamo is a historical embarrassment to America and its values, and it screams into your faces—you hypocrites, "What is the value of your signature on any agreement or treaty?"

(3) What we call you to thirdly is to take an honest stance with yourselves—and I doubt you will do so—to discover that you are a nation without principles or manners, and that the values and principles to you are something which you merely demand from others, not that which you yourself must adhere to. …

(5) We also advise you to pack your luggage and get out of our lands. We desire for your goodness, guidance, and righteousness, so do not force us to send you back as cargo in coffins.

(6) Sixthly, we call upon you to end your support of the corrupt leaders in our countries. Do not interfere in our politics and method of education. Leave us alone, or else expect us in New York and Washington.

If you fail to respond to all these conditions, then prepare for fight with the Islamic Nation. The Nation of Martyrdom; the Nation that desires death more than you desire life:

Think not of those who are killed in the way of Allah as dead. Nay, they are alive with their Lord, and they are being provided for. They rejoice in what Allah has bestowed upon them from His bounty and rejoice for the sake of those who have not yet joined them, but are left behind (not yet martyred) that on them no fear shall come, nor shall they grieve. They rejoice in a grace and a bounty from Allah, and that Allah will not waste the reward of the believers. [Quran 3:169-171]

The Nation of victory and success that Allah has promised:

It is He Who has sent His Messenger (Muhammad peace be upon him) with guidance and the religion of truth (Islam), to make it victorious over all other religions even though the Polytheists hate it. [Quran 61:9]

Allah has decreed that "Verily it is I and My Messengers who shall be victorious." Verily Allah is All-Powerful, All-Mighty. [Quran 58:21]

The Islamic Nation that was able to dismiss and destroy the previous evil Empires like yourself; the Nation that rejects your attacks, wishes to remove your evils, and is prepared to fight you. You are well aware that the Islamic Nation, from the very core of its soul, despises your haughtiness and arrogance.

If the Americans refuse to listen to our advice and the goodness, guidance, and righteousness that we call them to, then be aware that you will lose this Crusade Bush began, just like the other previous Crusades in which you were humiliated by the hands of the Mujahideen, fleeing to your home in great silence and disgrace. If the Americans do not respond, then their fate will be that of the Soviets who fled from Afghanistan to deal with their military defeat, political breakup, ideological downfall, and economic bankruptcy.

In my mind it is critical to understand the depth and scope of these words. Indeed, these are not only words. They reflect literally generations of frustration, anger, and commitment. As reflected in these words, the cause of the conflict is a religious worldview grounded on a particular aversion to the "modern lifestyle." The "roots" of this conflict go back to the Crusades—and the historical conflicts between religions. Those who believe that we can somehow resolve these deepseated beliefs are simply delusional. This is why we must find bridges with moderate Muslims who have a stake in the modern world. As described earlier in this chapter, however, making these relationships and sustaining them are extraordinarily difficult. This does not mean we should not try. It also does not mean that the "solution" simply entails talk and hope. It will require more. It will require blood and treasure along with talk and hope. If we are not ready for the former (blood and treasure), the latter (talk and hope) will be useless folly. With this background established, please now consider Table 8.1 and its related discussion.

As to "goal," each war is, in the end, a struggle for world domination.[65] While this may seem dramatic to some readers, this is because many people do not take the rhetoric of extremists seriously. Indeed, prior to World War II, Hitler told the world his intentions in the book, *Mein Kampf.* When he commenced to execute his intentions during the late 1930s and early 1940s, many were stunned. They sought to appease him at every turn. These futile attempts did not work, because he had a larger goal—world domination. Many refused to believe he actually believed his "insane" plan. Those few who recognized the seriousness of the situation were criticized and ostracized. Today we see Winston Churchill as a great statesman and a great leader. During the 1930s, he was roundly ignored—and even hated. Why? Because he told people what they did not want to hear. He told people that they had to fight Hitler—not appease him. Indeed, to this day, some people still write off Hitler as an insane maniac. Although he was an evil man, he had the mental lucidity to execute his goal.

Today, George Bush is criticized and ostracized. He has confronted radical Islam in a way that the "appeasers" find frightening—even criminal. Bush has been demonized as a "liar" for taking action against a perceived threat. The people

Table 8.1   Cold War versus Holy War

	COLD WAR	*HOLY WAR*
GOAL	World Domination	World Domination
IDEOLOGY	Communism vs. Capitalism	Radical Islam vs. Modernity
STRATEGY	Expansion (Domino Theory)	Submission (Allah)
METHODS	Military/Political Conquest	Religious/Political Conquest
TACTIC	Conventional Warfare (Armies + Nuclear Threat)	Asymmetric Warfare (Terrorism + WMD Threat)
DETERRENCE	M.A.D. (Mutually Assured Destruction) and S.T.A.R. Wars vs. Unilateral Disarmament	War (Military/Pre-emption) vs. Crime (Arrest/Prosecution)
INTERNAL and EXTERNAL CONSEQUENCE	"Godless" State vs. Market/Globalization	Islam (Moderate vs. Radical: al Qaeda vs. Iran) vs. Modernity (Secular vs. Judeo-Christian)
RESOLUTION	Enter Treaties/State Controlled Détente	Destroy Cells/State Supported Terrorism
ULTIMATE SOLUTION	State Control vs. Individual Freedom	Fanaticism (State control) vs. Freedom (Individual Rights)

who echoed his words five years previously (and immediately prior to the Iraq War), now call him a threat worse than the "enemy" (see Appendix for statements about Iraq and WMD). My, how history has a way of repeating itself! To those who take the time to read, listen, and watch the rhetoric of the "enemy," one would be hard-pressed to deny that the radical Islamist ideologies desire world domination. A large part of the problem is that many people have not been exposed to these ideologies. Hopefully this book will help address this ignorance. Please consider that ignorance does not equate with intelligence. Instead, it is about being informed. Unfortunately, being informed, while critical, is only part of the problem. The larger problem is, how do we resolve the ongoing threat? This question will soon be manifested in the Obama Administration.

As to "ideology," each war is, in the end, a struggle over ideas. Some, like Telhami, emphasize that the battle of ideas is more important than military battles.[66] This is why I devote much of this book to the study of the ideologies of extremist groups. It is my belief that movements require ideology. It is the "fuel" that lights and maintains the "fire." Without the "logic" and the "facts" derived from ideologies, the movement will soon lose steam. It will not be sustainable. The ideology of radical Islam is substantial. It has a worldwide reach. It has the ability to motivate people to give their lives for the "cause" (or for Allah). Indeed, those who were willing to die for Hitler did so for a man—not a god. How much more compelling—and dangerous—is the willingness to die for Allah? I believe it is unquestionably more dangerous. The danger is illustrated by these rhetorical questions: Are we, in the West, who represent modernity, willing to die for a larger cause? Is freedom worth dying for? Is freedom free? Does the "just war" concept within Christianity "justify" a "holy war" with radical Islam? The significance of this situation, which compares the vision of the West versus the vision of radical Islam, is powerfully contrasted by the following statement:[67]

> Islamic belief that "this mortal life" of ours, on this Earth, is but a stage, a test, and that our true life begins after death. This perspective contrasted with materialism of the West, whose purpose of life is to attain happiness now, or in the future, and there is no thought given to life-after-death and being judged by God (or Allah), and no belief in this life as a test. In exchange for their lives and their goods, Allah has given those who believe Paradise. Thus will they fight in Allah's cause, and thus will they kill, and be killed. [Quran 9:111]

As to "strategy," the contemporary approach is to cause submission to Allah. The historical, Cold War approach was to expand Communism through the "domino theory." In essence, the goal is the same: one step, one person, one country at a time. This is why each explosion, each attack, each "front" in the overall war is seen by the radical Islamists as part of the larger goal: submission to Allah through the establishment of the caliphate. As long as the intellectual elites fail to connect the dots, we will continue to see each incident in a myopic fashion. If we do not see the common threads for each group, each explosion, each theater, then we will be constantly disadvantaged in the overall strategy of the war.

As to "methods," the approaches are similar. The goal is political conquest. The distinction is that, during the Cold War the focus was on military means. In the Holy War, the focus is on religious means. In this way, religion is the means to the end! Indeed, religion may be both the means and the end. Religion provides the basis for the fight. It also provides the belief in Allah (or God for Christian extremists), who provides the ultimate "solution."

As to "tactic," the approaches are quite different. In the Cold War, the tactic was through conventional warfare, using armies and the threat of nuclear weaponry.

In the Holy War, the tactic is asymmetric warfare, using terrorism and the threat of WMD. As can be seen in this chapter, the application of terrorism is powerful. It has great psychological, operational, economic, and political implications. However, the use of terrorism is a "double-edged sword." If this tactic is used indiscriminately, it can backfire against those who kill too many, or more accurately, kill the "wrong" people (read sympathizers).

As to "deterrence," there are some significant distinctions. The key deterrence approaches in the Cold War era was MAD (mutually assured destruction), and then later STAR wars. These factors are often seen as both maintaining a tenuous "peace" between the two superpowers, and later giving the United States the edge in the waning years of the era.[68] In the Holy War, deterrence may have little impact to those who seek to "cleanse" the world for Allah. Mass death and destruction is not viewed as a "negative." Indeed, for some it is an incentive. In order for this Islamic "Messiah" to return, the world has to be in chaos—and on the brink of destruction. Consequently, there is a perverse incentive to create chaos and destruction in order to facilitate the return of this Islamic savior.

Based on this belief, the ability to "deter" through "mutually assured destruction" is highly questionable. This raises the notion of deterrence to another level. Can deterrence be achieved by preemption? As illustrated by the intelligence failures of the Iraq War, one would be hard-pressed to advocate this approach. Taking this approach off the table, however, may have disastrous consequences. Hence, the question of deterrence, just as in the Cold War, is controversial. Many in the Cold War, typically liberals, advocated "unilateral disarmament," hoping that this symbolic act would inspire the Soviets to do the same. In the Holy War, the question of whether the "war on terrorism" should be fought as a war or as crime is also a hot ideological debate. As previously developed, this question separates the political parties. The "solution" in my mind, and in others, is some balance between the two approaches. The "right" balance, however, is difficult to discern and maintain. Indeed, it is a "moving target" that takes great judgment based on factual analysis.

As to "internal and external consequence," the distinction between the eras is significant. In the Cold War era, the struggle was cleaner than today. Back then, the struggle was from a "Godless" state (Communism) versus a market-based global system (capitalism). This was a substantial struggle, but it was represented by rather distinct alternatives: either the system was run by the state or it was run by the market. While there were some internal disputes within the superpower positions, the struggle was largely one dominant position versus the other. In contemporary times, the competition is both an internal and external struggle. In Islam, the struggle is reflected by the competition between moderate and radical thought. According to Telhami, the radical thinkers are on the "offensive," while the moderate thinkers are on the "defensive."[69]

Within this struggle is another struggle, which is manifested in a battle between radical Islamic sects. On one hand is the radical Sunni sects (such as Wahhabism) led by al Qaeda. On the other is the Iranians dominated by a radical

Shiite movement, represented by Hezbollah and al-Sadr's Mahdi Army. Hence, the battle is twofold. The radicals struggle for control between two opposing versions of Islam, while they simultaneously attack and intimidate moderate Muslims, who simply want to live in peace and worship Allah. This struggle within Islam is not just in the Middle East. For example, some estimate that up to 80 percent of all mosques in the United States are managed by Saudi-funded Wahhabi clerics. As evidence of such, the American Center for Religious Freedom conducted a study of religious literature distributed in the 12 largest mosques in the United States. The study provided some disconcerting conclusions:[70]

- The literature provides that it is a "religious obligation" for Muslims to hate Christians and Jews.
- The literature notes that befriending, helping, or taking part in Christian or Jewish festivities is strictly forbidden.
- The literature instructs viewing democratic (non-Islamic) societies with contempt.
- The literature states to treat non-Wahhabi Muslims as infidels.
- The literature advises to kill anyone converting out of Islam.

Similarly, the West is fragmented around an internal struggle, where secular thought often competes, and even conflicts, with Judeo-Christian values and customs. Here the struggle is for control of the culture. This is a significant factor for a few reasons. First, the secular elites and the larger secular culture of the United States will never quite understand the implications of a holy war. This is because they have little, or no, concept of a God or of religious devotion. In my mind, this is dangerous because one of the key tenets of warfare is to understand your enemy. Almost by definition, secular progressives will not—or cannot—understand the enemy. Second, the culture conflict between secular progressives and Judeo-Christians also greatly impacts our will to fight an enemy that is an enigma to many in this country. Indeed, for years many saw the real enemy as George Bush. Well, he is now gone and largely irrelevant. Now what? Who will be the source of the blame going forward? We can only blame Bush for so long. Sooner or later, we must "define" who the enemy is. While some may ask, why define anyone as an enemy, my answer is this: When groups declare war on you, your choices are limited. You can either declare war or you can ignore the declaration of war. We have previously ignored two different declarations of war issued by al Qaeda-affiliated groups during the 1990s. How did that work out for us?

Overarching these internal struggles is the larger struggle between Islam and modernity. These are substantial and momentous battles fought on many fronts and in many ways. Clearly, this is not simply a military struggle. It is a struggle for the "hearts and minds" of the world. Ironically, while this momentous struggle takes place, many—possibly even most—of the Westernized world does not even recognize that the struggle exists. Even more ironically, the Chinese are largely unconnected to the struggle. They play both sides, and are often simply content to sit back and watch the "show" while they develop their own future strategies for domination. To those who believe in God, this is the kind of "chess match" that only God can plan. It is truly an extraordinary set of circumstances.

As to "resolution," the earlier era sought treaties and détente. In the current era the resolution is to destroy terrorist cells and state-supported terrorism. In this way, the resolution leads to the ultimate solution. The difficulty in this era is that treaties and détente are impossible when the battle is largely against non-state actors. For example, pretend that al Qaeda has finally determined that their grand struggle is over. Pretend that they want to quit the battle. What do we do? Sign a "peace treaty" with bin Laden? How about al-Zawahiri; maybe we can get him to sign? Even if each of their signatures would have any lasting value, what would the other Islamists do? Would they all quit because bin Laden and al-Zawahiri desired to quit? I trust the reader would recognize the obvious answer. Indeed, even if we could coax every member of al Qaeda to quit, what about Hamas (Islamic Resistance Movement), Hezbollah (Party of God, aka Islamic Jihad), Egyptian Islamic Jihad, al-Gama'at al-Islamiyya, the Islamic Movement of Uzbekistan, the Harakat ul-Mujahidin, the Palestine Liberation Front (PLF), Palestine Islamic Jihad (PIJ), Jaish-e-Mohammed (JEM), Abu Sayyaf Group (ASG), and the Muslim Brotherhood?

You get the picture. This is a war against a multifaceted movement. Therefore, the only real resolution available is to take down each radical cell. Of course, this is next to impossible. Simply stated, there will always be another small group of people who seek your destruction. This is why I believe changing the dynamic of the Middle East is critical to the long-term "resolution." In this way, Obama's assertion that "you don't defeat a terrorist network that operates in 80 countries by occupying Iraq"[71] misses the point. If you can implant a democracy that Muslims around the world can model, then you may not have to deal with each cell in each network in 80 different countries. In my mind, we will not be able to win this global battle cell by cell. While it is an extraordinarily complicated task, I contend that the larger answer is freedom and democracy—not rooting out cells. Instead, as described below, the key is creating a world where people desire to coexist in a peaceful manner. Obviously, this is the goal of all reasonable people. Accomplishing this goal, however, will not occur through peace treaties and agreements. Indeed, agreements are typically only useful with state actors. Even then, some treaties are not worth the paper they are written on. Consider North Korea and Iran—how well have we done negotiating agreements with these countries?

As to the "ultimate solution," in the end, the "grand struggle" can only be won by the determination of the basic premises contained in the ideologies. In the Cold War, the basic premise was the "State" controlled the lives and destinies of humans within the world (or at least certain countries). In the Holy War, the prophetic battle is between those who advocate a fanatical control of the individual by Allah (represented by the caliphate) versus those who advocate that individual freedom is God's purpose for mankind. In this way, the "holy terrorist" sees the primary audience as the deity. To reach this audience, terrorists must become visible—and must either conquer all or be extinguished.[72] In my mind, this is the titanic struggle represented in the biblical verse that says,[73]

> *Our struggle is not against flesh and blood, but against the rulers, against the powers, against the world forces of darkness, against the spiritual forces of wickedness in the heavenly places.*

This biblical view is similar to the Shia belief of the twelfth imam (or the Mahdi—which is an Islamic "Messiah"). This Mahdi would eventually emerge to lead a "Holy War" (Jihad) against the orthodox establishment to cleanse Islam.[74] In order for the return of this Islamist "savior," the world has to be in chaos—and on the brink of destruction. Consequently, there is a perverse incentive to create chaos and destruction in order to facilitate the return of the Mahdi or the twelfth imam.[75]

Hopefully, Table 8.1 helps to flesh out a worldview that may help you make sense of the years ahead. When you hear of a direct action by a particular group, consider the tenets of this table. When you assess the goals of a particular movement, consider the tenets of this table. Those who attempt to "explain" the "solutions" without considering these larger tenets will not be able to achieve success. You have the choice. See it as most do and "hope" that we can solve this dilemma. Or you can think of this "Holy War," with all its complexities and its implications. Of course, the assertions made in this book do not paint a pretty picture. As I have stated earlier, I would rather see a clear picture than a pretty picture. Let the future determine how accurate this picture is! I will leave this thought with an observation from Bernard Lewis, a highly regarded expert on Islam and the Middle East. He stated that the "grievances" asserted by the Islamists against the West (and the Great Satan) are simply "baseless charges, excuses, propaganda, and pretexts." According to Lewis, the real problem is that[76]

> Islam cannot reconcile itself to the rise of the "house of unbelief" and to the loss of what it considers its natural, God given right to dominate the world to the "enemies of God."

In closing, Figure 8.2 combines the extremist groups discussed in Chapter 3 with the notion of a "Holy War." Consider the ideologies of these groups. Each group has a "spiritual" basis—even if it is an "antireligious" spirituality. For example, anarchists view violence and destruction as a "cleansing" whereby some utopian society will develop. The Aryan Brotherhood adheres to the Odinist "religion," which is based on Nordic beliefs. Odinists believe that Christianity allowed its message to be adversely impacted by the introduction of blacks, Hispanics, and other nonwhites. Similarly, Black Liberation combines black Muslims, black Israelites, and black Christian churches to forward a "race conscious" notion of religion and society. Environmentalists in their extreme form view "Mother Nature" or the

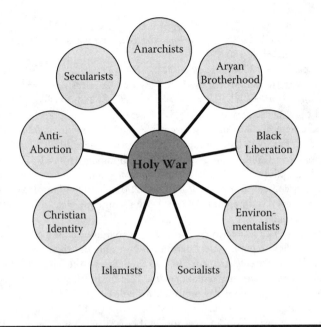

Figure 8.2   Copyright, James F. Pastor, 2009.

earth in a spiritual realm and as a source of devotion. Socialists see geopolitical ideologies as the ultimate goal of humankind. Islamists, as discussed in this chapter, see the solution to the world's problem as a caliphate—or by Allah's direct intervention of the twelfth imam or Mahdi. Similarly, Christian Identity advocates "Holy War" against the "forces of evil," namely blacks, Jews, and other nonbelievers. Antiabortionists seek to violently, but narrowly, advocate God's purpose by killing and defeating those who advocate and perform abortions. Finally, secularists disregard—and disavow—any notion of God or religion. They seek to remove God from society. Conversely, those who believe in God will push back. In the end, these groups represent a struggle for control. They will act for their deity—whether it is "God," "cleansing violence," "Mother Nature," or some "political ideology." They are "true believers" in their cause.

Those who do not acknowledge God—or understand His purpose—will not understand how to make sense of the years ahead. Many will be confused and deceived. My hope and prayers are that you are not one of those lost sheep. It is my desire to help make sense of this world—and the dramatic times ahead. As the old Chinese adage pointedly asserts, "May you live in interesting times!" You, indeed, live in interesting times!

Endnotes

1. Yungher, Nathan I. (2008). *Terrorism: The Bottom Line.* Upper Saddle River, NJ: Pearson/Prentice Hall, 150.
2. Yungher, Nathan I. (2008), op. cit., 150.
3. Lifton, Robert Jay (2005). "In the Lord's Hands: America's Apocalyptic Mindset," in *Violence and Terrorism.* Ed. Thomas J. Badey. McGraw-Hill/Dushkin, 145.
4. Lifton, Robert Jay (2005), op. cit., 145.
5. For an excellent account of these events, see the documentary *Inside 9/11* (2005). Produced by Towers Production, Inc., for National Geographic.
6. Whitlock, Craig (2008). "Probe of USS Cole Bombing Unravels: Plotters Freed in Yemen; U.S. Efforts Frustrated," *The Washington Post.* http://www.washingtonpost.com/wp-dyn/content/article/2008/05/03/AR2008050302047.html, May 4.
7. Ibid. http://www.washingtonpost.com/wp-dyn/content/article/2008/05/03/AR2008050302047.html.
8. The impact of 9/11 related to civilian deaths is well known. What is less understood is the loss of life by public safety personnel. Not only did thousands of civilians die on 9/11, the city's fire department lost 343 firefighters—the largest loss of life in one day in history for emergency responders; the Port Authority police suffered 37 deaths, the largest loss of life in one day in history for police; the NYPD itself lost 23 officers, the second-largest loss historically. See Miller, Judith (2007). "On the Front Line in the War on Terrorism: Cops in New York and Los Angeles Offer America Two Models for Preventing Another 9/11," *City Journal* Summer. http://www.city-journal.org/html/17_3_preventing_terrorism.html (retrieved on May 9, 2008).
9. http://ap.google.com/article/ALeqM5ihmILMXDSyifnMSZu2NK3vNWSazgD937DBSO0 (retrieved on September 19, 2008).
10. http://www.chicagobreakingnews.com/2008/10/obama-comments-on-pakistan-prompt-local-protest.html (retrieved on October 9, 2008).
11. Ibid, on October 9, 2008.
12. http://www.foxnews.com/ (retrieved on August 3, 2007).
13. http://www.foxnews.com/photoessay/0,4644,2164,00.html#1_0 (retrieved on August 5, 2007).
14. Stern, Jessica (2008), op. cit., 167.
15. Stern, Jessica (2008), op. cit., 167.
16. http://www.foxnews.com/projects/pdf/bin_laden_transcript.pdf (retrieved on September 7, 2007).
17. Yungher, Nathan I. (2008), op. cit., 151.
18. http://www.nytimes.com/slideshow/2008/04/25/nyregion/20080425BELL_11.html, April 26, 2008; juicyscoop.blogspot.com, April 26, 2008; and http://www.newsday.com/news/local/newyork/ny-nystre0426,0,3138952.story, April 26, 2008.
19. Nafisi, Azar (2004). "They the People: Our Abandoned Muslim Allies," in *The New Era of Terrorism: Selected Readings.* Ed. Gus Martin. Sage Publications, 276.
20. http://www.foxnews.com/story/0,2933,270241,00.html (retrieved on May 6, 2007).
21. Warikoo, Niraj. *Detroit Free Press.* http://www.freep.com/apps/pbcs.dll/article?AID=/20080425/NEWS02/80425047/1003/news (retrieved on April 25, 2008).
22. http://www.foxnews.com/story/0,2933,352689,00.html, April 26, 2008.

23. When considering the sources of terrorism, the "link between terrorism and nationalist, ethnic, religious and tribal conflict is far more tangible [than other so-called sources of such violence]," as asserted by Laqueur, Walter (2004), The Terrorism to Come, *Policy Review* 126. www.policyreview.org/aug04/laqueur_print.html (retrieved on November 1, 2004).

24. http://news.bbc.co.uk/2/hi/south_asia/7616429.stm, September 15, 2008.

25. Yungher, Nathan I. (2008), op. cit., 160.

26. President Obama's inauguration speech. http://www.msnbc.msn.com/id/28754569/ (retrieved on January 21, 2009).

27. http://news.yahoo.com/s/nm/20070907/wl_nm/algeria_bomb_toll_dc;_ylt=ApUU9 vUQE4FkN6TkUeO7NJK96Q8F (retrieved on September 8, 2007).

28. http://www.foxnews.com/photoessay/0,4644,2864,00.html#13_0 (retrieved on December 11, 2007).

29. https://www.osac.gov/Reports/report.cfm?contentID=70865 (retrieved on July 14, 2007).

30. http://www.foxnews.com/story/0,2933,307843,00.html (retrieved on November 3, 2007).

31. Brown, Vahid (2007). "Cracks in the Foundation: Leadership Schisms in al Qaeda from 1989–2006," Harmony Project, Combating Terrorism Center at West Point, West Point, NY.

32. Brown, Vahid (2007), op. cit., 42.

33. http://news.bbc.co.uk/2/hi/africa/7731839.stm (retrieved on November 17, 2008).

34. Ibrahim, Mohammed (2009). "Insurgents in Somalia Take Over Police Posts," *Associated Press*, January 3. http://www.nytimes.com/2009/01/04/world/africa/04somalia.html?_ r=1&ref=world.

35. Duhul, Salad (2009). "Last Ethiopian Troops Leave Somalia's Capital," *Associated Press,* January 15. http://news.yahoo.com/s/ap/20090115/ap_on_re_af/af_somalia; _ylt=AmsGq0Q6OG_tdiWHHpyTxOK96Q8F.

36. http://www.timesonline.co.uk/tol/news/world/middle_east/article5443427.ece.

37. 1 Kings 13.

38. Psalms 122:6.

39. http://ap.google.com/article/ALeqM5ihmILMXDSyifnMSZu2NK3v NWSazgD937DBSO0 (retrieved on September 19, 2008).

40. President Obama's inauguration speech. http://www.time.com/time/politics/arti-cle/0,8599,1872715-3,00.html (retrieved on January 21, 2008).

41. http://www.expatica.com/actual/article.asp?subchannel_id=81&story_id=37544 and http://www.foxnews.com/photoessay/0,4644,1928,00.html#8_0 (retrieved on June 22, 2007).

42. For a photo of the protests demanding South Korean troops leave Afghanistan see http://www.foxnews.com/photoessay/0,4644,2115,00.html, July 26, 2007.

43. http://news.bbc.co.uk/2/hi/south_asia/6910461.stm, July 22, 2007.

44. See, for example, Ayman al-Zawahri's assertion. http://www.chron.com/disp/story.mpl/ap/ world/4947209.html (retrieved on July 6, 2007); and bin Laden's assertion. http://www. foxnews.com/projects/pdf/bin_laden_transcript.pdf (retrieved on September 6, 2007).

45. Nafisi, Azar (2004), op. cit., 277; and see also Telhami, Shibley (2005). "Understanding the Challenge." in *Violence and Terrorism*. Ed. Thomas J. Badey. McGraw-Hill/Dushkin, 161.

46. http://ap.google.com/article/ALeqM5grQY9IZlnRcXplTJ05FsxTclBWfgD8VE65M06 (retrieved on March 17, 2008).

47. http://ap.google.com/articleALeqM5ihmILMXDSyifnMSZu2NK3vNWSazgD937D BSO0 (retrieved on September 19, 2008).

48. Ibid, http://ap.google.com/article/ALeqM5ihmILMXDSyifnMSZu2NK3vNWSazgD 937DBSO0 (retrieved on September 19, 2008).
49. http://www.msnbc.msn.com/id/20188364/ (retrieved on August 9, 2007).
50. http://news.bbc.co.uk/2/hi/middle_east/6994823.stm (retrieved on September 14, 2007).
51. http://www.foxnews.com/story/0,2933,296897,00.html (retrieved on September 15, 2007).
52. Brown, Vahid (2007), op. cit., 70.
53. Brown, Vahid (2007), op. cit., 70.
54. Yungher, Nathan I. (2008), op. cit., 147.
55. http://www.foxnews.com/story/0,2933,290291,00.html (retrieved on July 22, 2007).
56. http://yalibnan.com/site/archives/2007/08/99_iraqi_attack.php (retrieved on August 9, 2007).
57. http://www.foxnews.com/story/0,2933,305686,00.html (retrieved on October 27, 2007).
58. http://www.foxnews.com/story/0,2933,342111,00.html (retrieved on March 27, 2008).
59. http://news.yahoo.com/s/ap/20080410/ap_on_re_mi_ea/iraq_shifting_the_enemy;_ ylt=AhgSqPZIpuVWpe4yDDkYUtkLewgF (retrieved on April 11, 2008).
60. http://www.foxnews.com/story/0,2933,352066,00.html (retrieved on April 22, 2008).
61. *Security Management* (2007), December:94.
62. "Iran Remains Most Active State Sponsor of Terrorism: US" (2008). *Agence France Presse,* posted on April 30. http://afp.google.com/article/ALeqM5h116nr_azlHR5A-gajA5naaLnJBOg (retrieved on May 6, 2008).
63. "National Strategy for Homeland Security" (2007). Homeland Security Council, Office of the President of the United States, October.
64. bin Laden's "Letter to America," November 24, 2002. http://www.guardian.co.uk/world/2002/nov/24/theobserver/print (retrieved on November 25, 2008).
65. Yungher, Nathan I. (2008), op. cit., 152; and "NYPD Radicalization in the West: The Homegrown Threat" (2007):7, 43.
66. Telhami, Shibley (2005), op. cit., 160.
67. http://abdulhaqq.jeeran.com/operations.html (retrieved on August 10, 2007).
68. Ingraham, Laura (2007). *Power to the People.* Washington, DC: Regnery Publishing.
69. Telhami, Shibley (2005), op. cit., 160.
70. Yungher, Nathan I. (2008), op. cit., 143–144.
71. Barack Obama's acceptance speech, August 28, 2008. http://www.nytimes.com/2008/08/28/us/politics/28text-obama.html?pagewanted=1&_r=1 (retrieved on January 22, 2009).
72. Rapoport, David C. (2008). "Fear and Trembling: Terrorism in Three Religious Traditions," in *Terrorism in Perspective,* 2nd ed. Eds. Mahan, Sue and Pamela L. Griset. Thousand Oaks, CA: Sage Publications, 49, 60.
73. Ephesians 6:12.
74. Rapoport, David C. (2008), op. cit., 53.
75. Jeremiah, David (2008). *What in the World is Going On: 10 Prophetic Clues You Cannot Afford to Ignore.* Nashville, TN: Thomas Nelson Publishers, 88.
76. Yungher, Nathan I. (2008), op. cit., 156–157.

Chapter 9

Tipping Points—Public Policy "Triggers"

This chapter attempts to explain "why" extremism and terrorism are inevitable. In coming to this conclusion, you will have discerned certain themes presented throughout this book. These themes are built around ideologies and the resultant balkanization. A useful way to conceptualize how these factors may come together is illustrated by the recent best-selling book, *The Tipping Point*.[1] In my mind, the principles articulated by Gladwell are simple, yet powerful. He contends three principles combine to create phenomena. These principles are:[2]

1. Contagious behavior
2. Little changes create big effects
3. Change occurs at one dramatic moment

These principles can be demonstrated by the impact and implications of terrorism. As described earlier, the application of terroristic violence occurs at one dramatic moment—when the incident happens, when the bomb explodes. This violence can create responses from opposing groups, from police, and from the larger society. These responses have a certain momentum, resulting in what can be characterized as contagious behavior. This behavior revolves around fear—which is the underlying goal of terrorism. As this dynamic plays out, the little changes that are made by all affected people can have a dramatic effect on the larger society. While Gladwell's principles are not directly applicable to terrorism, one can envision how the continuum from ideology to terroristic violence to balkanization can result. The "missing link" in this continuum is the "trigger." The trigger will build on existing ideologies, which will act as the "fuel for the fire." When activated, violence will occur. When violence occurs, balkanization will result. In making this assertion, however, I must make clear certain caveats.

First, this chapter deviates from the overall approach of this book. I trust by now the reader has noted that this book has been heavily sourced and researched. The extent of research was designed to illustrate that the "wave is approaching." The *perfect storm* is coming. Whether or not you agree with my vision, I trust that you will acknowledge that the book is well researched and supported with numerous citations by many authors. This chapter, however, will be a bit different. By this I mean that I will not use extensive citations to build a case in support of my assertions. Instead, I will make my assertions based on my vision, my logic, and my insight. You have every right to reject my assertions. Indeed, I expect some percentage of you will do so. Those who reject my vision will surely have excellent reasons for doing so. In this sense, this is not a debate. You may be "proven" right. Then again, I may be "proven" right. In any event, the future will validate our respective opinions. This chapter, therefore, is my vision.

The second caveat is related to the initial one. The "triggers" I identify that may lead to extremism and terrorism are not designed to be "causally" connected. By this I mean the "triggers" may contribute to increases in extremism and terrorism. Taken individually each "trigger" is not necessarily the "cause" of the problem. Stated another way, I do not contend that each "trigger" is designed as "cause" and "effect" relationships. Indeed, I recognize that the world is very complex. People do things for many reasons. Committing crimes, based on extremist notions and ideologies, involves many factors. Sometimes these factors are more obvious than other times. This is particularly true when one is attempting to assess larger movements, which in the end are the result of many aggregate individual motivations and incentives. If there are "definitive" causes of such, then I will leave it to the statistical, psychological, and other experts to assert. For me, however, I see the problem from a larger perspective. I look for public policy issues that have little, or no, real compromises. I look for emotional—and basic—drivers that motivate people to act out violently. While many other factors may contribute to this violence, I see the "tipping point" to be societal factors. These societal factors, therefore, *contribute* to the resultant violence.

Finally, my assertions are not intended to be based on "normative" assessments. By this I mean the triggers are not designed to "blame" someone or some group for the problem. They are not designed to say one side is right and the other side is wrong. While we all have our biases, these triggers do not imply fault. Instead, I realize that these issues represent deeply held beliefs—and biases—that do not bode well for effective compromises. This is why I call them "triggers." They are emotional. They represent the worldviews of large segments of society. They represent what people care about. Many of these triggers may be worth dying—and killing—for! Given these assertions, how can I blame someone—or some group— for the problem? While I have my sense of what constitutes "good public policy," I readily admit that others will disagree. Instead, I simply seek to present issues that may contribute to the coming violence. I will attempt to explain the complexities related to these triggers, but I will do so without assigning fault. In the few instances when I do editorialize, I do so without criticism. Hence, when I "name names," I do so without "throwing stones." Consequently, my intention is not to harm. My intention, instead, is to warn. If there are "compromises" to these triggers, then hopefully this analysis will serve to facilitate such.

With these caveats established, please allow me to make a larger point about the below listed triggers. Each issue, which may result in violence, has strong attachments. These attachments may be based on philosophical, religious, moral, political, economic, intellectual, and/or ethnic or racial explanations. These attachments are critical to each person's worldview. They are critical to each person's identity. They are critical to each person's vision of what this country stands for. In short, these are deeply held beliefs. In my mind, the problem is not that people place great value on certain issues. The problem is that many—if not most—of these issues leave little room for effective compromise. Even deeper than this problem is this question: Who (or what group) will relent on any of these issues? This question presupposes another question: Why should anyone relent when they are right? This is the key to understanding the impact of these triggers. That is, each side is right! Why should anyone relent when they are right? When asked to relent on deeply held beliefs, it is particularly unreasonable to assume that this will occur. So I ask the question again, who (or what side) will relent? The question is rhetorical. The answer is obvious. Neither side will "give." That is why violence will occur. To make my point, let's look at some specific triggers. We will start with some obvious examples and then build from these to more controversial—and complicated—issues.

Abortion

The question of abortion is a classic example of precious little room for compromise. Some assert the "solution" to this issue is to make abortion less common by advocating certain alternatives, such as adoption, contraception, and education. These are all important. They contribute to the reduction in the incidence of abortion. The problem, however, is not the frequency of abortion. To the true believers, the problem is whether it should exist at all. Pro-choice advocates will not accept any reduction in the legal availability of abortion. Pro-life advocates will not accept the existence of legalized abortion. Indeed, both sides have debated over variations of abortion legislation, including "partial birth" abortion. The Obama Administration is also likely to expand international funding for abortion and for government funding of stem cell research. In the end, one side sees it as a "right," the other sees it as unethical or immoral. One side sees it as a "crime" to prevent abortion, the other sees it as a "crime" to perform abortion.

My prediction is this: abortion-related violence will increase—possibly dramatically in the years ahead. You may wonder why this is so? My answer is that the past several years have seen very little violence related to abortion. I believe this was due to the fact that "pro-lifers" believed that the Bush Administration would be able to appoint enough U.S. Supreme Court justices to swing the court toward reversing *Roe v. Wade*. This did not happen. With the Obama Administration in place, the pro-lifers know that the Obama appointments will be proabortion. Consequently, from the point of view of pro-lifers, their legal options are over—at least for years to come. This is particularly relevant when you consider that Obama may have two or three appointments in his first term. They know that the court's makeup will only change in *favor* of legalized abortion. This may result in more discretion to institute abortion. It may also result in more international funding for abortion from the Obama Administration. These are conclusions that many in the antiabortion movement will resent. Consequently, be prepared for more abortion-related violence.

The Economy

There are a number of factors that could trigger violence from a poor economy. Much of this is common knowledge. Poverty and unemployment have been argued as "causes" of crime for years. In addition to making criminals more desperate, a poor economy often forces cities to cut crime-prevention programs due to budgetary concerns.[3] Depending upon your view of these "causes," this may be "expected" or not. In any event, I envision a problematic economy for quite some time. It may be years before the economy is robust and vibrant. The level of violence will be related to how long and deep the recession actually is. Indeed, my concern is that the United States may have come to a point where the structural cracks in the system may make it impossible to compete in the world economy as we have grown accustomed to. The trillions of dollars being printed by the government will inevitably result in deeper, even more serious inflationary pressures on the dollar and the economy. While I do not fully understand the complexities of these issues, I do understand that many structural economic and fiscal problems are present. Exactly how this plays out is beyond the scope of this book.

My expertise is focused on crime—particularly extremist and terroristic violence. Even "normal" crime increases will further pressure already constrained policing agencies. We should expect to see an increase in crime rates in the months and years ahead. Some of this crime will be based on lack of employment and frustrations related to being unemployed. Look for substantial increases in workplace violence incidents. Look for violent acts from individuals who are angry with "the system." Many of these people will be frustrated from the lack of opportunity or tangible benefits as compared to their "high expectations" from the Obama election. Simply stated, the ability to deliver on expectations will be extraordinarily difficult—particularly since the "expectation bar" has been set so high.

It is likely that the economy will particularly exacerbate the relations of low- to mid-level workers. The ability of these individuals to obtain viable employment in the years ahead is questionable—at best. Unless these jobs are provided by government infrastructure projects, I contend that jobs for these workers will be difficult to obtain. This is particularly due to competition from international workers and markets. If these jobs are hard to come by, then competition for these jobs will be intense. Intense competition can be healthy. Yet it can bring out many negative emotions. Greed, jealousy, duplicity, frustration, desperation, and anger could resonate among large segments of the population. These individuals, who have traditionally been connected to "the system," may be less inclined to buy into the notion of the American dream. Indeed, they may increasingly see their prospects as dismal, even "hopeless."

This circumstance is particularly problematic given the juxtaposition of the expectations of "hope and change" derived from the Obama candidacy. It is a well-recognized psychological tenet that people will react to their circumstance partly— or even largely—from what they expect. If you do not expect much, you will not be too disappointed. If your expectations are high, however, your reaction may be severe. Stated another way, it is harder to accept less when you have been promised much! Those who currently believe that things will change for the better may have to accept that this may not be true. This may be a hard reality to accept. It may lead to frustration, disillusionment, anger, and ultimately to violence.

As I draft these words, the key issue for the Obama Administration is to pass the "stimulus bill." This bill, which totals about $1 trillion, was passed by Congress— without one Republican vote. Democrats contend the money is needed—and it is targeted to "stimulate" the economy. Republicans contend the bill is loaded with "pork," designed to repay Democratic interest groups. They also assert the bill will vastly increase the size of government. While I see more credence in the latter critique than the former, the larger point is that this "debate" is setting the tone for the months and years ahead. The tone will be about two very different views of the economy, the role of government, and the viability of the market. In the end it is a debate over the structural and philosophical underpinnings of the economy, the government, and the society. This is an extraordinarily substantive "debate." It is likely the most invasive undertaking of "the system" since the New Deal era. Indeed, prior to his election, news magazines trumpeted whether Obama will create a "new" New Deal. Based on the "bank bailout" plan instituted by the Bush Administration, coupled with the "stimulus bill" proposed by the Democratic-led Congress, it appears that this approach is, indeed, forthcoming.

Put aside the merits of this approach. Also put aside the reasons for how and why we arrive at this threshold. Simply look ahead. What is likely to transpire as we go forward? Look for both sides to blame each other for the crisis—and for the laggard recovery. As the months play out, the blame and the criticism will become increasingly political—and personal. Look for accusations to become more frequent and volatile. Watching our "leaders" become more emotional and disrespectful will result in "common people" being increasingly disillusioned and resentful.

This will further frustrate and balkanize society. The poor—and those who "represent" the poor—will increasingly blame the "rich" for the causes and the continuance of the fiscal mess. There will be many reasons trumpeted. Indeed, tax dollars spent on huge bonuses, lavish "retreats," corporate jets, and "excessive" salaries will fuel the resentment. Those with money will be targeted for attack—both figuratively and literally. Rich people will seek to "wall themselves out" of society. They will live in gated communities, avoid fancy restaurants, and live less conspicuous lifestyles. They will also buy security for more and more aspects of their lives. In short, the friction between rich and poor will be acute. The "blame game" will abound. Violence will result. More consequently, however, is that more and more people—particularly the great and stable middle class—will lose faith in "the system." Once people lose faith in the system, the "hope" that many had with the election of Barack Obama will wane—or be lost. I am afraid that the "change" they will advocate will be revolution to take down the capitalistic system! Of course, this goal has been advocated by a host of extremist groups—including al Qaeda, right-wing groups, environmental groups, and leftist/anarchist groups.

In summary, we are in the early stages where the impact of the economy will "inspire" violence by extremist groups. For example, some federal agents are warning that the threat from hate groups and splinter organizations connected to the Klan should not be underestimated, especially at a time of economic unrest. The concern is as the nation's economic troubles widen, it will give white supremacists a potent new source of discontent to exploit among potential recruits.[4] It is important to consider that many right-wing groups *wanted* Obama elected. They believe that his election—and his policies—will finally inspire the race war they have long advocated.

There is some evidence even prior to this election that this message was resonating with a certain percentage of the population. Since the year 2000, the number of hate groups has increased by 48 percent to about 888, according the Southern Poverty Law Center, an organization that monitors extremist movements. A pointed warning related to right-wing extremist groups was provided by another federal agent:[5] "These three things—the Internet, immigration and the economic crisis—that is the molten mixture for these guys," said the chief of the ATF's Nashville office. "That is the furnace of hate. As we speak, this is happening."

Energy and the Environment

The potential for violence related to energy and the environment is substantial. Like the variations noted above regarding the economy, there are many uncertainties as to how big a trigger this will be. The key variables going forward will be how energy and the environment play into these three potentialities: the price of oil, energy disruptions as a strategy to cripple the economy, and as a factor in the politics of energy.

Let's start with the price of oil. The question of how this relates to extremist violence will be largely based on cost. This will, in turn, trigger the scope and amount of exploration for resources conducted in the United States. If the price of oil stays low (as of the time of this writing) then the impact of this factor will be minimal. This will be due to very little pressure to exploit the expendable (oil, gas, coal, etc.) resources we possess. On the other hand, if the price of oil rises, then there will be increased pressure to drill for oil and gas. It will also result in increases in the use of coal and nuclear fuel. If this occurs, which I expect is the most likely result, a backlash against the increased exploration and production of such energy sources will occur. This backlash will include sabotage and targeted explosions. These will be directed against pipelines, production facilities, distribution facilities, and vehicles used for transportation of these products. An example of this violence can be found in British Columbia, Canada, where four bombings in three months targeting a firm called EnCana's natural gas production and distribution system. These attacks have caused the Royal Canadian Mounted Police (RCMP) to characterize the attacks as "increasingly violent."[6]

It is inevitable that these types of attacks will increase. This will be particularly true if the price of oil increases. The cycle of this logic is as follows: As the price of oil increases, the pressure to explore energy sources in the United States will also increase. This is exactly what occurred in the spring and summer of 2008. As the price of oil declined throughout the fall, the pressure to explore correspondingly decreased. In any event, any substantial increase in oil will reintroduce the pressure to explore. If exploration does increase, then the potential for attacks on energy firms and systems will increase. This violence will be conducted by radical environmentalists, anarchists, and leftists.

To those who advocate the increased use of solar, wind, and other renewable energy sources, there are at least two problems with these alternatives. First, I do not believe we can operationalize these sources quickly enough to cushion ourselves from the inevitable increases in oil prices. By this I mean, even if we move forward with these renewable resources, the price of oil will still be fluid enough to create pressures on an already unstable economy. Second, there is opposition to the widespread establishment of the systems needed to operationalize renewable resources. By this I do not necessarily mean the "usual suspects" (oil and auto firms). Ironically, many have resisted renewable resources because they do not want them in their "backyard." While almost everyone wants renewable energy, many do not want the noise and the disruption associated with it. For example, many communities have resisted the placement of wind turbines due to the noise from the blades. In addition, a recent news report shows the difficulties associated with the implementation of these energy sources. In California, environmentalists have litigated for years against solar, wind, and geothermal energy projects because the power lines would have to run through "pristine" wilderness areas.[7]

This is not to say that these matters cannot be worked out. My point, however, is that time is of the essence. Time is critical. We have precious little time to waste. Based on the conflicting interests involved, I believe the longer it takes to operationalize these renewable energy sources, the more likely extremists will utilize violence to "resolve" the matter. Indeed, this situation raises certain questions: When does the desire for energy production override the desire to maintain pristine areas? Isn't this the same argument made related to the Arctic National Wildlife Refuge (ANWR) in Alaska? This has been stalemated for about two decades. Should we expect better and quicker results when dealing with renewable resources?

The other aspect of this issue relates to using violence against energy as a means to cripple the economy. This strategy is as follows: For various reasons, extremists could target energy supplies as a means to disrupt the economy—and to create mass damages. Consider a couple of examples. In what became known as the Kennedy Airport plot, an employee at the airport and three other men with ties to Guyana, Trinidad, and Pakistan have been charged with plotting to blow up the airport's fuel tanks and pipelines. This planned terror attack was aimed at causing greater destruction than the September 11 attacks. The plotters planned to neutralize security personnel before blowing up the airport's fuel tanks and a section of a 40-mile fuel pipeline operated by Buckeye Partners.[8] Another case involved a Pennsylvania man, Michael Curtis Reynolds, who plotted to blow up U.S. energy installations in a bid to drive up gas prices and prompt a U.S. withdrawal from Iraq. According to prosecutors, the man was a sympathizer of al Qaeda. The defendant believed gasoline prices could hit "astronomical" levels if he succeeded in attacking the Alaska pipeline or the Transcontinental Pipeline connecting the Gulf of Mexico and the U.S. Northeast.[9] In my mind, these examples illustrate that the threat exists. Whether these spectacular plots could have been "successful" is another matter. In any event, as the below examples illustrate, this approach has its merits.

There is a disconcerting example south of the border that we should pay attention to. On September 11, 2007, ironically, a shadowy leftist guerrilla group took credit for a string of explosions that ripped apart at least six Mexican oil and gas pipelines. These explosions rattled financial markets and caused hundreds of millions of dollars in lost production. It was the second time in three months that the so-called People's Revolutionary Army (EPR) claimed responsibility for a pipeline attack. These attacks were said to be part of its "prolonged people's war" against "the anti-people government."[10]

The above example may illustrate both a strategy to disrupt the economy and a political message. In any case, the example should give us pause. Beyond these attacks, the larger political aspects of energy provide ripe opportunities for direct action. Think about the political rhetoric around energy during the 2004 presidential election (Kerry's attack on "big oil"), and during the spring and summer of 2008 when the Democratic-led Congress called executives of several oil companies to be grilled about their role in the price of oil. Most economists would agree the price of oil is a function of a number of factors. These include supply/demand, speculators, OPEC policies, profit margins, and many other factors. Just as with the economy, I am not qualified to make the case over the "causes" of the price. The approach by some politicians, however, seems geared more toward creating demagogues rather than actually working toward a solution. In any event, pay attention to the criticisms. In my mind, the more criticisms rise against "big oil" and other "villains," the more likely extremists will act out on this anger. This rhetoric will lead to violence against real or imagined "enemies."

On the other side of this issue, there is a growing movement to attribute the fear of "global warming" to a more insidious motivation. This movement is centered on the belief that environmentalism is designed to usurp the sovereignty of the United States in favor of a global government. This theory brings together an interesting mixture of hard-line, right-wing Christian organizations and anti-"new world order" groups. Advocates of this theory assert that the "environment is not about saving nature," but instead is "about a revolutionary coup in America." It is designed to "establish global governance and abandon the principles of natural law." These proponents further contend that sustainable development policies will require a "police state" that will ultimately "turn America into a globally governed homeland where humans are treated as biological resources."[11]

The basic thesis pushed by this movement is that the Security and Prosperity Partnership (SPP), a trade agreement between Canada, Mexico, and the United States, is part of a nefarious and secret plan to merge the United States, Canada, and Mexico into something called the "North American Union" (NAU). A Google search of this term will result in a substantial body of information—correct or imagined. In essence, those who fear the NAU insist that it will bring with it global government—and sustainable development policies. In their thinking, sustainable development is the real evil lurking in the shadows of global government. In this thinking, environmental policies actually exist to destroy individual freedoms and the U.S. system of government. The extent of the fury within this movement was encapsulated by a leader of an affiliated group, Tom DeWeese, who stated, "This is not some nice little debate, this is war." The war is against Western culture, and the Judeo-Christian and Islamic religions. In this thinking the world theology is pantheism, that is, "Nature is God." Included with this pantheism is a blend of communistic tenets including the reallocation of property rights and redistribution of assets. With this logic, the desire to save the environment is actually an insidious plot to destroy the country! Indeed, the purpose is not about weaning the country from foreign oil, or about protecting the environment. Instead, these people believe it is fostering a new "false religion" that advocates "worshipping the Earth."[12]

As these examples illustrate, those who seek to save the environment—or the world—may be pitted against those who seek to save the economy, the country, and even traditional religion. These are obviously substantial—and critical—interests. Interspersed with these interests is the need to maintain a modern lifestyle—which needs energy. The operative question is, can we meet the energy needs of our society while simultaneously respecting the interests of these deep-seated causes? As you can predict, I am doubtful.

Technology

The impact of technology related to potential violence may be boiled down to two key factors: weapons and the Internet. Think first about weapons. Over the last few years, the ability of small groups to conduct terrorism has shown radical improvements in "productivity." This productivity is based on substantial increases in the lethality and availability of weapons. The result is an exponential increase in the capacity to inflict economic, physical, psychological, and moral damage.

According to Robb, these improvements in lethality are just the beginning. He characterizes this as an "arc of productivity ... that lets small groups terrorize at ever-higher levels of death and disruption [which] stretches as far as the eye can see."[13] With this thinking, Robb asserts that eventually "one man may even be able to wield the destructive power that only nation-states possess today." This circumstance is occurring at a time when wars between states are receding. This "perverse twist of history" provides small groups the ability to create mass destruction with the use of sophisticated weapons. The potential for mass casualties and chaos, using only small arms, was aptly illustrated in the Mumbai attacks. Indeed, beyond isolated attacks like Mumbai, Robb asserts that Iraq is a "petri dish" for modern conflict. Iraq is where small groups are learning to fight modern militaries and modern societies. The likeliest point of origin and the most likely destination for these attacks are cities. As a result, we can expect to see "systems disruption" used again and again in modern conflict—particularly against megacities in the developing world. This threat is also against those in the developed West, as we have already seen in London, Madrid, and Moscow.[14]

Another key factor is the use of the Internet. It is hard to underestimate the impact of this technology. The significance of these radical Web sites was noted in the NYPD radicalization report that characterized the Internet as a "virtual incubator of its own."[15] Internet sites distribute everything from extremist literature to bomb making instructions. They provide photos of potential targets. They contain videos of security procedures. They illustrate—and trumpet—the aftermath of terrorist incidents. Indeed, the implications of the Internet are substantial. As mentioned earlier, the Internet is used to communicate al Qaeda's global ideology.[16]

The significance of the Internet can be illustrated by a couple of examples. Right-wing groups have been early proponents of the Internet. They have used the Internet for fund raising, propaganda, and recruitment. In recent years, the racist hate movements have veered away from large-scale, Klan-type gatherings. Instead, followers come together online at Web sites such as www.CreativityMovement.net and stormfront.org, which attracts an estimated 150,000 registered users who view instruction manuals, learn movement history, and exchange stories.[17] Similarly, as we saw in Chapter 3, radical animal and environmental groups have effectively used Web sites to communicate their ideologies to interested persons.

This same approach has been used by radical Islamists for years. While most of these Islamist sites are in Arabic, sites in English are increasingly appearing that are dedicated to communicating radical messages. Some of these Web sites are based in the United States. Sites such as www.RevolutionMuslim.com and www. Revolution.Muslimpad.com promote pro-jihad messages aimed at radicalizing readers. According to cyberterrorism expert Rabbi Abraham Cooper, part of the power of these Web sites comes from the context and interpretation of the radical messages. These messages offer dangerous inspiration. These types of sites plug into the "hardcore ideology that Al Qaeda espouses," said Jarret Brachman, director of research at West Point's Combating Terrorism Center. In this thinking, such Web sites have been compared to a "gateway drug."[18]

The goal is to hook people, just as a relatively harmless drug hooks people. It is designed to communicate radicalized thought to people in this country. The purpose is to see the world through the lens of al Qaeda. In the "About Us" section of one Web site, their mission was described as attempting to "bring to our readers the reality on the ground in the lands of Jihad, and exposing the lies and deceptions of the disbelievers, hypocrites, and tyrannical Governments." While these Web sites do not directly advocate jihad, "by implication the entire ideology does demand violence," said Brachman, who added that "this guy [Web site creator] is not just a consumer of this ideology, he's a producer of it." While the number of the viewers is not known, as mentioned above, the need to directly connect to a mass movement is not necessary, as the lethality of weaponry allows a small number of people to change history.

Police Shootings

As illustrated by the above "triggers," there are many factors that may create the incentive for violence. It is hard to deny that police shootings are a potential powder keg. This is particularly true when a white police officer shoots a black individual. Since I have represented many police officers in shooting incidents, and because I have personally experienced many volatile situations as a police officer, I will provide the perspective of police officers to these incidents. Since many readers may not have been faced with these experiences, I hope this provides some insight into the complexity and volatility inherent in these situations.

The Sean Bell case, mentioned earlier, is instructive. The officers in this case were accused of racism and were called "murderers." Why are these police officers accused of being racist—and KKK members? It may be helpful to provide a brief overview of the facts in this case. At about 4:00 am, a confrontation occurred in a strip club. The police were called. A police vehicle responding to the scene was involved in an accident with Bell's vehicle. Someone in Bell's vehicle allegedly made a furtive movement. Accusations were exchanged between occupants in the vehicles. At some point, the police officers opened fire on the vehicle, killing Sean Bell. Fifty shots were fired by four different police officers. Let me be clear. This was a tragic case. Firing 50 rounds is undeniably problematic. However, the accusations leveled against the officers were questionable—at best. Was this the result of racism? Is there evidence that the officers intended to murder Sean Bell? In my mind, this speaks more to lack of discipline and improper training then it does illegal conduct or racism.

Without getting into the conflicting accounts of the incident, the above circumstance was tragic, yet expected. It was tragic because an unarmed man was killed on his wedding day. Clearly, the emotions derived from the pending marriage helped drive the sentiment against the police. The police officers, of course, did not know this fact. By all accounts, they did not even know Sean Bell or his companions. Nor did they know if they were armed with weapons. They were simply trying to do their job in a tense and potentially dangerous situation. To assert that they are "murderers" or that they are "racists" from the facts of this case are simply wrong—and inflammatory.

Regardless of the "judgments" and arguments made by those who desire to make this case into a racial litmus test, some facts may illustrate the difficulties inherent in these encounters. Let's look at some statistics that may help shed light on the perceived dangers faced by the police. While it is not widely reported, FBI statistics reveal that a disproportionately large number of assaults on police are from black offenders. From 1996 to 2005, the FBI statistics reveal that anywhere from one third to more than one half of all police officers who were feloniously murdered were killed by black offenders.[19] For example, in 2004 there were 58 police officers killed in the line of duty by felonious means. Of these 58 killings, 30 were by black offenders and 28 were by white offenders.[20] Similarly, in 1996 there were 85 police officers killed in the line of duty by felonious means. Of these 85 killings, 41 were by black offenders, 35 by white offenders, three by Asian/Pacific Islander offenders, two by American Indian/Alaskan natives, and in four the race was not reported. These statistics vary from year to year. Some years, like 2000, show a greater proportion of white offenders—46 out of 66 killings, with blacks "only" accounting for 20 of the 66 killings.[21] Since blacks make up only about 12–13 percent of the overall population, these data—by any statistical measure—reveal a much greater proportion of police officers being killed by blacks than any other race.

My intention is not to characterize black offenders as being the only threat to police officers. This would be an incorrect and inflammatory assertion. My desire in presenting these data is to give some sense of what police officers must deal with. Police officers must assess the nature and intention of individuals they encounter. They must do so while being cognizant of the probabilities—or the likelihood—that the individual may pose some danger to their safety. An example may help make sense of my point. It is statistically correct to say males pose a much greater threat to police than females. Using FBI data, females committed only 10 killings of the 652 police officers killed in the line of duty by felonious means from 1996 to 2005.[22] This means that over a 10-year period, females accounted for only about 1.5 percent of all police killings. Since females make up roughly 50 percent of the total population, the statistical likelihood that a police officer will be killed by a female versus a male is extraordinarily disproportionate. Using these simple statistics, the threat posed by females to the safety of police officers pales in comparison to the threat posed by males.

Similarly, the data of those who are more likely to commit murder is also instructive. Consider that between 2002 and 2006, there was a 52 percent increase in murders committed by teenage African American males, with much of that violence gang related. This increase in gang violence has also led to an increase in the number of police officers killed in the line of duty. In 2007, 186 officers across the country were killed, the highest number since 1989 if the 2001 terrorist attacks are excluded.[23] Further, while the overall murder rate has been dropping for several years, the murder rate for African Americans is on the rise. African Americans make up just 13 percent of the country's population but almost half of all murder victims are black.[24]

Additional data provide some insight. According to the Uniform Crime Report (UCR) data, in 2006 there were 17,399 homicides committed in this country. Of the homicides where the offender was known (12,477), 6,843 were black, 5,339 were white, and 295 were classified as "other."[25] These data reveal that more than half (almost 55%) of the known homicide offenders in 2006 were black. Even assuming that none of the unknown offenders were black—which would be a highly suspect assumption—still, about 39 percent of all homicide offenders in 2006 were black. Similar percentages are also seen in 2005 homicide data. In 2005, there were 17,029 homicides committed in this country. Of the homicides where the offender was known (12,130), 6,379 were black, 5,452 were white, and 299 were classified as "other."[26] These data reveal that more than half (about 52.5%) of the known homicide offenders in 2005 were black. Even assuming that none of the unknown offenders were black, still about 37 percent of all homicide offenders in 2005 were black.

These data are consistent with statistics from 2004 and 2003. In 2004, there were 15,935 homicides committed in this country. Of the homicides where the offender was known (11,218), 5,608 were black, 5,339 were white, and 271 were classified as "other."[27] These data reveal that about half (49.9%) of the known homicide offenders in 2004 were black. Even assuming that none of the unknown offenders were black, still about 35 percent of all homicide offenders in 2004 were black. In 2003, there were 16,043 homicides committed. Of the homicides where the offender was known (11,169), 5,729 were black, 5,132 were white, and 308 were classified as "other."[28] Data from previous years exhibit similar ratios of black homicide offenders. In addition, data for black violent crime rates also reveal a disproportionate ratio of black offenders.[29]

So what do these data represent? The statistics plainly reveal that black males are much more likely to kill police officers. Blacks are also more likely to commit murder and to be murdered. The larger point, however, is more subtle. I do not mean to imply that police officers should ignore the threat posed by whites or even of females. Nor do I imply that police should overemphasize the potential threat posed by black males. Indeed, these statistics are simply the aggregate of many tragic situations. These data also do not imply that police should ignore the individualized cues and indicators posed in encounters with citizens. Indeed, these individualized perceptions and indicators are critical. They represent the key to officer safety—and to the legal standards developed by the U.S. Supreme Court. I contend this factor, appropriately characterized as "officer safety," is assessed through the experience factor of the officer. Indeed, the race of the suspect remains "below the surface" when courts review police use of force cases. Consequently, I have no quarrel with courts not explicitly making race an affirmative factor in use of force cases, as it can adequately be assessed in conjunction with other "experiential" factors.

These data and the related logic raise the provocative notion of perception both before and after a police shooting. Prior to the decision to pull the trigger, police officers must assess numerous facts, observations, stimuli, and the like. Some of these factors may be correctly noted and processed, some may be incorrectly perceived. The standard shaped by the U.S. Supreme Court is of "objective reasonableness." This standard is assessed by the officer at the time of the incident. This assessment requires the court or the jury to step into the "shoes of the officer" at the time of the incident. Hence, what the officer sees, hears, feels, smells, and perceives during the incident should be included in this assessment. While court decisions do not affirmatively include race or gender as a factor in this assessment, the emphasis on the experience of the police officer is of critical consideration. Of course, the experiences of police officers differ—often greatly. They can differ in many factors, including training, years on the job, numbers and types of arrests, type of agency (urban, suburban, rural, etc.), specific positions, background characteristics (military, education, gender, race, etc.), and a host of other factors.

However important these factual—and perceptive—indicators are, the statistics revealed above will inevitably factor into the minds of individual police officers. When faced with a potentially dangerous situation, numerous thoughts go through your mind. These thoughts may shape your perception. They flow through your mind in fractions of seconds. Your mental computer records numerous "facts" and perceptions. These are processed and result in a response—or a decision. Does the gender of the individual (or suspect) matter in these situations? At some level, the answer is likely that it does. Does the race of the individual (or suspect) matter? At possibly a deeper level, the answer is likely that it does matter. Can one quantify how much gender and race factor into a decision? This is an extraordinarily difficult assessment.[30] Hence, one factor that may be assessed, in a subtle way, is the relationship between experience and race. While this is another provocative assessment, I contend that it must be accounted for.

While I am quite sure that some will criticize my recantation of the above data, my intention is not to blame blacks for crime. Indeed, the mere fact that these data are included in this book will subject me to the charge of being a "racist." I realize this charge will be made. Instead of defending myself from these inevitable attacks, I think the better approach is to explain the purpose of these data. This is to expound upon what experience tells a police officer. Experience will dictate that blacks commit a disproportionate amount of violent crime. The reasons for this fact are debatable. Some will argue that the cause is socioeconomic factors, such as poverty, lack of education (or quality education), family structure, drugs and alcohol, racism, and numerous other "causes" of crime. I do not seek to dispute the validity of these factors as they are beyond the scope of this book. Instead, I approach this question for another purpose, that is, to speak to the experiences of police officers. As mentioned in previous chapters, police officers are ill equipped to affect the root causes of crime. They cannot change the economic system. They cannot make the educational system more equitable, effective, or efficient. They cannot inspire families to raise their children properly, nor restrain teens from having sex at a young age and without birth control methods. They also cannot prevent individuals from choosing to consume drugs and alcohol. They cannot stop racists from being racists. Indeed, the best they can do is fairly, honestly, and equitably deal with the *effects* of crime, that is, to do their job as best as they can, and to treat all citizens with respect, dignity, and equality.

Do all police officers accomplish these laudable goals? Of course not! Name one other job—in any sector or in any country—in which a person can achieve anywhere near perfection in his or her job functions. It is impossible—and honest people will admit this. However, let a police officer fail to achieve these goals, and it becomes "news." Should it be "newsworthy" each time an employee in any job fails to live up to standards? Of course not! While I accept the fact that police officers have a special role in society, I cannot accept the notion that they are inherently corrupt, racist, or any other characterization that many in this society are all too happy to tag them with.

Those who place these tags on police officers cannot explain away why such a large percentage of blacks commit violent crimes. Even if they could by using socioeconomic "evidence," or by condemning the "racist society," these factors—even if they are valid—mean precious little to a police officer who has to make a split-second decision in a potentially volatile situation. What I seek to make clear is police officers, like all human beings, are biologically inclined toward self-defense. Indeed, the law specifically affords police the right to self-defense. When police officers make the wrong decision, it does no good to make them into "murderers" and "racists." All it serves are the self-interests of some "race baiters," and those who are seeking to divide society around a racial/nationalist agenda.

This brings us to the *aftermath* of police shooting cases, such as the Sean Bell case. Instead of acknowledging the legitimate concerns that are sometimes posed to the safety of police officers, some are quick to turn a tragic shooting into a "racial incident." These racial provocateurs seem driven to insert a racial component into the decision making of the officer. Conversely, they are almost always devoid of the impact of the statistical data presented above. In essence, the provocateurs advocate that the police used race as part of the decision to shoot. They refuse to acknowledge, however, that the data demonstrably illustrate that race may be a factor in the danger posed to the officer. Hence, the logic is to use the race of the victim to foster the notion that police are racists, while they ignore the statistical data that suggest that race may be a factor in assessing the danger posed to the officer. In my mind, you cannot have it both ways. If race matters, then it should matter to both mitigate and aggravate the perspective of the officer.

This logic leads to the inevitable, yet provocative, question: If blacks commit a disproportionate number of police killings—and of homicides—is it inappropriate for police to be more guarded in certain encounters with black males? Those who will be offended by this question are likely—and ironically—to be the same people who will strongly advocate using race in employment decisions, college enrollment, government contracts, and the like. Consider this logic. The underlying basis for affirmative action programs relates to past discrimination. The underlying basis for crime statistics relates to past criminal conduct. Both are based on aggregated historical evidence—meaning affirmative action decisions do not require evidence of past discrimination against a particular individual. Why then is criminal history aggregated in historical data inapplicable to street cops? This is particularly true when they must make split-second, life and death decisions. How should we fairly answer these questions? I have no dispute with people who desire to work toward fairly addressing these vexing and controversial questions. However, I do have a quarrel with the race provocateurs who want it both ways. They want to pretend that race (through crime statistics) should not matter in life and death situations, while they assert that race (through affirmative action programs) should matter in hiring decisions. In my mind, this is both unfair and dangerous—to both the officer and to the larger society.

There are two broad consequences to this discussion. First, it may cause police officers to "disengage" from potentially dangerous circumstances. By this I mean police officers may be inclined not to intervene, or at least delay involvement, in situations that may require police action. For example, the officers in Bell's case could have decided not to go to the call, or they could have delayed approaching the scene in a manner that would have resulted in Bell's vehicle being gone before the arrival of the police. This "disengagement strategy" is particularly relevant in circumstances where police proactively engage citizens—such as in traffic and street stops. Some of the best police work is done in circumstances where police initiate the stop. If police are apprehensive because they may be called "murderers" or "racists" for making an incorrect split-second decision, would not a rational response be to avoid making stops that may lead to difficult decisions? The logic becomes, why risk the consequences? Let the vehicle drive on—regardless of what crime the occupants may have committed, or are committing. To be clear, I do not advocate this "disengagement strategy." However, if police officers are going to be made pawns in a dangerous political/racial game, it will be hard to deny that some officers will take this inappropriate, but inevitable response.

The other likely consequence is that police officers will become increasingly detached from the community. While I do not advocate such detachment, it may be hard to prevent. In this light, it is critical that all people of good will seek to break down the barriers and the hardened positions between the community and the police. While I am not optimistic that those with the "agendas" will be overcome by good people, I still hope this will occur. Although this book is not sufficient to break down these barriers, hopefully it will illustrate where we are headed—if we continue on the current path. In my mind, the key to this goal is best understood in the application of perception. Since all parties to this "play" called "life" see it from their perspective, we must be cognizant of how this influences our attitudes and decisions.

In essence, the way police officers see their circumstance influences their decisions. This is particularly relevant in the larger question of the militarization of police. In this sense, militarized police represent the epitome of use of force. Think of the impact assault weapons and armored vehicles have on an already angry community. Think of this impact on police officers who are armed with assault rifles but are "gun shy" because they have seen other officers being criminally charged—and made to be political examples—because they incorrectly reacted to a perceived dangerous situation. At the same time, these same police officers see themselves increasingly as targets for criminals and extremists who seek to "kill racist cops" or destroy the capitalist system. These are dangerous mixtures of fear and self-defense. We must take this dynamic into account.

As I drafted this book another police shooting caused widespread rioting in Oakland. In this case, it appears a transit police officer brazenly shot an unarmed man. To be clear, if the facts are correct in the Oakland incident, then I have no sympathy for the police officer. If the officer shot the individual as he lay prone on the ground, then the officer should be prosecuted. If, indeed, prosecutors can make a case for murder, they should pursue this charge.

Notwithstanding the potential criminal prosecution, many sought to take the law into their own hands. More than 300 businesses and hundreds of cars were damaged as rioters fanned through downtown Oakland. These rioters were "protesting" the New Year's Day fatal shooting. Police arrested about 105 people. Oakland residents recalled a night of *terror* and frustration as they wondered why rioters vented their rage on seemingly random, innocent victims. In my mind, the answer was articulated in a quote by an Oakland resident who asserted, "There's this anger just under the surface that's always waiting to bubble over."[31] This rioting continued the following day, when unruly protesters smashed store windows, burned cars, and vandalized an Oakland police vehicle. Police in riot gear shut down a main thoroughfare in Oakland after protesters tried to stop cars and threw trash cans into the street. An organizer of the protest said a group of *anarchists* not associated with the organizations hosting the rally had smashed a police vehicle before setting a garbage can on fire—triggering the rioting.[32]

This blatant shooting incident is the exception rather than the rule. In the typical case, when an officer has to make a split-second judgment, it is done to protect rather than to murder. If these judgments lead to riots, it has a chilly effect on police officers—and a detrimental impact on society. Police officers will say, it could have

332 ■ *Terrorism and Public Safety Policing*

been me. What would I do if it were me? What will happen to my career, my family, my house, my dreams? These are difficult—and emotional—issues that most people outside the "police world" do not see nor seem to care about. They are, nonetheless, real concerns to police. I submit if these are concerns to the police, then society should take notice—because in the long run they will be affected by them.

An example of this consequence can be seen in the killing of four Oakland police officers on March 21, 2009.[33] The shooter was killed by the police. The shooter was viewed as a "hero" by a sizable portion of the black community.[34] The potential impact of this incident is both disconcerting and telling. As I have attempted to demonstrate throughout this book, the "hardening" of positions by potentially opposing groups is dangerous. Consider what police–community relations will be like going forward. Can the anger be stemmed? Will police officers be able to do their jobs when faced with the potential of being targeted by certain citizens? Will citizens respond with fear or anger when confronted by police officers? Who will bridge the growing divide between the police and the community? I do not know these answers. Some see this incident as an indication of larger societal consequences. Consider this quote from an "advocate" of the police killer, who calls on[35]

> all progressive-minded people to stand against the brutal, long-standing, publicly supported policies of police containment that keep the African community under the grip of a colonial occupation for which the Oakland Police Department (OPD) is the front line of assault. The deaths of four members of the OPD on March 21, 2009, were the result of these relentless policies, which are manifested daily in the cold-blooded police murders, brutality and harassment of African men and women … by the heavily armed, military style Oakland police force. African people in Oakland have a right to struggle against this government-imposed terror. This is exactly what our brother Lovelle Mixon did.

Can we expect to go forward without more tragic and problematic examples of police use of force? Even deeper concerns come to mind: How do we stop these riots and address this anger? In my mind, the reason this anger "exists below the surface" is extraordinarily deep seated. It comes from historical discrimination coupled with contemporary racial provocateurs. It continues through a mix of reality and perception. It is difficult to "prove," yet easy to assert. Because of these factors, it is extremely difficult to "cure." Indeed, with the election of President Obama (see below discussion), I contend it will be even more difficult to effectively address the racial components of police shootings. These vexing—and hardening—positions will result in more rioting. It is inevitable. Each time this occurs, it serves as another example that will be trumpeted by the extremists—and an example that all police officers will assess. This dynamic will only be made more difficult—and volatile— with assault weapons and tactics.

Race, Religion, and Politics

Given that this analysis is on extremist ideologies, it is inevitable that we address underlying factors that lead to such thinking. Three of the most pervasive motivating factors—race, religion, and politics—come together in this section. Most people would avoid these issues, since they can be perceived as the "third rail." Those who step on the third rail get electrocuted. Even though I am cognizant of this implication, I feel that avoiding this issue does not do justice to the larger theme of this book, that extremist and terrorist violence will substantially increase.

The historic presidency of Barack Obama has set in motion an unprecedented opportunity for America and for the world. As mentioned in the first chapter, this is an extraordinary time. His presidency could be so memorable that it will impact the future direction of the country for years to come. This impact could be both extraordinarily positive and frighteningly negative. As I have traced certain trends in this book, I tend to believe the latter is more likely than the former. Since I believe the potentially adverse impact of race, religion, and politics is significant, please allow me to flesh out the basis for this conclusion. Before doing so, it may be useful to remind the reader that the essence of politics is that it is a battle of ideas. Many of these ideals are strongly held.

To put contemporary America—and the Obama Administration—in context, it may be useful to think back to his extraordinarily well received speech before the 2004 Democratic Convention. This is the speech that put Barack Obama on the national stage. He delivered a stirring speech, entitled "The Audacity of Hope." He stated, in pertinent part,[36]

> Now even as we speak, there are those who are preparing to divide us—the spin masters, the negative ad peddlers who embrace the politics of "anything goes." Well, I say to them tonight, there is not a liberal America and a conservative America—there is the United States of America. There is not a Black America and a White America and Latino America and Asian America—there's the United States of America.
>
> The pundits, the pundits like to slice-and-dice our country into Red States and Blue States; Red States for Republicans, Blue States for Democrats. But I've got news for them, too. We worship an "awesome God" in the Blue States, and we don't like federal agents poking around in our libraries in the Red States. We coach Little League in the Blue States and yes, we've got some gay friends in the Red States. There are patriots who opposed the war in Iraq and there are patriots who supported the war in Iraq. We are one people, all of us pledging allegiance to the stars and stripes, all of us defending the United States of America.

> In the end—In the end—In the end, that's what this election is about. Do we participate in a politics of cynicism or do we participate in a politics of hope?

The power of these words is substantial. They cut to the core of how we should live and think about each other. The dilemma for President Obama—and the country—is, how do we make this happen? It is easier to say this than to do it. Indeed, some may think I am being cynical by even raising this question. A couple of pointed comments may illustrate my larger concern. Both of these examples took place at the very start of the Obama presidency. On the day following the Obama inauguration, conservative talk show host Rush Limbaugh was asked if he wanted President Obama to succeed. He responded by stating, in pertinent part,[37]

> Success can be defined two ways … if he is going to do a *new* New Deal, why would I want him to succeed? … If he is going to implement a far left agenda … I don't believe in that … why would I want Socialism to succeed?

The night before this interview aired, two rappers, Young Jeezy and Jay-Z, were performing at an Obama inauguration party. During their performance, they made the following comments:[38]

> I wanna thank two people. I wanna thank the motherf----- overseas that threw the two shoes at George Bush. And I want to thank the motherf----- who helped them move their shit up out of the White House. Keep it moving, bitch, before my President is motherf----- black, nig--- … I don't want no more Bush. No more war. No more Iraq. No more white lies, my President is black.

Think about both of these comments. Will either of these individuals agree on anything related to the political system? Indeed, they are so far apart that it may be impossible to find any common ground. The problem is not these people. The problem is that they represent the worldviews of millions of people. They also speak to millions of people. Do you think this will be the last time we will hear such rhetoric? Given these statements were made—and aired—on the first day of the presidential term, I see this as a sign of things to come.

With the commencement of the new administration, the dilemma for President Obama will be how to deal with the mutually inconsistent positions illustrated by the above statements. At the earliest stage of the Obama Administration, it was my observation that President Obama will try to balance these competing extremes. While he clearly ran his campaign on the left, he has made some overturns to the middle. Indeed, he has met with conservative thinkers, he has retained Defense Secretary Gates, and he has appealed to comity from both political parties. Here is the problem. The extremes will not let him find the middle. Consider this example: When Obama picked evangelical preacher Rick Warren to say the prayer at his inauguration, he inflamed the secular left. In response, Obama chose gay Episcopal bishop Gene Robinson to deliver the invocation to kick off inauguration week.[39]

Please understand my purpose for presenting this example. First, it illustrates that President Obama may try to "please everyone." Of course, by selecting these two ministers, he succeeded in making both sides angry. Second, while I see the choice of these ministers to be largely irrelevant, many are deeply concerned about what they represent. Warren represents an "antigay" agenda to some, while to others Robinson represents the advocacy of the gay agenda. This is a very emotional and controversial matter. Do you think there is a solid middle ground in this issue? In my mind, while many in the middle could care less about gay rights—and gay marriage—many on both sides of the political spectrum feel strongly about this matter. The fact that President Obama attempted to "thread this needle" says to me that he may be well intended, but he will inevitably have to "pick sides." Simply stated, both sides will force him to do so. Once he picks sides, he will make the "losing side" angry.

This is the same with the Limbaugh/Jay-Z example used above. While Limbaugh argued more on a political analysis, he freely admitted that he does not want the president to succeed. If the president does not succeed, then what happens to the country? Does the country not also fail to succeed if the president fails? Remember Hillary Clinton's impassioned assertion that Bush *required* people to agree with him about the Iraq War—or they were not patriotic. Mrs. Clinton's response was that criticism of wrong policies was, indeed, the *definition* of patriotism! This logic was echoed and advocated by numerous liberal thinkers during the Bush Administration. Will this same logic remain during the Obama Administration?

Moreover, does Limbaugh's desire to have the first black president fail mean he is racist? This is particularly true for people like Jay-Z, who has clearly communicated that his worldview is embedded with racial overtones. The larger point is whether policy critics of President Obama become racist simply from their criticism. To Obama's credit, he has tried to rise above race. Will he—or can he—continue to do so? While I will address this issue more deeply below, the point at this juncture is whether Obama will critique—and criticize—comments like those made by Jay-Z. Does it matter that Jay-Z called the president the N-word? Does it matter that he also disrespected the former president on the inauguration night of a "historic" presidency? In my mind, neither are appropriate—to say the least. Consider that Obama has advocated bringing the political parties together. If he fails to rebuke Jay-Z (which is what I predict), what does this say about his desire to bring the country together?

What you can readily discern is that a dilemma is developing that will inevitably become much more difficult to resolve. President Obama has essentially two choices: either rebuke partisan and racist comments or stay silent. While I do not expect Obama to be one of the "bomb throwers," there are plenty of these on both sides of the fence. When these inevitable comments are made, what does he do? If he rebukes his "side," then it will be like "shooting himself in the foot." If he does so, particularly if the rebuked person is black, then how long will it take before he is criticized as being an "Uncle Tom"? Remember, while the media, his supporters, and the "thinkers" consider Barack Obama as "black," thereby making his presidency "historic," the fact is he is half white. If he sides with the "other side," how long will it take to be attacked as "Uncle Tom" and other divisive words? Remember words count. History dies hard. On the other "side," some might see this as "the final insult—a black man in the White House." [40]

Consider also an editorial by Joseph C. Phillips. In writing for blackamerica.com, he asserts that Obama's presidential run has always been about race. He contends that it not "race" as we most often envision it. It is not race-"ism." He pointedly asserts, as I do, that most Americans are tired of race and are looking to move beyond it in a concrete way. Part of the excitement around Obama was the potential to realize a vision of an America that finally lives up to her promise—"a promise that is impossible so long as we are stratified by color and class consciousness."[41] What Americans believe in is his ability to bring us one step closer to the embodiment of our national motto "E pluribus unum"—out of many, one. According to Phillips, however, the irony is that Obama needs race. He asserts that without it "the emperor has few clothes." The key question is whether Obama "is committed to the idea of racial non-discrimination and that his vision of an America moving beyond the old conversations about race." I contend that in order to demonstrate this commitment he will have to confront racial provocateurs and racial preferences. He cannot do so because, if he does, he will sever his own party. By failing to do so, he will then prove to the "other side" that it is, indeed, all about race. Consequently, Phillips concludes[42]

> … so finally it must come down to race—not the ethnicity of either candidate, but their willingness to transcend old conversations of race in this country. At the same time, his support of preferences based on race belies the nobility of his speech and the vision that made him a star.

Ironically, race was used in the controversy over replacing Obama's senate seat. During this controversy, many made the case that his senate seat "must" be filled by another black. When the Illinois governor was arrested for allegedly attempting to sell the seat to the highest bidder, he effectively turned the tables and appointed Roland Burris. Although Burris is black, he was not backed by the "political machine." When the senate leadership threatened not to allow Burris to be seated, congressman and former Black Panther Bobby Rush stated, "I would ask you to not hang or lynch the appointee. … And I don't think any senators want to go on the record to deny an African-American from taking a seat in the U.S. Senate." This thinly veiled threat caused *Chicago Tribune* columnist John Kass, who has made a career out of investigating the Chicago "political machine," to state the obvious: "Isn't that the old politics of race that Obama was to have transcended for us?"[43]

Regardless of the fact that many well-intentioned people desire to rise above race, any belief that this presidency will be "post-racial" is to deny reality. Indeed, I contend the opposite will occur. Race will be used as a sword and as a shield. As a sword, it will be used to attack the "racists" whenever it is convenient. As a shield, it will be used to divert criticism from policy adversaries. The tag of "racist" will be used against those who disagree. You may think I am overstating the point. I hope I am. I also realize some of you have decided I am a "racist" because I address this subject. I expect that. It is part of the deep-seated nature of race in this country. I expect this will be the "reward" I get for my desire to warn. I will be happy to live with this tag as I attempt to deliver this message!

Now take it even deeper. Combine religion into this racial and political mix. Religion becomes relevant for two reasons. First, it equates with the "Holy War" developed in this book. While I have largely focused on Islamists in this Holy War analysis, the fact remains that both white and black nationalistic churches also are part of this larger war.

In this light, consider what I view as an extraordinary—and dangerous—precept to a predicted increase in extremism, that is, the fact that President Obama's former church, Trinity United Church of Christ, had an overt underlying racial orientation. If Barack Obama had not been a member of this church, it would have little, if any, national attention—or consequence. However, he was a member for 20 years. He quit the church and renounced Reverend Wright during the spring of 2008. This occurred when the Obama campaign was being criticized for the provocative words of the good reverend. In my mind, the words of Reverend Wright were a sideshow. Like any other long-time minister, he has made thousands of sermons over the course of a long career on the pulpit. His provocative words do not trouble me nearly as much as the nature of the church. Indeed, those who argue that Reverend Wright's inflammatory sermons were taken "out of context," are hard-pressed to explain away the underlying premises of the church. To look at their Web site, it is hard not to come to the conclusion that race is an underlying premise of the organization.

Trinity United Church of Christ is based on a black nationalistic message— otherwise known as "black liberation theology." To get a sense of the larger worldview of this church, view its beliefs posted on its Web site. It states, in pertinent part, as follows[44] (emphasis added):

> We are a congregation which is Un-ashamedly *Black* and Unapologetically Christian. ... Our roots in the *Black* religious experience and tradition are deep, lasting and permanent. We are an African people, and remain "true to our native land," the mother continent, the cradle of civilization. God has superintended our pilgrimage through the days of slavery, the days of segregation, and the long night of racism. It

is God who gives us the strength and courage to continuously address injustice as a people, and as a congregation. We constantly affirm our trust in God through cultural expression of a *Black* worship service and ministries which address the *Black* Community.

Let me explain the significance of my concern. Any religion that has a racially polarizing orientation will serve to balkanize society around deeply held "spiritual" justifications. I will introduce this assertion by asking this question: What makes racial nationalistic churches problematic? Consider two books: *Black Theology and Black Power* and *The White Man's Bible*. Ask yourself, which one is acceptable? Why?

Whatever your answer to my provocative questions, consider the source of these books. *Black Theology and Black Power* is on sale at the Trinity United Church of Christ. Indeed, this book is not simply "for sale" at the church. The church's Web site trumpets this book as the basis of its beliefs. To use their words,[45]

> The vision statement of Trinity United Church of Christ is based upon the systematized liberation theology that started in 1969 with the publication of Dr. James Cone's book, *Black Theology and Black Power*.

In its Web site, the church also advocated a "black value system." They explain that "African-centered thought, unlike Euro-centrism, does not assume superiority and look at everyone else as being inferior."[46] I see their message as essentially saying "we are right" because our value system does not advocate superiority, unlike those Eurocentrism people, who believe they are superior. While I agree on one level, some groups (as below) believe they are indeed superior, I assert that the "black value system," even if not explicitly designed to signify "superiority," is inevitably separatist. Indeed, the church adopted these values in 1981. In both May 2005 and November 2006, the church's Web site included the following language:[47]

> We believe in the following 12 precepts and covenantal statements. These Black Ethics must be taught and exemplified in homes, churches, nurseries and schools, wherever Blacks are gathered. They must reflect on the following concepts [emphasis added]:

> 1. Commitment to God
> 2. Commitment to the *Black* Community
> 3. Commitment to the *Black* Family
> 4. Dedication to the Pursuit of Education
> 5. Dedication to the Pursuit of Excellence
> 6. Adherence to the *Black* Work Ethic
> 7. Commitment to Self-Discipline and Self-Respect
> 8. Disavowal of the Pursuit of "Middleclassness"

9. Pledge to make the fruits of all developing and acquired skills available to the *Black* Community
10. Pledge to Allocate Regularly, a Portion of Personal Resources for Strengthening and Supporting *Black* Institutions
11. Pledge allegiance to all *Black* leadership who espouse and embrace the *Black* Value System
12. Personal commitment to embracement of the *Black* Value System.

Consider the overt racial nature of these values. Why does the church focus on black, instead of simply focusing on people? Does God focus on the color of your skin? In my mind, when an organization—particularly a church—uses race as an underlying basis of its creed, it can become a source of division and divisiveness. Three points on this latter assertion: First, if a church used the term "white" each time Trinity United Church of Christ used the term "black," how would the white church be viewed? I am quite certain it would be viewed as "racist." If this standard applies to a white church, why does it not apply to the black church? Second, if this "black value system" is not problematic, why did they remove it from their Web site shortly after their ideology was revealed during the presidential campaign? Indeed, after Reverend Wright's comments during his sermons at this church became part of the Obama campaign, the 12-point "Black Value System" was removed from the Trinity United Church of Christ Web site. Checking the Web site on May 3, 2008, revealed the above 12 precepts had been removed.[48] Ironically, sometime *after* the election of President Obama, the black value system was placed back on the Web site.[49] Is this simply a coincidence? I am doubtful. In my eyes, these facts speak volumes.

Finally, if a white politician had been a 20-year member of a church that maintained a "white value system," do you think that politician would have even a remote chance to be president? Alternatively, what do the premises of Trinity United Church of Christ say about Barack Obama's mindset? It is particularly ironic that if these racially oriented premises, subscribed to by his long-time church, are compared to the "unifying" message of the Obama campaign, it leads one to ask the obvious question: Can you advocate national "unity" while being a member of a church that openly advocates black centrist and black nationalist messages? This question is best left answered by the reader.

This leads to the question posed earlier: When and if it is acceptable to advocate a separatist and balkanized society. Some would argue it is acceptable for blacks, but not for whites—because of slavery and the effects of historical and contemporary discrimination.

This assertion, however, must also deal with the implications of opposing views, such as those advocated by the readers of the *White Man's Bible,* which was published by the founder of the Church of the Creator. Also included in this group ideology are other infamous books including *The Struggle Facts* and *What the Government and the Media Don't Want You To Know.*

This white supremacist "church" openly advocates racial separation. The Church of the Creator (also known as "Creativity") advocates[50]

> the proposition that the white race is "nature's highest creation" and that "white people are the creators of all worthwhile culture and civilization." Followers of the WCOTC do not believe in God, heaven, hell or eternal life. They consider Jews and nonwhites, whom they refer to as "mud races," to be the "natural enemies" of the white race. They follow the "Golden Rule" which means what is good for the white race is the highest virtue. What is bad for the white race is the ultimate sin.

The Creativity Movement, whose motto is "RaHoWa" (Racial Holy War), proclaims that its belief system, Creativity, "is a racial religion" whose primary goal is the "survival, expansion, and advancement of [the] White Race exclusively." Their view of religion is simple: "Our race is our religion."[51] To these people, race is everything: the white race is "nature's highest creation." Their ideology provides extremist rhetoric. Indeed, to them "every issue, whether religious, political or racial ... [should be] viewed through the eyes of the White Man and exclusively from the point of view of the White race as a whole." Ultimately, WCOTC hopes to organize white people to achieve world domination, "free from alien control and free from pollution of alien races. ... Only on the basis of recognizing our enemies, destroying and/or excluding them and practicing racial teamwork can a stable lasting government be built."[52] The extremist ideology of this group may be best illustrated from this quote from the *White Man's Bible,* which says,[53]

> We of the CHURCH OF THE CREATOR are not hypocrites. We openly state that some people need killing, that killing has always been with us and will always be with us. ... Killing our enemies, too, is under certain circumstances a necessary measure for the survival of our own race. Therefore we condone it, and it, too, is no sin in our religion.

This "racial religion's" commitment to race can be viewed through the notion that loyalty to the race is the greatest of honors. Conversely, they view racial treason as the worst of crimes. This movement is gaining steam. The scope of these white supremacist movements is growing with the election of President Obama.[54] In an attempt to gain membership, a theme of the group speaks to these implications: "White people awake! Save the white race!"[55] This blatant attempt to use race to induce both fear and identity is dangerous.

Given these juxtapositions, I ask the question again: Which one of these books is acceptable? In my mind, the only consistent answer is, neither is acceptable. If your answer is different than mine, then I respectfully say that your answer is part of the problem. I do not ask that you believe me, just consider the words of Dr.

Martin Luther King, who so powerfully stated, "I have a dream that my four little children will one day live in a nation where they will not be judged by the color of their skin but by the *content of their character*." In short, the more we justify "group think" based on *color of the skin,* the more likely racial groups will oppose each other. Now add politics back into the mix. The emotion, power, and implications of politics *will add violence to the implications of group think.* I know that this statement will offend some. More than likely the same people offended by this statement are those who will justify one of the above books—while condemning the other! To those who think this way, my response is you cannot have it both ways. Can you criticize my views, while ignoring the implications of your views? Nonetheless, I am quite sure you have "justified" your views and the error of my "inflammatory rhetoric." I answer these likely criticisms with four provocative questions. I will view these as rhetorical in nature, as the "answers" to these questions are likely to have little consensus—and provoke some consternation and controversy. Please think about your "answers" to these questions:

- Question #1: Do you think racial nationalistic religions are "innocent"?
- Question #2: Do you think they can incite violence?
- Question #3: Can we be "unified" and racially nationalistic at the same time?
- Question #4: Can we have one standard for white nationalistic religions and another for black nationalistic religions? If so, what implications does this portend?

Hopefully you see my provocative prose as a way of making a point. The larger point, in my mind, is that the failure to move away from racial and nationalistic identities will inevitably result in conflict. A classic example of the emphasis on group identity is seen in the much-trumpeted notion of "diversity" along with its related legal mandate of affirmative action. Think about the underlying basis of diversity and affirmative action. While some of the principles inherent in these are sound and powerful, I believe many are using these concepts to further racial, gender, and nationalistic identities. While this assertion may be controversial, please consider my logic related to diversity and affirmative action.

First, when was the last time you heard the term "the melting pot"? The principle inherent in this term was designed to bring many diverse cultures together around a larger American identity. This notion recognized that in order to maintain a peaceful, cohesive society, there must be some "glue" or larger purpose that holds diverse cultures together.

Second, I am respectful and fascinated by various cultural norms, foods, customs, languages, and the like. These traditions are wonderful and should be maintained. I believe that some advocates of diversity, however, are not interested in the larger American culture. These individuals do not desire the "melting pot." Instead, they seek to enhance their own group identity. If you believe this assertion is incorrect, why do we have racial and ethnic groups of all stripes and types, from student groups to bar associations; from community groups to congressional caucuses; from industry associations to educational curricula? If these groups are interested in blending into American society, why do we still need balkanized associations? Over 40 years after historic civil rights legislation was passed, balkanized groups still find it necessary to have their "own" associations. Is it necessary that black students have their own student groups and even their own proms? Surely some of these groups are innocent, inconsequential, and even appropriate. To illustrate the balkanizing implications of this logic, consider this question: What would be the response if white groups decided to have their own "white only" groups and "white only" proms? Would the "civil rights," cultural, and political leaders justify such segregation? Would these groups be defended and advocated by the compelling need for diversity?

The larger public policy concern, however, is that diversity—and affirmative action—is grounded on group identity. The very nature of these concepts advocates "group consciousness." They require people to think about group identity. They advocate using race, nationality, gender, and other group identity as a way of promoting "diversity" and as a way of providing opportunities in the workplace or in government contracts. In my mind, this will not promote a unified society. It will not promote a "post-racial" society. Indeed, when group consciousness is promoted by legal and cultural standards, the more logical result is a balkanized society. When group consciousness is promoted by the power of law and by the "thought leaders" within the society, is it unreasonable to believe that this may contribute to the separation of groups around racial, cultural, and gender-based interests? Let me answer my own question: These group consciousness or group identity approaches will inevitably promote a balkanized society.

If one plays out the logical conclusion of diversity and affirmative action, it may be useful to think of the "end game." Ask yourself how these questions are going to be answered: When does the logic of discriminating against one group (whites) for past discrimination against another group (blacks) result in a level playing field? When do we know that equity has been achieved? How does one know when the playing field has been leveled? Who makes this determination? Some will assert that the courts, particularly the U.S. Supreme Court, have the power to make that determination. While this may be technically true, is any such decision going to be embraced? When shall those on either side of the affirmative action debate come to accept any decision that is adverse to their interests? Under what circumstances will we know when this should occur? Of course, these questions bring together racial, legal, and political implications. They bring together this combustible mixture at a time when the economy and political system can ill afford to "resolve" these vexing questions. Indeed, polling during the campaign by the Quinnipiac University Polling Institute suggested that Obama's continued support for racial preferences will hurt him.[56] While this did not affect the presidential campaign, as I pointed out above, it will be an issue during his presidency. In this way, those who advocate the balkanizing effects of diversity and affirmative action must be prepared for the implications of such. Of course, those who have an interest in maintaining these "group think" concepts will not recognize that they may be precursors to violence.

As problematic as this mixture is, there are some group associations that are even more dangerous. Consider the impact of a racial nationalist religion. Is a white or black centric church as harmless as a student association? I think not. The typical student is usually more concerned with grades, parties, and other activities. Conversely, the depth of emotion and commitment from religion far exceeds those of a group of students. As developed in this book, the election of Barack Obama has set in motion an interesting—and potentially dangerous—mix of race, religion, and politics. Please do not reject this assertion outright.

Indeed, this is the "third rail" of American society. Many people are even afraid to mention that this "exists." Many, if not most, Americans have been taught not to talk about these issues as they will inevitably alienate or offend people. This should illustrate how intense these feelings are. It should also illustrate that these issues involve interests and power. In developing this book, I tried to be very careful and objective in even raising these issues, as I understand the impact of them. Consequently, this is exactly why they should be considered "triggers."

The mere fact that most people shy away from these issues demonstrates that we must confront them. For example, when the "Reverend Wright" controversy broke in the spring of 2008, Barack Obama gave a highly regarded speech on race. His speech was trumpeted by numerous pundits. It was hailed as the *definitive speech on race*. Within a week or so after the speech, it seemed to disappear into the campaign. When is the last time you heard reference to this speech? The larger point is that the mixture of race, religion, and politics is so divisive that people seem to naturally gravitate away from it. When it rears its ugly head, we deal with it—at some level—and then let it go as quickly as we can. This is, in my mind, what happened to the *definitive speech on race* delivered by then candidate Obama. As developed in this section, I am not optimistic that we will be able to effectively deal with this combustible mixture of race, religion, and politics. Regardless of your race, your religion, or your party, we all need to be cognizant of these implications.

Law and the Political System

Since every extremist group justifies its violence based on some notion that they are following a "higher law," it is critical that we consider the implications of the legal and political system. There are two key components of this thinking. First, the notion that "we are a country of laws, not of men," is becoming increasingly important. By this I mean the system of law must guide our policies and our social fabric. It is critical that we adhere to legal principles, and strictly avoid any impression that laws favor one group or class more than any other. Unfortunately, as important as this is, as inferred in the above discussion, this is easy to say and difficult to achieve. Please allow me to develop this point.

As an attorney I am quite familiar with questions often posed by clients who are trying to get a sense of the legal system. Their questions typically sound something like these examples: What does the law say about this? Is this legal? How can the judge make this decision when the *law* does not support that? These questions are grounded on the notion that the law is some mechanical device that one only needs to apply to certain facts. The reality is the law is often very subjective. This is particularly true for large public policy issues that have some political component. Issues such as abortion, affirmative action, discrimination, harassment, civil rights violations, and the like are embedded with a subjective component. While each of these legal theories has certain tests and standards to assess the cause of action, in the end these tests and standards cannot be completely objective. The classic example is the notion of "reasonableness." Attorneys argue this concept hundreds of times per day. Courtrooms and court briefs are literally riddled with competing arguments over this concept. No matter how persuasive, no matter how precise, no matter how pointed one's argument is, the decision on what is "reasonable" in any case is often based on degrees of nuance.

While it is beyond the scope of this book to go much deeper into this assertion, suffice it to say that critical *legal* assessments are based less on the law than on a particular decision maker's assessment of the "best" public policy. In this sense, the law shapes public policy, which is often determined by the subjective worldview of the court (i.e., judge, jury, panel). This is not meant to criticize our legal system. I believe this system is as good as humans can create. However, it is flawed because it is operated by humans—and humans are flawed. My larger point, however, is that critical public policy decisions are often made under the guise of a particular *black letter law,* when in fact they are simply subjective policy decisions.

The question of abortion is a classic example. Whatever your opinion of the appropriateness of abortion, the question of its *legality* is really a question of whose rights will prevail. Do the mother's rights trump those of the fetus? This question was decided in *Roe v. Wade*, and its progeny, in the affirmative. Part of the logic of the decision was that the fetus has not yet become a "person." Unless—and until—the fetus becomes a "person," no "rights" are availed. This is so because the constitution only provides rights to "persons." Ironically, the animal rights advocates are pushing the envelope in the opposite direction. They seek to define animals as "persons." This status gives them the basis to enforce their "rights" to object to being caged and subsequently killed by humans. Indeed, they advocate *speciesism* to complain that humans are destroying the animal population, similar to how humans who destroy a particular human population are guilty of *genocide.*

This is the same "logic" used to deny slaves rights under the Constitution. Back then, slaves were not quite "persons." Instead they were considered only three fifths of a "person." Consider the lasting impact of this "compromise." It has caused terrible human suffering for generations of blacks who were treated as "property" by slave owners. It has contributed to a pervasive prejudice against a race of people due almost exclusively to their skin color. It has resulted in numerous legal and public policy decisions that segregated people along racial lines. It has contributed—or resulted—in a bloody civil war. It has contributed to another hundred years of resentment and hostility between two landmark events: emancipation and the civil rights legislation. In short, one is struck by the magnitude of attempting to "resolve" irretractable issues by way of "compromise." This same dilemma presents itself in the triggers outlined in this chapter.

I trust you see where I am going with this argument. In the end, *the law* is what the decision makers say it is. In the context of extremism and terrorism, the key concern is whether we as a society can "justify" that our laws are, indeed, worth adhering to. Said another way, can our legal system prevail over the "higher law" that some extremist group advocates? This question is often based on who has the higher moral standing. Who has the "right" to assert which law should prevail? In a civilized society, this "right" belongs to the government—and its legal system. As we have seen throughout this book, many groups have developed ideologies that directly compete with this notion. Indeed, one of the key characteristics of terrorism is that it challenges the notion that the government is valid. It also challenges the notion that laws derived from government are valid.

The most obvious example of this competing ideology is with radical Islam (also see the section Constitution versus Sharia Law below). The "logic" of the Islamists is that the Koran and Sharia law equate with their Constitution. When any human law conflicts with these Allah-inspired writings, the human law is of no avail. If your human law does not relent to Allah-inspired law then it can be ignored. If any human *system or government* stands in the way of implementing Allah laws then it can be *legally* suppressed or destroyed. Take this logic one step further. Those who kill and die in a jihad[57] (holy war) are rewarded with paradise. This reward is *guaranteed* to those engaged in jihad. Therefore, in this war for Allah, killing and dying is not a crime. Instead, it is the ultimate sacrifice that deserves the highest recognition and reward. Ultimately, Allah's will and laws trump the legal and political system devised by humans.

Similar logic has been used throughout history. Aristotle instructed that it was one's *civic duty* to kill a despot ruler. Caesar, Lincoln, McKinley, and others died by this logic. Similar logic also prevails in contemporary America. Think of the white supremacists who see the system as corrupt. Think of the black nationalists who see the system as racist. Think of the environmentalists and the animal rights advocates who see the capitalistic system as killing the planet and innocent animals. Think of the antiabortionists who view the U.S. Supreme Court as "murderers." Against these competing ideologies—and within an increasingly competitive world that is vying for limited resources—this country must accomplish the extraordinarily delicate duty of maintaining the legitimacy of law. It must do so by accounting for the interests of myriad and often competing groups. As this book has made clear, this is an increasingly difficult task.

The significance of this challenge may be illustrated by a few examples. Consider gay marriage in terms of the *black letter law*. When one looks to the "law," the definition of marriage is quite clear: one man and one woman. In terms of the meaning of the language, this is not too difficult to comprehend. However, in terms of the interests involved, it is much more difficult. Whatever your opinion of the merits of this issue, you must agree that this is a "trigger." Neither side of the debate will be satisfied. Based on some of the incidents following the recent Proposition Eight decision in California, you must also agree that violence may result. Indeed, it already has. Also consider the continued application of affirmative action, particularly in an economy where fewer jobs are available and where people may become increasingly desperate. Regardless of the merits of law, can you envision this being a "trigger," especially during the current administration? The logic will sound like this: Minorities will resent it if the law is changed. Whites will resent it if the law is not changed. Ironically, whites are or will soon be statistical "minorities." How does this impact the viability of the law?

The second point related to this section relates to the interplay between politics and the law. Based on the two previous elections (2000 and 2004), the country was almost "perfectly" divided. The election of Barack Obama, who won by a handsome margin, changed the percentages to about 52–48 percent. Even with this ratio, the country is still politically divided. As mentioned earlier, President Obama has a substantial challenge if he is truly interested in bringing the parties together. Remember, words count: "There is not a liberal America and a conservative America—there is the United States of America. There is not a Black America and a White America and Latino America and Asian America—there's the United States of America."[58] As a leader, President Obama will have the burden of achieving this goal of bringing the country together. When Bush promised to "change the tone in Washington," he was castigated because he failed to do so. Indeed, the mantra that "he was a divider, not a uniter" was like a mantle hanging on his administration. While I have my opinion as to who was most accountable for this division, suffice it to say the tables are now turned. The burden is on the leader to make unity happen. It will be interesting to see how "unified" our politicians become—and who gets the blame if they are not "united."

An interesting early test of this question has to do with the desire of some Democrats to investigate certain Bush Administration officials—possibly including Bush for allegedly committing crimes related to the "war on terror." Indeed, Representative John Conyers, the powerful chairman of the House Judiciary Committee, announced he wants to set up a commission to look into whether the Bush Administration broke the law by taking the nation to war against Iraq and instituting aggressive antiterror initiatives. The Michigan Democrat called for an "independent criminal probe into whether any laws were broken in connection with these activities." To the date of this writing, President Obama appears, again, to be trying to "thread the needle." He stated, "I don't believe that anybody is above the law," but he added, "On the other hand, I also have a belief that we need to look forward as opposed to looking backwards." House speaker Nancy Pelosi was a bit more assertive. She stated that "the law might compel" Democrats to press forth on some prosecutions of Bush Administration officials, saying they may not "have a right to ignore" the allegations.[59] If they decide they cannot "ignore" these allegations and move forward with prosecutions it will create a political free-for-all—and possibly a constitutional crisis. Space does not allow me to flesh out the implications of this issue. One brief point on this note: If these "policy" decisions become a source of criminal investigation, we will abandon a long-standing precedent from one administration to another. Suffice it to say, if you want comity you must exercise discretion.

Whether or not these investigations take place, it would be wise to critically assess how bridges can be built between the parties. This will only be accomplished by working on compromises for issues that are ripe for such, and by disagreeing on principle for issues that are not ready for compromise. The critical consideration is that *both* parties must avoid demonizing each other. Watch how this plays out. If Washington politicians cannot get along, how do you expect those who are struggling to find a job and pay the bills will feel about the government? Why would these people find common ground when the "leaders" fail to do so?

Finally, pay attention to corruption in government. While I cannot statistically validate this sense, it seems that the number of government corruption cases have increased in recent years. Maybe I am wrong. Of course, the fact that I live in Chicago may have some impact on my thinking. While it may give you some sense to list the names of recently "affected" politicians, it may be suffice to simply state the obvious: If political leaders do not follow the law, then we should not expect those disconnected from "the system," to do so! As we go forward, pay attention to both the criminal and ethical misdeeds of our elected and appointed leaders. This particularly includes police officers and police officials. While I have much regard for police officers and the difficulties of police work, I do not excuse police corruption. An example of the corrupting and corrosive influences of police corruption was illustrated in the powerful movie titled *Pride and Glory*.[60] The impact of "law enforcement" corruption can result in widespread implications—both within policing and in the larger society. Remember this adage: Terrorists adhere to a "higher law." If our legal system is deemed corrupt, then those who seek to ignore the law—or to destroy "the system"—are much more powerful. This also makes the destruction of the system much more likely!

Constitution and Sharia Law

As described above, the potential conflicts between the constitution and Sharia law are not only likely, they are to be expected. A classic example is with daily prayer. Each Muslim is required to pray five times a day. It is one of the five required "pillars" of Islam.[61] These prayers are to take place at regular intervals. It stands to reason that these daily prayers must be implemented into an individual's daily regimen. In some circumstances this may be readily accomplished. As a public school student, however, these prayers present a potential for constitutional conflicts. For example, at Carver Elementary School in San Diego, controversy rose when it was learned that school administrators had instituted an afternoon "recess" to allow Muslim students to pray. Since the U.S. Constitution specifically prohibits any public school to "sanction" prayer, the San Diego school was forced to rescind this practice. A similar situation occurred in Minnesota.

Some may be asking, what is the big deal? Why prohibit this prayer? The obvious answer is that the legal system cannot preclude prayer for some religions, while allowing it for others. The principle of "equal protection" would preclude such. Therefore, unless the U.S. Supreme Court reverses its long-standing principle of "separation of church [or mosque] and state," then the practice of sanctioning prayers in public schools is prohibited. Further, if schools attempt to get "creative" to allow some informal prayer time, then they risk a backlash from the followers of Christianity, Judaism, and other religions. I would remind the reader that this issue is very potent. Many people hold prayer very dearly. As a society, we need to be cognizant of this fact. We would be on a very slippery slope if we attempted to find legal or even informal "accommodations" around this issue. As stated above, if it appears that *the law* is really a "moving target" without any principled basis, then it will invite disrespect for the law. Consequently, this is an issue without balance. It has to be applied strictly—or not at all. Indeed, if the constitutional principle were changed, it would be perceived as designed to accommodate Muslim practices. This would also be a dangerous change to make. Hence, this is a classic "damned if you do and damned if you don't" situation.

Another difficult balance relates to another First Amendment right. This deals with freedom of speech. An example of this issue can be seen in Europe. In the Netherlands, a Freedom Party leader named Geert Wilders produced a film called *Fitna*. This film juxtaposed verses from the Koran against a background of violent film clips and images of terrorism by Islamic radicals. The publication of the film caused uproar in many European and Middle Eastern countries. An Amsterdam appeals court recently ruled against Wilders, saying that he could be criminally prosecuted for the film. The court further decided that the film contained "one-sided generalizations ... which can amount to inciting hatred." This ruling reversed a decision last year by the public prosecutor's office, which said Wilders' film and interviews were painful for Muslims but not criminal. On his behalf, Wilders told Dutch media "it was a black day for myself and for freedom of speech."[62]

The appeals court decision rested on weighing Wilders' anti-Islamic rhetoric against his right to free speech. This "legal test," of course, is on its face subjective. The court ruled he had gone beyond the normal leeway given to politicians. While judges in the Netherlands generally are loath to become involved in public debate, the court said it was making an exception in this case. The court explained the rationale for this exception. It stated, "The court considers this so insulting for Muslims that it is in the *public interest* to prosecute Wilders" (emphasis added). This decision set the stage for what will likely be a highly charged trial. It will touch on declining Dutch tolerance toward a large immigrant population from Muslim countries.[63]

I trust that the reader can discern the freedom of speech issues raised by this case. Do you have any concern that courts may seek to weigh the balance against freedom of speech in order to facilitate public order and safety? Is this good or bad? Could this occur in the United States? I believe it will.

Another issue that will likely create a legal challenge deals with an inmate's right to access religious instruction. In this regard, please consider the discussion about imams within the prison system from the previous chapter. The concern was that radical imams may act as "spiritual sanctioners" to inspire inmates toward a radicalized version of Islam. Whether or not you consider this a legitimate threat, the question is this: Can correctional officials restrict an inmate's access to religious teachings and services without violating the inmate's constitutional right to freedom of religion?[64] This requires a delicate balance between monitoring the beliefs, backgrounds, and teachings of imams (or other ministers) against the privacy and sanctity of religious prayer, study, and worship. These are substantial and compelling issues. These legal and operational questions are evolving, and they promise to become more prominent in the years ahead. It will be a challenge to legally and safely effectuate this balance.

Finally, the potential implications of Sharia law and the U.S. legal system are larger than the Bill of Rights. Indeed, common law and legislatively enacted statutes relating to divorce, spousal rights and abuse, women's rights, clothing and privacy norms, and a host of other potential issues may present legal challenges. My only caution here is if "exceptions" are made from legal norms and principles, then we must be prepared for increasing disrespect for the law. As seen in the Wilders case, "exceptions" from established law for the benefit of a specific group may result in widespread questions as to the nature of the system. These questions will result in reduced trust and adherence to the legal and political system. It is a slippery slope, indeed, to try to balance the interests of specific groups with those of the larger society. We must be very careful as this slope has great "downside" potential!

Sovereignty

The notion of sovereignty is embedded in a number of contemporary issues. Consider that each of these issues impacts the notion of sovereignty: immigration, the "new world order," environmentalism, and even the approach to international relations. The international relations aspect largely relates to the question of when and why we need support to make decisions. There are strong opinions on both sides of this issue. It is beyond the scope of this book to debate the merits of this assertion. It is important to consider, however, that this issue strikes at powerful notions of sovereignty and patriotism versus the desire to live as a "community of nations."

The environmentalism aspects of sovereignty were outlined above in the Energy and the Environment section. Beyond these points, the Kyoto treaty is an excellent example of the pointed arguments made on this question. In essence, the debate is centered on whether this country should make energy and emissions decisions based on a self-interested view of what is good for our economy. Conversely, should these decisions be tied to a larger world community? Similarly, those in opposition to the "new world order" include an interesting mix of liberal, conservative, religious, secular, labor, anarchist, anti-WTO (World Trade Organization), environmental, and a host of other "interest groups" who fear the pending world government. The fact that such diverse groups could coalesce around this issue is rather amazing (for additional discussion of these groups see Chapter 3). This is especially pointed since these groups would likely disagree on almost every other public policy issue. In my mind, the fact that the fear of the new world order crosses these ideology spectrums makes it a ripe issue for violence. Indeed, the WTO riots in Seattle were a clear example of this.

Similarly, the immigration debate encompasses a number of interrelated factors, including economics, culture, language, religion—and sovereignty. The gist of these arguments were captured by the below public commentary. It was allegedly written by Barry Loudermilk, an Air Force veteran who sent it to the *Bartow Trader* newspaper in Georgia in 2005.[65] Some feel these remarks are "dead on," while others consider it racist. Regardless of where you stand on the issue, this has become one of the most popular rants about what many perceive as political correctness run amok.[66] The relative merits of this commentary, or how it fits into your worldview, are somewhat irrelevant. In short, one is hard-pressed to deny that these are strong sentiments. The significance of such is that strong sentiments can—or will—equate to direct action. With that said, the commentary is as follows:

> I, for one, am quite disturbed by these actions of so-called American citizens; and I am tired of this nation worrying about whether or not we are offending some individual or their culture.
>
> Since the terrorist attacks on September 11, we have experienced a surge in patriotism by the majority of Americans. However, the dust from the attacks had barely settled in New York and Washington D.C. when the "politically correct" crowd began complaining about the possibility that our patriotism was offending others.
>
> I am not against immigration, nor do I hold a grudge against anyone who is seeking a better life by coming to America. In fact, our country's population is almost entirely composed of descendants of immigrants; however, there are a few things that those who have recently come to our country, and apparently some native Americans, need to understand.
>
> First of all, it is not our responsibility to continually try not to offend you in any way. This idea of America being a multicultural community has served only to dilute our sovereignty and our national identity. As

Americans, we have our own culture, our own society, our own language, and our own lifestyle. This culture, called the "American Way" has been developed over centuries of struggles, trials, and victories by millions of men and women who have sought freedom.

Our forefathers fought, bled, and died at places such as Bunker Hill, San Juan, Iwo Jima, Normandy, Korea, Vietnam. We speak English, not Spanish, Arabic, Chinese, Japanese, Russian, or any other language. Therefore, if you wish to become part of our society—learn our language! "In God We Trust" is our national motto. This is not some off-the-wall, Christian, Right Wing, political slogan—it is our national motto. It is engraved in stone in the House of Representatives in our Capitol and it is printed on our currency. We adopted this motto because Christian men and women, on Christian principles, founded this nation; and this is clearly documented throughout our history. If it is appropriate for our motto to be inscribed in the halls of our highest level of Government, then it is certainly appropriate to display it on the walls of our schools. God is in our pledge, our National Anthem, nearly every patriotic song, and in our founding documents. We honor His birth, death, and resurrection as holidays, and we turn to Him in prayer in times of crisis. If God offends you, then I suggest you consider another part of the world as your new home, because God is part of our culture and we are proud to have Him.

We are proud of our heritage and those who have so honorably defended our freedoms. We celebrate Independence Day, Memorial Day, Veterans Day, and Flag Day. We have parades, picnics, and barbecues where we proudly wave our flag. As an American, I have the right to wave my flag, sing my national anthem, quote my national motto, and cite my pledge whenever and wherever I choose. If the Stars and Stripes offend you, or you don't like Uncle Sam, then you should seriously consider a move to another part of this planet.

The American culture is our way of life, our heritage, and we are proud of it. We are happy with our culture and have no desire to change, and we really don't care how you did things where you came from. We are Americans, like it or not, this is our country, our land, and our lifestyle.

Our First Amendment gives every citizen the right to express his opinion about our government, culture, or society, and we will allow you every opportunity to do so. But once you are done complaining, whining, and griping about our flag, our pledge, our national motto, or our way of life, I highly encourage you to take advantage of one other great American freedom, the right to leave. If you agree, pass this onto other Americans!! It is time to take action.

It is my hope that these examples alert the reader to potential extremist triggers. Let's end with one proposition that we can all agree on: Many, if not all, of the triggers described above are embedded with strongly held convictions or interests. Regardless of your personal beliefs, it is fair to say that many people have strong views on abortion, energy and the environment, the economy, police shootings, the Constitution, and the sovereignty of American society. In my mind, these are taken as a "given." The next chapter provides recommendations for ways to minimize the impact of these triggers—and discusses some implications of extremism for the larger society.

Endnotes

1. Gladwell, Malcolm (2002). *The Tipping Point*. New York: Little Brown and Company.
2. Gladwell, Malcolm (2002), op. cit., 9.
3. Fields, Gary (2008). "Murder Spike Poses Quandary," *Wall Street Journal*, May 6, A16.
4. Johnson, Carrie (2009). "Bad Economy May Fuel Hate Groups, Experts Warn," *Washington Post*, January 11, A4.
5. Johnson, Carrie (2009), op. cit., A4.
6. Drake, Laura (2009). "Fear and Loathing over B.C. Pipeline Blasts," *Edmonton Journal*, January 10. http://www.canada.com/topics/news/national/story.html?id=1164587.
7. "Green Energy Problem," *Fox News Channel*, January 15, 2009.
8. Faiola, Anthony and Steven Mufson (2007). "N.Y. Airport Target of Plot, Officials Say," *Washington Post*, June 3, A1; and "Terror Incidents in the U.S. Since the 9/11 Attacks" (2008). *Counter-Terrorism* 1, no. 1 (May/June):53.
9. "Man Accused of Plotting to Blow Up Pipelines," *Reuters*, July 9, 2007.
10. http://news.yahoo.com/s/ap/20070911/ap_on_re_la_am_ca/mexico_pipeline_explosions;_ ylt=As7RaBpyvVpL0dX8FG5BvwC3IxIF, September 11, 2007.
11. Smith, Janet (2008). "Earth Worship: Environmentalism Seen as Police State Precursor," *Intelligence Report* Winter. http://www.splcenter.org/intel/intelreport/article.jsp?aid=968 (retrieved on December 10, 2008).
12. Smith, Janet (2008), op. cit.
13. Robb, John (2007). "The Coming Urban Terror: Systems Disruption, Networked Gangs, and Bioweapons," *City Journal* Summer. http://www.city-journal.org/html/17_3_urban_terrorism.html (retrieved on May 16, 2008).
14. Robb, John (2007), op. cit., 2.
15. NYPD (2007). "Radicalization in the West: The Homegrown Threat":20.
16. Morgenstern, Henry (2008). "From Virtual Jihad to Real Jihad," *The Counter Terrorist* 1, no. 1 (May/June):27.
17. Johnson, Carrie (2009). "Bad Economy May Fuel Hate Groups, Experts Warn," *Washington Post*, January 11, A4.
18. "North Carolina Web Site Said to Be 'Gateway Drug' To Terror," *Fox News*, May 16, 2008. www. foxnews.com.
19. Federal Bureau of Investigation (FBI) (2006). *Law Enforcement Officers Killed and Assaulted 2005*. U.S. Department of Justice, October. www.fbi.gov (retrieved on March 7, 2008).

20. Ibid, FBI (2006). www.fbi.gov (retrieved on March 7, 2008).
21. Ibid, FBI (2006). www.fbi.gov (retrieved on March 7, 2008).
22. Ibid, FBI (2006). www.fbi.gov (retrieved on March 7, 2008).
23. Marks, Alexandra (2008). "Key Factor in Murder Trends: Youth, Gang Violence," *Christian Science Monitor,* January 4, 1.
24. Fields, Gary (2008), op. cit., A16.
25. Uniform Crime Report (UCR) for year 2006, compiled by the Federal Bureau of Investigation, September 2007. http://www.fbi.gov/ucr/cius2006/offenses/expanded_information/data/shrtable_03.html (retrieved on May 11, 2008).
26. Uniform Crime Report (UCR) for year 2005, compiled by the Federal Bureau of Investigation, September 2006. http://www.fbi.gov/ucr/05cius/offenses/expanded_information/data/shrtable_03.html (retrieved on May 11, 2008).
27. Uniform Crime Report (UCR) for year 2004, compiled by the Federal Bureau of Investigation, September 2005. http://www.fbi.gov/ucr/cius_04/offenses_reported/violent_crime/murder.html (retrieved on May 11, 2008).
28. Uniform Crime Report (UCR) for year 2004, compiled by the Federal Bureau of Investigation, September 2005. http://www.fbi.gov/ucr/cius_03/xl/03tbl2-5.xls (retrieved on May 11, 2008).
29. See, for example, White, Michael D. (2002). "Identifying Situational Predictors of Police Shootings Using Multivariate Analysis," *Policing: An International Journal of Police Strategies and Management* 25, no. 4:726–51.
30. White, Michael D. (2002), op. cit., 726–51.
31. Jones, Carolyn (2009). "Oakland Storekeepers Tell of Night of Terror," *San Francisco Chronicle*, January 9, A12. http://www.sfgate.com/cgi- bin/article.cgi?f=/c/a/2009/01/09/MNC3155VI6.DTL&hw=Storekeepers+Tell+of+Terror&sn=001&sc=1000.
32. "2nd Night of Violent BART Protests in Oakland," KPIX 5 San Francisco, Associated Press, and BCN (California), January 9, 2009. http://cbs5.com/local/BART.shooting.protest.2.902981.html.
33. Harris, Harry and Kamika Dunlap (2009) "Three Oakland Police Officers Killed, One Critically Wounded after Traffic Stop, Shootout," *Oakland Tribune.* http://www.mercurynews.com/centralcoast/ci_11968175 (retrieved on April 1, 2009). Note: Three officers died on the scene and the fourth officer died a few days later.
34. http://www.sfgate.com/cgi-bin/article.cgi?f=/c/a/2009/03/25/MNDD16N9VP.DTL, March 26, 2009.
35. http://uhurunews.com/story?resource_name=stop-the-genocidal-war-on-the-african-community-now-economic-and-social-justice-for-the-african-community (retrieved on March 27, 2009).
36. Barack Obama speech at 2004 Democratic Convention. http://www.americanrhetoric.com/speeches/convention2004/barackobama2004dnc.htm (retrieved on January 22, 2009).
37. Rush Limbaugh interview with Sean Hannity, *Fox News.* http://www.foxnews.com/ (retrieved on January 22, 2009).
38. http://www.foxnews.com/ (retrieved on January 22, 2009).
39. Gilgoff, Dan (2008). "With Rick Warren Flap, Gay Activists Say Obama Has Long Been a 'Mixed Bag,'" *U.S. News and World Report,* December 18. http://www.usnews.com/blogs/god-and-country/2008/12/18/with-rick-warren-flap-gay-activists-say-obama-has-long-been-a-mixed-bag.html (retrieved on January 22, 2009).

40. Johnson, Carrie (2009), op. cit., A4.
41. Phillips, Joseph C. (2008). "Barack Obama Can't Win as Long as He Continues to Play That Tired, Dog-Eared Race Card." http://www.blackamericaweb.com/site.aspx/sayitloud/phillips819 (retrieved on August 27, 2008).
42. Phillips, Joseph C. (2008), op. cit.
43. Kass, John (2008). "For Sheer Brazenness, Nobody Surpasses Rod," *Chicago Tribune*, December 31. http://www.chicagotribune.com/news/columnists/chi-kass-burris-31-dec31,0,1367315.column.
44. http://www.tucc.org/about.htm (retrieved on April 25, 2008).
45. http://www.tucc.org/store/index.cfm?action=catbrowse&catid=69 (retrieved on April 25, 2008).
46. http://www.tucc.org/about.htm (retrieved on April 25, 2008).
47. http://web.archive.org/web/20050404190242/www.tucc.org/about.htm, from May 7, 2005, and November 12, 2006 (as retrieved on May 3, 2008, at http://www.archive.org/index.php).
48. See http://www.tucc.org (retrieved on May 3, 2008).
49. See http://www.tucc.org (retrieved on March 31, 2009).
50. www.adl.org and State and Local Anti-Terrorist Training (SLATT), 21.
51. White, Jonathan R. (2008). "A Theology of Anti-government Extremism," *Terrorism in Perspective,* 2nd ed. Eds. Mahan, Sue and Pamela L. Griset. Thousand Oaks, CA: Sage Publications, 193.
52. http://www.adl.org/Learn/ext_us/WCOTC.asp?xpicked=3&item=17 (retrieved on May 5, 2008).
53. http://www.adl.org/Learn/ext_us/WCOTC.asp?xpicked=3&item=17 (retrieved on May 5, 2008).
54. "Neo-Nazi Materials Found Outside Homes in N.C." http://hamptonroads.com/2009/01/neonazi-materials-found-outside-homes-nc (retrieved on January 16, 2009).
55. Shay, Becky (2009). "Billings Group Wants to Change Image of White Supremacists," *Billings Gazette (Montana).* http://www.missoulian.com/articles/2009/01/08/bnews/br60.txt (retrieved on January 8, 2009).
56. Phillips, Joseph C. (2008). "Barack Obama Can't Win as Long as He Continues to Play That Tired, Dog-Eared Race Card." http://www.blackamericaweb.com/site.aspx/sayitloud/phillips819 (retrieved on August 27, 2008).
57. There are two characterizations of the term "jihad." Greater jihad entails an inner struggle that an individual goes through in order to submit to Allah's will. The lesser jihad entails an outward struggle to defend the Islamic community. See, for example, Jeremiah, David (2008). *What in the World is Going On: 10 Prophetic Clues You Cannot Afford to Ignore.* Nashville, TN: Thomas Nelson Publishers, 79.
58. Barack Obama speech at 2004 Democratic Convention, op. cit.
59. Sammon, Bill (2009). "Pelosi Open to Prosecution of Bush Administration Officials." http://www.foxnews.com/politics/2009/01/18/pelosi-open-prosecution-bush-administration-officials/ (retrieved on January 18, 2009).
60. *Pride and Glory* (2008). New Line Cinema, Solaris Entertainment, and O'Connor Brothers Producers.
61. Jeremiah, David (2008), op. cit., 79.
62. Corder, Mike (2009). "Dutch Court: Prosecute Anti-Islamic Lawmaker," *Associated Press*, January 21. http://news.yahoo.com/s/ap/20090121/ap_on_re_eu/eu_netherlands_hate_speech;_ylt=Ar85.P8mhejAroTgvwLp0DZ0bBAF.

63. Corder, Mike (2009), op. cit.
64. Lefkowitz, Josh (2008). "Terrorists Behind Bars," May 5. www.nefafoundation.org.
65. For an account of how this commentary was drafted and circulated see the below Web site. Since the Web site critiqued and seemed to invalidate some examples that appeared with the commentary, I struck these examples from the commentary. The commentary that appears in the narrative, therefore, does not include these examples. If you desire to view the examples, and the critique, please see http://www.truthorfiction.com/rumors/f/flagoffense.htm (retrieved on January 24, 2009).
66. http://www.breakthechain.org/exclusives/beamerican.html (retrieved on January 24, 2009).

Chapter 10

Recommendations and Implications

This chapter provides an outline of key issues related to the predicted increase in extremist violence. As the reader knows, this predicted increase will spur the formation of a new policing model. Of course, the previous chapter discussed the triggers that will foster such violence. I do not pretend to provide answers to these vexing triggers. Instead, this chapter will attempt to address the "solutions" related to policing a violent society. The new policing model, of course, will not be a panacea. It is simply a pragmatic response to societal circumstances. Trying to understand the larger societal implications of this policing model is, in my mind, the only approach where actual "solutions" can be applied. In this way, we will focus on the "responses," not the causes of the circumstances. I will leave the resolution of the causes—the triggers—to policy makers and political leaders. I hope this book will alert and articulate the implications of failing to adequately address these triggers. In any event, we will focus on specific recommendations and the implications of *Public Safety Policing*.

As implied in the above discussion, this new model of policing is a challenge, complicated by a number of factors. These factors will be addressed:

1. Order maintenance
2. Private policing
3. Search and seizure
4. Intelligence methods
5. Investigations and interrogations
6. Use of force
7. Security versus rights

Order Maintenance

The key principles related to order maintenance have been effectively developed within the *National Strategy for Homeland Security*. This strategy outlines three key principles. The first principle is a culture of preparedness. This strategy articulates the difficulties of balancing responses to terrorism. Specifically, it states,[1]

> As individual citizens we must guard against complacency, and as a society we must balance the sense of optimism that is fundamental to the American character with a sober recognition that future catastrophes will occur. The certainty of future calamities should inform and motivate our preparedness, and we will continue to emphasize the responsibility of the entire nation to be flexible and ready to cope with a broad range of challenges.

The second principle takes this thinking to the next level. It stresses the importance of countering biases toward "reactive responses and approaches." This thinking seeks to avoid simply maintaining the status quo until something happens. When an incident occurs, policy makers scramble to develop reactive "solutions." The strategy, therefore, advocates encouraging and rewarding innovation. It seeks "new ways of thinking." It seeks to "align authority and responsibility so that those who are responsible for a mission or task have the authority to act." As with any problem, opportunities for new ways of thinking, innovative techniques, and thoughtful solutions must be used. Finally, the third principle is that "individual citizens, communities, the private sector, and non-profit organizations each perform a central role in homeland security."[2] This notion has been a key theme of this book.

These principles are applicable in the new policing model. We seek to develop new ways of thinking to address the threat of terrorism and extremist violence. As previously stated, the current policing model, *Community Policing*, will not be sufficient to counter these eventualities. A key aspect of this model is the use of order maintenance provisions. In its application, terrorism risk management measures should be rigorously reexamined to ensure adequacy. These measures include, but are not limited to, physical security perimeters, isolation of mail and delivery areas, setback distances between security fences and key buildings, and barricades. In addition, citizens should be alert to and immediately report any situation that appears to constitute a threat or suspicious activity.

One way to articulate what to watch for is the acronym known as PAIN. This means pre-attack indicators. As this book has made clear, terrorist attacks are typically preceded by certain threats or suspicious activities. In developing these pre-attack indicators, one is often inundated with myriad factors that are difficult to discern. Indeed, these factors are even more difficult to distinguish between "innocent" and "suspicious." This is partly because they are so common. However, if these factors can be effectively organized—or categorized—then the potential to discern and distinguish common activities may be enhanced. In this light, I have developed the following categories designed to enhance the ability to effectively "understand" innocent activities from suspicious activities:[3]

Surveillance/reconnaissance
- Parking, loitering, standing in same area over multiple days
- Individuals who stay at bus stops or train stations for extended time
- Increase in the frequency and nature of suspected surveillance incidents
- Prolonged static surveillance using operatives disguised as panhandlers, shoe shiners, news agents, street sweepers, and food or flower vendors who were not previously seen in the area
- Inspection, photography, or observation of entry points, access controls, or perimeter barriers, such as doors, fences, and walls (note: *what* is the focus of the photo)
- Evidence of foot or mobile surveillance of two or three individuals who appear to be working together
- Individuals pacing off distances
- Unusual behavior by individuals who stare or quickly look away from security personnel
- Inquiries or documentation of police/security personnel and their procedures
- Deliberate penetration attempts into secured, private, sensitive areas
- Cameras/videotape and other observation equipment
- GPS units, night vision, high-mag lenses, and tracking devices
- Maps, photos, diagrams, sketches, blueprints

Vehicles
- Rental, theft, or purchase of a one-ton (or larger) truck or van
- Modification of truck/van with heavy-duty springs to handle heavier load
- Suspicious rental or theft of limousine
- Theft or access to emergency vehicles
- Homemade or missing license plates (UCC, British West Indies)
- Theft of license plates, particularly government plates

Weapons/weapons training
- Theft or unusual sale of weapons or ammunition
- Reports of automatic weapons firing
- Signs or reports of paramilitary training
- Theft or sale of protective body armor
- Nonmilitary persons stopped with military-style weapons, clothing, and equipment

Explosives/chemicals
- Reports of small explosions in remote or rural wooded areas (may be testing)
- Emergency room reports of chemical burns or treatment for missing hands/fingers
- Reports of chemical fires, toxic odors, brightly colored stains, or rusted metal fixtures in apartments, hotel/motel rooms, or self-storage units
- Disposing/dumping chemicals
- Dead plants or animals (mice, rats, rabbits)
- Explosives theft or sale of large amounts of explosive powder, blasting caps, or high-velocity explosives
- Large sales of ammonium nitrate (fertilizer)
- Theft or sale of containers (i.e., propane bottles, propane tanks)
- Rental of storage units for storage of nontraditional or suspicious items (i.e., fertilizer, fuel oil, propane)
- Complaints of strange smells around recently rented self-storage facilities
- Reports of chemical deliveries directly from the manufacturer to a self-storage facility or unusual deliveries of chemicals to residential or rural addresses

Literature
- Documents asserting claims of conspiracy
- Radical/revolutionary literature
- Extremist pamphlets, communiqués, flyers, etc.
- Terrorist literature and training manuals
- Bomb-making manuals
- Law enforcement/police training manuals
- Military training manuals

Testing/operational planning
- A pattern or series of false events requiring law enforcement and/or emergency response (unattended bags/boxes, bomb threats, false alarms, etc.)
- Abandoned devices that could contain explosives, such as vehicles, suitcases, bags, and the like
- Increase in the number of telephone or e-mail threats
- Reports of computer hackers attempting to access sites with personal identification, maps, or other targeting examples

Suicide bomber indicators
- Carrying heavy luggage or wearing a backpack
- Clothing is loose or out of sync with environment or weather
- Repeatedly patting their upper body/rigid midsection
- Sweating, mumbling (prayers), unusually calm
- Eyes focused and vigilant

- Strange "chemical" odors or heavy colognes
- Pale face from recently shaved beard
- Protruding bulges or exposed wires under clothes
- Walking with deliberation, usually alone
- Tightened hands (holding detonation device?)

Contraband cigarettes
- Shipping case concealed inside an outer case
- Cigarettes in plain, unmarked cases
- Cartons and packs stored or wrapped in plastic bags
- Misspellings on packs or cartons ("Please Oon's Litter")
- Clear film wrapping over cartons
- Cigarettes with foreign writing on packaging
- Cigarette packs with out of state or no tax stamps

Just as in the development of PAIN factors, there are certain recommendations typically used to interdict potential terrorist acts. These factors are designed to control and harden the environment. They include such factors as rearranging exterior vehicle barriers, and using traffic cones and roadblocks to alter traffic patterns near facilities to reduce straight "runways." These traffic and vehicle security methods would be enhanced by instituting a robust vehicle inspection program such as checking under the undercarriage, under the hood, and in the trunk of vehicles. In addition, security experts recommend implementing highly visible vehicle, foot, and roving security patrols that vary in size, timing, and routes. Vehicle inspection training should be provided to security personnel. Of course, it is wise to approach all illegally parked vehicles in and around facilities, questioning drivers and directing them to move immediately. If an owner cannot be identified, have the vehicle towed. It is also recommended to limit the number of access points and strictly enforce access control procedures. Certain security technologies are also recommended. These include increasing parameter lighting, and installing visible security cameras and motion sensors. Coupled with the use of appropriate technology, it is recommended to remove view-restricting vegetation in and around perimeters. Finally, conducting vulnerability studies focusing on physical security, structural engineering, infrastructure engineering, power, water, and air infiltration is recommended. In the end, this principle is applicable: "Look for things that are there that should not be, and things that should be there but are not."

In addition to these recommendations, certain other precautions are typically considered by security professionals:

■ Keep complete records of all official identification cards, badges, decals, uniforms, and license plates distributed, documenting any unusual activities or events, and canceling access to items that are lost or stolen.

- Protect and account for all uniforms, patches, badges, ID cards, and other forms of official identification to protect against unauthorized access to facilities, including stripping all decommissioned vehicles slated for resale and/or salvage of all agency identifying markings and emergency warning devices.
- Use new and improved tamper-proof identification card technology to eliminate reuse or unauthorized duplication.
- Notify your uniform store vendors of the need to establish and verify the identities of individuals seeking to purchase uniform articles.
- Ensure all personnel are provided a security briefing regarding present and emerging threats.

Private Policing

Much of the aforementioned order maintenance provisions will be performed by private police. The underlying reasoning for such rests with the logic of order maintenance. That is, extremist violence will be the overriding concern for private policing arrangements. As previously developed, there are a number of functions that are currently being performed by private police. Notwithstanding the cooperative efforts and favorable data, many people—including police officers—are not totally convinced of the merits of private policing. The notion of private policing can be summarized by the following questions: Is it appropriate for "clients," who are citizens of a governmental entity, to pay a private firm for public safety services? Indeed, my answer is made plain with this rhetorical question: Is it wrong to pay for personal protection? Stated another way, if public police cannot or will not provide for your personal protection, is it wrong to pay a security firm to do so? It is my belief that no reasonable person should deny this right of self-defense. Notwithstanding the answers to these questions, the following statement sums up the concern of private policing: "In the eyes of the police, guards [security personnel] seem to occupy a confusing gray area between public official and private citizen that many cops find disconcerting."[4]

This perception, however, is not universal. Ample evidence exists that private citizens and property owners do not seem as concerned with these issues. Indeed, such matters as government sovereignty and legal niceties are often superseded by concerns for *security and safety*, not these "esoteric" issues like the government and the law.[5] According to Carlson, many business owners simply care about their own security. Some even claim that regardless of the cost paid for these services, the protection received is well worth it.[6] In this sense, I contend that the tension between personal security and constitutional rights will typically err on the side of security. One can reasonably speculate that the desire for security will be much more pronounced in the years ahead. Given this reality or this perception, the question that naturally follows is, how should these arrangements be structured?

Let me first answer this question initially in a broad manner. I contend that private security and municipal policing will require a bridge that joins these seemingly complimentary, but often conflicted, entities. This requires more than "partnerships" between security and policing. It requires a structural approach, in which security personnel and municipal police are joined together within the organizational chart—and the organizational cultures of the respective entities. As illustrated by the arrangements in the synergy chapter (Chapter 7), policy makers should look to successful public-private models for insight and direction. These arrangements are the result of decades designed to foster better relations between law enforcement and the security industry. Many of these relationships have been built on individuals moving from one profession (usually from law enforcement) and obtaining employment in the other profession (usually to the security industry). Over time, many meaningful professional relationships developed as individuals interacted with their counterparts in the other industry. Innovations like Operation Cooperation have been instrumental in this development.

Operation Cooperation is, in essence, a goal and a program. From the perception of its goals, the goal is to articulate and communicate certain partnership models, where security and police work together to combat crime and to deliver public safety services. From a programmatic perspective, the Law Enforcement Liaison Council (LELC) of Asis International in conjunction with other entities published a document, titled "Operation Cooperation," which outlines the history of public–private partnerships and advocates for future cooperative work. This document describes some of the most effective programs illustrated by the stated goals and principles of cooperative public/private policing arrangements. These include the Business/Law Enforcement Alliance (BLEA) in California, the Area Police-Private Security Liaison (APPL) program in New York City, and the Downtown Detroit Security Executive Council (DDSEC) in Detroit, Michigan. These models act as templates from which additional partnerships can be instituted.[7]

As effective as these partnerships have been, their value will be limited unless more concrete ties are developed between private security and public police. It is becoming increasingly necessary to build upon these partnerships. In my mind, the time has come to institutionalize the efforts of security and police personnel to enhance the coordination and cooperation of public safety services. This should be done through structural and contractual relationships. Indeed, without more definitive structural or contractual ties, partnerships will be too dependent upon informal personal relationships. Personal relationships can be fickle. While these are important, they are not sufficient without more concrete ties. Unfortunately, innovative partnerships have not completely broken down the barriers between the two groups of professionals. Attitudes and histories often die hard. Despite some ongoing differences and societal trends, the insidious motivations of terrorists necessitate the acceleration of the structural cooperation of security and policing.[8] The details of this future relationship need to be articulated and fleshed out. One thing is certain, however—enhanced structural coordination would not be possible without the tireless efforts of those professionals who developed and built foundational partnerships.[9]

The development of these sophisticated public–private arrangements requires addressing key related questions. These relate to the following: What are the legal and constitutional limitations of private police? What licensing, training, and accountability guidelines are appropriate? These and other key questions will be developed below.

These questions point to the distinction between public and private policing. They raise many implications. For example, the legal questions point to philosophical implications. This relates to the fact—or at least a perception—that security personnel do not carry the same sense of legal and moral authority as public police officers. This may or may not relate to the extent of police powers. In this sense, the level of perceived authority could affect how the private officers perform their jobs. A classic example is when a private police officer directs someone to refrain from loitering. The willingness to adhere to this directive may relate to whether the officer has the authority, either legal or moral, to force compliance. The answer may not be clear-cut. Consequently, the level of perceived versus actual authority is extraordinarily important.[10] Both of these are grounded in the notion of legal authority.

There are two basic issues relating to legal authority. Although we will deal with each separately, it is important to note that legal authority and constitutional protections are often interrelated. For example, if a private security officer makes an arrest, his or her authority to make the arrest may be questioned. Typically, this inquiry points to the legal power to effect the arrest. Conversely, in the prosecution of the arrestee, there will often be an inquiry as to whether any search or seizure of the arrestee is constitutionally proper.[11] In this inquiry, the question is not about the power to effect the arrest, but whether the search and seizure conforms to the confines of the Fourth Amendment. While this seems like splitting hairs, it is a rather distinct legal inquiry. In the former example relating to the power of arrest, the legal inquiry typically points to whether the private security officer had the power to arrest the individual. In the latter example relating to the search and seizure, the legal inquiry points to whether the search and seizure of the arrestee was constitutionally proper. With this caveat established, these issues will be examined separately.

A. Constitutional Protections

It is generally understood that the constitutional prohibitions contained in the Bill of Rights were designed to limit the power of the government. These rights are applicable only when government is involved. In legal parlance, the applicability of these protections is triggered when a "state actor" was involved in the arrest. State actor is a legal term to describe government employees, agents, or officials, such as a police officer or some other law enforcement official. The initial legal question one must ask is whether private police are state actors. The answer to this question points to whether constitutional provisions will be applicable to the actions of private police. Simply stated, constitutional protections are only applicable to government. Unless private police officers are considered "state actors," they are not deemed part of government.

If they are not part of government, particular constitutional protections, such as the Fourth Amendment prohibitions against unreasonable searches and seizures, will not be applicable to private police. While there is often confusion over this question, in my earlier research, I concluded that private police within the Marquette Park arrangement (see Chapter 7) were indeed state actors.[12]

Historically, such constitutional protections did not apply to private police.[13] However, courts are now apt to extend constitutional protections to include actions by private security personnel. Typically for constitutional protections to apply to security personnel, one must show their actions have a connection to government or with sworn police officers. While this is a factually driven determination, one way to understand this legal question is by assessing the respective functions of the private police in each arrangement. This is important, in part, because the goal(s) of the client in the specific arrangement may drive how the private police officers perform their job. For example, a client could desire aggressive and extensive security measures. This may result in practices markedly similar to the functions of public police. In a public environment, this may include aggressive enforcement of criminal laws and crime prevention techniques such as order maintenance. In this context, clients may expect them to "act like the police," thereby enforcing laws and public order. This conclusion was echoed by Clifford, who asserted that "the application of the law enforcement (Fourth Amendment) standard to security professionals is inevitable as the scope of security increases."[14]

This assertion begs the obvious question: When does a private police officer act as a state actor? This is not as clear-cut as it may appear. When this involves police and law enforcement officials performing a public function, the answer is usually straightforward: Constitution protections are applicable. When private security personnel are involved, the answer is more complicated. There are a number of criteria that courts use to assess if security personnel acted as a "state actor," including:[15]

1. Whether the security personnel are licensed by a governmental entity
2. Whether the security personnel acted in cooperation with or by the supervision of public police
3. Whether the security personnel were actually police officers working secondary employment (moonlighting)
4. Whether the security personnel were designated with "special police" powers
5. Whether a "nexus" exists, meaning a significant connection or contact with government

6. Whether security personnel were performing a public function. This question typically hinges on whether the individual was
   a. Acting to enforce the law versus merely serving a private interest
   b. Wearing a "police-like" uniform, firearm, and other police equipment
   c. Whether the individual was identified as the "police"
   d. The location of the arrest, either on private or public property

The applicability of constitutional prohibitions is determined by these factors. If the individual is deemed to have acted under the color of law (as a state actor) then constitutional protections apply. The next inquiry is to assess if governmental immunity applies. Generally, government officials performing discretionary functions typically are granted qualified immunity. Qualified immunity is available to state actors, generally if:[16]

1. The action was not a breach of clearly established rights at that time, and
2. The individual's conduct was objectively reasonable.

Whether qualified immunity applies is a question of law for courts to consider. If qualified immunity does attach, then no liability exposure will result. If qualified immunity does not attach, then various statutory remedies are available to the plaintiff in civil cases. In a criminal context, the remedy is to prevent evidence obtained in violation of the constitution from being used at trial. This is known as the exclusionary rule, which is designed to exclude evidence that was improperly— or illegally—obtained. This rule seeks to prevent, or at least diminish, the incidence of constitutionally violative actions by not rewarding bad police conduct. The aim is to dissuade police from such conduct by excluding the evidence at trial. The logic is that police will be less likely to commit bad acts if they are prevented from using the fruits of the constitutional violation, such as a coerced confession or illegally recovered contraband, from being used at the trial. In this sense, the remedy is defensive in that it protects the integrity of the trial (and constitutional violations) by refusing to allow tainted evidence in a criminal proceeding.[17]

In a civil context, the remedy is to assert causes of actions against the offending officer(s) and the employing entity. These causes of action seek compensatory and punitive damages, injunctions, changes in policy and practice, and other relevant remedies. Here the aim is to "make the plaintiff whole" by awarding compensatory damages, or to punish and deter bad actions through the assertion of punitive damages. Typically, the lawsuit asserts some deprivation of rights, either statutory or constitutional.

The most common statutory claim is Title 42 Section 1983, which states,[18]

> Every person, who under color of any statute, ordinance, regulation, custom, or usage, of any State or territory, subjects, or causes to be subjected, any citizen of the United States or other persons within the

jurisdiction thereof to the deprivation of any right, privilege, or immunity secured by the Constitution and laws, shall be liable to the party injured in the action at law, suit in equity, or other proper proceeding for redress.

To state a Section 1983 claim, the plaintiff must allege the violation of a constitutional right, and show that the alleged violation was committed by a person acting under color of state law. Acting under color of state law requires that the defendant exercise power possessed by virtue of state law, and made possible only because he or she is clothed with the authority of state law. In the context of private security, common allegations relate to searches and seizures and improper use of force. To defend against these Fourth Amendment claims typically requires establishing probable cause for the arrest. Probable cause means that the facts and circumstances within the officer's knowledge are sufficient to warrant a prudent person, or one of reasonable caution, to believe, in the circumstances shown, that the suspect has committed, is committing, or is about to commit an offense. Establishing probable cause also requires that the arresting officer articulate concrete and objective facts from which he or she inferred criminal conduct.

B. Arrest Powers

The power of arrest is often a legal question for the court. This inquiry typically points to the power, not the conduct, of the person making the arrest. Conversely, the conduct related to search and seizure is typically a fact question based on legal standards. As inferred in the above discussion, the ability to make an arrest is inevitably tied to the authority of the state. The notion of making a "citizen's arrest" is illustrative of this point. Government has long allowed, and often encouraged, citizens to act to effect an arrest when warranted. Upon the advent of public police, this practice was slowing and inevitably discouraged. After many generations, the incident of citizen arrests is now quite rare. However, with the rise of private security personnel, the frequency of arrests by security personnel is much more frequent. Consequently, there appear to be two trends going in opposite directions.[19]

As the average citizen is less inclined to make an arrest, the inclination of security personnel to make arrests becomes more common. Although I make this assertion, I do not necessarily see a correlation between them. Instead, the increase in the number and scope of private security personnel may be the key factor in any increase in the number of arrests. Indeed, the more security personnel employed, the more likely arrests will be made. It becomes a function of probability based on the sheer size and scope of the security industry. Further, consider the number of shoplifting arrests that occur on an annual basis. It is safe to assume that many, if not most of these arrests are made by security personnel. In any case, whenever an arrest is made, it inevitably involves the power of the state. The arrestee is typically processed by the police, charged by prosecutors, and tried in a state or federal court.

Even when one understands that the power of arrest is available to all citizens, it is commonly believed that the police have broad arrest powers, while private citizens have much more limited powers. This is generally false. While each state has differing laws relating to the power to effect arrest, there is some commonality throughout the country. Almost all states give citizens power to effect arrests for felonies, and for misdemeanors committed in their presence. Indeed, the slight distinction relating to arrest powers between the police and private citizens can be illustrated by the language of arrest powers for all citizens:[20]

> Any person may arrest another when he has reasonable grounds to believe that an offense other than an ordinance violation is being committed.

The legal powers derived from this statute reveal the following elements: First, the timing of the arrest—"is being committed"—entails while the criminal act is in progress, or immediately after the criminal act has been completed.[21] Second, private citizens can arrest for a felony and a misdemeanor, but not an ordinance violation. Obviously, this gives private citizens (read security personnel) wide authority for making an arrest. This is particularly true when one considers most ordinance violations relating to criminal acts also have a corresponding misdemeanor charge. In this sense, there is little distinction between arrest powers of ordinances and misdemeanors. A classic example of this empty distinction is disorderly conduct, which is often sanctioned in both municipal ordinances and in state misdemeanor statutes. Consequently, the most common distinction between the arrest powers of police and security is that police can arrest on the authority of court-issued warrants and after the crime has been committed.

Given this analysis, it is recommended that private police officers be vested with some governmental authority. Currently, there are three basic alternatives, as shown in Figure 10.1. Consider this figure as a continuum. At one extreme are private citizen arrest powers. At the other extreme are peace officer (police) arrest powers. In the middle, are special police. This status provides for the enforcement and arrest powers of peace officers though the individual is actually employed by a private firm.[22] This combines private citizen (i.e., not an employee of government) with the arrest powers of a peace officer (public police officer).[23] Peace officer arrest powers are only available to the special police officer when he or she is "on duty."

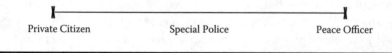

Figure 10.1   **Legal/arrest power continuum (Copyright, James F. Pastor, 2009).**

This limitation is not deemed to be problematic as it does not affect the work they are paid to perform.[24]

Without instituting this "special police" designation, private police officers will have the same arrest powers as a private citizen. One way to distinguish the arrest powers of citizens and private police is through practical implications. While they possess the same inherent powers, in practice "private police are occupationally disposed to use powers that a citizen may rarely, if ever, invoke.[25] Because of this, Joh asserts that "private police are more like public police, and less like private citizens."[26] In addition, as discussed above, while there is not typically a great distinction in arrest powers, there are certain benefits of being "blessed" by government. This includes a certain moral and legal authority that most citizens tend to respect. In this way, the pronouncements and actions of an officer with some governmental authority is much more likely to be complied with. For example, the common response, "I don't have to listen to you, you are not the police," would be largely negated with this official connection to governmental authority. Without this designation, these encounters would constitute one private citizen (i.e., private police officer) telling another private citizen what to do.

Consequently, it is recommended that the "special police" designation be used for private police officers to address the issue of moral and legal authority. Special police officers have full police powers as peace officers *while performing their job.* This "on-duty" aspect would give municipal police departments a larger "police force" without the economic and operational constraints caused by employing more police officers. The special police designation would also give the private police officers a much greater level of moral and legal authority, which is often an important element of an effective police officer. An example of this approach can be found in the Cincinnati Private Police. Pursuant to its municipal code, the city allows private police to perform special police duties.[27]

This special police designation may carry with it the protection of "qualified immunity." Qualified immunity is essentially a shield against liability. It protects the officer (and his or her employer) from civil lawsuits. While this shield is not available for reckless or malicious conduct, it does serve to protect the reasonable and prudent officer who makes a mistake in judgment or behavior. Further, having qualified immunity attached to private police officers serves to reduce the legal exposure of the security firm and, accordingly, the insurance costs associated with the service provision.[28] On the other side, the city can reduce—or even negate—its liability exposure by developing indemnification and hold harmless provisions into the contract with the security firm. These provisions place the liability exposure on the security firm instead of the city. While these provisions may not completely absolve the city from liability, they are effective in reducing the liability exposure from the special police designation.

C. Licensing Standards

Licensing standards directly relate to the issue of legal authority. In order to perform the work of the "police," private police officers should be trained and selected in a manner commensurate with their functional work product. Stated another way, training and selection standards must prepare these officers for the complexities of policing. Indeed, the largest security association in the world, ASIS International, has recognized this fact. In furtherance of this goal, "The Private Security Officer Selection and Training Guideline" has been promulgated. In this guideline, the authors note that "security officers … must also be able to work closely and effectively with public safety personnel."[29] This is directly in line with the thesis of this book—and of the *Public Safety Policing* model.

This guideline is, by far, the most comprehensive approach to addressing the training and selection needs of security officers. While this guideline is designed for private security officers generally, it has direct application to private police officers. Simply stated, the guideline is both relevant and pointed. This guideline recommends state regulation in such areas as background investigations, training, continuing education, insurance, licensing, and oversight bodies. In addition, the guideline suggests certain selection criteria for new hires, including criminal history, education, citizenship, fingerprinting, photographs, drug screening, and other personal information related to the applicant.[30] Without getting into the details of these criteria, suffice it to say that each of these factors will go a long way toward establishing more professionalism in the security industry generally, and in those private police officers who operate within the public realm. Indeed, since the actions of private police officers are likely to be much more visible in the public realm, the need to meet or exceed these criteria is of critical importance.

This being said, it is not necessary that the training and selection standards are equivalent to that of a public police officer—who typically receive 600 to 800 hours of training. Instead, the best practice would be to develop a training curriculum that focuses on the particular role or function to be performed. The different levels and types of training would then be regulated by a particular type of license issued by the state (or other government entity).

The proposed training and licensing continuum could be illustrated as shown in Table 10.1. In this model, the key is to assess both the functionality and critical nature of the job. As the functional complexity of the work increases, or as the critical nature of the task increases, the level of training and licensing should also increase. An excellent example of this continuum can be found in vehicle licensing standards. For passenger vehicles, the typical training and licensing requirements are rather basic. As the nature of the vehicle becomes more complicated to operate (i.e., larger tractor trailers), or as the nature of the cargo becomes more sensitive to protect (i.e., passengers in a bus or dangerous chemicals in a tank car), the need for better trained and higher skilled drivers also increases.

Table 10.1   Training and Licensing Continuum

Functionality/Criticality Continuum				
<——————— *Training Hours* ——————>				
Public	Traffic control	CSO	Patrol officer	Tactical officer	SWAT HBT
Private	Traffic control	Ambassador	Hybrid patrol officer	Armed/ proactive patrol officer	Nuclear utility SWAT
License	*A*	*B*	*C*	*D*	*E*

Copyright, James F. Pastor, 2009.

In this sense, the key is to train and license the security officer in a manner that adequately prepares them for the expected work product. For example, the tasks of a traffic control aide vary substantially from the tasks of security officers at a nuclear power plant. Each should be trained and licensed at a different level. The licensing should range from class "A" to "D" or "E," depending upon the particular legislative approach. Similarly, training should range from 20 or 40 hours minimum, and rise to 200 to 600 hours for street patrols and utility/critical infrastructure security.[31]

Similarly, the skills and job description of the Ambassador (i.e., Atlanta, Seattle, Minneapolis, etc.) can be compared to those of the Community Service Officer (CSO) in the public sector. The patrol officer in the public sector can be compared to the "hybrid" private patrol officer. These hybrid officers should have more training than the Ambassador. They will also perform certain duties similar to police patrol officers. They will make occasional arrests, they will take reports, and they will perform various order maintenance functions. Tactical police officers are typically more trained than patrol officers. They tend to be much more proactive, looking to engage suspicious persons and make arrests when appropriate. Similarly, the armed/proactive private patrol officer will receive more training than the hybrid patrol officer. They also will make more arrests, and conduct themselves in a more proactive manner. They will look to engage suspicious persons, yet they will still perform various order maintenance functions (e.g., Hollywood BID, Marquette Park, etc.). Finally, the respective sectors will also have their SWAT components. In the public sector, these officers will be a proportionately larger percentage of public policing personnel. These SWAT officers (and to some extent tactical officers as well) will represent the "militarization" aspects of the new policing model. In the private sector, these SWAT officers can be compared to those performing security functions in Iraq, such as Blackwater and Triple Canopy.

D. Accountability Standards

Finally, the issue of accountability of private police should be addressed. While this is a large undertaking, it is critical that private police be perceived as accountable to the community, the law, and to the larger society. This must be more than a perception. Real and specific mechanisms must be in place. Indeed, one of the most telling conclusions from my research of privatized policing arrangements is that formal accountability standards and methods must be developed.[32]

There are several avenues to enhancing accountability. These must go beyond potential liability in civil courts. As mentioned above, civil and constitutional sanctions are available to remedy misconduct. This discussion goes beyond these sanctions. First and foremost, specific operating procedures must be developed that address the realities of the job. Just as post orders are critical to the security of a protected facility, so is the need for policies and procedures that will guide the private police officer through the expectations of the work. Without specific guidance, there is simply too much discretionary decision making in the fluid environment of the "street." Indeed, discretion without judgment formed through proper guidance and experience is a recipe for disaster.

Second, the police chief, the police commission, or a community-based board should oversee the operations of the private policing firm(s).[33] In my mind, the community-based board in conjunction with police officials is the best way to facilitate accountability. This approach parallels the logic of *Community Policing*. Just as *Community Policing* is designed to get the community involved in the day-to-day operations of the police, this oversight board can work with administrators of the security firm for direction and guidance in addressing the problems within the community. Unlike *Community Policing*, however, a contracted relationship provides for a more authentic "client-based service" because the security firm can be fired. The police agency does not face this ultimate "sanction." Consequently, this model would actually give the community decision-making powers relative to the work product of the private policing services. Additionally, local police administrators should also work with this oversight board, thereby helping to coordinate the activities of both the public and private police officers.

The last critical element of accountability is to have some well-defined process to address citizen complaints. This should be done by a separate board specifically mandated with investigatory and quasi-judicial powers to impose discipline and other sanctions. This board should be vested with subpoena powers and the ability to conduct hearings. These hearings should be designed to assess the substance of any allegation or complaint. The board should also have the legal authority to levy warnings, fines, and other employment and contractual remedies. Such board authority could be empowered to a number of existing governmental agencies, including the Department of Professional Regulation or a civilian oversight board that monitors police misconduct. However this board is constituted, it must be able to deal with the type of complaints common to police departments.[34]

The challenges ahead present a massive potential market for security firms. Just as the new asymmetric form of warfare is changing the way the military confronts and combats terrorism, so too police agencies must reinvent the way of policing. This transformation will leave a void, or at least a gap, in how public safety services are delivered to communities. Security firms are uniquely prepared to bridge this gap and deliver needed order maintenance and related services. This service must be deployed in a systematic and professional fashion. Simply stated, too much is at stake. Public safety and constitutional protections will be affected—positively or negatively—by how this new policing model is ultimately implemented. While we can expect mistakes to occur, the level of professionalism exhibited by those charged with public safety will be a key indicator in the level of success. In this sense, wrestling with these identifiable deficiencies constitutes a critical yet basic subject that needs to be further addressed and explored.

The desire for professionalism within private policing must center on even more basic purposes: the safety of individuals and communities, and the stability of our way of life. It is important to remember that the threat of terrorism is designed not only to kill people and damage property, but also to destroy the very fabric of the country. Those in the security industry, especially those protecting public environments, trophy or symbolic buildings, and the critical infrastructure, will be on the front lines of this asymmetric conflict. Advancing standards and principles of professionalism is our best defense.[35]

One way to assess standards that will foster professionalism can be illustrated in Table 10.2. In this table, the training standards vary depending upon specific state requirements. Some states do not even have requirements. In order to generalize the wide-ranging state "requirements," the table presents the current standards as 20/40. This means 20 training hours for unarmed guards, and 40 training hours for armed guards. These training standards represent the current norm. As noted

Table 10.2 Private Police Recommendations

Issue	Current	Consider
Training	20/40	A–E license
Education	HS/GED	Function specific
Drug screening	Industry specific	Function specific "safety sensitive"
Intelligence data	No private access/ imminent harm	Criticality access
Legal authority	Private citizen	Special police

Copyright, James F. Pastor, 2009.

above, however, these requirements fall far below those of public police. Police typically receive 600–800 hours of academy training plus ongoing "in-service" training. As presented in this table, I advocate licensing standards from "A" to "E" similar to vehicle licensing.

Considering education standards, current practice is largely confined to minimum levels, such as high school or GED equivalent. I propose raising these education standards in accord with the specific job function. In this way, education, as with training, is designed to fit the actual work to be performed by the officer. Similarly, current drug screening standards are largely dependent on the specific industry or even the particular company policy. As with education and training, I contend the appropriate approach is to tailor the practice of drug screening toward specific industries. In particular, I believe the legal standard of "safety sensitive" should prevail. This standard is deemed an exception to the warrant requirement. In the application of this standard, those individuals who perform "safety-sensitive" functions, such as police officers, transit workers, and truck drivers, are subject to random drug screens. The essence of this standard is that those who perform safety-sensitive functions are so important that they must relinquish some individual privacy rights for the well-being of others. Hence, security personnel should be subject to drug screening due to their particular "public safety" functions.

As to intelligence data, typically there is little or no access for private security personnel. I believe this must change. Consider Project Griffin and NYPD SHIELD. Both of these programs have a robust information flow from and to public and private entities. While much of this information may not be deemed "intelligence" or even "law enforcement sensitive," the current legal standard of "imminent harm" likely prevents adequate communication. As such, I believe that this standard needs to be changed to a lesser standard. This "critical access" standard would allow communication to select private security personnel who protect critical infrastructure. These may include transportation, food, utilities, educational, financial, and other key public safety functional areas. These individuals must submit to an appropriate level of background checks. They also should be subject to various controls related to the information (see intelligence methods discussion in Chapter 5 and below). In any event, it is critical that information and data be disseminated to these "partners" in public safety.

Finally, as noted above, in many cases it may be necessary to have private police officers vested with "special police" powers. As Table 10.2 illustrates, the typical current circumstance is to limit private police to "private citizen" arrest powers. While I demonstrate that the distinction in these arrest powers is not substantial, the larger message this sends is that private police are vested with the power of government. This is often critical to obtain compliance. It is also critical to maintain the perception of professionalism. In the end, the "special police" status enhances both the perceived and legal power of private police. I believe this will be critical to appropriately perform order maintenance—and law enforcement—functions on the public way.

Accomplishing these dual principles of professionalism and safety will require a delicate balance between individual rights and security provisions. This will not be easy. The fluidity of the street and the unpredictable nature of the committed terrorist make this a very delicate balance. There are contemporary examples of this delicate balance. Consider the use of private security firms in Iraq. Defense Secretary Robert Gates said he is concerned "whether there has been sufficient accountability and oversight in the region over the activities of these security companies." The Defense Department released a memo to U.S. commanders in response to growing concerns, instructing them to "disarm, apprehend, and detain" any private security officials involved in illegal conduct. This new policy signaled the end of immunity for defense contractors currently shielded from oversight by U.S. law.[36]

In the end, the liability exposure requires a substantial level of professionalism. This entails being sensitive to clients, and at the same time being committed to the larger mission. While mistakes will be made, the mission must go on. We cannot fail. With this in mind, F. Thomas Braglia, the former president of the Illinois Association of Chiefs of Police, noted that in the current climate what was once considered a "professional relationship" between the public and private sectors has now because a "professional necessity."[37] This professional necessity presents the largest increase in business opportunities for security firms since the 1850s, when security personnel "policed" the American "wild west." This opportunity, however, is a double-edged sword, replete with pitfalls for the unwary. This is likely where the greatest opportunities for the security industry exist. Ironically, this is where most of the problems and pitfalls reside. Hopefully this book will help us find the appropriate balance between security and rights.

If these approaches are not developed, then the result will be a dual system of policing. Private and public police must come together in a structured manner, or they will continue as two separate entities. While this has been the historical norm, the problem going forward is that as private police increase their scope and sophistication, the implications related to a dual system become more problematic. In this way, the rich will hire their own police. The poor will have to rely on the public police. While this has been traditionally the norm, the new dynamic will be increased extremism and terroristic violence. This will motivate people to buy more and more protection. If these protective services are not connected together this dual system will result in significant societal implications. I will close this section with an observation by Trojanowicz who spoke to these implications:[38]

> Few people recognize the full implications, which is that the affluent can afford to buy as much extra protection as they want and need, while the rest must rely exclusively on public police … the irony—or perhaps the result—is that the poor are the most likely to be the victims of crime and the least likely to be able to buy more police protection.

Search and Seizure

If extremist violence increases, so will the application of search and seizure methods. These methods will substantially increase within the public realm, particularly in crowded areas such as trains and buses. An excellent example of this methodology can be found in the Metro transportation system in Washington, D.C. Metro officials have instituted random searches in their 86 rail stations and over 12,000 bus stops. Random searches will be conducted of backpacks, purses, and other bags carried by passengers before they enter a rail station or board a bus. The search will focus on detecting explosives. Metro officers receive training to perform these searches.

Although it is difficult to measure the success of the search policy, it does let the public know that police are taking steps to combat terrorism. The policy does not require advance notice to passengers. Passengers do have the right to refuse a search, though they will not be allowed to board the bus or enter the station if they do so. To reduce inconvenience, searches are supposed to last between 8 and 15 seconds. Although police will be looking for explosives, if any illegal items are found, they will be confiscated and the bag's carrier will be arrested. Passengers will be randomly chosen, though police officers will have the right to stop people who are acting suspiciously.[39]

The inspection protocol used in these searches can be outlined as:

- The searches will take place only when police determine that circumstances—such as an elevated threat level—warrant heightened vigilance.
- No advance notice will be given, but just before inspections begin, police will post signs alerting riders. Inspections will be conducted by five to eight police officers and a police dog trained to sniff for explosives. Officials said searches would last 8 to 15 seconds.
- Police will only inspect areas of bags that are capable of concealing explosives. Police will not be viewing the content of papers or other reading material.
- If illegal items such as drugs are found, they will be confiscated as evidence, and police will cite or arrest the individual. Those who refuse to have their bags searched will not be allowed to enter. Police will not arrest people who refuse to have their bags inspected.
- In the searches, police will randomly choose a number. Then they will ask riders with bags who correspond to that number to step aside for an inspection before boarding a bus or entering a rail station. If others are acting suspiciously, Transit Police have the right to stop a person not selected for inspection.

While I contend that this protocol is useful for physical searches, it does not address privacy issues related to camera and security technologies. As a general rule, the Fourth Amendment protections are triggered when a person has a reasonable expectation of privacy.[40] If a person does not have reasonable expectation of privacy, the Fourth Amendment does not apply.[41] Courts have upheld surveillance cameras on public streets.[42] There are certain principles that must be assessed and protected in these surveillance programs. Since there has been a much longer history of camera use in the United Kingdom, it may be useful to assess how privacy rights and public safety are balanced. In the United Kingdom, the Data Protection Act limits processing of personal data in order to protect privacy of individuals, using eight statutory principles:[43]

1. Fairly and lawfully processed in accordance with applicable statutory conditions
2. Obtained and processed only for specified, lawful purposes
3. Adequate, relevant, and not excessive in relation to the purpose for which they are processed
4. Accurate data
5. Not kept longer than necessary
6. Processed in accordance with the data subjects' rights
7. Secure storage
8. Not transferred to countries outside the European Economic Area without adequate protection of personnel data

Intelligence Methods

As with privacy concerns in a search and seizure context, there are a number of key principles to consider in establishing an intelligence operation. The Los Angeles Police Department (LAPD) provides some excellent insight into this undertaking. Of course, establishing an intelligence unit can be controversial. The potential for infringement upon civil liberties is the most obvious concern. As presented in Chapter 5, the benefits of establishing an intelligence unit are substantial. The overall goals of the intelligence operation should be to ensure accountability and focused investigations designed to protect the specific interests of the department and the larger municipality. Sharing information is based on building trusting relationships with counterparts throughout the region and the country. Building appropriate working relationships with other local and state agencies is a critical component of any municipal intelligence operation.[44]

Once the need for an intelligence unit has been justified and a mission clearly articulated, it is critical that comprehensive guidelines governing its operation be established. The guidelines should not simply restate the procedures followed by all employees. Indeed, the intelligence function is unique and must be controlled to a greater degree than other department functions. Guidelines governing operations, personnel selection, equipment, logistics, dissemination of information procedures, reporting procedures, and file security must all be of equal importance in establishing and managing such a unit. At a minimum, the guidelines should provide for these functional criteria:[45]

- Opening and maintaining an investigation
- Limitations and prohibitions concerning investigative methods
- Dissemination of intelligence information
- Control and management of sources
- Undercover and surveillance activities
- Control of intelligence files
- Personnel administration
- Auditing and oversight
- Public access to information

Beyond these guidelines, it is also necessary to maintain oversight of the intelligence operations. In order to ensure appropriate oversight, the number of management levels between the unit and the oversight manager should be reduced to an absolute minimum. Regularly scheduled briefings should be provided by the unit to the oversight manager. These guidelines and their procedures should be subject to an annual comprehensive audit. In addition, the operation should also be subject to unannounced audits. These audits should cover all aspects of the unit's operation. It is important, of course, to ensure that the independent auditors of the intelligence unit are closely scrutinized and subject to comprehensive background investigations.[46]

Personnel selection within the intelligence operation is a key ingredient in determining the level of its success. Personnel assigned must clearly understand this concept. They also must learn the ideologies and cultures of targeted groups in order to anticipate their actions. Investigators who tend to become easily frustrated or measure success by arrests are probably not fit for intelligence. When selecting personnel a careful screening process must take place. This should include an oral interview, a detailed review of the application and related documents, interviews of the candidate's previous supervisors, and a detailed background investigation, including a polygraph examination. Individuals who are sympathetic to a particular targeted group or ideology should quickly be screened from this assignment. It is also typical for all personnel assigned to the intelligence operations to obtain a Secret (or Top Secret) clearance through the FBI. Even clerical staff must go through the screening process, though they do not need a Secret clearance if they do no have access to intelligence files and related information. Overall, the process of selecting and screening personnel is lengthy and tedious. It pays great dividends, however, in maintaining the confidentiality of the unit's data as well as ensuring a mature, loyal staff.[47]

Finally, LAPD guidelines note that it is extremely important for supervisors to perform objective oversight. They must not completely rely on a neutral auditor to insure adherence to mandated procedures. They should proactively provide leadership and demonstrate active interest in cases. They should participate in surveillance activities, meet with sources developed by their subordinates, conduct random audits, and ensure total compliance with established guidelines. In addition, supervisors should participate in planning operations and counterterrorism strategies, conducting formal/informal briefings, assessing threats, performing officer safety bulletins, analyzing trends, and the like.[48]

In summary, while intelligence plays a critical role in public safety, there are a number of legal and administrative requirements that may cause concerns. While it is understandable that these concerns would exist, they should not prevent intelligence from being properly utilized. In the end, intelligence is an important tool; use it correctly but do not be afraid of it! In order to make this process more manageable, these plain language and summary requirements may be useful:

1. Audit trails are required.
2. Records shall note to whom information is released, why it is released, and the date of dissemination.
3. Records shall note sensitivity and confidence levels, and the identities of submitting agencies and control officials.
4. Procedures to ensure that all information has relevancy shall be drafted and adhered to.
5. Procedures for the periodic review of information shall be drafted and adhered to.
6. Information that is misleading, obsolete, or unreliable shall be purged and destroyed.
7. Use common sense and review legal principles.
8. Remember "need to know" and "right to know" access for dissemination.
9. Maintain control and consistently assess your files.
10. Communicate with security firms, businesses, and local, state, and federal agencies on a regular basis.
11. Integrate law enforcement intelligence into the overall mission of your agency.
12. Operate agency with a bottom-up/top-down flow of information.

Investigations and Interrogations

While these aspects of policing are not directly related to the elements of *Public Safety Policing*, I believe that a couple of critical points need to be made. These points relate to the legal and operational issues related to investigations and interrogations. In some ways, the investigation and interrogation of terrorism is the same as with "normal" criminals. In some ways, it is quite different. While I do not have definitive recommendations related to these distinctions, I hope this discussion provides some benefit. In order to more fully comprehend the distinctions—or the possible distinctions—the following examples may inform your thinking.

In the United Kingdom, a special committee is considering a proposal that would extend the amount of time that police can detain terror suspects without charging them. Currently police can hold suspects for 28 days without charging them. The proposal seeks to extend this time frame to 42 days. Metropolitan Police Commissioner Sir Ian Blair argued that officers needed more time to detain suspects because planned attacks are very complex. As would be expected, this proposal has been criticized by some who believe that the current limit is sufficient and an extension would send the wrong message to Britain's Muslim community.[49]

These laws relating to detention have been amended due to the impact of terrorism. Prior to 9/11, U.K. police were allowed 14 days to hold suspects without charging. This was expanded to 28 days following the July 7, 2005, train bombings.[50] Data from these detentions are instructive. Between 9/11 and the end of 2006, a total of 1,162 people were detained under suspicion of terrorism offenses. The impact of these detentions may be best demonstrated by the 2006 trans-Atlantic airline plot. When this plot was uncovered, 24 people were held pending further investigation. While these individuals were being held, British police conducted an extensive investigation involving 200 cell phones, 400 computers, 8,000 CD/DVD/computer discs, and 70 homes, businesses, and open spaces.[51] The scope and breadth of this investigation could not have been possible in the United States (see discussion below).

In the United States, President Obama is poised to make rather dramatic changes to interrogation policies. CIA Director Leon Panetta said in his confirmation hearings that he would support the prosecution of some *agents* who used torture when interrogating terrorism suspects. In his remarks, Panetta noted that agents who deliberately violated the law by using torture should be prosecuted. While he does not support the prosecution of agents who were "given high-level guidance" allowing the use of techniques such as waterboarding, Panetta added that the Senate Intelligence Committee would be a good place for an inquiry into the CIA's use of torture. Panetta further asserted that he would do everything he could to cooperate with such an investigation. Contrast this thinking with that of former CIA Director Michael Hayden. He did not support congressional inquiries into his agency's use of torture because he believed that agents would be intimidated in their performance if they felt legally vulnerable. Further, Panetta also discussed the approach the Obama Administration would take regarding the use of torture. He noted that if necessary he would ask the president to allow harsher interrogation techniques than those allowed by the *Army Field Manual*, which has been established as the standard for interrogations. However, Panetta said he would inform Congress if President Obama were to authorize a departure from those standards.[52]

In my mind, these examples speak volumes as to what lies ahead for policing—and for public safety. First, the police in the United Kingdom have the ability to hold suspects without charging for 28 *days* without charging them with a crime.

This allows the police to pursue investigative leads for almost one month before charging or releasing the terrorism suspect. It also allows the police to interrogate the suspect during this time frame. Think of the significance of this legal standard. If a terrorist plot is imminent, the police could hold terrorism suspects, investigate individuals from known cells, and generally follow related investigative leads. They are able to do this for one month. Now think of American police practices. Police in the United States are limited to 48 *hours* before they must charge or release a suspect. The distinction between the United States and the United Kingdom is dramatic. In my mind, 48 hours is woefully too short when one considers the potential implications of failing to interdict a pending terrorist plot. Indeed, police in the United Kingdom desire to increase their power by 50 percent to 42 days. I contend—and predict—American police must reassess these time constraints. Simply stated, if we do not do so, we will take a significant tool away from the police.

The other example relates to the changes that are or will take place related to CIA interrogations. Based on the example provided above, it is my assertion that the Obama Administration will move away from some of the interrogation methods used by the Bush Administration. The stated reason for these changes is to increase our moral and legal standards. While I respect the desire to raise the bar—both morally and legally—we must realize that dangerous consequences exist. As I will develop in the Security versus Rights section below, the fact is we cannot have optimal levels of security and rights.

The last issue related to investigations relates to the age-old notions of "motive," "means," and "opportunity." In the typical criminal investigation, these issues have been well developed. Motive relates to why someone would want to commit the crime. Here investigators look for reasons why someone would be inclined to kill another. Motives such as greed, revenge, heat of passion, jealousy, and the like are typically analyzed. Similarly, means in a criminal case typically relates to how the crime was committed. For example, a gun was used to shoot the person, a vehicle was used for transportation, a crowbar was used to access the premises, and the like. Finally, opportunity typically relates to who had the ability to commit the crime. It further relates to where the opportunity presented itself. When focusing on both who and where the crime was committed, it narrows the opportunity to a select number of people.

In terrorism investigations, "motive," "means," and "opportunity" are still important, yet the focus of these techniques is different (Figure 10.2). Motive in a terrorism investigation points to the ideology of the group or cause. A clear example of this is with a bombing of an abortion clinic. This target is so limited that it often points directly to antiabortion groups—and specific individuals within these groups. Further, since the "direct action" is often combined with a communiqué (remember terrorism is primarily theater), the motive of the action will be made clear in the communiqué. The motive and the ideology of the group must be analyzed and reconciled. Investigators must assess whether these make sense. As to means, the "how" or the operational tactics and methods used is also critical. For example, some terrorist groups have been known to use specific types of bombs. If

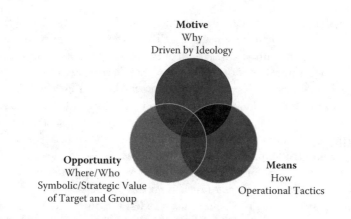

Figure 10.2 Terrorism investigation recommendations (Copyright, James F. Pastor, 2009).

this "signature" of the group does not equate with the communiqué, then one must be cautious about making rash conclusions. A classic example of this is the train bombings in Spain. When the bombings took place, the separatist group ETA took immediate credit for the attack. However, the nature of the attack did not equate with the historical methods used by ETA. This group tended to avoid mass casualties. It typically called in a warning prior to the explosion. The Spain train bombings did not correspond with these approaches. This caused investigators to quickly turn their attention away from ETA to al Qaeda.

Opportunity assesses the "where" and "who" questions in terms of the strategic and symbolic values. This relates to both the target and the offending group. This entails considering what strategic and symbolic value the target represents. It also entails considering what benefits a particular group's strategic and symbolic interests are represented in the direct attack. The key here is that the target and the ideology of the group must correspond. While it is true that "random" attacks on soft targets may represent widespread strategic and symbolic value, it is important to keep this approach in mind as a way to analyze who benefits and why from the direct action.

Finally, once these investigative principles are assessed, it is recommended that an "enterprise" approach is used to counter terrorist groups. This approach uses intelligence-driven investigative techniques to "identify the full scope of a criminal organization."[53] This approach avoids arrests against low-level operatives. Instead, it seeks to work the case as deep into the criminal organization as possible. An example of this approach is seen in Israel. When Israeli police encounter low-level crimes, such as prostitution, minor drug offenses, and the like, they seek to determine the source and motivation of the larger criminal organization. Consequently, the desire is not simply to arrest and prosecute individual members of the group. The larger goal is to take down the entire organization.

Use of Force: Model and Training

One of the most controversial aspects of this new policing model involves whether the "use of force" model currently used in policing should be amended. At the outset, let me give my opinion. The current use of force model will need to be modified or at least clarified to account for suicide bombers. In order to get a sense of where I am going with this assertion, it may be useful to consider some guidance from DHS training manuals. Consider this language:[54]

> If the suicide bomber is moving in the direction of his/her target, immediate action should be taken to stop or slow the approach. ... In most cases, lethal force is the only alternative. Using *intermediate* options on the use of force continuum will likely cause the bomber to detonate his/her IED. ... To complicate matters, you may be forced to operate on suspicion rather than hard evidence. Using lethal force against a suspicious, yet innocent, individual is an example of the worst possible scenario for an event of this kind. ... Once the decision is made to use lethal force, the officer designated to fire should attempt to kill the individual with one shot. ... A more dangerous shot to the head may be required ...

These guidelines have real life application. On July 7, 2005, four young men committed suicide bombings against London trains and a bus, killing 52 people. On July 21, 2005, another attempt was made to bomb the London transportation system. These bombs failed to explode. On July 22, 2005, Jean Charles de Menezes is seen running on a London train platform. Police chase the suspect. He is subsequently shot in the head and killed. Tragically, the suspect was not a terrorist.[55] A subsequent year-long investigation by the Crown Prosecution Service resulted in a decision not to prosecute the officers. A London court subsequently found the department liable, but not the individual officers.

Another incident illustrates this difficult dynamic. In June 2006 in the London neighborhood of Forest Gate, police raided a Muslim home acting on an intelligence tip about a "dirty bomb." Police tactically enter the home using stun grenades. During the entry, however, police accidentally shot a man. No dirty bomb was found. Two other men were subsequently released without being charged.[56] Following the incident, London Metropolitan Police Chief Blair stated that "there has to be an acceptance of *robust* techniques when the threat is very real" (emphasis added).[57]

Both of these examples portend what will occur in the United States. In both cases, the police were faced with the possibly of an imminent and substantial threat. In both cases they were wrong. In both cases innocent people were killed. Both cases were tragic, yet predictable. Consider the alternatives. What if the individual killed on the train was, indeed, a suicide bomber? What would have happened if individuals in the Forest Gate home possessed a "dirty bomb?" If these individuals were killed by police prior to exploding their devices, would those in the "audience" have applauded the actions of the police officers? Of course, they would. But since the police were wrong, the predictable accusations are leveled at the officers and at the larger department. Is this fair? Do you think this will not occur in the United States? It will happen here. Inevitably, the "brilliant" people in the audience will be dismayed with such "trigger happy," even "racist" police officers. With these predictable accusations, do you think a police officer will take the chance of being wrong? Just as in my arguments related to police shootings, the inevitable response from police is to "disengage." Simply stated, if police are not supported when they make critical, split-second decisions in an attempt to avoid catastrophic events, then they will tend to avoid these circumstances—and fail to take timely action. In any case, these decisions will have societal implications.

The legal standard to assess whether the force used was "reasonable" requires a careful assessment of objective facts as perceived by the officer at the time of the incident. The court in *Graham v. Connor* framed the analysis as follows:[58]

> Reasonableness of particular use of force must be judged from perspective of reasonable officer on the scene, and the calculus of reasonableness must allow for fact that police officers are often forced to make split-second judgments, in circumstances that are tense, uncertain and rapidly evolving, about amount of force that is necessary in a particular situation.

This is a very fact-driven assessment. The fact finder is supposed to put themselves in the shoes of the officer at that moment in time. The assessment of what is reasonable depends upon many facts and circumstances. These include "the severity of the crime, whether the suspect poses an immediate threat to the safety of the officers or others, and whether the suspect is actively resisting arrest or attempting to evade arrest by flight."[59] In addition, what is reasonable "must be judged from the perspective of a reasonable officer on the scene, rather than with the 20/20 vision of hindsight."[60]

In this way, the "Monday-morning quarterbacking" or the 20/20 hindsight arguments must be tempered by the facts and perceptions as they were at the time of the incident. Sometimes this assessment can literally require a reaction based on a second, or even in fractions of a second. This is particularly true in shooting incidents. As one can image, this is a difficult assessment to make. Numerous stimuli and perceptions must be processed quickly and accurately. This must be accomplished under tense and dangerous situations. Fortunately, courts have articulated some factors to help determine the appropriateness of the extent and level of force. These factors include:

- Seriousness of the threat
- Immediacy of the threat (in terms of time and distance)
- Weapons used (or threatened to be used) by the suspect

- Whether escape or retreat was possible
- Safety of innocent third parties (the public at large)

With this legal standard in mind, the application of suicide bombers to the use of force model presents some unique problems. Let's start with a simple assertion. The key determination is what level of force (if any) is reasonable under the circumstances. In order to assess the reasonableness of force, models have been developed to illustrate the appropriate application of force.[61] These models are designed to illustrate the reasonable officer's perception against the reasonable officer's appropriate response. The model provides specific characterizations of perceptions and appropriate responses (responses are in parentheses): compliant (cooperative controls) to passive resistant (contact controls) to active resistant (compliance techniques) to assaultive (defensive tactics) to serious assaultive (deadly force).[62]

As illustrated by Figure 10.3, in most cases, these models require a corresponding relationship between perception and response. Typically this requires that the officer's response commence at the lowest corresponding level as compared to the officer's perception. Stated another way, the model usually does not commence with the use of deadly force. Even in circumstances where deadly force is appropriate, officers are typically trained to take cover and engage the suspect in verbal commands. These commands typically involve such responses as "drop the gun," "put your hands up," or "get on the ground." While these commands are being made, officers are trained to not unduly put themselves in harm's way. If, during these verbal commands, the suspect appears ready to fire the gun, then the officer has the legal authority to fire *before* being fired upon. As dynamic and complex as these situations can be, they pale by comparison to those of the suicide bomber.

The application of this model related to suicide bombers will be very tenuous. Consider these facts. An individual is seen wearing a large, loose-fitting, out of season jacket walking nervously in a crowded street fair. The individual has wires protruding from under his jacket. His eyes are intense. He has a distinct and heavy odor of cologne. He appears to be holding something in his left hand, which is held

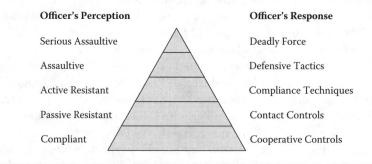

Officer's Perception	Officer's Response
Serious Assaultive	Deadly Force
Assaultive	Defensive Tactics
Active Resistant	Compliance Techniques
Passive Resistant	Contact Controls
Compliant	Cooperative Controls

Figure 10.3   Use of force model considerations (Copyright, James F. Pastor, 2009).

tightly against his body. In the backdrop of this street fair, intelligence analysts had previously warned that an extremist group was going to make a "big statement." You are an officer assigned to the street fair. What do you do? The most respected legal and operational policies suggest that[63]

> lethal force is justified if the suspect represents a significant threat of death or serious injury to an officer or others. … Officers should be reminded that the law does not require that the threat of death or serious injury be *imminent*, as is sometimes noted in police use of force policies [emphasis in original].
>
> One [officer] need not wait until a suicide bomber makes a move or takes other action potentially sufficient to carry out the bombing when officers have reasonable basis to believe that the suspect has the capability to detonate a bomb. The *threat* of such use is, *in most instances* [emphasis added], sufficient justification to employ deadly force. An officer need only determine that the use of deadly force is objectively reasonable under the circumstances [emphasis in original].

Consider this guidance in light of the above scenario. The guidelines provide the legal authority to use deadly force when the officer objectively believes that the circumstances warrant it. In this scenario, as I presented the facts, the officer may objectively believe that the individual may be a suicide bomber. In this circumstance, the officer has few options. First, do nothing and "hope" the individual is not a threat, that he is simply homeless or "down on this luck." Second, attempt to inconspicuously move bystanders away from the path of the individual. Third, confront the individual and ask him to drop the object in his hand. Fourth, shoot the individual in the head.[64]

Ironically, the established guidelines would not advise using technique two or three. Consider the alternatives. The second technique, while it may be appropriate in some circumstances, is risky since the individual may observe the officer attempting to remove bystanders from his path. Also, the bystanders are not likely to silently and dutifully respond to the officer's discreet attempts to seek immediate compliance. Similarly, the third technique is also obviously risky. If the individual is a suicide bomber, confronting him will likely be the last thing the officer ever does. So too for the bystanders who happen to be nearby.

In the end, the options may often boil down to two alternatives: do nothing and hope, or shoot the individual in the head. I trust the reader will acknowledge this extraordinarily difficult circumstance. Mark my words, this will occur in the United States.[65] It will occur frequently! Indeed, this will occur because the use of suicide bombers is inexpensive and effective. According to Hoffman, it is the "ultimate smart bomb." Perhaps more importantly, suicide bombings are "coldly efficient" in that they tear at the fabric of trust that holds societies together."[66] As this section makes clear, however, the operational impact on public safety providers will be severe. If I am correct, we need to amend—or at least clarify—the use of force models.

A contemporary example may illustrate how difficult it will be to codify such precise judgment under intense circumstances. Consider the use of private security personnel in Iraq. From 2006 to 2007, the number of weapons used by private security nearly doubled to 207 compared to 115 the previous year. The military acknowledges that the coordinating and enforcing discipline among thousands of contractors moving around the battlefield has been a challenge. These private security personnel are required to use the same procedures as the military when encountering a threat. They are supposed to progressively "escalate force" by issuing warnings verbally and/or with hand signals before shooting to kill.[67]

What does this example illustrate and portend? While I cannot prove this assertion, my experience tells me that these data illustrate that some individuals may have shot instead of signaled. Think about the time frame of these data. This was at the height of the Iraq "civil war." As events got more violent, my sense is that the private security personnel were more likely to shoot. Did they appropriately escalate force prior to shooting? I cannot answer this question definitively. I can say, however, if people are fearful, they will respond to their perceived threat and act in self-defense. More importantly, what these data portend is if extremist violence becomes commonplace in this country, look for significant increases in deadly force incidents by police and security personnel.

While it is beyond the scope of this book to provide details of a model policy, suffice it to say that the model must emphasize the possibility of the immediate use of deadly force. Such force must be contemplated without any verbal command, or even hand signals. The policy should further instruct the officer to shoot into the head of the suspect—as aiming at the center mass (as is typical current training) will likely explode the explosive vest. In addition, this policy presupposes substantially more frequent and intense firearms training protocols. These training sessions should focus on "move and shoot" type training. This training should be as realistic as possible. It should include shooting on house entries, vehicle stops, and around crowded areas. These techniques are advocated instead of the rote standing and shooting at paper target approach currently used. Consequently, as I asserted in the "militarization" of police chapter, the training should be more reflective of tactical applications and military weaponry.

Security versus Rights

This section attempts to bring together the main themes of this book. I close this book with what I consider the most important principles facing this country—and any individual. Since the reader made it this far through the book, I presume that you have determined that my tendency is to err on the side of security as opposed to rights. While I readily admit to this tendency, I do not discount the incredibly important notion of rights—or more broadly, freedom or liberty. In my mind, freedom is one of the most important human ideals. It is what has driven people for generations. Millions of people have died for this ideal. It is, in short, what drives human souls to live a better life for themselves or for their children. The significance of this ideal may be best epitomized by the movie *Braveheart.*[68] The Scottish leader, William Wallace, fought against England, seeking freedom for his country. He was captured and asked to renounce this movement. He refused. As he was about to be hanged, he cried out "FREEEEE-DOMMMMMM" as his last words! The rest, as they say, is history.

My point is freedom is an extraordinarily powerful motivator. Indeed, in my analysis of the "Holy War," I believe the only way we can win this war is if freedom prevails over fanaticism. The war will be won, in the end, when more people are willing to die for freedom as opposed to those who are willing to die for a fanatical worldview. Put aside everything else you read in this book. Put aside every analysis you read or heard about in the "war on terrorism." I submit to you that this basic notion is stronger than any speech, any policy, any diplomatic effort, any politician—even any policing model! In the end, it is all about the reason you are living. Does your life have meaning larger than you? Are you willing to die for something? At the end of your life, do you "win" if you have the most toys, or a lasting and meaningful legacy?

Ironically, the value placed on freedom as the ultimate "solution" is partly tempered by the realities of the global conflict. In my mind, while the ultimate solution is that freedom must prevail over fanaticism, the reality is most people will not be willing to see it that way—or to have it that way. By this I mean the ultimate solution is only for the few who understand the nature of the conflict. As I stated earlier, since many in this country do not possess a belief in God, they will never accept the notion that a "Holy War" even exists. Indeed, they are even less likely to be part of the conflict. Most Americans simply want to be left alone. Unfortunately, the fanatics will not leave us alone—regardless of the wisdom or the folly of the Obama Administration policies. To reassert the statement made by Defense Secretary Gates, "We may not be interested in the long war, but the long war is interested in us."[69]

Since most Americans do not recognize or intend to be part of this war, I contend the only way we can hold off defeat is to secure ourselves from those who seek to do us harm. Interestingly, I find myself advocating for security over freedom because I do not believe the majority of Americans are ready for the nature of this conflict. If we as a country decide that this "war" is worth fighting, then the emphasis will likely shift to the notion that freedom is worth dying for. Until this time, if it indeed it ever occurs, I believe the best approach is to emphasize security in an attempt to maintain something close to the American ideal. I realize this statement may sound ambiguous—even contradictory. In some ways it is. In my mind the American ideal has always been more of a concept than a reality. We have many sins, many flaws. Our noblest ideals and principles, however, are real. Many have died for them. It seems to me that those on the political left, who tend to be the most critical of this country, are the very people who most ardently contend we must live up to the ideals of this country. In doing so, they strongly advocate for their rights, the rights of suspects, and the esteem of the world community. When they are not trumpeting these ideals, however, they seem more than happy to criticize this country as sexist, racist, imperialistic, selfish, and on and on. My point is this: Are those people who ardently advocate for their rights willing to die for them?

I will leave this rhetorical question for the reader. What is not rhetorical is that we go forward into history with a historic presidency at a time of great distress. As stated throughout this book, the policy changes and the circumstances of the times will result in increased extremist violence. The policy changes will shift from a security emphasis (as in the Bush Administration) to a rights emphasis in the Obama Administration. To be clear, I have every reason to believe that President Obama is a "true believer" in this approach. Indeed, his obvious love for his children and for this country would not allow him to intentionally put this country at risk. His policies, however, will do just that. As stated earlier, regardless of what people may say, there is no optimal level of security *and* rights. Liberty, by its very nature, allows for the free flow of people within society. In this sense, liberty, through the application of constitutional protections, allows citizens to interact, reside, conduct business, and move to and fro in a relatively unencumbered manner. The ability to do so, however, may provide opportunities or vulnerabilities to physical attack. Consequently, the conveniences and rights afforded to citizens of this country facilitate a perverse counter-objective—the destruction of people and property by those who are inclined to do so. Something has to give. I believe it will be our security.

The difficult dynamic between security and rights (or freedom) was thoughtfully analyzed by renowned constitutional attorney Stuart Taylor. He concisely stated, "When dangers increase, liberties shrink." According to Taylor it is preferable to adjust the rules and stop terrorism than to adhere to rigid laws and suffer the consequences. He made this larger point: "Preventing mass murder is the best way of avoiding a panicky stampede into truly oppressive 'police stateism,' in which measures now unthinkable could suddenly become unstoppable."[70] In this thinking it is better to avoid tragic and dramatic terrorist attacks *because* these attacks will lead to more draconian police and security practices. Hence, this "solution" is somewhat counterintuitive. It is necessary to proportionately reduce rights—and freedom—in order to prevent terrorist attacks. Lacking or at least minimizing terrorist attacks results in the protection of rights and freedoms. Consequently, one can make the argument that those who attempt to hold fast to each "small" freedom (see examples below) will actually experience the loss of significant freedoms. While those who advocate for rights will not see it this way, Posner notes that "the safer the nation feels the more weight judges will be willing to give to the liberty interest."[71] If society feels safe, judges will further liberty interests. If society is fearful, judges will further reduce rights in favor of security. A pointed analogy may help illustrate this dynamic: "A rattlesnake loose in the living room tends to end any discussion of animal rights."[72]

With these underlying principles established, let's observe and analyze the application of security versus rights in the world of policing. The new model of policing will be implemented in direct relation to the level of terroristic threat. This will foster competing desires of security and rights. Those who are fearful of crime and terrorism naturally desire more security. Just as fear is driving the need for security, it may also trump the quest for individual rights. In this sense, the desire for security will motivate people to advocate "militarized" police officers, hire private police officers, and use surveillance technologies. If these methods are not adequately restricted and controlled, they will lead to abuses. Furthermore, if tactical police units or private police personnel are not adequately trained and skilled, they are likely to violate our rights in the quest to keep us safe. Protecting people, however, usually requires control and surveillance, both of which are likely to affect the liberty and constitutional rights of the controlled or the surveilled.

Conversely, those who worry about liberty and constitutional rights will demand accountability and professionalism from public safety service providers. These goals, however, are often competing. In order to achieve the balance between security and rights, we must require higher levels of training, licensing standards, and more accountability. Particularly with private policing, this will require regulations, legitimatized legal authority, and increased expenditures for these services. Consequently, the relationship between the money expended and the services rendered creates a delicate balancing act. The optimal balance can only be achieved in relative calm, as opposed to the face of fear.

As developed in this book, the implementation of *Public Safety Policing* will not be a panacea. It is, instead, a pragmatic approach to vexing problems. As the above discussion makes clear, there are many conflicting views related to this policing model. The essence of these views is what principle should prevail: security or rights. It may be instructive to get a sense of how these views are articulated. Each of the elements of this policing model has at its core an underlying struggle between these critical principles.

In the placement of cameras in Denver, some residents voiced concerns about possible privacy violations. These concerns were dismissed by U.S. Senator Martinez who noted, "Police will be on guard against violating or impeding First and Fourth Amendment rights while using the cameras." He added, "It's not an Orwellian type of thing, it's a crime thing." The opposite assertion was aptly made by Mark Silverstein, legal director of the American Civil Liberties Union of Colorado, who contends that "there is something terribly invasive about police employees watching us with sophisticated cameras." This sense was echoed by a resident, who stated, "It seems like Big Brother is able to get closer and closer watching American citizens."[73] This concern was also made by a Washington, DC, lawyer who focuses on privacy issues, Melissa Ngo, who said using such technology could pave the way for "Big Brother" government spying. "If this technology ends up being deployed widely, it seems to be another step toward a society where you need to accept surveillance in every part of your life," Ngo added.[74] This was similarly asserted by U.K. sociologist Clive Norris, who concluded that cameras are becoming so "omnipresent that all Britons should assume their behavior outside the home is monitored."[75]

The debate between security versus rights is also relevant on an operational level. At this level, the question becomes whether the risk of reducing rights is justified by whether there is actually an increase in security. Stated another way, is there actually an increase in security by utilizing these methods? There is some evidence in the affirmative.

In Newark, New Jersey, Mayor Cory Booker believes the public sector surveillance system will lead to less crime. Statistics appear to bear this out. As of late August of 2008, there have been 37 murders, a 40 percent drop from 62 last year. Shooting incidents decreased by 19 percent. Within the last year, live or recorded video evidence led to 101 arrests. Booker hopes the gunshot detection technology will further lower those crime rates. To address privacy concerns, city officials have teamed up with the American Civil Liberties Union to establish a set of rules and standards, including not allowing cameras to look inside residences and only keeping footage for 30 days. Police officials credit the increased surveillance for the decrease in crime. These officials also attribute crime reduction to the department's overall strategy.[76]

According to Brooks, research has shown that CCTV provides a decrease in the levels of crime. This reduction in crime, however, may only be for a short period of time and in certain crime categories.[77] Despite a significant investment in closed-circuit television cameras, British police officials note that just three percent of street crimes in London are solved using the images. After spending billions of pounds installing cameras, police are trying to implement new procedures designed to increase the effectiveness of the cameras. These include the creation of a new national database of images, putting images of suspects on the Internet, and including pictures of convicted criminals in the database. Others contend that police need additional training because they often avoid analyzing images since it can be difficult.[78]

Another study of camera systems in the United Kingdom was conducted by Martin Gill. He analyzed 14 separate CCTV systems, interviewed more than 300 people, and observed 450 hours of CCTV video. This research revealed some interesting results. The study found that sometimes too many cameras were installed, making adequate surveillance nearly impossible. Conversely, sometimes too few cameras were installed, making coverage incomplete. In between these extremes, sometimes operators ignored their work, the images were too hazy, or camera positioning resulted in variations from glare, foliage, and other environmental factors. Other problems stem from the use of simple disguises, such as hats, hoods, wigs, and the like. Even if the camera system accounted for all these factors, sometimes people could not be swayed from committing a crime due to drugs, alcohol, rage, or other factors.[79]

Of course, cameras should not be expected to deter all crime. This would be an unrealistic expectation. Sometimes the camera may help to capture the criminal. This was done in the U.K. examples noted earlier. It also occurs on a much smaller scale. For example, on August 11, 2003, Chicago police made their first arrest after a camera image showed Marcus D. Jackson smoking marijuana in his parked vehicle.[80] In some communities, however, whether or not cameras actually prevent crime is often not the issue. To some it's the perception that counts. Brooks notes that although "the community may have some concerns with CCTV, they generally welcome the systems."[81]

Of course, not all would agree with Brooks. In a *USA Today* article on the implementation of cameras in Chicago, Colias noted that residents and lawmakers are divided over whether cameras are effective—and whether they are an invasion of privacy that "brands neighborhoods as ghettos." Despite the reductions in crime rates noted in the article, where narcotics calls dropped 76 percent over a seven-month period and minor crimes, such as property damage, declined by 46 percent, a state senator attacked the program as a "violation of people's civil liberties ... that people shouldn't be spied on by Big Brother." In response, an ACLU spokesperson conceded that the cameras were constitutional—as long as the "police use them only to monitor street crime."[82] Chicago Mayor Richard Daley weighed in on this long-standing question, stating,[83]

> It's not Big Brother ... if you live in a community plagued with guns, gangs and drugs, they're screaming out for any help, it will enable us to keep an eye on several different street corners at the same time with minimal additional manpower.

This dispute between crime and rights has also been seen in other cities. In recent testimony before the Washington, DC, Council, Police Chief Cathy L. Lanier said the cameras have caused a 19 percent reduction in violent crime in areas within 250 feet of the devices. DC Mayor Adrian Fenty also touted the program as an important step toward ensuring public safety. Of course, critics say the cameras will only displace crime and could infringe on citizens' civil liberties. "These little pieces—they grow," says Art Spitzer of the ACLU. "You put a camera here it's not so bad, you put a camera there it's not so bad. But then it turns out all of a sudden, we find out there are 5,200 cameras. That's a big number."[84] A big number indeed! This criticism is not unexpected. To this point, questions have been raised as to whether such technology is even necessary or ethical. Melissa Ngo of the electronic-watchdog group Electronic Privacy Information Center says in the years following 9/11, the Bush Administration has a record of "expansions into surveillance when there's no credible threat."

Notice here the problem is the Bush Administration, particularly when *"there's no credible threat."* To those who have read this book—and numerous other books on terrorism—it defies existing facts and appropriate logic to defend this statement. However, one theme of this book points to the easy "answer" to simply blame Bush, and to deny the existence of any threat. In my mind, this approach fails to even register on the radar screen. Indeed, it is too hard to deal in the merits of the issue—to substantively argue the delicate balance between security and rights. To some, like Ms. Ngo, it is easier to simply demonize Bush while pretending the threat does not exist. This "logic" does not provide any meaningful solution. It simply furthers a dangerous and divisive fiction. What will she say about this matter in the Obama Administration?

A better approach is to actually address the security and rights (or privacy) balance. For example, consider the DC camera system that some have criticized for insufficient privacy safeguards. In response to this concern, the DC attorney general's office is creating a policy to protect privacy rights. It demonstrates an attempt to balance these competing concerns.[85] Similarly, in Florida critics cite the murders of a mother and daughter in a Boca Raton mall parking lot to show surveillance cameras are not a substitute for more on-duty police officers. "We should not install surveillance cameras because the federal government is enticing local communities with federal dollars or because cameras are now cheap," says Howard Simon of the American Civil Liberties Union. The article cites research that suggests security cameras work best when security guards are on patrol and the cameras are placed in well-lit areas. Of course, this goes back, again, to rights and resources.[86] It also points to two key elements of *Public Safety Policing*.

In the end, advocates of security and advocates of rights are both correct. Each of these principles must be furthered. The movement toward a surveillance-based society, however, will not be stopped. Simply stated, the train has left the platform. The train will not turn back. As we have seen in this book, the trend toward increasing security controls will not be stopped. This fact has application both in the threat and in the perception. Let me develop this assertion. Please review Figure 10.4. This figure attempts to illustrate the delicate and difficult decision process that political and public safety leaders must assess. Let's analyze this process. Starting at the top, suppose that a universe of potential threats must be assessed. These threats can be something as simple as loitering or a package left on a street corner to the threat of a WMD attack. I will presume everyone wants to mitigate these potential threats. I will also presume that some will perceive the potential for threats differently than others. I will also presume people will differ as to how to best mitigate the potential threats. These are all reasonable expectations. The problem is how to reconcile or, more accurately, how to respond to these potential threats. When deciding how to respond, it is critical to consider balancing rights (freedoms) and security (safety). While it would be utopia to have complete freedom with no restrictions on our rights, all reasonable people will agree that this is impossible. Similarly, it would be utopia to achieve complete security with all threats mitigated. All reasonable people will agree that this is impossible. In this continuum, somewhat in the middle is the optimal balance. Here is where the decisions are made—and where the conflicts exist.

On your left side (ironically) are those who desire to err on the side of rights. This entails government underreacting to the potential threat. On your right side

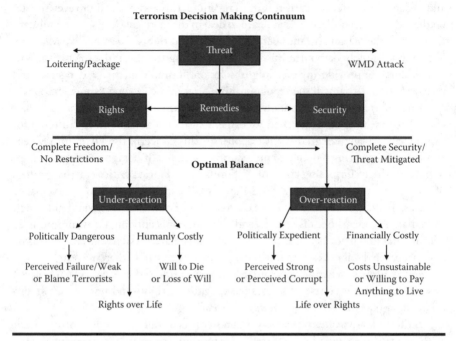

Figure 10.4   Terrorism decision-making continuum (Copyright, James F. Pastor, 2009).

(ironically) are those who desire to err on the side of security. This entails government overreacting to the potential threat. Understand that these are "judgment calls" based on the worldview and the biases of the decision makers. In the real world, it is almost impossible to have perfect knowledge as to the exact nature, timing, location, and method of a potential attack. It is seldom, if ever, that these factors are known with definitiveness before an actual attack occurs. In the few cases where this information is indeed known, chances are it would be derived from intelligence capabilities and practices. Of course, the extent and scope of intelligence are also based on the worldview and biases of the decision maker. In the end, this process is circular and subjective. Let's deal with each of these options individually.

An under-reaction entails doing less than necessary to mitigate the potential threat. This option is politically dangerous. If an attack occurs, the inevitable questions will result. Did the government do enough to protect us? How could this attack have been stopped? These and other questions are inevitable. As mentioned earlier, the government and the terrorist group both need to "spin" their story. However, the government needs its story to be spun beyond official proclamations. This requires media, opposition parties, and other thoughts leaders to advocate the government "line." If these critical information sources focus on the group's act—and condemn the source of the action—then the "masses" are likely to "understand" the cause as being the "bad" terrorists. This is what occurred in the days after 9/11. Conversely, if the media, opposition parties, and other thought leaders blame the government for failing to stop the attack, then the "masses" are likely to "understand" the cause as being a "weak" government. Hence, the perceived cause of the direct action is fluid and subjective. Because the country and the media are so bifurcated, it is likely that the "masses" will "understand" the perceived cause based on where they get their "news." In any event, it is potentially dangerous for politicians to be perceived as "weak." Hence, it is politically expedient to overreact to the potential threat.

On a more basic level, it is humanly costly to underreact to the threat of terrorism. Typically, the decision process is whether to impose security methods or to foster freedom. Security methods, while not a guarantee, will make it harder to successfully hit the target. Fostering freedom, conversely, will make it easier to successfully hit the target. Simply stated, if government policies do not adequately address and mitigate the threat, then attacks will occur. This will result in the loss of human life. Here the question is, do you actually desire to protect and foster your rights if you may have to die doing so? In this sense, we can enhance the rights of suspects. We can enhance the security of citizens. While I advocate seeking the "proper" balance between these two critical principles, it is vital not to kid ourselves. Let's not pretend that we can maximize rights and maximize security. Something has to take precedent. Something has to be prioritized. When we focus on rights, we will increase security risks. When we focus on security, we will decrease freedom standards. President Bush clearly focused on the latter. President Obama likely will focus on the former. As stated earlier, neither of these approaches are inherently "bad," "wrong," or "evil." Instead, it is based on a worldview. One worldview prefers rights over security, while the other prefers security over rights.

To those who desire rights over security, I add one cautionary note. If you desire this approach, it is necessary to acknowledge the potential for security risks. If you accept this increased risk voluntarily and willingly, then I commend your courage and resolve. If you truly value rights over your life, then my regards are with you. To those who parrot this notion without thinking through the implications, however, then I caution you to be careful what you ask for! Stated another way, if you are not prepared to increase your risk in relation to your desire to enhance and preserve freedom and rights, then I respectfully assert that you are simply denying reality.

In the end, this dynamic has two mirror-opposite implications. In a sustained terrorist campaign, people will either determine that their rights are so valuable that they are willing to die for them, or they will experience the loss of will and concede to the demands of the terrorists. Ultimately, advocates for freedom and rights, if they are truly convinced of this principle, will favor rights over life. In this sense, rights and security are like a balance—think of "Lady Justice" with the scales. If you do not acknowledge this dynamic, then I respectfully submit you are being deceived or simply have not thought through the implications of such. In any event, I believe the notion of "eyes wide open" works as an analogy for this issue. Take this "advice" for whatever it is worth!

On the opposite side of the continuum are those who favor security over rights. These political leaders will tend to overreact to the threat of terrorism. Here again, perception is more important than reality. The example of former President Bush is instructive. Those who saw his policies as an overreaction viewed him as corrupt—as desiring to take my rights away. Think of Ms. Ngo who criticized the Bush Administration's "expansions into surveillance when there's no credible threat." To a large number of Americans this assertion is right on point. The questions that are missed by those with this worldview are this: Is the fact that we have not experienced another terrorist attack since 9/11 evidence that no threat exists? Or does it manifest from the policies of the Bush Administration that mitigated the threat? Of course, to those with conflicting worldviews, the answer is either the former or the latter. As described throughout this book, terrorism has become so politicized that most people cannot let go of their bias to objectively assess "reality." Those who have labored through this book know my opinion. With all due respect to those with a worldview that supports those of Ms. Ngo, I will let time determine if the threat actually exists.

For now, former President Bush's policies have "convinced" many in this country that he indeed lied over WMD in Iraq (see Appendix) and imposed draconian—and "illegal"—practices designed to combat the threat of terrorism. The fact that this country has been safe for over seven and a half years (as of the time of this writing) seems to be of no consequence to some. Indeed, Bush receives no credit from many in society for this fact. While this may be partly due to Bush's inability to articulate the nature of the threat—and of his policies designed to address the threat—it also has much to do with the media pronouncement of daily "propaganda of the deed." It also has much to do with opposition party leaders who seemed content to blame Bush—instead of the "terrorists." While Bush made many mistakes, as discussed in this book, he also kept us safe. He took the fight to the enemy. He was sometimes flawed but he was resolute. He sought to protect the country even at the expense of some rights and conveniences. As you can discern from the framework of this book, I think in retrospect, history will see his policies more positively than negatively. Indeed, some may look back on the Bush era with respect. I predict his policies will increasingly be viewed as being based on a strong response to the threat of terrorism rather than the current and simplistic notion that he was a lying and corrupt leader.

The policies of the Bush Administration were indeed costly. The wars in Iraq and Afghanistan expended much blood and treasure. In this sense, I think it is fair to criticize Bush as having overreacted to the potential threat of WMD in Iraq. It is fair to say this decision was wrong. Because we have the benefit of hindsight, we can sound so wise and thoughtful in making this assertion. As pointed out in the Appendix, however, those who thought otherwise *prior* to the war were largely silent. Of course, one voice that did speak against the war was President Obama.

His opposition to the war has been made plain. He clearly spoke out against the war *prior* to the war. His voice, however, was coming from a state legislator. He had no vote or influence in the decision. He subsequently campaigned against the war. Largely due to his clear opposition, he defeated the favored Democratic candidate—Hillary Clinton.

Now that he is elected, he will have to make difficult decisions related to the war. Will he remove U.S. troops from Iraq within the 18-month time frame? If—and when—the troops are removed, will this manifest a free and friendly ally? Will the Iraqi government represent democratic principles and ideals? In my mind, this is the real reason why Bush invaded. Even if my sense is incorrect, we have an extraordinary opportunity to further freedom rather than fanaticism. Will we have the will to sustain this struggle? Will we have the will to foster freedom in a very dangerous—and critical—region? Think back to the chorus of naysayer and critical commentary. What are we doing in this civil war? Famously, the senate majority leader, Henry Reid, declared the Iraq War as lost in spring 2007. Specifically, Reid stated[87]

> I believe myself that the secretary of state, secretary of defense and—
> you have to make your own decisions as to what the president knows—
> (know) this war is lost and the surge is not accomplishing anything as
> indicated by the extreme violence in Iraq yesterday.

In February 2009, who is making this same assertion? Better yet, who held the Democratic leader accountable for being wrong? His words simply disappear into the void of the media. They are not so interested in Iraq anymore. The "news" is not as "interesting" as it was two and three years ago. Simply stated, as noted in Chapter 8, the "propaganda of the deed" is not as common as it was years ago. This should be trumpeted throughout society—and by freedom-loving people everywhere. Where is this chorus? The silence is deafening! In the end, the war in Iraq—as well as the larger "Holy War," will manifest the ultimate question to President Obama and to the American people, that is, do we have the will to sustain this conflict? Bush called this a "generational conflict." He was right. As asserted earlier, I do not believe that we are disposed to engaging in such a long conflict. This is particularly due to the nature and the complexity of the conflict. In the end, are we willing to do as former President Kennedy asked in his inauguration address in 1961:[88]

> Let every nation know, whether it wishes us well or ill, that we shall
> pay any price, bear any burden, meet any hardship, support any friend,
> oppose any foe, in order to assure the survival and success of liberty.

Unless we can muster these basic—yet powerful—ideals we will not win the fight against our adversaries. Stated another way, unless we are willing to pay any price, we will not succeed. This includes financial, societal, political, or personal costs. In the end, we must be willing to subordinate our rights over our lives—but be prepared to also pay with our lives. For good and for bad, our new president will be entrusted with innumerable decisions relative to this conflict. He needs prayers, wisdom, and support. He also needs to deeply understand the worldview of those who desire to kill us and to destroy the American empire—or the Great Satan. President Obama did not create this circumstance. It may not be fair to expect him to extricate us from it. History or providence has brought us to this point. Like one of President Obama's heroes, neither did Abraham Lincoln create the circumstances he inherited. Does President Obama have the wisdom, the faith, and the courage to lead us through the years ahead? Time will tell. I am greatly concerned. We, as a people, need to understand what we are up against. Hopefully this book will help flesh out how to think about these substantive issues facing this country.

One way to assess the underlying worldviews that lead people to favor security or rights is to understand this dynamic. How does one come to focus on security or rights? In times of calm and serenity, almost every reasonable person will favor rights over security. When violent events occur, some percentage of people will refocus their lives around security. If they happen to work in jobs that expose them to crime, violence, or war, then they will tend to err on the side of security. This is largely due to the exposure to the brutality of life. Those who have not lived these experiences will be less likely to discern this brutality. They may, therefore, be more inclined to focus on their rights.

In the end, I contend this dynamic is based at its core on this basic question: Are people inherently good or bad? While this does not have a straight line, constant answer, this core belief has significant implications. If you believe people are inherently good, then you will be much more likely to talk to them. This tendency will enable you to believe that people will "do the right thing." They can be reached by solid facts, good logic, and a supportive and friendly approach. In biblical terms, this approach is grounded on the famous sermon that advocates "turning the other cheek" and "love thy neighbor as thy self." Since most people live in a "civilized" world, this worldview is prominent with most people—particularly those who can be considered the "elites." These people are more likely to focus on their rights.

Conversely, those who see people as inherently bad are much more inclined to fight them. This tendency will enable you to believe that people must be watched, or at least not implicitly trusted. In this notion, "trust but verify" is a defining logic. In biblical terms, this approach is grounded on the Old Testament notion of "the fall." The fall is the original sin. From this sin, human nature was implanted in men and women. This belief recognizes that people are self-interested. They will do what is good for them. While some people will be able to overcome these tendencies, one must not assume they will do so. In order to foster a more selfless approach to life, the goal is to place appropriate incentives to direct human nature to its better proclivity.

In closing, I ask you to dig deep to wrestle with your own proclivity and your sense of the challenges we face ahead. It is my sense that our "Westernized" or "civilized" minds are deeply ambivalent about the notion of evil. Indeed, as an "intellectual," I find it often out of place in "academic" circles to even mention the word. To many the notion of evil is simplistic, a throwback to earlier eras of human development. Ironically, this "sophisticated" thinking is naïve. Even if you dismiss the underlying truth to this notion, one is hard-pressed to deny that our adversaries view us as evil. The left desires to simply critique our foreign policy as the source of this belief. If you actually listen to or read what is said, however, our adversaries critique many aspects of American society—including our perceived moral and spiritual decadence. Assuming we can "clean up" our foreign policy and offer sufficient reparations to "cure" our past faults, do you think they will ignore the "sins" of our culture and our lifestyle? The cold, hard fact is they will not forgive these "sins." Simply stated, they see us as "evil." Many of our most "enlightened" citizens and leaders cannot even acknowledge the concept of evil. Who has the upper hand in this thinking?

I think the answer is clear. In a worldview that seeks to separate "believers" from the infidels, our adversaries have a great incentive. This incentive leads some with the desire to fight to the death. Indeed, many of our adversaries value death more than we value life. The impact of this reality is clear—at least to those who understand the stakes. The implication of such was pointedly made by Laura Ingraham, who stated,[89]

> It is not enough for us to defend American soil or to maintain a thriving economy. It will all be in vain if we fail to nurture and refresh America's soul. And that is only possible through individual belief demonstrated through action. ...
>
> If we lose faith in God, it will be very difficult to keep faith with our duty to defend America—from without or within. ... If we find unity in faith, there is no challenge—internal or external—that can overwhelm us.

Indeed, the issue is not simply rights against security. The issue is what we stand for. If we see the "big picture" and understand the larger purpose of life, then the challenges that lie ahead are placed in proper perspective. The universal struggle our adversaries define as a "Holy War" has been asserted against us. Many in this country, either consciously or unwittingly, are allies in this struggle. Of course, no one is "wrong." Everyone sees their role as necessary and proper. People of good will disagree on principle. People with evil hearts and minds simply do not care. In the end, people will look at the legacy of our lives and ask, what did he or she live for? Were you part of the solution or the problem? This answer is both personal and provincial. I think I will let Matthew answer for me: "For whoever wants to save his life will lose it, but whoever loses his life for me will find it."[90]

I close this book with two pointed quotations. One speaks of war. The other advocates for peace. The first is from another North American president who spoke of hope prior to our current president: Vicente Fox, the former president of Mexico. In his book, *Revolution of Hope*, he powerfully asserts that[91]

Only when we are fully immersed in challenge can we forget our weakness and our fears and summon the courage, stamina, and strength to overcome all obstacles. ... In order to move mountains, first we must move souls. This is our challenge. This is how we become men and women for others. This is our revolution of hope.

The other quote is thousands of years old. It was made famous by the Sun Tzu. His work, *The Art of War*, has been a manual for commanders and military strategists for thousands of years. His approach to war is simple yet profound. As "civilized" and "sophisticated" people, we sometimes find these notions—like the concept of evil—so trite and even foolish. I say these principles have sustained the test of time not because they are trite or foolish. Instead, they have because they speak to the basic tenets of human existence and human nature. As you read these words, please juxtapose them with the quotes above. They all go to the same place. They all relate to why we live. They all relate to what we live for. I hope they touch you and stay with you in the months and years ahead. In any event, the message from Tzu is as follows:[92]

If you know the enemy and know yourself, you need not fear the results of a hundred battles. If you know yourself and not the enemy, for every victory gained, you will also suffer a defeat. If you know neither yourself or the enemy, you will succumb in every battle.

In the end, there are many "heroes" during peaceful times. When violence prevails, most of these "heroes" will forget their advocacy for "rights and the noble principle of human dignity." It is my belief that only during times of trouble are we able to discern the true character of people and societies. May this book provide you with the hope and courage to see the way through difficult times ahead.

Endnotes

1. *National Strategy for Homeland Security* (2007). Homeland Security Council, Office of the President of the United States, October, 41.
2. *National Strategy for Homeland Security*, 41.
3. These indicators were obtained from a number of open sources and commingled together for organization and presentation.
4. Carlson, Tucker (1995). "Safety Inc.: Private Cops Are There When You Need Them," *Policy Review* 73 (Summer):52–62.
5. Pastor, James F. (2003). *The Privatization of Police in America: An Analysis and Case Study*. Jefferson, NC: McFarland and Company.
6. Carlson, Tucker (1995), op. cit.
7. Pastor, James F. (2007). "Private Policing in Public Environments," *Protection of Assets Manual*, ASIS International, January.

8. Simeone, Matthew J. (2006). "The Power of Public-Private Partnerships P3 Networks in Policing," *The Police Chief,* May.

9. Pastor, James F. (2007), op. cit.

10. Pastor, James F. (2007), op. cit.

11. See Holtz, Larry E. (2001). *Contemporary Criminal Procedure,* 7th ed. Longwood, FL: Gould Publications.

12. Pastor, James F. (2003), op. cit., 110–163.

13. See, for example, Pastor, James F. (2006). *Security Law and Methods.* Burlington, MA: Butterworth-Heinemann; and Nemeth, Charles P. (1989). *Private Security and the Law.* Cincinnati: Anderson.

14. Clifford, March (2004). *Identifying and Exploring Security Essentials.* Upper Saddle River, NJ: Pearson/Prentice Hall, 279.

15. Pastor, James F. (2006), op. cit., 413–414.

16. Pastor, James F. (2006), op. cit., 414–415.

17. Pastor, James F. (2006), op. cit., 415.

18. Pastor, James F. (2006), op. cit., 415.

19. Pastor, James F. (2006), op. cit., 412–413.

20. See Chapter 39/107-3 of Illinois Compiled Statutes.

21. Nemeth, Charles P. (1989), op cit., 72–79; and Pastor, James F. (2003), op cit., 77–83.

22. See, for example, Maryland Public Safety Statute Section 3-307, which allows the special police officer to make arrests, issue traffic citations, and direct and control traffic.

23. The use of "special police" status is rather common, but not well publicized. For example, in the city of Boston, there are about 125 armed special police employed by the city with an additional 100 employed by private firms. Swidey, Neil (2006). "Private Eyes: In Boston, as in Iraq, Private Cops Are Now Patrolling Some of the Most Dangerous Beats: Is This the Best Way to Keep the City Safe?" *The Boston Globe,* April 9, 46.

24. Pastor, James F. (2006), op. cit., 424–425.

25. Joh, Elizabeth E. (2004). "The Paradox of Private Policing," *The Journal of Criminal Law and Criminology* 95, no. 1:49–132, 64.

26. Joh, Elizabeth E. (2004), op. cit., 112.

27. Cincinnati Municipal Code, Title VIII: Business Regulations, Section 887-1. http://216.196.232.226/1c/cppa/PAGE8.HTM (retrieved on March 20, 2006).

28. Pastor, James F. (2006), op. cit., 425–426.

29. "Private Security Officer Selection and Training" (2004). ASIS International.

30. Ibid, "Private Security Officer Selection and Training" (2004), op. cit.

31. Pastor, James F. (2006), op. cit., 426–427.

32. Pastor, James F. (2003), op. cit., 110–163.

33. See, for example, Cincinnati Municipal Code Chapter 887-9, 11, 13, and 15.

34. Pastor, James F. (2006), op. cit., 427–428.

35. Pastor, James F. (2007), op. cit.

36. Cole, August (2007). "Private Security Providers Become a Pentagon Focus," *Wall Street Journal,* September 27, A9; Lardner, Richard (2007). "Who Watches US Security Firms in Iraq?" *Associated Press,* September 19; Barrett, Barbara (2007). "House OKs Bill to Make Security Contractors Subject to Prosecution in U.S.," *Kansas City Star,* October 4; and Karp, Jonathan (2007). "Contractors in War Zone Face Legal Front," *Wall Street Journal,* March 8, A10. In this article Karp provided some interesting legal background regarding this issue. He stated that "[p]rivate security contractors who

serve with American troops in Iraq are facing the threat of liability claims over the deaths of private security guards and American soldiers. Due to a 1950 Supreme Court ruling and other forms of protection, U.S. soldiers and their relatives are prohibited from suing the U.S. government over injuries or deaths that occur during military service. But suits are being filed against private security contractors that could test whether the contractors can be held liable under civil tort law. One case in particular that could impact the private security industry involves a suit filed against affiliates of Blackwater USA over the deaths of three U.S. soldiers who died in Afghanistan in November 2004 aboard a transport plane being operated by the affiliates. Michael Socarras of McDermott, Will, and Emery, lead trial lawyer for the Blackwater affiliates, says that defense contractors will face a changed environment if the case is allowed to go forward. 'Here is what is so alarming about the case: Never before has tort liability been applied to operations on the battlefield.' Blackwater is facing another suit in North Carolina that centers on the deaths of four Blackwater security guards during a March 2004 ambush in Fallujah, Iraq. The North Carolina suit alleges wrongful death and "fraudulent misrepresentation in contract."

37. Braglia, F. Thomas (2004). "Public-Private Law Enforcement: A Win-Win Partnership," *Command*, Winter.
38. Trojanowicz, Robert C. (1988). "Serious Threats to the Future of Policing," *Footprints*, National Center for Community Policing, Fall/Winter:1–2.
39. Sun, Lena H. (2008). "Metro to Randomly Search Riders' Bags," *Washington Post*, A1. http://www.washingtonpost.com/wp-dyn/content/article/2008/10/27/AR2008102700767.html?hpid=moreheadlineslocal (retrieved on October 28, 2008).
40. Video Surveillance: Information on Law Enforcement's Use of Closed Circuit Television to Monitor Selected Federal Property in Washington, DC (2003). Government Accounting Office, GAO-03-748, June:7.
41. *Katz v. U.S.*, 389 U.S. 347 (1967).
42. *U.S. v. Jackson*, 213 F.3d 1269 (10th Cir., 2000).
43. Video Surveillance: Information on Law Enforcement's Use of Closed Circuit Television to Monitor Selected Federal Property in Washington, DC (2003), op. cit., 29.
44. Parks, Bernard C., Joseph Curreri, and Gary S. Williams (2004). Terrorism and the Municipal Police Department. http://www.lapdonline.org/search_results/content_basic_view/27421 (retrieved on January 3, 2009).
45. Parks, Bernard C., Joseph Curreri, and Gary S. Williams (2004), op. cit., 2.
46. Parks, Bernard C., Joseph Curreri, and Gary S. Williams (2004), op. cit., 3.
47. Parks, Bernard C., Joseph Curreri, and Gary S. Williams (2004), op. cit., 3.
48. Parks, Bernard C., Joseph Curreri, and Gary S. Williams (2004), op. cit., 4.
49. Edwards, Richard (2008). "Police Have Foiled 15 Terror Plots Since 7/7." www.telegraph.co.uk (retrieved on April 23, 2008).
50. Harwood, Matt (2008). "Fighting Terrorism in the U.K.," *Security Management*, January:48–55.
51. Harwood, Matt (2008), op. cit., 54.
52. Mikkelsen, Randall (2009). "Obama CIA Pick May Back 'Limited' Abuse Prosecution," *Reuters* (UK), February 5.
53. O'Neil, Siobhan (2007). "Terrorist Precursor Crimes: Issues and Options for Congress," *Congressional Research Service* May 24:20.

54. National Center for Bio/Medical Research and Training (2004). "Recognizing WMD on the Streets," *Law Enforcement Prevention and Deterrence of Terrorist Acts,* Version 1.0, 4–64.

55. http://edition.cnn.com/2005/WORLD/europe/07/27/menezes.brazil/ (retrieved on February 10, 2009).

56. Harwood, Matt (2008), op. cit., 48.

57. Harwood, Matt (2008), op. cit., 50.

58. *Graham v. Connor,* 490 U.S. 386 (1989). See also *Tennessee v. Gardner,* 471 U.S. 1 (1985), holding that use of force, including deadly force, is a "seizure" pursuant to the Fourth Amendment.

59. See *Graham* supra.

60. See *Johnson v. LaRabida,* 372 F. 3d 894 (2004).

61. Connor, G. (1995). *Law Enforcement Officer Use of Force Model,* Integrated Force Management.

62. Connor, G. (1995), op. cit.

63. Training Key #582, Suicide (Homicide) Bombers: Part II (2005). Alexandria, VA: International Association of Chiefs of Police.

64. Training Key #582, Suicide (Homicide) Bombers: Part II (2005), op. cit., 2.

65. Of course, I am not the only person with this opinion. See, for example, former FBI Director Robert S. Mueller, who warned in May 2002 that suicide bombings like those in Israel are "inevitable" in the United States. Tucker, Jonathan B. (2003). "Strategies for Countering Terrorism: Lessons from the Israeli Experience," *Journal of Homeland Security* March 26:4.

66. Hoffman, Bruce (2006). "Defining Terrorism," in *Terrorism and Counter-Terrorism: Understanding the New Security Environment.* Eds. Russell D. Howard and Reid L. Sawyer. Dubuque, IA: McGraw-Hill, 145.

67. Michaels, Jim (2007). "Private Security Contractors' Role Grows in Iraq," *USA Today.* http://www.usatoday.com/news/world/iraq/2007-09-03-contactor_N.htm?csp=34 (retrieved on January 3, 2008).

68. Gibson, Mel, Alan Ladd, Bruce Davey, and Stephen McEveety (producers) (1995). *Braveheart* [motion picture]. United States: Paramount Pictures and Icon Entertainment.

69. Grant, Greg (2008). *Government Executive.com,* April 22. http://www.govexec.com/story_page.cfm?articleid=39835&dcn=e_ndw (retrieved on April 25, 2008); and Bender, Bryan (2008). "Gates: US Military Must Retool to Fight Terrorism," *Boston Globe,* December 5.

70. Yungher, Nathan I. (2008). *Terrorism: The Bottom Line.* Upper Saddle River, NJ: Pearson/Prentice Hall, 265–266.

71. Yungher, Nathan I. (2008), op. cit., 266.

72. Yungher, Nathan I. (2008), op. cit., 270.

73. Nicholson, Kieran (2008). "Denver Weighs Security vs. Privacy as Cops Focus Cameras on Crime," *The Denver Post.* http://www.denverpost.com/news/ci_10613181 (retrieved on October 3, 2008).

74. http://www.usatoday.com/news/nation/2008-09-17-car-scanner_N.htm?csp=34 (retrieved on September 19, 2008).

75. GAO, op. cit., 16.

76. Ante, Spencer E. (2008). "Newark and the Future of Crime Fighting," *BusinessWeek,* August 25.

77. Brooks, David Jonathon (2005). "Is CCTV a Social Benefit? A Psychometric Study of Perceived Social Risk," *Security Journal* 18, no. 2:20.
78. Bowcott, Owen (2008). "Closed-Circuit Television No Help in Solving British Crime." *Sydney Morning Herald* (Australia). http://www.smh.com.au/news/world/cctv-no-help-in-solving-british-crime/2008/05/06/1209839648170.html (retrieved on May 7, 2008).
79. Elliott, Robert (2007). "Britain's CCTV Surveilled." *Security Management* March:45.
80. Main, Frank (2003). "Camera's First Catch Gets Felony Drug Charge." *Chicago Sun-Times,* August 12.
81. Brooks, David Jonathon (2005), op. cit., 25.
82. Colias, Mike (2004). "Neighbors Divided Over Chicago's Crime Busting Cameras." *USA Today,* April 30, 15.
83. Spielman, Fran and Frank Main (2003). "City Deploys High-Tech Cameras to Fight Crime." *Chicago Sun-Times,* July 11.
84. Emerling, Gary (2008), op. cit.
85. Sheridan, Mary Beth (2008), op. cit.
86. Fooksman, Leon and Barbara Hijek (2008). "Cameras Keep Digital Eye Out of Trouble." *Fort Lauderdale Sun-Sentinel,* January 15, A1.
87. Roberts, Joel (2007). "Senator Reid On Iraq: 'This War Is Lost,' Democratic Majority Leader Says Troop Buildup Is Not Working," *CBS News,* April 20. http://www.cbsnews.com/stories/2007/04/20/politics/main2709229.shtml?source=RSSattr=HOME_2709229 (retrieved on February 20, 2009).
88. http://nothingbuttruth.com/maximum-crane/2008/03/let-every-nation-know/ (retrieved on February 20, 2009).
89. Ingraham, Laura (2007). *Power to the People.* Washington, DC: Regnery Publishing, 316–317.
90. Matthew 6:25.
91. Fox, Vicente and Rob Allyn (2007). *Revolution of Hope: The Life, Faith and Dreams of a Mexican President.* New York: Viking Penguin Press, New York,132, 355.
92. Tzu, Sun. *Art of War.* Trans. Lionel Giles. http://www.chinapage.com/sunzi-e.html (retrieved on February 20, 2009).

Bibliography

1 Kings 13.

"2nd Night of Violent BART Protests in Oakland" (2009). *KPIX 5 San Francisco, Associated Press,* and *BCN* (California), January 9. http://cbs5.com/local/BART.shooting.protest.2.902981.html.

2006 ASIS Security Industry Salary Survey. *Security Management*, August:20.

28 CFR Part 23.2.

44 Minutes: The North Hollywood Shoot-Out (2003). Twentieth-Century Fox Film Corporation.

Abbas, Rohma (2008). "Security Guards Hired for Early Morning Hours," *Stony Brook Independent*, October 30.

Adams, Duncan (2008). "In Its Garages, Roanoke Aims to Stop Threats—Real or Imagined," *Roanoke Times* (VA), July 21.

Aidi, Hisham (2005). "Jihadi's in the Hood: Race, Urban Islam and the War on Terror," in *Violence and Terrorism*. Ed. Thomas J. Badey: McGraw-Hill/Dushkin.

"Aiming To Protect and Serve" (2007). *Investor's Business Daily*, August 17.

Anderson, Kerby. "Arguments Against Abortion." http://www.leaderu.com/orgs/probe/docs/arg-abor.html (retrieved on May 2, 2008).

Anderson, Teresa (2008). "Cooperation Rules," *Security Management*, September:95–106.

Andrews International, Inc. (2007). "A Private Police Success Story," Andrews International, Inc., March:1.

Ante, Spencer E. (2008). "Newark and the Future of Crime Fighting," *BusinessWeek*, August 25.

Archibold, Randal C. (2009). "U.S. Plans Border 'Surge' Against Any Drug Wars," *New York Times*, January 8.

Asbury, John (2009). "Racial Beatings in San Jacinto Valley Linked to Obama Election," *The Press-Enterprise*, January 18. http://www.pe.com/localnews/hemet/stories/PE_News_Local_S_hate18.44d722b.html.

ASIS International (2004). *The Private Security Officer Selection and Training Guideline.*

Atlas, Randy I. (2008). "Fear of Parking," *Security Management*, February:54.

Avila, Oscar (2008). "Mexico City's Crime Rate Is Like Gold for Security Firms," *Chicago Tribune*, May 20.

Ayi, Mema (2004). "Cal City Police Use Cameras, Surveillance to Cut Crime," *Northwest Indiana Times*, August 30.

Azzam, Maha (2005). "Al Qaeda: The Misunderstood Wahhabi Connection and the Ideology of Violence," in *Violence and Terrorism*. Ed. Thomas J. Badey: McGraw-Hill/Dushkin.

Bagli, Charles V. (2008). "Police Want Tight Security Zone at Ground Zero," *New York Times.* August 12. http://www.dailynews.com/news/ci_8527308 (retrieved on March 17, 2008).

Bailin, Paul (2000). "Gazing into Security's Future." *Security Management,* November.

Barrett, Barbara (2007). "House OKs Bill to Make Security Contractors Subject to Prosecution in U.S.," *Kansas City Star,* October 4.

Barrie, Allison (2008). "Homeland Security Detects Terrorist Threats by Reading Your Mind," *Fox News,* September 23. http://www.foxnews.com/story/0,2933,426485,00.html.

Barstow, David (2004). "Security Companies: Shadow Soldiers in Iraq," *New York Times,* April 19, A1.

Bayley, David H. and Clifford D. Shearing (2001). "The New Structure of Policing: Description, Conceptualization and Research Agenda," N.I.J., NCJ# 187083, U.S. Department of Justice, July.

BBC News (2004). "Private 'Police' Confuse Public." May 23. www.bbc.co.uk/1/hi/uk/3664365.stm.

Bellman, Eric (2008). "A Traumatized Mumbai Seeks to Protect Itself," *Wall Street Journal,* December 18.

Bender, Bryan (2008). "Gates: US Military Must Retool to Fight Terrorism," *Boston Globe,* December 5.

Benson, Bruce L. (1990). *The Enterprise of Law: Justice Without State.* San Francisco, CA: Pacific Research Institute for Public Policy.

Benson, Bruce L. (1996). "Are There Trade Offs Between Costs and Quality in the Privatization of Criminal Justice?" *Journal of Security Administration* 19, no. 2:19–50.

Benson, Bruce L. (1997). *Privatization in Criminal Justice. National Institute of Justice.* Office of Justice Programs, U.S. Department of Justice.

Best, Steven and Anthony J. Nocella (2008). "Defining Terrorism." http://www.critical-animalstudies.org/JCAS/Journal_Articles_download/Issue_2/DefiningTerrorism.doc (retrieved on May 2, 2008).

Betten, Michael and Mitchell Mervosh (2005). "Should Police Respond to Alarms?" June 8. www.securitymanagement.com retrieved.

Bilik, Al (1992). "Privatization: Defacing the Community." *Labor Law Journal,* 338–43.

Blackstone, Erwin A. and Simon Hakim (2002). "A Market Solution for False Alarms," *Reason,* November 11.

Blakely, Edward J. and Mary Gail Snyder (1997). "Gating America." www.asu.edu/caed/proceedings97/Blakely (retrieved on October 28, 2004).

Blumenthal, Ralph (2008). "What the Mexicans Might Learn from the Italians," *New York Times.* http://www.nytimes.com/2008/06/01/weekinreview/01blumenthal.html?_r=2&ref=americas&oref=slogin&oref=slogin.

Blyskal, Jeff (1996). "Thugbusters." *New York* 28, no. 11 (March 16).

Booth, William (2009). "Gunmen Attack TV Offices in Mexico," *Washington Post,* January 8, A9.

Bourque, Julia (2004). "Chief: More Officers Mean Less Crime: Calumet City to Lure Reserve Police Officers," *Northwest Indiana Times,* July 2.

Bowcott, Owen (2008). "Closed-Circuit Television No Help in Solving British Crime." *Sydney Morning Herald* (Australia) http://www.smh.com.au/news/world/cctv-no-help-in-solving-british-crime/2008/05/06/1209839648170.html (retrieved on May 7, 2008).

Braglia, F. Thomas (2004). "Public-Private Law Enforcement: A Win-Win Partnership," *Command,* Winter.

Braveheart [motion picture] (1995). Gibson, Mel, Alan Ladd, Bruce Davey, and Stephen McEveety (producers). United States: Paramount Pictures and Icon Entertainment.

Brodzinsky, Sibylla (2008). "Is Colombia's Revolutionary Armed Forces of Colombia on the Ropes?" *Christian Science Monitor,* May 21:6.

Brooks, David Jonathon (2005). "Is CCTV a Social Benefit? A Psychometric Study of Perceived Social Risk," *Security Journal* 18, no. 2:20.

Brown, Cynthia (2004). "Outsourcing Police Jobs: Cops Replaced by Civilians to Cut Costs," *American Police Beat* XI, no. 12 (December).

Brown, Vahid (2007). "Cracks in the Foundation: Leadership Schisms in al Qaeda from 1989–2006," Harmony Project, Combating Terrorism Center at West Point, West Point, NY.

Bulwa, Demian (2008). "Richmond Installs 'Smart' Cameras," *San Francisco Chronicle,* May 15.

Bureau of Justice Assistance (BJA) (2005). "Engaging the Private Sector to Promote Homeland Security: Law Enforcement-Private Security Partnerships," September.

Burns, Robert (2007). "Tighter Control of Blackwater Agreed," *Associated Press,* December 6.

Carlson, Tucker (1995). "Safety Inc.: Private Cops Are There When You Need Them," *Policy Review* 73 (Summer).

Carroll, Timothy J. (2008). "Hoboken Gets First-of-Its-Kind Security System," *Hoboken Reporter,* October 13.

CBS News (2005). "Miami Police Take New Tack against Terror." November 29.

Chanken, Marcia, and Jan Chaiken (1987). "Public Policing—Privately Provided." National Institute of Justice. Office of Justice Programs, U.S. Department of Justice, June.

Cincinnati Municipal Code, Title VIII: Business Regulations, Section 887-1. http://216.196.232.226/1c/cppa/PAGE8.HTM (retrieved on March 20, 2006).

Cincinnati Municipal Code, Chapter 887-9, 11, 13, and 15.

"City Cameras to Catch Every Car" (2008). *BBC News,* May 20.

"City Launches Security Training." www.nynewsday.com (retrieved on April 27, 2005).

Clemow, Brian (1992). "Privatization and the Public Good." *Labor Law Journal,* 344–49.

Clifford, Mary (2004). *Identifying and Exploring Security Essentials.* Upper Saddle River, NJ: Pearson/Prentice Hall.

Clotfelter, Charles T. (1977). "Public Services, Private Substitutes and the Demand for Protection Against Crime." *The American Economic Review* 67, no. 5876–76.

Cloud, David S. (2007). "Ex-Commander Says Iraq Effort Is 'a Nightmare,'" *The New York Times* http://www.nytimes.com/2007/10/13/washington/13general.html (retrieved on February 3, 2009).

Clutterbuck, Richard (1975). "The Police and Urban Terrorism," *The Police Journal.*

Cohen, Lawrence E. and Marcus Felson (1979). "Social Change and Crime Rate Trends." *American Sociological Review* 44:588–607.

Cole, August (2007). "Private Security Providers Become a Pentagon Focus," *Wall Street Journal,* September 27, A9.

Cole, Bradley (2003). "Merrillville Cop Chief Wants OK for Camera to Nab Traffic Violators," *Post-Tribune,* December 11.

Colias, Mike (2004). "Neighbors Divided Over Chicago's Crime Busting Cameras." *USA Today,* April 30, 15.

Colson, John (2008). "RFTA Bus Security Armed With Stun Guns," *Aspen Times,* January 10.

"Community and City Services Problem Strategies" (2000). Chicago Alternative Policing Strategy (CAPS), Chicago Police Department, December 12:1–14.

Connor, G. (1995). "Law Enforcement Officer Use of Force Model." Integrated Force Management.

Cooke, Leonard G. and Lisa R. Hahn (2006). "The Missing Link in Homeland Security," *The Police Chief* 73, no. 11 (November).

Cooper, H. H. A. (2008). "Terrorism: The Problem of Definition," *Terrorism in Perspective*, 2nd ed. Thousand Oaks, CA: Sage Publications.

Corder, Mike (2009). "Dutch Court: Prosecute Anti-Islamic Lawmaker," *Associated Press*, January 21. http://news.yahoo.com/s/ap/20090121/ap_on_re_eu/eu_netherlands_hate_speech;_ylt=Ar85.P8mhejAroTgvwLp0DZ0bBAF.

Correll, DeeDee (2007). "Colorado Springs May Change Gun Rules for Guards," *Los Angeles Times*, December 15, A17.

Coulter, Ann (2003). *Treason: Liberal Treachery from the Cold War to the War on Terrorism.* New York: Crown Forum.

Covington, Jeanette and Ralph B. Taylor (1991). "Fear of Crime in Urban Residential Neighborhoods: Implications of Between and Within Neighborhood Sources for Current Models." *The Sociological Quarterly* 32, no. 2.

Cox, Steven M. (1990). "Policing into the 21st Century." *Police Studies* 13, no. 4:168–77.

Crenshaw, Martha, ed. (1983). *Terrorism, Legitimacy and Power: The Consequence of Political Violence.* Middleton, CT: Wesleyan University Press.

Cruickshank, Ken (1994). "Frenchman's Creek Provides the Ultimate in Security." *Manager's Report* 8 (November).

Cruz, Claudio (2009). *Associated Press*. http://www.dallasnews.com/sharedcontent/dws/news/world/mexico/stories/DN-mexviolence_04int.ART.State.Edition2.4a508fe.html.

Csepiga, Melanie (2004). "Local Director Says Grants are Drying Up and County Will Get No Money Without Plan," *NW Times*, November 24.

Cunningham, William C., John J. Strauchs and Clifford W. Van Meter (1991). "Private Security: Patterns and Trends," National Institute of Justice. Office of Justice Programs. U.S. Department of Justice, August.

Cunningham, William C. and Todd H. Taylor (1994). "The Growing Role of Private Security." National Institute of Justice. Office of Justice Programs, U.S. Department of Justice, October.

Dallas Morning News (2007). "Police: Security Guard with Assault Rifle Kills 2 Suspected Robbers," October 4.

Dalton, Dennis R. (1993). "Contract Labor: The True Story." *Security Management*, January.

Daniels, Rhianna (2008). "Dallas Passes Convenience Store Security Ordinance," *Security Director News*, September 10.

Davies, Heather J. and Gerald R. Murphy (2002). "Protecting your Community from Terrorism: Strategies for Law Enforcement, Working with Diverse Communities," *Community Oriented Policing Services* and *Police Executive Research Forum*.

Davis, James R. (1982). *Street Gangs: Youth, Biker and Prison Groups.* Dubuque, IA: Kendall-Hunt.

Davis, Robert C. and Sarah Dadush (2000). "The Public Accountability of Private Police: Lessons from New York, Johannesburg, and Mexico City." Vera Institute of Justice, August.

Delk, James D. (1995). *Fires and Furies: The L.A. Riots.* Palm Springs, CA: ETC Publications.

DeStefano, Anthony M. (2007). "New Role for the Bravest," *Newsday* (retrieved on November 24, 2007).

Dilulio, John J. (1995). "Ten Facts About Crime." National Institute of Justice. Office of Justice Programs. U.S. Department of Justice, January 16.

Donahue, John D. (1989). *The Privatization Decision.* New York: Basic Books.

Doyle, Sue (2008). "Metro Gets $16.1 Million for Gates," *Los Angeles Daily News*, July 15.

Drake, Laura (2009). "Fear and Loathing over B.C. Pipeline Blasts," *Edmonton Journal*, January 10. http://www.canada.com/topics/news/national/story.html?id=1164587.

DuCanto, Joseph N. (1999). Establishment of Police and Private Security Liaison. Manuscript presented at the 45th Annual Seminar of the American Society for Industrial Security, Las Vegas, Nevada, September 27–30.

Duhul, Salad (2009). "Last Ethiopian Troops Leave Somalia's Capital," *Associated Press*, January 15. http://news.yahoo.com/s/ap/20090115/ap_on_re_af/af_somalia;_ylt=AmsGq0Q6OG_tdiWHHpyTxOK96Q8F.

Edwards, Richard (2008). "Police Have Foiled 15 Terror Plots Since 7/7'" www.telegraph.co.uk (retrieved on April 23, 2008).

Eisenberg, Carol (2007) "NYC Counter-Terror Chief Urges Stiffer Subway Protection." www.newsday.com (retrieved on March 7, 2007).

Elliott, Robert (2007). "Britain's CCTV Surveilled." *Security Management,* March.

Emerling, Gary (2008). "5,000 Monitoring Cameras Opened to D.C. Police," *Washington Times,* April 9.

Ephesians 6:12.

Ezeldin, Ahmed Galal (1987). *Terrorism and Political Violence.* Chicago: University of Illinois at Chicago Press.

Faiola, Anthony and Steven Mufson (2007). "N.Y. Airport Target of Plot, Officials Say," *Washington Post,* June 3, A1.

Farah, Joseph (1997). "The Militarization of the Domestic Police," WorldNetDaily.com, November 6. http://www.wnd.com/news/article.asp?ARTICLE_ID=14363 (retrieved on May 6, 2008).

Farnham, Alan (1992). "U.S. Suburbs Are Under Siege." *Fortune*, December 28.

Feibel, Carolyn (2008). "Houston Will Tackle Convenience Store Crimes," *Houston Chronicle,* March 10.

Feliton, John R. and David B. Owen (1994). "Guarding Against Liability." *Security Management*, September.

Felson, Marcus (2002). *Crime and Everyday Life.* Thousand Oaks, CA: Sage Publications.

Fenton, Mike (2008). "Discouraging Loiterers by Design." *Security Management* 52, no. 5 (May):68.

Fields, Gary (2008). "Murder Spike Poses Quandary," *Wall Street Journal*, May 6, A16.

Fisher, Bonnie and Jack L. Nasar (1995). "Fear Spots in Relation to Microlevel Physical Cues: Exploring the Overlooked." *Journal of Research in Crime and Delinquency* 32, no. 2:214–39.

Fooksman, Leon and Barbara Hijek (2008). "Cameras Keep Digital Eye Out of Trouble," *Fort Lauderdale Sun-Sentinel,* January 15, A1.

Forero, Juan (2009). "Obama and Chávez Start Sparring Early," *Washington Post,* January 19, A15. http://www.washingtonpost.com/wp-dyn/content/article/2009/01/18/AR2009011802325.html.

Fox, Vicente and Rob Allyn (2007). *Revolution of Hope: The Life, Faith and Dreams of a Mexican President.* New York: Viking Penguin Press.

"Fusion Centers Should Work With ISAC's" (2007). *Security Management* 51, no. 11 (November):34.

Gladwell, Malcolm (2002). *The Tipping Point.* New York: Little Brown and Company.

Ganor, Boaz (2005). "Terror as a Strategy of Psychological Warfare," in *Violence and Terrorism.* Ed. Thomas J. Badey: McGraw-Hill/Dushkin.

Gardham, Duncan (2008). "Counter Terrorism: Police Disrupt 13 Terror Networks in Last Year." http://www.telegraph.co.uk/news/uknews/2450020/Counter-terrorism-Police-disrupt-13-terror-networks-in-last-year.html (retrieved on July 23, 2008).

Garza, Mariel (2002). "Alarm Plan: Police May Quit Reacting," *L.A. Daily News,* December 2. www.freerepublic.com (retrieved on May 13, 2004).

Geyelin, Milo (1993). Hired Guards Assume More Police Duties as Privatization of Public Safety Spreads. *The Wall Street Journal,* June 1.

Gibbs, Jack P. and Maynart L. Erickson (1976). "Crime Rates of American Cities in an Ecological Context." *American Journal of Sociology* 82:605–20.

Gilgoff, Dan (2008). "With Rick Warren Flap, Gay Activists Say Obama Has Long Been a 'Mixed Bag,'" *U.S. News and World Report.* December 18. http://www.usnews.com/blogs/god-and-country/2008/12/18/with-rick-warren-flap-gay-activists-say-obama-has-long-been-a-mixed-bag.html (retrieved on January 22, 2009).

Goldberg, Ceil (1994). "New Roles for Private Patrols," *Security Management,* December.

Goldman, G., and R. Shusett (executive producers) (2002). *Minority Report* [motion picture]. United States: 20th Century Fox and Dreamworks, LLC.

Goonan, Peter (2009). "Affidavit Provides Details of Macedonia Church Fire Probe," *The Republican Newsroom* (MA), January 19. http://www.masslive.com/news/index.ssf/2009/01/affidavit_provides_details_of.html?category=Crime&category=Fires&category=Springfield.

Gorder, Pam Frost (2009). "Smart Cameras Are Watching You," *The Lantern* (Ohio State University), January 9. http://media.www.thelantern.com/media/storage/paper333/news/2009/01/09/Campus/smart.Cameras.Are.Watching.You-3582772.shtml.

Gordon, Corey and William Brill (1996). "The Expanding Role of Crime Prevention Through Environmental Design in Premises Liability." National Institute of Justice, April.

Graham, Thomas and Ted Gurr, eds. (1971). *History of Violence in America.* Princeton, NJ: Princeton University Press.

Graham v. Connor, 490 U.S. 386 (1989).

Grant, Greg (2008). Government Executive.com, April 22. http://www.govexec.com/story_page.cfm?articleid=39835&dcn=e_ndw (retrieved on April 25, 2008).

"Green Energy Problem" (2009). *Fox News Channel,* January 15.

Greisman, H. C. (1979). "Terrorism and the Closure of Society: A Social Impact Projection." *Technological Forecasting and Social Change* 14.

Griffin, Joel (2008). "Toledo Requires Closed-Circuit Television Systems in C-Stores, Small Restaurants," June 2. SecurityInfoWatch.com.

Grimm, Andy (2005). "Gary Approves Surveillance Camera Purchase," *Post-Tribune,* June 17.

Hall, Mimi (2008). "Rethink Spending on Anti-Terrorism, Report Says," *USA Today,* 1A. http://www.usatoday.com/news/washington/2008-10-01-terrormoney_N.htm (retrieved on October 3, 2008).

Hall, Mimi (2008). "Surveillance System Raises Privacy Concerns," *USA Today,* February 29, 3A.

Hall, Mimi (2008). "Amtrak Expands Security Sweeps," *USA Today,* July 11, 1A on July 11.

Hall, Mimi (2007). "Feds Work on Detecting Bombs in USA," *USA Today,* November 27, A3.

Hamblen, Matt and Patrick Thibodeau (2008). "IT Deputized to Help Take a Bite Out of Crime," *Computerworld,* March 3.

Hamm, Mark S. (2007). "Terrorist Recruitment and Radicalization in Prison," NIJ Conference, July.

Hans Heitman and Thomas Linnane v. City of Chicago, 04 C 3304, U.S. District Court for Northern District of Illinois, Eastern Division, order issued on September 11, 2007.

Harcourt, Bernard E. (2002). "Policing Disorder: Can we Reduce Serious Crime by Punishing Petty Offenses?" *Boston Review.*

Harwood, Matt (2008). "Fighting Terrorism in the U.K.," *Security Management*, January:48–55.

Hawley, Chris (2007). "Security Business Booms in Mexico," *Arizona Republic*, May 3.

Hays, Tom (2007). "New York City Police Eye Trucks as Potential Vehicles for Terrorists," *Seattle Times*, June 12.

Hazelkorn, Bud (2003). "Privatization of Police: Making Crime Pay," *San Francisco Chronicle*, August 17.

Hebdon, R. (1995). "Contracting Out in New York State: The Story the Lauder Report Chose Not to Tell." *Labor Studies Journal* 20 no. 1:3–24.

Herbeck, Dan (2008). "Private Army of Contractors Carries a Heavy Load in Iraq," *Buffalo News*, March 31.

Heredia, Christopher (2008). "Oakland May Hire Armed Security Guards," *San Francisco Chronicle*, April 16, B2.

Herold, Noam (2008). "Nuclear Terrorism: A 21st Century Threat." *The Counter Terrorist* 1, no. 1 (May/June).

Higgins, Andrew (2004). "Contract Cops: As It Wields Power Abroad, US Outsources Law and Order Work," *Wall Street Journal*, February 2.

Hilliker, Joel (2009). "Can He Deliver, Why There Is Reason for Hope," *Trumpet*. http://www.thetrumpet.com/index.php?q=5693.0.110.0 (retrieved on January 17, 2009).

Hoffman, Bruce (2006). "Defining Terrorism," in *Terrorism and Counter-Terrorism: Understanding the New Security Environment*. Eds. Russell D. Howard and Reid L. Sawyer. Dubuque, IA: McGraw-Hill.

Hoffman, Bruce (2004). "Rethinking Terrorism and Counter-Terrorism Since 9/11," in *The New Era of Terrorism: Selected Readings*. Ed. Gus Martin. Thousand Oaks, CA: Sage Publications.

Holtz, Larry E. (2001). *Contemporary Criminal Procedure*, 7th ed. Longwood, FL: Gould Publications.

Homeland Security Act (HSA) of 2002, Pub. L. No. 107-296, 116 Stat. 2135 (November 25).

"Homeland Security and Anti-Terrorism Preparations," Chicago Police Department, General Order 04-04, December 6, 2004.

Hopkins, Kyle (2008). "City Plans to Arm Security Guards," *Anchorage Daily News*, February 26.

Houreld, Katharine (2008). "Private Security Firms to Take on Pirates," *Associated Press*, October 27.

House of Representatives for the United States Congress, H.R. 2996, 104th Congress, Law Enforcement and Industrial Security Cooperation Act of 1996, introduced by Rep. McCollum on February 29.

Howard, Jacqueline (2008). "Shots Fired at Private Police Employee," January 23. http://www.wcpo.com/news/local/story.aspx?content_id=0123b69a-aa51-4c74-a0d9-de485f871737.

Hsu, Spencer S. and Ann Scott Tyson (2008). "Pentagon to Detail Troops to Bolster Domestic Security," *Washington Post*, A01. http://www.washingtonpost.com/wp-dyn/content/article/2008/11/30/AR2008113002217_pf.html (retrieved on December 2, 2008).

Hyde, David (2001). "A Theory of Evolution," *Canadian Security* 23, no. 5 (June/July).

Ibrahim, Mohammed (2009). "Insurgents in Somalia Take Over Police Posts," *Associated Press,* January 3. http://www.nytimes.com/2009/01/04/world/africa/04somalia. html?_r=1&ref=world.

Illinois Compiled Statutes, Chapter 39/107-3.

Indiana Code 10-19-10-2.

Ingraham, Laura (2007). *Power to the People.* Washington DC: Regnery Publishing.

"Innovative Surveillance" (2007). *Security Technology and Design* 17, no. 11 (November).

Inside 9/11 (2005). Produced by Towers Production, Inc., for National Geographic.

Intersec (2008). 18, no. 4 (April).

Ioffe, Karina (2005). "Cameras Aim to Boost Sense of Security." www.recordnet.com (retrieved on April 10, 2005).

IOMA (2001). *Security Director's Report,* May.

"Iran Remains Most Active State Sponsor of Terrorism: US" (2008). *Agence France Presse,* April 30. http://afp.google.com/article/ALeqM5h116nr_azlHR5AgajA5naaLnJBOg (retrieved on May 6, 2008).

Islamic Radicalization in State and Local Prisons: NJTTF Correctional Intelligence Initiative Assessment of Radicalization and Recruitment (2006). FBI Counter-Terrorism Division, Intelligence Assessment, August 20.

Ist, Ians (2009). "Mumbai Attacks Call for New Counter Terrorism Strategy: Obama," *Economic Times of India,* January 12.

Jackson, Pamela Irving (1984). "Opportunity and Crime: A Function of City Size." *Sociology and Social Research* 68, no. 2:173–93.

Jeremiah, David (2008). *What in the World is Going On: 10 Prophetic Clues You Cannot Afford to Ignore.* Nashville, TN: Thomas Nelson Publishers.

Joh, Elizabeth E. (2004). "The Paradox of Private Policing," *The Journal of Criminal Law and Criminology* 95, no. 1:49–132.

Joh, Elizabeth E. (2005). "Conceptualizing the Private Police," *Utah Law Review,* October:574–617.

Johnson, Carrie (2009). "Bad Economy May Fuel Hate Groups, Experts Warn," *Washington Post,* January 11, A4.

Johnson, Kevin (2003). "Federal, Local Cuts Pull Cops Off Streets," *USA Today,* December 2.

Johnson, Kevin and Frank Thomas (2008). "Mumbai Attacks Refocus U.S. Cities," *USA Today,* December 5, 1A.

Johnson, Thomas H. and M. Chris Mason (2008). "All Counterinsurgency Is Local," *The Atlantic,* October.

Johnston, Les (1992). *The Rebirth of Private Policing.* London: Routledge.

Johnson v. LaRabida, 372 F. 3d 894 (2004).

Jones, Carolyn (2009). "Expecting More Protests, City to Hire Guards," *San Francisco Chronicle,* January 16, B5.

Jones, Carolyn (2009). "Oakland Storekeepers Tell of Night of Terror," *San Francisco Chronicle,* January 9, A12 http://www.sfgate.com/cgi- bin/article.cgi?f=/c/a/2009/01/09/ MNC3155VI6.DTL&hw=Storekeepers+Tell+of+Terror&sn=001&sc=1000.

Kaplan, Robert (1994). "The Coming Anarchy," *Atlantic Monthly*, February.

Karp, Jonathan (2007). "Contractors in War Zone Face Legal Front," *Wall Street Journal,* March 8, A10.

Kass, John (2008). "For Sheer Brazenness, Nobody Surpasses Rod," *Chicago Tribune,* December 31. http://www.chicagotribune.com/news/columnists/chi-kass-burris-31-d ec31,0,1367315.column.

Katz v. U.S., 389 U.S. 347 (1967).

Kearney, Pat (2000). "Going Private Downtown: Business Hire Their Own Police," 9, no. 49. www.thestranger.com (retrieved on May 1, 2004).

Keen, Judy (2006). "Daley Wants Security Cameras at Bars," *USA Today,* February 14.

Kelling, George (1995). "Reduce Serious Crime by Restoring Order." *The American Enterprise,* May/June.

Kelling, George and William H. Sousa (2002). "Do Police Matter: An Analysis of the Impact of New York City's Police Reforms," Manhattan Institute, Center for Civic Innovation, 22 (December).

Kelling, G. L. and C. M. Coles (1996). *Fixing Broken Windows: Restoring Order and Reducing Crime in Our Communities.* New York: Simon and Schuster.

King, Paula (2008). "Tight Security Promised for Streets of Brentwood," *Mercury News,* November 4.

Kinzer, Stephen (2004). "Chicago Moving to 'Smart' Surveillance Cameras," *New York Times,* September 21.

Kirkup, James (2008). "Police Prepare Terror Attack Warning for Restaurants and Cinemas," *London Telegraph,* August 4.

Kolderie, Ted (1986). "The Two Different Concepts of Privatization." *Public Administrative Review* 10, no. 2:285–90.

Kolpacki, Thomas A. (1994). "Neighborhood Watch: Public/Private Liaison." *Security Management,* November.

Konzol, Mark J., Allison Hantschel and Alice Hohl (2003). "The Police Are Watching: Chicago Force Unveils Camera System That Will Record Activity on the Streets," *Daily Southtown,* July 11.

Kouri, Jim (2008). "Homeland Security and Justice Departments Providing More Info to Local Officers," *National Ledger* (NC), November 16. http://www.nationalledger.com/ artman/publish/article_272623792.shtml.

Kraska, Peter and Victor Kappeler (1997). "Militarizing American Police: The Rise and Normalization of Paramilitary Units," *Social Problems* 44.

Landman, Karina (2003). National Survey of Gated Communities in South Africa. www. gatedcomsa.com (retrieved on June 20, 2006).

"LAPD Buys 'Dirty Bomb' Detectors" (2007). *Daily Breeze,* September 10.

Laqueur, Walter (2004). "The Terrorism to Come," *Policy Review* 126. www.policyreview. org/aug04/laqueur_print.html (retrieved on November 1, 2004).

Lardner, Richard (2007). "Who Watches US Security Firms in Iraq?" *Associated Press,* September 19.

Laverty, Deborah (2003). "Merrillville Chief, Councilman Want More Cops," *The Times,* November 18.

"Law Enforcement Officers Killed and Assaulted 2005." U.S. Department of Justice, Federal Bureau of Investigation, released on October 2006. www.fbi.gov (retrieved on March 7, 2008).

"Law Enforcement Prevention and Deterrence of Terrorist Acts." Department of Homeland Security, Version 1.0, 2/9.

Lee, Jennifer (2005). "Caught on Tape, Then Just Caught," *New York Times,* May 22.

Lefkowitz, Josh (2008). "Terrorists Behind Bars." www.nefafoundation.org (retrieved on May 5, 2008).

Leicester, John (2007). "British 'Big Brother' System of CCTV Surveillance Impresses Neighbors in Europe and in the U.S.," *Associated Press,* July 11.

Leiser, Ken (2008). "Guards' Visibility Reassures Riders," *St. Louis Post-Dispatch,* September 21.

Levin, Gregg (2007). "Dallas PD Fights Crime with Video Surveillance," *Security Technology and Design* 17, no. 7 (July).

Lewis, Dan A. and Michael G. Maxfield (1980). "Fear in the Neighborhoods: An Investigation of the Impact of Crime," *Journal of Research in Crime and Delinquency* July:160–89.

Lifton, Robert Jay (2005). "In the Lord's Hands: America's Apocalyptic Mindset," in *Violence and Terrorism.* Ed. Thomas J. Badey: McGraw-Hill/Dushkin.

Lindell, Rebecca (2003). "Traffic Nightmare," *Kellogg,* Summer.

Linowes, David F. (1988). *Report of the President's Commission on Privatization. Privatization: Toward More Effective Government.* Washington, DC: U.S. Government Printing Office.

Liska, Allen E., Joseph J. Lawrence, and Andrew Sanchirico (1982). "Fear of Crime as a Social Fact," *Social Forces* 60, no. 3:760–70.

Litsikas, Mary (1994). "Security System Installations Up in 1994." *Security Distributing and Marketing,* September.

Lowrey, Michael (2003). "Incentives, Privatization Help City Police: Charlotte Addresses Burglar Alarm Abuse through Creative Program," *Carolina Journal Online,* November 17. www.carolinajournal.com/issues/display_story.html?id=1197 (retrieved on March 7, 2004).

Lucadamo, Kathleen and Pete Donohue (2007). "Bloomberg: Get Surveillance Cameras for Buses, Trains," *New York Daily News,* October 3.

Lyall, Sarah (2007). "Britain Plans New Security Measures," *New York Times,* November 15.

Mahan, Sue and Pamela L. Griset (2008). *Terrorism in Perspective,* 2nd ed. Thousand Oaks, CA: Sage Publications.

Main, Frank (2003). "Camera's First Catch Gets Felony Drug Charge." *Chicago Sun-Times,* August 12.

Main, Frank and Fran Spielman (2003). "New Police Gang Effort Comes up Big," *Chicago Sun-Times,* December 11.

"Man Accused of Plotting to Blow Up Pipelines" (2007). *Reuters,* July 9.

Marks, Alexandra (2008). "Key Factor in Murder Trends: Youth, Gang Violence," *Christian Science Monitor,* January 4, 1.

Marks, Paul (2007). "Can a Government Remotely Detect a Terrorist's Thoughts," *New Scientist* 195, no. 2616 (August 11).

Maryland Public Safety Statute Section 3-307.

Matthew 6:25.

Mazzetti, Mark and William Glaberson (2009). "Obama Will Shut Guantanamo Site and C.I.A. Prisons," *New York Times,* January 22, A1.

McEwen, Tom, Deborah Spence, Russell Wolff, Julie Wartell, and Barbara Webster (2003). *Call Management and Community Policing: A Guidebook for Law Enforcement.* Institute for Law and Justice, U.S. Department of Justice, February.

McGoey, Chris E. (1999). "Gated Communities: Access Control Issues." www.crimedoctor.com/gated.htm (retrieved on June 20, 2006).

McKenzie, Evan (1994). *Privatopia: Homeowner Associations and the Rise of Residential Private Government.* New Haven: Yale University Press.

McKenzie, Sarah (2005). "Business, City Join to Fight Crime Downtown," *Minneapolis/St. Paul Business Journal.* www.msnbc.msn.com/id/7541911/ (retrieved on April 17, 2005).

McLain, Jennifer (2008). "Police: Beef Up Security at Club," *San Gabriel Valley Tribune* (CA), September 29.

McLennan, Barbara N., ed. (1970). *Crime in Urban Society*. London: Cambridge University Press.

McLeod, Ross (2002). *Para-Police*. Toronto: Boheme Press.

Meadows, Robert J. (1991). "Premises Liability and Negligent Security: Issues and Implications." *Journal of Contemporary Criminal Justice* 7, no. 3:112–25.

Meserve, Jeanne and Mike M. Ahlers (2007). "FDNY Anti-Terror Plans Spark Fears of Witch Hunts," *CNN* (retrieved on December 5, 2007).

"Mexico Drug Gang Killing Surge" (2008). *BBC News,* December 9. http://news.bbc.co.uk/2/hi/americas/7772771.stm.

Michaels, Jim (2007). "Private Security Contractors' Role Grows in Iraq," *USA Today*. http://www.usatoday.com/news/world/iraq/2007-09-03-contactor_N.htm?csp=34 (retrieved on January 3, 2008).

Mikkelsen, Randall (2009). "Mumbai-Like Attack Could Happen in US—Bush Aide," *Reuters* (UK), January 8.

Mikkelsen, Randall (2009). "Obama CIA Pick May Back 'Limited' Abuse Prosecution," *Reuters* (UK), February 5.

Miller, Joel (2002). "Cops at War: The Drug War and the Militarization of Mayberry," December 30. http://www.rutherford.org/oldspeak/articles/law/oldspeak-cops.asp (retrieved on May 6, 2008).

Miller, Judith (2007). "On the Front Line in the War on Terrorism: Cops in New York and Los Angeles Offer America Two Models for Preventing Another 9/11," *City Journal,* Summer. http://www.city-journal.org/html/17_3_preventing_terrorism.html (retrieved on May 9, 2008).

Miller, Wilbur R. (1977). *Cops and Bobbies: Police Authority in New York and London, 1830–1870*. Chicago: University of Chicago Press.

Miranda, Rowan A. (1993). "Better City Government at Half the Price, in *Chicago's Future in a Time of Change,* Richard Simpson, ed. Stipes.

Mokwa, Joseph and Terrence W. Stoehner (1995). "Private Security Arches Over St. Louis," *Security Management,* September.

Moore, Mark H. and Robert C. Trojanowicz (1988). "Perspectives on Policing: Corporate Strategies for Policing," National Institute of Justice, Office of Justice Programs. U.S. Department of Justice, no. 6 (November).

Morgan, David R. (1992). "The Pitfalls of Privatization: Contracting Without Competition," *American Review of Public Administration* 22, no. 4:251–68.

Morgenstern, Henry (2008). "From Virtual Jihad to Real Jihad," *The Counter Terrorist* 1, no. 1 (May/June).

Muhlhausen, David B. (2001). "Do Community Oriented Policing Services Grants Affect Violent Crime Rates?" *The Heritage Foundation* CDA01-05, May 25.

Municipal Code of the City of Chicago Section 4-60-130, and General Provisions Section 4-60-205.

Mroue, Bassem (2007). "Blackwater License Being Pulled in Iraq," *Associated Press,* September 17.

Nacos, Brigitte (2005). "Terrorism as Breaking News: Attack on America," in *Violence and Terrorism*. Ed. Thomas J. Badey: McGraw-Hill/Dushkin.

Nafisi, Azar (2004). "They the People: Our Abandoned Muslim Allies," in *The New Era of Terrorism: Selected Readings*. Ed. Gus Martin. Thousand Oaks, CA: Sage Publications.

Nalla, Mahesh and Graeme R. Newman (1991). "Public Versus Private Control: A Reassessment," *Journal of Criminal Justice* 19:414–36.

National Center for Bio/Medical Research and Training (2004). "Recognizing WMD on the Streets," *Law Enforcement Prevention and Deterrence of Terrorist Acts,* Version 1.0, 4–64.

National Policy Summit: Building Private Security/Public Policing Partnerships to Prevent and Respond to Terrorism and Public Disorder (2004). National Institute of Justice, Office of Community Oriented Policing Services.

"National Strategy for Homeland Security" (2007). Homeland Security Council, Office of the President of the United States, October.

Nedoroscik, Jeffrey A. (2005). "Extremist Groups in Egypt," in *Violence and Terrorism.* Ed. Thomas J. Badey: McGraw-Hill/Dushkin.

Nemeth, Charles P. (1989). *Private Security and the Law.* Cincinnati, OH: Anderson.

"Neo-Nazi Materials Found Outside Homes in N.C." http://hamptonroads.com/2009/01/neonazi-materials-found-outside-homes-nc (retrieved on January 16, 2009).

Newton, Paula (2008). "New Security Camera Can 'See' Through Clothes," *CNN International,* April 16.

Nicholson, Kieran (2008). "Denver Weighs Security vs. Privacy as Cops Focus Cameras on Crime," *The Denver Post.* http://www.denverpost.com/news/ci_10613181 (retrieved on October 3, 2008).

"North Carolina Web Site Said to Be 'Gateway Drug' To Terror" (2008). *Fox News,* May 16. www. foxnews.com.

Nuttall, Jeremy (2008). "Ferry Rides to See Tougher Security," *Globe and Mail* (CAN), July 22. http://www.theglobeandmail.com/servlet/story/LAC.20080722.BCFERRIES22/TPStory/National on July 22.

"NYPD Opens New Counterterrorism Nerve Center" (2008). November 18. http://www.wjla.com/news/stories/1108/570988.html.

"NYPD Radicalization in the West" (2007). The Homegrown Threat.

O'Malley, Jaclyn (2005). "Homeland Security Grants Add Infrared Gear," *Reno Gazette-Journal,* March 1.

O'Neil, Siobhan (2007). "Terrorist Precursor Crimes: Issues and Options for Congress," *Congressional Research Service,* May 24, 1, May 24.

Olick, M. (1994). "Private Response: The No Response Solution." *Security News,* December.

Oliver, Willard M. (2004). *Community-Oriented Policing: A Systematic Approach to Policing.* Upper Saddle River, NJ: Prentice Hall.

"Operation Cooperation," (2004). Bureau of Justice Assistance, U.S. Department of Justice, the Institute of Law and Justice, and Hallcrest Division of Science Applications International Corporation. www.ilj.org/securitypartners/coop_paper_old.html (retrieved on October 28, 2004).

Ortiz, Christopher W., Nicole J. Hendricks and Naomi F. Sugie (2007). "Policing Terrorism: The Response of Local Police Agencies to Homeland Security," *Criminal Justice Studies* 20, no. 2 (June):91–109.

Palango, Paul (1998). "On the Mean Streets: As the Police Cut Back, Private Cops Are Moving In." *MacLeans* 111, no. 2 (January 12).

Parks, Bernard C., Captain Joseph Curreri, as updated by Captain Gary S. Williams, Commanding Officer of Major Crimes Division. "Terrorism and the Municipal Police Department." http://www.lapdonline.org/search_results/content_basic_view/27421 (retrieved on January 3, 2009).

Parry, Marc (2008). "New View of Campus Watch," *Albany Times Union* (NY), March 8, A1.

Pastor, James F. (2003). *The Privatization of Police in America: An Analysis and Case Study.* Jefferson, NC: McFarland.

Pastor, James F. (2005). "Public Safety Policing," *Law Enforcement Executive Forum* 5, no. 6 (November):13–27.

Pastor, James F. (2005). "Terrorism and Public Safety Policing," *Crime and Justice International* 21, no. 85 (March/April):4–8.

Pastor, James F. (2006). *Security Law and Methods.* Burlington, MA: Butterworth-Heinemann.

Pastor, James F. (2007). "Private Policing in Public Environments" in *Protection of Assets Manual.* Alexandria, VA: ASIS International.

Patterson, Julien (1995). "Forging Creative Alliances," *Security Management,* January.

Perez, Evan (2002). "Demand for Security Still Promises Profit," *Wall Street Journal,* April 9.

Perkins, Nancy and Amy Joi O'Donoghue (2008). "Heavily Armed Sect Raid Pleased Officials," *The Desert Morning News,* April 16. http://www.policeone.com/police-products/vehicles/specialty/articles/1684847-Heavily-armed-sect-raid-pleased-officials (retrieved on May 6, 2008).

Phillips, Joseph C. (2008). "Barack Obama Can't Win as Long as He Continues to Play That Tired, Dog-Eared Race Card." http://www.blackamericaweb.com/site.aspx/sayitloud/phillips819 (retrieved on August 27, 2008).

Pillar, Paul R. (2001). "Is the Terrorist Threat Misunderstood?" *Security Management,* May.

Plushnick-Masti, Ramit (2008). "U.S. Police Departments Deploying Heavy Armor," May 13. http://www.policeone.com/police-products/vehicles/specialty/articles/1244834-U-S-police-departments-deploying-heavy-armor (retrieved on May 6, 2008).

Poland, James M. (2005). *Understanding Terrorism: Groups, Strategies and Responses.* Upper Saddle River, NJ: Pearson/Prentice Hall.

Posner, Richard (2006). *Not a Suicide Pact: The Constitution in a Time of National Emergency.* London: Oxford University Press.

Practical Guide to Intelligence-Led Policing (2006). New Jersey State Police.

Prenzler, Tim (2005). "Mapping the Australian Security Industry," *Security Journal* 18, no. 4:51–64.

Pride and Glory (2008). New Line Cinema, Solaris Entertainment and O'Connor Brothers [producers].

Psalms 122:6.

Quirk, Matthew (2008). "How to Grow a Gang," *The Atlantic,* May.

Radford, Dean (2008). "Renton Transit Center Beefs Up Security with Guards on Bikes," *Renton Reporter,* July 16. http://www.pnwlocalnews.com/news/25411819.html.

Rapoport, David C. (2008). "Fear and Trembling: Terrorism in Three Religious Traditions," in *Terrorism in Perspective,* 2nd ed. Eds. Mahan, Sue and Pamela L. Griset. Thousand Oaks, CA: Sage Publications.

Ratcliff, Jerry H. (2008). *Intelligence-Led Policing.* Devon, UK: Willian Publishing.

Reid, Betty (2008). "Security at County Colleges to Begin Carrying Guns," *Arizona Republic,* January 7.

Reiman, Jeffrey (2004). *The Rich Get Richer and the Poor Get Prison: Ideology, Class and Criminal Justice.* Boston, MA: Pearson, Allyn and Bacon.

"Renton, Wash., Beefing Up Downtown Security" (2007). *Puget Sound Business Journal* (Seattle), November 25.

Reppetto, Thomas (1974). *Residential Crime.* Cambridge: Ballinger.

Reynolds, Morgan O. (1994). "Using the Private Sector to Deter Crime." National Center for Policy Analysis, March.

Richardson, Valerie (2005). "FBI Targets Domestic Terrorists," in *Violence and Terrorism.* Ed. Thomas J. Badey: McGraw-Hill/Dushkin.

Ridler, Keith (2008). "Arms Race with Criminals Has Police Toting Heavy-Duty Rifles," March 23. http://www.signonsandiego.com/news/nation/20080323-0837-police-weapons.html (retrieved on May 6, 2008).

Robb, John (2007). "The Coming Urban Terror: Systems Disruption, Networked Gangs, and Bioweapons," *City Journal,* Summer. http://www.city-journal.org/html/17_3_urban_terrorism.html (retrieved on May 16, 2008).

Robbins, Stephen P. (2003). *Organizational Behavior.* Upper Saddle River, NJ: Prentice Hall.

Roberts, Joel (2007). "Senator Reid On Iraq: 'This War Is Lost,' Democratic Majority Leader Says Troop Buildup Is Not Working," *CBS News,* April 20. http://www.cbsnews.com/stories/2007/04/20/politics/main2709229.shtml?source=RSSattr=HOME_2709229 (retrieved on February 20, 2009).

Roberts, Marta (2004). "Working in a War Zone," *Security Management*, November.

Robinson, Frank W. (1996). "From Blight to Bliss," *Security Management*, February.

Robinson, Matthew (1997). "Why the Good News on Crime," *Investor's Business Daily*, April 30.

Root, Jay (2008). "Mexican Army Can't Stop Drug Lords' War on Cops," *McClatchy Newspapers,* May 8. http://www.mcclatchydc.com/226/story/36404.html (retrieved on May 8, 2008).

Rosen, Marie (2006). "A Gathering Storm—Violent Crime in America," Police Executive Research Forum, October.

Rozas, Angela (2007). "Anti-Terror Center Adds Crime Focus," *Chicago Tribune,* December 28.

Rozenberg, Barry (2004). "Protecting the City of Angels," *Homeland Security*, March. www.mcgraw-hillhomelandsecurity.com.

Sammon, Bill (2009). "Pelosi Open to Prosecution of Bush Administration Officials." http://www.foxnews.com/politics/2009/01/18/pelosi-open-prosecution-bush-administration-officials/ (retrieved on January 18, 2009).

Sanchez Jr., Jose L. (2008). "Radiation Detection Devices to Be Installed at Harbor," *Ventura County Star* (CA), June 6. http://www.venturacountystar.com/news/2008/jun/06/radiation-detection-devices-to-be-installed-at/.

Sandler, Larry (2008). "Police May Now Order Security Cameras in Milwaukee Bars," *Milwaukee Journal Sentinel,* September 16.

Sarre, Rick (2005). "Researching Private Policing: Challenges and Agendas for Researchers," *Security Journal* 18, no. 3:57–70.

Savas, E. S. (2000). *Privatization and Public-Private Partnerships.* Chatham House.

Schine, Eric, Richard S. Dunham, and Christopher Farrell (1994). "America's New Watchword: If It Moves, Privatize It," *Business Week*, December 12.

Schmerler, Karin, Matt Perkins, Scott Phillips, Tammy Rinehart, and Meg Townsend (2002). "Problem Solving Tips: A Guide to Reducing Crime and Disorder through Problem-Solving Partnerships," Office of Community Oriented Policing Services, U.S. Department of Justice, June.

Schwartz, Jeremy (2008). "Drug Violence in Atlanta Tied to Several Cartels," *Atlanta Journal-Constitution,* July 31.

Scott, Michael S. and Herman Goldstein (2005). "Shifting and Sharing Responsibilities for Public Safety Problems: Problem Oriented Guides for Police Response," Guide Series No. 3, Office of Community Oriented Policing Services, U.S. Department of Justice, August:1–53.

Seamon, Thomas M. (1995). "Private Forces for Public Good," *Security Management*, September.

Seattle Police Department (2004). November 22. www.seattle.gov.

Sedensky, Matt (2008). "AK-47s Are Turning Up More in US," *Newsweek*, March 26.

Seyler, Stephen (2008). "2008 Final Report for Hollywood and Sunset Business Improvement Districts," Andrews International, BID Security Director, 1-1-08 through 12-28-08.

Shay, Becky (2009). "Billings Group Wants to Change Image of White Supremacists," *Billings Gazette (Montana)*. http://www.missoulian.com/articles/2009/01/08/bnews/br60.txt (retrieved on January 8, 2009).

Shearing, Clifford D. and Philip C. Stenning (1983). "Private Security: Implications for Control," *Social Problems* 30, no. 5:493–506.

Shelman, Jeff (2007). "To Deter Crime at U, These Eyes Never Blink," *Star Tribune (MN)*, November 24.

Shenk, D. (2003). "Watching You: The World of High-Tech Surveillance," *National Geographic*, November:4–29.

Shenk, Joshua Wolf (1995). "The Perils of Privatization," *The Washington Monthly*, May.

Sheridan, Mary Beth (2008). "D.C. Forging Surveillance Network," *Washington Post*, May 1, A1.

Short, Vicky (2001). "Kent County Council Creates Its Own Private Police Force." www.wsws.org (retrieved on May, 23, 2006).

Simeone, Matthew J. (2006). "The Power of Public-Private Partnerships P3 Networks in Policing." *The Police Chief*, May.

Simon, Steven (2004). "The New Terrorism: Securing the Nation Against a Messianic Foe," in *The New Era of Terrorism: Selected Readings*. Ed. Gus Martin. Thousand Oaks, CA: Sage Publications.

Simonsen, Clifford E. and Jeremy R. Spindlove (2000). *Terrorism Today: The Past, The Players, The Future*. Upper Saddle River, NJ: Pearson/Prentice Hall.

Smith, Brent L. and Kelly R. Damphousse (2002). "The American Terrorism Study: Patterns of Behavior, Investigation and Prosecution of American Terrorists," *N.I.J.*, Final Report in Grant #1999-IJCX-0005, January 18.

Smith, Janet (2008). "Earth Worship: Environmentalism Seen as Police State Precursor," *Intelligence Report*, Winter. http://www.splcenter.org/intel/intelreport/article.jsp?aid=968 (retrieved on December 10, 2008).

Smith, Lynn Newhart and Gary D. Hill (1991). "Victimization and Fear of Crime," *Criminal Justice and Behavior* 18, no. 2:217–40.

Spadanuta, Laura (2008). "Patrols Gone Private," *Security Management*, August:20–22.

Spalding, Tom (2004). "IPD to Arm Officers with M-16s," *Indianapolis Star*, August 27.

Spencer, Suzy (1997). "Private Security." Phoenix Mosaic Group. onpatrol.com/cs.privsec.html.

Spielman, Fran (2004). "Daley Wants Bigger Traffic Management Corps," *Chicago Sun-Times*, November 12.

Spielman, Fran and Frank Main (2008). "Cops to Get Rifles to Compete with Gangs," *Chicago Sun-Times*, April 26.

Spielman, Fran and Frank Main (2003). "Elite Police Unit to Flood Streets in City's Hot Spots," *Chicago Sun-Times*, June 24.

Spielman, Fran and Frank Main (2003). "City Deploys High Tech Cameras to Fight Crime," *Chicago Sun-Times,* July 11.

Spitzer, Steven and Andrew T. Scull (1977). "Privatization and Capitalist Development: The Case of the Private Police," *Social Problems* 25, no. 1:18–28.

State and Local Anti-Terrorist Training (SLATT) Manual, Domestic Terrorist Groups, 13. \content\section3domestic\pdfs\narrative.pdf.

Steinhauser, Paul (2009). "Poll Finds Great Expectations for Obama." http://www.cnn.com/2008/POLITICS/11/13/poll.obama/index.html (retreived on January 17, 2009).

Stephens, Gene (2005). "Policing the Future: Law Enforcement's New Challenges," *The Futurist* 39, March/April.

Stern, Jessica (2008). "The Ultimate Organization: Networks, Franchises and Freelancers," in *Terrorism in Perspective,* 2nd ed. Eds. Mahan, Sue and Pamela L. Griset. Thousand Oaks, CA: Sage Publications.

Straw, Joseph (2008). "Fusion Centers and Civil Rights," *Security Management.* http://www.securitymanagement.com/article/fusion-centers-and-civil-rights-004447 (retreived on September 12, 2008).

Sun, Lena H. (2008). "Metro to Randomly Search Riders' Bags," *Washington Post,* A1. http://www.washingtonpost.com/wp-dyn/content/article/2008/10/27/AR2008102700767.html?hpid=moreheadlineslocal (retreived on October 28, 2008).

Swidey, Neil (2006). "Private Eyes: In Boston, as in Iraq, Private Cops Are Now Patrolling Some of the Most Dangerous Beats: Is This the Best Way to Keep the City Safe?" *The Boston Globe,* April 9, 46, April 9.

Swonk, Diane (2003). *The Passionate Economist: Find the Power and Humanity Behind the Numbers.* New Yrok: John Wiley and Sons.

Telhami, Shibley (2005). "Understanding the Challenge," in *Violence and Terrorism.* Ed. Thomas J. Badey. McGraw-Hill/Dushkin.

Tennessee v. Gardner, 471 U.S. 1 (1985).

"Terror Incidents in the U.S. Since the 9/11 Attacks" (2008). *Counter-Terrorism* 1, no. 1 (May/June):53.

Testimony of Donald Van Duyn, Deputy Assistant Director, Counterterrorism Division, Federal Bureau of Investigation, before the Senate Committee on Homeland Security and Governmental Affairs, September 19, 2006.

Testimony of Robert S. Mueller, III, Director, Federal Bureau of Investigation, before the Senate Committee on Intelligence of the United States Senate, February 16, 2005.

Testimony of Javed Ali, Senior Intelligence Officer, Office of Intelligence and Analysis, Department of Homeland Security, before the Senate Committee on Homeland Security and Government Affairs, September 19, 2006.

Thomas, Frank (2007). "TSA to Test New Thermal Cameras in Rail Stations," *USA Today,* October 4.

Thurston, Timothy W. II (2007). The Military's Role in Domestic Terrorism, Unpublished masters thesis at Naval Postgraduate School, Monterey, CA, December.

Tobacco and Terror: How Cigarette Smuggling Is Funding our Enemies Abroad (2008). Legislative report prepared by the Republican Staff of the U.S. House Committee on Homeland Security, U.S. Rep. Peter T. King (R-NY), Ranking Member.

Tolchin, Martin (1985). "Private Guards Get New Role in Public Law Enforcement," *New York Times,* November 29.

Training Key #582, Suicide (Homicide) Bombers: Part II (2005). Alexandria, VA: International Association of Chiefs of Police.

Traynor, Ian (2003). "The Privatization of War: $30 Billion Goes to Private Military, Fears Over Hired Guns' Policy," *The Guardian* (UK), December 10.

Trojanowicz, Robert C. (1988). "Serious Threats to the Future of Policing," *Footprints*, National Center for Community Policing, Fall/Winter:2.

Trojanowicz, Robert C. and David L. Carter (1990). "The Changing Face of America," *FBI Law Enforcement Bulletin*, January.

Tucker, Jonathan B. (2003). "Strategies for Countering Terrorism: Lessons from the Israeli Experience," *Journal of Homeland Security*, March 26.

Tzu, Sun (date unknown). *Art of War.* Trans. Lionel Giles. http://www.chinapage.com/sunzi-e.html (retrieved on February 20, 2009).

Uchitelle, Louis and John Markoff (2004). "Terrorbusters, Inc.: The Rise of the Homeland Security Industrial Complex," *New York Times,* October 17.

Uniform Crime Report (UCR) for year 2006. Compiled by the Federal Bureau of Investigation, September 2007. http://www.fbi.gov/ucr/cius2006/offenses/expanded_information/data/shrtable_03.html (retrieved on May 11, 2008).

Uniform Crime Report (UCR) for year 2005. Compiled by the Federal Bureau of Investigation, September 2006. http://www.fbi.gov/ucr/05cius/offenses/expanded_information/data/shrtable_03.html (retrieved on May 11, 2008).

Uniform Crime Report (UCR) for year 2004. Compiled by the Federal Bureau of Investigation, September 2005. http://www.fbi.gov/ucr/cius_04/offenses_reported/violent_crime/murder.html (retrieved on May 11, 2008).

Uniform Crime Report (UCR) for year 2004. Compiled by the Federal Bureau of Investigation, September 2005. http://www.fbi.gov/ucr/cius_03/xl/03tbl2-5.xls (retrieved on May 11, 2008).

U.S. Department of Justice (2004). "Crime in the United States." www.fbi.gov/ucr/cius_04/offenses_reported/violent_crime/index.html (retrieved on June 23, 2006).

U.S. Department of Justice and U.S. Department of Defense (1997). "Department of Justice and Department of Defense Joint Technology Program: Second Anniversary Report." Washington, DC: U.S. Department of Justice, February.

U.S. Department of Labor Statistics from May 2004. Cited in *Security Director's Report* (2006). March, 7. www.ioma.com.

U.S. v. Jackson, 213 F.3d 1269 (10th Cir., 2000).

Valero, Rafael Enrique (2008). "Hired Guns," *National Journal,* January 7.

Vernon-Sparks, Lisa (2006). "Special Guard Squad's Debut Showcases Commando-Style Protection," *Providence Journal.* August 3. http://www.projo.com/ri/coventry/content/projo_20060803_cv3team.1ee9eeb.html (retrieved on August 3, 2006).

Video Surveillance: Information on Law Enforcement's Use of Closed Circuit Television to Monitor Selected Federal Property in Washington D.C. (2003). Government Accounting Office, GAO-03-748, June.

Wadman, Robert C. and William Thomas Allison (2004). *To Protect and To Serve: A History of Police in America.* Upper Saddle River, NJ: Pearson/Prentice Hall.

Walinsky, Adam (1993). "The Crisis of Public Order," *The Atlantic Monthly*, July.

Walmington, Joe (2005). "Good Guys Must Seize and Control Turf," *The Toronto Sun,* December 31. www.torontosun.com (retrieved on June 25, 2006).

Walsh, William F., Edwin J. Donovan, and James F. McNicholas (1992). "The Starrett Protective Service: Private Policing in an Urban Community," in *Privatizing the United States Justice System.* Eds. Gary W. Bowman et al. Jefferson, NC: McFarland, 157–77.

Wardlaw, Grant (1982). *Political Terrorism: Theory, Tactics and Counter-Measures*. Cambridge: Cambridge University Press.

Warikoo, Niraj (2008). *Detroit Free Press*. http://www.freep.com/apps/pbcs.dll/article?AID=/20080425/NEWS02/80425047/1003/news (retrieved on April 25, 2008).

Warner, Frank (2007). "The New York Times Left Out Gen. Richardo Sanchez' Attack on News Reporting That Results in Killing Americans." http://frankwarner.typepad.com/free_frank_warner/2007/10/the-new-york-ti.html (retrieved on February 3, 2009).

Waugh, William L. (1982). *International Terrorism*. Salisbury, NC: Documentary Publications.

Wayne, Leslie (2004). "Security for the Homeland, Made in Alaska," *New York Times*, August 12.

"Weapons of Mass Destruction Student Manual AWR-160," U.S. Department of Homeland Security, Preparedness Directorate, Office of Grants and Training, Center for Domestic Preparedness.

Weathers, William A. (2008). "Terrorism? Zoom In," *Cincinnati Enquirer*, February 28.

Weber, Diane Cecilia (1999). "Warrior Cops: The Ominous Growth of Para-Militarism in American Police Departments," Cato Institute. August 26. http://www.tysknews.com/Depts/The_Law/paramilitarism_in_police2.htm (retrieved on May 6, 2008).

Webster, Barbara (2008). "Combat Deployment and the Returning Police Officer," U.S. Department of Justice, Office of Community Oriented Policing Services and Institute for Law and Justice, 2005-HS-WX-K005, August.

Wessel, Robert H. (1995). "Privatization in the United States," *Business Economics*, October.

West, Marty L. (1993). "Get a Piece of the Privatization Pie," *Security Management*, March.

White, Jonathan R. (2008). "A Theology of Anti-government Extremism," in *Terrorism in Perspective*, 2nd ed. Eds. Mahan, Sue and Pamela L. Griset. Thousand Oaks, CA: Sage Publications.

White, Michael D. (2002). "Identifying Situational Predictors of Police Shootings Using Multivariate Analysis," *Policing: An International Journal of Police Strategies and Management* 25, no. 4:726–51.

Whitlock, Craig (2008). "Probe of USS Cole Bombing Unravels: Plotters Freed in Yemen; U.S. Efforts Frustrated," *The Washington Post*, May 4. http://www.washingtonpost.com/wp-dyn/content/article/2008/05/03/AR2008050302047.html.

Widdowson, Anna (2008). "Urban Shield Tests Police Ability," *Daily Californian*, September 15.

Wilkinson, Paul (1986). *Terrorism and the Liberal State*. Washington Square, NY: New York University Press.

Williams, Dave (2008). "Businesses Face Crime Wave," *Atlanta Business Chronicle*, July 28.

Williams, Juan (2009). "Judge Obama on Performance Alone: Let's Not Celebrate More Ordinary Speeches," *The Wall Street Journal*, January 20. http://online.wsj.com/article/SB123249791178500439.html.

Wilson, James Q. and George L. Kelling (1982). "Broken Windows," *The Atlantic*, March.

Winton, Richard and David Pierson (2007). "LAPD Reviews Terror Threat at Nightclubs," *Los Angeles Times*, July 4.

Witkowski, Michael J. (2004). "The Gang's All Here," *Security Management*, May.

WKOW.com (Madison, Wis.) (2008). "Armed Security Guards Becoming Industry Standard," August 5. http://www.wkowtv.com/global/story.asp?s=8794528&ClientType=Printable.

Wolf, John B. (1981). *Fear of Fear: Survey of Terrorist Operations and Controls in Open Societies*. New York: Plenum.

Wood, Laurie (2007). *Intelligence Report* Fall:56–57.

Woods, Christina M. (2008). "Club Safety May Draw New Laws," *Wichita Eagle* (KS), September 8.

WSOC-TV (2006). "Private Police Patrols Begin in Charlotte," May 23. www.wsoctv. com/news/7561311/detail.html.

Young, Bob (2008). "Surveillance Cameras Installed in Seattle's Cal Anderson Park," *Seattle Times*, April 22.

Young, R. (1977). "Revolutionary Terrorism, Crime and Morality," *Social Theory and Practice* 4.

Youngs, Al (2004). "The Future of Public/Private Partnerships," *FBI Law Enforcement Bulletin*, January.

Yungher, Nathan I. (2008). *Terrorism: The Bottom Line.* Upper Saddle River, NJ: Pearson/ Prentice Hall.

Zavis, Alexandra (2007). "Iraqi Official: Blackwater Exit Not Feasible," *Los Angeles Times*, September 24.

Zielinski, Mike (1999). "Armed and Dangerous: Private Police on the March," *Covert Action Quarterly*. Caq.com/caq/caq54p.police.html.

Web Site Sources

Emergency Response/Management

http://www.citizencorps.gov/ (retrieved on February 1, 2009).

http://www.citizencorps.gov/cert/ (retrieved on February 1, 2009).

www.nydailynews.com (retrieved on October 11, 2007).

Media

http://www.freerepublic.com/focus/f-news/1145998/posts (retrieved on February 3, 2009).

http://www.truthorfiction.com/rumors/f/flagoffense.htm (retrieved on January 24, 2009).

http://www.breakthechain.org/exclusives/beamerican.html (retrieved on January 24, 2009).

http://www.cnn.com/US/9802/04/us.un.iraq/ (retrieved on February 4, 2009).

http://www.americanthinker.com/2007/07/saluting_the_white_flag.html (retrieved on February 21, 2009).

http://www.truthorfiction.com/rumors/b/bushlied.htm (retrieved on February 21, 2009).

Press release from Nancy Pelosi. http://www.house.gov/pelosi/priraql.htm (retrieved on April 30, 2008).

http://www.truthorfiction.com/rumors/b/bushlied.htm (retrieved on February 4, 2009).

Clinton, Bill (2004). *Time*, June. Quoted by the *Wall Street Journal*, November 18, A16.

Kinsella, Jack. http://hallindsey.org/index.php?option=com_content&task=view&id=241& Itemid=1 (retrieved on February 29, 2008).

Politics—Obama

http://www.huffingtonpost.com/2008/11/04/obama-victory-speech_n_141194.html (retrieved on January 19, 2009).

http://www.chicagobreakingnews.com/2008/10/obama-comments-on-pakistan-prompt-local-protest.html (retrieved on October 9, 2008).

Kennedy, John F. Inauguration speech. http://nothingbuttruth.com/maximum-crane /2008/03/let-every-nation-know/ (retrieved on February 20, 2009).

Obama, Barack. Inauguration speech. http://www.msnbc.msn.com/id/28754569/ (retrieved on January 21, 2009).

Obama, Barack. Inauguration speech. http://www.time.com/time/politics/article/0,8599,1872715-3,00.html (retrieved on January 21, 2009).

Obama, Barack (2008). Acceptance speech, August 28. http://www.nytimes.com/2008/08/28/us/politics/28text-obama.html?pagewanted=1&_r=1 (retrieved on January 22, 2009).

Obama, Barack (2004). Speech at 2004 Democratic Convention. http://www.americanrhetoric.com/speeches/convention2004/barackobama2004dnc.htm (retrieved on January 22, 2009).

Obama, Barack (2009). Executive Order—Review and Disposition of Individuals Detained at the Guantánamo Bay Naval Base and Closure of Detention Facilities, January 22. http://www.whitehouse.gov/the_press_office/ClosureOfGuantanamoDetentionFacilities/.

Police

http://www.msnbc.msn.com/id/19116778/ (retrieved on August 24, 2007).

www.cityoflondon.police.uk (retrieved on June 10, 2008).

http://www.foxnews.com/story/0,2933,340748,00.html (retrieved on March 23, 2008).

http://www.killology.com/index.htm (retrieved on March 7, 2008).

Balko, Radley (2007). Testimony on our militarized police departments before the House Subcommittee on Crime, June 21. http://www.reason.com/news/show/121169.html (retrieved on May 6, 2008).

http://www.foxnews.com/story/0,2933,340748,00.html (retrieved on March 23, 2008).

http://www.usatoday.com/news/washington/2007-01-26-militarygiveaways_x.htm (retrieved on May 6, 2008).

Star-Telegram (2007). February 26. www.dfw.com/mld/dfw/news/16786386.htm (retrieved on August 17, 2007).

http://www.nypd.org (retrieved on December 2, 2008).

http://www.nypdshield.org/public/about.aspx (retrieved on December 2, 2008).

http://www.nypdshield.org/public/nexus.nypd (retrieved on December 2, 2008).

http://www.nypdshield.org/public/initiatives.nypd (retrieved on December 2, 2008).

http://www.lapdonline.org/search_results/content_basic_view/6502 (retrieved on January 3, 2009).

Racial Relations/Incidents

http://www.foxnews.com/story/0,2933,330504,00.html (retrieved on February 10 and 12, 2008).

http://www.themilitant.com/index.shtml (retrieved on September 23, 2007).

http://www.foxnews.com/story/0,2933,297731,00.html (retrieved on September 23, 2007).

http://www.foxnews.com/story/0,2933,270241,00.html, May 6, 2007 (retrieved on April 28, 2008).

http://www.lewrockwell.com/blog/lewrw/archives/020008.html (retrieved on March 16, 2008).

http://elections.foxnews.com/2008/03/16/obama-pastors-church-fires-back/ (retrieved on March 16, 2008).

http://www.houmatoday.com/article/20080422/APA/804221036 (retrieved on April 27, 2008).
Various accounts of the Sean Bell case: http://www.nytimes.com/2008/04/28/nyregion/28bell.
    html?ref=nyregion, and http://www.nydailynews.com/topics/Sean+Bell.
http://www.nytimes.com/slideshow/2008/04/25/nyregion/20080425BELL_11.html
    (retrieved on April 26, 2008).
juicyscoop.blogspot.com (retrieved on April 26, 2008).
http://www.newsday.com/news/local/newyork/ny-nystre0426,0,3138952.story   (retrieved
    on April 26, 2008).
Rush Limbaugh interview with Sean Hannity, *Fox News*. http://www.foxnews.com/ (retrieved
    on January 22, 2009).
http://www.foxnews.com/ (retrieved on January 22, 2009).
http://www.tucc.org/about.htm (retrieved on April 25, 2008).
http://www.tucc.org/store/index.cfm?action=catbrowse&catid=69 (retrieved on April 25, 2008).
http://web.archive.org/web/20050404190242/www.tucc.org/about.htm, May 7, 2005, and
    November 12, 2006 (as retrieved on May 3, 2008, at http://www.archive.org/index.php).
http://www.tucc.org (retrieved on May 3, 2008).

Technology/Intelligence

http://www.manhattan-institute.org/html/cb_43.htm (retrieved on October 16, 2007).
http://www.latimes.com/news/local/la-me-counterterror14apr14,1,5682393.story (retrieved
    on April 16, 2008).
"Video Cameras on the Lookout for Terrorists." www.cnn.com (retrieved on September 1,
    2006 at http://edition.cnn.com/2006/tech/08/07/terrorism.technology.ap).
"Eye on Video: Adding Audio Intelligence." SecurityInfoWatch.com (retrieved on July
    22, 2008).
http://www.airvisual.com/intelliviewer.htm (retrieved on April 7, 2008).
http://www.usatoday.com/news/nation/2008-09-17-car-scanner_N.htm?csp=34   (retrieved
    on September 19, 2008).
www.seattle.gov (retrieved on November 22, 2004).
www.ebscohost.com (retrieved on March 26, 2008).
http://www.venturacountystar.com/news/2008/jun/06/radiation-detection-devices-to-be-
    installed-at/ (retrieved on June 6, 2008).
http://www.reuters.com/article/wtMostRead/idUSN1026252120070811   (retrieved   on
    August 14, 2007).
http://www.usatoday.com/news/nation/2008-09-17-car-scanner_N.htm?csp=34   (retrieved
    on September 19, 2008).

Security/Private Police

http://www.pinkertons.com/timesharing/timesharing1.asp (retrieved on March 12, 2003).
www.securitas.com (retrieved on June 10, 2008).
http://www.govexec.com/story_page.cfm?articleid=40050&dcn=e_hsw
www.sfpatrolspecpolice.com (retrieved on December 10, 2008).
http://www.atlantadowntown.com/ambassador.asp (retrieved on November 12, 2008).
http://findarticles.com/p/articles/mi_qa3676/is_/ai_n8805715 (retrieved on November
    12, 2008).

Cherry Hill Courier-Post (New Jersey). http://www.courierpostonline.com/article/20081227/ NEWS01/812270323/1006 (retrieved on December 27, 2008).

Intelligarde. www.intelligarde.org (retrieved on June 25, 2006).

http://www.thebostonchannel.com/news/11143266/detail.html (retrieved on March 1, 2007).

http://www.manhattan-institute.org/html/cb_43.htm (retrieved on October 16, 2007).

Terrorism

For definition of terrorism see http://www.fbi.gov/congress/congress02/jarboe021202.htm (retrieved on May 2, 2008).

For examples of the particular goals of terrorism, see http://www.isvg.org/ and www.txdps.state.tx.us.

For explanation of the Terrorist Surveillance Act, please see press release at http://www.usdoj.gov/opa/documents/nsa_myth_v_reality.pdf (retrieved on January 31, 2009).

http://icasualties.org/oif/IraqiDeaths.aspx (retrieved on June 7, 2008).

www.cdi.org/terrorism/terrorist-groups.cfm (retrieved on July 27, 2006).

http://www.guardian.co.uk/egypt/story/0,129630,00.html (retrieved on July 19, 2007).

http://www.insideprison.com/prison_gang_profile_JUIIS.asp (retrieved on February 1, 2009).

Information related to the Dearborn, Michigan, indictment can be found at a number of Web sites, including http://www.milnet.com/terr-prosecutions/2006-08-23_ybakri.pdf (retrieved on February 1, 2009).

"Gang Activity in the U.S. Military." http://usmilitary.about.com/od/justicelawlegislation/a/gangs.htm (retrieved on July 27, 2006).

http://www.armyofgod.com/Paulhillindex.html (retrieved on May 2, 2008).

http://www.armyofgod.com/EricRudolphHomepage.html (retrieved on May 2, 2008).

http://www.fbi.gov/congress/congress02/jarboe021202.htm (retrieved on May 2, 2008).

http://www.earthliberationfront.com/main.shtml (retrieved on May 2, 2008).

http://www.salvationinc.org/archives/2004_08.html on May 2, 2008).

www.cdi.org/terrorism/terrorist-groups.cfm (retrieved on May 2, 2008).

http://www.csmonitor.com/2008/0328/p07s03-woam.html (retrieved on May 16, 2008).

http://www.knowgangs.com/gang_resources/profiles/ms13/ (retrieved on June 12, 2007).

www.kkk.com/intro.htm (retrieved on August 17, 2007).

www.adl.org (retrieved on August 17, 2007).

http://www.newblackpanther.com (retrieved on May 5, 2008).

http://www.startribune.com/484/story/1459843.html (retrieved on October 9, 2007).

http://www.dc.state.fl.us/pub/gangs/prison.html (retrieved on May 5, 2008).

http://www.splcenter.org/intel/intelreport/article.jsp?aid=569 (retrieved on May 5, 2008).

http://www.washingtonpost.com/wp-dyn/content/article/2008/06/04/AR2008060401636.html (retrieved on June 5, 2008).

http://www.theyeshivaworld.com/article.php?p=20633 (retrieved on July 4, 2008).

http://www.foxnews.com/projects/pdf/bin_laden_transcript.pdf (retrieved on September 7, 2007).

http://www.foxnews.com/ (retrieved on August 3, 2007.

http://www.foxnews.com/story/0,2933,270241,00.html (retrieved on May 6, 2007).

http://news.yahoo.com/s/nm/20070907/wl_nm/algeria_bomb_toll_dc;_ylt=ApUU9vUQE 4FkN6TkUeO7NJK96Q8F (retrieved on September 8, 2007).

http://www.foxnews.com/story/0,2933,352689,00.html on April 26, 2008).

http://news.bbc.co.uk/2/hi/south_asia/7616429.stm on September 15, 2008.

http://www.foxnews.com/photoessay/0,4644,2864,00.html#13_0 (retrieved on December 11, 2007).

https://www.osac.gov/Reports/report.cfm?contentID=70865 (retrieved on July 14, 2007).

http://www.foxnews.com/story/0,2933,307843,00.html (retrieved on November 3, 2007).

http://www.timesonline.co.uk/tol/news/world/middle_east/article5443427.ece.

http://ap.google.com/article/ALeqM5ihmILMXDSyifnMSZu2NK3vNWSazgD937 DBSO0 (retrieved on September 19, 2008).

http://news.bbc.co.uk/2/hi/africa/7731839.stm (retrieved on November 17, 2008).

http://ap.google.com/article/ALeqM5ihmILMXDSyifnMSZu2NK3vNWSazgD937 DBSO0 (retrieved on September 19, 2008).

http://www.expatica.com/actual/article.asp?subchannel_id=81&story_id=37544.

http://www.foxnews.com/photoessay/0,4644,1928,00.html#8_0 (retrieved on June 22, 2007).

http://news.bbc.co.uk/2/hi/south_asia/6910461.stm on July 22, 2007).

Ayman al-Zawahri's assertion: http://www.chron.com/disp/story.mpl/ap/world/4947209.html (retrieved on July 6, 2007).

bin Laden's assertion taken on September 6, 2007: http://www.foxnews.com/projects/pdf/bin_laden_transcript.pdf.

http://ap.google.com/article/ALeqM5grQY9IZlnRcXplTJ05FsxTclBWfgD8VE65M06 (retrieved on March 17, 2008).

http://ap.google.com/article/ALeqM5ihmILMXDSyifnMSZu2NK3vNWSazgD937 DBSO0 (retrieved on September 19, 2008).

Ibid @ http://ap.google.com/article/ALeqM5ihmILMXDSyifnMSZu2NK3vNWSazgD937 DBSO0 (retrieved on September 19, 2008).

http://www.msnbc.msn.com/id/20188364/ (retrieved on August 9, 2007).

http://news.bbc.co.uk/2/hi/middle_east/6994823.stm (retrieved on September 14, 2007).

http://www.foxnews.com/story/0,2933,296897,00.html (retrieved on September 15, 2007).

http://www.foxnews.com/story/0,2933,290291,00.html (retrieved on July 22, 2007).

http://yalibnan.com/site/archives/2007/08/99_iraqi_attack.php (retrieved on August 9, 2007).

http://www.foxnews.com/story/0,2933,305686,00.html (retrieved on October 27, 2007).

http://www.foxnews.com/story/0,2933,342111,00.html (retrieved on March 27, 2008).

http://news.yahoo.com/s/ap/20080410/ap_on_re_mi_ea/iraq_shifting_the_enemy;_ylt=Ah gSqPZIpuVWpe4yDDkYUtkLewgF (retrieved on April 11, 2008).

http://www.foxnews.com/story/0,2933,352066,00.html (retrieved on April 22, 2008).

http://abdulhaqq.jeeran.com/operations.html (retrieved on August 10, 2007).

bin Laden's "Letter to America" on November 24, 2002. http://www.guardian.co.uk/world/2002/nov/24/theobserver/print (retrieved on November 25, 2008).

http://news.yahoo.com/s/ap/20070911/ap_on_re_la_am_ca/mexico_pipeline_explosions;_ylt=As7RaBpyvVpL0dX8FG5BvwC3IxIF (retrieved on September 11, 2007).

http://www.adl.org/Learn/ext_us/WCOTC.asp?xpicked=3&item=17 (retrieved on May 5, 2008).

http://edition.cnn.com/2005/WORLD/europe/07/27/menezes.brazil/ (retrieved on February 10, 2009).

Appendix

Since WMD have been so hotly politicized by the Iraq War, it may be interesting to note that some of the same people who criticized President Bush had echoed similar assertions about the presence of WMD in Iraq. The following information relative to WMD in Iraq was stated during the Clinton Administration.

In the intervening months during 1998, President Clinton, his administration, and key Democrat leaders made bold statements about the threat posed by Iraq. For example, even prior to the bombing and his nationally publicized speech, President Clinton stated on February 4, 1998,[1]

> One way or the other, we are determined to deny Iraq the capacity to develop weapons of mass destruction and the missiles to deliver them. That is our bottom line.

Following this speech, Secretary of State of Madeline Albright stated on February 18, 1998 (emphasis added),[2]

> Iraq is a long way from here, but what happens there matters a great deal here. For the risks that the leaders of a rogue state will use nuclear, chemical or biological weapons against us or our allies is the *greatest security threat* we face.

Later that same year, Democratic Senators Carl Levin, Tom Daschle, and John Kerry sent a letter to President Clinton dated October 8, 1998, which stated,[3]

> We urge you, after consulting with Congress, and consistent with the U.S. Constitution and laws, to take necessary actions (including, if appropriate, air and missile strikes on suspect Iraqi sites) to respond effectively to the threat posed by Iraq's refusal to end its weapons of mass destruction programs.

Nancy Pelosi, a member of the House Intelligence Committee, issued a press release on December 16, 1998, which stated,[4]

> I am keenly aware that the proliferation of chemical and biological weapons is an issue of grave importance to all nations. Saddam Hussein has been engaged in the development of weapons of mass destruction technology, which is a threat to countries in the region, and he has made a mockery of the weapons inspection process.
>
> The responsibility of the United States in this conflict is to eliminate weapons of mass destruction, to minimize the danger to our troops, and to diminish the suffering of the Iraqi people. The citizens of Iraq have suffered the most for Saddam Hussein's activities; sadly, those same citizens now stand to suffer more. I have supported efforts to ease the humanitarian situation in Iraq and my thoughts and prayers are with the innocent Iraqi civilians, as well as with the families of U.S. troops participating in the current action.
>
> I believe in negotiated solutions to international conflict. This is, unfortunately, not going to be the case in this situation, where Saddam Hussein has been a repeat offender, ignoring the international community's requirement that he come clean with his weapons program. While I support the president, I hope and pray that this conflict can be resolved quickly and that the international community can find a lasting solution through diplomatic means.

Shortly thereafter, on December 18, 1998 (after three days of sustained bombing of Iraq), President Clinton said the following about the WMD threat from Iraq:[5]

> Heavy as they are, the cost of action must be weighed against the price of inaction. If Saddam defies the world and we fail to respond, we will face a far greater threat in the future. Saddam will strike again at his neighbors. He will make war on his own people. And mark my words, he will develop weapons of mass destruction. He will deploy them and he will use them.

Prior to the war numerous Democratic leaders made bold statements about the presence of WMD in Iraq. For example, Al Gore stated the following on September 23, 2002:[6] "Iraq's search for weapons of mass destruction has proven impossible to deter and we should assume that it will continue for as long as Saddam is in power." In addition, Senator Ted Kennedy stated the following at a speech at Johns Hopkins University on September 27, 2002:[7] "We have known for many years that Saddam Hussein is seeking and developing weapons of mass destruction." There are substantially more quotations in a similar vein by Democratic leaders. The evidence is all over the Web. Since this information is so readily available, does it not strike you as troubling that these quotes were not presented to these "leaders" when they later boldly claimed Bush was lying?

Now let's briefly describe the circumstances in Iraq. First, to those who blame the war on Bush lying about WMD, I believe the quotations made by Democratic leaders during the Clinton Administration make a mockery of this mantra. I included these quotes because these assertions were made when intelligence was derived from the Clinton Administration. You certainly cannot blame Bush for lying about intelligence three years prior to taking office. Further, even after the Iraq War started, Bill Clinton was on record essentially saying that unaccounted for WMD existed in Iraq. Here is Clinton's assertion during an interview with *Time* magazine, published in June 2004:[8]

> You know, I have repeatedly defended President Bush against the left on Iraq, even though I think he should have waited until the U.N. inspections were over ...
>
> After 9-11, let's be fair here, if you had been president, you'd think, well, this fellow bin Laden just turned three airplanes full of fuel into weapons of mass destruction, right? Arguably they were super-powerful chemical weapons. Think about it that way ...
>
> But you also have to say, well my first responsibility now is to try everything possible to make sure that this terrorist network and other terrorist networks cannot reach chemical and biological weapons or small amounts of [nuclear] material. ... That's why I supported the Iraq thing. There was a lot of stuff unaccounted for ...

By any fair standard, it is simply wrong to hang the tag of "liar" on President Bush for the lack of WMD recovered in Iraq. Given the assertions made by Clinton, coupled with those Democrats who warned that Iraq had WMD, it is disingenuous, at best, to now assert that the failure to recover WMD amounts to a lie. To those who desire to think logically about this issue, consider this. When Saddam Hussein kicked the U.N. inspectors out of Iraq in 1998, was it more or less likely that he would restart the weapons program in the intervening five years (from 1998 to the invasion in 2003)? Further, consider that the Iraq Survey Group reported in October 2004 that Saddam himself was "lying" about the existence of WMD. Apparently he was more worried about Iran than about the pending U.S. invasion. He evidently did not believe that the United States would actually invade and take down this government.

Finally, in February 2008, CBS's *60 Minutes* interviewed George Piro, the FBI interrogator who spent nearly seven months questioning Saddam Hussein after his capture. In this interview, Piro also asserted that Saddam was running a bluff because he was certain the United States would not invade. Saddam expected something more along the lines of the four-day aerial attack that occurred in December 1998. Indeed, according to Kinsella, George Piro made this compelling point:[9]

He [Saddam] survived that one and he was willing to accept that type of attack. Saddam wanted Iran to believe he had nuclear weapons because he feared an Iranian attack. If he admitted to the West that he didn't, the US and its allies might stand down, but he was convinced that Iran would seize the moment and launch their own invasion. Evidently, Saddam was less worried about his chances with the Americans than he was with the Iranians. Saddam fooled Western intelligence because he convinced even his top generals that Iraq had both a stockpile of WMD and an ongoing nuclear program.

Instead of honestly presenting these statements in the public debate, the issue of terrorism has been "politicized" around simplistic cliches, such as "Bush lied and people died." While the Bush Administration has made numerous mistakes—and strategic miscalculations—in Iraq, the cold, hard facts are that every intelligence service in the world believed that Iraq had WMD prior to the Iraq War. This fact is well known, by members of both political parties. It was confirmed and validated by the Iraq Survey Group, which reported findings to the Senate Intelligence Committee on October 7, 2004. In the report, the leader of the group, Charles Duelfer, stated that Saddam actively sought to maintain the perspective that he had WMD. He did this because[10]

the Iranian threat was very, very palpable to him [Saddam], and he didn't want to be second to Iran, and he felt he had to deter them. So he wanted to create the impression that he had more than he did.

There is substantial other evidence available in public sources to further validate this assertion. For example, a leader of al Qaeda was asked in 1998 if he had nuclear or chemical weapons, and he responded, "Acquiring weapons for the defense of Muslims is a religious duty." In this light, the CIA had intelligence reports from senior Arab intelligence officials that in October 1998 bin Laden had obtained one or two nuclear suitcase weapons from a Central Asian republic in return for $30 million in cash and two tons of heroin worth $70 million—a deal brokered by the Chechen mafia. Others asserted that bin Laden paid millions of dollars to stockpile these portable weapons at a hideout near Kandahar in southern Afghanistan.[11] In August 2001, bin Laden and his deputy, al-Zawahiri, met Pakistani scientists from a group called Umma Tameer-E-Nau to discuss how al Qaeda could build a nuclear device. Later in June 2002, Sulaiman Abu Ghaith, a Kuwaiti-born cleric, posted a statement on the Internet saying that "al Qaeda has the 'right' to kill 4 million Americans."[12]

These are dangerous and complicated factors. I do not have definitive facts. Neither do you. The solution, to some people, is to simply make Bush a "liar." This is both unfair and disingenuous. It is also dangerous—as we will likely distrust our own intelligence reports to our own detriment. We will live to regret this.

Endnotes

1. http://www.cnn.com/US/9802/04/us.un.iraq/ (retrieved on February 4, 2009).
2. http://www.americanthinker.com/2007/07/saluting_the_white_flag.html (retrieved on February 21, 2009).
3. http://www.truthorfiction.com/rumors/b/bushlied.htm (retrieved on February 21, 2009).
4. Press release from Nancy Pelosi. http://www.house.gov/pelosi/priraql.htm (retrieved on April 30, 2008).
5. *Wall Street Journal* (2005). November 18, A16.
6. http://www.truthorfiction.com/rumors/b/bushlied.htm (retrieved on February 4, 2009).
7. http://www.truthorfiction.com/rumors/b/bushlied.htm (retrieved on February 4, 2009).
8. President Clinton, June 2004 (from *Time* magazine), as quoted by the *Wall Street Journal*, November 18, 2005, A16.
9. Jack Kinsella. http://hallindsey.org/index.php?option=com_content&task=view&id=241&Itemid=1 (retrieved on February 29, 2008).
10. Kinsella, Jack. February 29, 2008. http://hallindsey.org/index.php?option=com_content&task=view&id=241&Itemid=1.
11. This information came from a PowerPoint slide obtained from the U.S. Attorney's Office.
12. Herold, Noam (2008). "Nuclear Terrorism: A 21st Century Threat." *The Counter Terrorist* 1, no. 1 (May/June):11.

Index

435

Umma Tameer-E-Nau, 432
Unclassified data, 163
"Uncle Tom," 336
Unified efforts, 346
Uniform Crime Report (UCR), 327
United Kingdom
    assume behavior monitoring, 391
    detaining terror suspects, 380
    growth in security industry, 32
    public environment cameras, 179
    public-private cooperative methods, 236
    soft targets, 261, 262
    surveillance programs, 377
    threats against, 292
    transformation of policing, 32
United States, *see also* Great Satan (United
      States)
    Capitol shooting incident of 1954, 94
    detaining/releasing suspects, 381
    public environment cameras, 179–180
    Security and Prosperity Partnership, 323
    use of force, 383
UNITY OF THE RANKS audiotape, 289
Universal Islamic Society, 110
Universities, 187, 228n63, *see also specific*
      university
University of Minnesota, 187
Uno Technology, 222
Urban Area Security Initiative, 159
Urban Shield, 248
U.S. Army War College's Center for Strategic
      Leadership, 143
U.S. State Department, *xviii*
USA Today, 392
USS Cole attack, 275
Utah, 219
Utilities, 51–52, 179

V

Van Duyn, Donald, 76, 78, 84n101
Vehicles, 359
Venezuela, 282, *see also* Chávez (Venezuelan
      President)
Vice Lords, 72
Victory, peace instead of, 292
VIDA, *see* Visitor Information and Downtown
      Assistance (VIDA)
Video Interoperability for Public Safety (VIPS)
      program, 183
Violence
    council to minimize excessive, 295, 296

designed to produce fear, 47
extremist ideologies impact, 16–24
goals of, 46–50
group think, 341
implications of terroristic, 139–152
as message, 56–57
randomness, 46
Violent Crime Control and Law Enforcement
      Act, 28
Virginia Jihad Network, 111
Virginia Tech massacre, 45, 136, 248
Visitor Information and Downtown Assistance
      (VIDA), 252
Volya, Narodnaya, 94

W

Wackenhut Security, 259
"Wag the dog" approach, 275
Wahhabi extremism, 77, 307–308
Wainstein, Ken, 137
"Walk of the Stars" (Hollywood Walk of Fame),
      248
Wallace, William, 388
Wall Street Journal, 53
War by proxy, 150
Ward, Richard, *xiv, xv, xx*
War on terror declaration, 12, 56
Warren, Rick, 335
Washington, D.C.
    camera surveillance, 185
    clearance levels, 176
    closed-circuit video systems, 183
    police personnel reduction, 29
    Public Safety Policing Model, 237
Washington Post, 53, 178
Washington (state)
    camera surveillance, 186
    model synergy, 256
    private security, 252
    public environment cameras, 181
Water pipe (hookah) bars, incubators, 66
WCOTC, *see* World Church of the Creator
      (WCOTC)
Weapons and weapons training
    acquiring as religious duty, 432
    order maintenance, 359
    transfers, timing of, 128
Weather Underground, 17, 94
Web sites sources, *xviii,* 423–427, *see also*
      Internet
Webster studies, 147